The REMARRIED EMPRESS

Art by **SUMPUL**  ❦  Adapted by **HereLee**  ❦  Original story by **Alphatart**

2

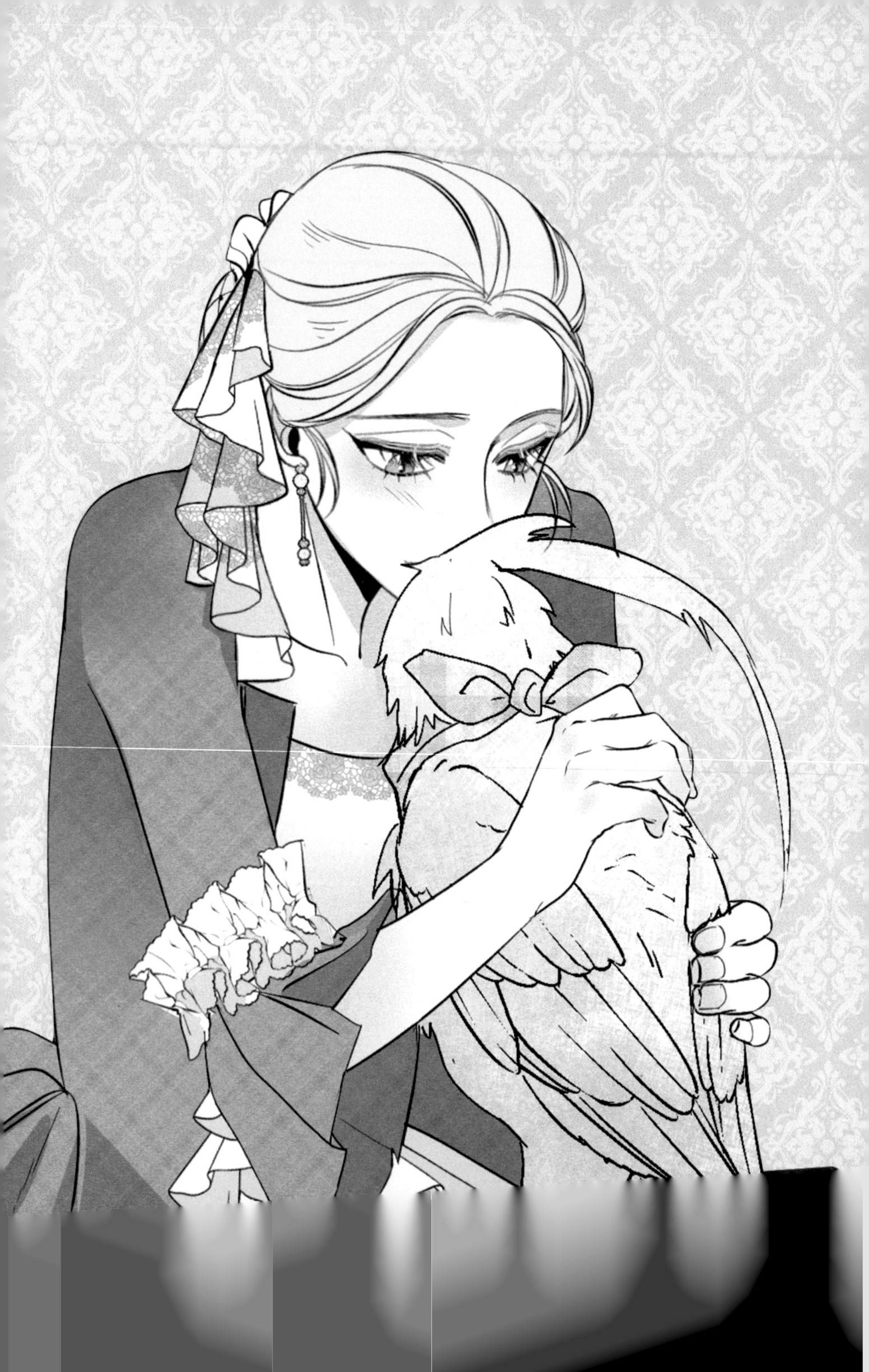

# The Remarried Empress

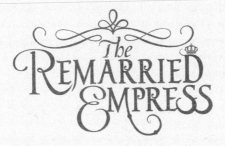

## - Table of Contents -

# The Remarried Empress

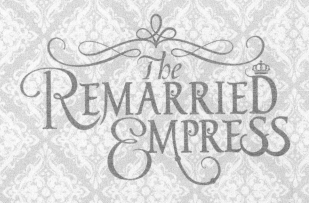

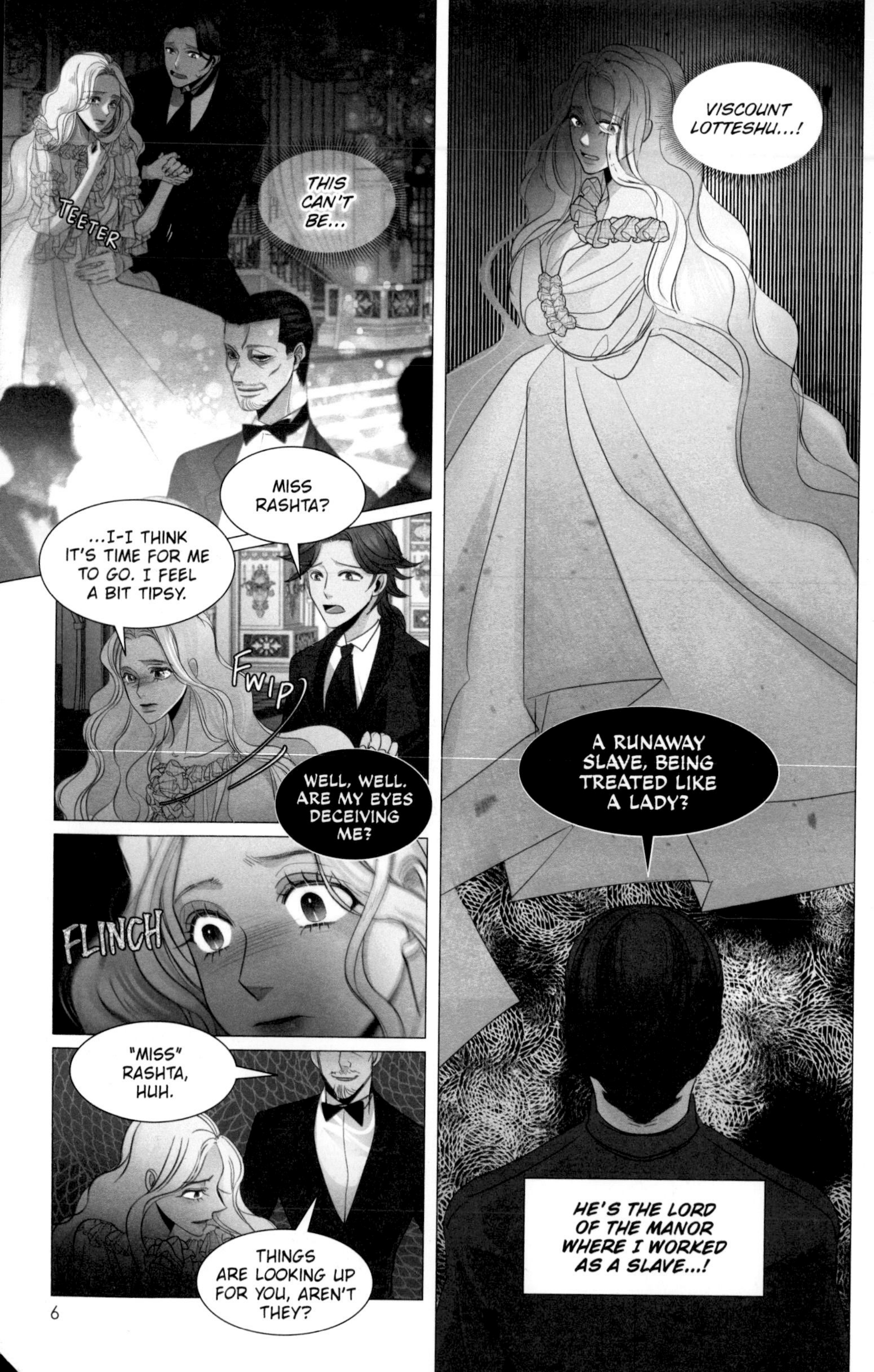
THIS CAN'T BE...
TEETER
MISS RASHTA?
...I-I THINK IT'S TIME FOR ME TO GO. I FEEL A BIT TIPSY.
FWIP
WELL, WELL. ARE MY EYES DECEIVING ME?
FLINCH
"MISS" RASHTA, HUH.
THINGS ARE LOOKING UP FOR YOU, AREN'T THEY?
VISCOUNT LOTTESHU...!
A RUNAWAY SLAVE, BEING TREATED LIKE A LADY?
HE'S THE LORD OF THE MANOR WHERE I WORKED AS A SLAVE...!

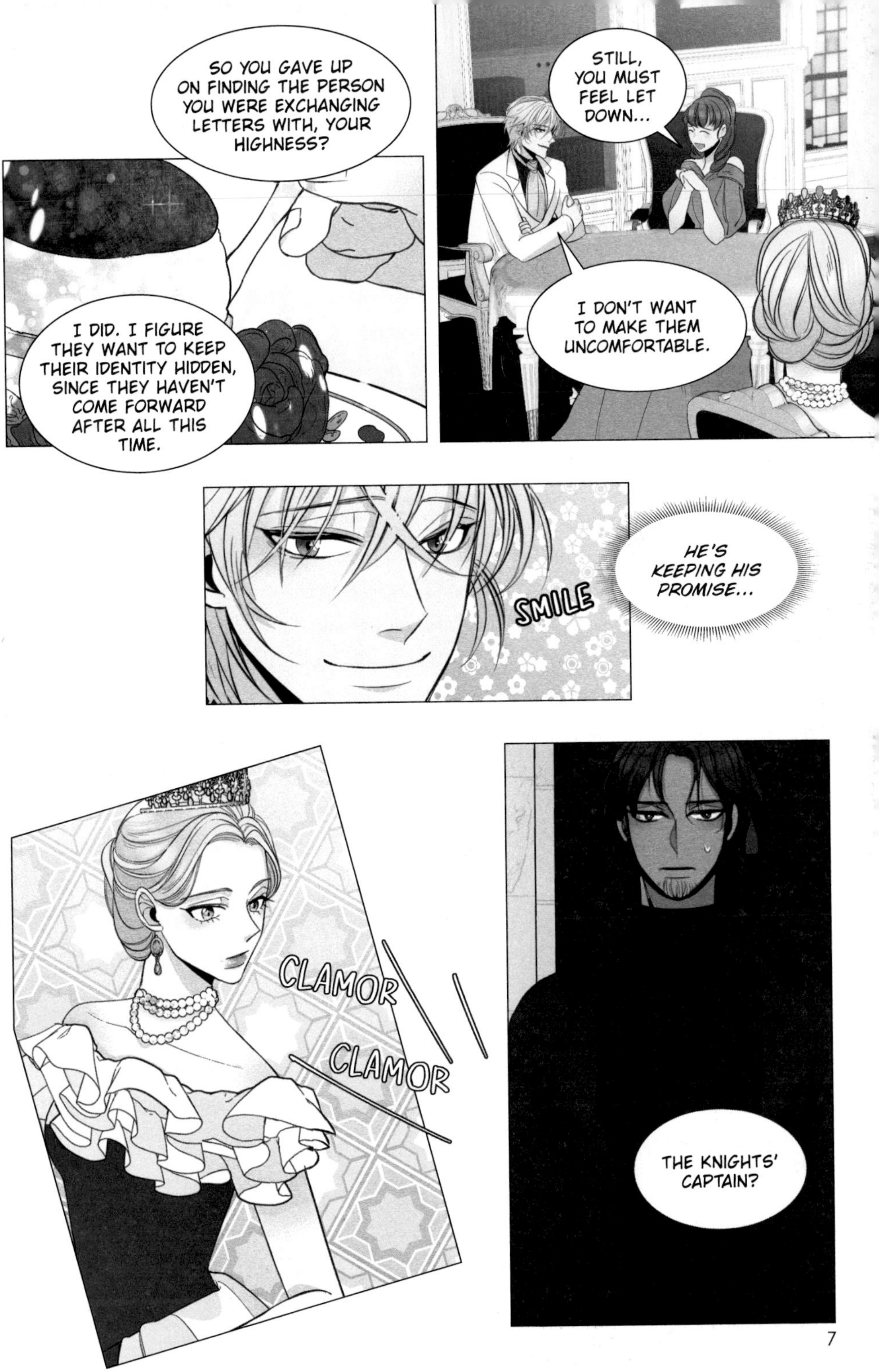
SO YOU GAVE UP ON FINDING THE PERSON YOU WERE EXCHANGING LETTERS WITH, YOUR HIGHNESS?
I DID. I FIGURE THEY WANT TO KEEP THEIR IDENTITY HIDDEN, SINCE THEY HAVEN'T COME FORWARD AFTER ALL THIS TIME.
STILL, YOU MUST FEEL LET DOWN...
I DON'T WANT TO MAKE THEM UNCOMFORTABLE.
SMILE
HE'S KEEPING HIS PROMISE...
CLAMOR
CLAMOR
THE KNIGHTS' CAPTAIN?

IT SEEMS YOU'RE NEEDED BRIEFLY IN THE GRAND BANQUET HALL, YOUR MAJESTY.

WHAT'S THE MATTER?

HESITATE

...WELL.

LET'S GO.

DID SOMETHING HAPPEN?

HE WOULD'VE TOLD ME IF I WAS NEEDED AS WELL.

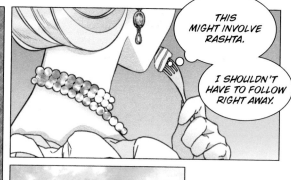

THIS MIGHT INVOLVE RASHTA.

I SHOULDN'T HAVE TO FOLLOW RIGHT AWAY.

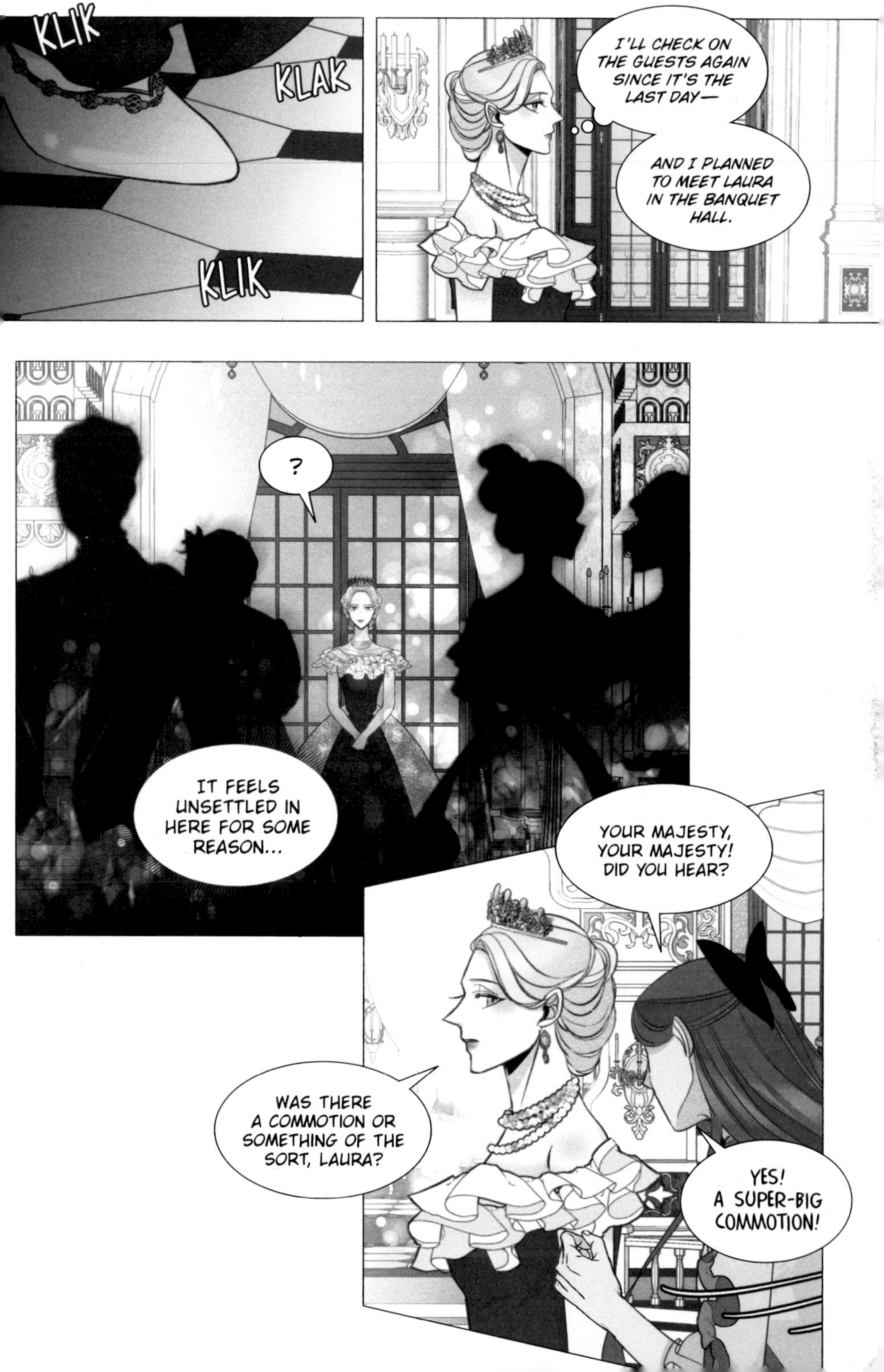
KLIK
KLAK
KLIK
I'LL CHECK ON THE GUESTS AGAIN SINCE IT'S THE LAST DAY—
AND I PLANNED TO MEET LAURA IN THE BANQUET HALL.
?
IT FEELS UNSETTLED IN HERE FOR SOME REASON...
YOUR MAJESTY, YOUR MAJESTY! DID YOU HEAR?
WAS THERE A COMMOTION OR SOMETHING OF THE SORT, LAURA?
YES! A SUPER-BIG COMMOTION!

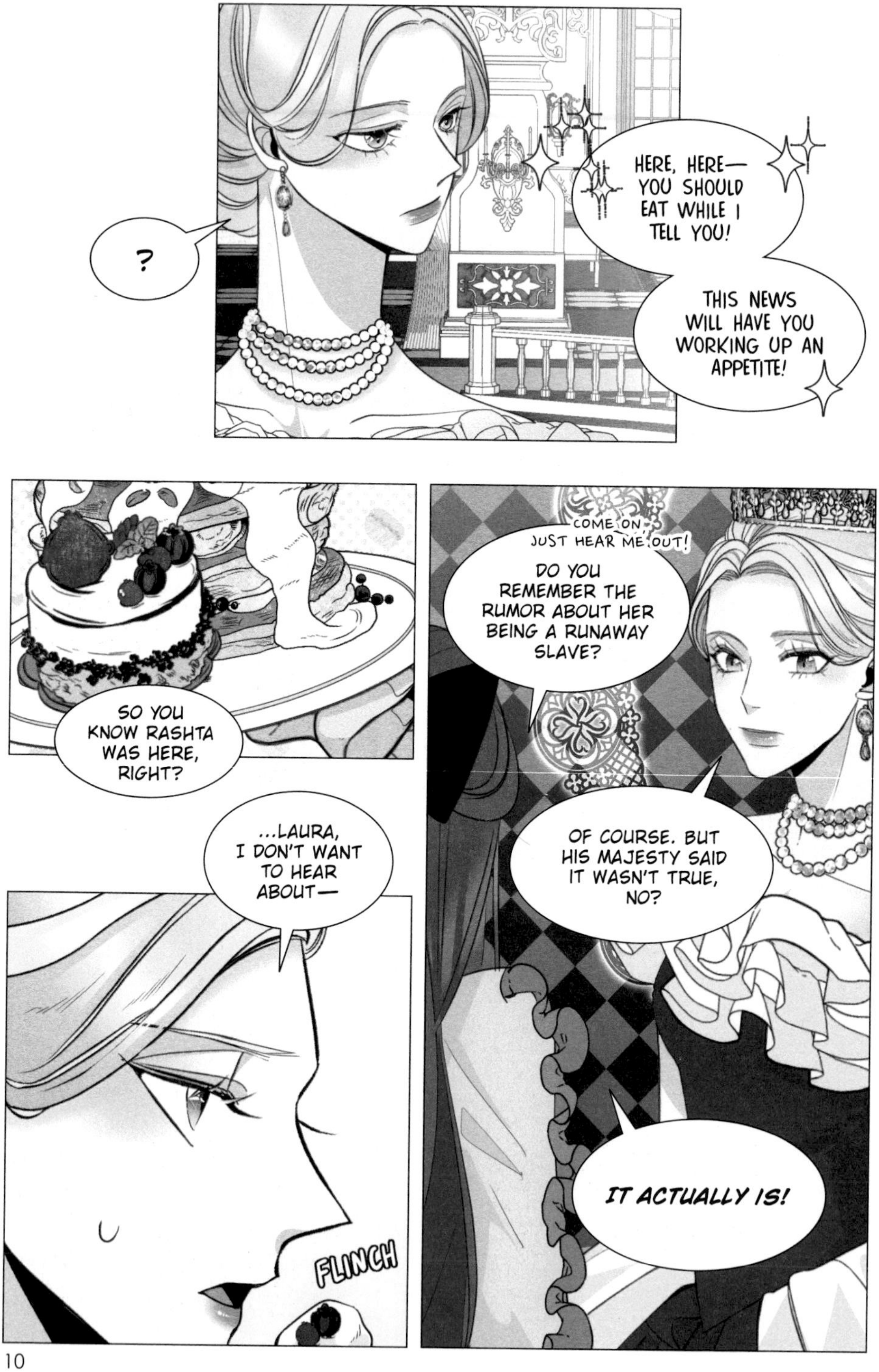
?
HERE, HERE— YOU SHOULD EAT WHILE I TELL YOU!
THIS NEWS WILL HAVE YOU WORKING UP AN APPETITE!
SO YOU KNOW RASHTA WAS HERE, RIGHT?
COME ON, JUST HEAR ME OUT!
DO YOU REMEMBER THE RUMOR ABOUT HER BEING A RUNAWAY SLAVE?
...LAURA, I DON'T WANT TO HEAR ABOUT—
FLINCH
OF COURSE. BUT HIS MAJESTY SAID IT WASN'T TRUE, NO?
IT ACTUALLY IS!

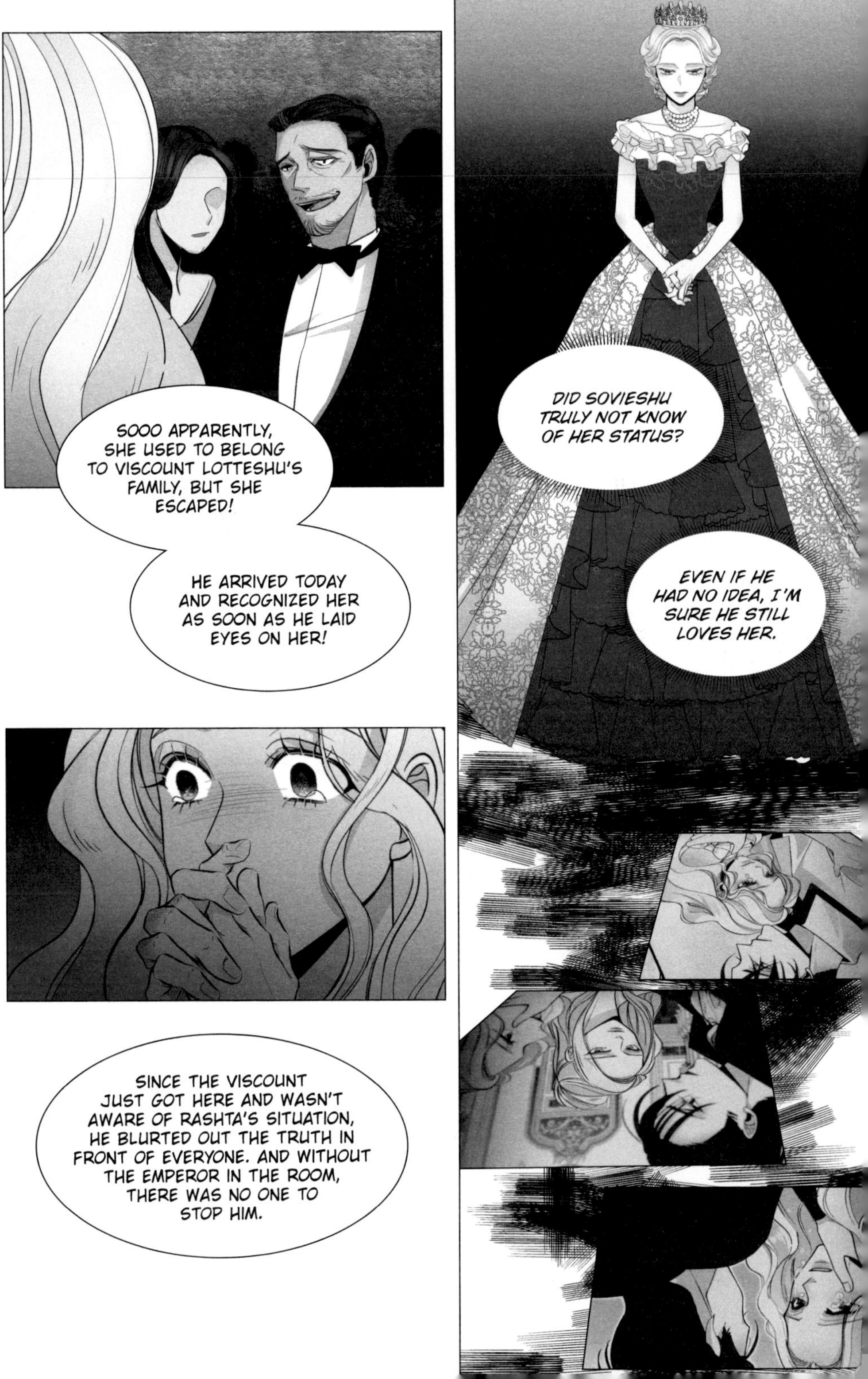
SOOO APPARENTLY, SHE USED TO BELONG TO VISCOUNT LOTTESHU'S FAMILY, BUT SHE ESCAPED!
HE ARRIVED TODAY AND RECOGNIZED HER AS SOON AS HE LAID EYES ON HER!
SINCE THE VISCOUNT JUST GOT HERE AND WASN'T AWARE OF RASHTA'S SITUATION, HE BLURTED OUT THE TRUTH IN FRONT OF EVERYONE. AND WITHOUT THE EMPEROR IN THE ROOM, THERE WAS NO ONE TO STOP HIM.
DID SOVIESHU TRULY NOT KNOW OF HER STATUS?
EVEN IF HE HAD NO IDEA, I'M SURE HE STILL LOVES HER.

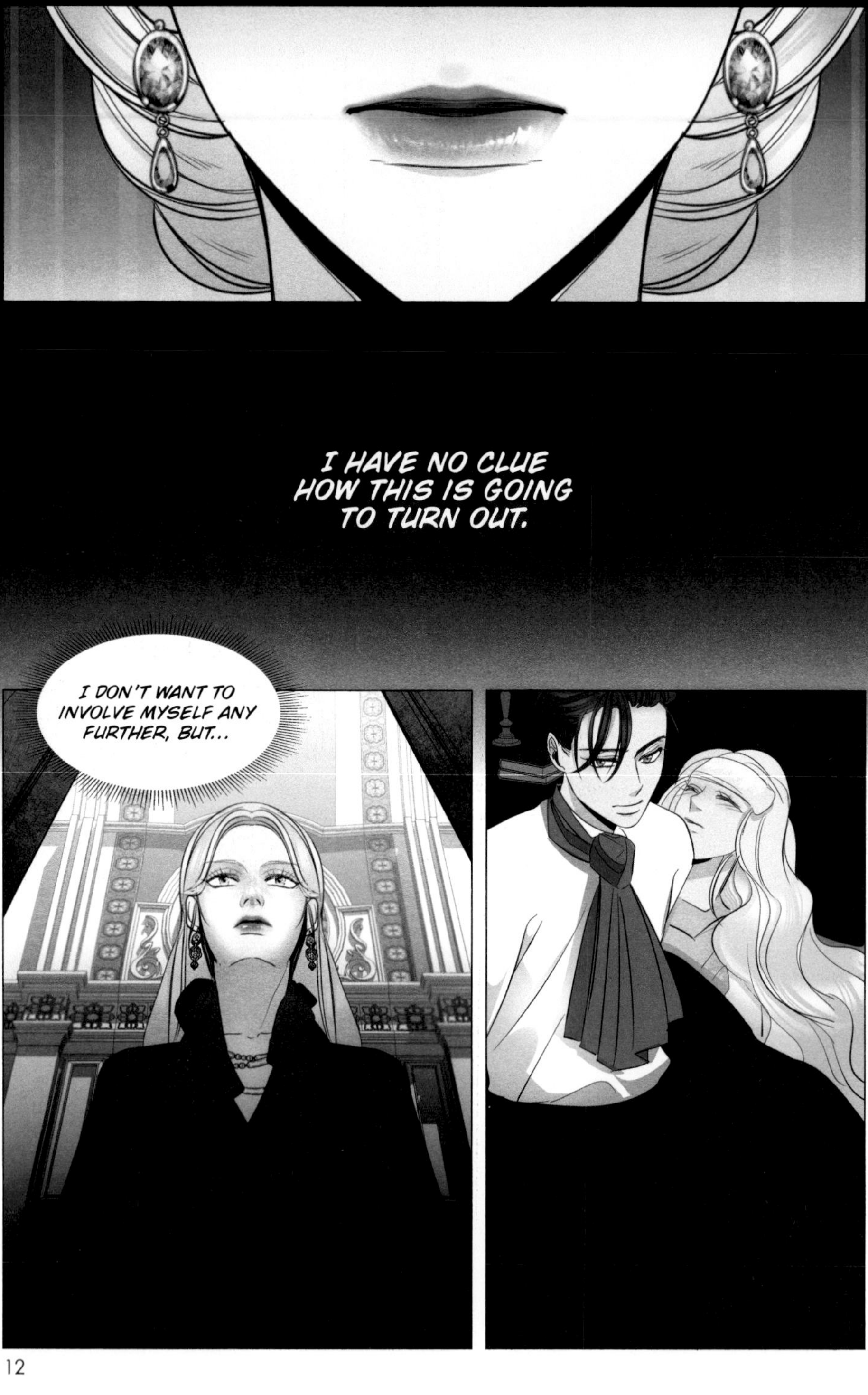
I HAVE NO CLUE HOW THIS IS GOING TO TURN OUT.
I DON'T WANT TO INVOLVE MYSELF ANY FURTHER, BUT...

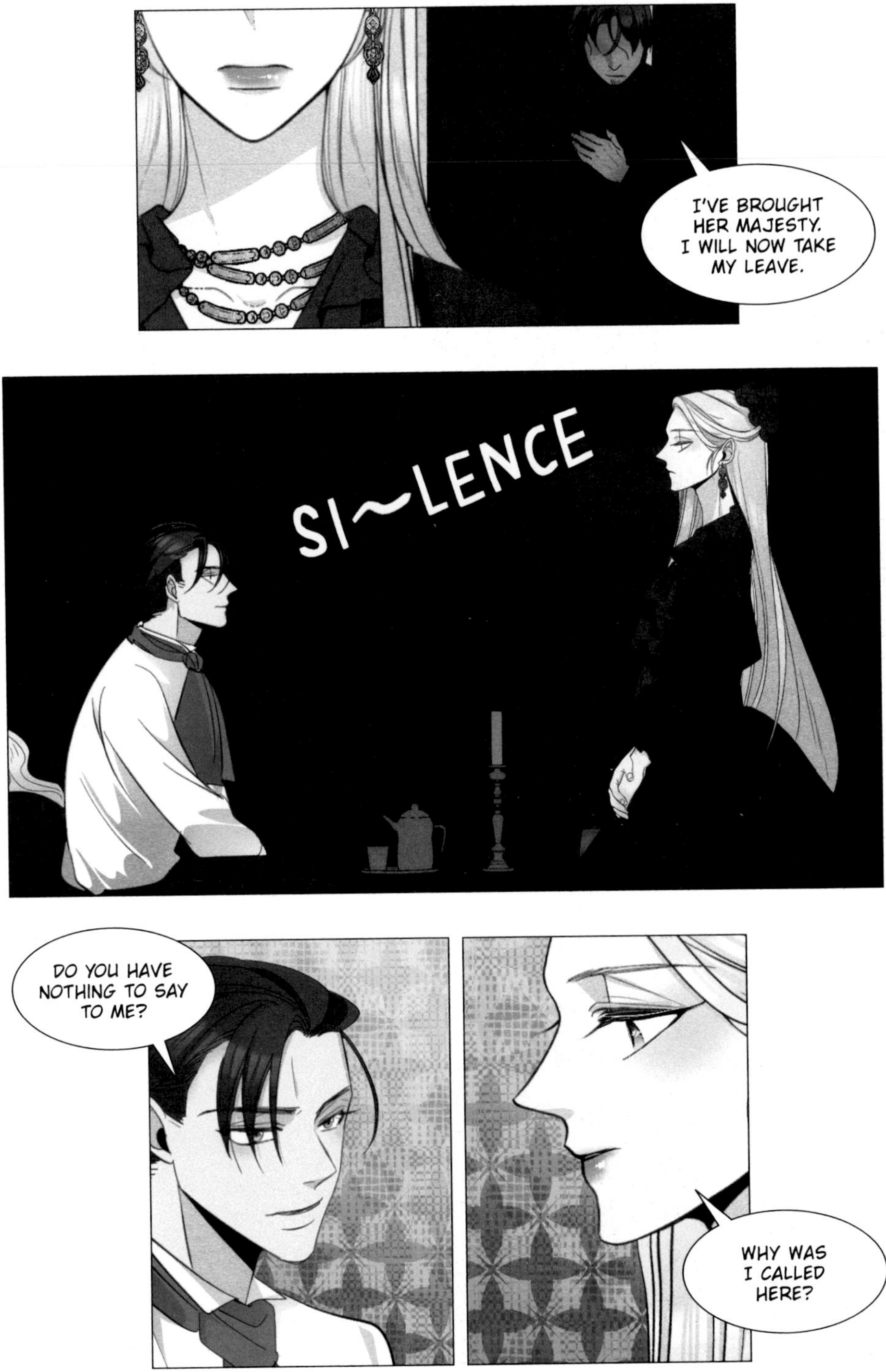
I'VE BROUGHT HER MAJESTY. I WILL NOW TAKE MY LEAVE.
SI~LENCE
DO YOU HAVE NOTHING TO SAY TO ME?
WHY WAS I CALLED HERE?

I SEE YOU'RE NOT FAZED IN THE SLIGHTEST BY RECENT EVENTS.

YOU WERE BORN THE DAUGHTER OF A HIGH-RANKING NOBLE FAMILY.

IS THAT HOW IT LOOKS TO HIM?

YOU HAVE WEALTH, POWER, WIT, AND LOOKS. AND NOW, YOU ARE EVEN THE EMPRESS.

I MUST NOT BE LETTING ANYTHING SHOW ON MY FACE.

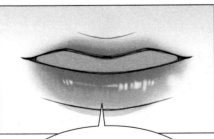

ON THE OTHER HAND, RASHTA STARTED OUT WITH NOTHING.

I HEARD ABOUT WHAT HAPPENED WITH MISS RASHTA. I UNDERSTAND YOUR MAJESTY IS UPSET, BUT THERE'S NO REASON TO TAKE IT OUT ON ME.

SHE IS CLEVER AND BEAUTIFUL, BUT NEVER HAD AS MUCH AS A CHANCE TO SHOW IT.

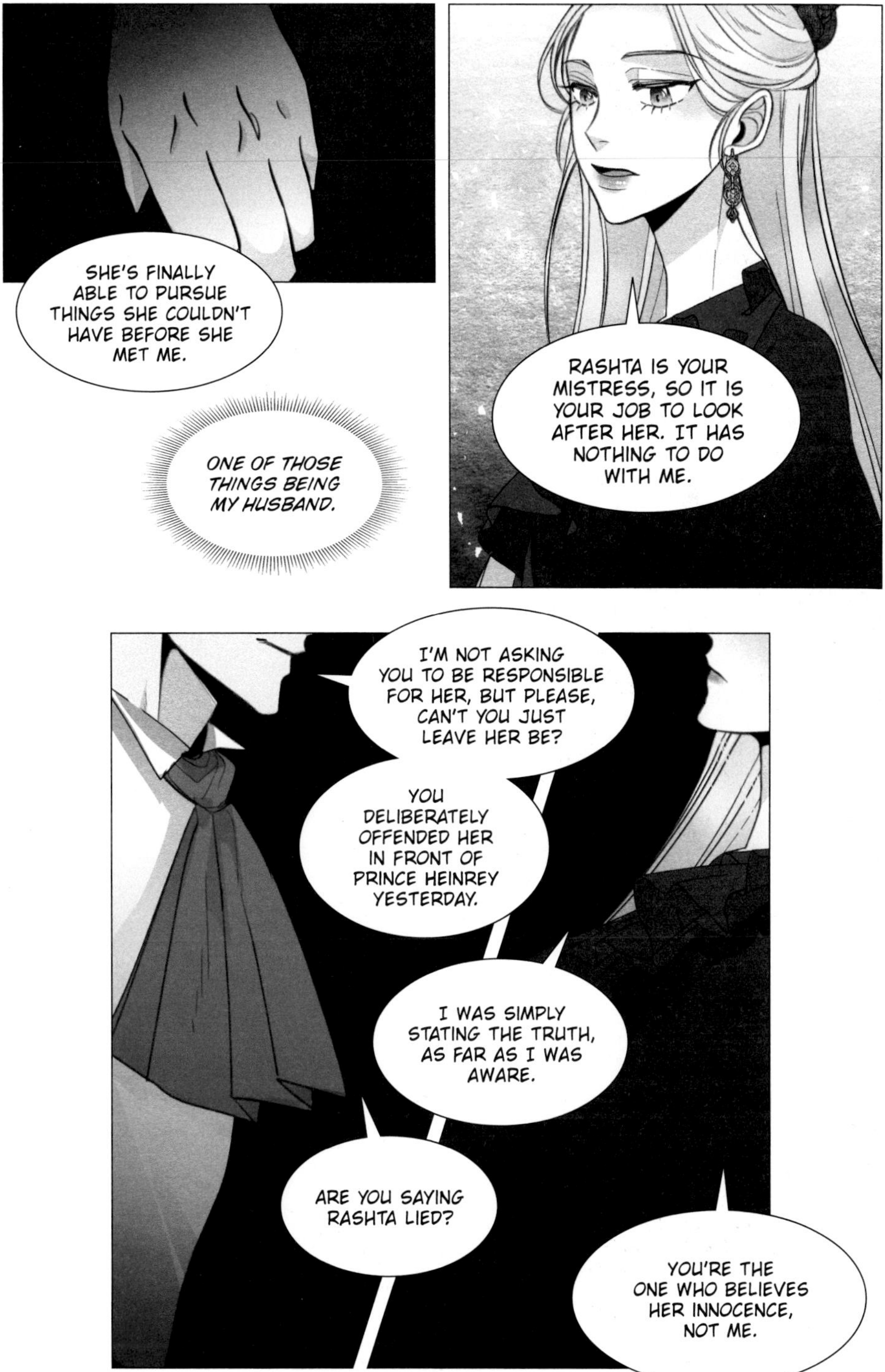
SHE'S FINALLY ABLE TO PURSUE THINGS SHE COULDN'T HAVE BEFORE SHE MET ME.
ONE OF THOSE THINGS BEING MY HUSBAND.
RASHTA IS YOUR MISTRESS, SO IT IS YOUR JOB TO LOOK AFTER HER. IT HAS NOTHING TO DO WITH ME.
I'M NOT ASKING YOU TO BE RESPONSIBLE FOR HER, BUT PLEASE, CAN'T YOU JUST LEAVE HER BE?
YOU DELIBERATELY OFFENDED HER IN FRONT OF PRINCE HEINREY YESTERDAY.
I WAS SIMPLY STATING THE TRUTH, AS FAR AS I WAS AWARE.
ARE YOU SAYING RASHTA LIED?
YOU'RE THE ONE WHO BELIEVES HER INNOCENCE, NOT ME.

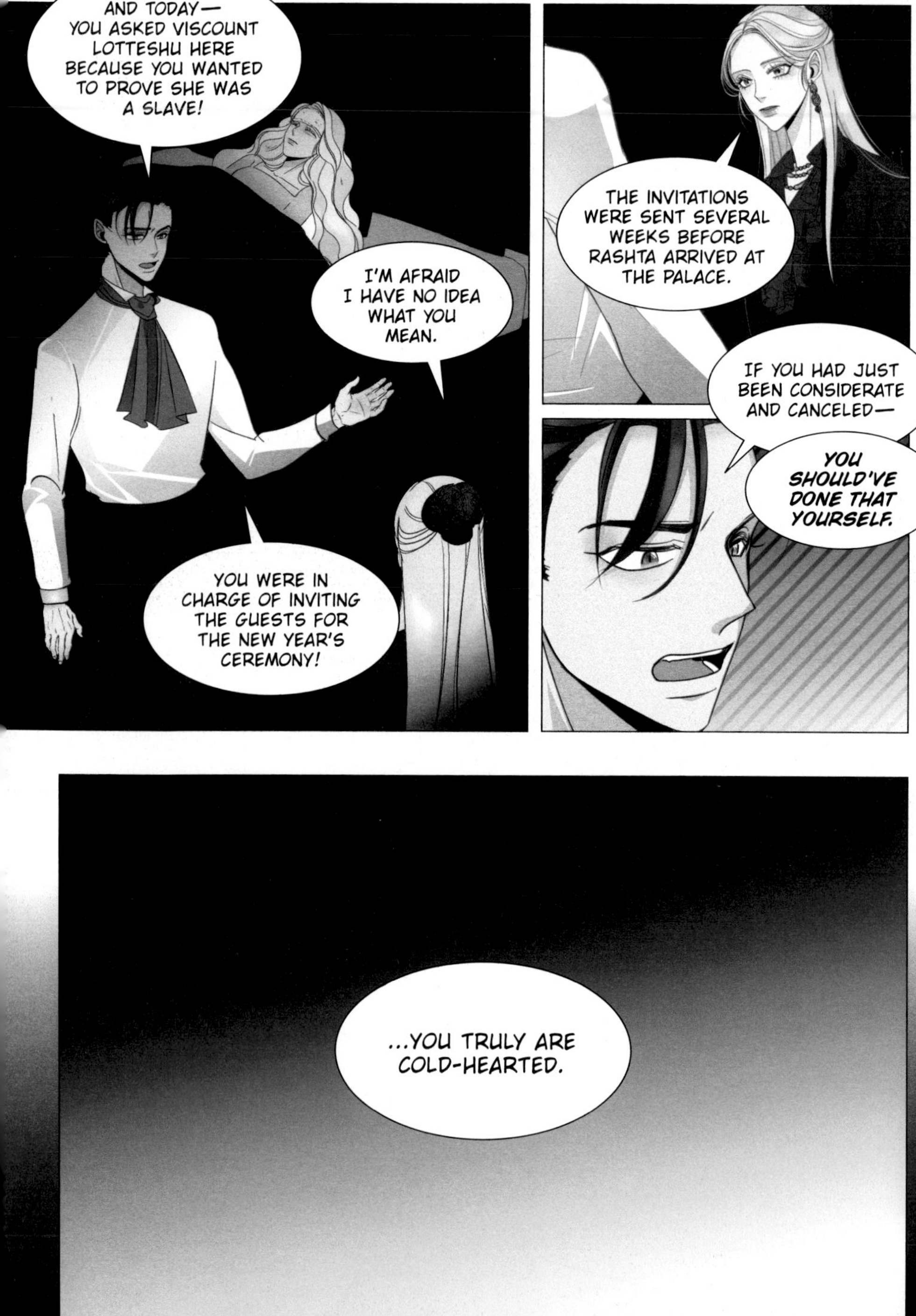
AND TODAY— YOU ASKED VISCOUNT LOTTESHU HERE BECAUSE YOU WANTED TO PROVE SHE WAS A SLAVE!
I'M AFRAID I HAVE NO IDEA WHAT YOU MEAN.
YOU WERE IN CHARGE OF INVITING THE GUESTS FOR THE NEW YEAR'S CEREMONY!
THE INVITATIONS WERE SENT SEVERAL WEEKS BEFORE RASHTA ARRIVED AT THE PALACE.
IF YOU HAD JUST BEEN CONSIDERATE AND CANCELED—
*YOU SHOULD'VE DONE THAT YOURSELF.*
...YOU TRULY ARE COLD-HEARTED.

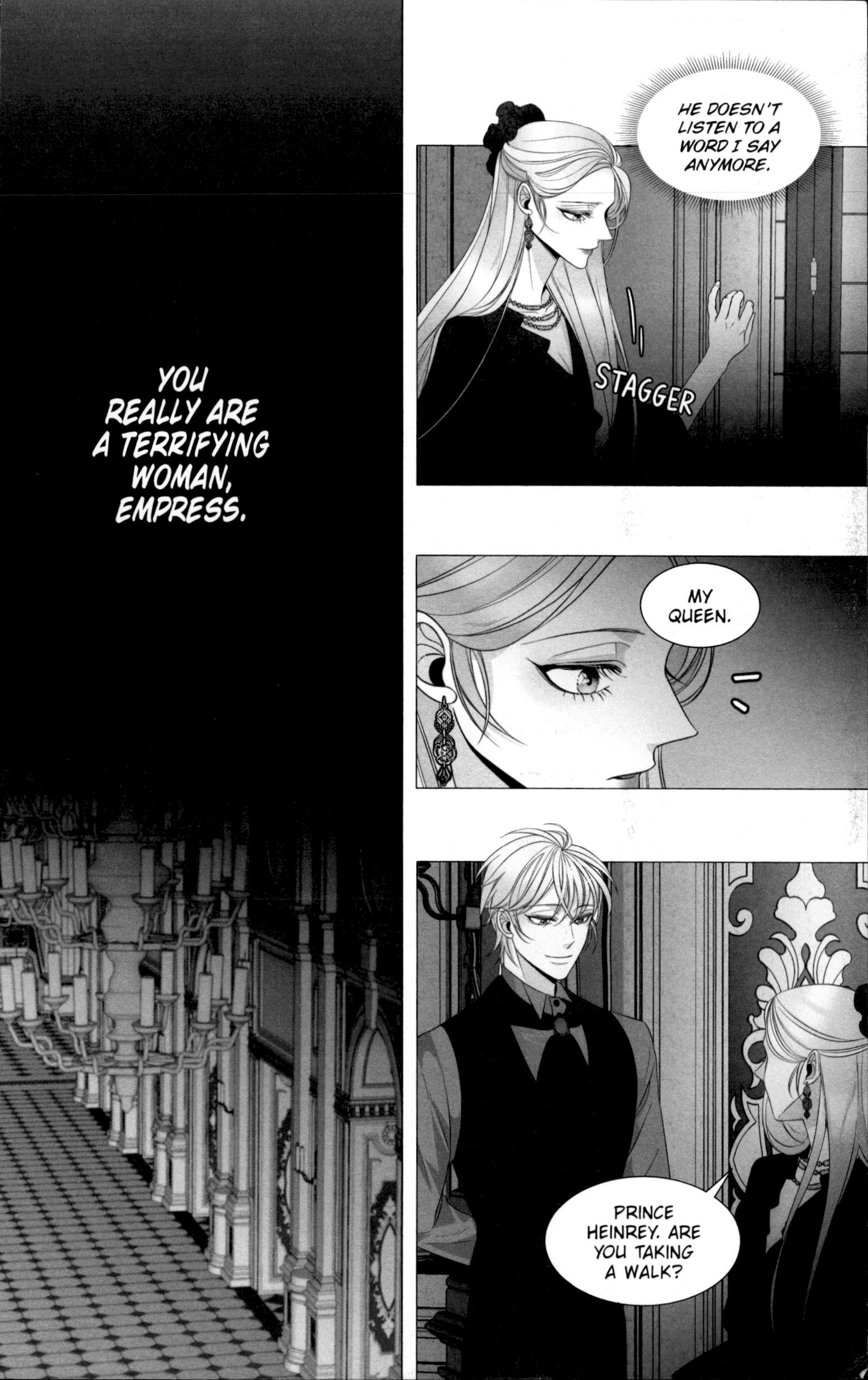
YOU REALLY ARE A TERRIFYING WOMAN, EMPRESS.
HE DOESN'T LISTEN TO A WORD I SAY ANYMORE.
STAGGER
MY QUEEN.
PRINCE HEINREY. ARE YOU TAKING A WALK?

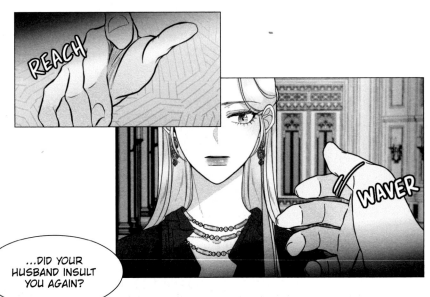

REACH

WAVER

...DID YOUR HUSBAND INSULT YOU AGAIN?

SQUEEZE

"AGAIN"?

I SHOULD'VE MET YOU FIRST.

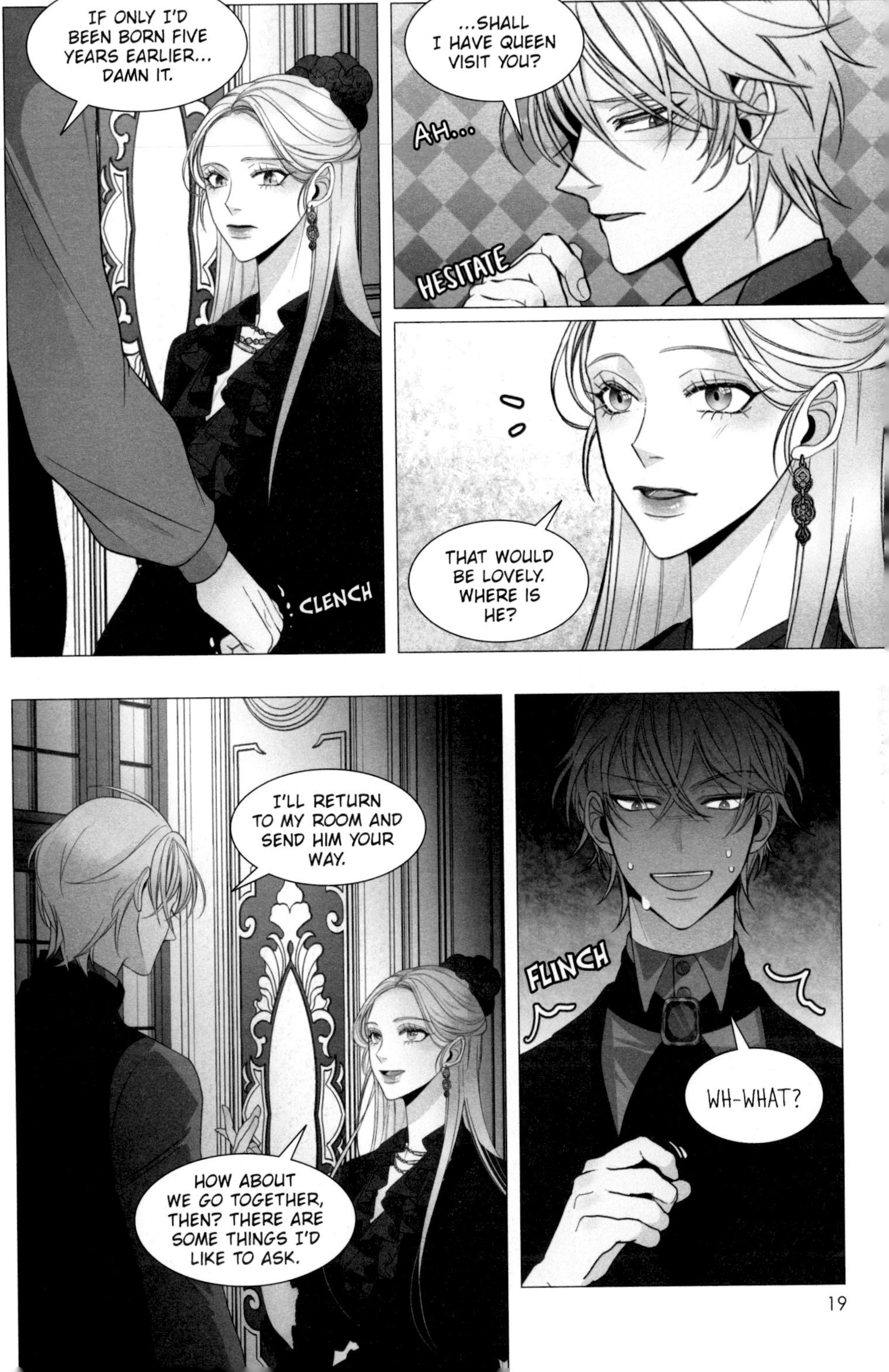
IF ONLY I'D BEEN BORN FIVE YEARS EARLIER... DAMN IT.
CLENCH
...SHALL I HAVE QUEEN VISIT YOU?
AH...
HESITATE
THAT WOULD BE LOVELY. WHERE IS HE?
I'LL RETURN TO MY ROOM AND SEND HIM YOUR WAY.
HOW ABOUT WE GO TOGETHER, THEN? THERE ARE SOME THINGS I'D LIKE TO ASK.
FLINCH
WH-WHAT?

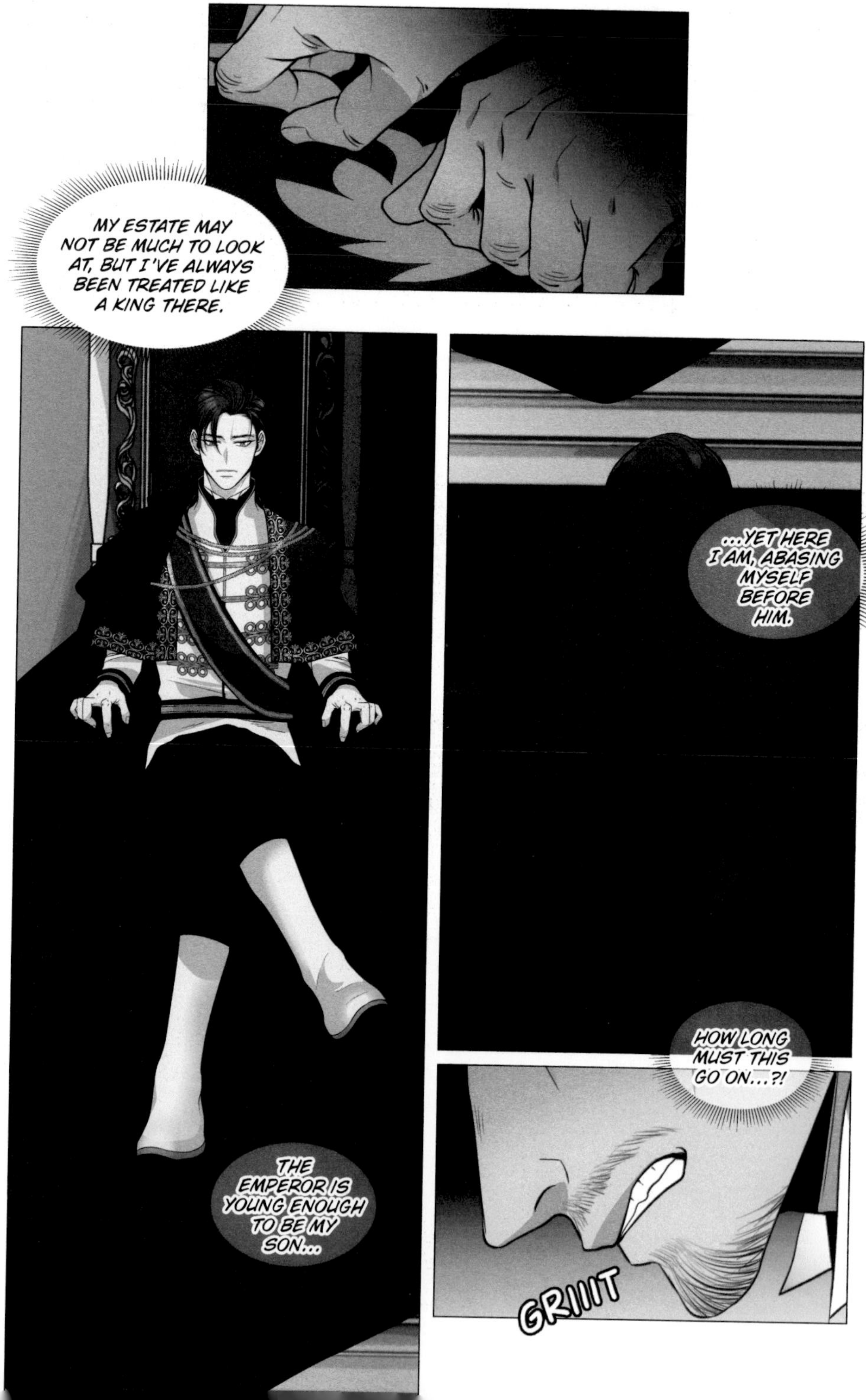
MY ESTATE MAY NOT BE MUCH TO LOOK AT, BUT I'VE ALWAYS BEEN TREATED LIKE A KING THERE.
THE EMPEROR IS YOUNG ENOUGH TO BE MY SON...
...YET HERE I AM, ABASING MYSELF BEFORE HIM.
HOW LONG MUST THIS GO ON...?!
GRIIIT

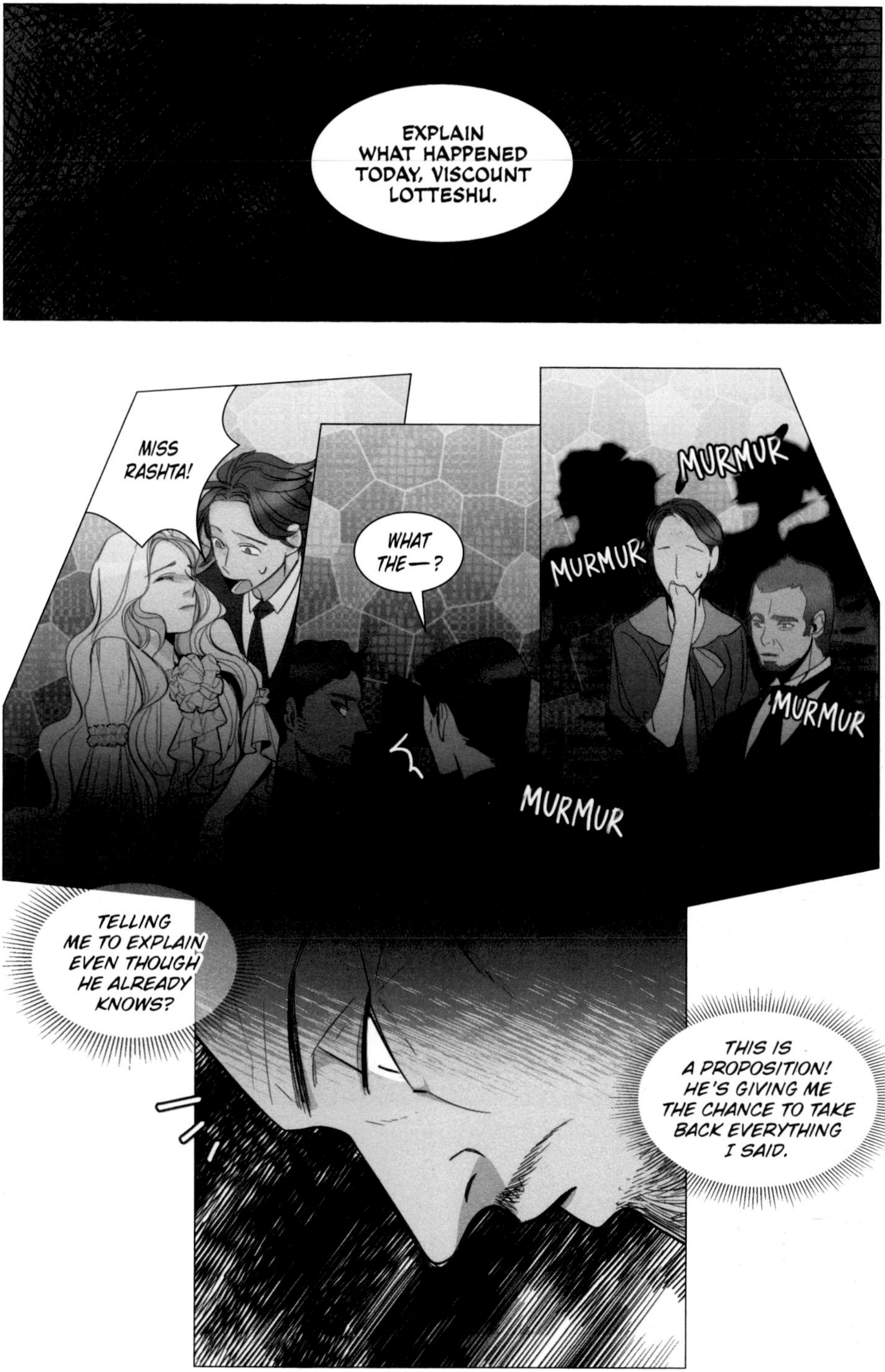
EXPLAIN WHAT HAPPENED TODAY, VISCOUNT LOTTESHU.
MISS RASHTA!
WHAT THE—?
MURMUR
MURMUR
MURMUR
MURMUR
TELLING ME TO EXPLAIN EVEN THOUGH HE ALREADY KNOWS?
THIS IS A PROPOSITION! HE'S GIVING ME THE CHANCE TO TAKE BACK EVERYTHING I SAID.

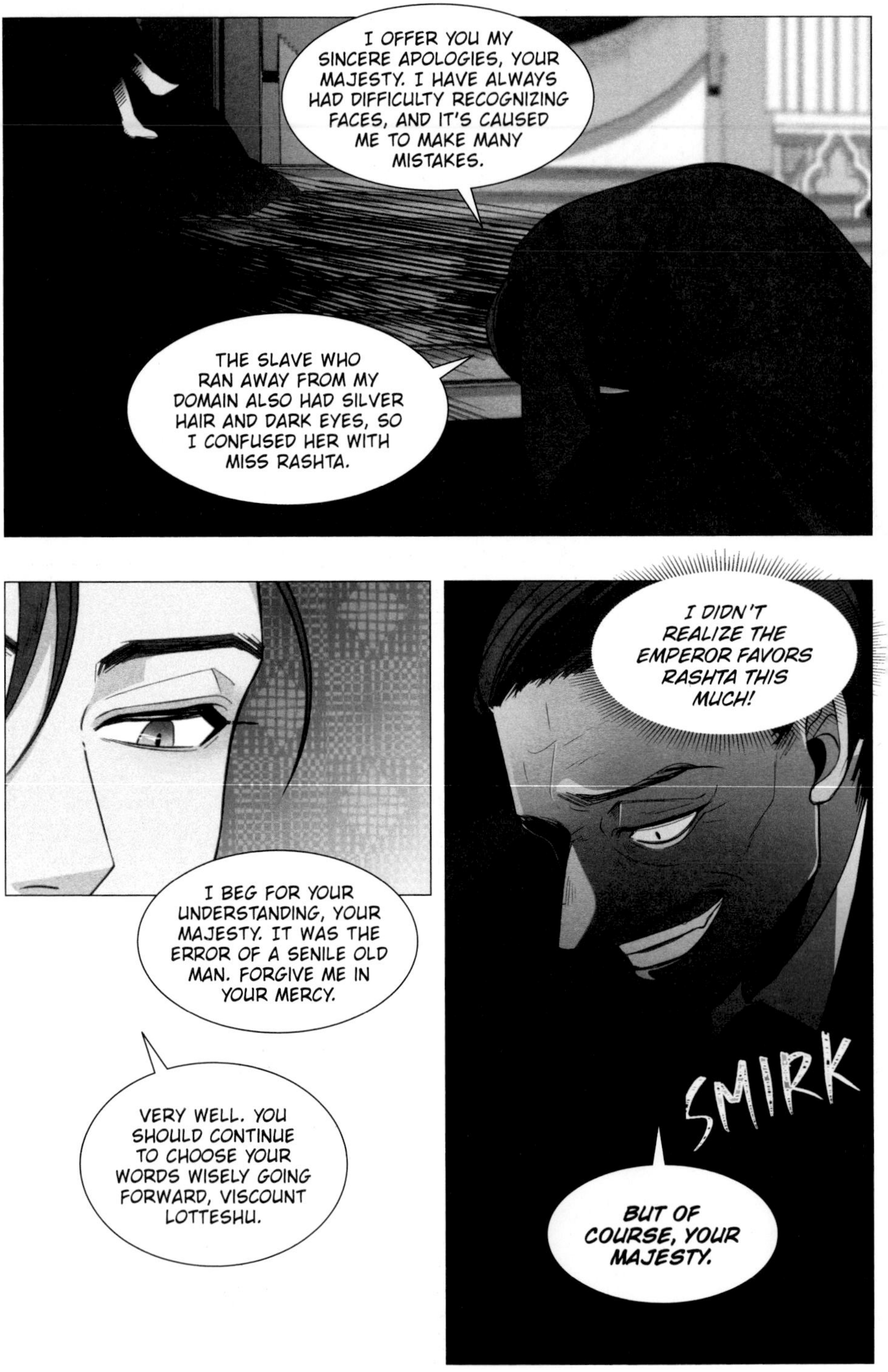
I OFFER YOU MY SINCERE APOLOGIES, YOUR MAJESTY. I HAVE ALWAYS HAD DIFFICULTY RECOGNIZING FACES, AND IT'S CAUSED ME TO MAKE MANY MISTAKES.
THE SLAVE WHO RAN AWAY FROM MY DOMAIN ALSO HAD SILVER HAIR AND DARK EYES, SO I CONFUSED HER WITH MISS RASHTA.
I BEG FOR YOUR UNDERSTANDING, YOUR MAJESTY. IT WAS THE ERROR OF A SENILE OLD MAN. FORGIVE ME IN YOUR MERCY.
VERY WELL. YOU SHOULD CONTINUE TO CHOOSE YOUR WORDS WISELY GOING FORWARD, VISCOUNT LOTTESHU.
I DIDN'T REALIZE THE EMPEROR FAVORS RASHTA THIS MUCH!
SMIRK
BUT OF COURSE, YOUR MAJESTY.

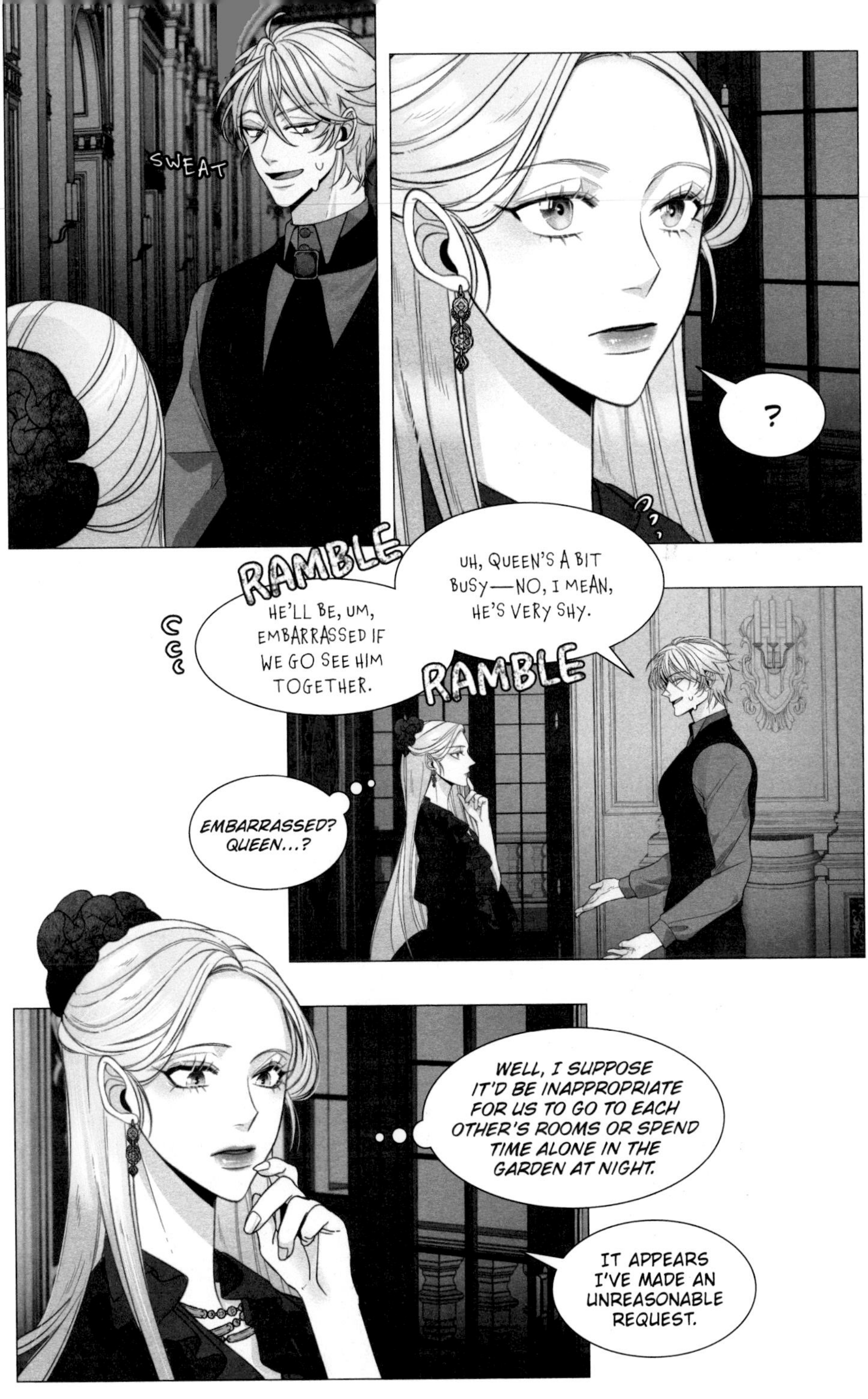
SWEAT
?
RAMBLE
UH, QUEEN'S A BIT BUSY—NO, I MEAN, HE'S VERY SHY.
HE'LL BE, UM, EMBARRASSED IF WE GO SEE HIM TOGETHER.
RAMBLE
EMBARRASSED? QUEEN...?
WELL, I SUPPOSE IT'D BE INAPPROPRIATE FOR US TO GO TO EACH OTHER'S ROOMS OR SPEND TIME ALONE IN THE GARDEN AT NIGHT.
IT APPEARS I'VE MADE AN UNREASONABLE REQUEST.

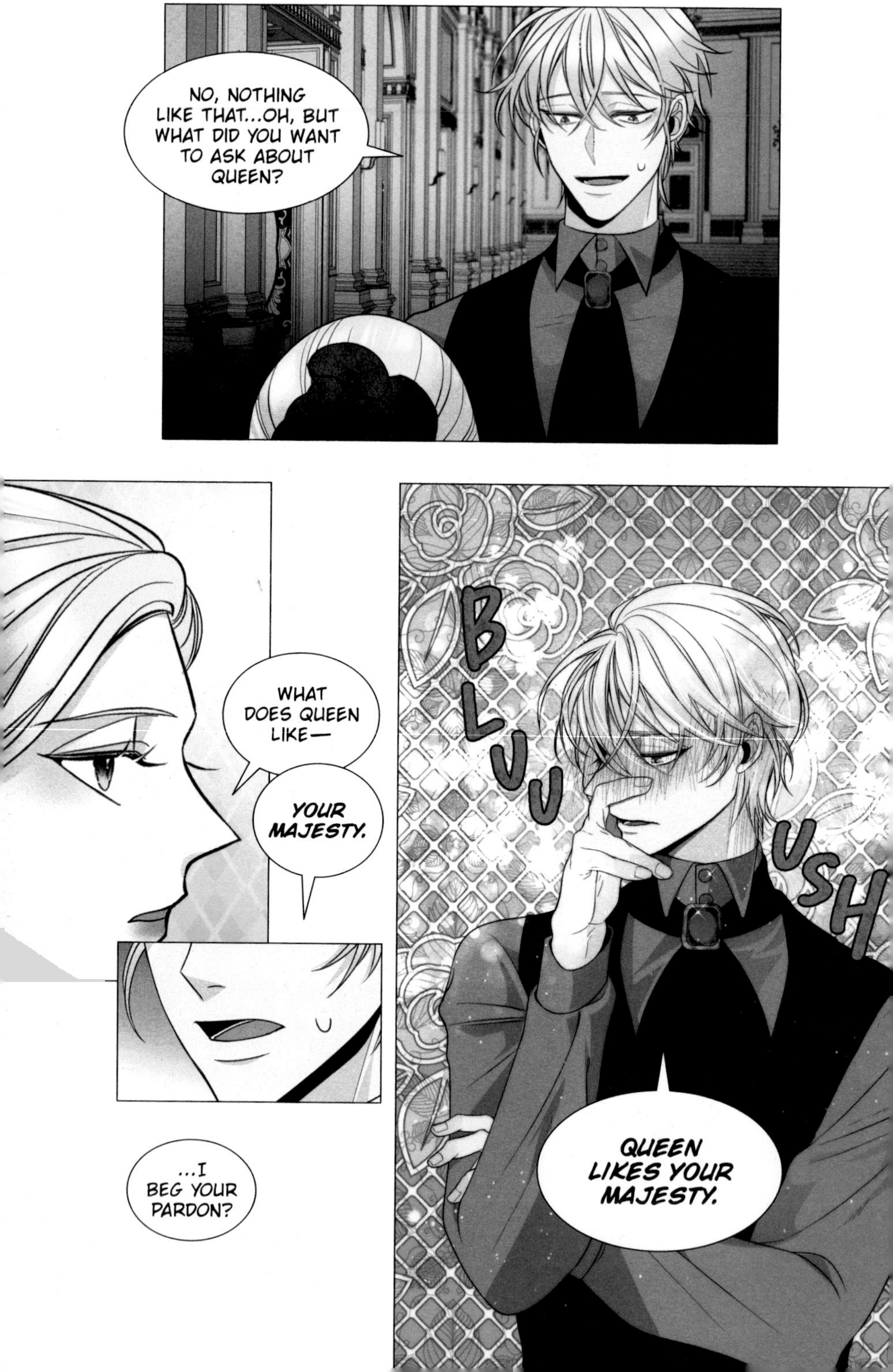
NO, NOTHING LIKE THAT...OH, BUT WHAT DID YOU WANT TO ASK ABOUT QUEEN?
WHAT DOES QUEEN LIKE—
YOUR MAJESTY.
...I BEG YOUR PARDON?
BLUUUSH
QUEEN LIKES YOUR MAJESTY.

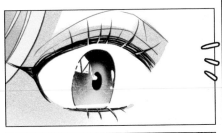

FLUSH

I WANTED TO KNOW WHAT QUEEN LIKES *TO EAT.*

OH... TO EAT.

HEH.

HE MUST BE FLUSTERED, DESCRIBING A BIRD LIKE A HUMAN.

PLEASE TELL HIM I APPRECIATE IT. BUT THAT WASN'T WHAT I INTENDED TO ASK.

QUEEN'S A GOOD BIRD, SO HE'LL LIKE WHATEVER YOUR MAJESTY GIVES HIM.

HUH? BUT STILL...

I'LL GO SEND HIM TO YOU NOW.

AH, OKAY...

25

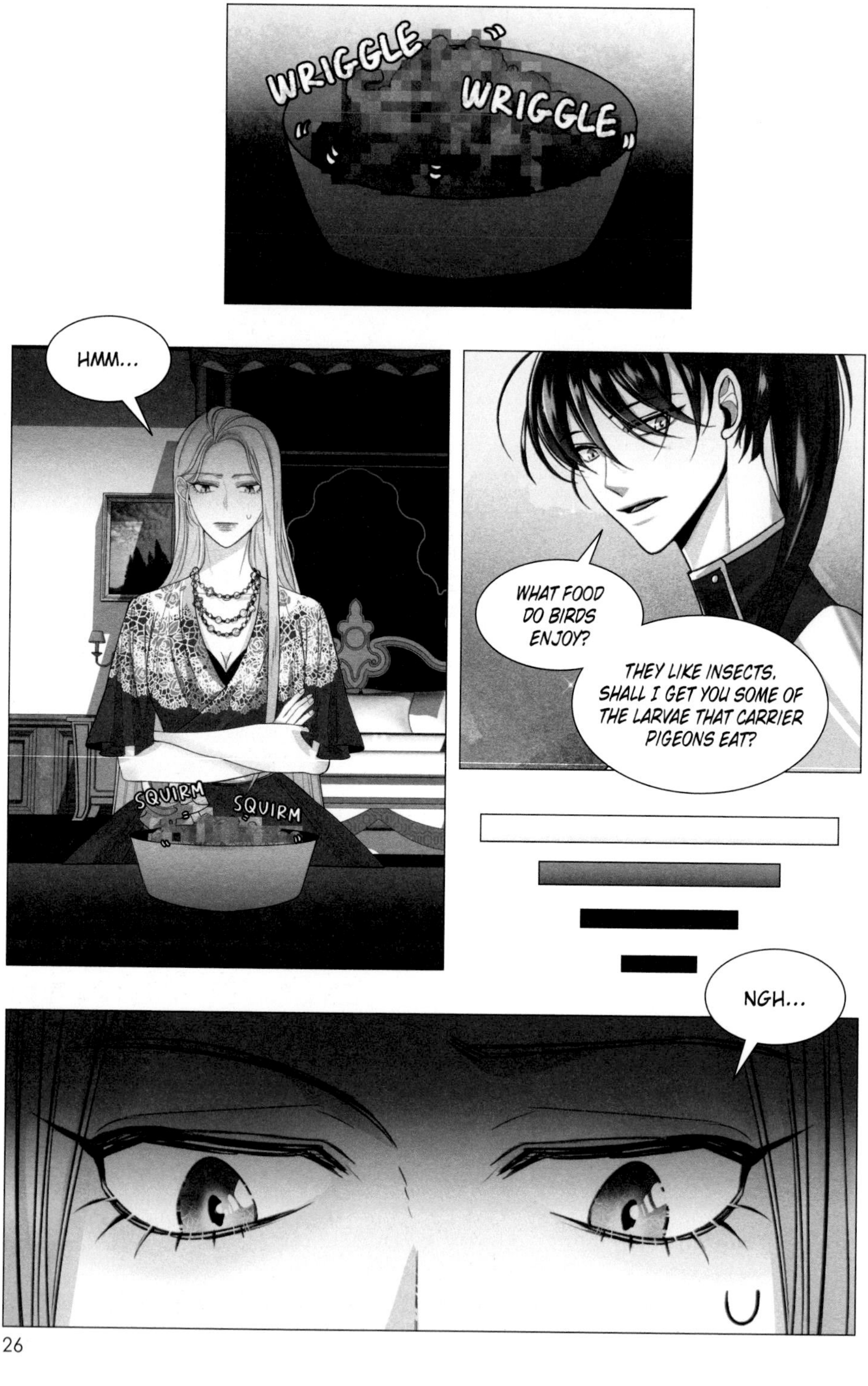
WRIGGLE
WRIGGLE
HMM...
SQUIRM
SQUIRM
WHAT FOOD DO BIRDS ENJOY?
THEY LIKE INSECTS. SHALL I GET YOU SOME OF THE LARVAE THAT CARRIER PIGEONS EAT?
NGH...

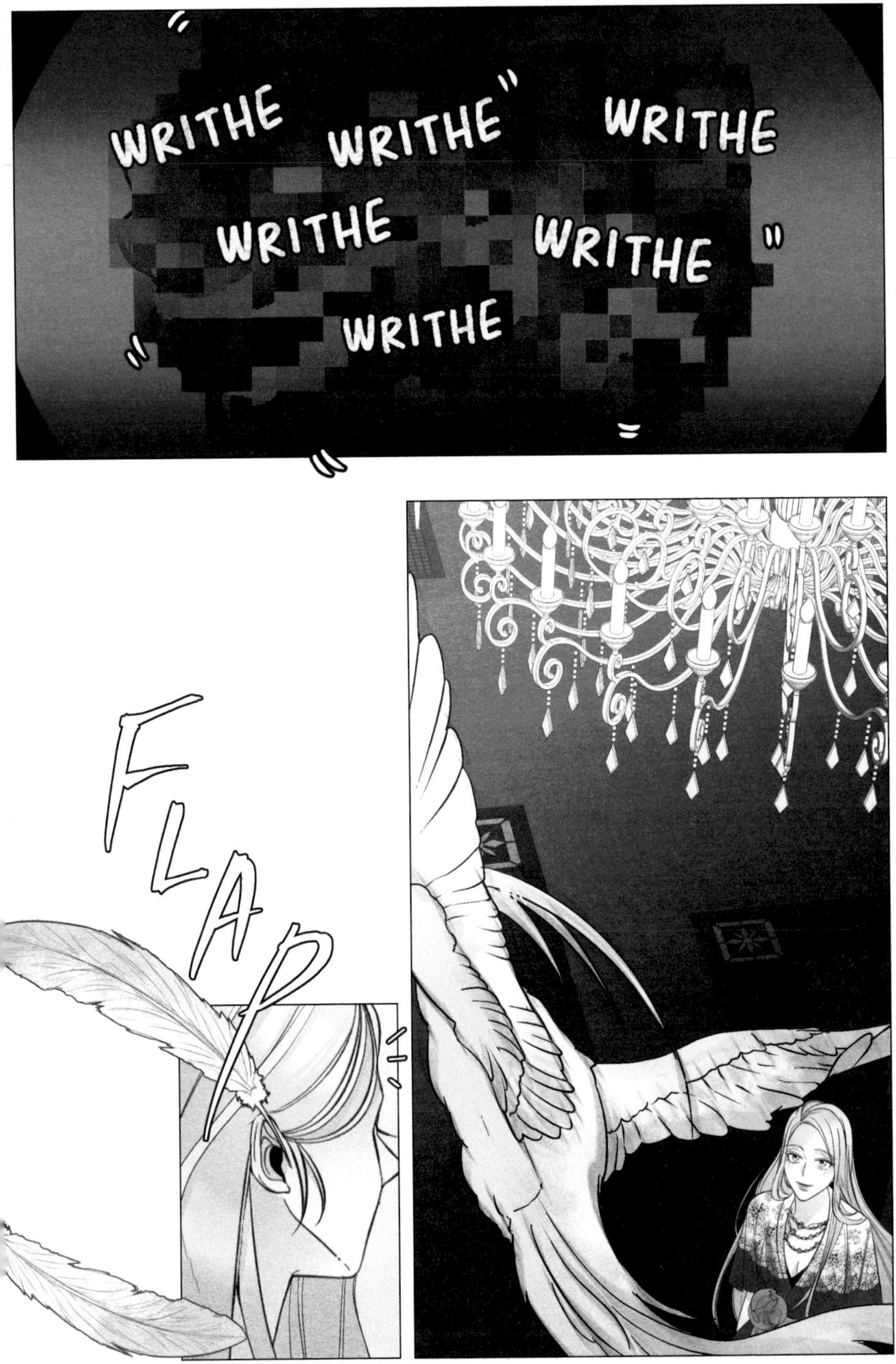
WRITHE
WRITHE
WRITHE
WRITHE
WRITHE
WRITHE
FLAP

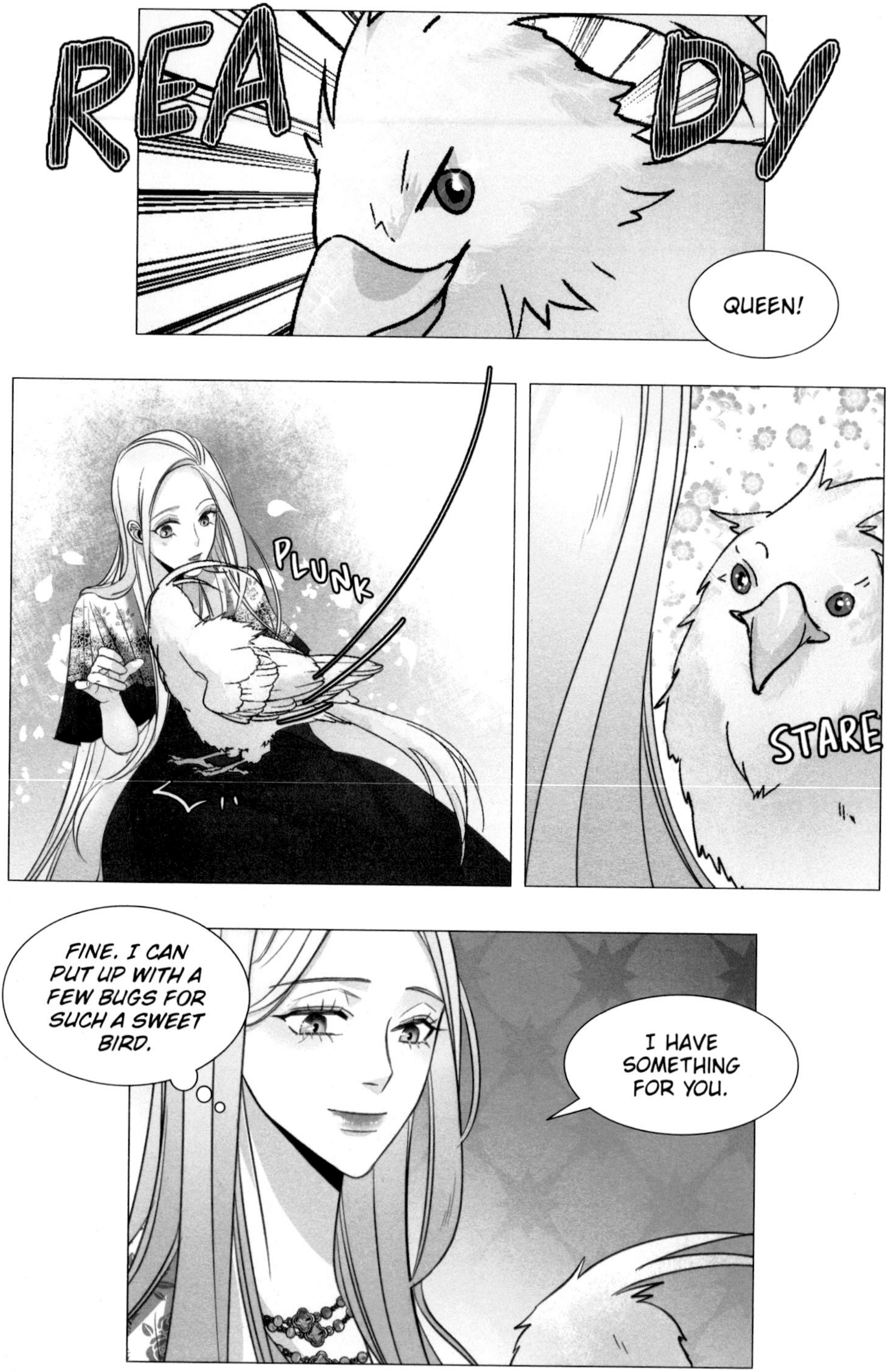
READY
QUEEN!
PLUNK
STARE
FINE. I CAN PUT UP WITH A FEW BUGS FOR SUCH A SWEET BIRD.
I HAVE SOMETHING FOR YOU.

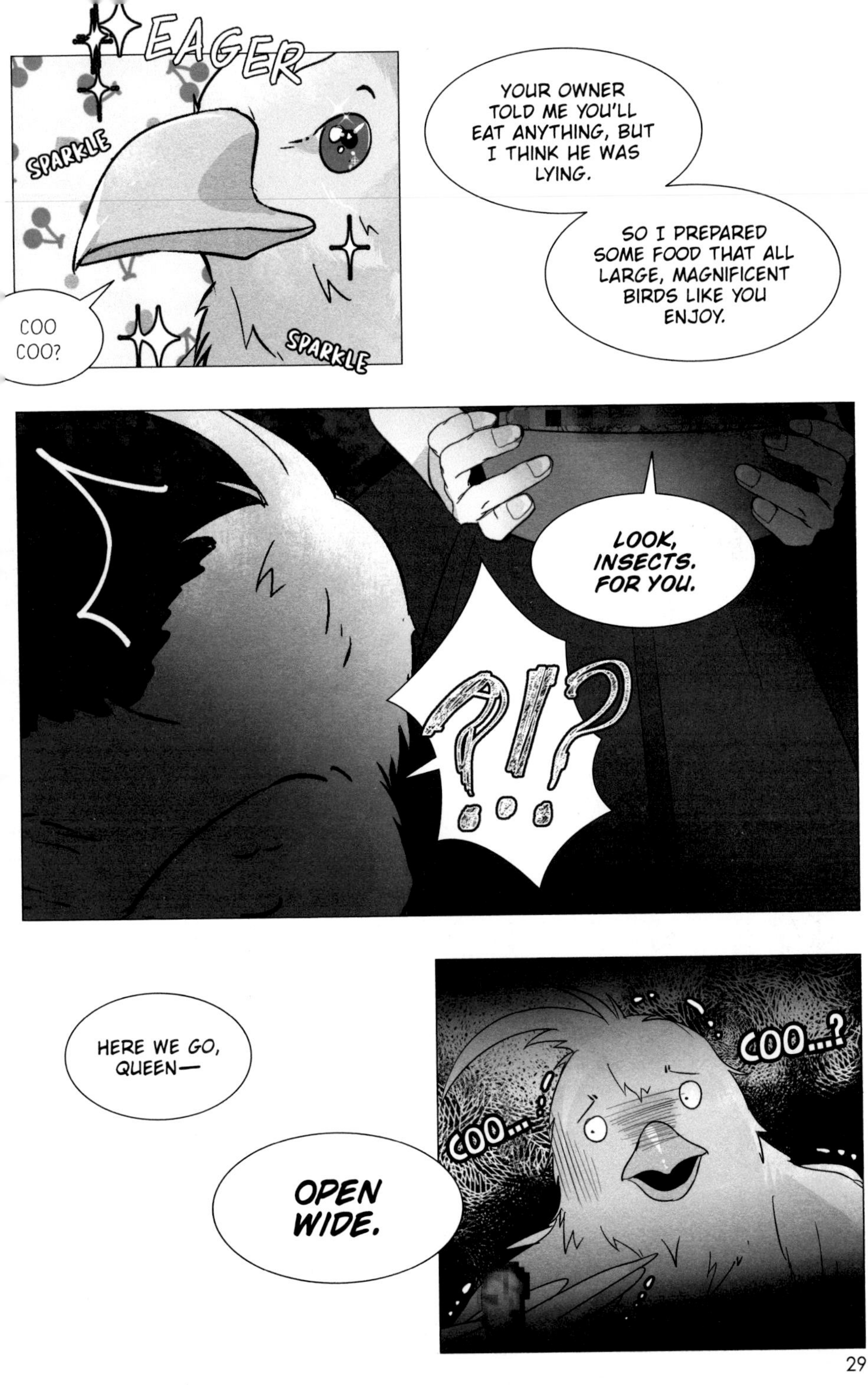
EAGER
SPARKLE
SPARKLE
COO COO?
YOUR OWNER TOLD ME YOU'LL EAT ANYTHING, BUT I THINK HE WAS LYING.
SO I PREPARED SOME FOOD THAT ALL LARGE, MAGNIFICENT BIRDS LIKE YOU ENJOY.
LOOK, INSECTS. FOR YOU.
?!?...
HERE WE GO, QUEEN—
OPEN WIDE.
COO...?
COO...

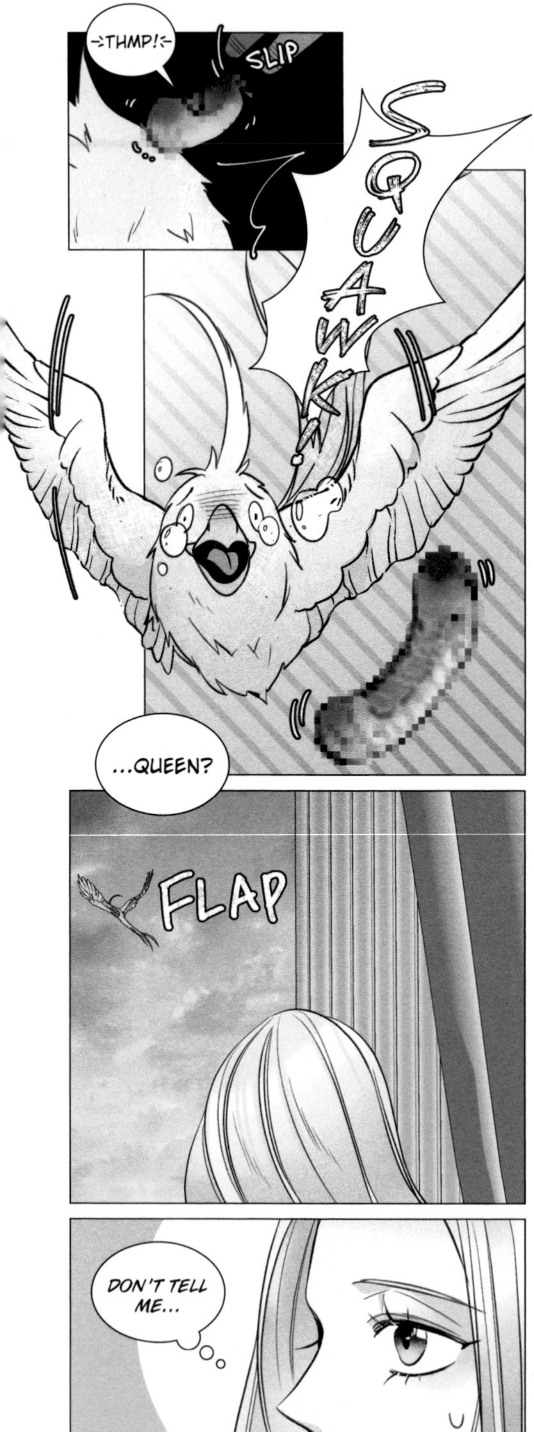
THMP!
SLIP
SQUAWK!
...QUEEN?
FLAP
DON'T TELL ME...

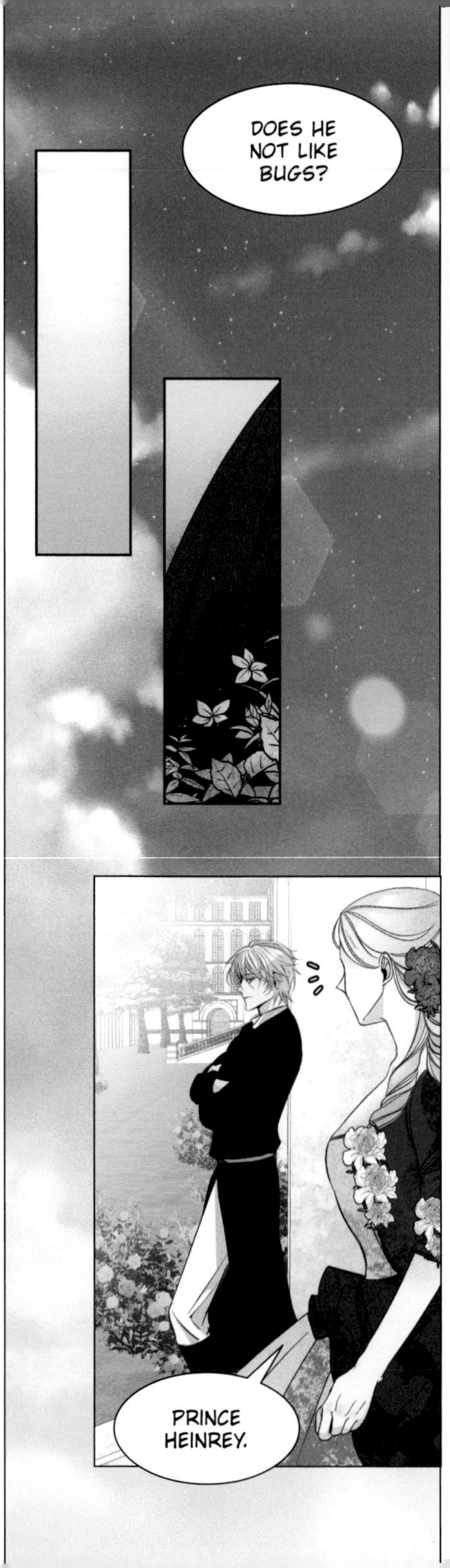
DOES HE NOT LIKE BUGS?
PRINCE HEINREY.

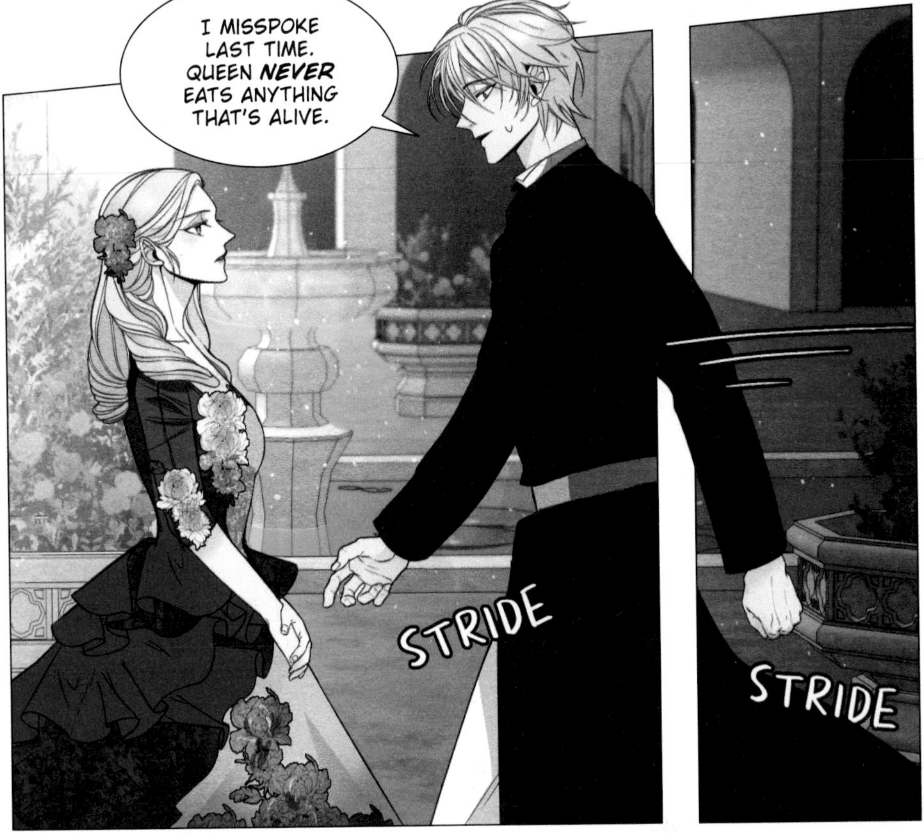
I MISSPOKE LAST TIME. QUEEN **NEVER** EATS ANYTHING THAT'S ALIVE.
STRIDE
STRIDE

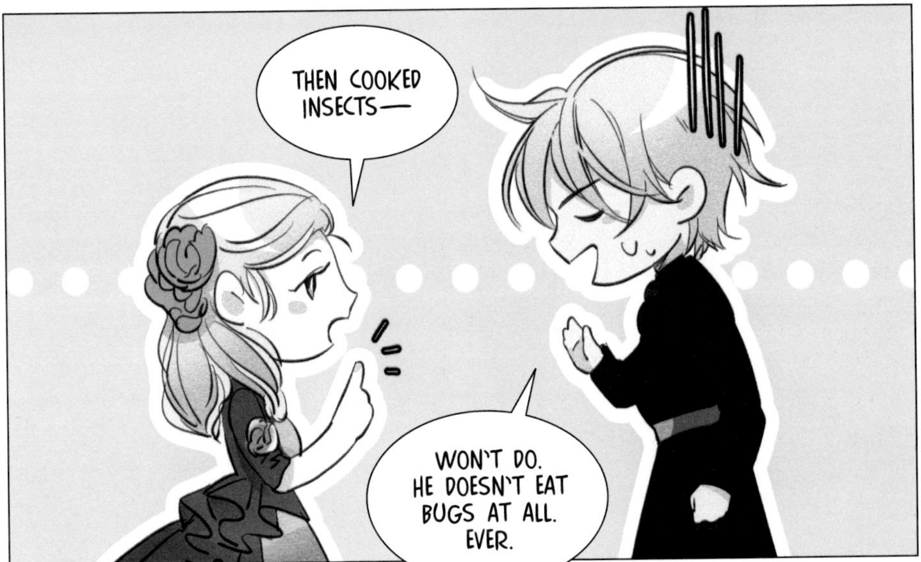
THEN COOKED INSECTS—
WON'T DO. HE DOESN'T EAT BUGS AT ALL. EVER.

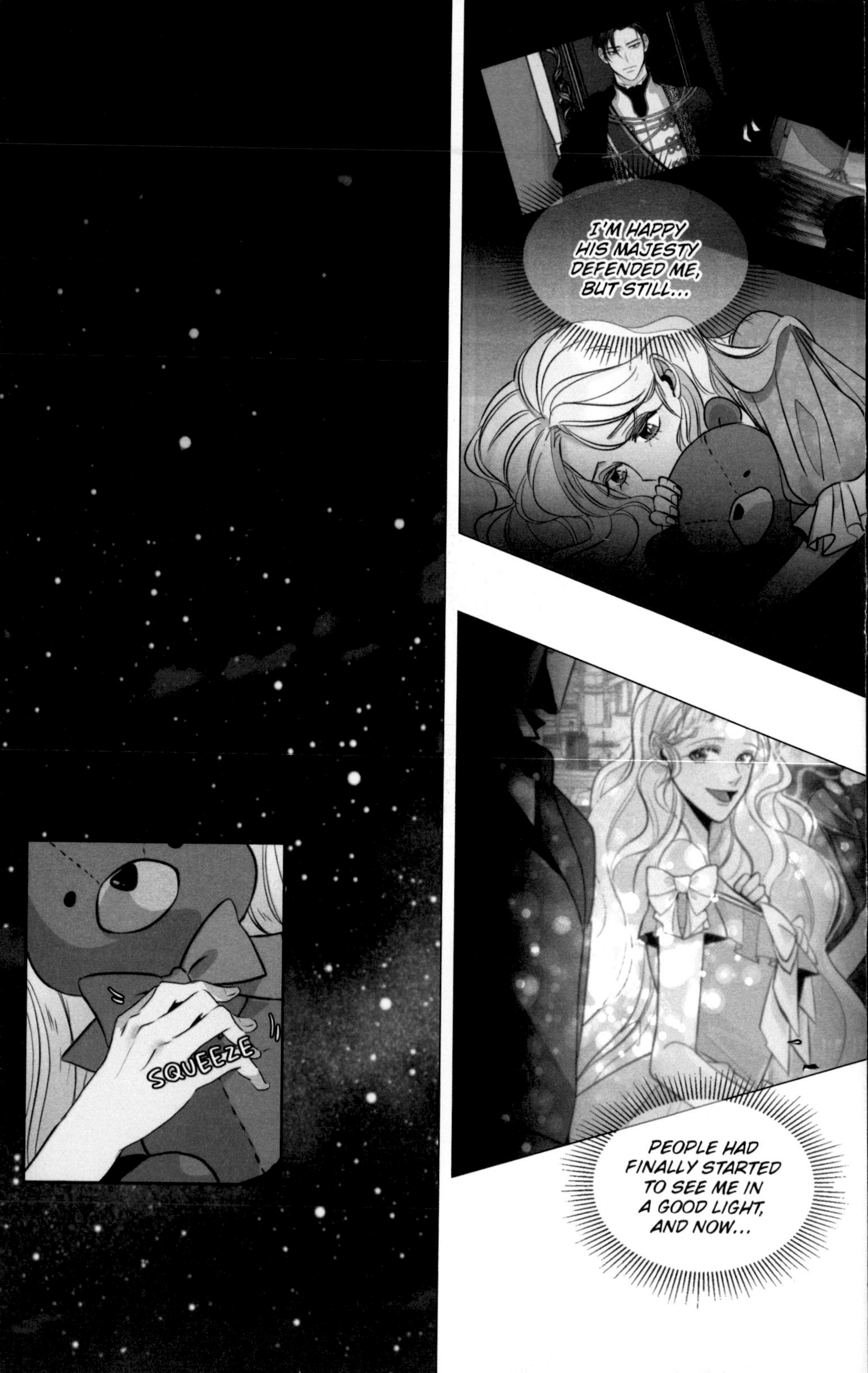
I'M HAPPY HIS MAJESTY DEFENDED ME, BUT STILL...
PEOPLE HAD FINALLY STARTED TO SEE ME IN A GOOD LIGHT, AND NOW...
SQUEEZE

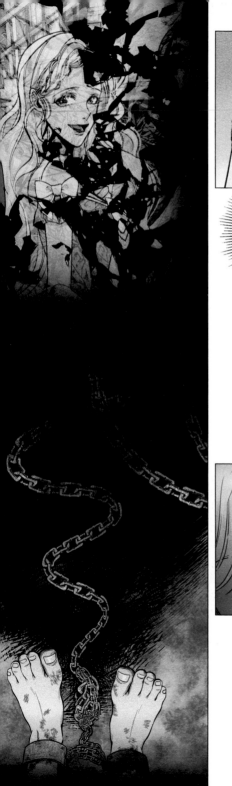

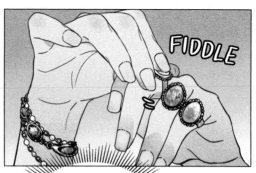

FIDDLE

NO. EVEN THOUGH I WAS ONCE A SLAVE, I'M THE EMPEROR'S MISTRESS NOW. EVERYTHING'S FINE.

MISS RASHTA.

VISCOUNT LOTTESHU HAS COME TO SEE YOU. WHAT SHOULD I DO?

MY LORD IS HERE?!

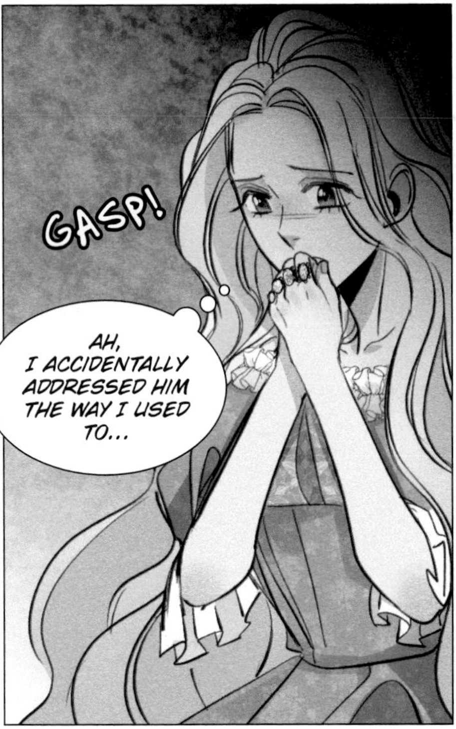
GASP!
AH, I ACCIDENTALLY ADDRESSED HIM THE WAY I USED TO...

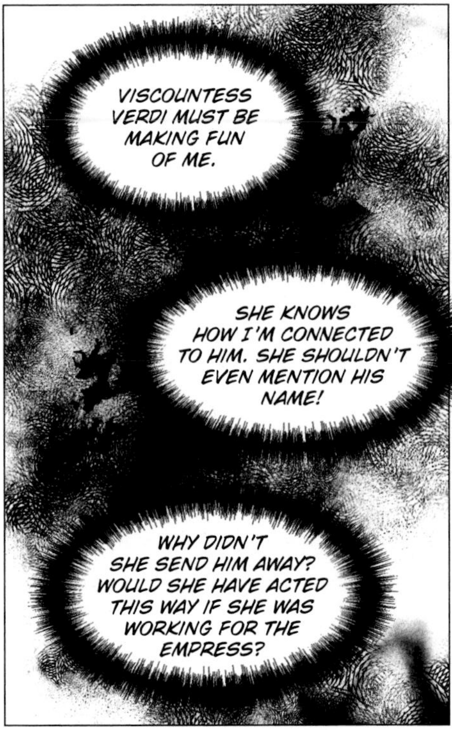
VISCOUNTESS VERDI MUST BE MAKING FUN OF ME.
SHE KNOWS HOW I'M CONNECTED TO HIM. SHE SHOULDN'T EVEN MENTION HIS NAME!
WHY DIDN'T SHE SEND HIM AWAY? WOULD SHE HAVE ACTED THIS WAY IF SHE WAS WORKING FOR THE EMPRESS?

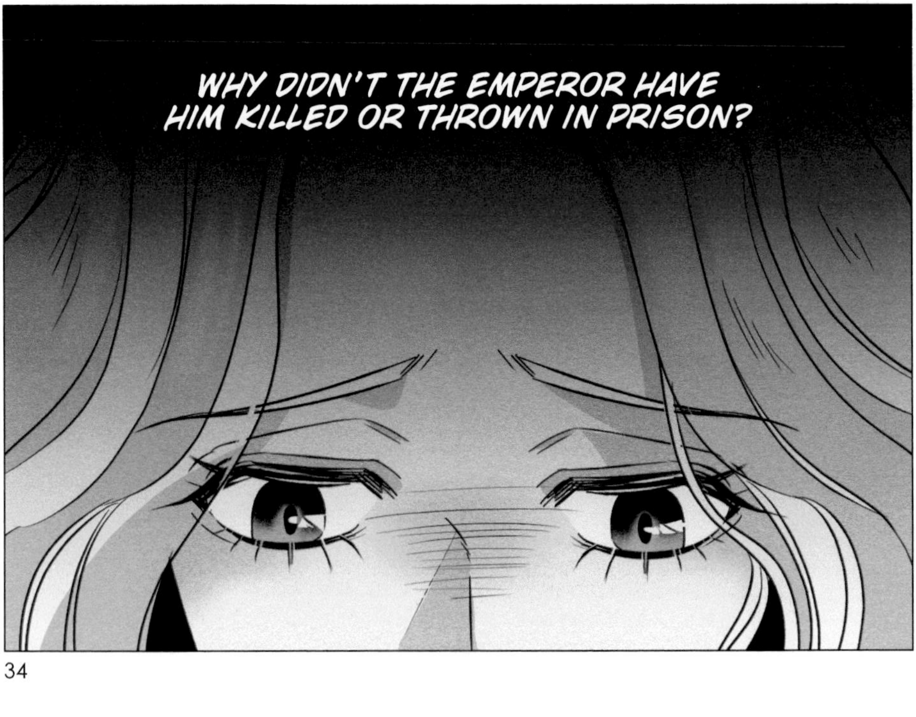
WHY DIDN'T THE EMPEROR HAVE HIM KILLED OR THROWN IN PRISON?

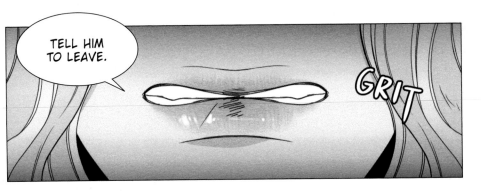

TELL HIM TO LEAVE.

GRIT

RAGE

TREMBLE

...UM, I'M AFRAID HE SAID IF YOU DIDN'T AGREE TO MEET HIM, YOU MAY REGRET IT...

THEN TELL HIM TO COME IN! LET ME SEE THAT SHAMELESS MUG OF HIS!

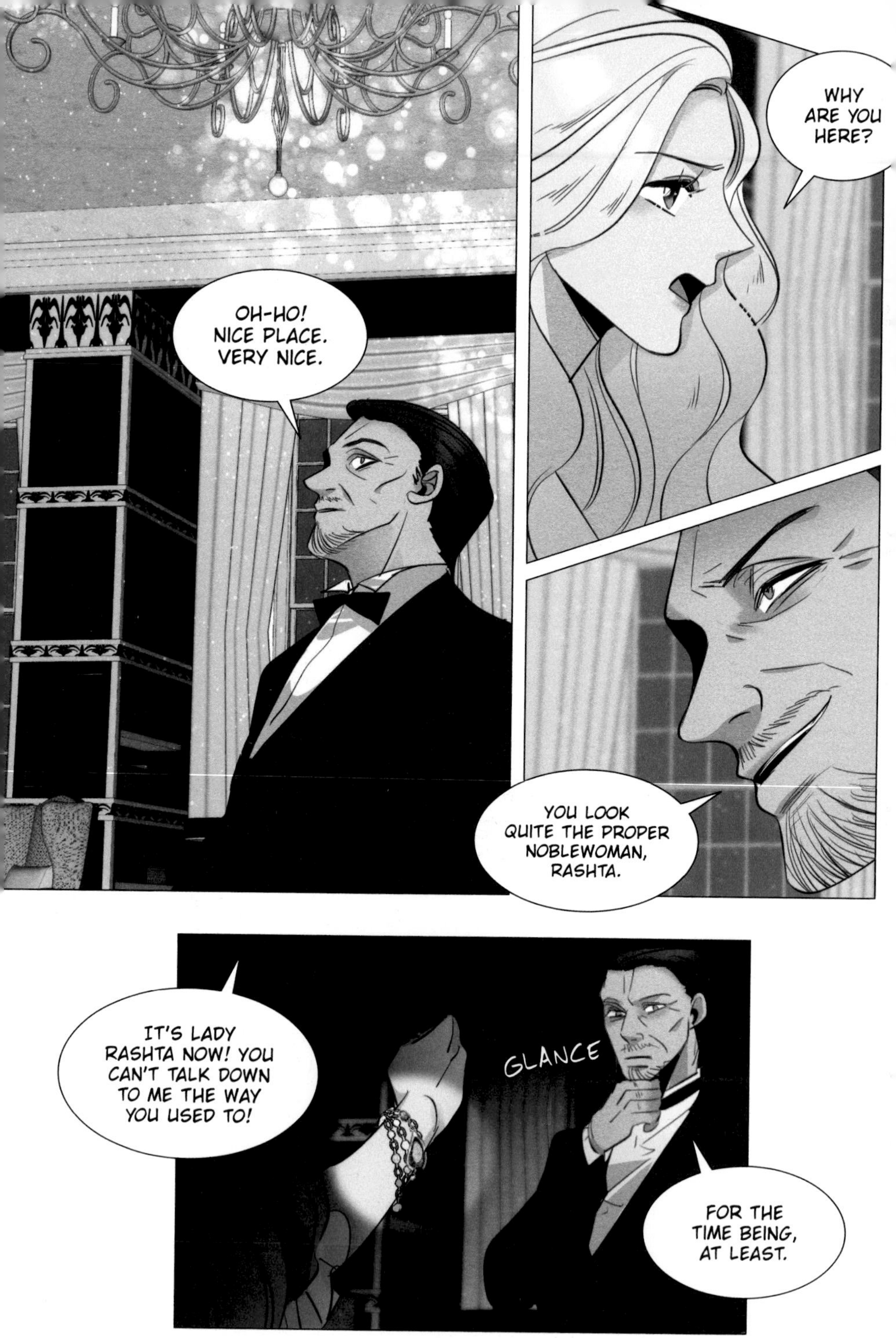
OH-HO! NICE PLACE. VERY NICE.
WHY ARE YOU HERE?
YOU LOOK QUITE THE PROPER NOBLEWOMAN, RASHTA.
IT'S LADY RASHTA NOW! YOU CAN'T TALK DOWN TO ME THE WAY YOU USED TO!
GLANCE
FOR THE TIME BEING, AT LEAST.

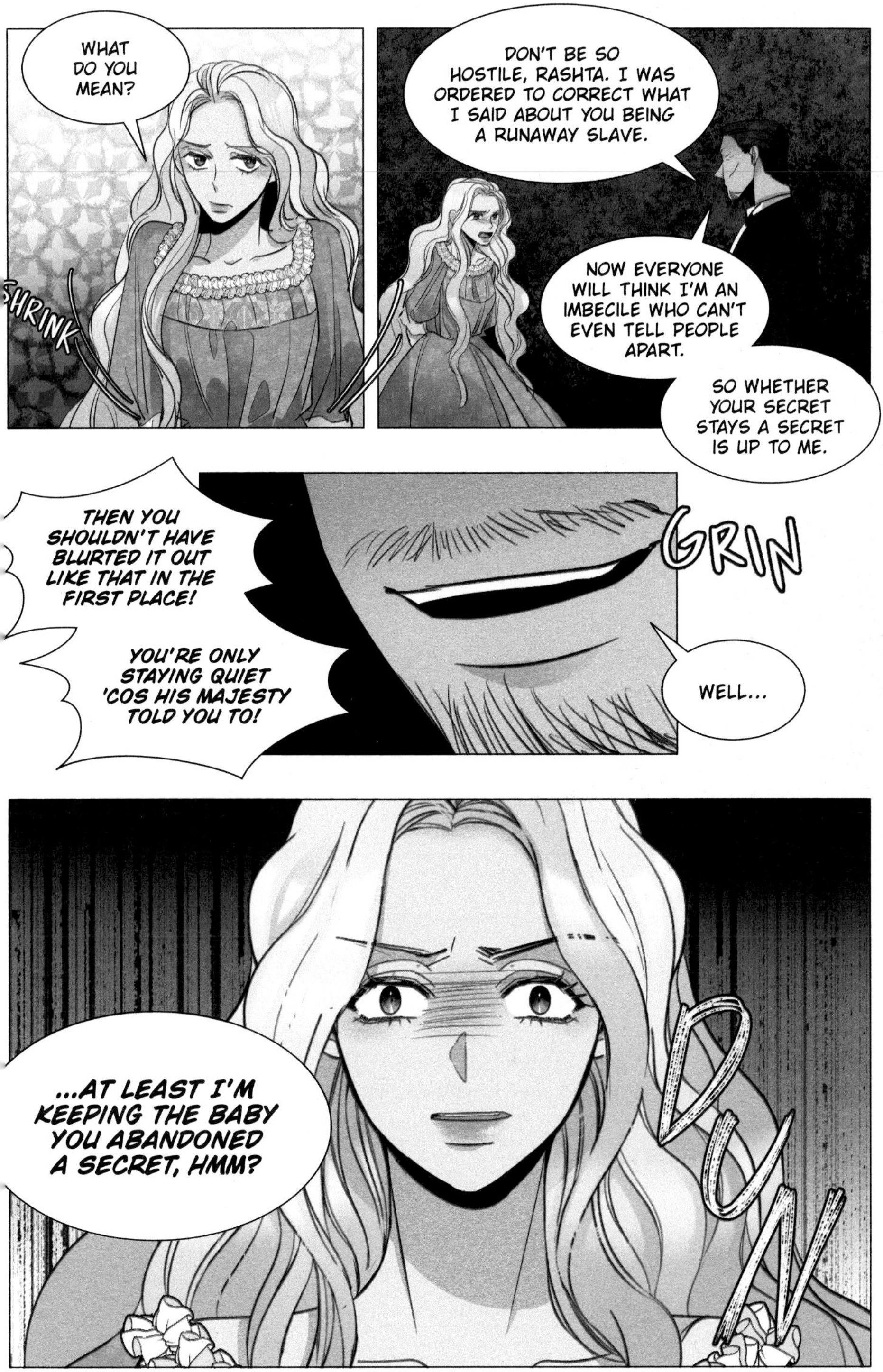
WHAT DO YOU MEAN?
SHRINK
DON'T BE SO HOSTILE, RASHTA. I WAS ORDERED TO CORRECT WHAT I SAID ABOUT YOU BEING A RUNAWAY SLAVE.
NOW EVERYONE WILL THINK I'M AN IMBECILE WHO CAN'T EVEN TELL PEOPLE APART.
SO WHETHER YOUR SECRET STAYS A SECRET IS UP TO ME.
THEN YOU SHOULDN'T HAVE BLURTED IT OUT LIKE THAT IN THE FIRST PLACE!
YOU'RE ONLY STAYING QUIET 'COS HIS MAJESTY TOLD YOU TO!
GRIN
WELL...
...AT LEAST I'M KEEPING THE BABY YOU ABANDONED A SECRET, HMM?
DUN

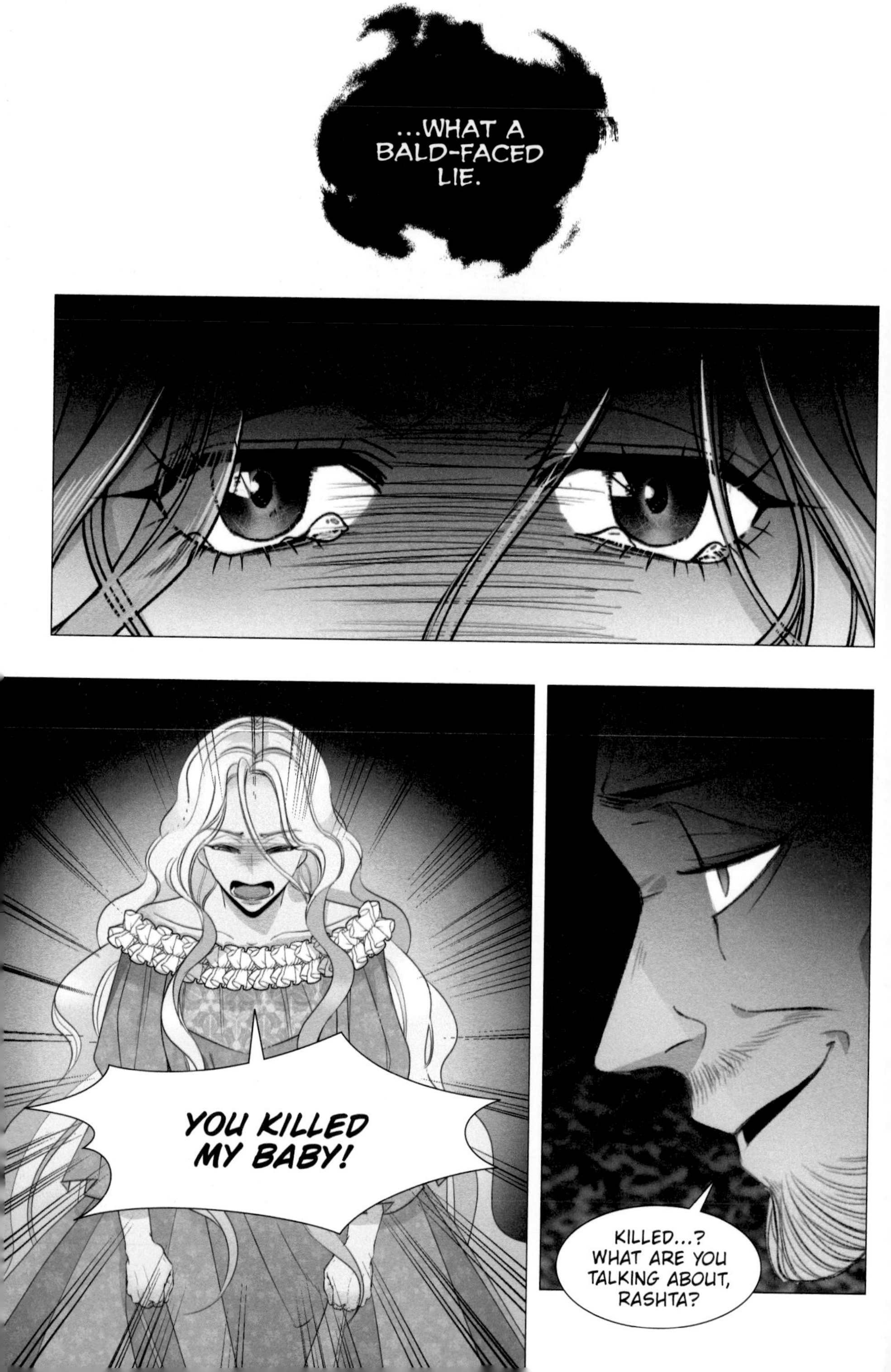
...WHAT A BALD-FACED LIE.
YOU KILLED MY BABY!
KILLED...? WHAT ARE YOU TALKING ABOUT, RASHTA?

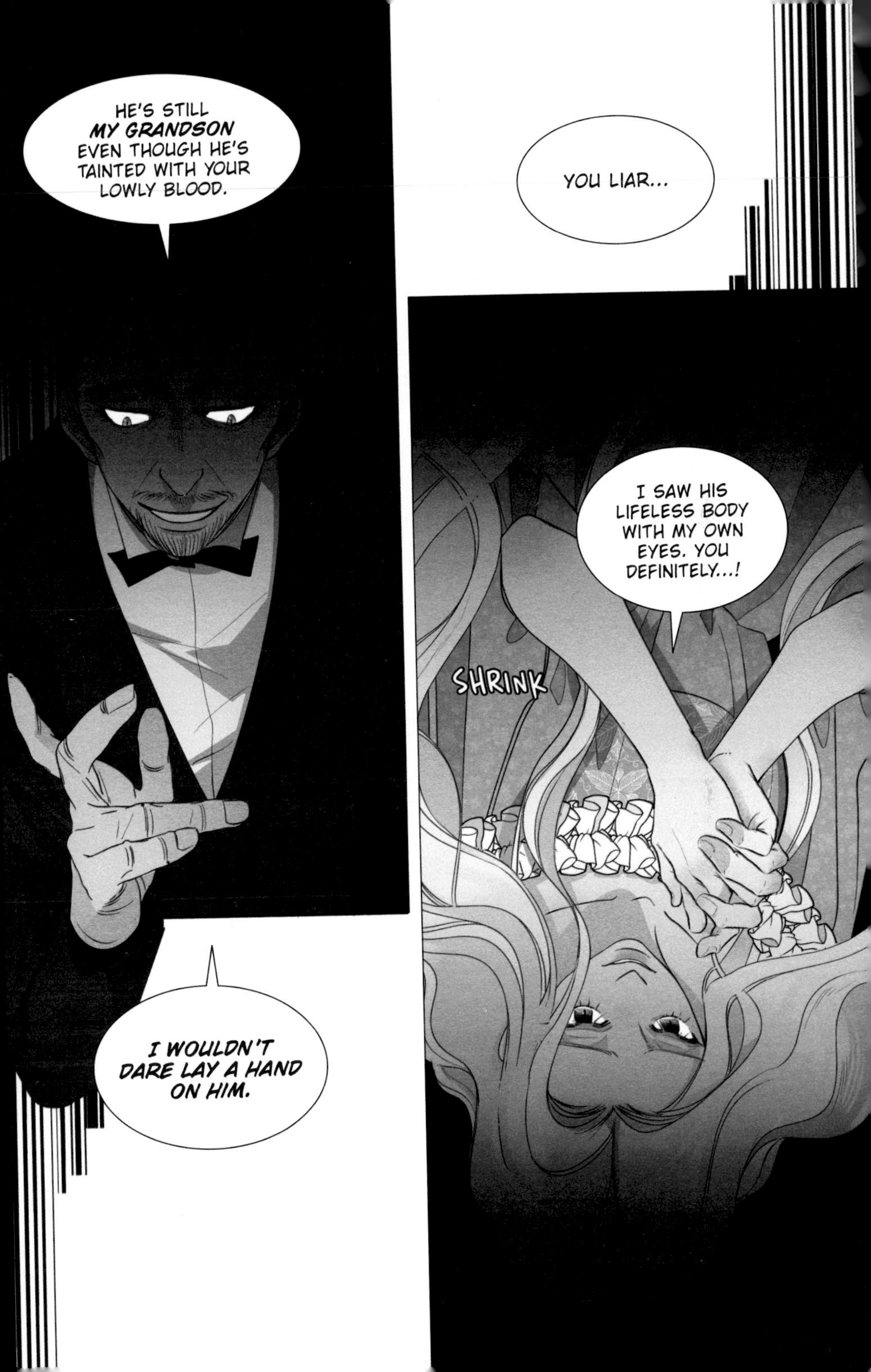
HE'S STILL MY GRANDSON EVEN THOUGH HE'S TAINTED WITH YOUR LOWLY BLOOD.
I WOULDN'T DARE LAY A HAND ON HIM.
YOU LIAR...
I SAW HIS LIFELESS BODY WITH MY OWN EYES. YOU DEFINITELY...!
SHRINK

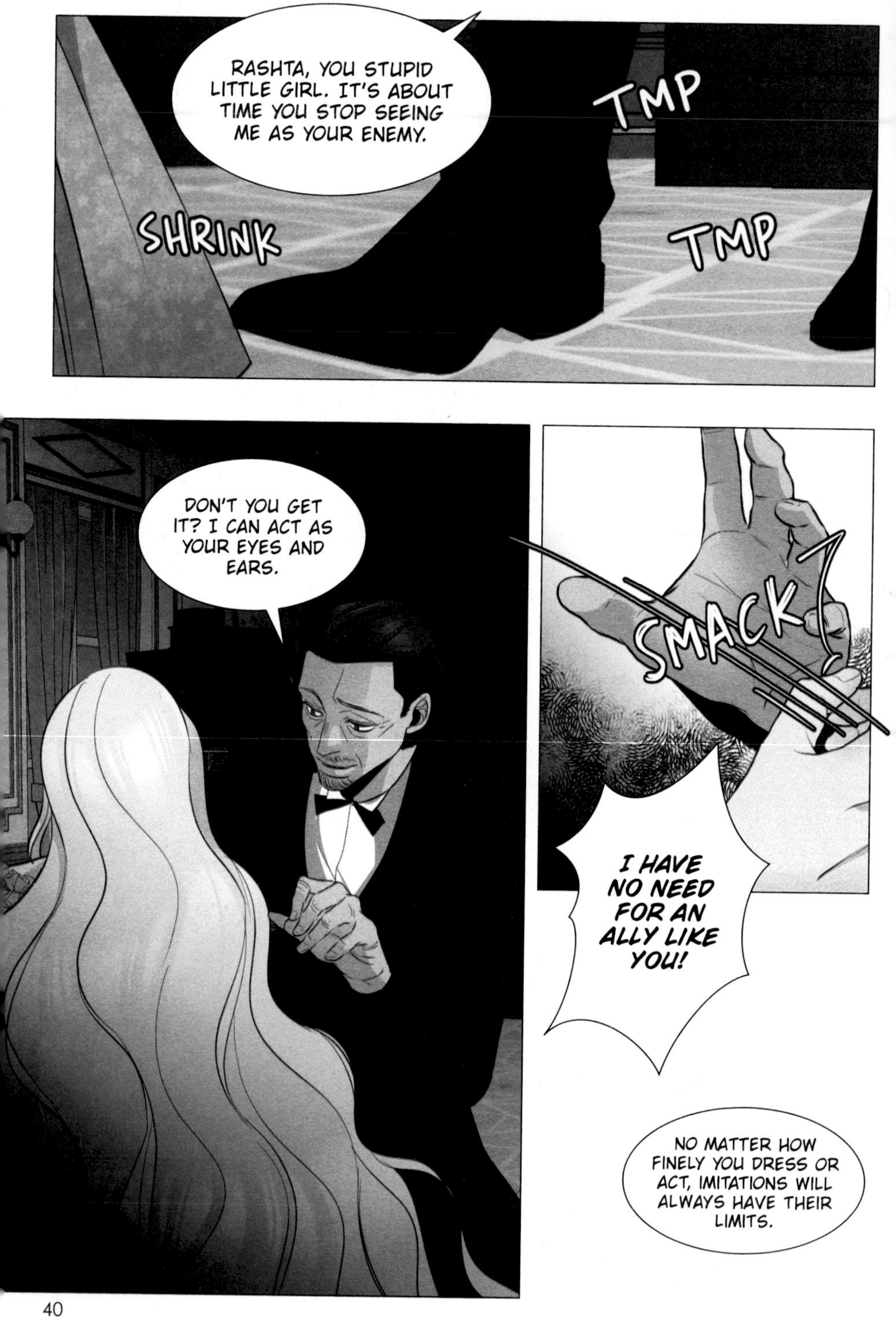
RASHTA, YOU STUPID LITTLE GIRL. IT'S ABOUT TIME YOU STOP SEEING ME AS YOUR ENEMY.
TMP
SHRINK
TMP
DON'T YOU GET IT? I CAN ACT AS YOUR EYES AND EARS.
SMACK
I HAVE NO NEED FOR AN ALLY LIKE YOU!
NO MATTER HOW FINELY YOU DRESS OR ACT, IMITATIONS WILL ALWAYS HAVE THEIR LIMITS.

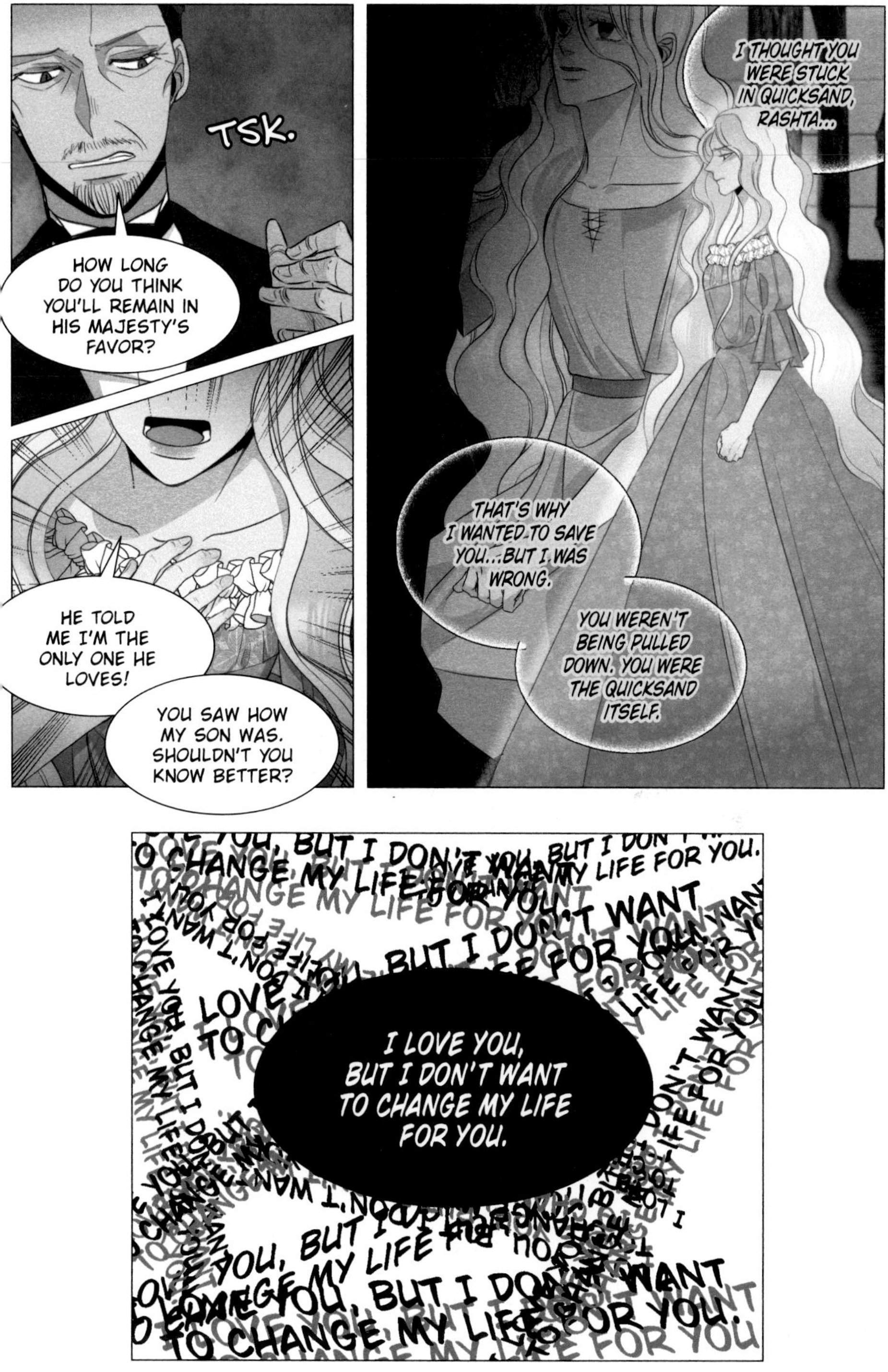

TSK.
HOW LONG DO YOU THINK YOU'LL REMAIN IN HIS MAJESTY'S FAVOR?
HE TOLD ME I'M THE ONLY ONE HE LOVES!
YOU SAW HOW MY SON WAS. SHOULDN'T YOU KNOW BETTER?
I THOUGHT YOU WERE STUCK IN QUICKSAND, RASHTA...
THAT'S WHY I WANTED TO SAVE YOU...BUT I WAS WRONG.
YOU WEREN'T BEING PULLED DOWN. YOU WERE THE QUICKSAND ITSELF.
I LOVE YOU, BUT I DON'T WANT TO CHANGE MY LIFE FOR YOU.

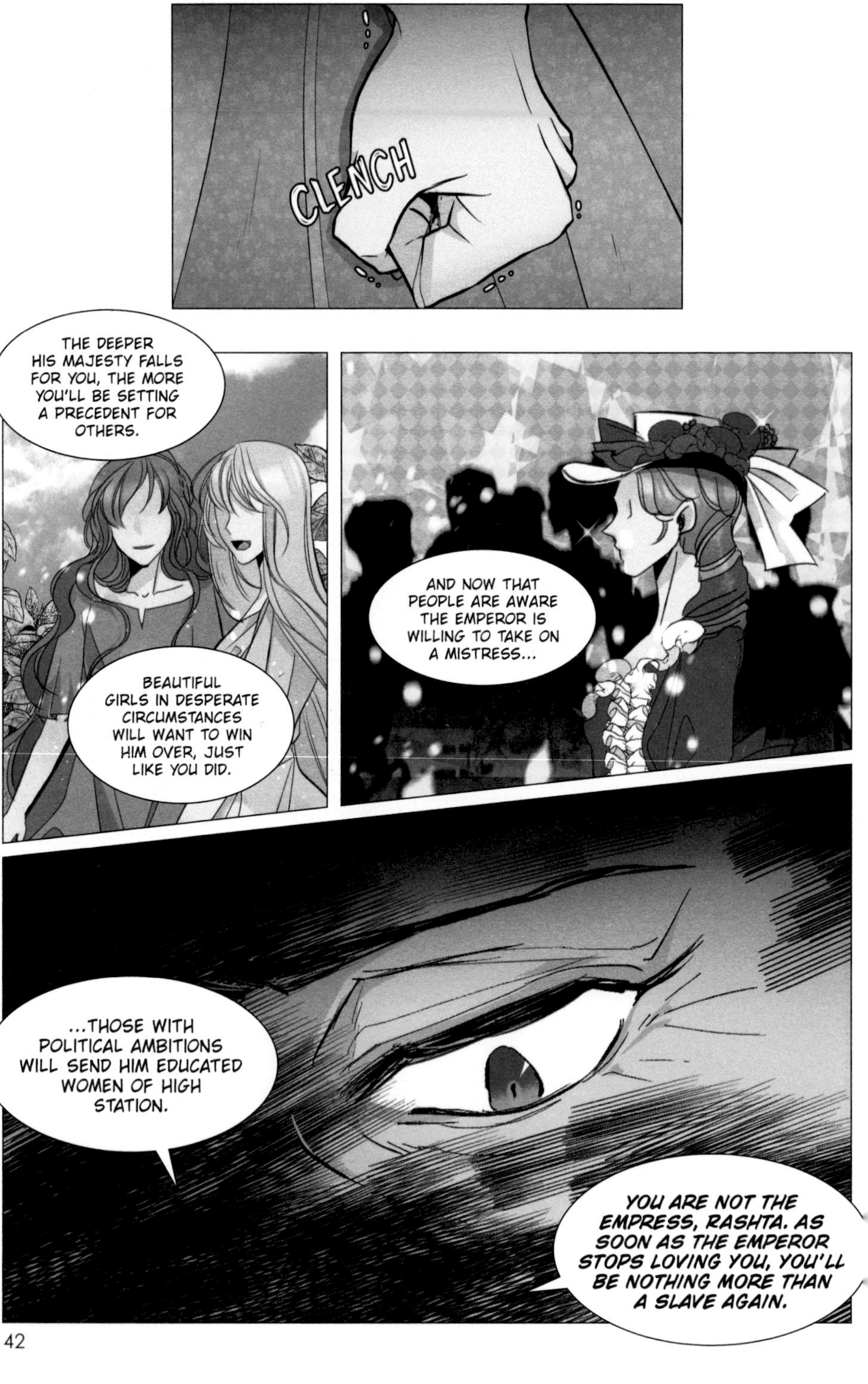
CLENCH
THE DEEPER HIS MAJESTY FALLS FOR YOU, THE MORE YOU'LL BE SETTING A PRECEDENT FOR OTHERS.
BEAUTIFUL GIRLS IN DESPERATE CIRCUMSTANCES WILL WANT TO WIN HIM OVER, JUST LIKE YOU DID.
AND NOW THAT PEOPLE ARE AWARE THE EMPEROR IS WILLING TO TAKE ON A MISTRESS...
...THOSE WITH POLITICAL AMBITIONS WILL SEND HIM EDUCATED WOMEN OF HIGH STATION.
YOU ARE NOT THE EMPRESS, RASHTA. AS SOON AS THE EMPEROR STOPS LOVING YOU, YOU'LL BE NOTHING MORE THAN A SLAVE AGAIN.

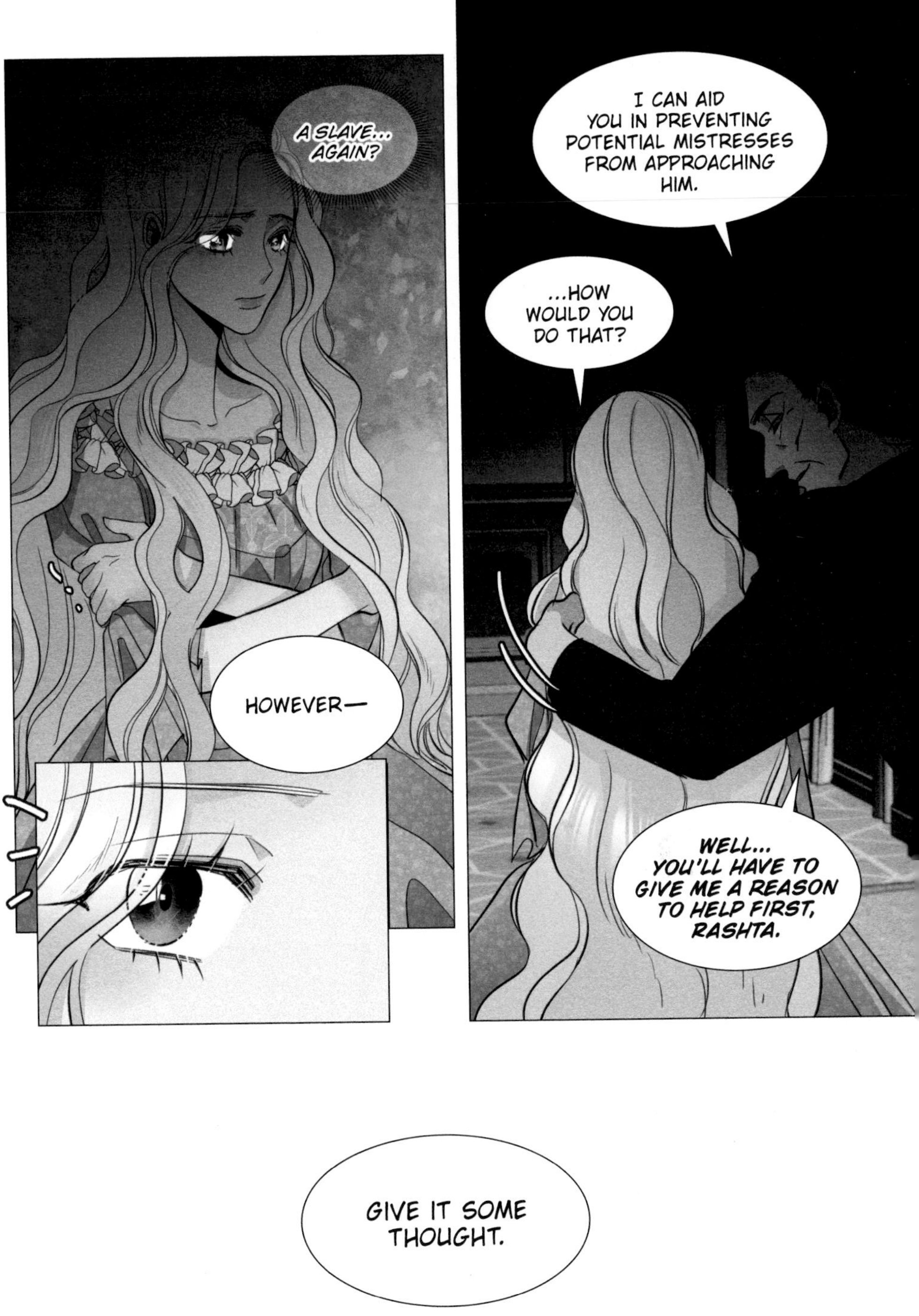
A SLAVE... AGAIN?
HOWEVER—
I CAN AID YOU IN PREVENTING POTENTIAL MISTRESSES FROM APPROACHING HIM.
...HOW WOULD YOU DO THAT?
WELL... YOU'LL HAVE TO GIVE ME A REASON TO HELP FIRST, RASHTA.
GIVE IT SOME THOUGHT.

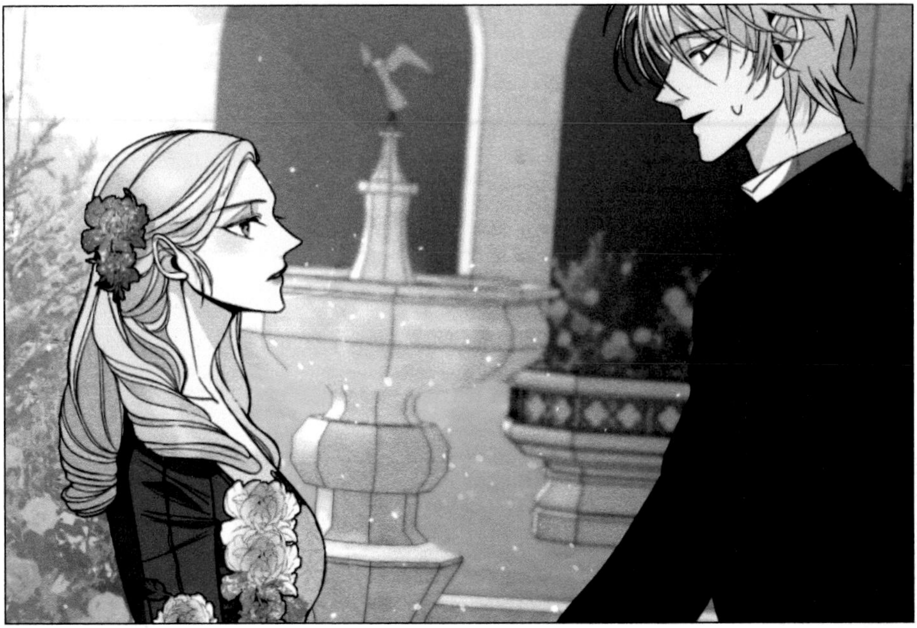

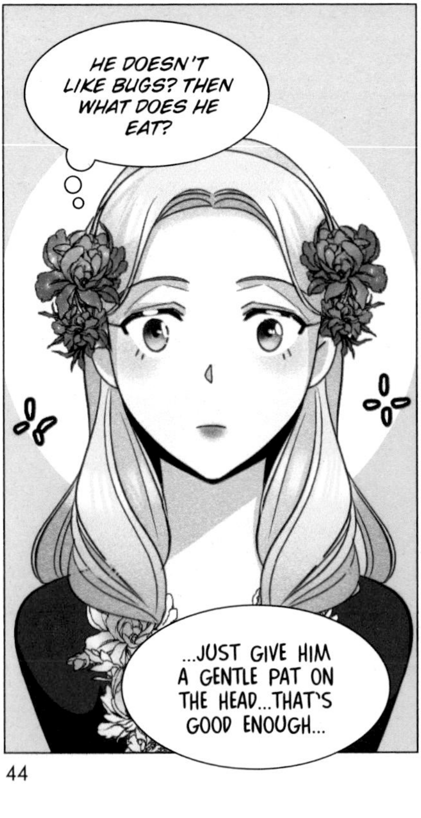
HE DOESN'T LIKE BUGS? THEN WHAT DOES HE EAT?
...JUST GIVE HIM A GENTLE PAT ON THE HEAD...THAT'S GOOD ENOUGH...

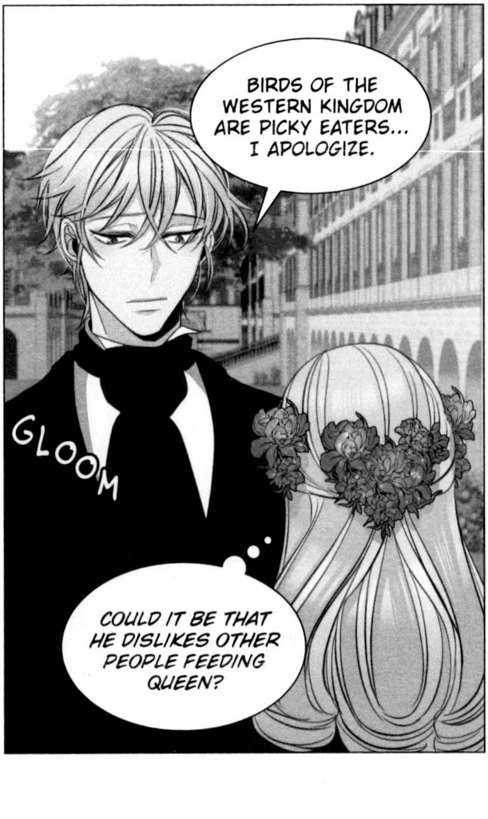
BIRDS OF THE WESTERN KINGDOM ARE PICKY EATERS... I APOLOGIZE.
GLOOM
COULD IT BE THAT HE DISLIKES OTHER PEOPLE FEEDING QUEEN?

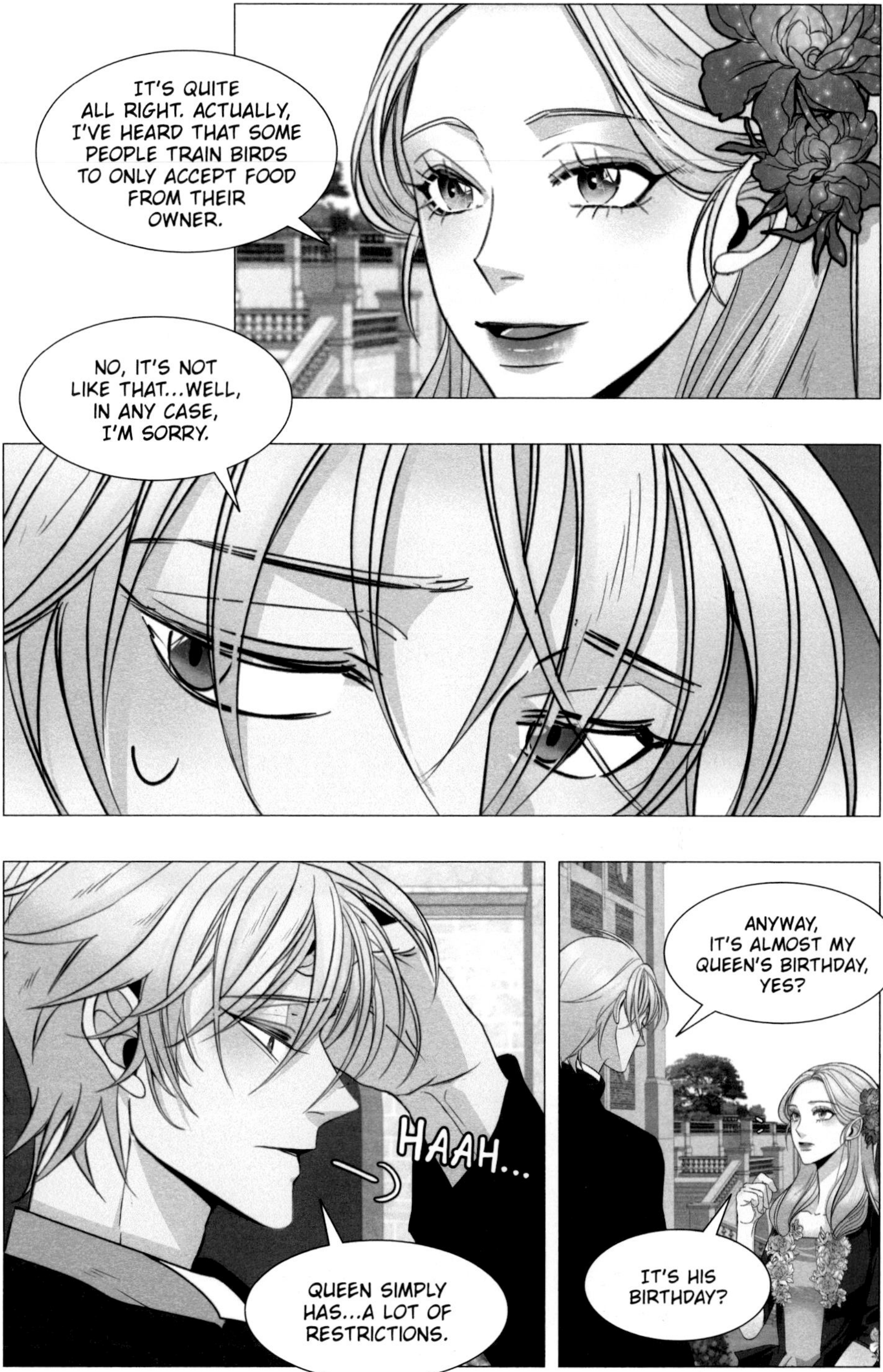
IT'S QUITE ALL RIGHT. ACTUALLY, I'VE HEARD THAT SOME PEOPLE TRAIN BIRDS TO ONLY ACCEPT FOOD FROM THEIR OWNER.
NO, IT'S NOT LIKE THAT...WELL, IN ANY CASE, I'M SORRY.
HAAH...
QUEEN SIMPLY HAS...A LOT OF RESTRICTIONS.
ANYWAY, IT'S ALMOST MY QUEEN'S BIRTHDAY, YES?
IT'S HIS BIRTHDAY?

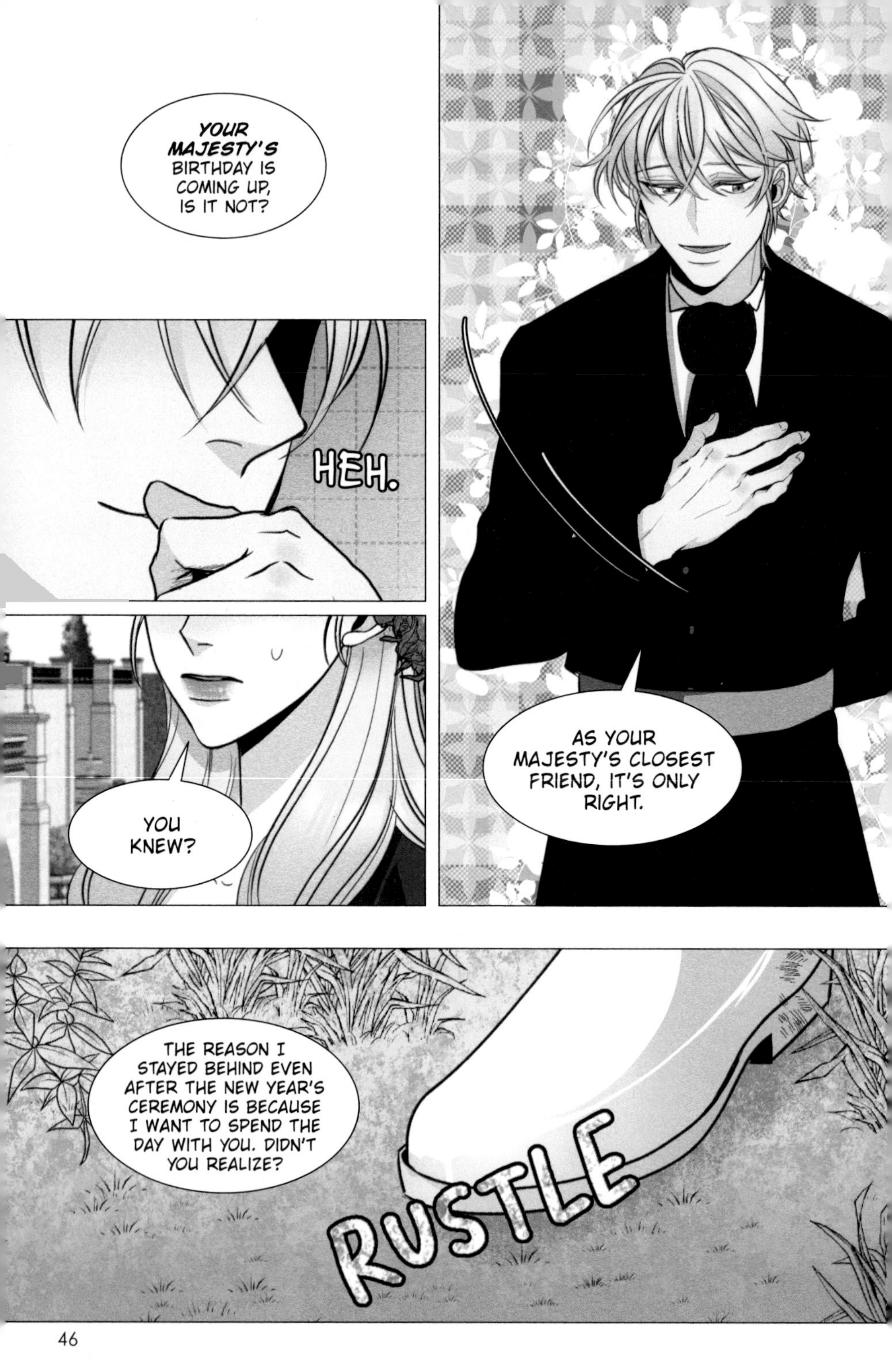
YOUR MAJESTY'S BIRTHDAY IS COMING UP, IS IT NOT?
HEH.
YOU KNEW?
AS YOUR MAJESTY'S CLOSEST FRIEND, IT'S ONLY RIGHT.
THE REASON I STAYED BEHIND EVEN AFTER THE NEW YEAR'S CEREMONY IS BECAUSE I WANT TO SPEND THE DAY WITH YOU. DIDN'T YOU REALIZE?
RUSTLE

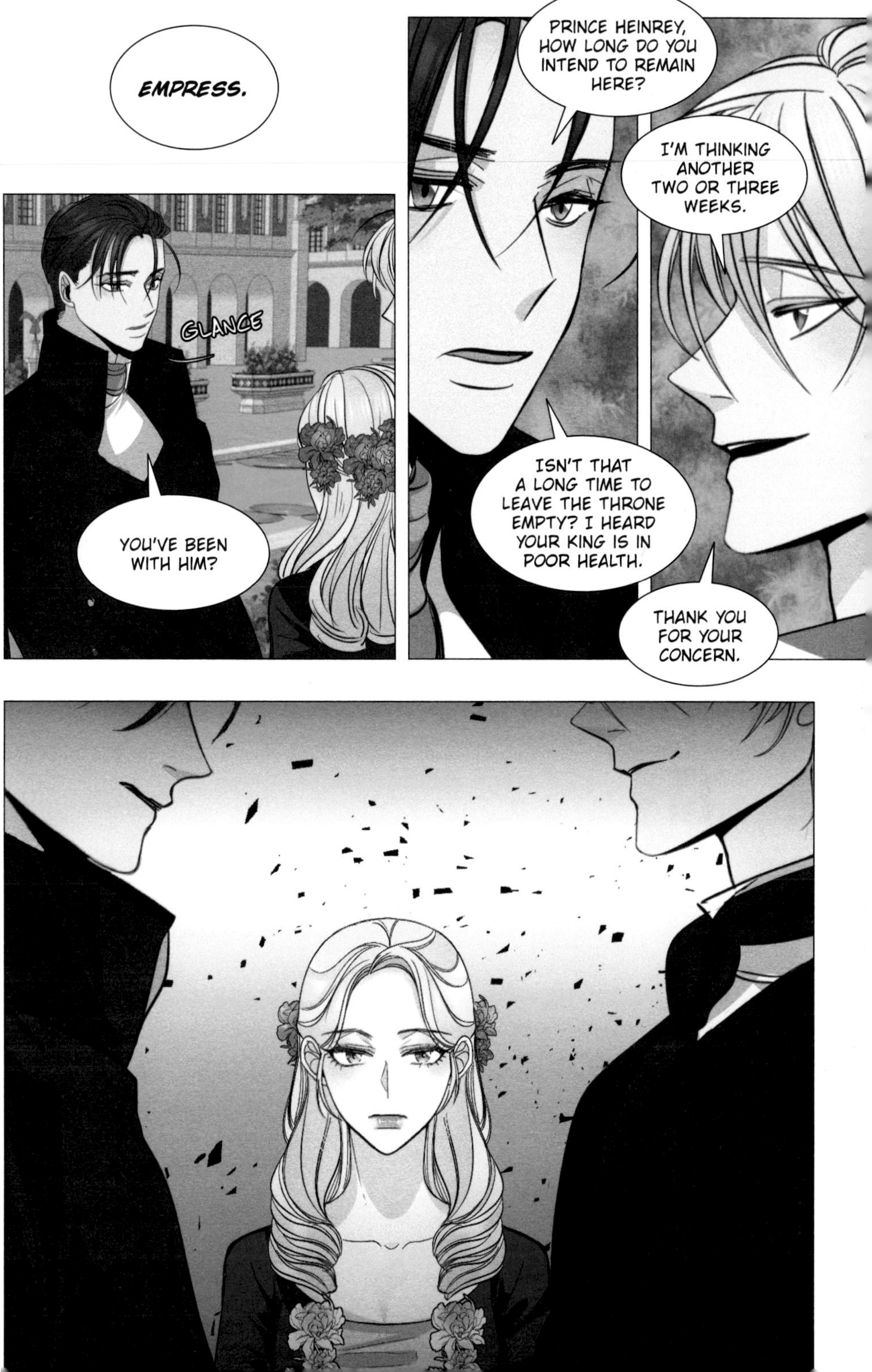
EMPRESS.
GLANCE
YOU'VE BEEN WITH HIM?
PRINCE HEINREY, HOW LONG DO YOU INTEND TO REMAIN HERE?
I'M THINKING ANOTHER TWO OR THREE WEEKS.
ISN'T THAT A LONG TIME TO LEAVE THE THRONE EMPTY? I HEARD YOUR KING IS IN POOR HEALTH.
THANK YOU FOR YOUR CONCERN.

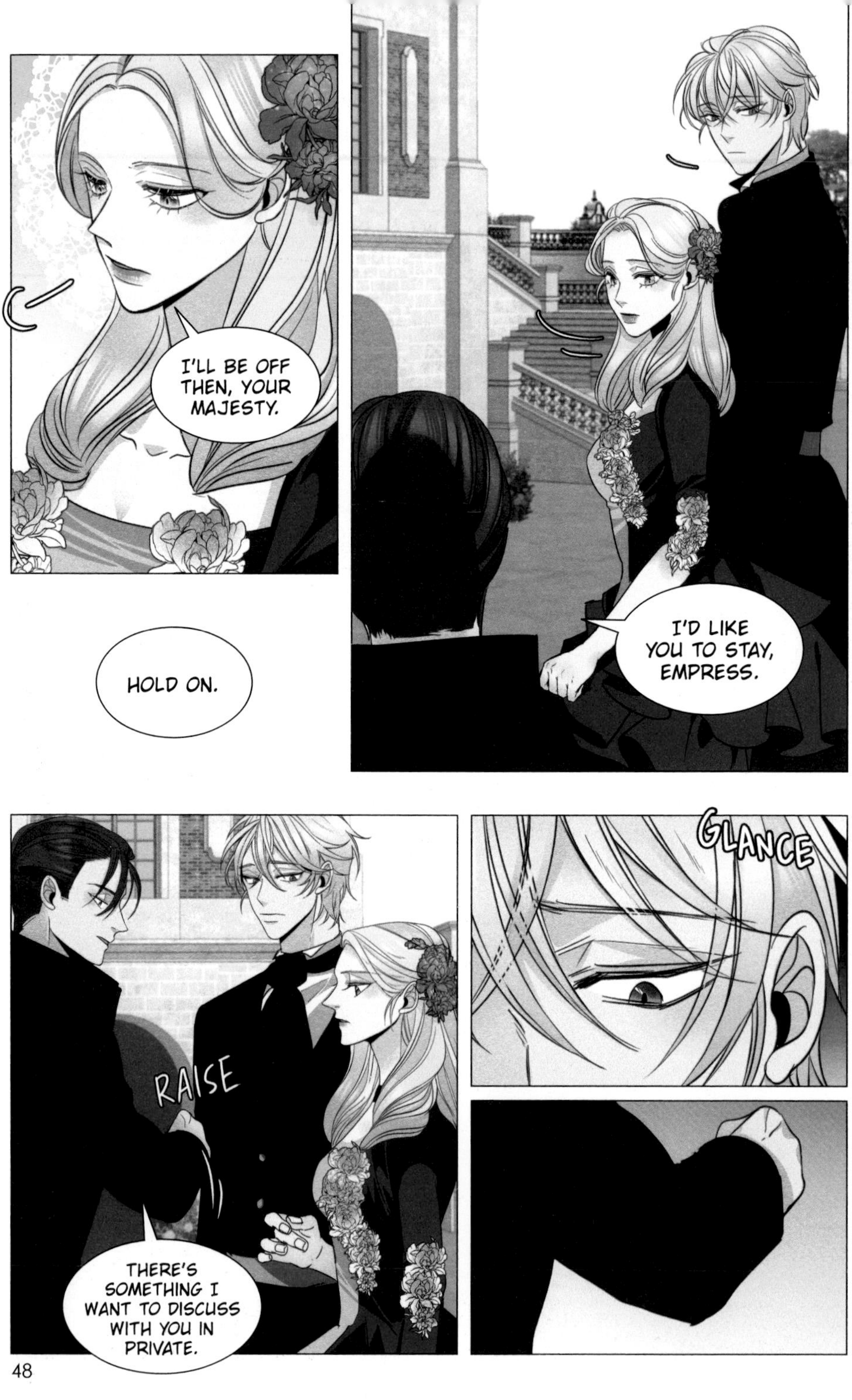
I'LL BE OFF THEN, YOUR MAJESTY.
HOLD ON.
I'D LIKE YOU TO STAY, EMPRESS.
RAISE
THERE'S SOMETHING I WANT TO DISCUSS WITH YOU IN PRIVATE.
GLANCE

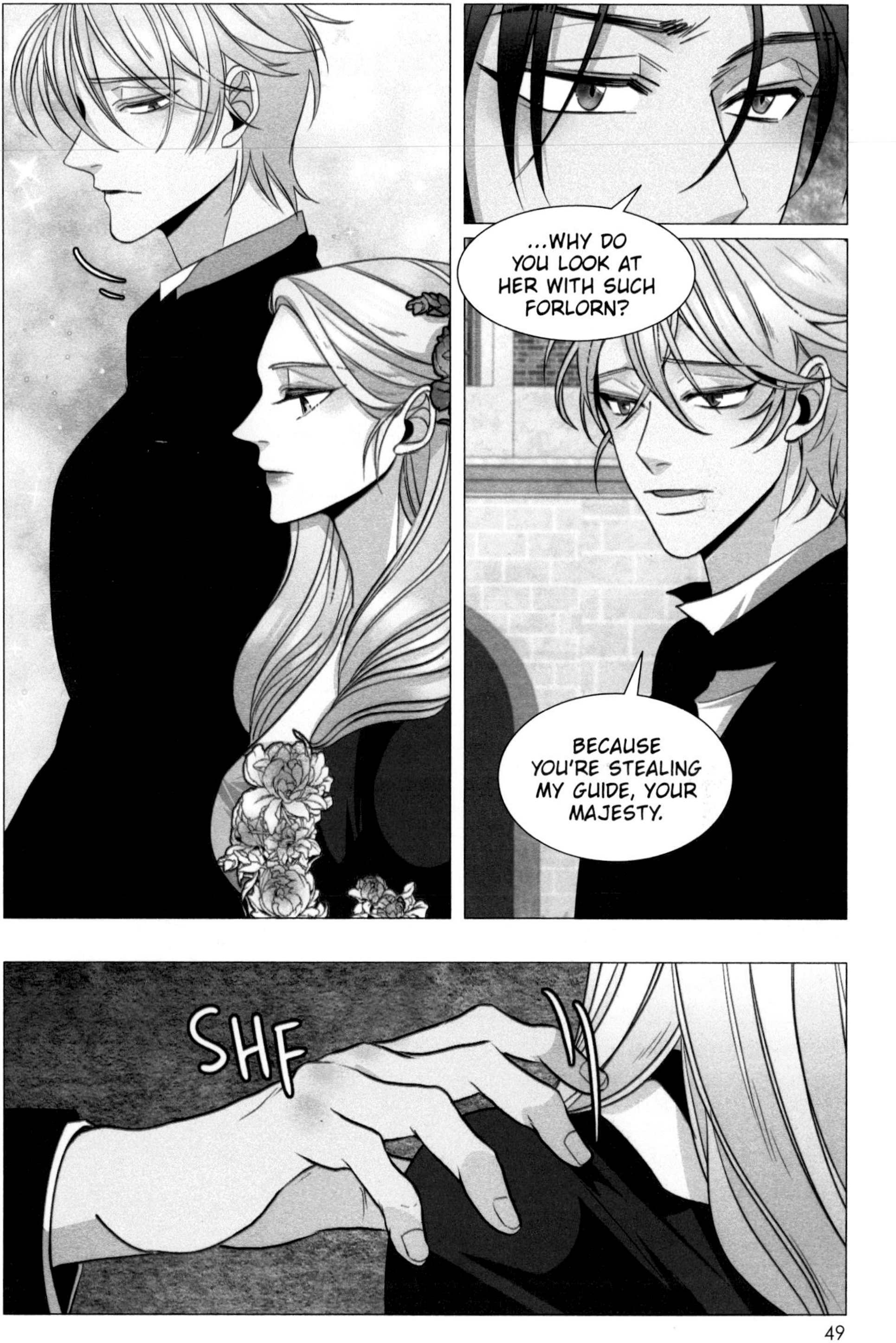

...WHY DO YOU LOOK AT HER WITH SUCH FORLORN?
BECAUSE YOU'RE STEALING MY GUIDE, YOUR MAJESTY.
SHF

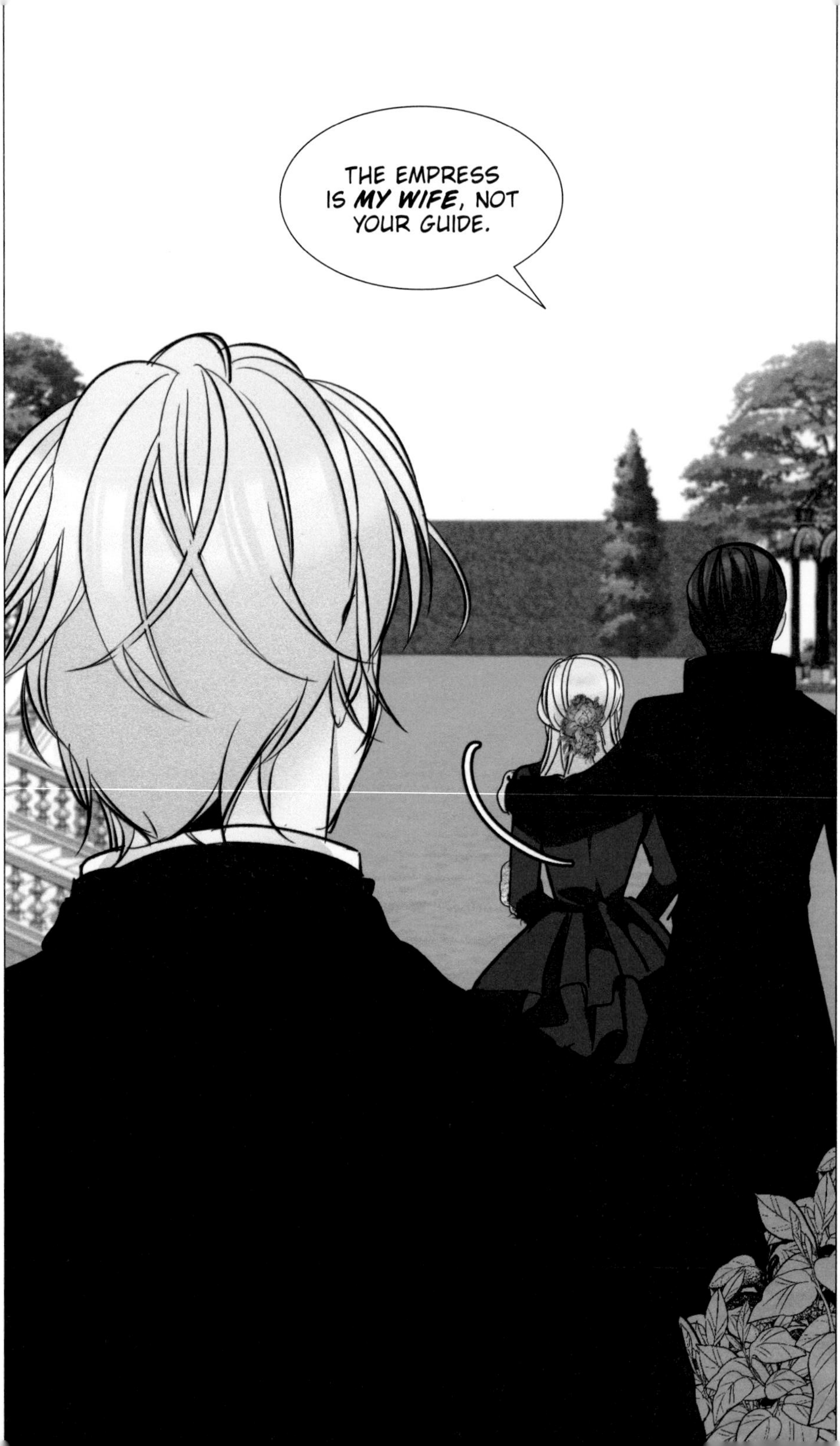
THE EMPRESS IS MY WIFE, NOT YOUR GUIDE.

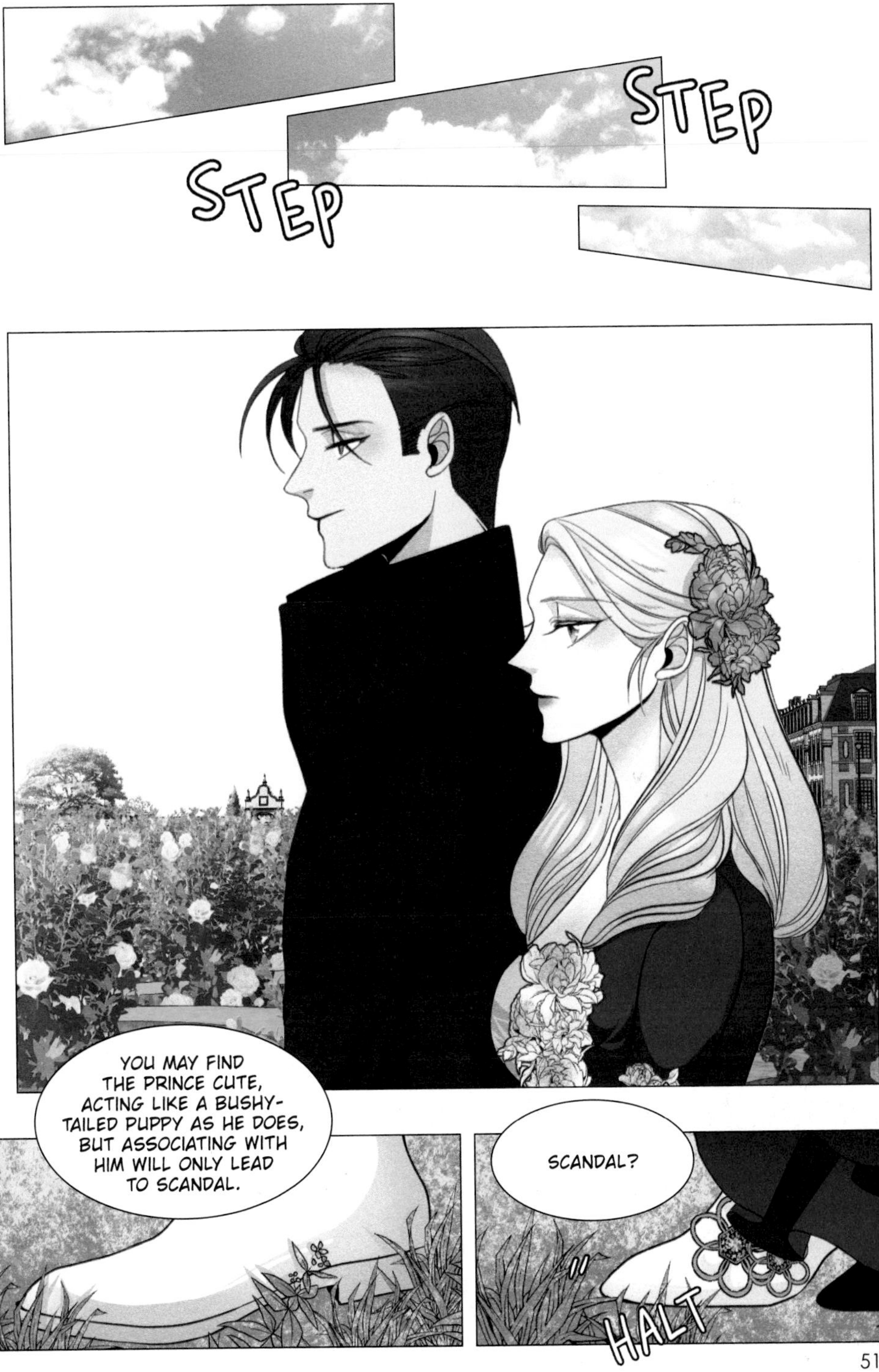
STEP
STEP
YOU MAY FIND THE PRINCE CUTE, ACTING LIKE A BUSHY-TAILED PUPPY AS HE DOES, BUT ASSOCIATING WITH HIM WILL ONLY LEAD TO SCANDAL.
SCANDAL?
HALT

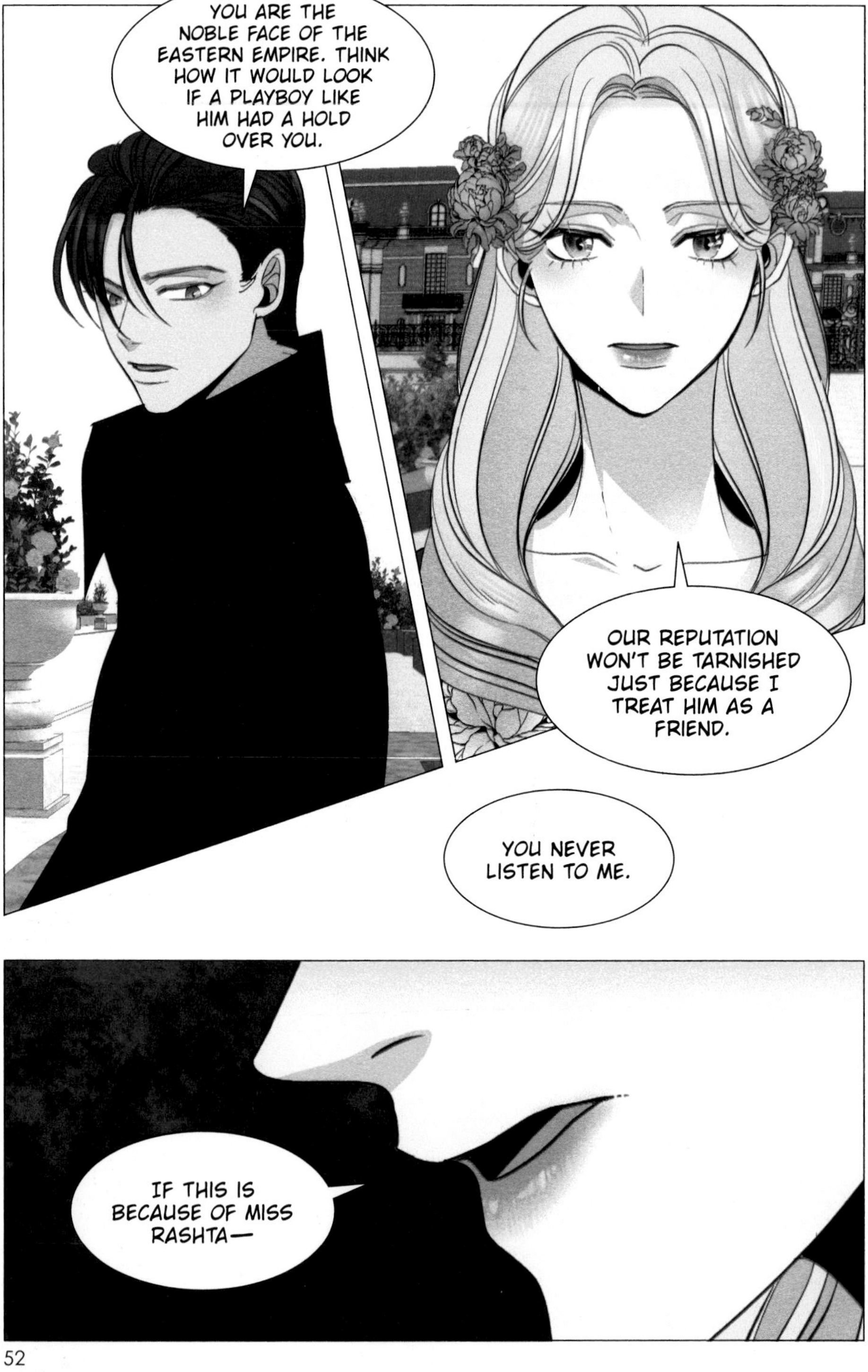
YOU ARE THE NOBLE FACE OF THE EASTERN EMPIRE. THINK HOW IT WOULD LOOK IF A PLAYBOY LIKE HIM HAD A HOLD OVER YOU.
OUR REPUTATION WON'T BE TARNISHED JUST BECAUSE I TREAT HIM AS A FRIEND.
YOU NEVER LISTEN TO ME.
IF THIS IS BECAUSE OF MISS RASHTA—

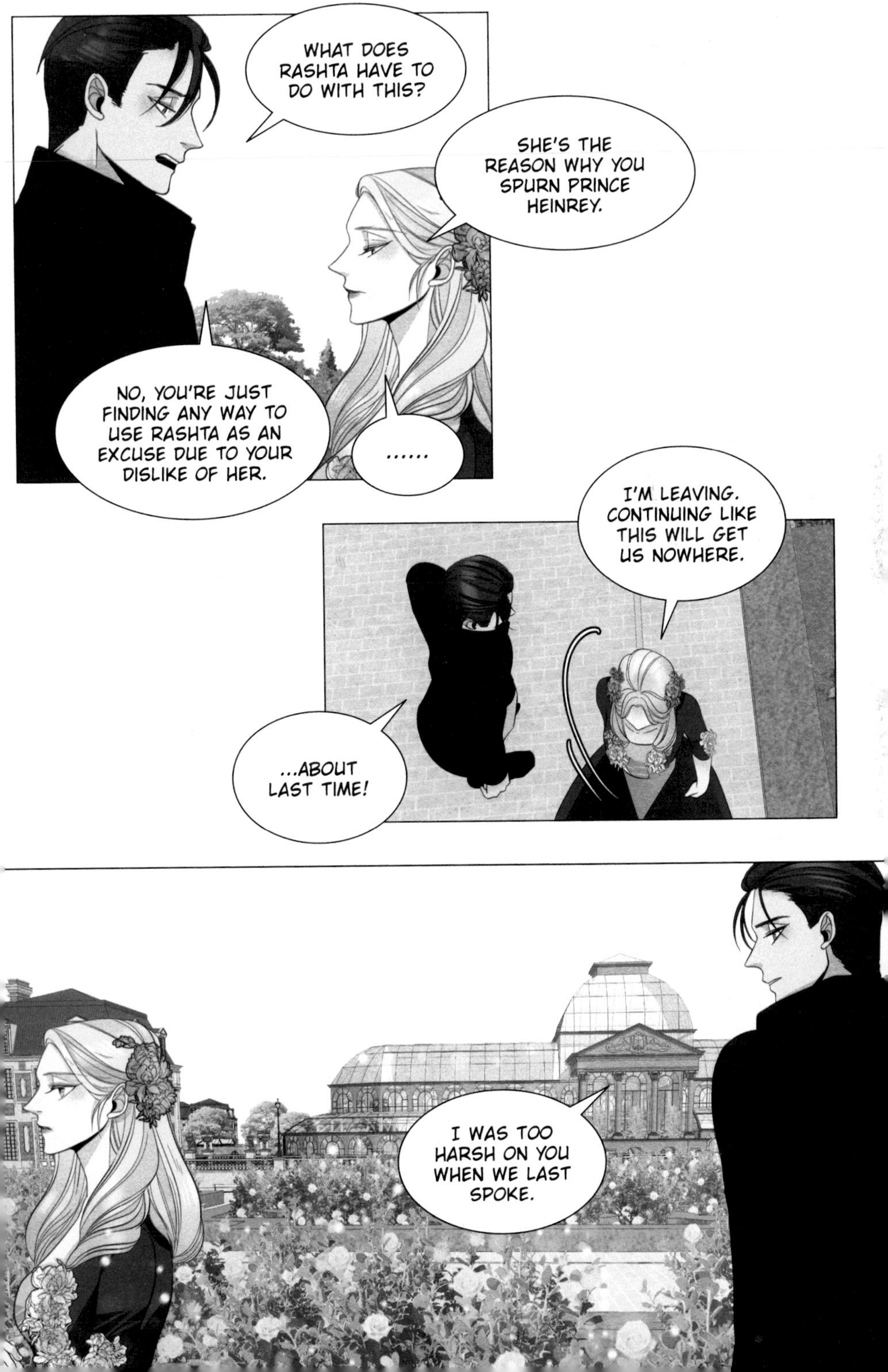
WHAT DOES RASHTA HAVE TO DO WITH THIS?
SHE'S THE REASON WHY YOU SPURN PRINCE HEINREY.
NO, YOU'RE JUST FINDING ANY WAY TO USE RASHTA AS AN EXCUSE DUE TO YOUR DISLIKE OF HER.
......
I'M LEAVING. CONTINUING LIKE THIS WILL GET US NOWHERE.
...ABOUT LAST TIME!
I WAS TOO HARSH ON YOU WHEN WE LAST SPOKE.

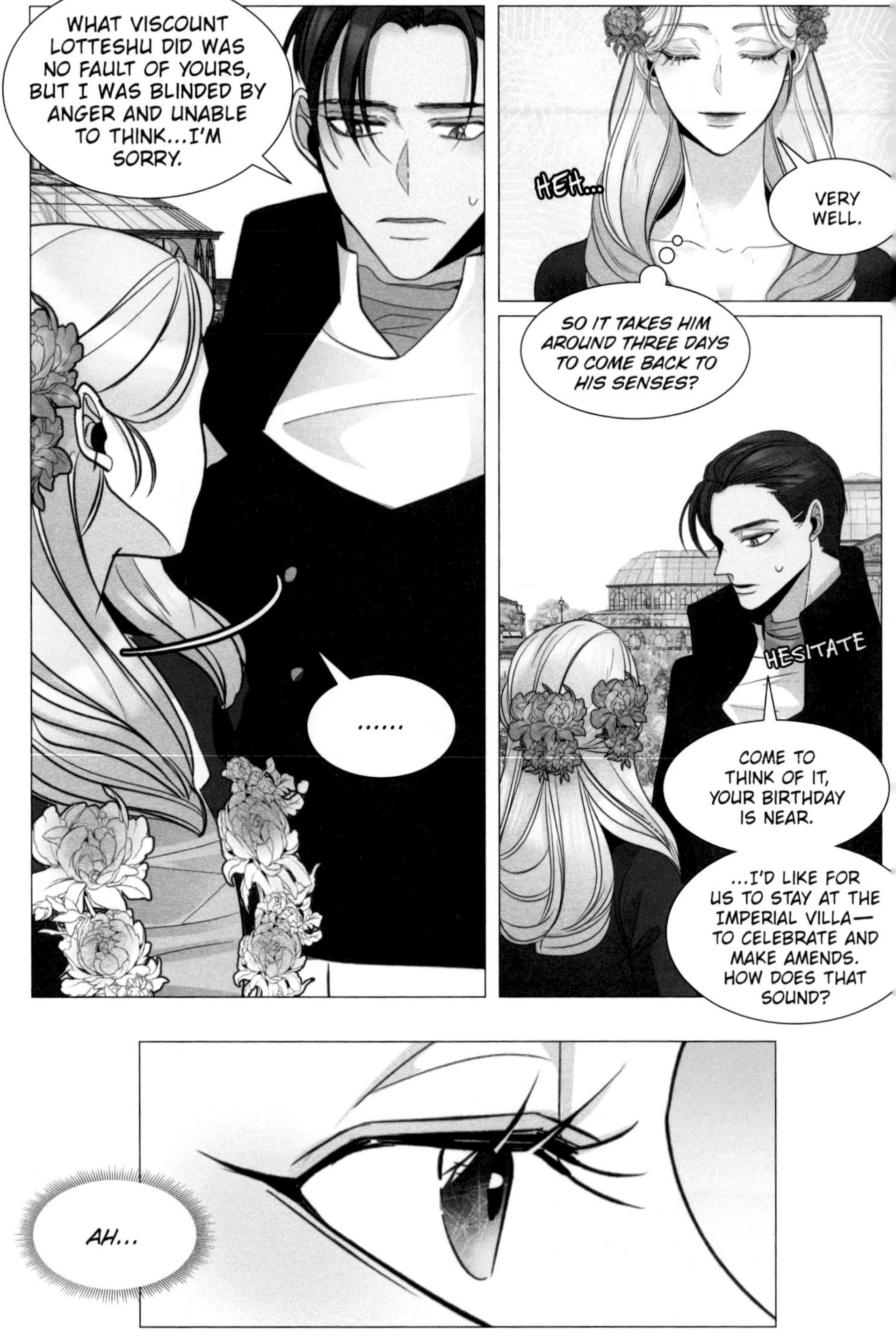
WHAT VISCOUNT LOTTESHU DID WAS NO FAULT OF YOURS, BUT I WAS BLINDED BY ANGER AND UNABLE TO THINK...I'M SORRY.
......
HEH...
VERY WELL.
SO IT TAKES HIM AROUND THREE DAYS TO COME BACK TO HIS SENSES?
HESITATE
COME TO THINK OF IT, YOUR BIRTHDAY IS NEAR.
...I'D LIKE FOR US TO STAY AT THE IMPERIAL VILLA—TO CELEBRATE AND MAKE AMENDS. HOW DOES THAT SOUND?
AH...

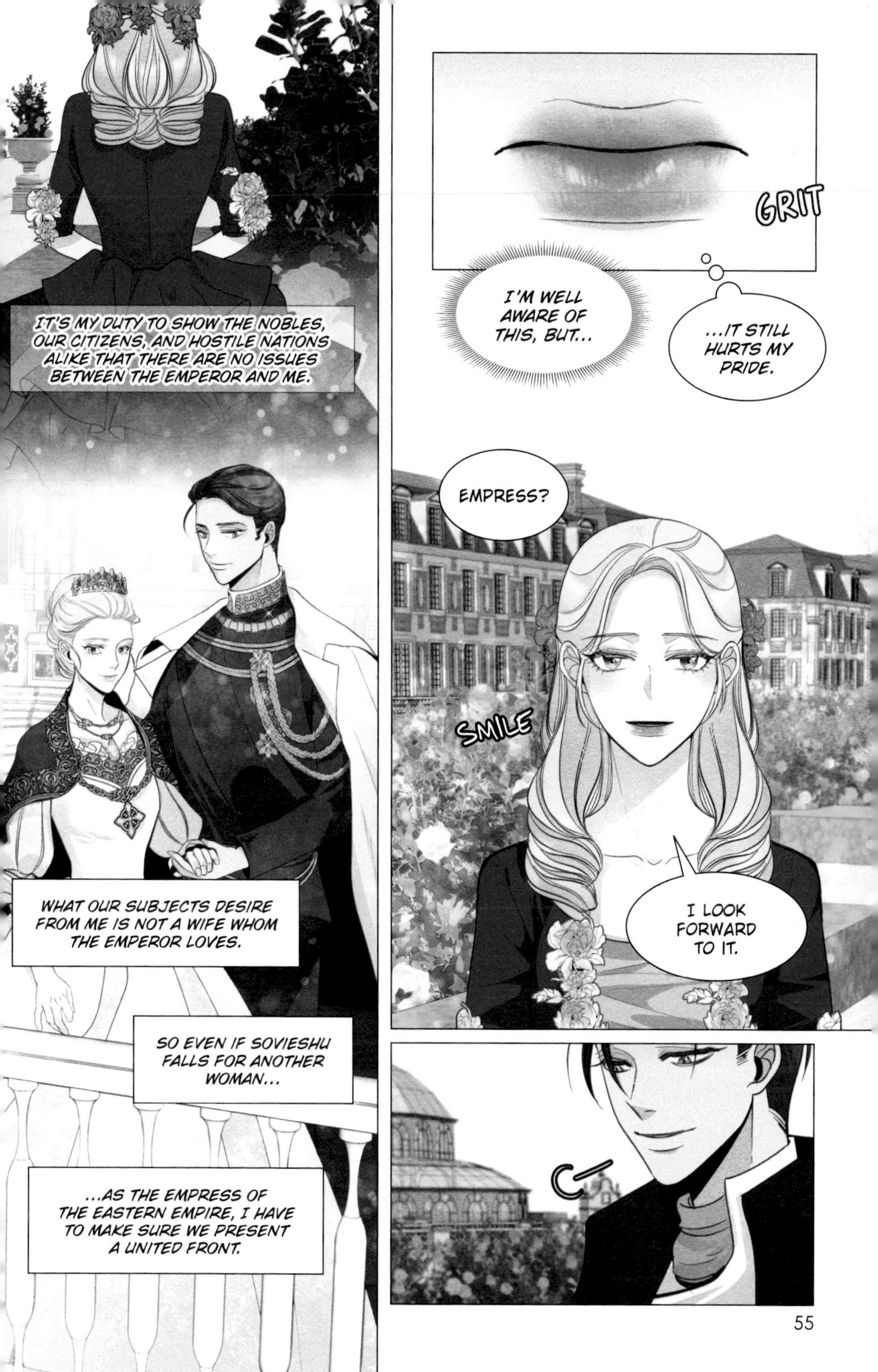
IT'S MY DUTY TO SHOW THE NOBLES, OUR CITIZENS, AND HOSTILE NATIONS ALIKE THAT THERE ARE NO ISSUES BETWEEN THE EMPEROR AND ME.
WHAT OUR SUBJECTS DESIRE FROM ME IS NOT A WIFE WHOM THE EMPEROR LOVES.
SO EVEN IF SOVIESHU FALLS FOR ANOTHER WOMAN...
...AS THE EMPRESS OF THE EASTERN EMPIRE, I HAVE TO MAKE SURE WE PRESENT A UNITED FRONT.
GRIT
I'M WELL AWARE OF THIS, BUT...
...IT STILL HURTS MY PRIDE.
EMPRESS?
SMILE
I LOOK FORWARD TO IT.

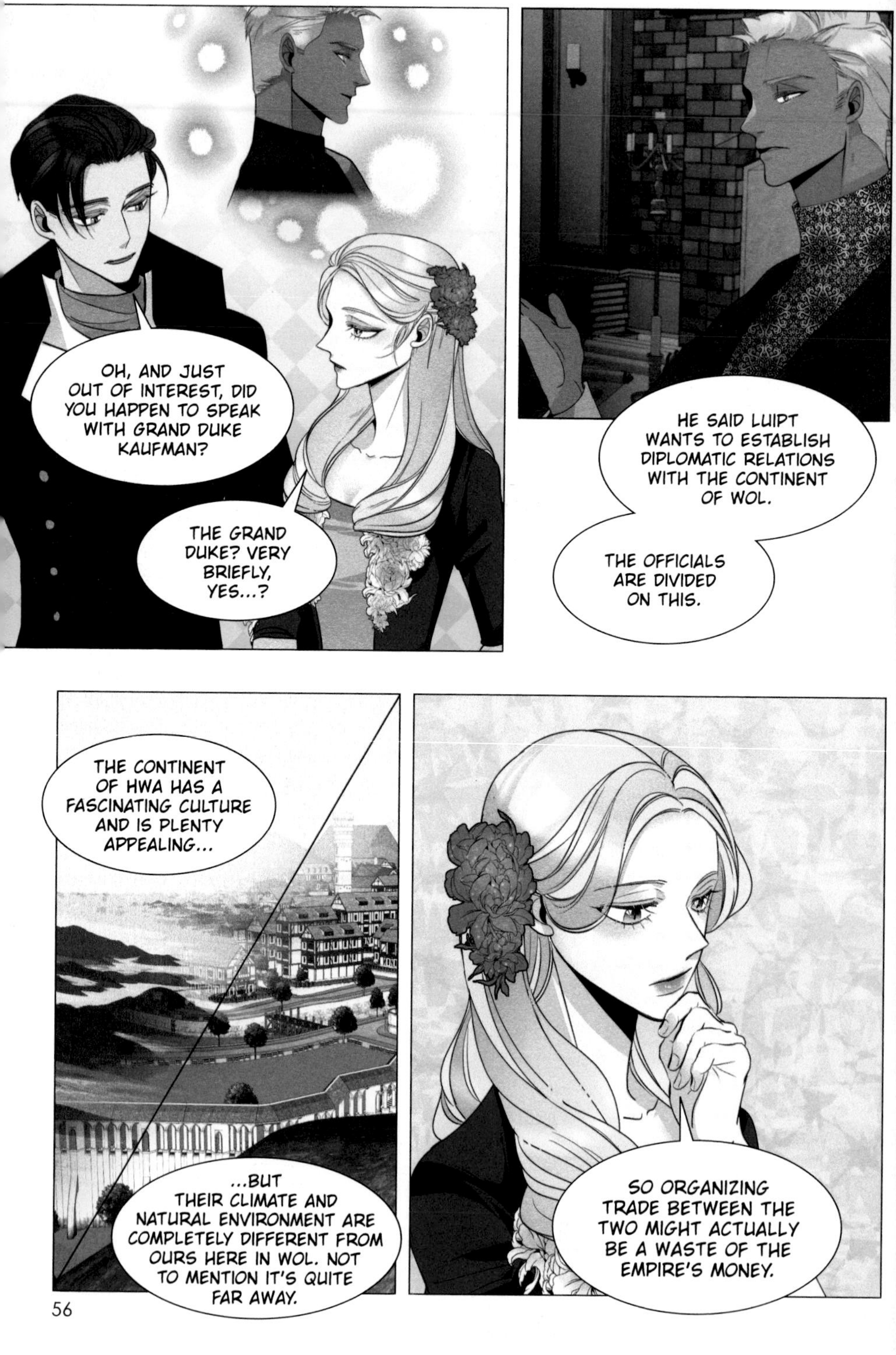
OH, AND JUST OUT OF INTEREST, DID YOU HAPPEN TO SPEAK WITH GRAND DUKE KAUFMAN?
THE GRAND DUKE? VERY BRIEFLY, YES...?
HE SAID LUIPT WANTS TO ESTABLISH DIPLOMATIC RELATIONS WITH THE CONTINENT OF WOL.
THE OFFICIALS ARE DIVIDED ON THIS.
THE CONTINENT OF HWA HAS A FASCINATING CULTURE AND IS PLENTY APPEALING...
...BUT THEIR CLIMATE AND NATURAL ENVIRONMENT ARE COMPLETELY DIFFERENT FROM OURS HERE IN WOL. NOT TO MENTION IT'S QUITE FAR AWAY.
SO ORGANIZING TRADE BETWEEN THE TWO MIGHT ACTUALLY BE A WASTE OF THE EMPIRE'S MONEY.

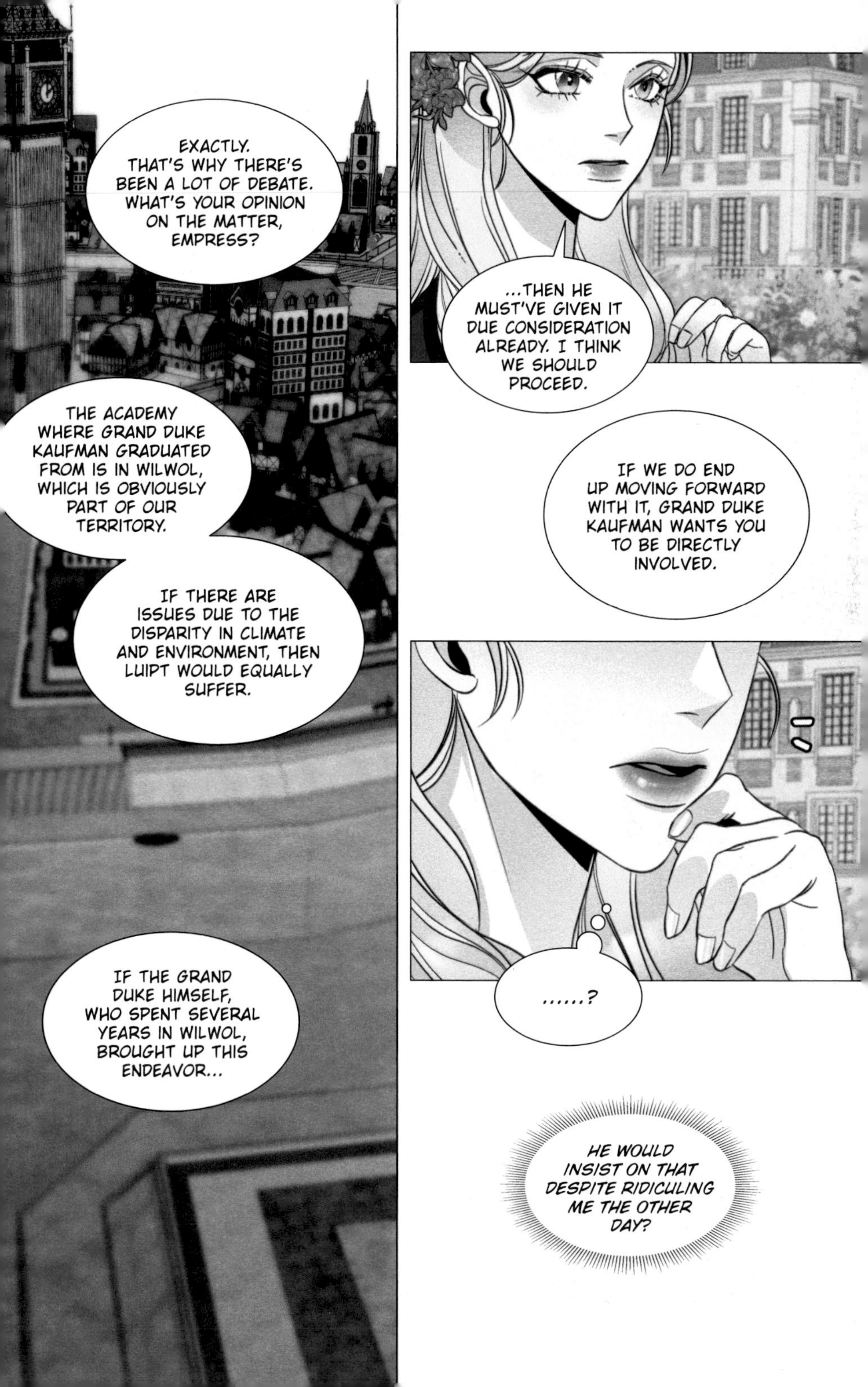
EXACTLY. THAT'S WHY THERE'S BEEN A LOT OF DEBATE. WHAT'S YOUR OPINION ON THE MATTER, EMPRESS?
THE ACADEMY WHERE GRAND DUKE KAUFMAN GRADUATED FROM IS IN WILWOL, WHICH IS OBVIOUSLY PART OF OUR TERRITORY.
IF THERE ARE ISSUES DUE TO THE DISPARITY IN CLIMATE AND ENVIRONMENT, THEN LUIPT WOULD EQUALLY SUFFER.
IF THE GRAND DUKE HIMSELF, WHO SPENT SEVERAL YEARS IN WILWOL, BROUGHT UP THIS ENDEAVOR...
...THEN HE MUST'VE GIVEN IT DUE CONSIDERATION ALREADY. I THINK WE SHOULD PROCEED.
IF WE DO END UP MOVING FORWARD WITH IT, GRAND DUKE KAUFMAN WANTS YOU TO BE DIRECTLY INVOLVED.
......?
HE WOULD INSIST ON THAT DESPITE RIDICULING ME THE OTHER DAY?

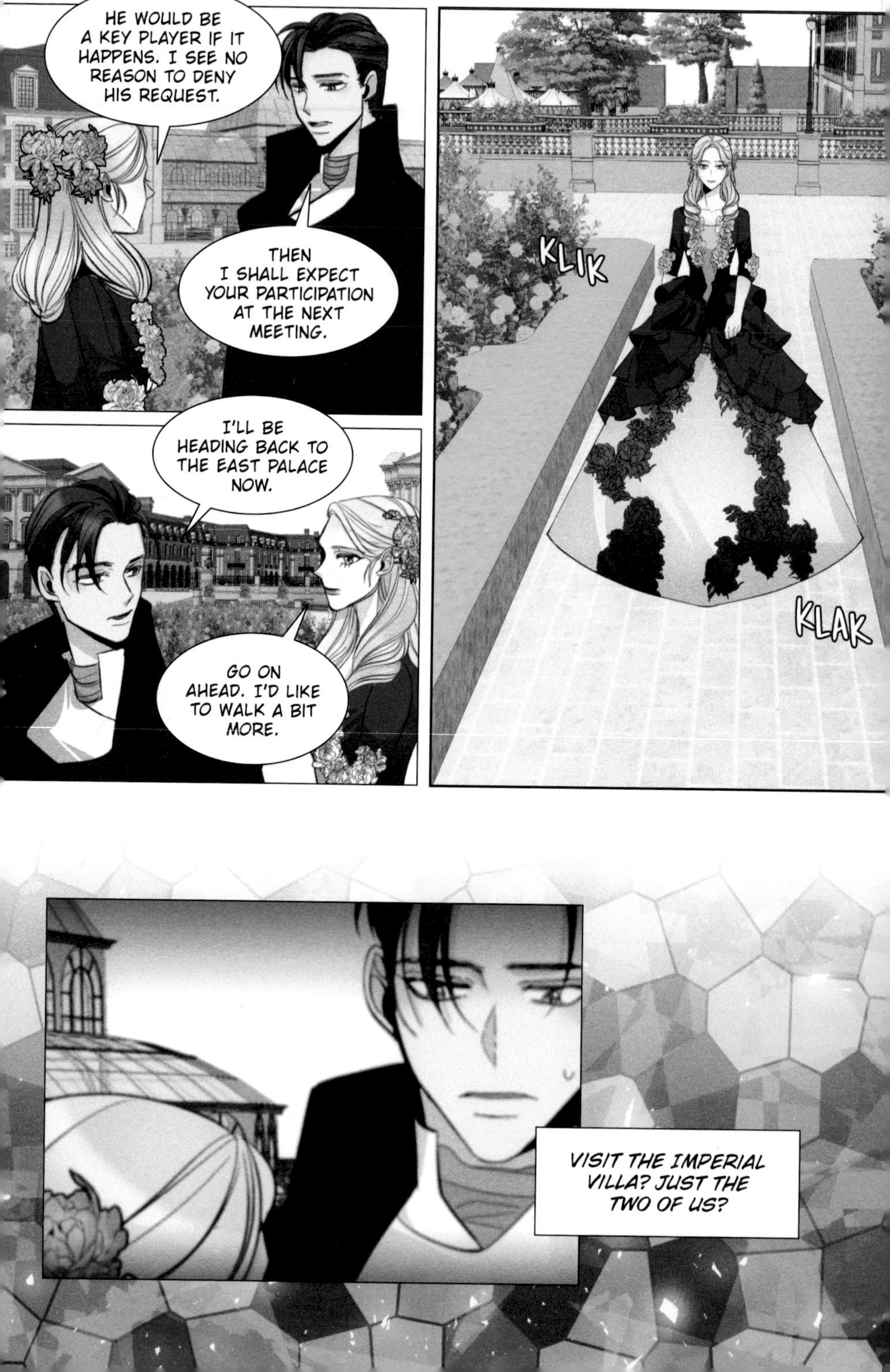
HE WOULD BE A KEY PLAYER IF IT HAPPENS. I SEE NO REASON TO DENY HIS REQUEST.
THEN I SHALL EXPECT YOUR PARTICIPATION AT THE NEXT MEETING.
I'LL BE HEADING BACK TO THE EAST PALACE NOW.
GO ON AHEAD. I'D LIKE TO WALK A BIT MORE.
KLIK
KLAK
VISIT THE IMPERIAL VILLA? JUST THE TWO OF US?

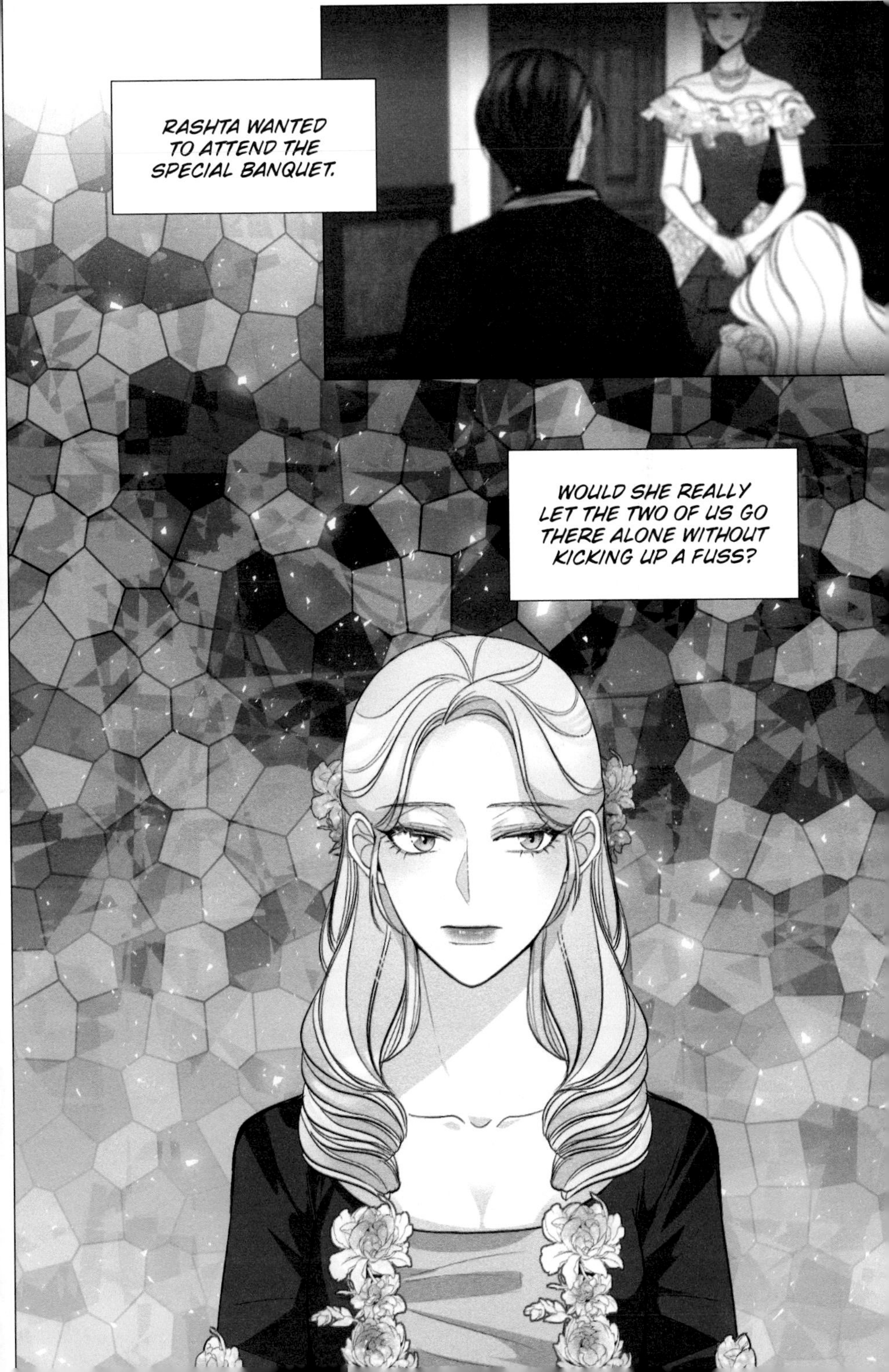
RASHTA WANTED TO ATTEND THE SPECIAL BANQUET.
WOULD SHE REALLY LET THE TWO OF US GO THERE ALONE WITHOUT KICKING UP A FUSS?

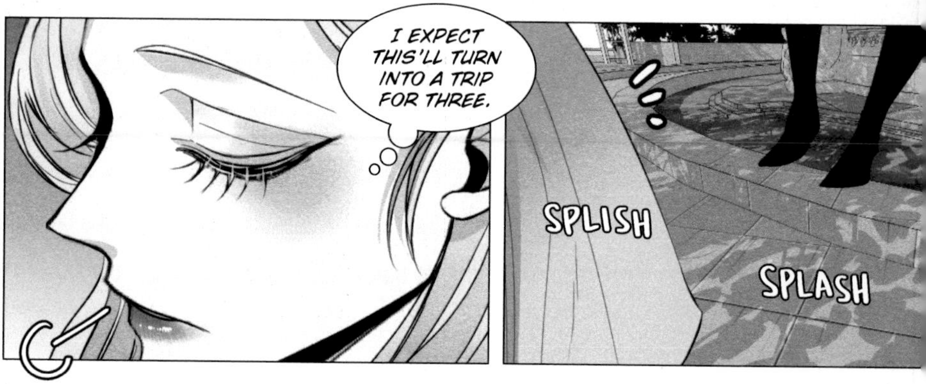
I EXPECT THIS'LL TURN INTO A TRIP FOR THREE.
SPLISH
SPLASH

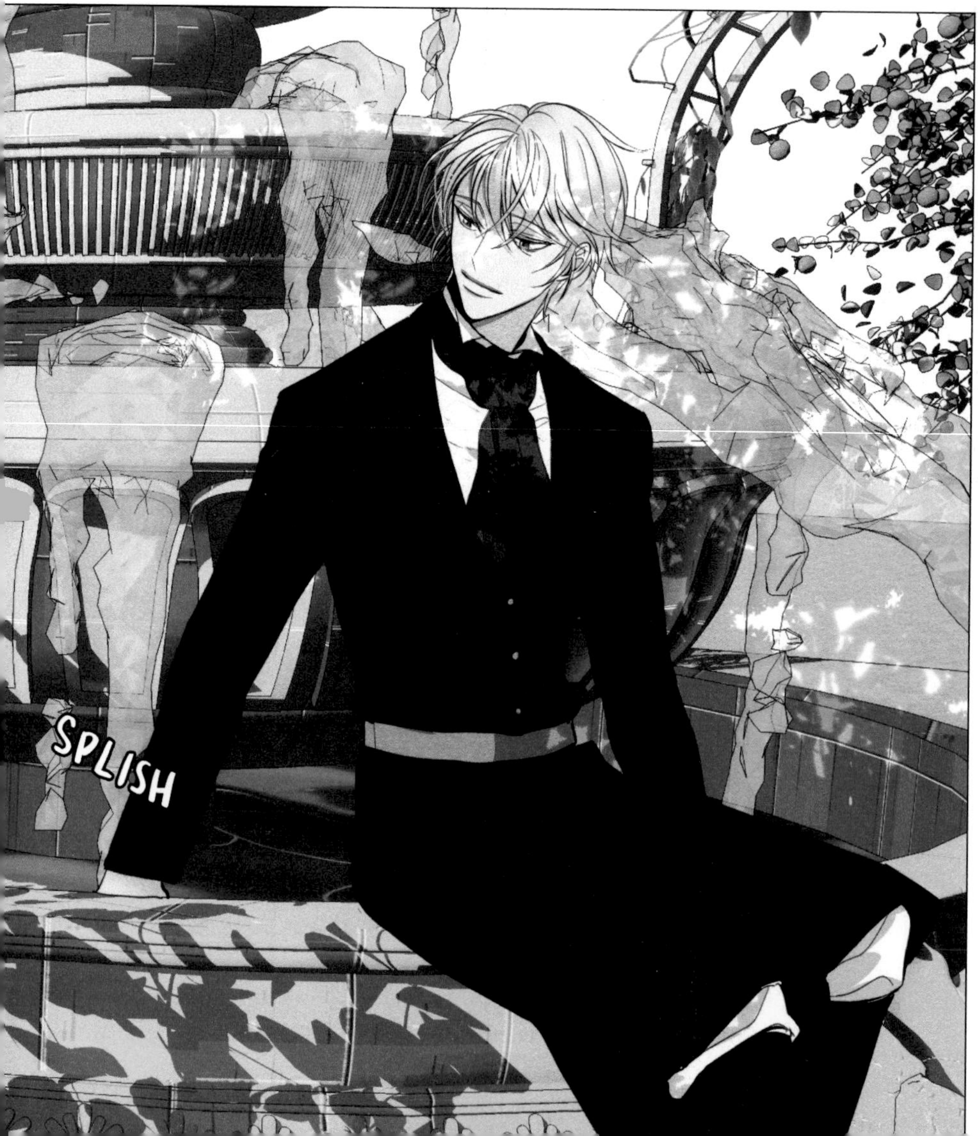
SPLISH

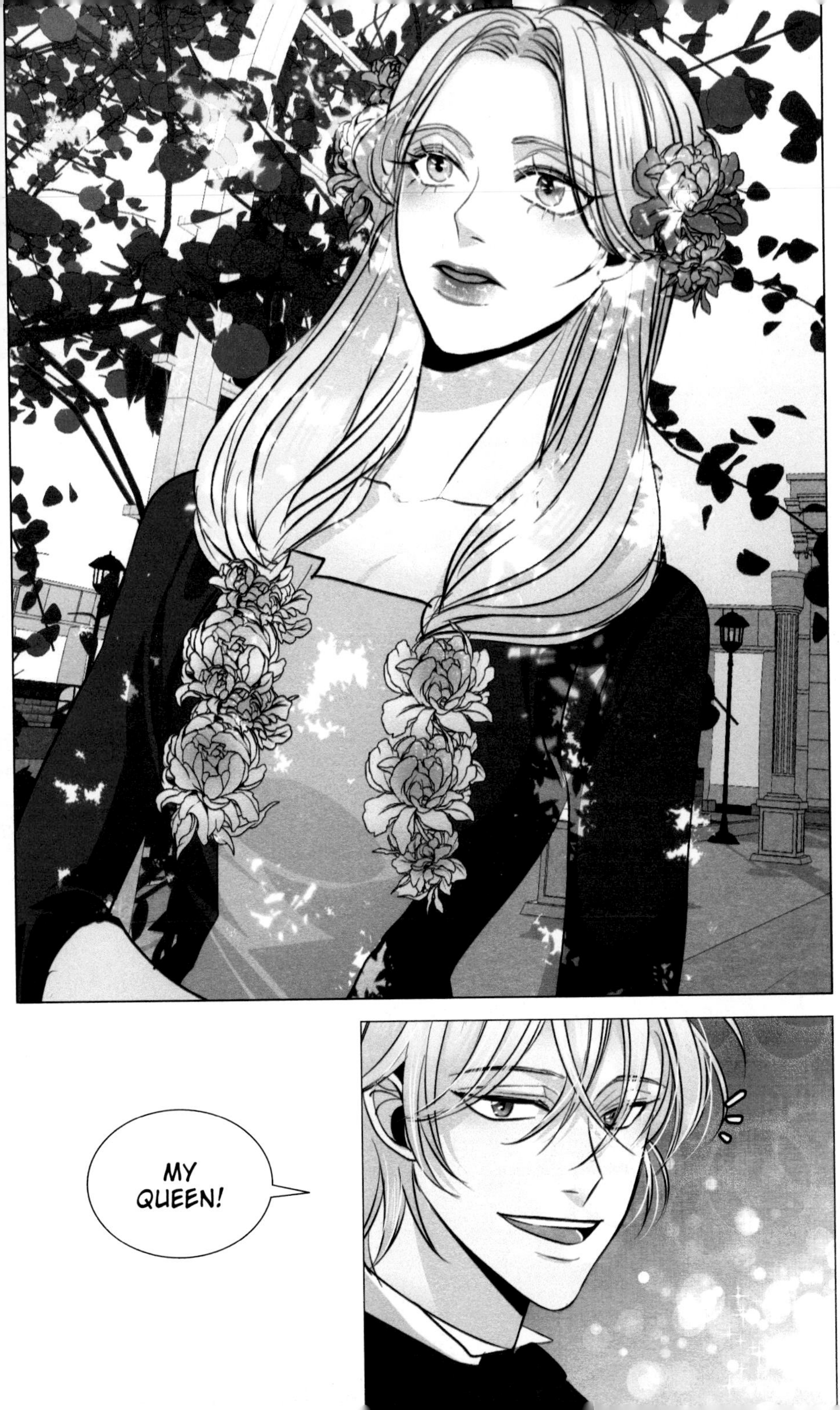
MY QUEEN!

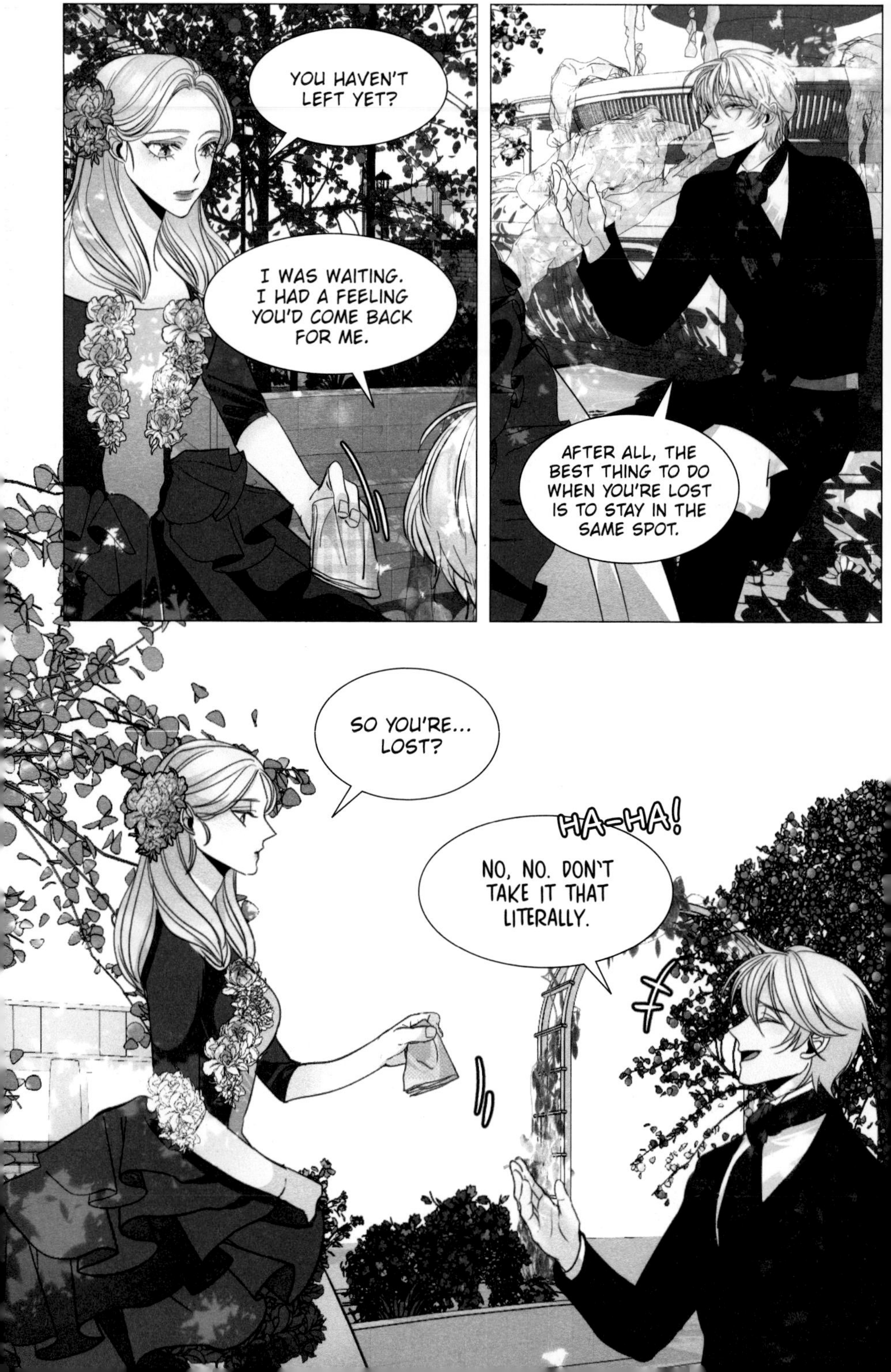
YOU HAVEN'T LEFT YET?
I WAS WAITING. I HAD A FEELING YOU'D COME BACK FOR ME.
AFTER ALL, THE BEST THING TO DO WHEN YOU'RE LOST IS TO STAY IN THE SAME SPOT.
SO YOU'RE... LOST?
HA-HA!
NO, NO. DON'T TAKE IT THAT LITERALLY.

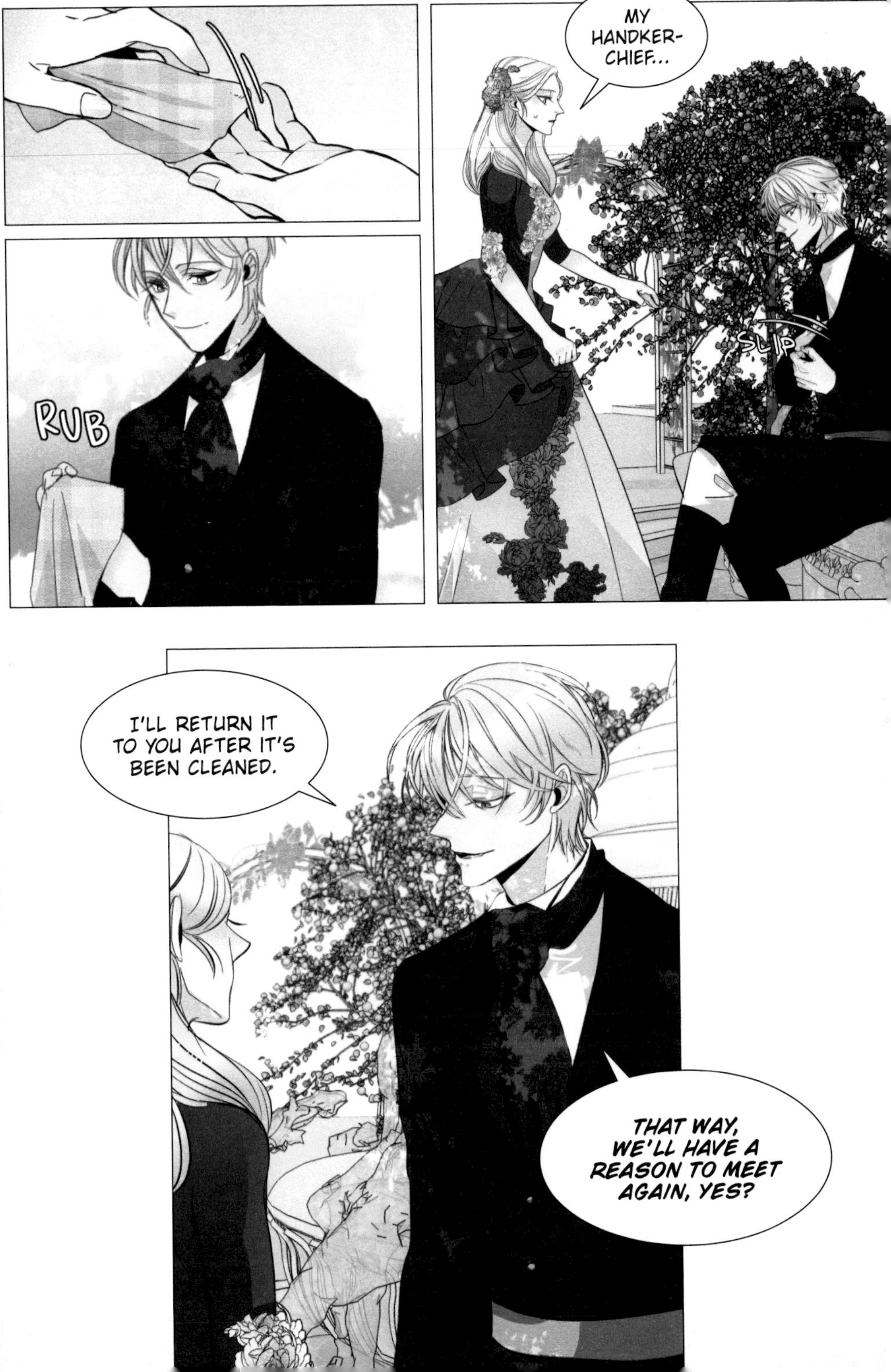
RUB
MY HANDKER-CHIEF...
SLIP
I'LL RETURN IT TO YOU AFTER IT'S BEEN CLEANED.
THAT WAY, WE'LL HAVE A REASON TO MEET AGAIN, YES?

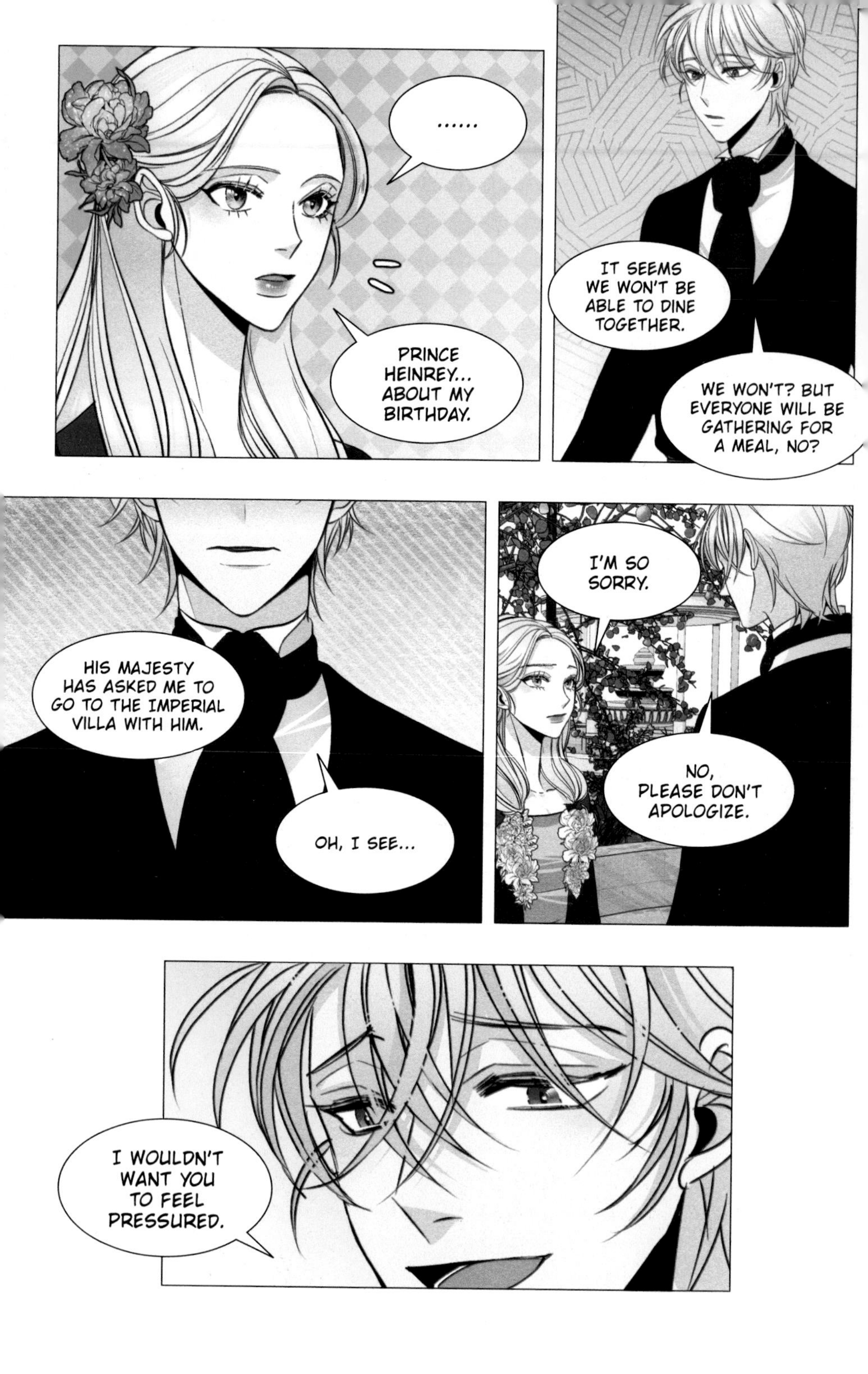
......
PRINCE HEINREY... ABOUT MY BIRTHDAY.
IT SEEMS WE WON'T BE ABLE TO DINE TOGETHER.
WE WON'T? BUT EVERYONE WILL BE GATHERING FOR A MEAL, NO?
HIS MAJESTY HAS ASKED ME TO GO TO THE IMPERIAL VILLA WITH HIM.
OH, I SEE...
I'M SO SORRY.
NO, PLEASE DON'T APOLOGIZE.
I WOULDN'T WANT YOU TO FEEL PRESSURED.

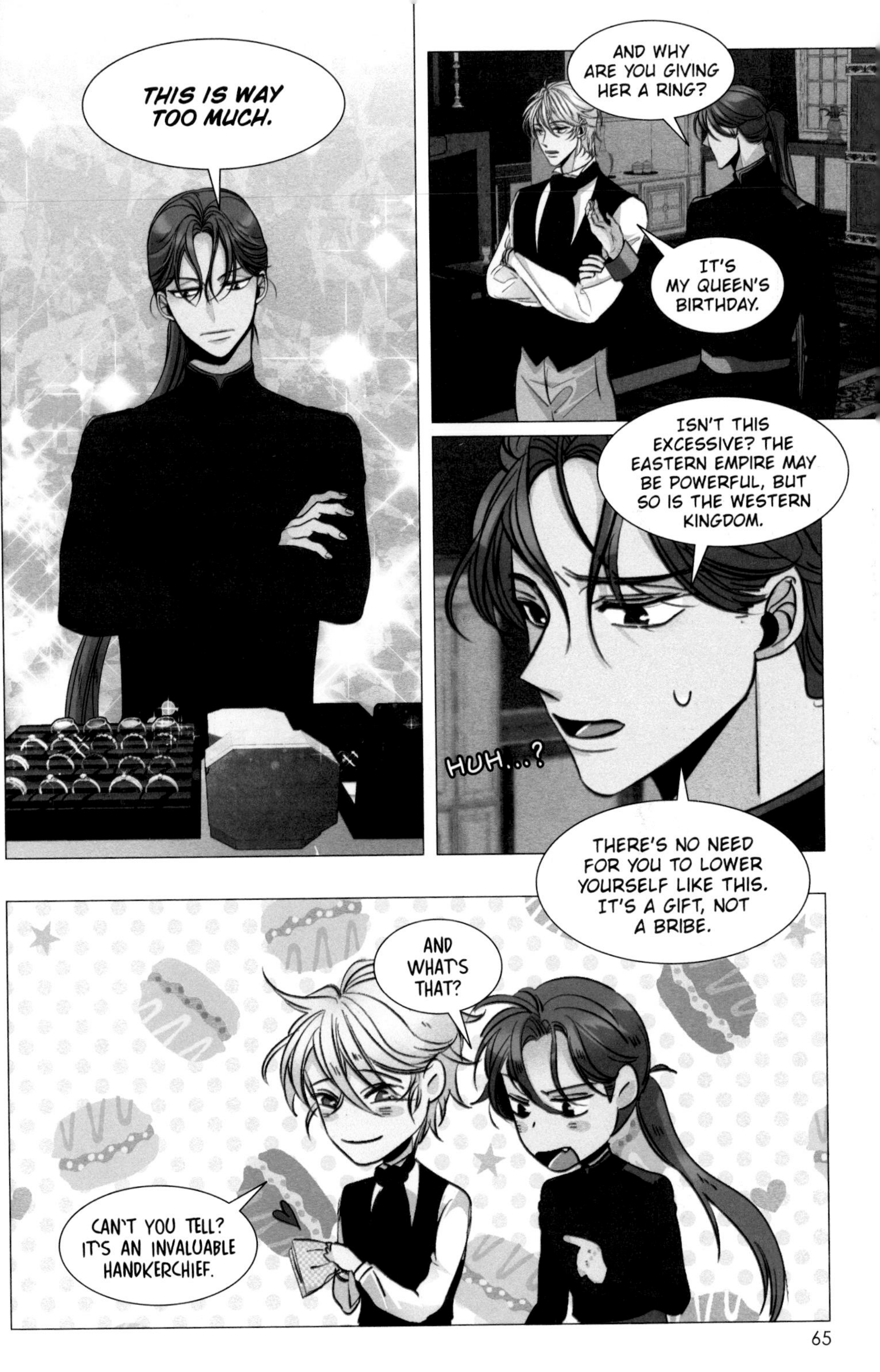
THIS IS WAY TOO MUCH.
AND WHY ARE YOU GIVING HER A RING?
IT'S MY QUEEN'S BIRTHDAY.
ISN'T THIS EXCESSIVE? THE EASTERN EMPIRE MAY BE POWERFUL, BUT SO IS THE WESTERN KINGDOM.
HUH...?
THERE'S NO NEED FOR YOU TO LOWER YOURSELF LIKE THIS. IT'S A GIFT, NOT A BRIBE.
AND WHAT'S THAT?
CAN'T YOU TELL? IT'S AN INVALUABLE HANDKERCHIEF.

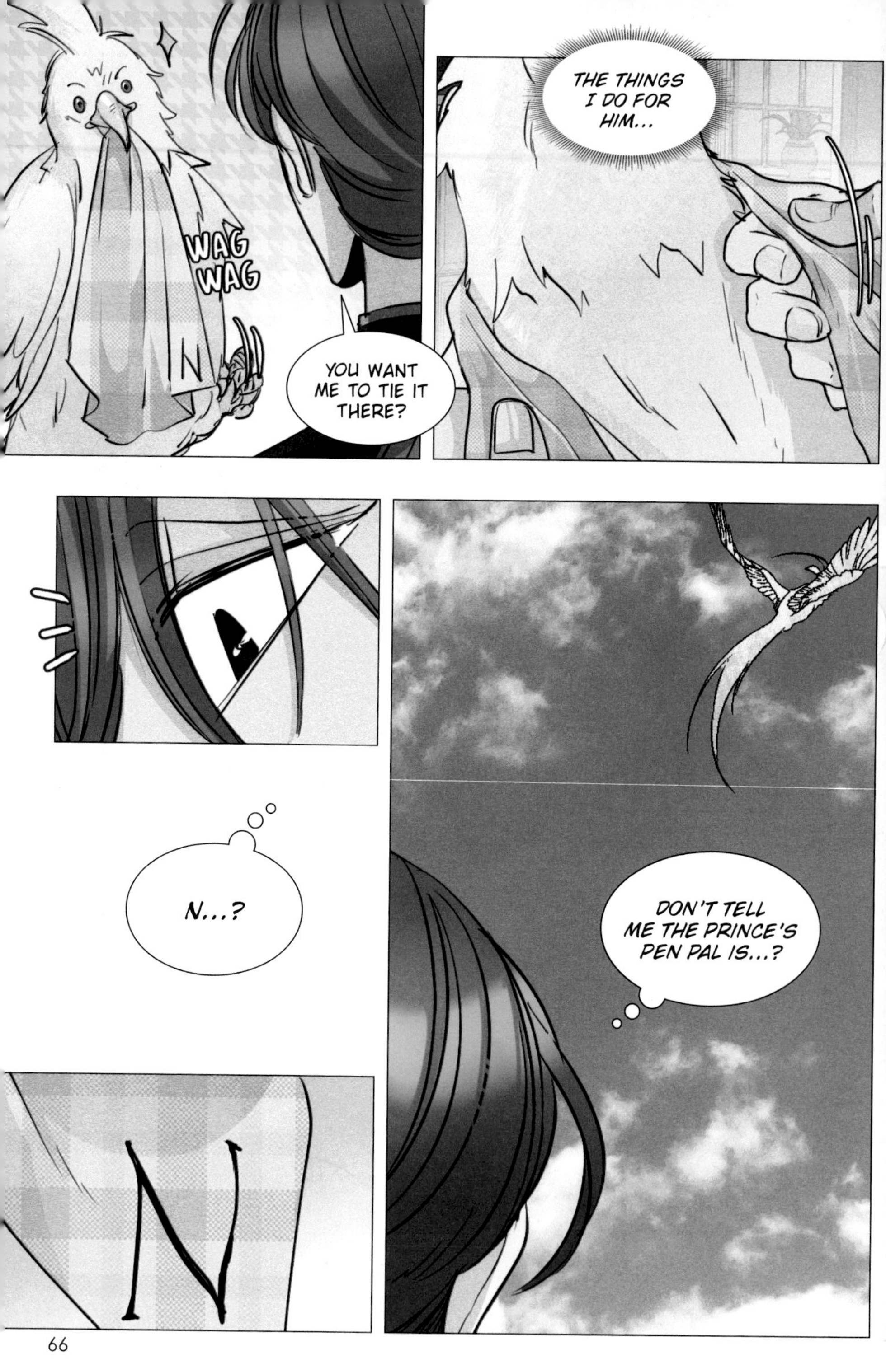
WAG
WAG
YOU WANT ME TO TIE IT THERE?
THE THINGS I DO FOR HIM...
N...?
DON'T TELL ME THE PRINCE'S PEN PAL IS...?
N

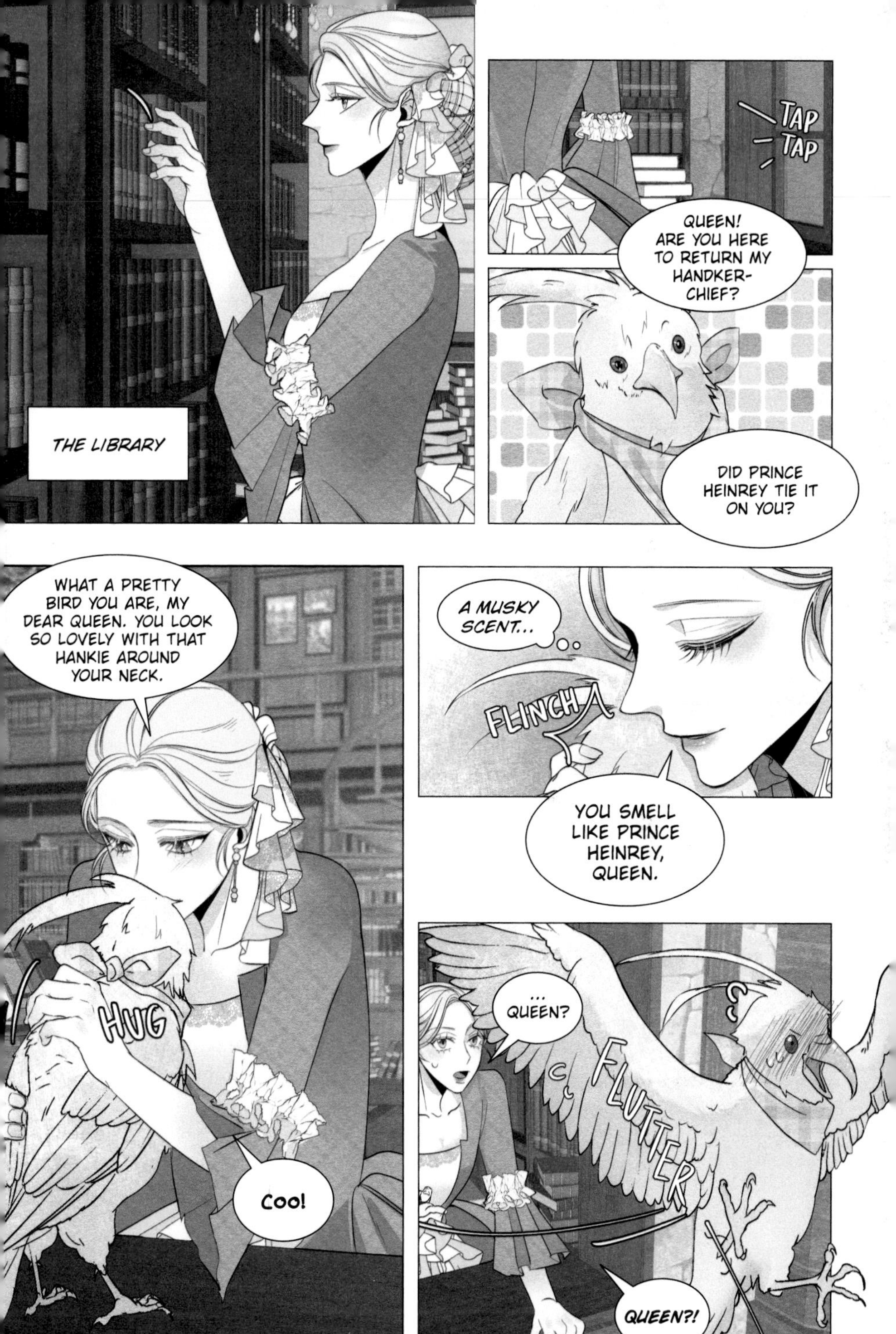
THE LIBRARY
TAP TAP
QUEEN! ARE YOU HERE TO RETURN MY HANDKER-CHIEF?
DID PRINCE HEINREY TIE IT ON YOU?
WHAT A PRETTY BIRD YOU ARE, MY DEAR QUEEN. YOU LOOK SO LOVELY WITH THAT HANKIE AROUND YOUR NECK.
HUG
COO!
A MUSKY SCENT...
FLINCH
YOU SMELL LIKE PRINCE HEINREY, QUEEN.
... QUEEN?
FLUTTER
QUEEN?!

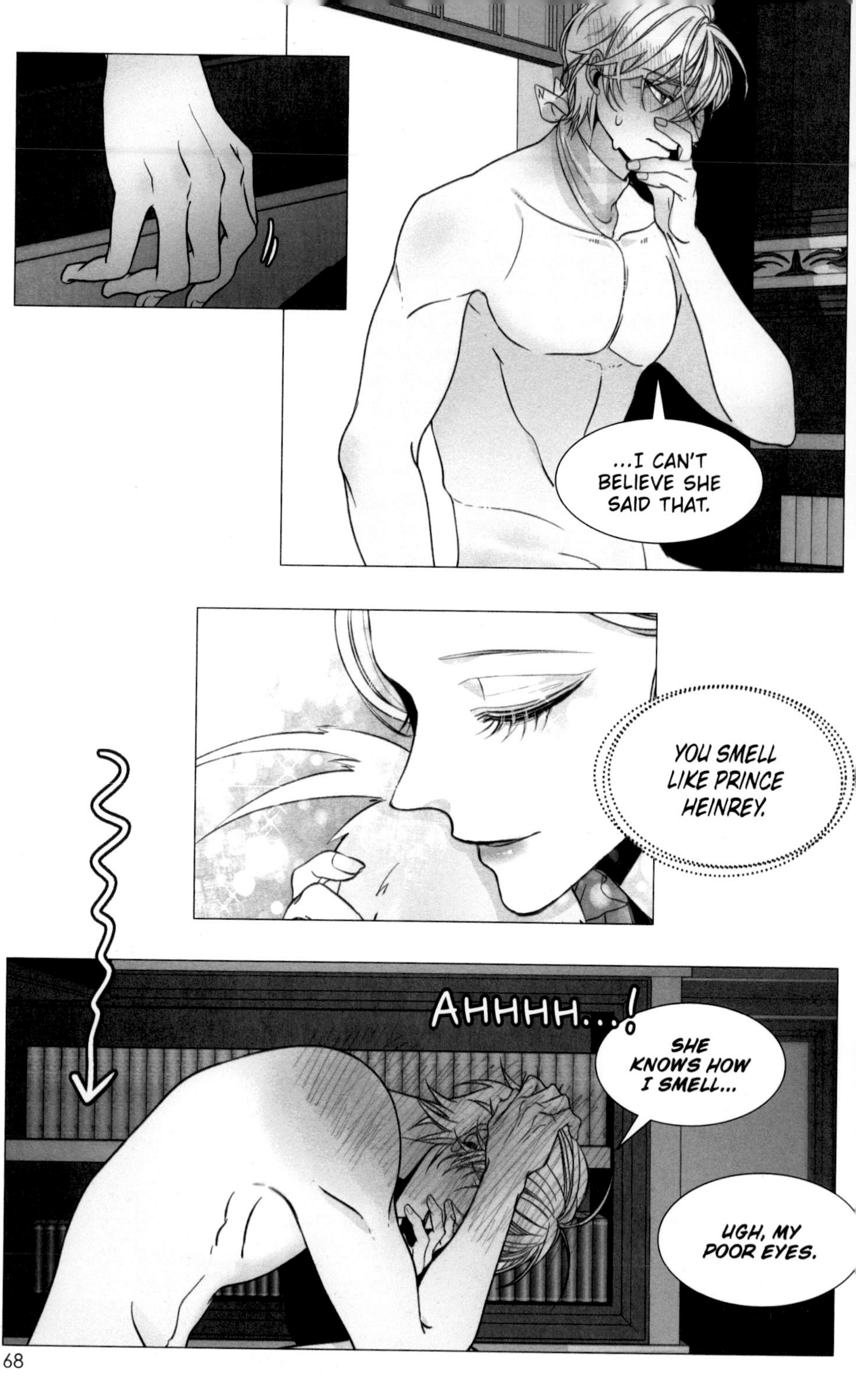
...I CAN'T BELIEVE SHE SAID THAT.
YOU SMELL LIKE PRINCE HEINREY.
AHHHH...!
SHE KNOWS HOW I SMELL...
UGH, MY POOR EYES.

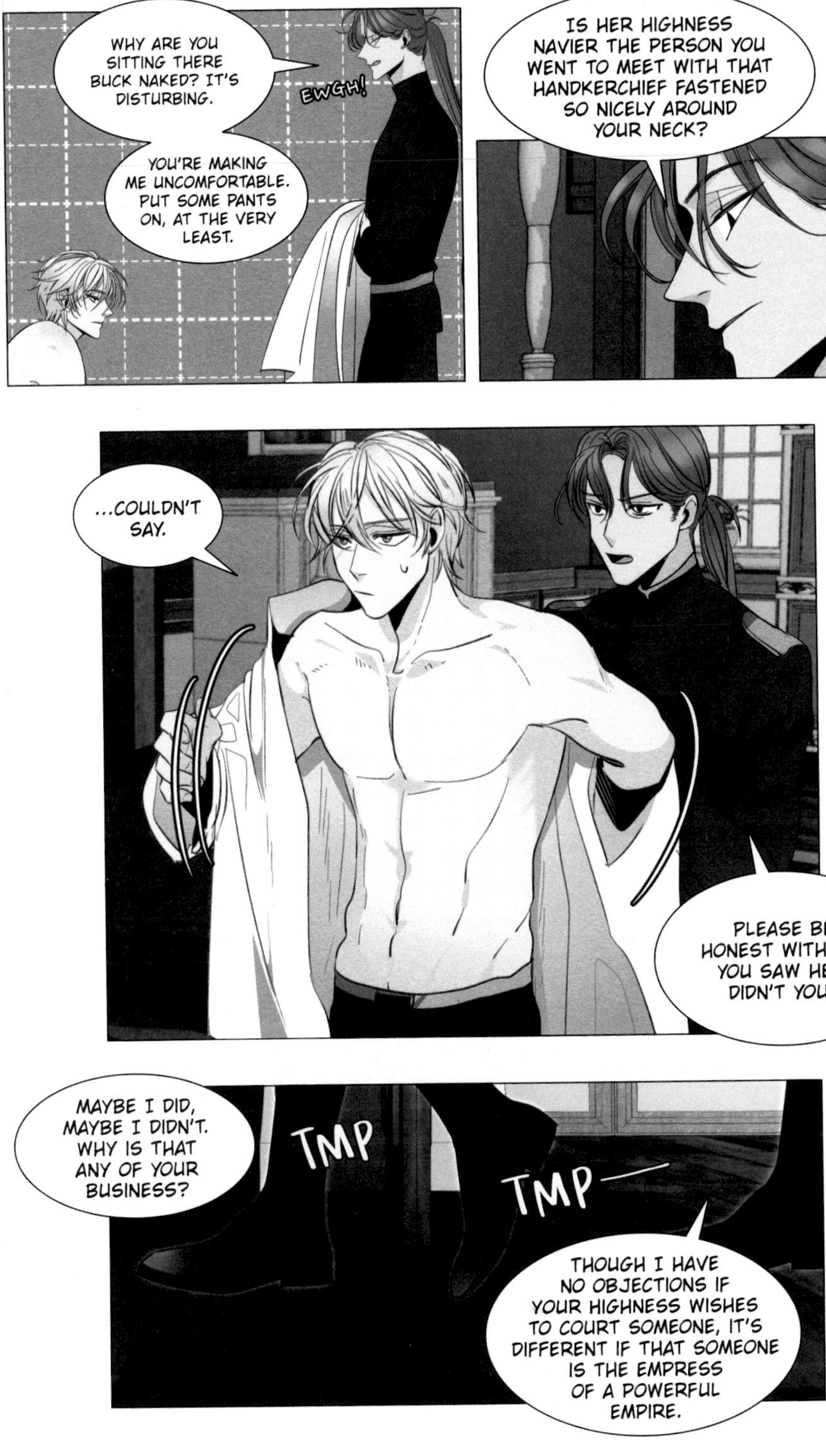
WHY ARE YOU SITTING THERE BUCK NAKED? IT'S DISTURBING.
EWGH!
YOU'RE MAKING ME UNCOMFORTABLE. PUT SOME PANTS ON, AT THE VERY LEAST.
IS HER HIGHNESS NAVIER THE PERSON YOU WENT TO MEET WITH THAT HANDKERCHIEF FASTENED SO NICELY AROUND YOUR NECK?
...COULDN'T SAY.
PLEASE BE HONEST WITH ME. YOU SAW HER, DIDN'T YOU?
MAYBE I DID, MAYBE I DIDN'T. WHY IS THAT ANY OF YOUR BUSINESS?
TMP
TMP—
THOUGH I HAVE NO OBJECTIONS IF YOUR HIGHNESS WISHES TO COURT SOMEONE, IT'S DIFFERENT IF THAT SOMEONE IS THE EMPRESS OF A POWERFUL EMPIRE.

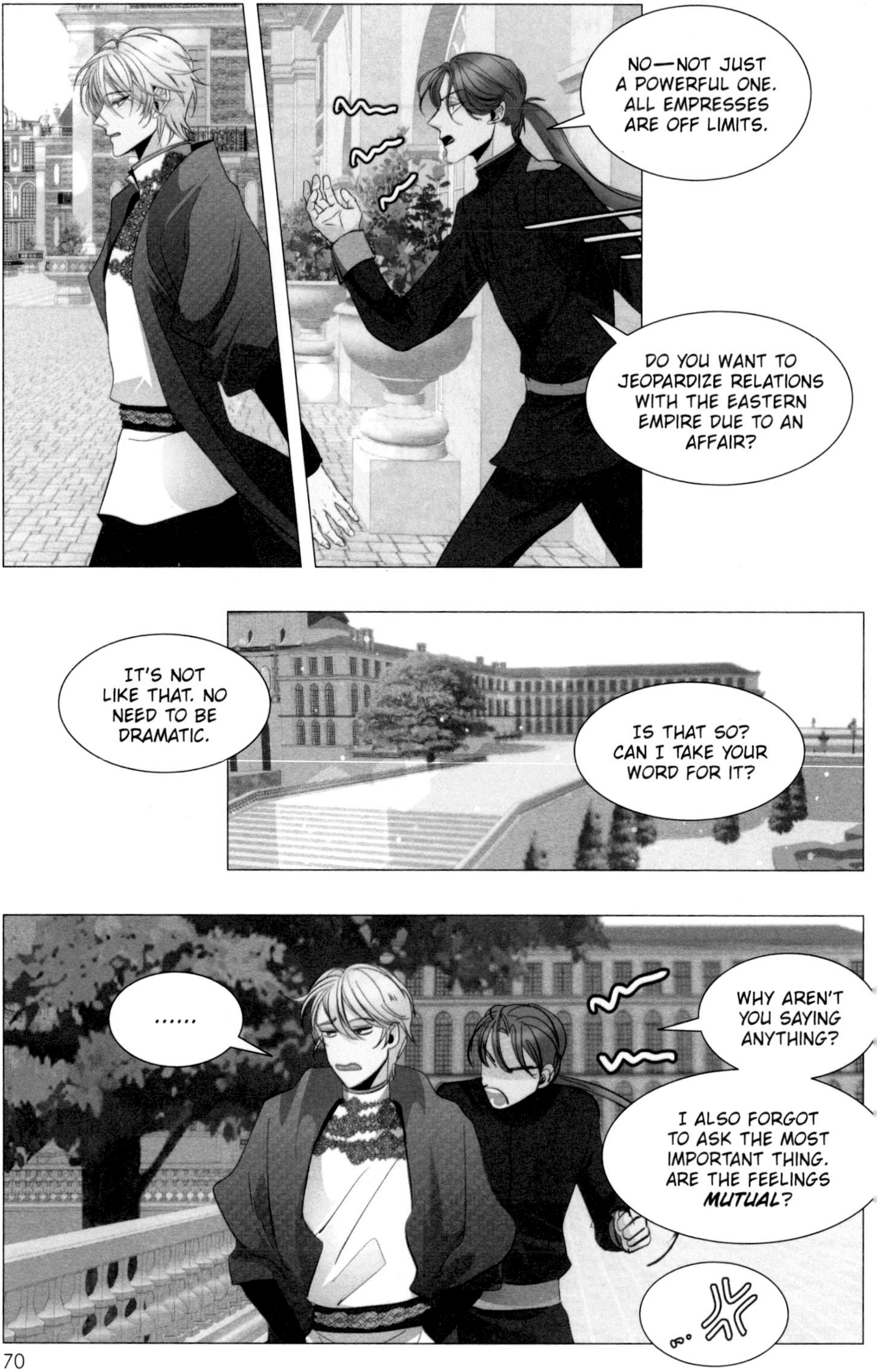

NO—NOT JUST A POWERFUL ONE. ALL EMPRESSES ARE OFF LIMITS.
DO YOU WANT TO JEOPARDIZE RELATIONS WITH THE EASTERN EMPIRE DUE TO AN AFFAIR?
IT'S NOT LIKE THAT. NO NEED TO BE DRAMATIC.
IS THAT SO? CAN I TAKE YOUR WORD FOR IT?
......
WHY AREN'T YOU SAYING ANYTHING?
I ALSO FORGOT TO ASK THE MOST IMPORTANT THING. ARE THE FEELINGS MUTUAL?

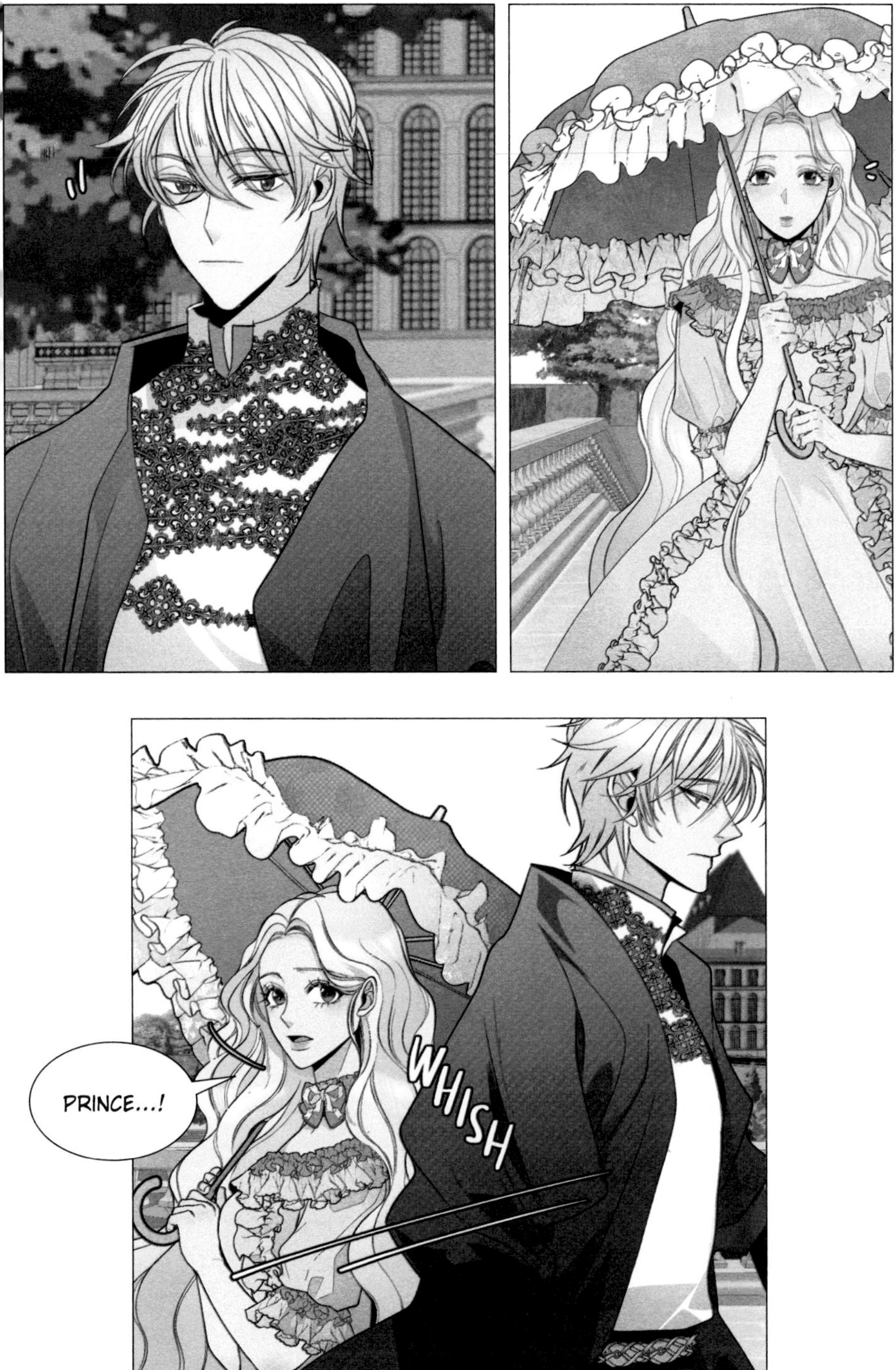
PRINCE...!
WHISH

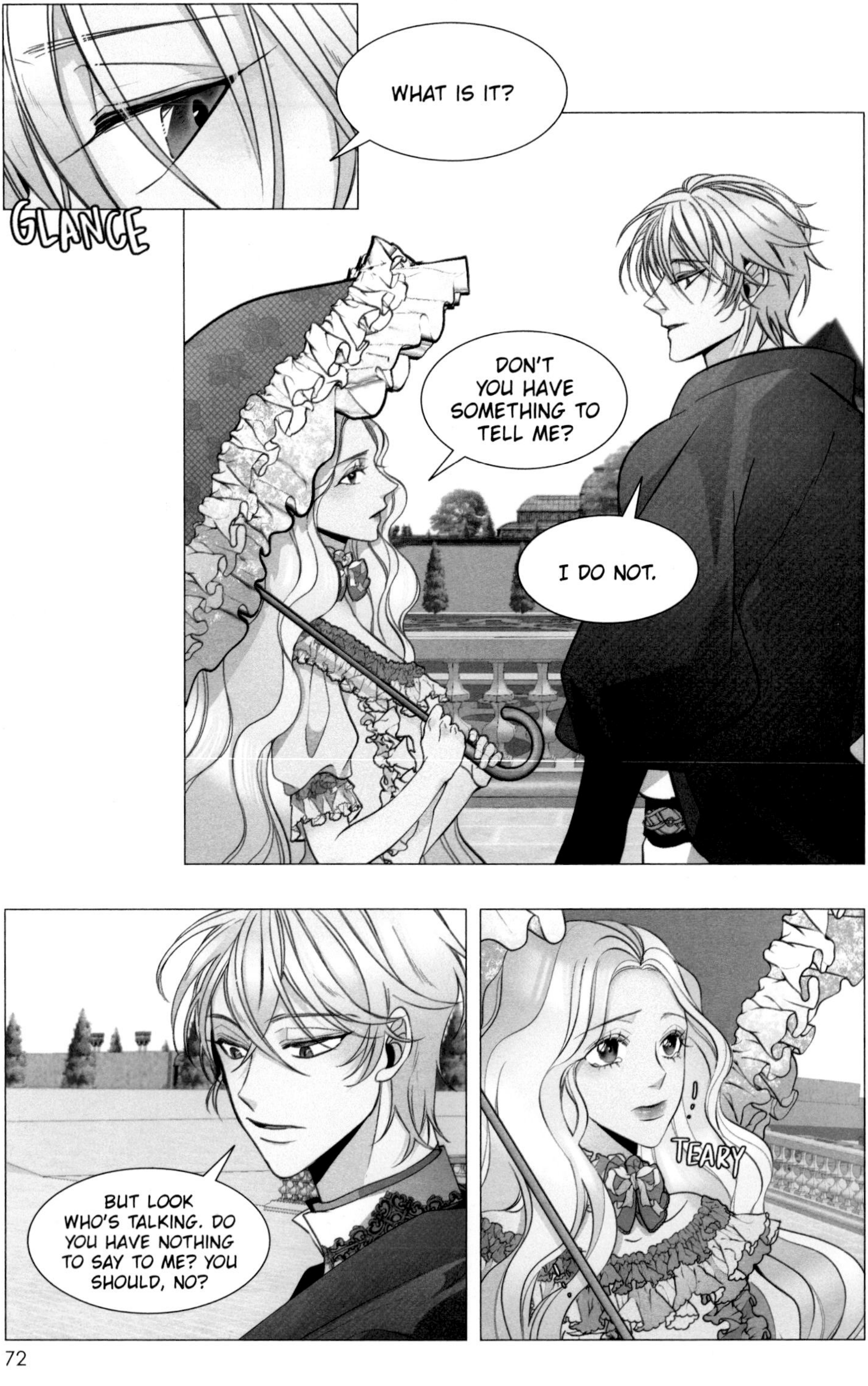
WHAT IS IT?
GLANCE
DON'T YOU HAVE SOMETHING TO TELL ME?
I DO NOT.
BUT LOOK WHO'S TALKING. DO YOU HAVE NOTHING TO SAY TO ME? YOU SHOULD, NO?
!
TEARY

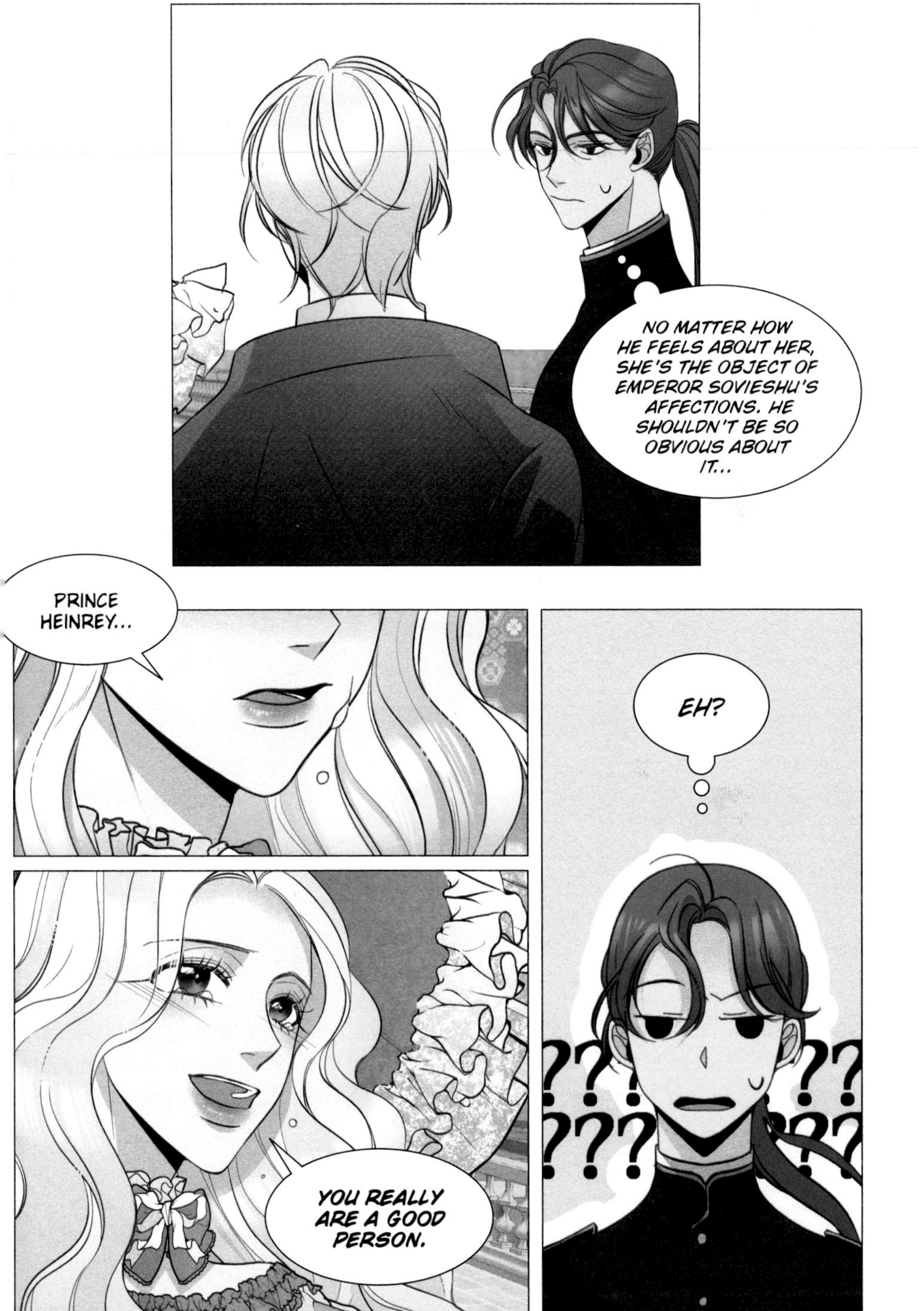
NO MATTER HOW HE FEELS ABOUT HER, SHE'S THE OBJECT OF EMPEROR SOVIESHU'S AFFECTIONS. HE SHOULDN'T BE SO OBVIOUS ABOUT IT...
PRINCE HEINREY...
EH?
YOU REALLY ARE A GOOD PERSON.
???
???

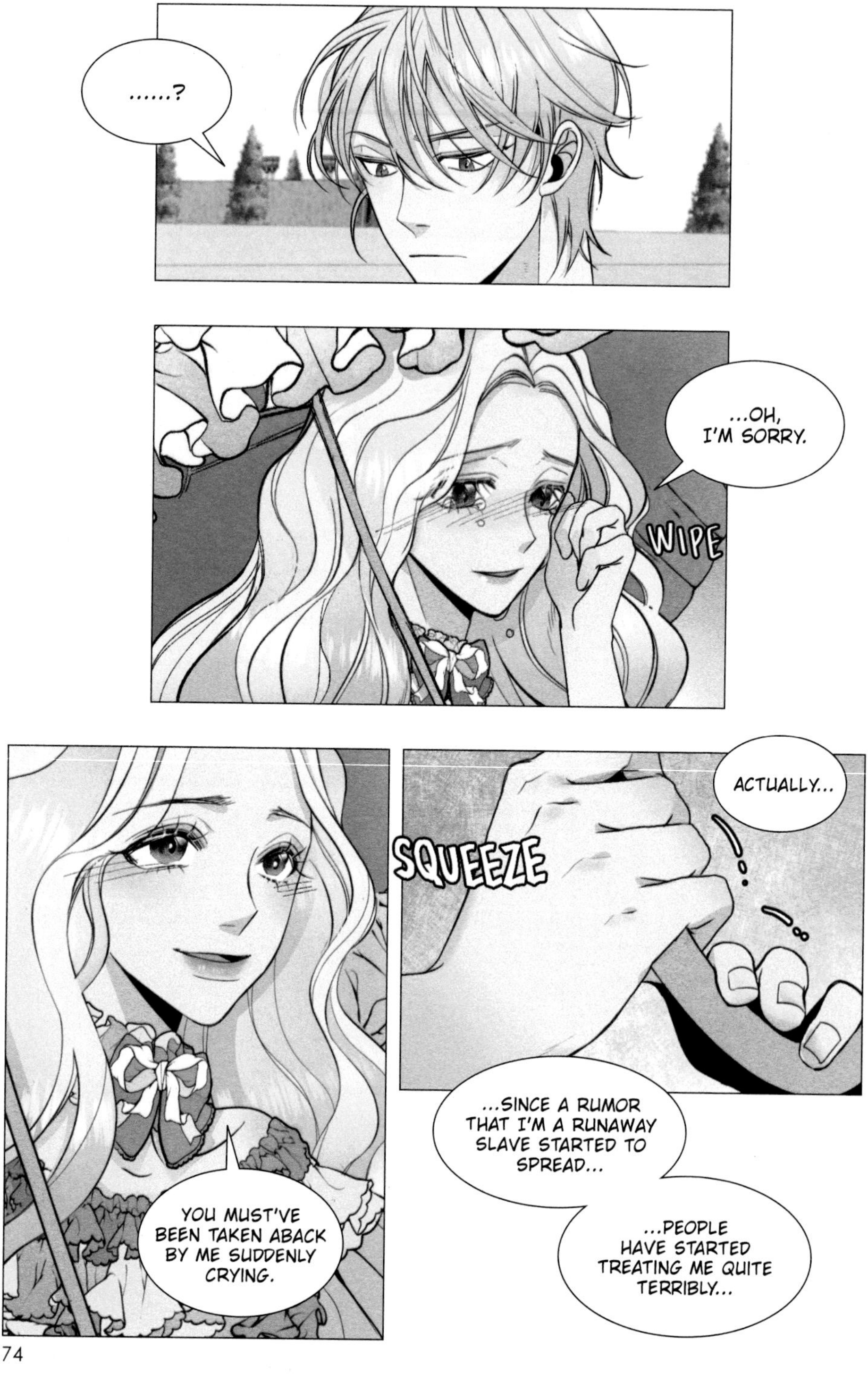
......?
...OH, I'M SORRY.
WIPE
YOU MUST'VE BEEN TAKEN ABACK BY ME SUDDENLY CRYING.
ACTUALLY...
SQUEEZE
...SINCE A RUMOR THAT I'M A RUNAWAY SLAVE STARTED TO SPREAD...
...PEOPLE HAVE STARTED TREATING ME QUITE TERRIBLY...

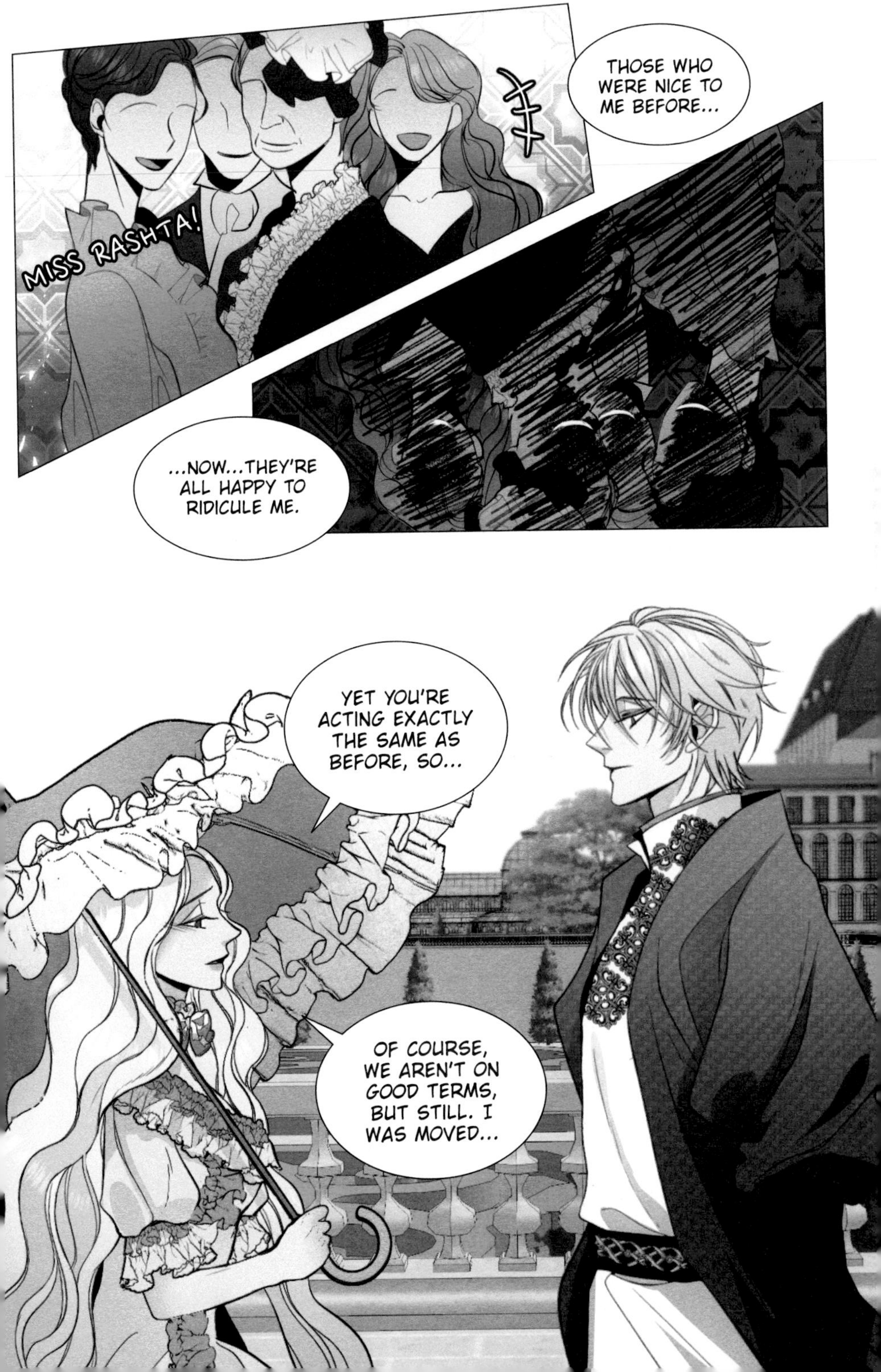
MISS RASHTA!
THOSE WHO WERE NICE TO ME BEFORE...
...NOW...THEY'RE ALL HAPPY TO RIDICULE ME.
YET YOU'RE ACTING EXACTLY THE SAME AS BEFORE, SO...
OF COURSE, WE AREN'T ON GOOD TERMS, BUT STILL. I WAS MOVED...

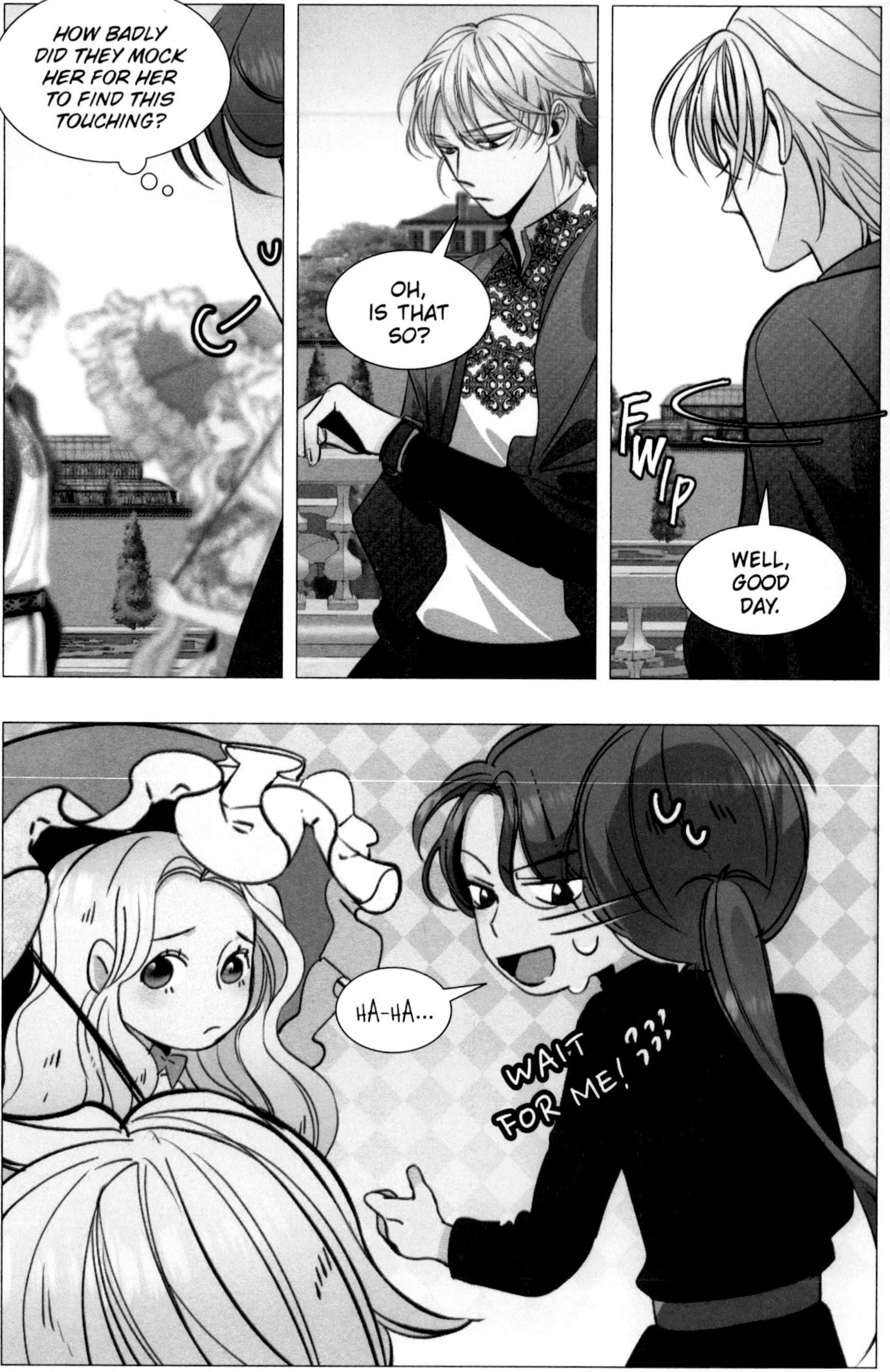
HOW BADLY DID THEY MOCK HER FOR HER TO FIND THIS TOUCHING?
OH, IS THAT SO?
FWIP
WELL, GOOD DAY.
HA-HA...
WAIT FOR ME!

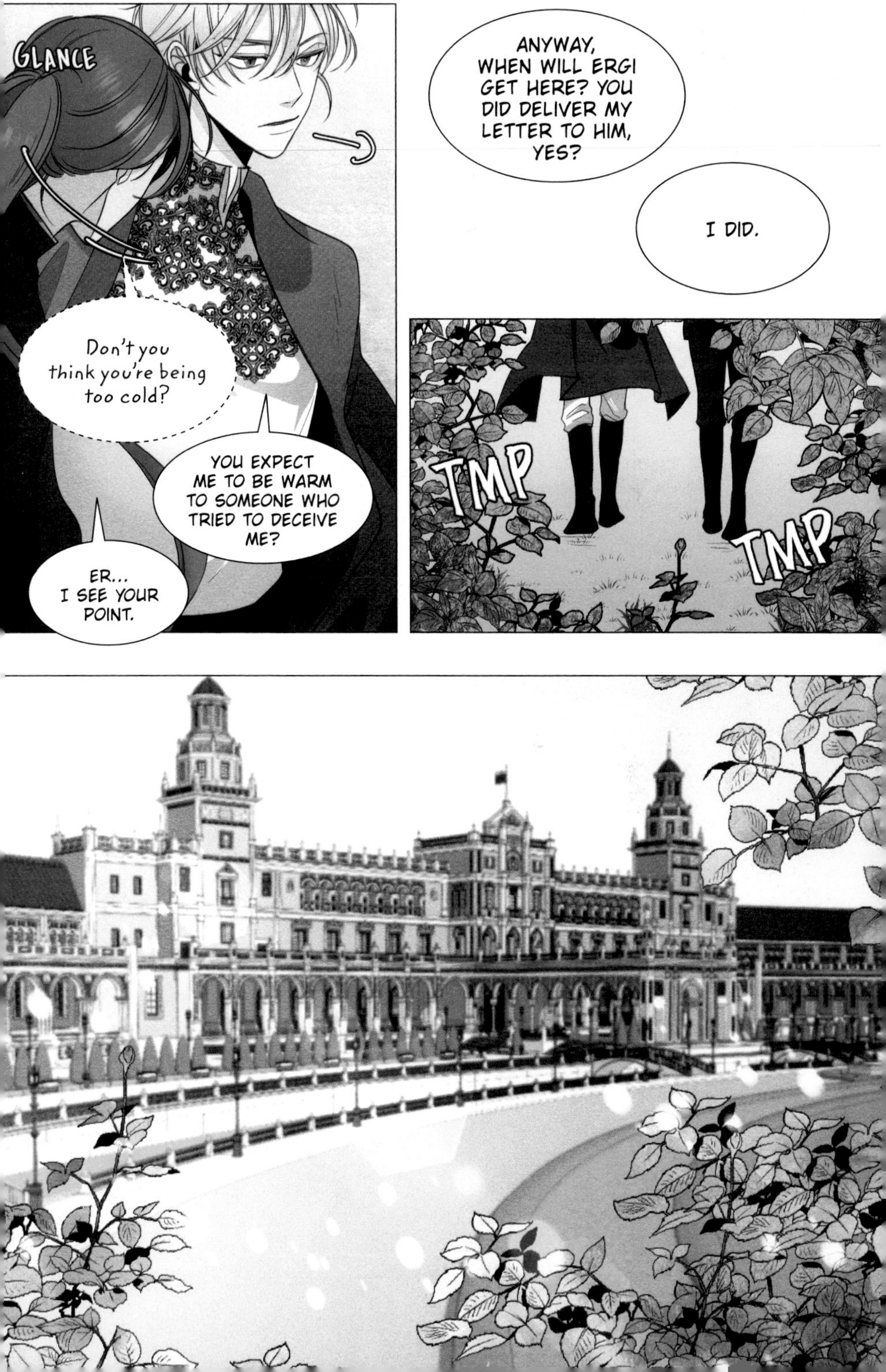
GLANCE
Don't you think you're being too cold?
YOU EXPECT ME TO BE WARM TO SOMEONE WHO TRIED TO DECEIVE ME?
ER... I SEE YOUR POINT.
ANYWAY, WHEN WILL ERGI GET HERE? YOU DID DELIVER MY LETTER TO HIM, YES?
I DID.
TMP
TMP

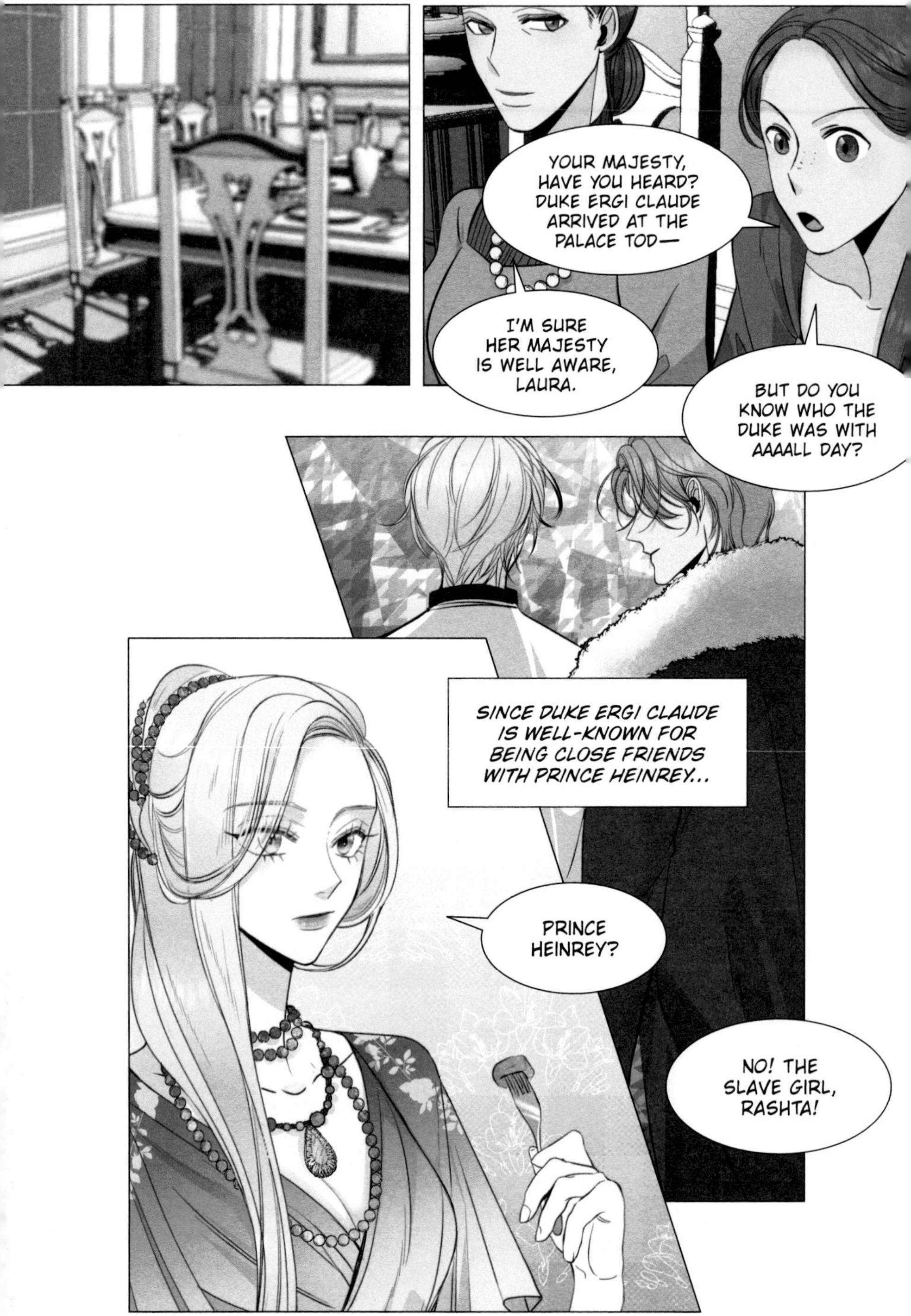

YOUR MAJESTY, HAVE YOU HEARD? DUKE ERGI CLAUDE ARRIVED AT THE PALACE TOD—
I'M SURE HER MAJESTY IS WELL AWARE, LAURA.
BUT DO YOU KNOW WHO THE DUKE WAS WITH AAAALL DAY?
SINCE DUKE ERGI CLAUDE IS WELL-KNOWN FOR BEING CLOSE FRIENDS WITH PRINCE HEINREY...
PRINCE HEINREY?
NO! THE SLAVE GIRL, RASHTA!

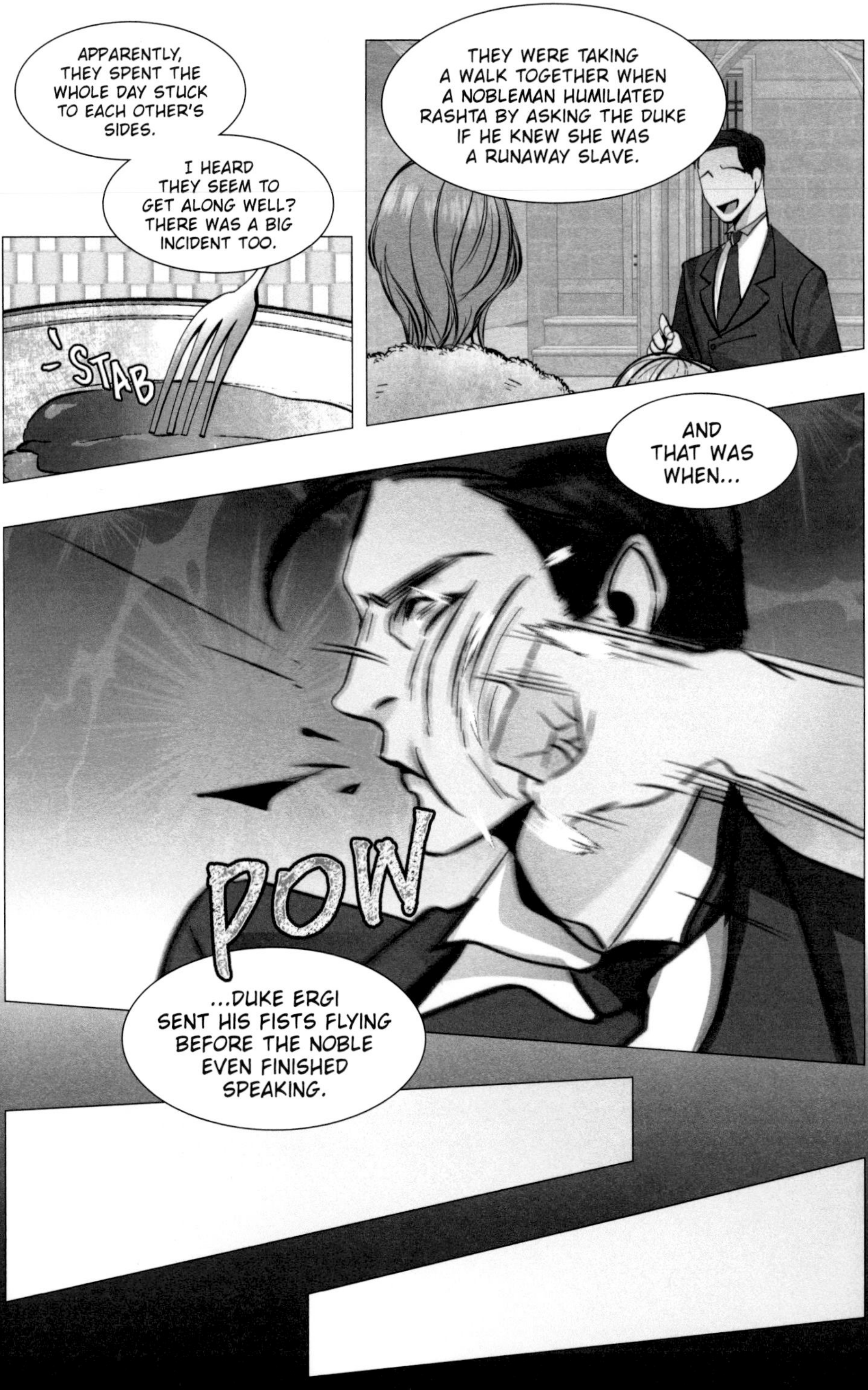
APPARENTLY, THEY SPENT THE WHOLE DAY STUCK TO EACH OTHER'S SIDES.
I HEARD THEY SEEM TO GET ALONG WELL? THERE WAS A BIG INCIDENT TOO.
STAB
THEY WERE TAKING A WALK TOGETHER WHEN A NOBLEMAN HUMILIATED RASHTA BY ASKING THE DUKE IF HE KNEW SHE WAS A RUNAWAY SLAVE.
AND THAT WAS WHEN...
POW
...DUKE ERGI SENT HIS FISTS FLYING BEFORE THE NOBLE EVEN FINISHED SPEAKING.

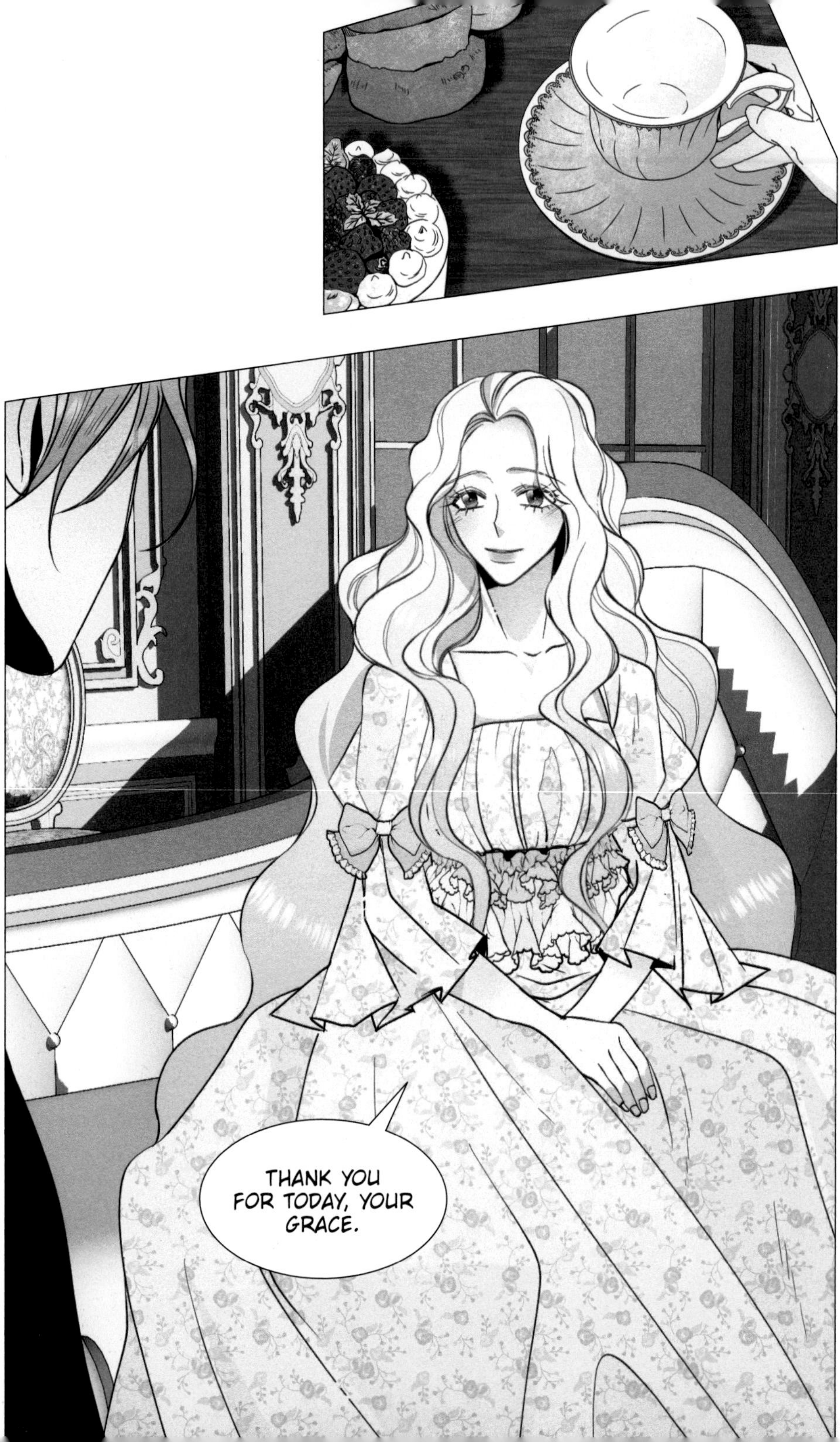
THANK YOU FOR TODAY, YOUR GRACE.

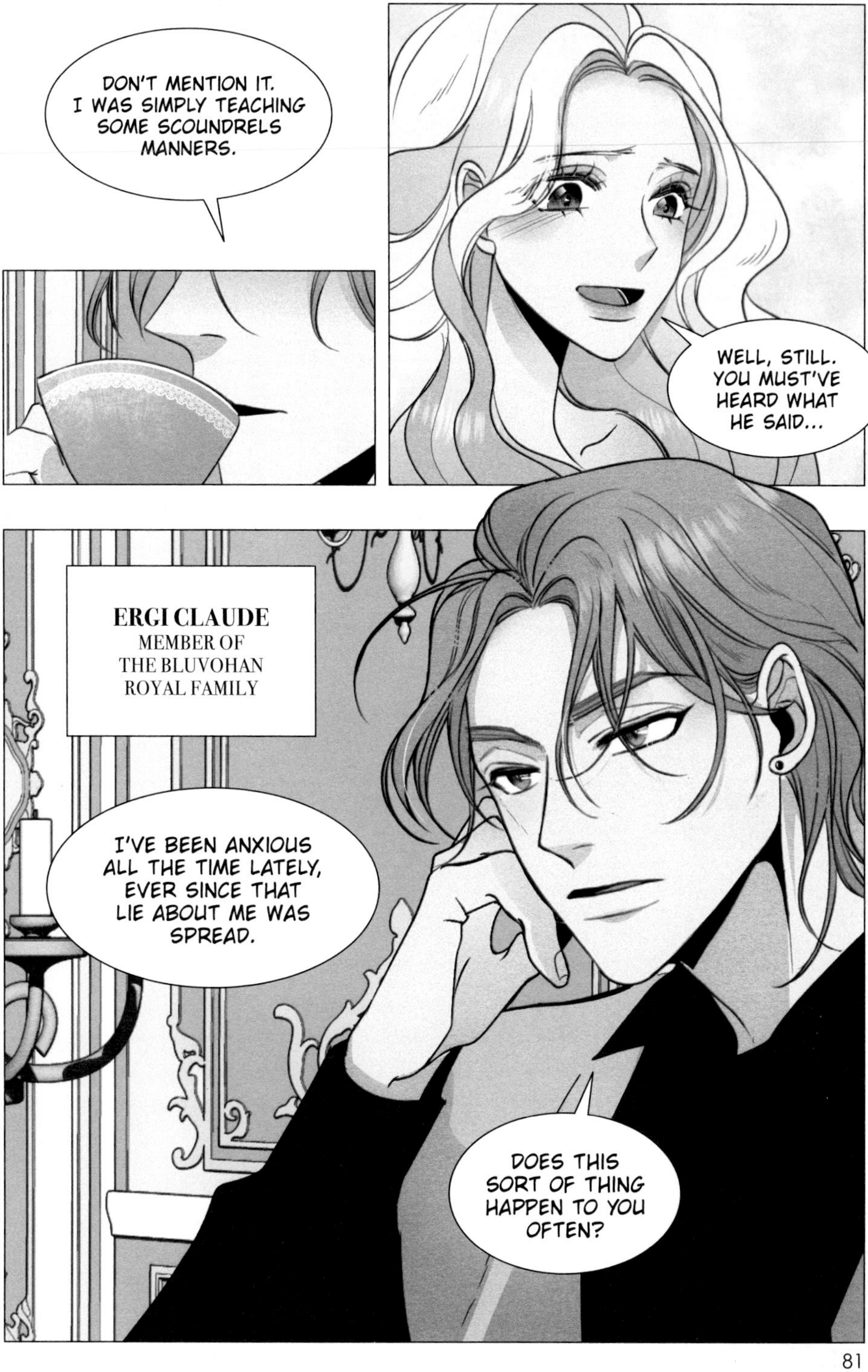
DON'T MENTION IT. I WAS SIMPLY TEACHING SOME SCOUNDRELS MANNERS.
WELL, STILL. YOU MUST'VE HEARD WHAT HE SAID...
ERGI CLAUDE MEMBER OF THE BLUVOHAN ROYAL FAMILY
I'VE BEEN ANXIOUS ALL THE TIME LATELY, EVER SINCE THAT LIE ABOUT ME WAS SPREAD.
DOES THIS SORT OF THING HAPPEN TO YOU OFTEN?

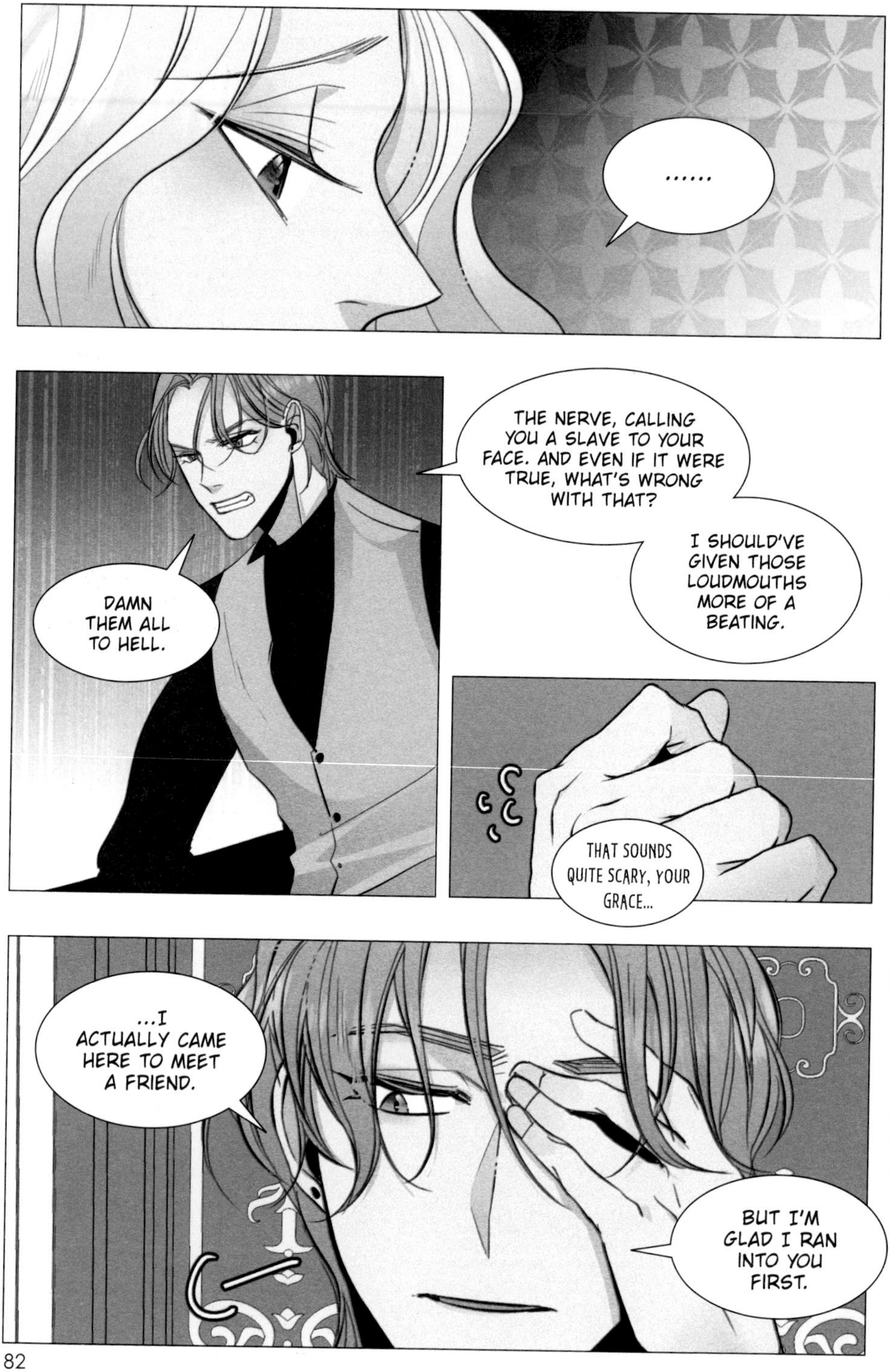
......
THE NERVE, CALLING YOU A SLAVE TO YOUR FACE. AND EVEN IF IT WERE TRUE, WHAT'S WRONG WITH THAT?
I SHOULD'VE GIVEN THOSE LOUDMOUTHS MORE OF A BEATING.
DAMN THEM ALL TO HELL.
THAT SOUNDS QUITE SCARY, YOUR GRACE...
...I ACTUALLY CAME HERE TO MEET A FRIEND.
BUT I'M GLAD I RAN INTO YOU FIRST.

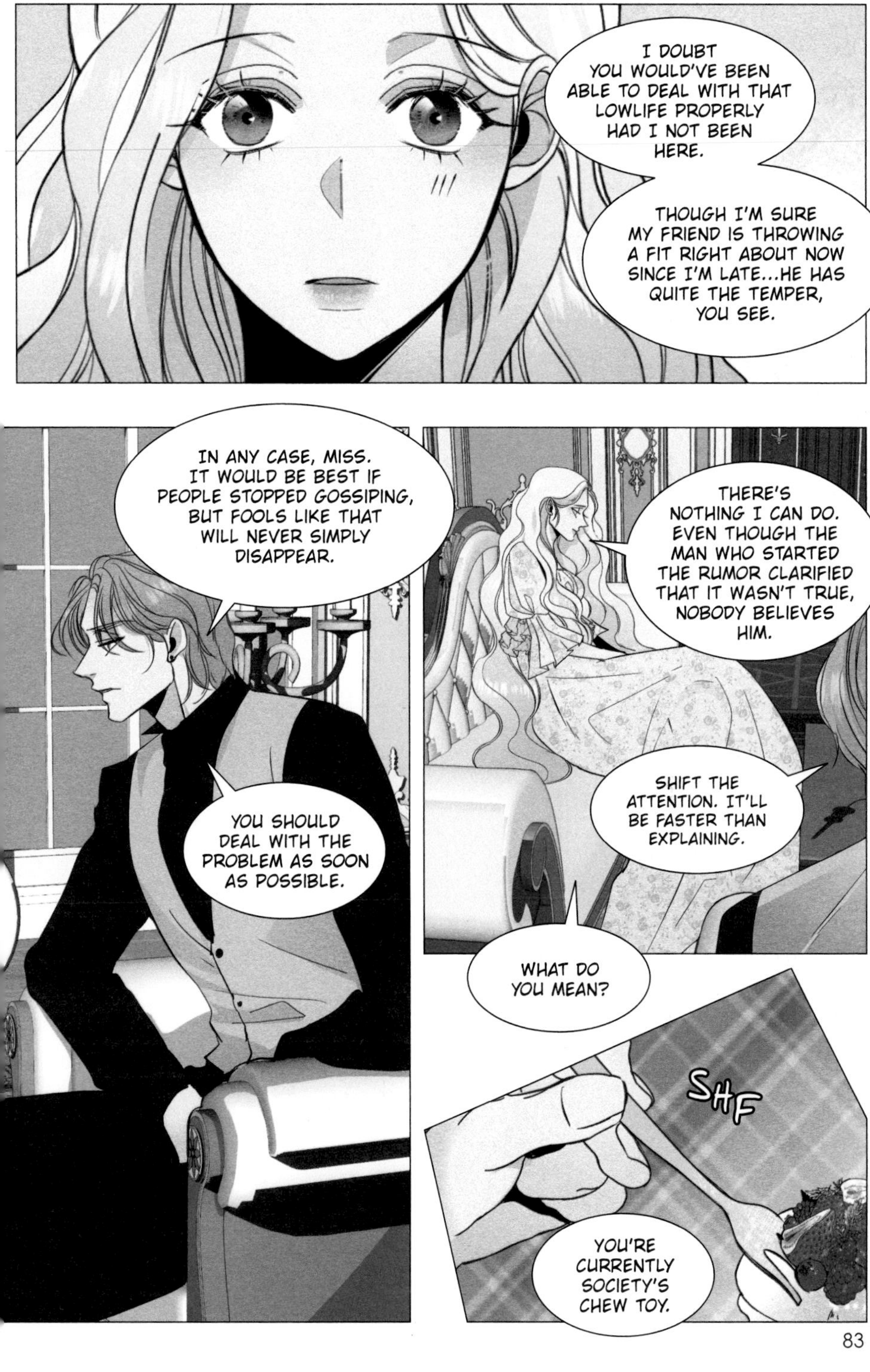
I DOUBT YOU WOULD'VE BEEN ABLE TO DEAL WITH THAT LOWLIFE PROPERLY HAD I NOT BEEN HERE.
THOUGH I'M SURE MY FRIEND IS THROWING A FIT RIGHT ABOUT NOW SINCE I'M LATE...HE HAS QUITE THE TEMPER, YOU SEE.
IN ANY CASE, MISS. IT WOULD BE BEST IF PEOPLE STOPPED GOSSIPING, BUT FOOLS LIKE THAT WILL NEVER SIMPLY DISAPPEAR.
YOU SHOULD DEAL WITH THE PROBLEM AS SOON AS POSSIBLE.
THERE'S NOTHING I CAN DO. EVEN THOUGH THE MAN WHO STARTED THE RUMOR CLARIFIED THAT IT WASN'T TRUE, NOBODY BELIEVES HIM.
SHIFT THE ATTENTION. IT'LL BE FASTER THAN EXPLAINING.
WHAT DO YOU MEAN?
SHF
YOU'RE CURRENTLY SOCIETY'S CHEW TOY.

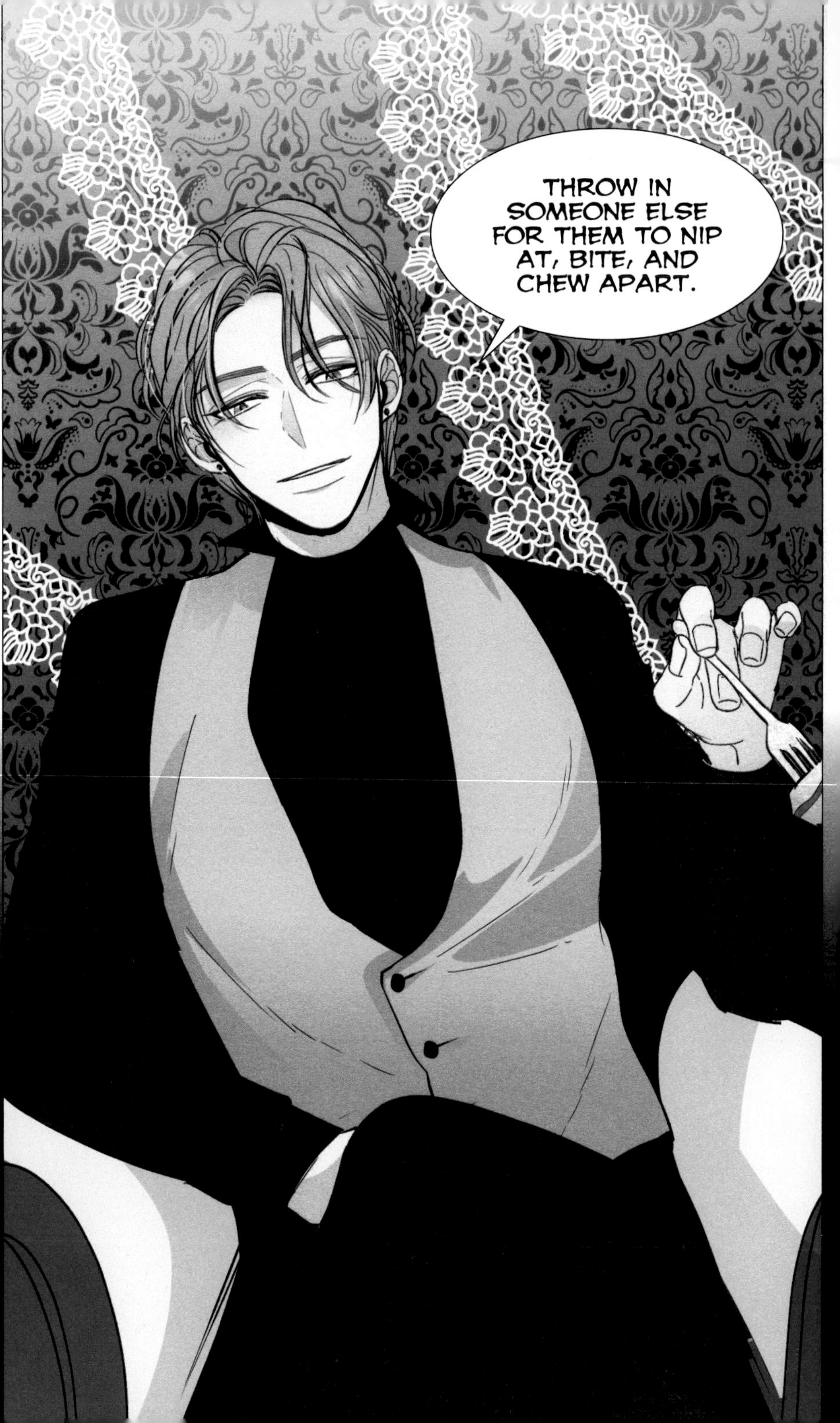
THROW IN SOMEONE ELSE FOR THEM TO NIP AT, BITE, AND CHEW APART.

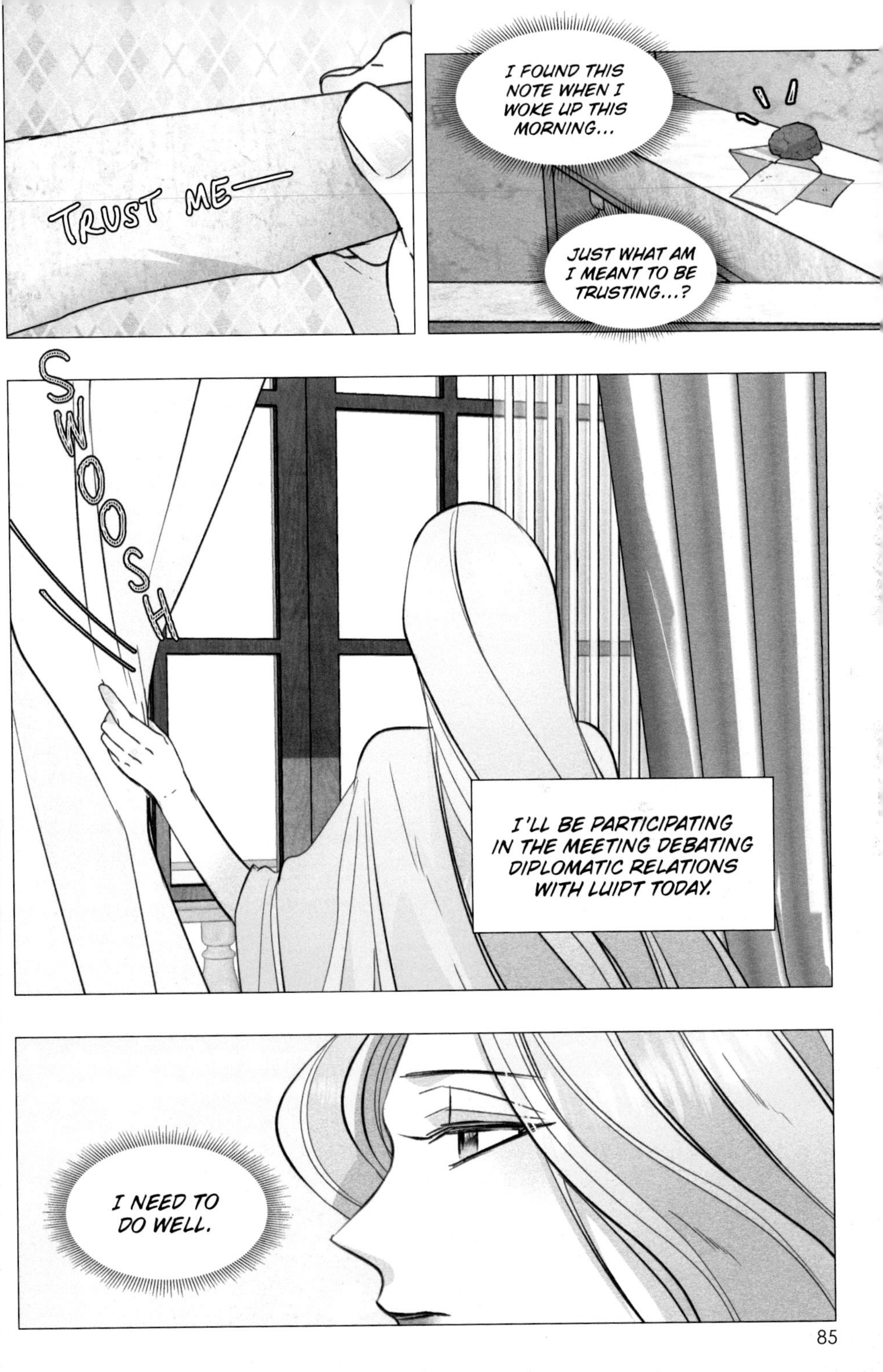
TRUST ME—
I FOUND THIS NOTE WHEN I WOKE UP THIS MORNING...
JUST WHAT AM I MEANT TO BE TRUSTING...?
SWOOSH
I'LL BE PARTICIPATING IN THE MEETING DEBATING DIPLOMATIC RELATIONS WITH LUIPT TODAY.
I NEED TO DO WELL.

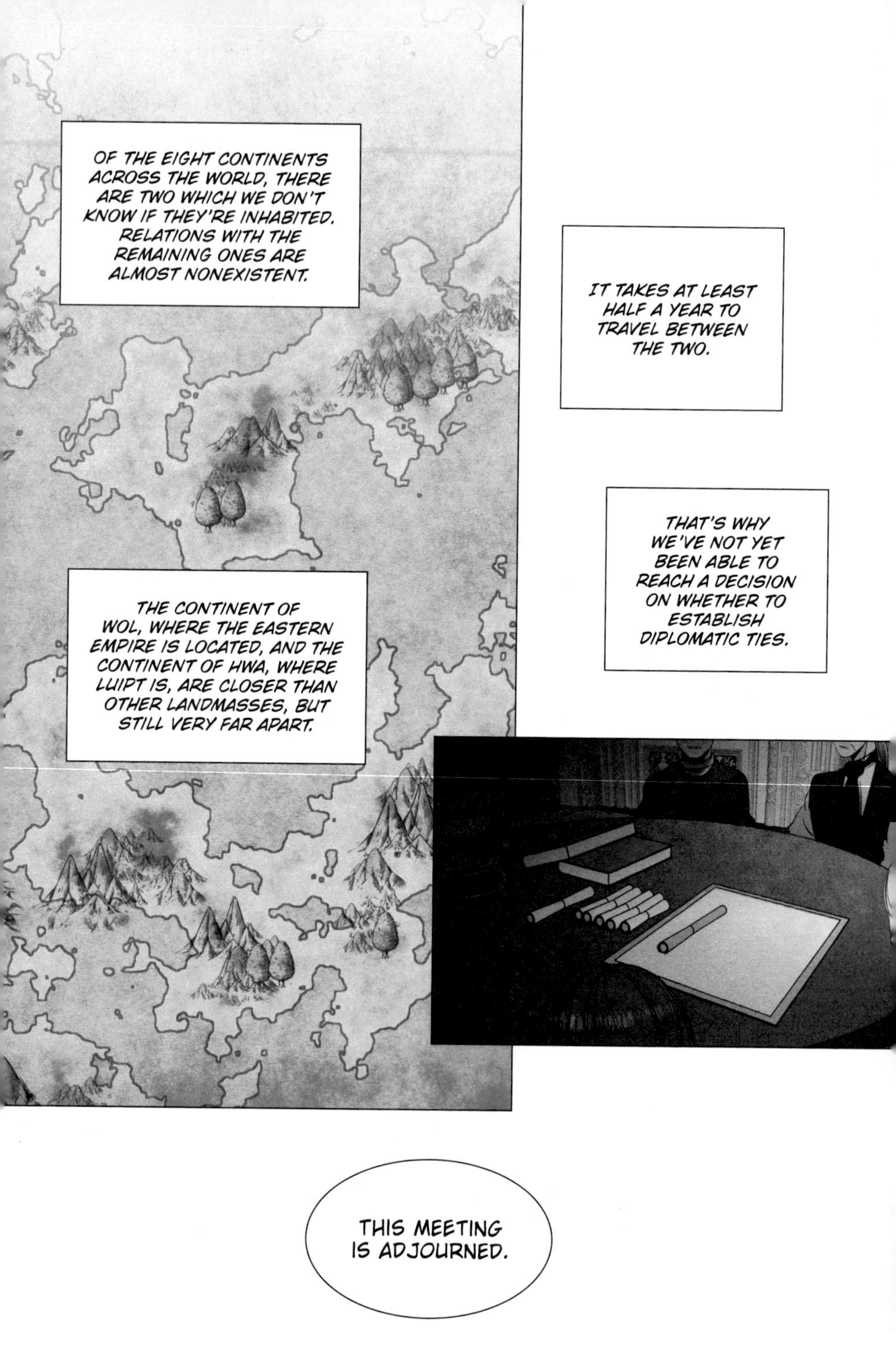
OF THE EIGHT CONTINENTS ACROSS THE WORLD, THERE ARE TWO WHICH WE DON'T KNOW IF THEY'RE INHABITED. RELATIONS WITH THE REMAINING ONES ARE ALMOST NONEXISTENT.
IT TAKES AT LEAST HALF A YEAR TO TRAVEL BETWEEN THE TWO.
THE CONTINENT OF WOL, WHERE THE EASTERN EMPIRE IS LOCATED, AND THE CONTINENT OF HWA, WHERE LUIPT IS, ARE CLOSER THAN OTHER LANDMASSES, BUT STILL VERY FAR APART.
THAT'S WHY WE'VE NOT YET BEEN ABLE TO REACH A DECISION ON WHETHER TO ESTABLISH DIPLOMATIC TIES.
THIS MEETING IS ADJOURNED.

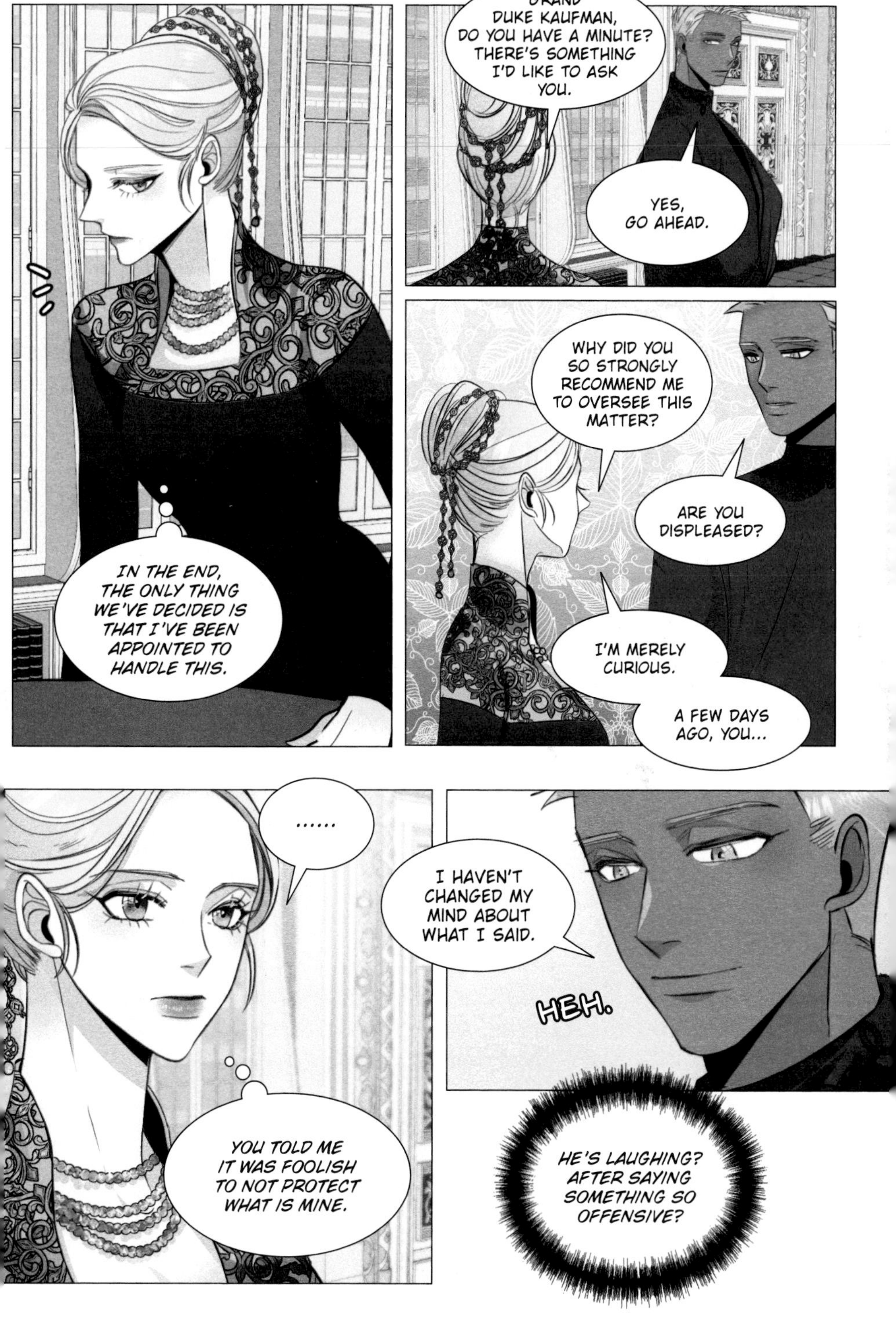

IN THE END, THE ONLY THING WE'VE DECIDED IS THAT I'VE BEEN APPOINTED TO HANDLE THIS.
GRAND DUKE KAUFMAN, DO YOU HAVE A MINUTE? THERE'S SOMETHING I'D LIKE TO ASK YOU.
YES, GO AHEAD.
WHY DID YOU SO STRONGLY RECOMMEND ME TO OVERSEE THIS MATTER?
ARE YOU DISPLEASED?
I'M MERELY CURIOUS.
A FEW DAYS AGO, YOU...
......
YOU TOLD ME IT WAS FOOLISH TO NOT PROTECT WHAT IS MINE.
I HAVEN'T CHANGED MY MIND ABOUT WHAT I SAID.
HEH.
HE'S LAUGHING? AFTER SAYING SOMETHING SO OFFENSIVE?

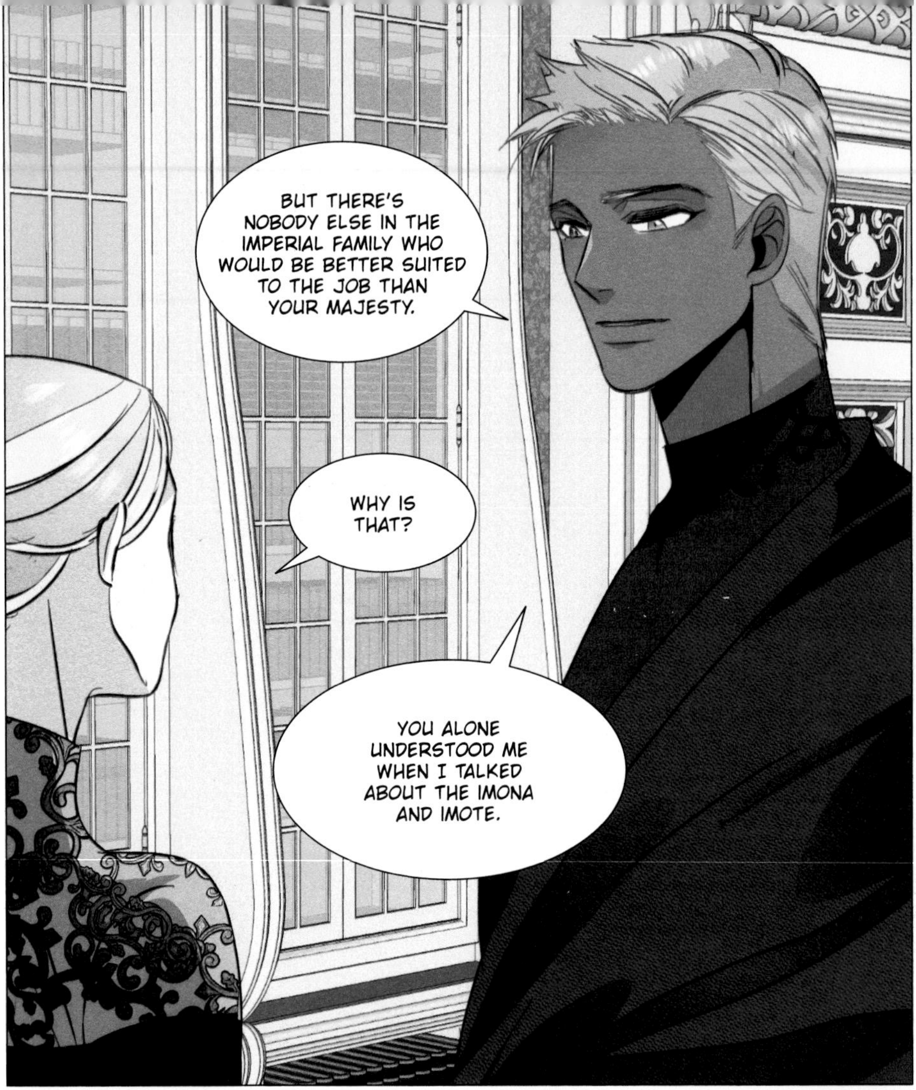
BUT THERE'S NOBODY ELSE IN THE IMPERIAL FAMILY WHO WOULD BE BETTER SUITED TO THE JOB THAN YOUR MAJESTY.
WHY IS THAT?
YOU ALONE UNDERSTOOD ME WHEN I TALKED ABOUT THE IMONA AND IMOTE.
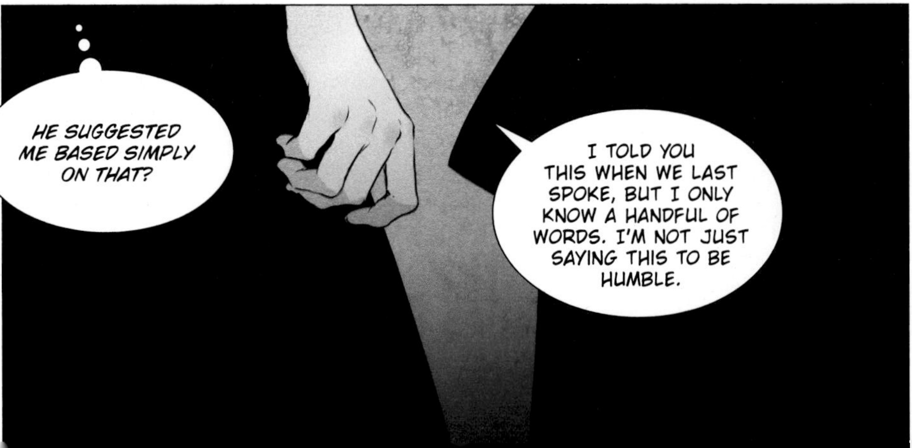
HE SUGGESTED ME BASED SIMPLY ON THAT?
I TOLD YOU THIS WHEN WE LAST SPOKE, BUT I ONLY KNOW A HANDFUL OF WORDS. I'M NOT JUST SAYING THIS TO BE HUMBLE.

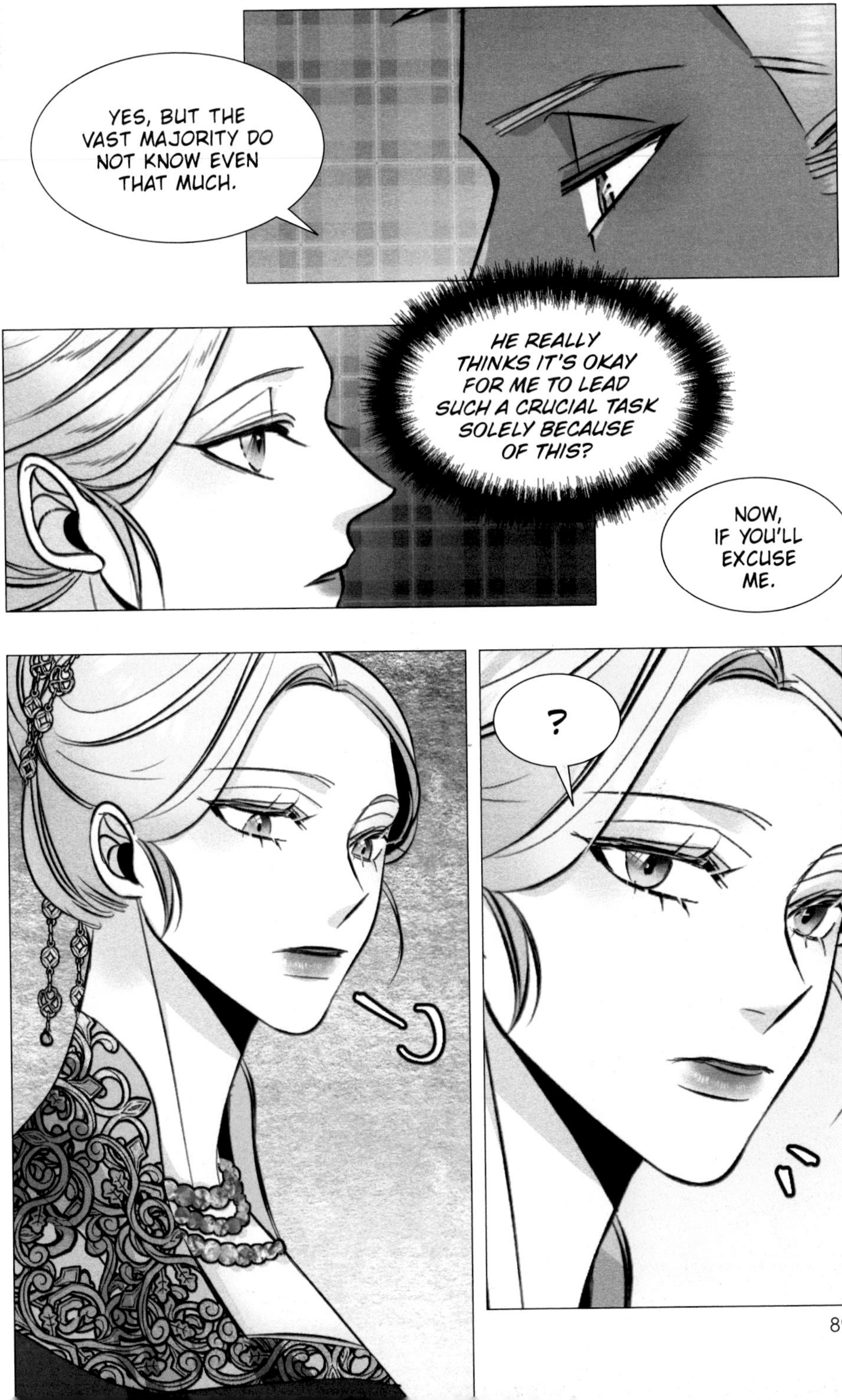
YES, BUT THE VAST MAJORITY DO NOT KNOW EVEN THAT MUCH.
HE REALLY THINKS IT'S OKAY FOR ME TO LEAD SUCH A CRUCIAL TASK SOLELY BECAUSE OF THIS?
NOW, IF YOU'LL EXCUSE ME.
?

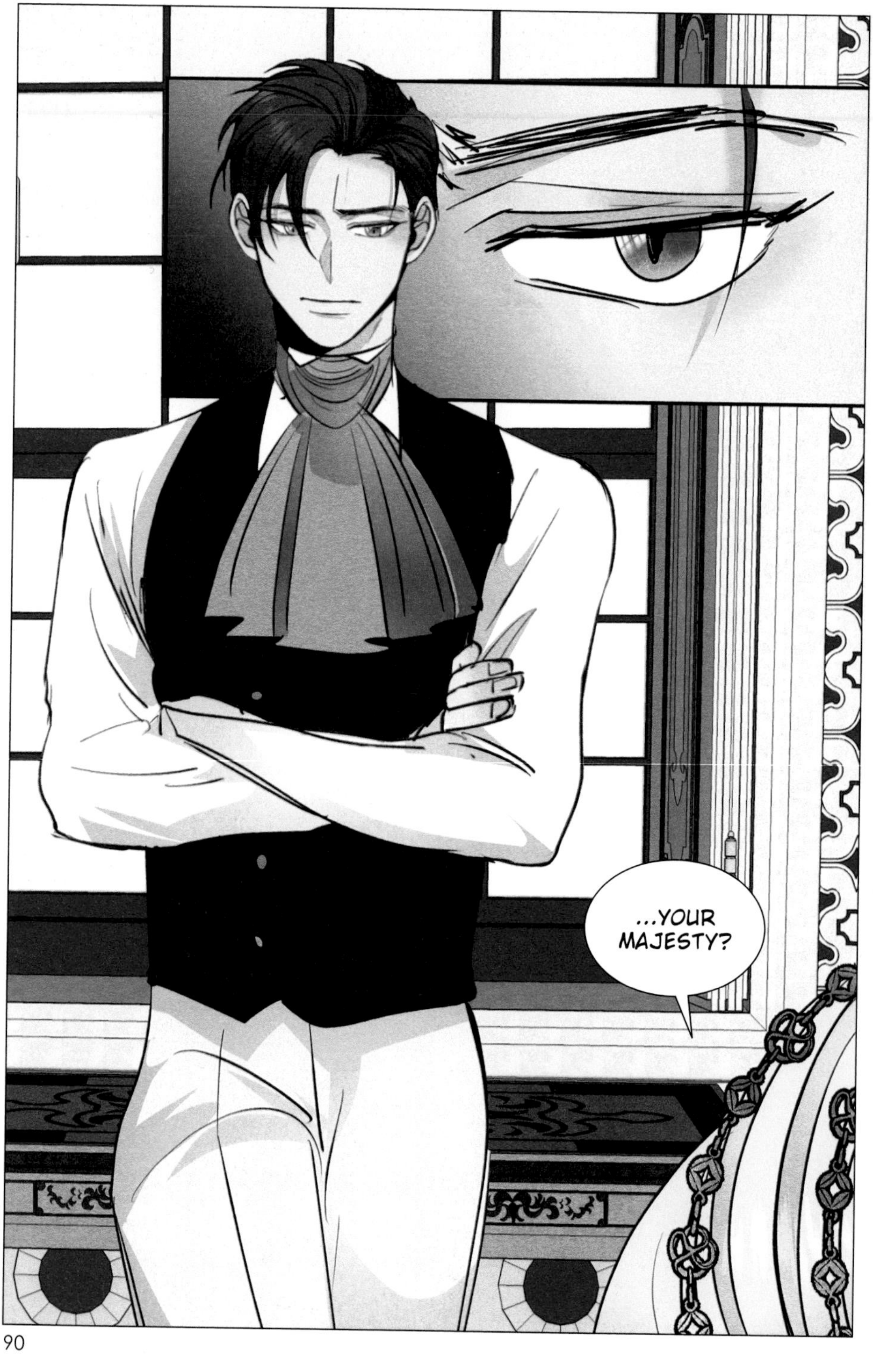
...YOUR MAJESTY?

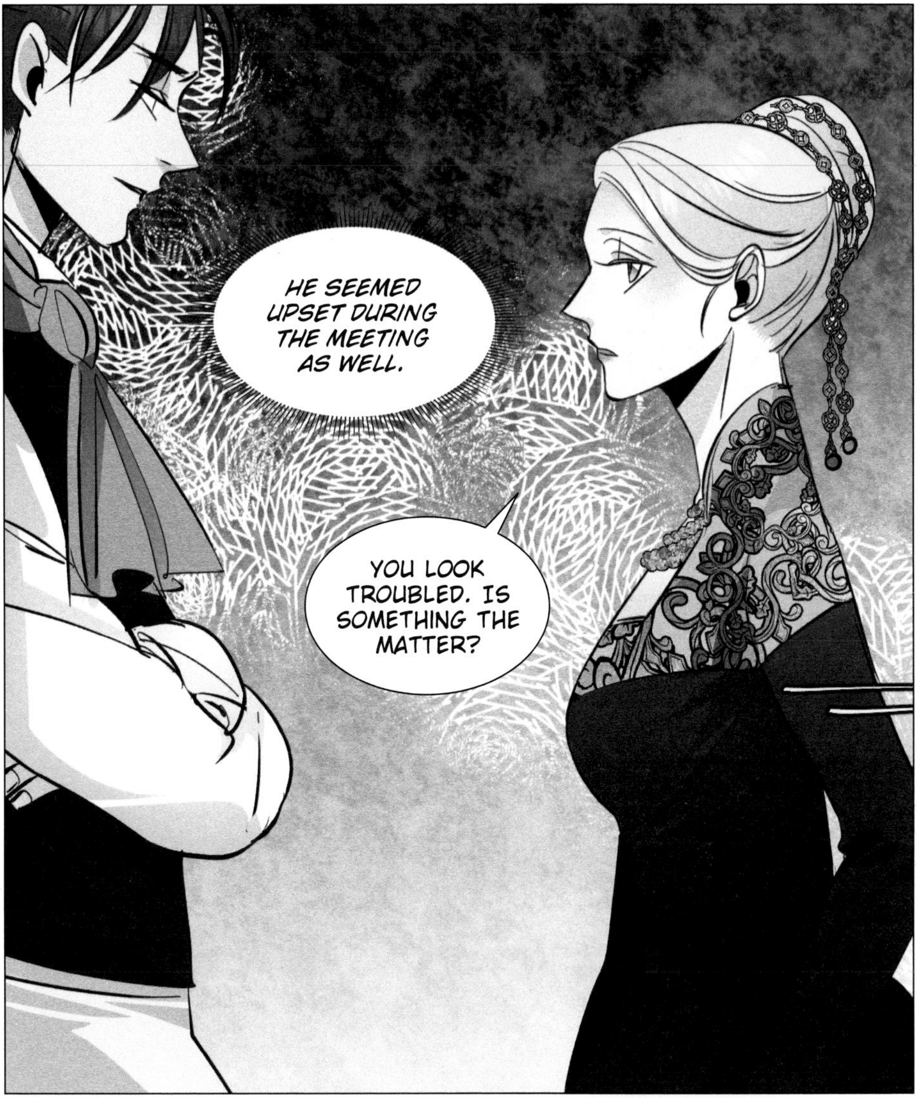
HE SEEMED UPSET DURING THE MEETING AS WELL.
YOU LOOK TROUBLED. IS SOMETHING THE MATTER?

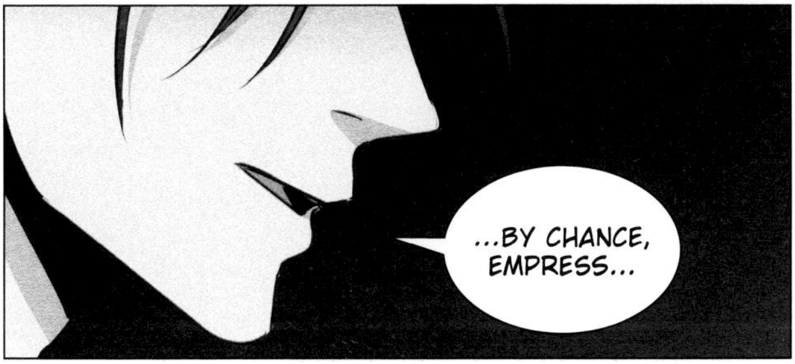
...BY CHANCE, EMPRESS...

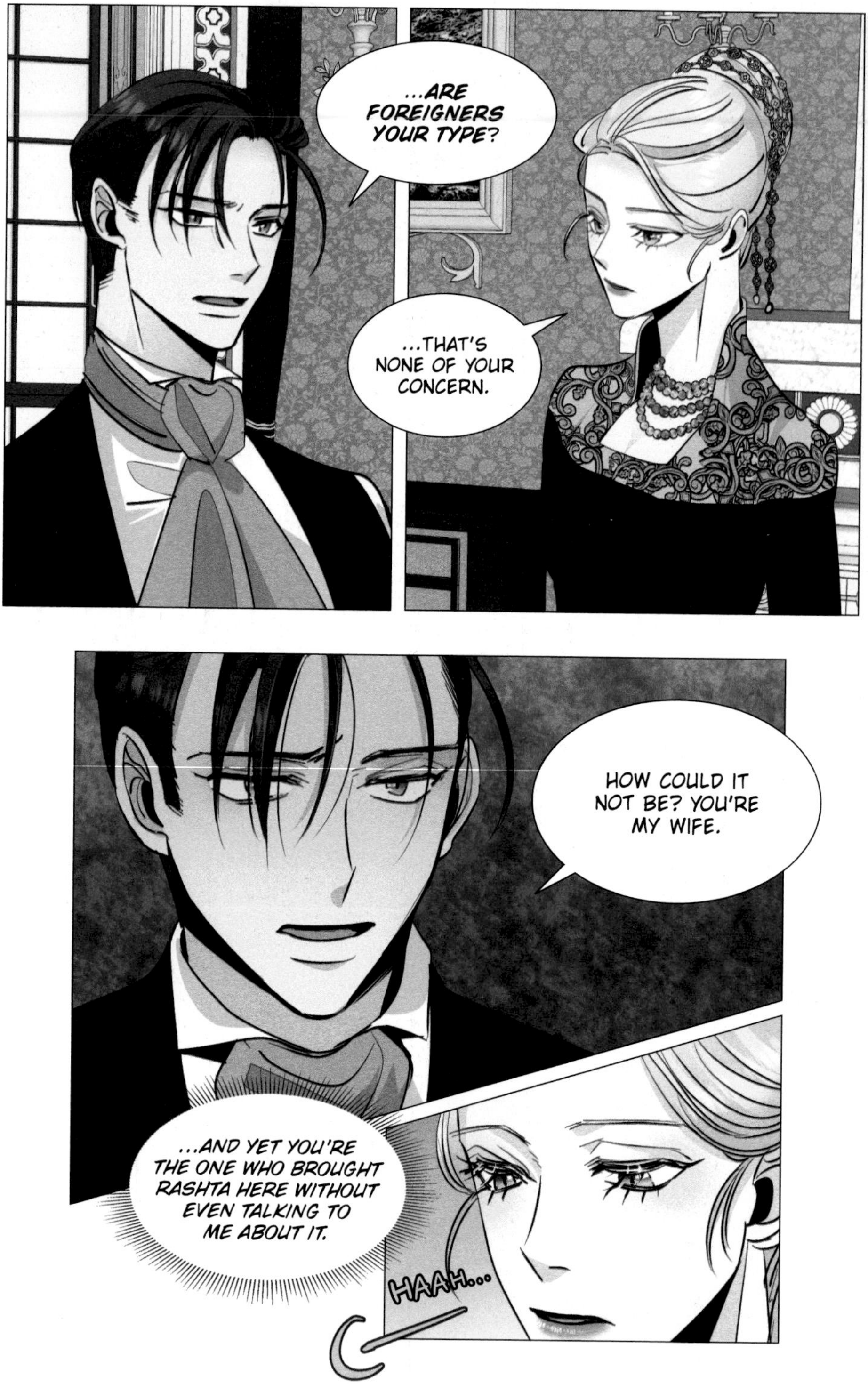
...ARE FOREIGNERS YOUR TYPE?
...THAT'S NONE OF YOUR CONCERN.
HOW COULD IT NOT BE? YOU'RE MY WIFE.
...AND YET YOU'RE THE ONE WHO BROUGHT RASHTA HERE WITHOUT EVEN TALKING TO ME ABOUT IT.
HAAH...

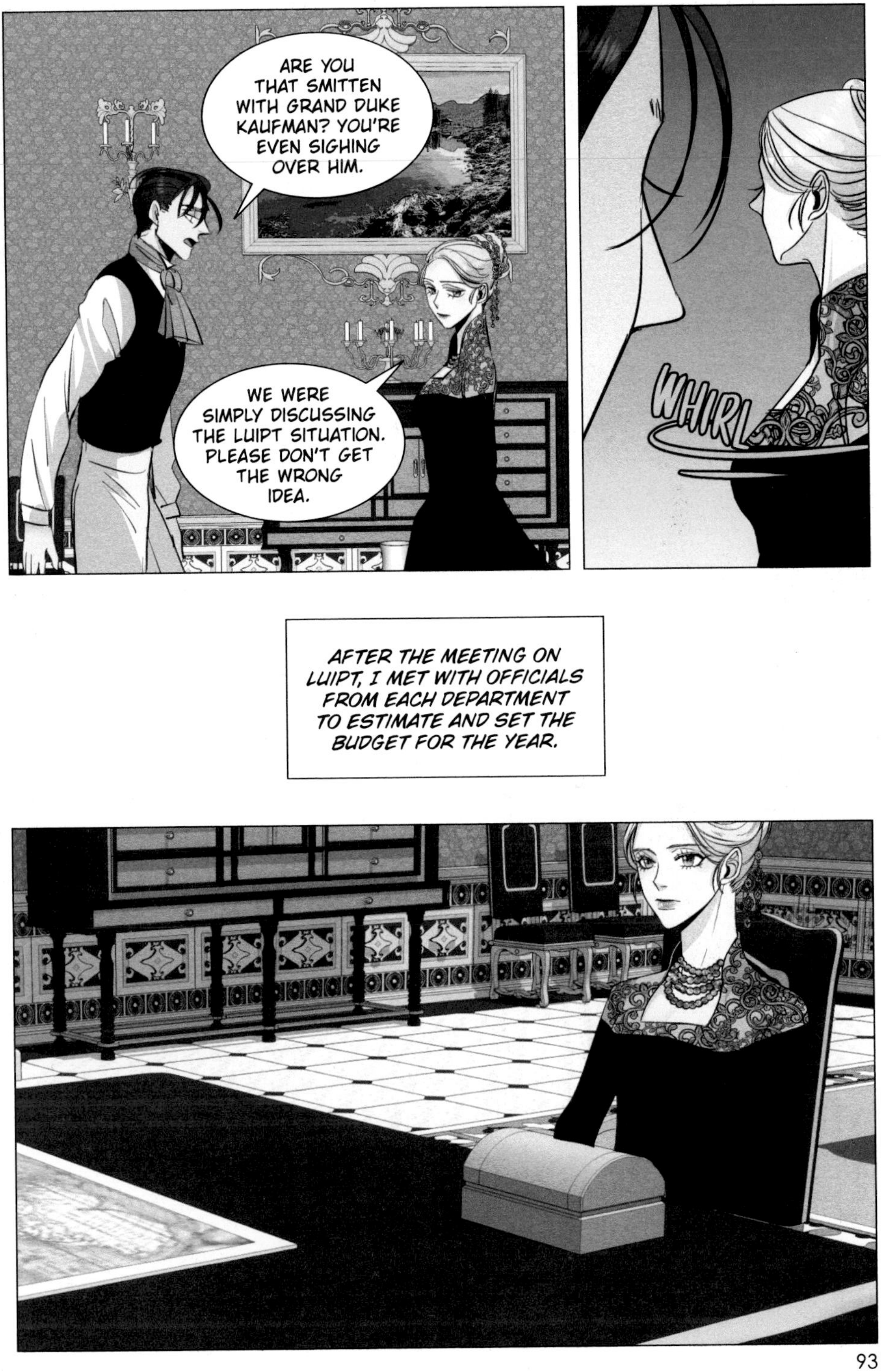
ARE YOU THAT SMITTEN WITH GRAND DUKE KAUFMAN? YOU'RE EVEN SIGHING OVER HIM.
WE WERE SIMPLY DISCUSSING THE LUIPT SITUATION. PLEASE DON'T GET THE WRONG IDEA.
WHIRL
AFTER THE MEETING ON LUIPT, I MET WITH OFFICIALS FROM EACH DEPARTMENT TO ESTIMATE AND SET THE BUDGET FOR THE YEAR.

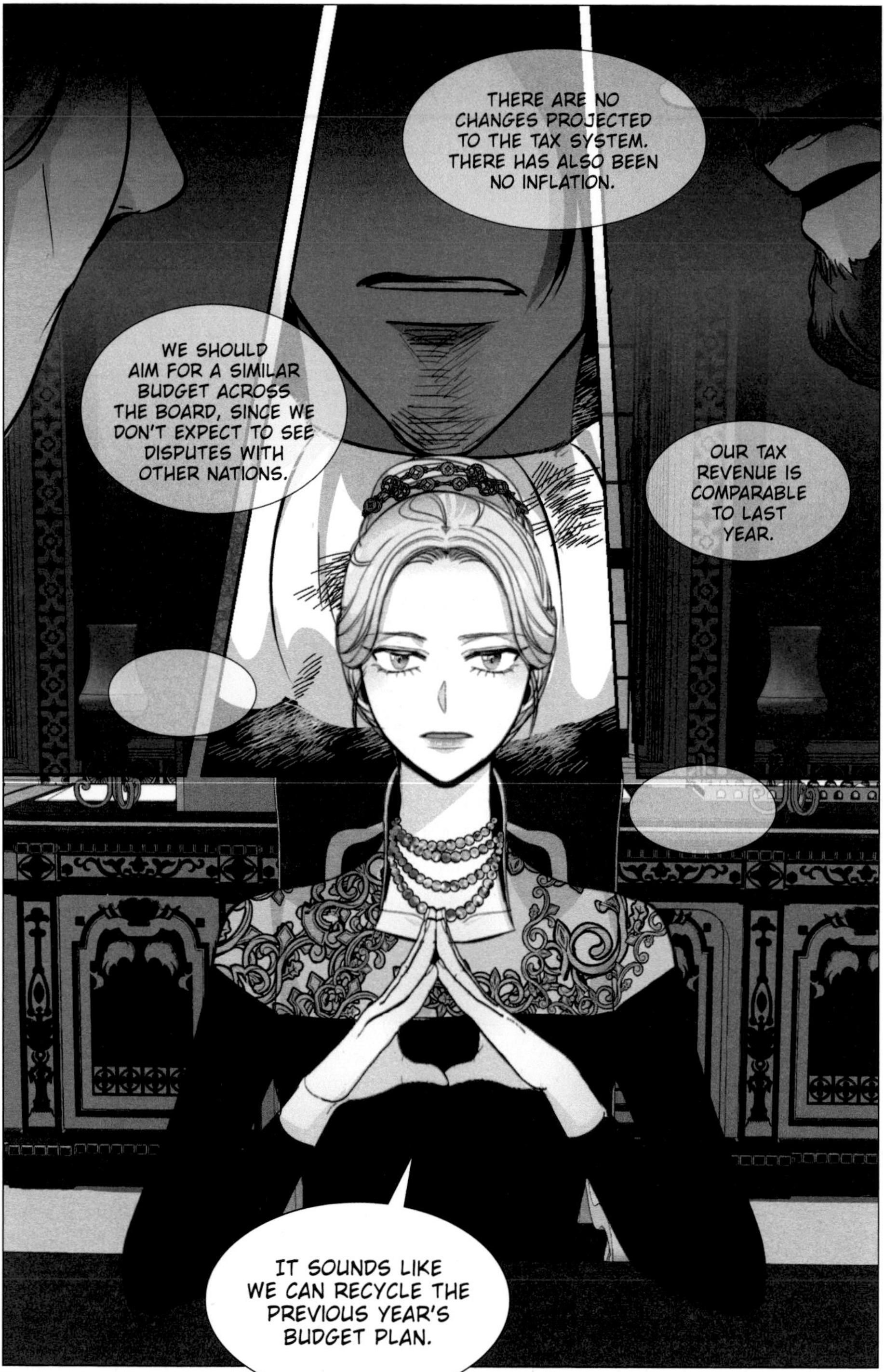
THERE ARE NO CHANGES PROJECTED TO THE TAX SYSTEM. THERE HAS ALSO BEEN NO INFLATION.
OUR TAX REVENUE IS COMPARABLE TO LAST YEAR.
WE SHOULD AIM FOR A SIMILAR BUDGET ACROSS THE BOARD, SINCE WE DON'T EXPECT TO SEE DISPUTES WITH OTHER NATIONS.
IT SOUNDS LIKE WE CAN RECYCLE THE PREVIOUS YEAR'S BUDGET PLAN.

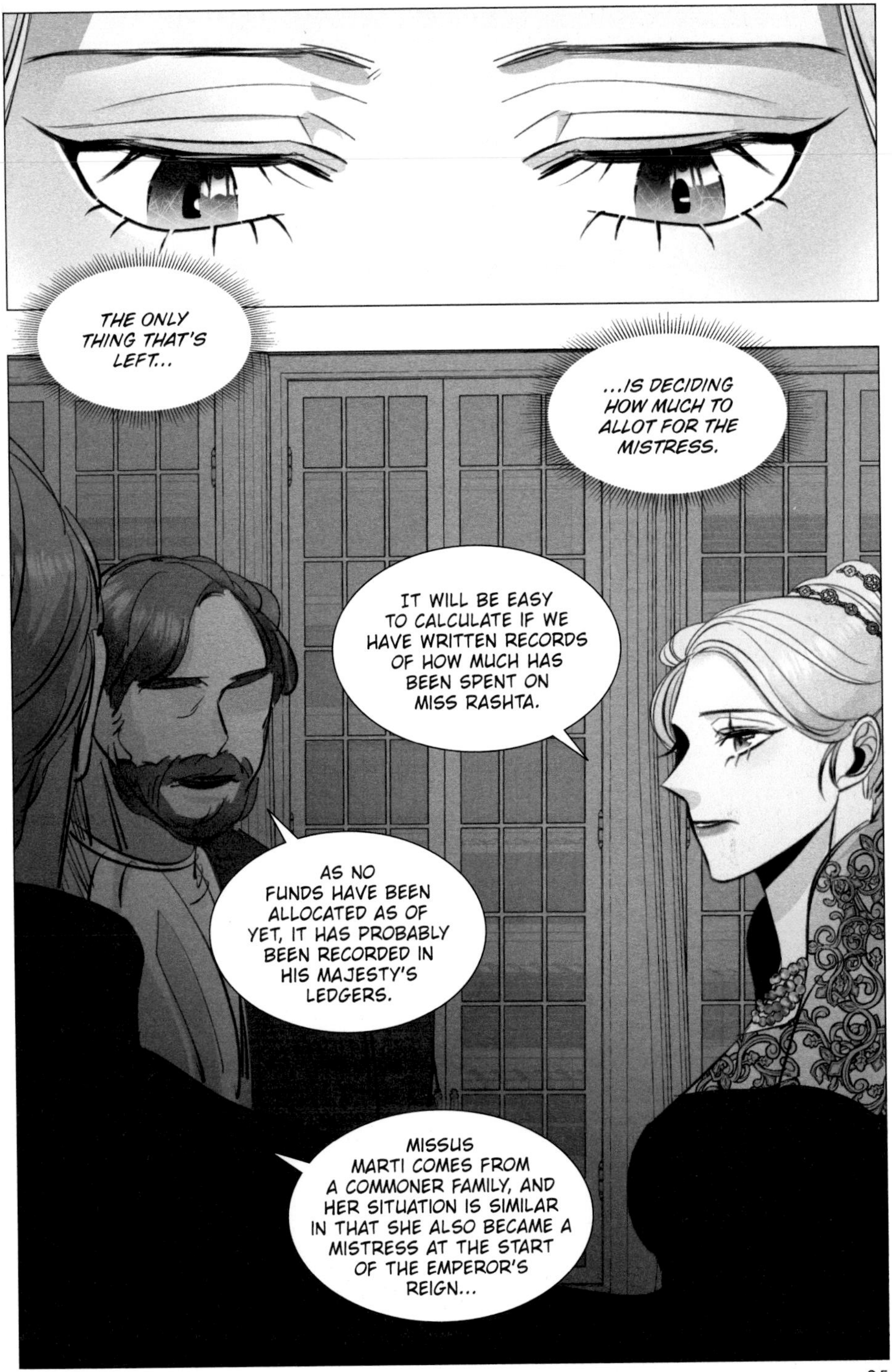
THE ONLY THING THAT'S LEFT...
...IS DECIDING HOW MUCH TO ALLOT FOR THE MISTRESS.
IT WILL BE EASY TO CALCULATE IF WE HAVE WRITTEN RECORDS OF HOW MUCH HAS BEEN SPENT ON MISS RASHTA.
AS NO FUNDS HAVE BEEN ALLOCATED AS OF YET, IT HAS PROBABLY BEEN RECORDED IN HIS MAJESTY'S LEDGERS.
MISSUS MARTI COMES FROM A COMMONER FAMILY, AND HER SITUATION IS SIMILAR IN THAT SHE ALSO BECAME A MISTRESS AT THE START OF THE EMPEROR'S REIGN...

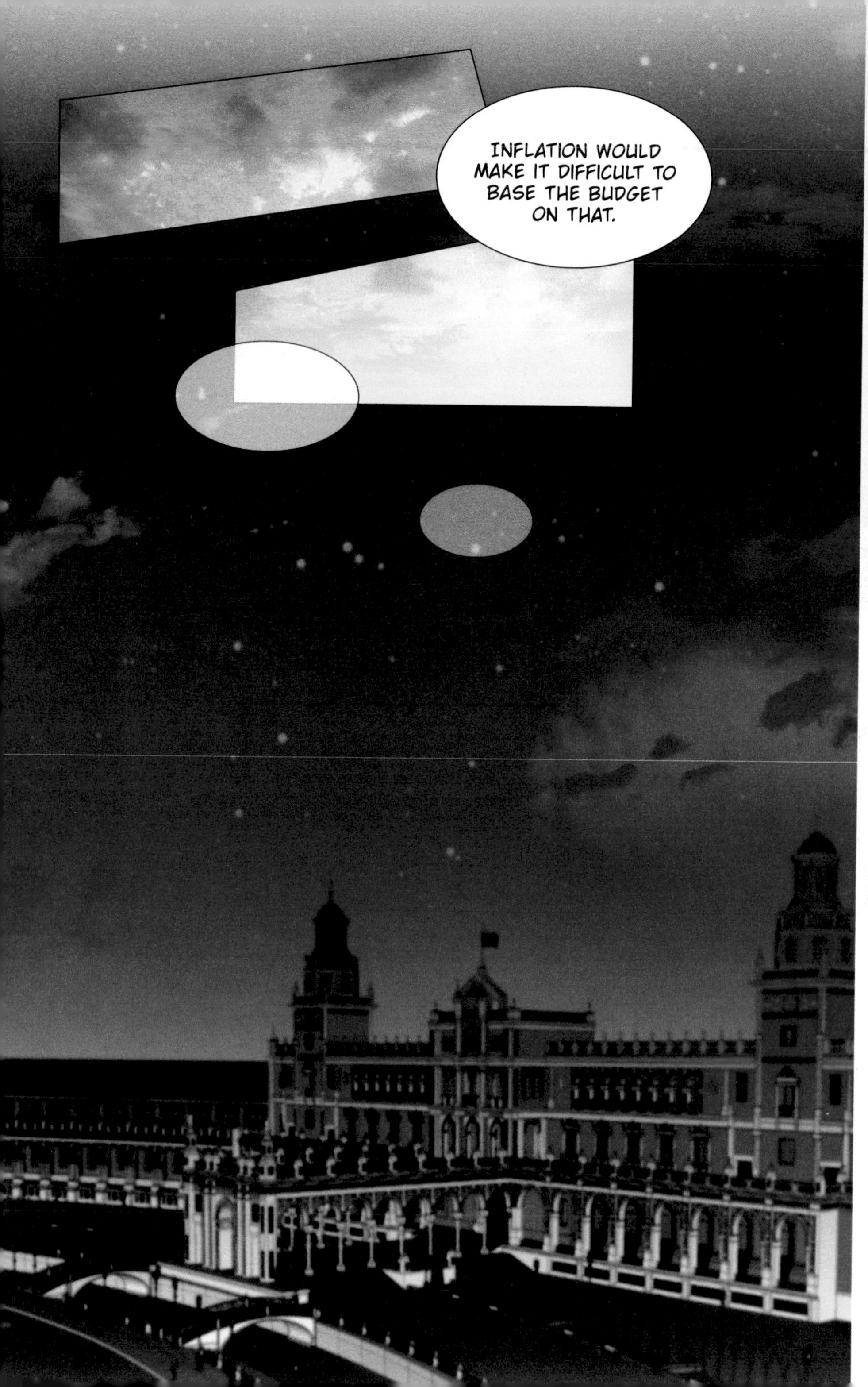
INFLATION WOULD MAKE IT DIFFICULT TO BASE THE BUDGET ON THAT.

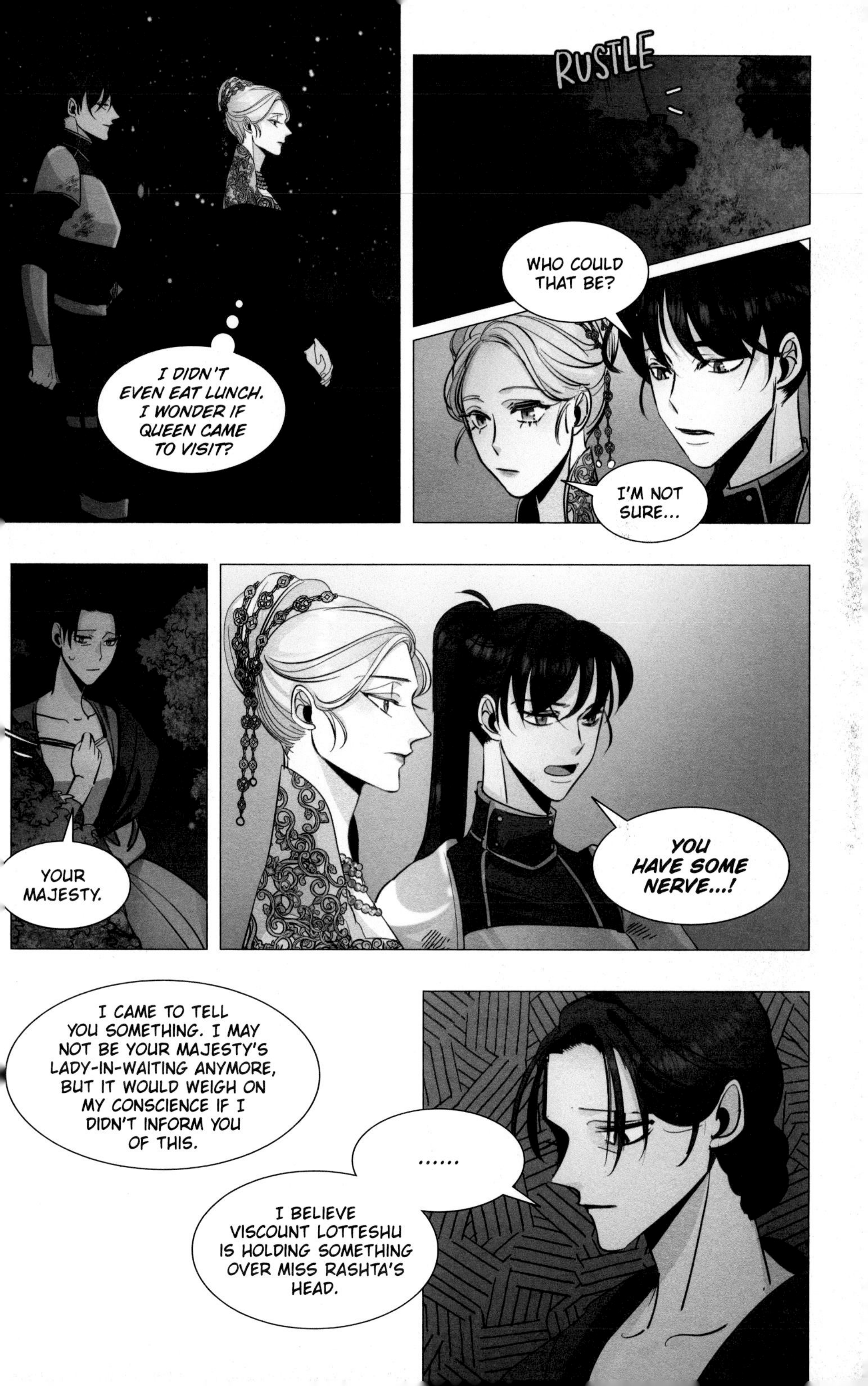
I DIDN'T EVEN EAT LUNCH. I WONDER IF QUEEN CAME TO VISIT?
RUSTLE
WHO COULD THAT BE?
I'M NOT SURE...
YOUR MAJESTY.
YOU HAVE SOME NERVE...!
I CAME TO TELL YOU SOMETHING. I MAY NOT BE YOUR MAJESTY'S LADY-IN-WAITING ANYMORE, BUT IT WOULD WEIGH ON MY CONSCIENCE IF I DIDN'T INFORM YOU OF THIS.
......
I BELIEVE VISCOUNT LOTTESHU IS HOLDING SOMETHING OVER MISS RASHTA'S HEAD.

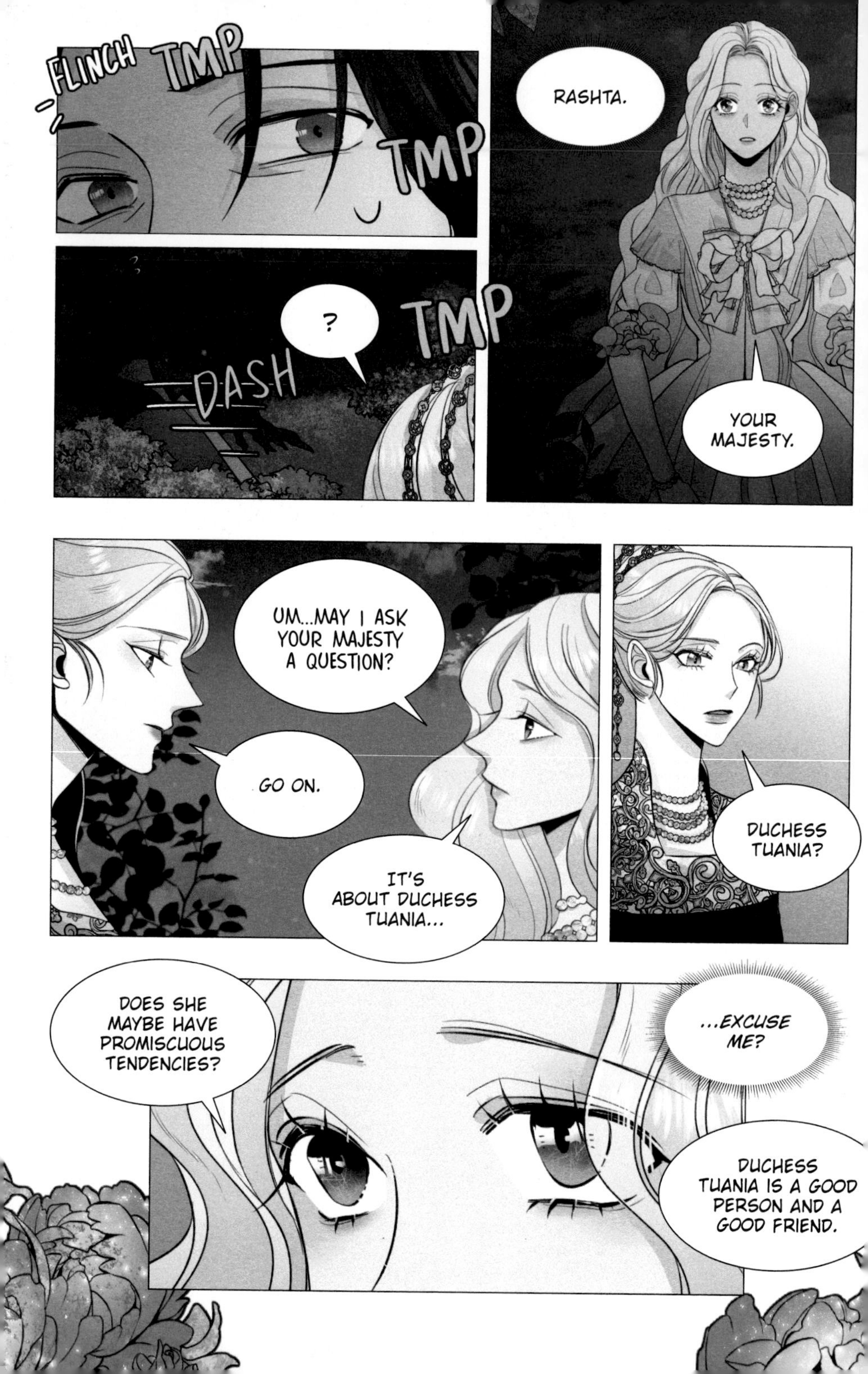
FLINCH
TMP
TMP
?
DASH
TMP
RASHTA.
YOUR MAJESTY.
UM...MAY I ASK YOUR MAJESTY A QUESTION?
GO ON.
IT'S ABOUT DUCHESS TUANIA...
DUCHESS TUANIA?
DOES SHE MAYBE HAVE PROMISCUOUS TENDENCIES?
...EXCUSE ME?
DUCHESS TUANIA IS A GOOD PERSON AND A GOOD FRIEND.

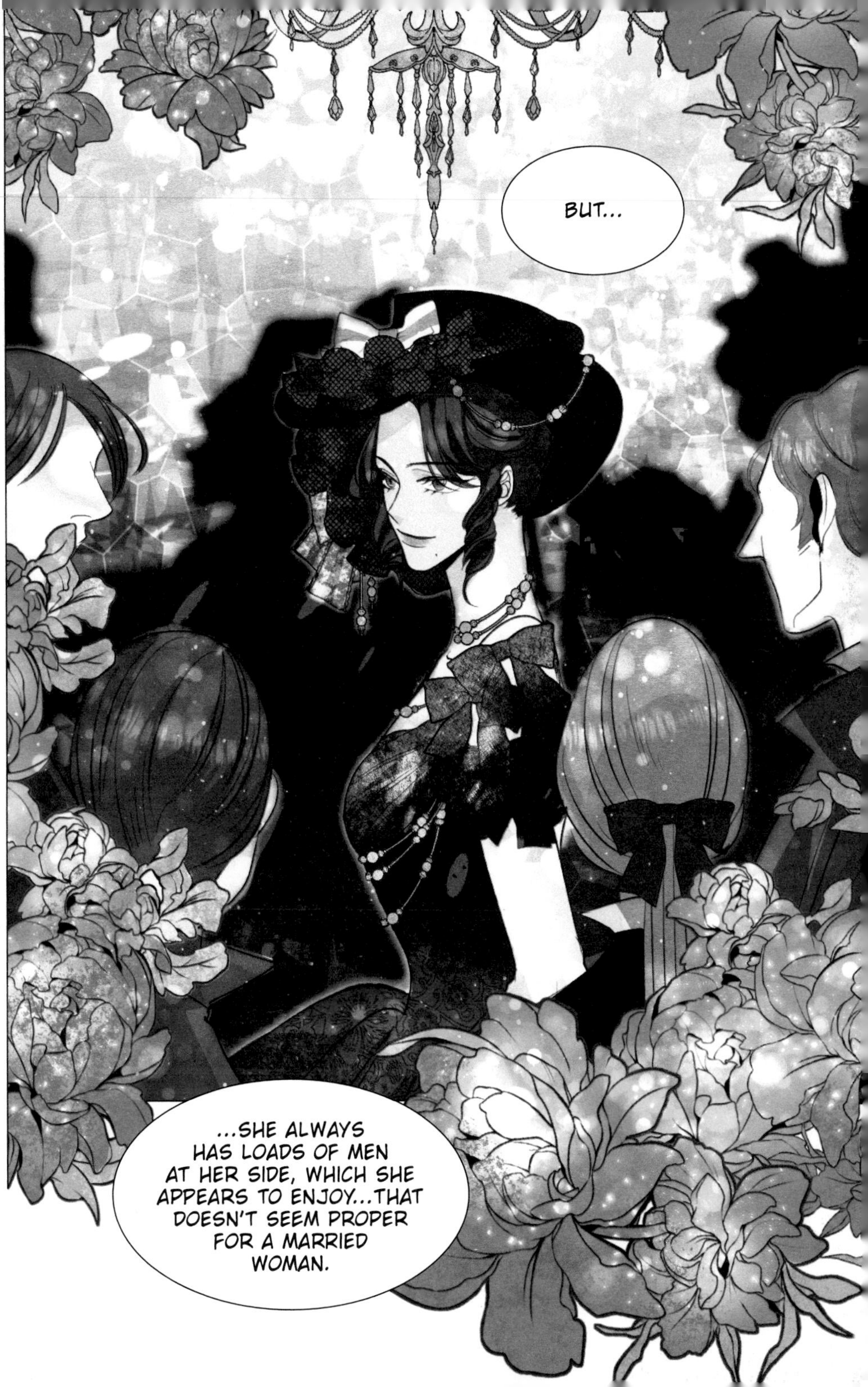
BUT...
...SHE ALWAYS HAS LOADS OF MEN AT HER SIDE, WHICH SHE APPEARS TO ENJOY...THAT DOESN'T SEEM PROPER FOR A MARRIED WOMAN.

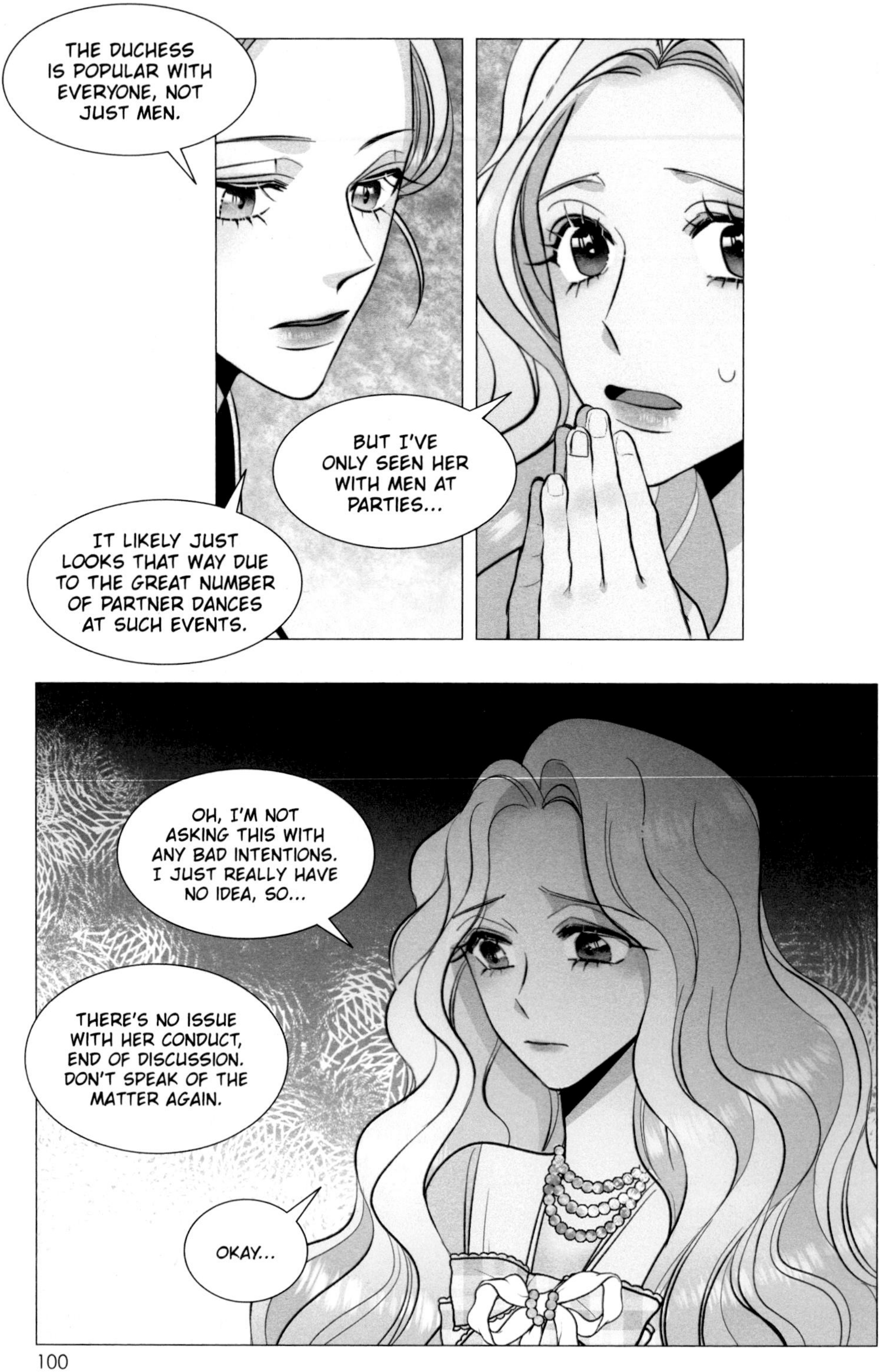
THE DUCHESS IS POPULAR WITH EVERYONE, NOT JUST MEN.
BUT I'VE ONLY SEEN HER WITH MEN AT PARTIES...
IT LIKELY JUST LOOKS THAT WAY DUE TO THE GREAT NUMBER OF PARTNER DANCES AT SUCH EVENTS.
OH, I'M NOT ASKING THIS WITH ANY BAD INTENTIONS. I JUST REALLY HAVE NO IDEA, SO...
THERE'S NO ISSUE WITH HER CONDUCT, END OF DISCUSSION. DON'T SPEAK OF THE MATTER AGAIN.
OKAY...

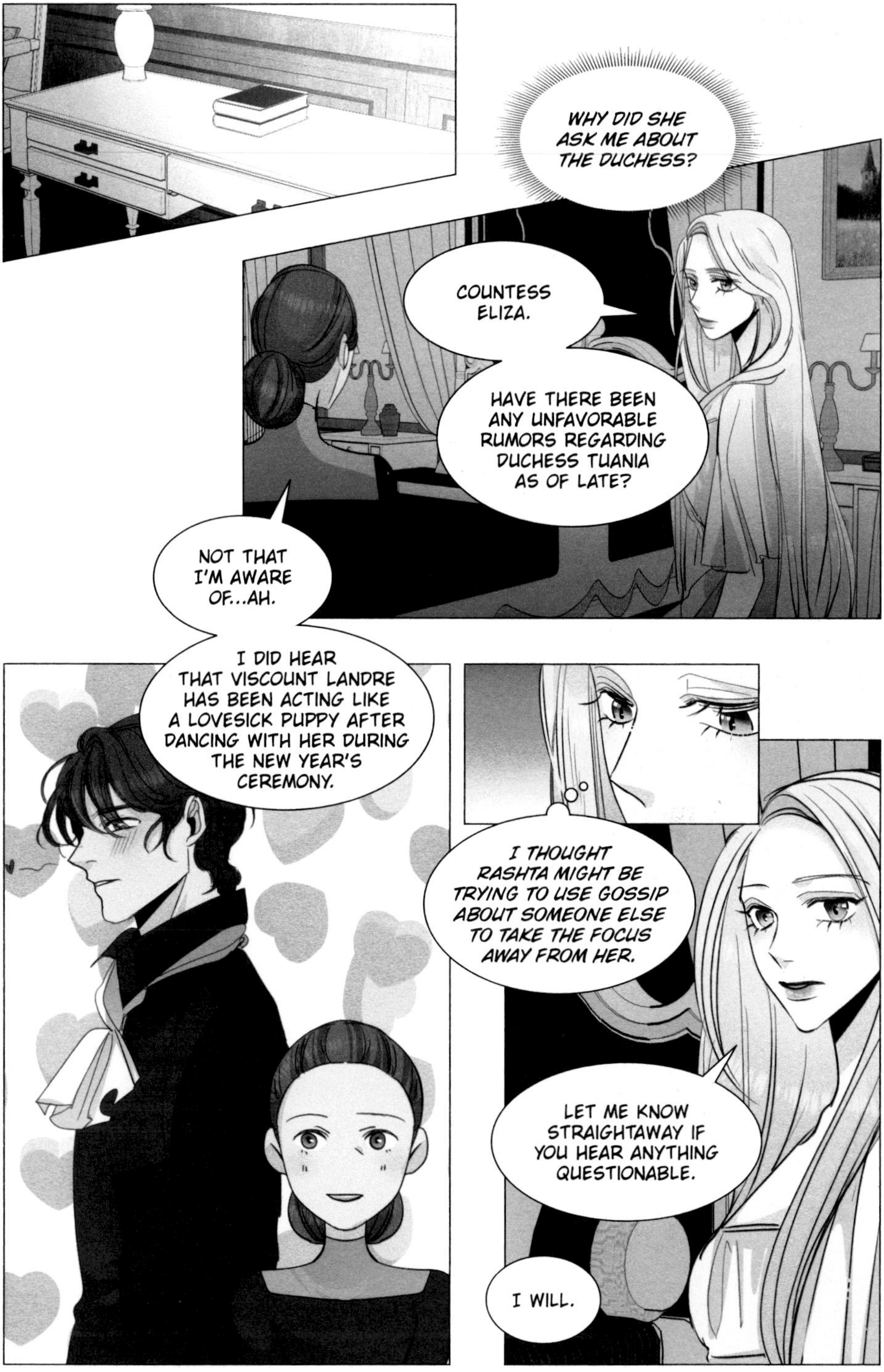
WHY DID SHE ASK ME ABOUT THE DUCHESS?
COUNTESS ELIZA.
HAVE THERE BEEN ANY UNFAVORABLE RUMORS REGARDING DUCHESS TUANIA AS OF LATE?
NOT THAT I'M AWARE OF...AH.
I DID HEAR THAT VISCOUNT LANDRE HAS BEEN ACTING LIKE A LOVESICK PUPPY AFTER DANCING WITH HER DURING THE NEW YEAR'S CEREMONY.
I THOUGHT RASHTA MIGHT BE TRYING TO USE GOSSIP ABOUT SOMEONE ELSE TO TAKE THE FOCUS AWAY FROM HER.
LET ME KNOW STRAIGHTAWAY IF YOU HEAR ANYTHING QUESTIONABLE.
I WILL.

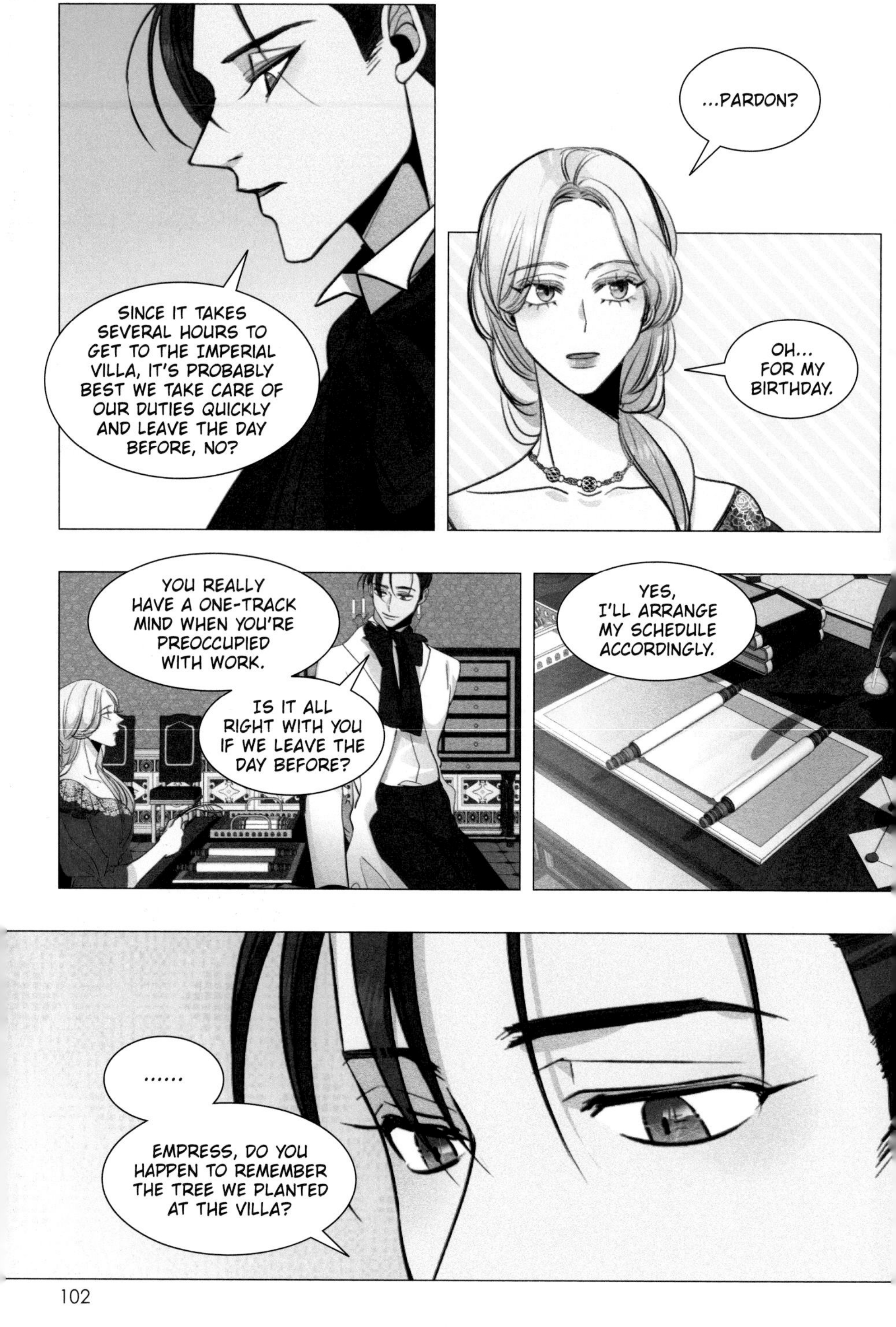
SINCE IT TAKES SEVERAL HOURS TO GET TO THE IMPERIAL VILLA, IT'S PROBABLY BEST WE TAKE CARE OF OUR DUTIES QUICKLY AND LEAVE THE DAY BEFORE, NO?
...PARDON?
OH... FOR MY BIRTHDAY.
YOU REALLY HAVE A ONE-TRACK MIND WHEN YOU'RE PREOCCUPIED WITH WORK.
IS IT ALL RIGHT WITH YOU IF WE LEAVE THE DAY BEFORE?
YES, I'LL ARRANGE MY SCHEDULE ACCORDINGLY.
......
EMPRESS, DO YOU HAPPEN TO REMEMBER THE TREE WE PLANTED AT THE VILLA?

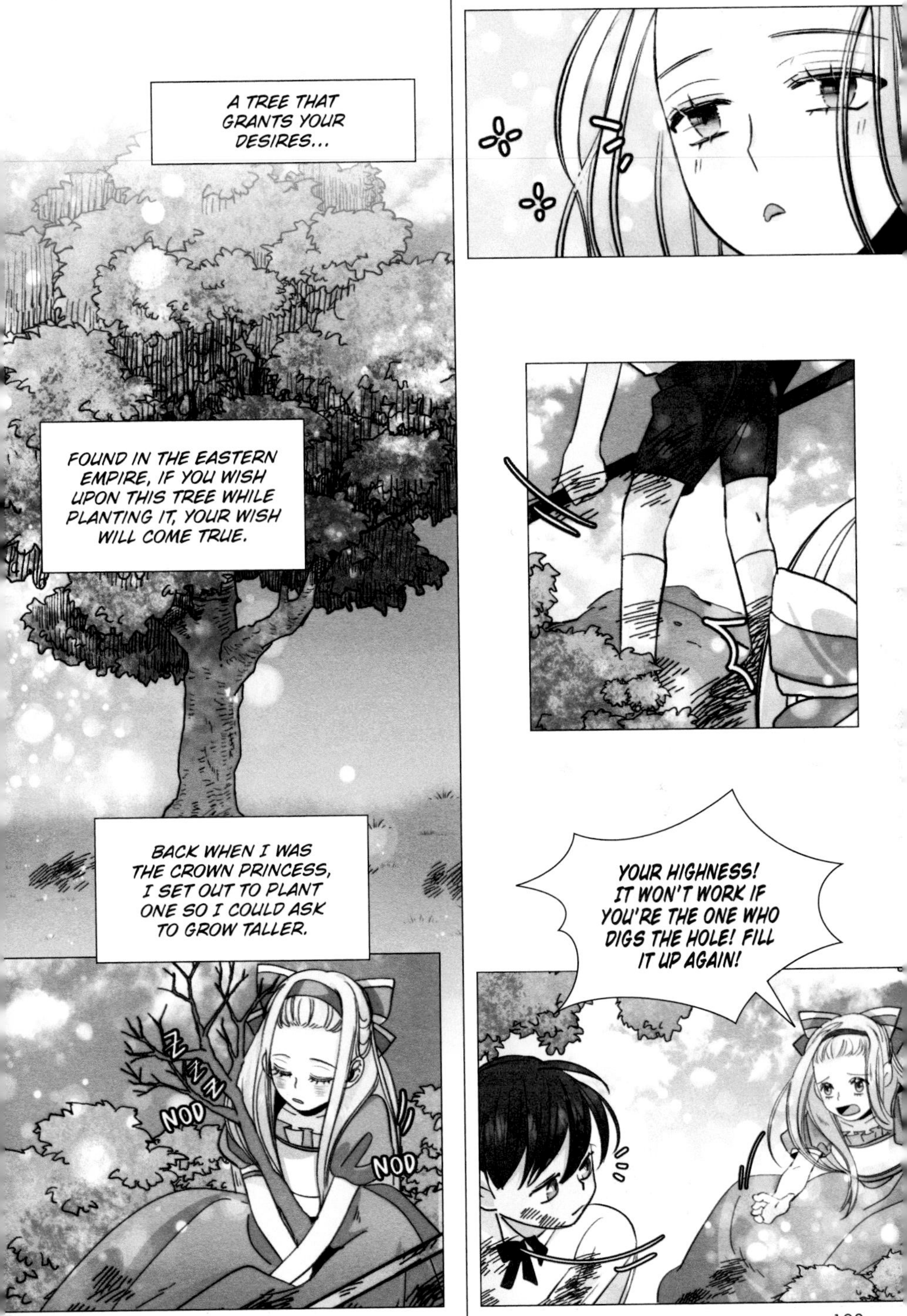
A TREE THAT GRANTS YOUR DESIRES...
FOUND IN THE EASTERN EMPIRE, IF YOU WISH UPON THIS TREE WHILE PLANTING IT, YOUR WISH WILL COME TRUE.
BACK WHEN I WAS THE CROWN PRINCESS, I SET OUT TO PLANT ONE SO I COULD ASK TO GROW TALLER.
NOD
NOD
YOUR HIGHNESS! IT WON'T WORK IF YOU'RE THE ONE WHO DIGS THE HOLE! FILL IT UP AGAIN!

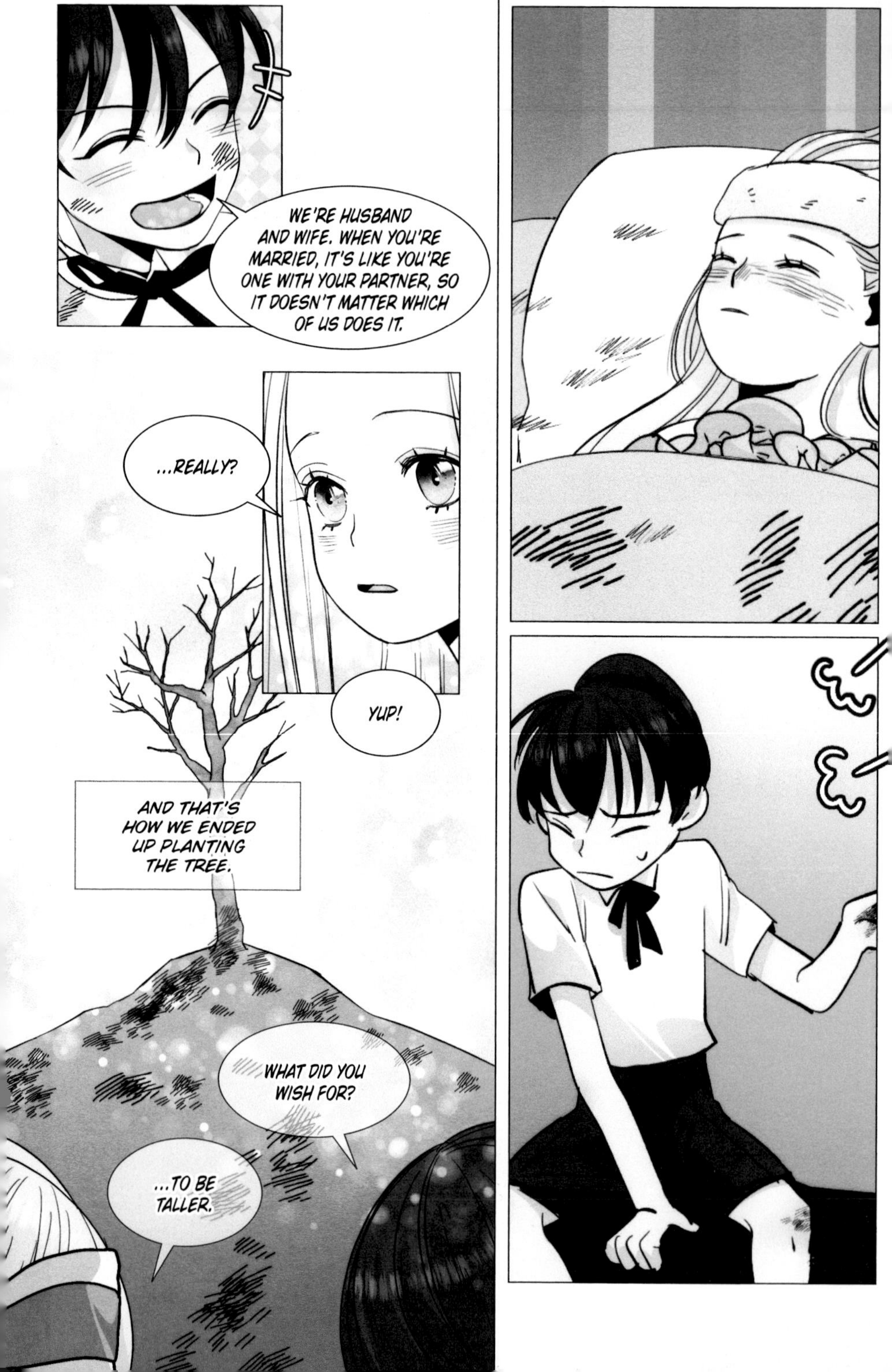
WE'RE HUSBAND AND WIFE. WHEN YOU'RE MARRIED, IT'S LIKE YOU'RE ONE WITH YOUR PARTNER, SO IT DOESN'T MATTER WHICH OF US DOES IT.
...REALLY?
YUP!
AND THAT'S HOW WE ENDED UP PLANTING THE TREE.
WHAT DID YOU WISH FOR?
...TO BE TALLER.

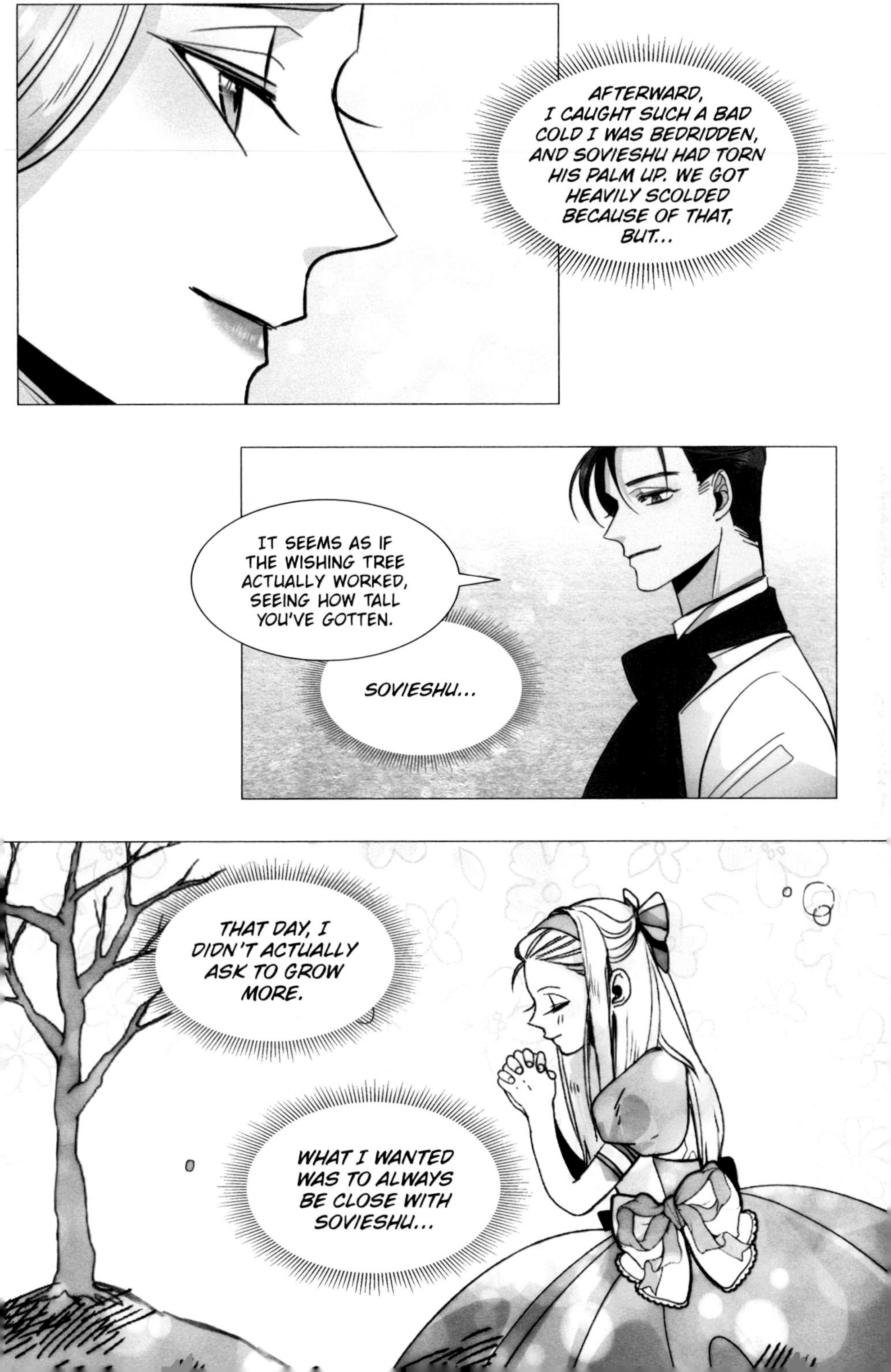
AFTERWARD, I CAUGHT SUCH A BAD COLD I WAS BEDRIDDEN, AND SOVIESHU HAD TORN HIS PALM UP. WE GOT HEAVILY SCOLDED BECAUSE OF THAT, BUT...
IT SEEMS AS IF THE WISHING TREE ACTUALLY WORKED, SEEING HOW TALL YOU'VE GOTTEN.
SOVIESHU...
THAT DAY, I DIDN'T ACTUALLY ASK TO GROW MORE.
WHAT I WANTED WAS TO ALWAYS BE CLOSE WITH SOVIESHU...

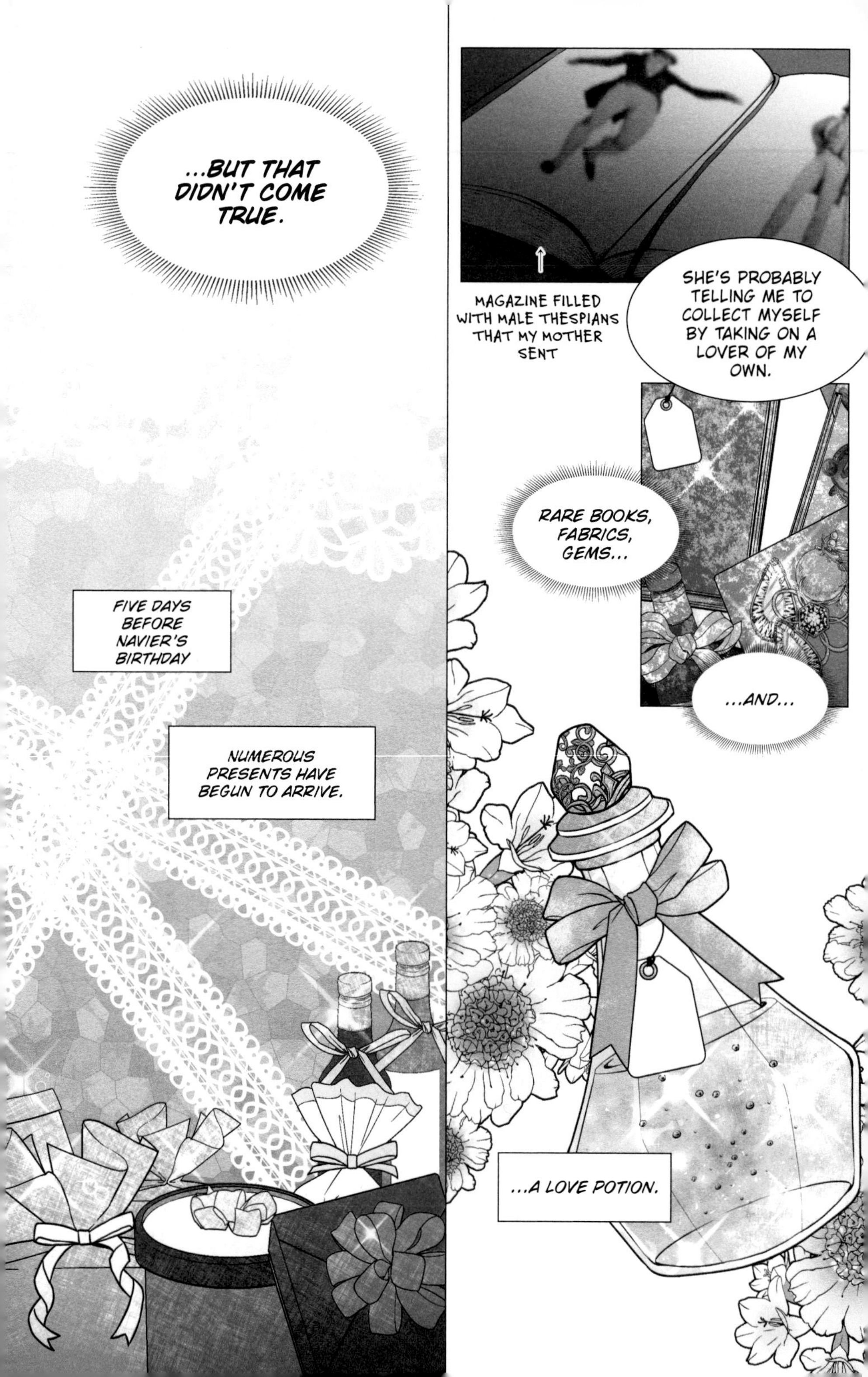
...BUT THAT DIDN'T COME TRUE.
FIVE DAYS BEFORE NAVIER'S BIRTHDAY
NUMEROUS PRESENTS HAVE BEGUN TO ARRIVE.
MAGAZINE FILLED WITH MALE THESPIANS THAT MY MOTHER SENT
SHE'S PROBABLY TELLING ME TO COLLECT MYSELF BY TAKING ON A LOVER OF MY OWN.
RARE BOOKS, FABRICS, GEMS...
...AND...
...A LOVE POTION.

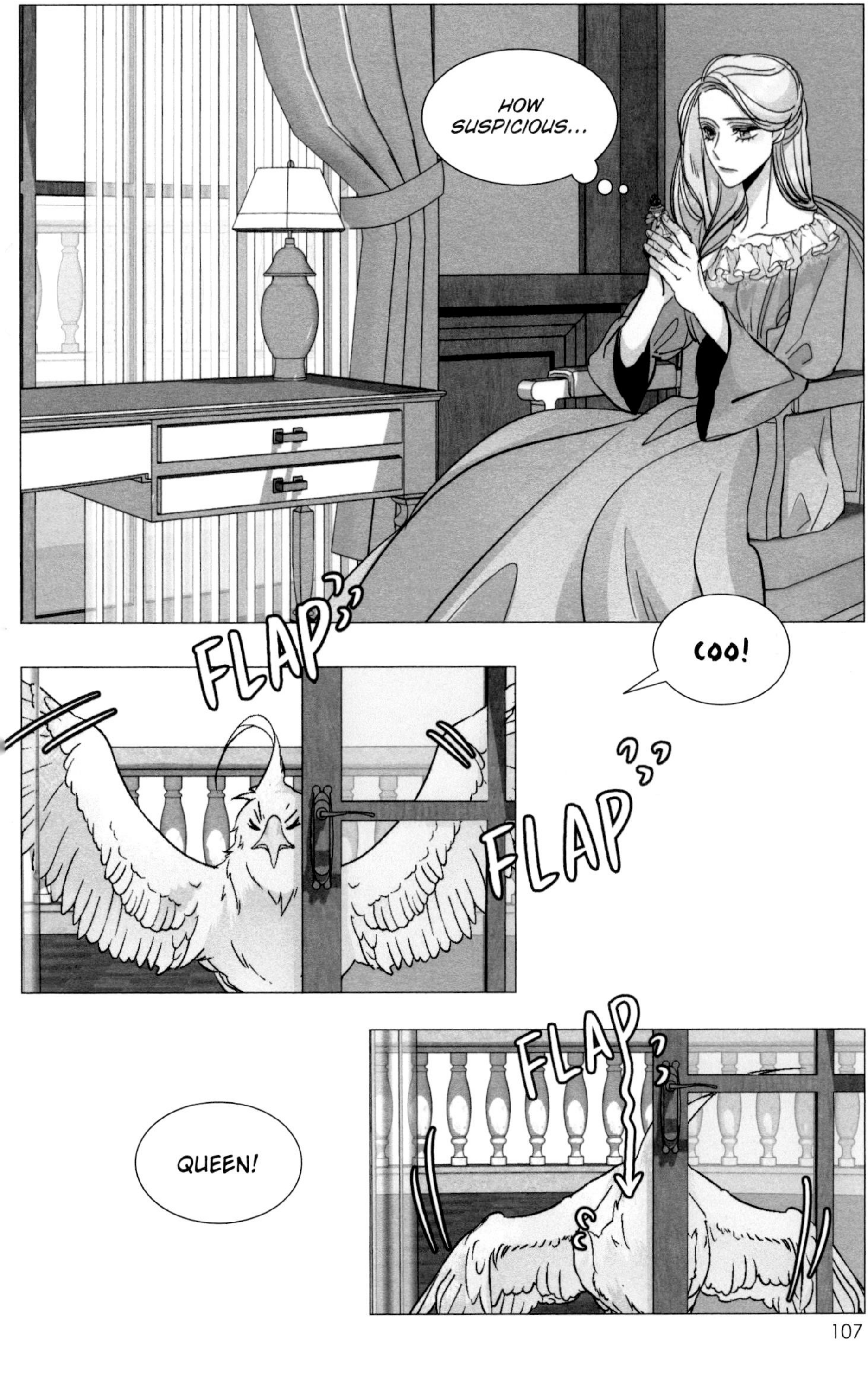
HOW SUSPICIOUS...
FLAP,,,
COO!
FLAP,,,
FLAP,,
QUEEN!

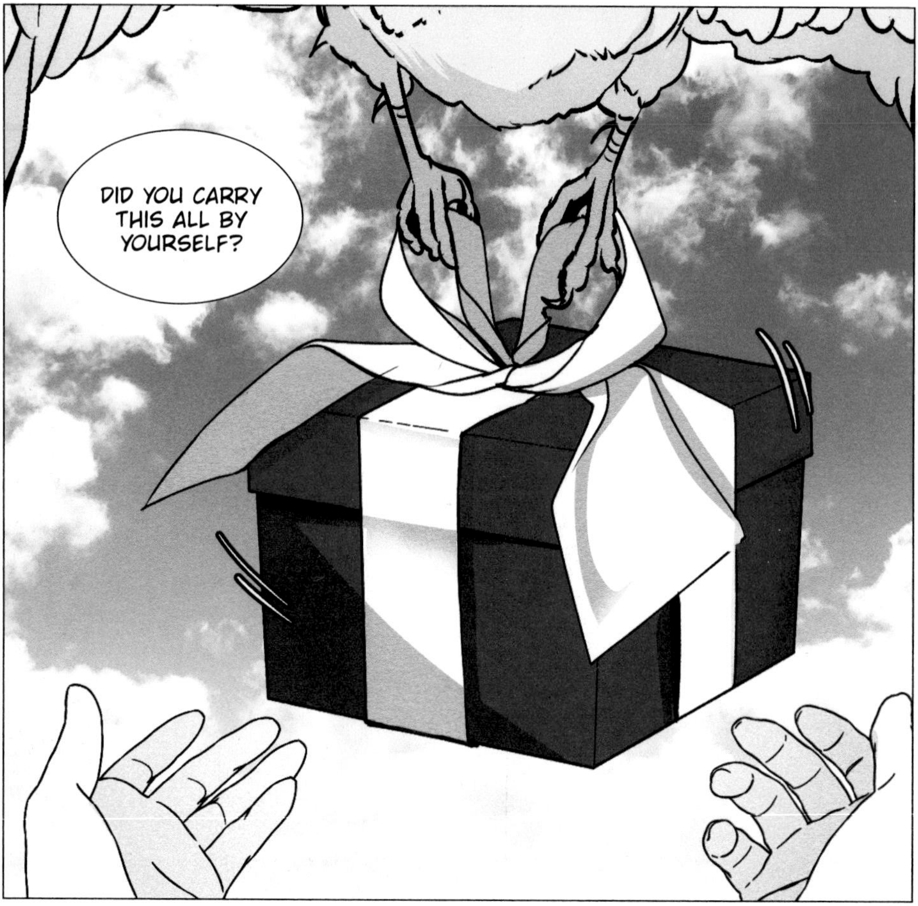
DID YOU CARRY THIS ALL BY YOURSELF?

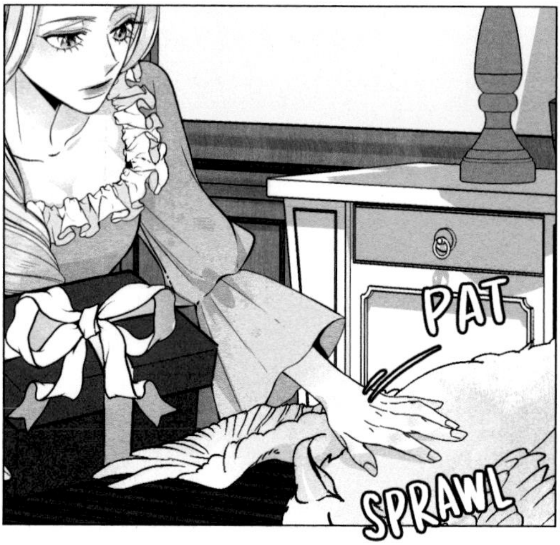
GOODNESS, I DIDN'T THINK PRINCE HEINREY WOULD BE SO CRUEL. HE SHOULD HAVE BROUGHT THIS OVER DIRECTLY OR SENT SOMEBODY ELSE.
PAT
SPRAWL

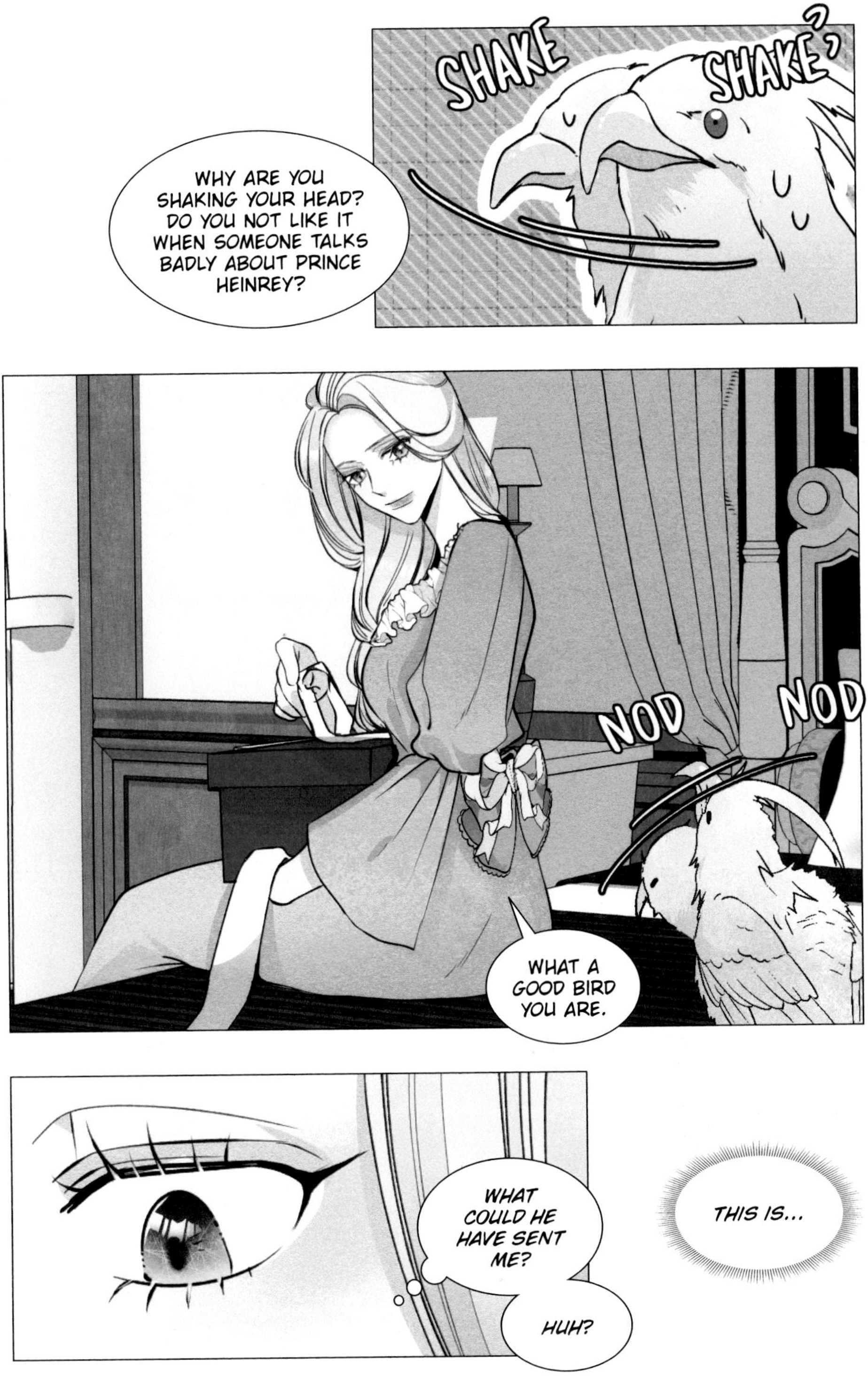
SHAKE
SHAKE
WHY ARE YOU SHAKING YOUR HEAD? DO YOU NOT LIKE IT WHEN SOMEONE TALKS BADLY ABOUT PRINCE HEINREY?
NOD
NOD
WHAT A GOOD BIRD YOU ARE.
WHAT COULD HE HAVE SENT ME?
HUH?
THIS IS...

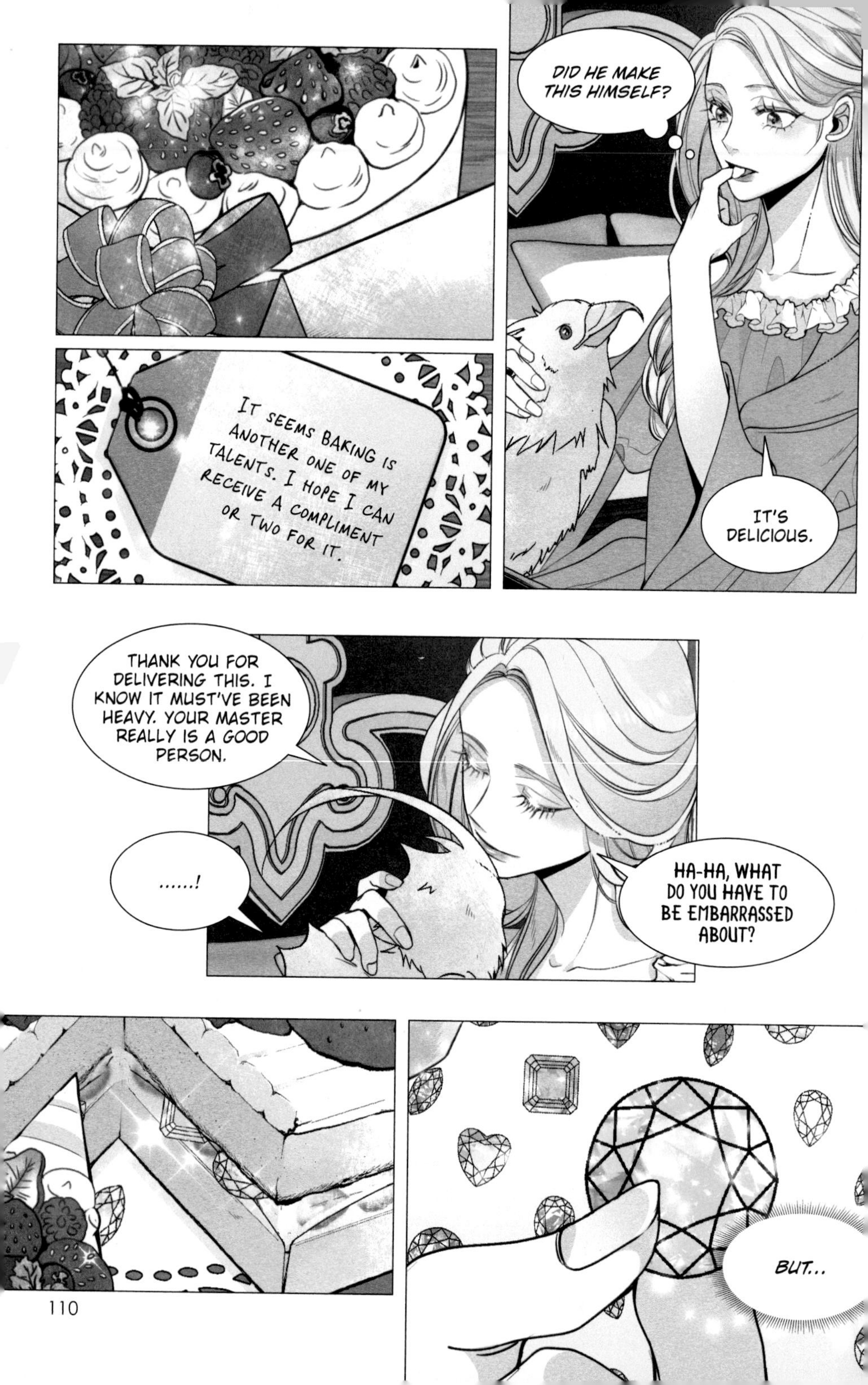
It seems baking is another one of my talents. I hope I can receive a compliment or two for it.
DID HE MAKE THIS HIMSELF?
IT'S DELICIOUS.
THANK YOU FOR DELIVERING THIS. I KNOW IT MUST'VE BEEN HEAVY. YOUR MASTER REALLY IS A GOOD PERSON.
......!
HA-HA, WHAT DO YOU HAVE TO BE EMBARRASSED ABOUT?
BUT...

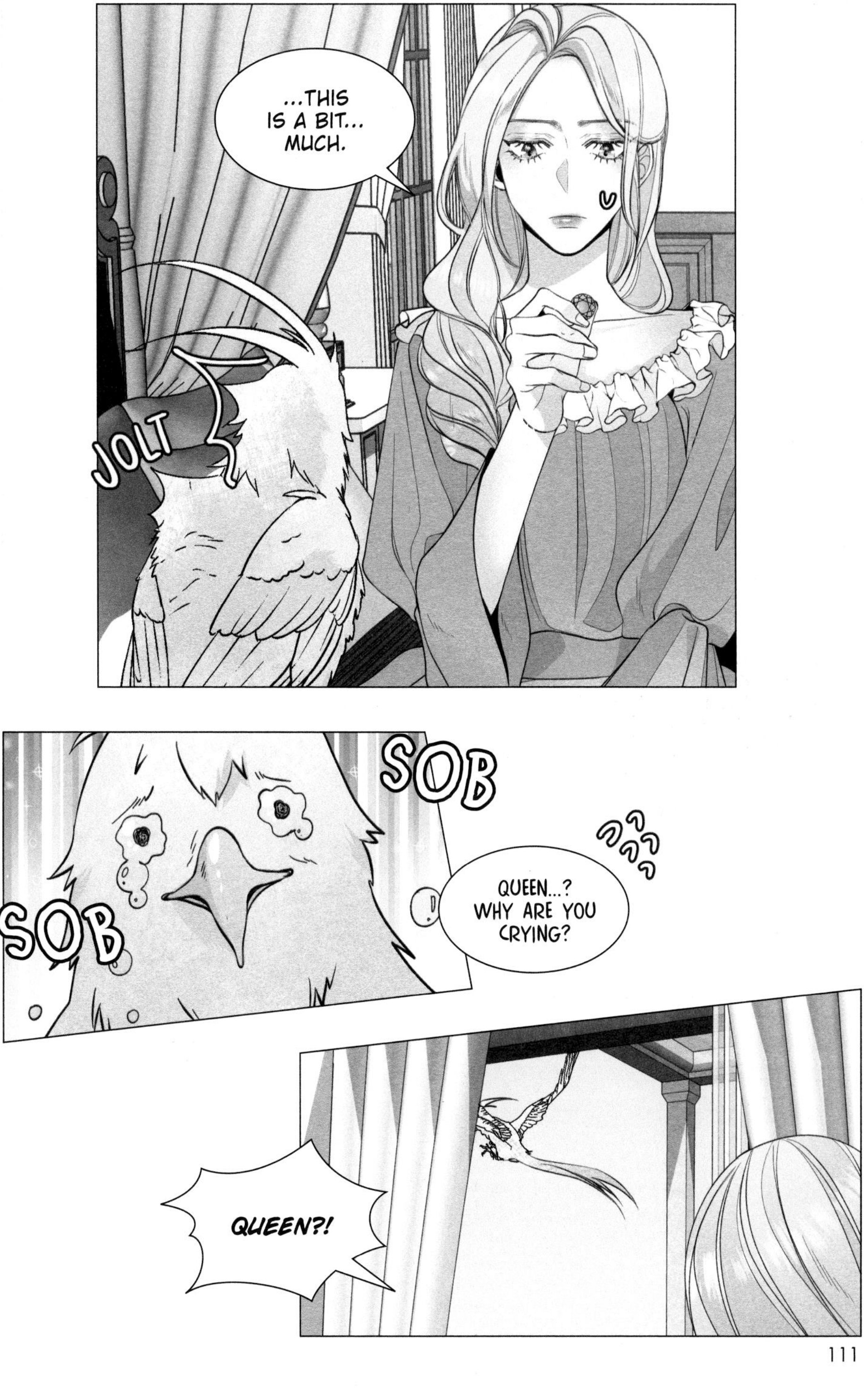
...THIS IS A BIT... MUCH.
JOLT
SOB
SOB
QUEEN...? WHY ARE YOU CRYING?
QUEEN?!

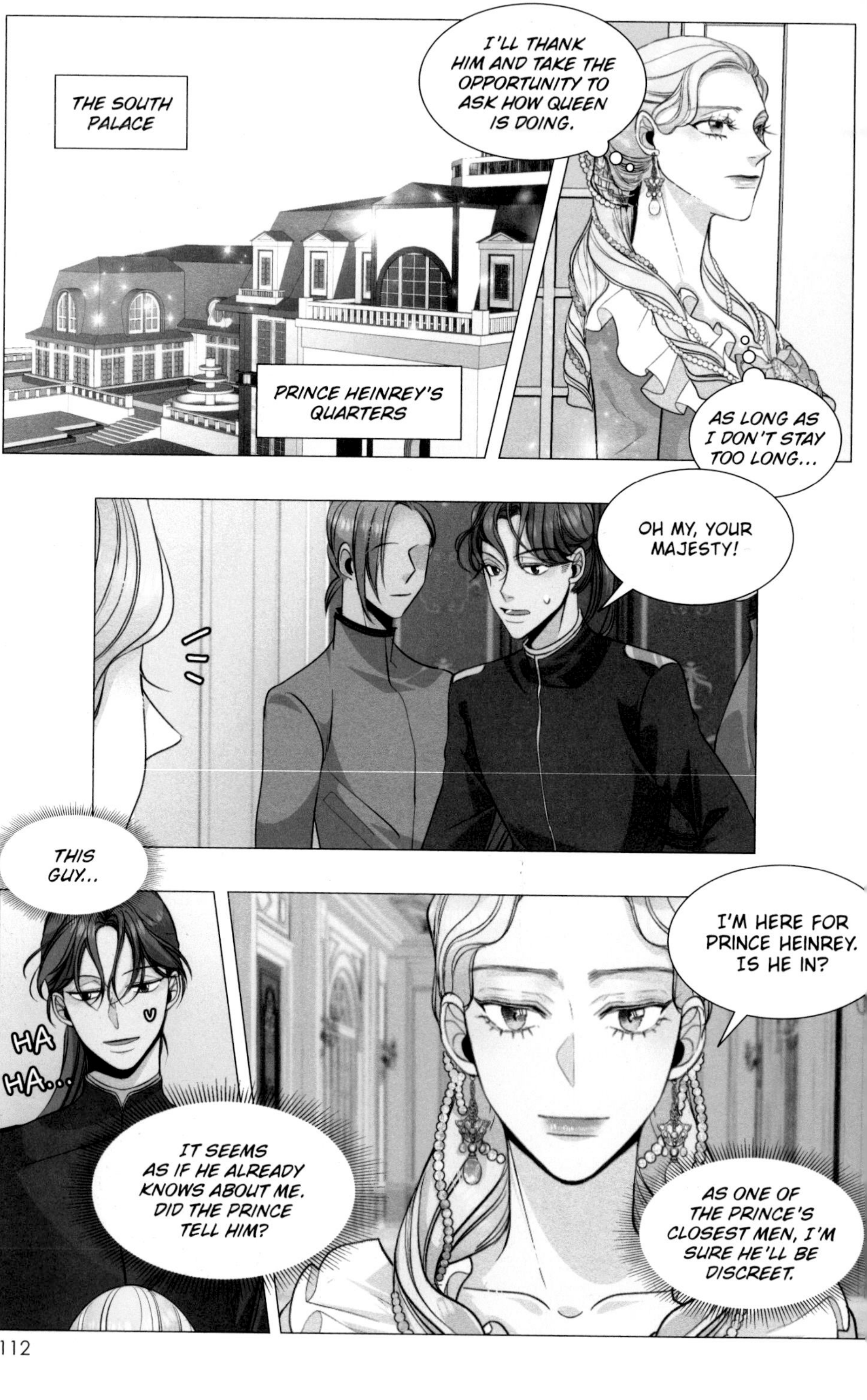
THE SOUTH PALACE
PRINCE HEINREY'S QUARTERS
I'LL THANK HIM AND TAKE THE OPPORTUNITY TO ASK HOW QUEEN IS DOING.
AS LONG AS I DON'T STAY TOO LONG...
OH MY, YOUR MAJESTY!
THIS GUY...
I'M HERE FOR PRINCE HEINREY. IS HE IN?
HA HA...
IT SEEMS AS IF HE ALREADY KNOWS ABOUT ME. DID THE PRINCE TELL HIM?
AS ONE OF THE PRINCE'S CLOSEST MEN, I'M SURE HE'LL BE DISCREET.

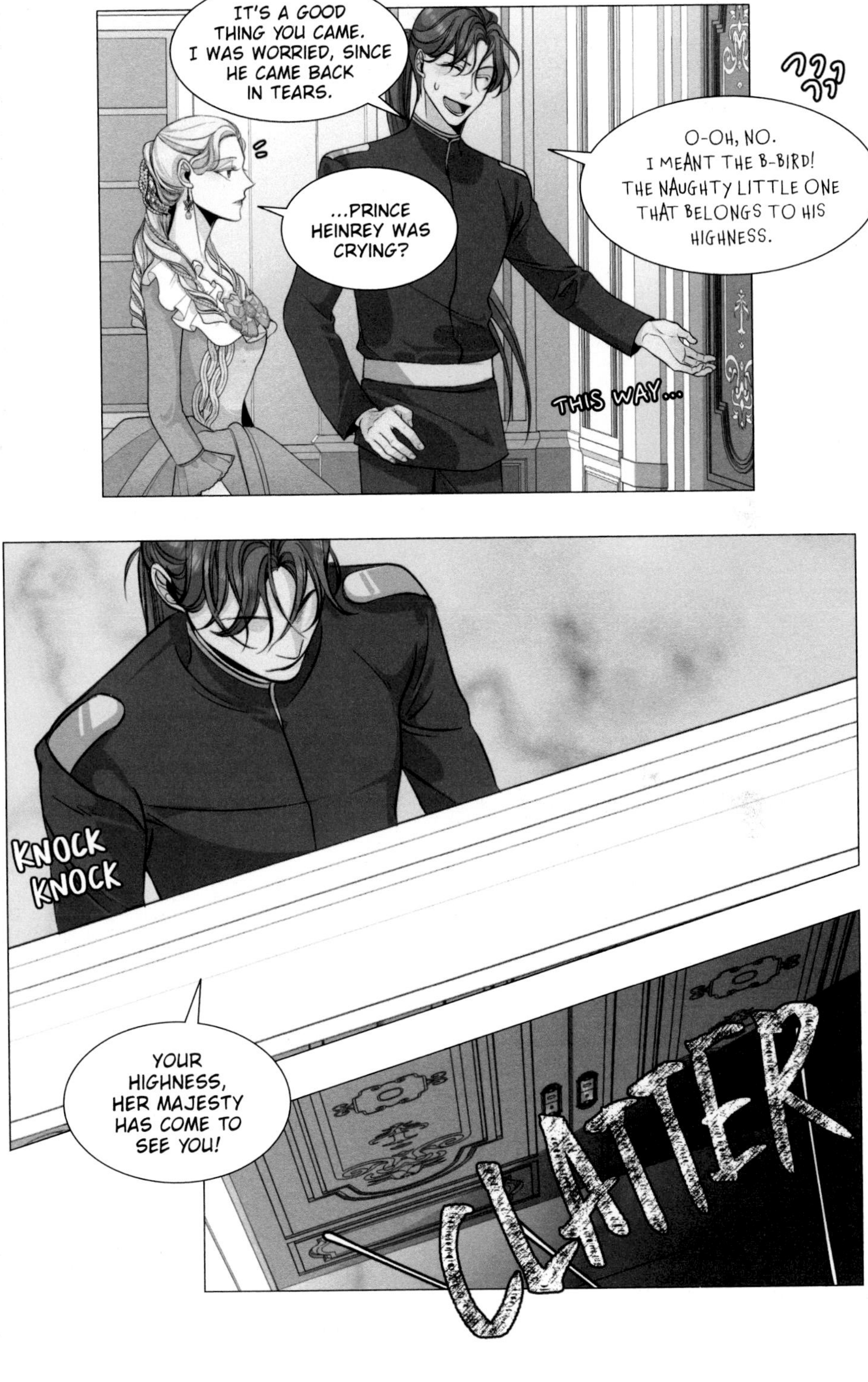
IT'S A GOOD THING YOU CAME. I WAS WORRIED, SINCE HE CAME BACK IN TEARS.
...PRINCE HEINREY WAS CRYING?
O-OH, NO. I MEANT THE B-BIRD! THE NAUGHTY LITTLE ONE THAT BELONGS TO HIS HIGHNESS.
THIS WAY...
KNOCK KNOCK
YOUR HIGHNESS, HER MAJESTY HAS COME TO SEE YOU!
CLATTER

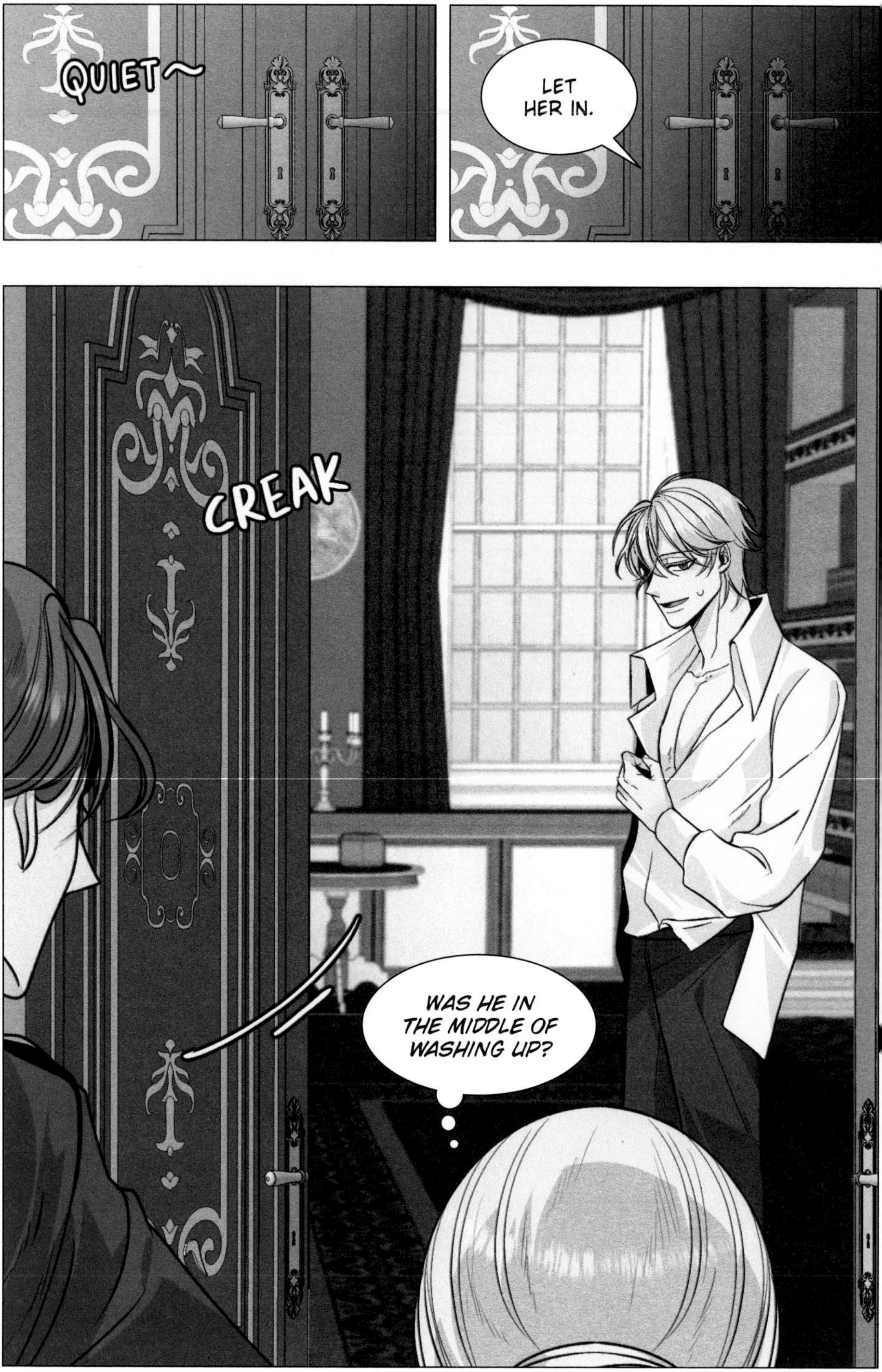
QUIET~
LET HER IN.
CREAK
WAS HE IN THE MIDDLE OF WASHING UP?

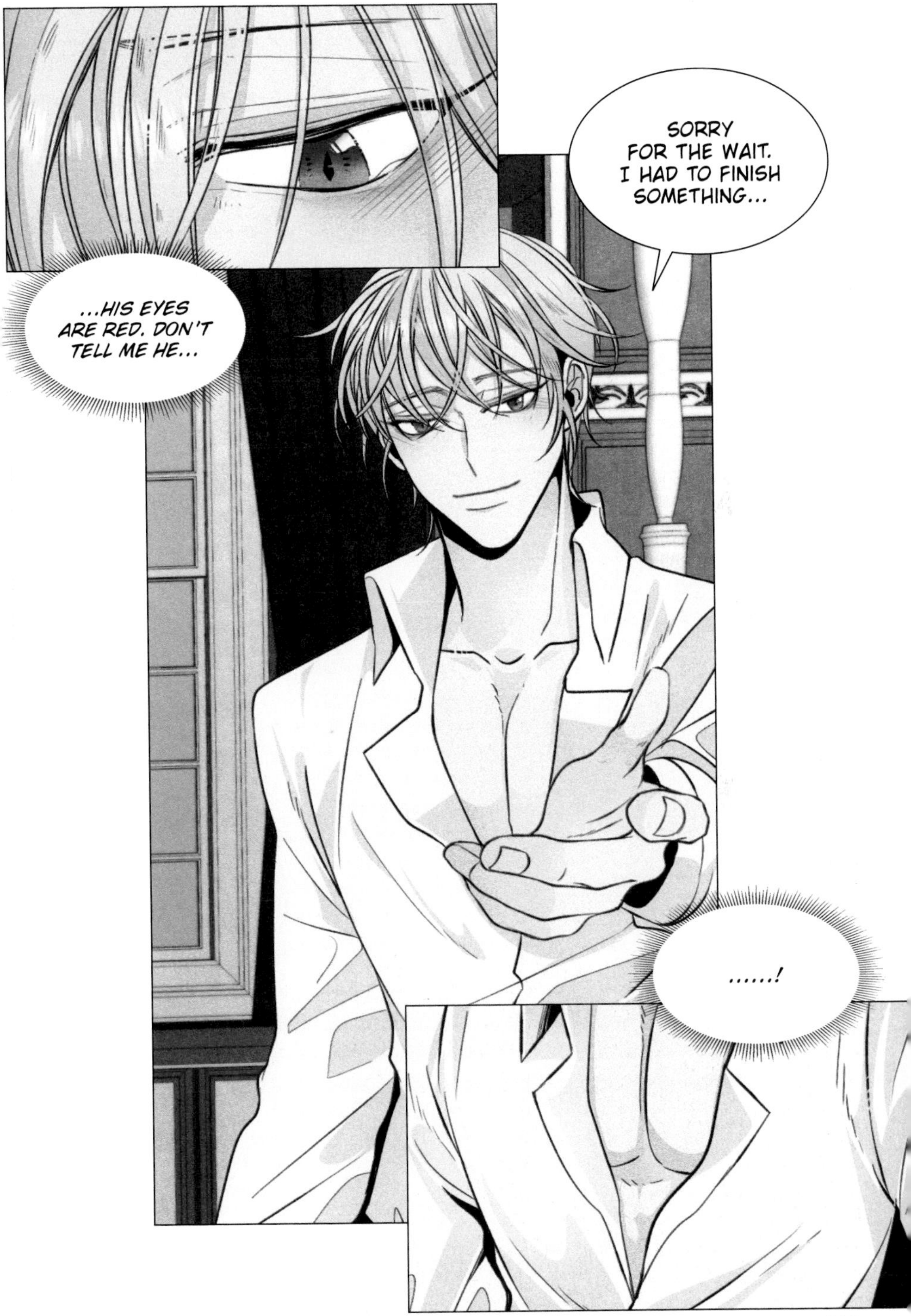
SORRY FOR THE WAIT. I HAD TO FINISH SOMETHING...
...HIS EYES ARE RED. DON'T TELL ME HE...
......!

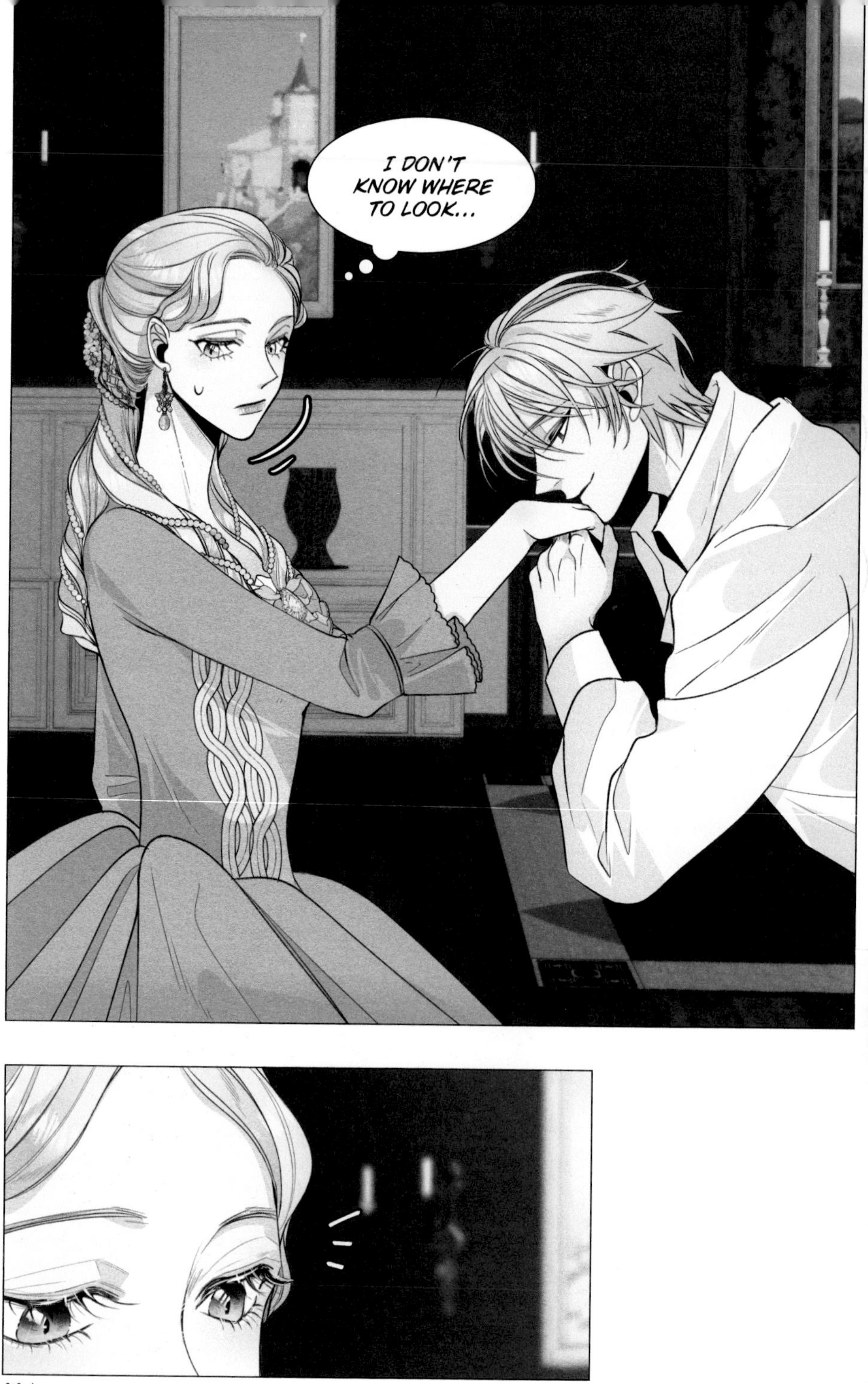
I DON'T KNOW WHERE TO LOOK...

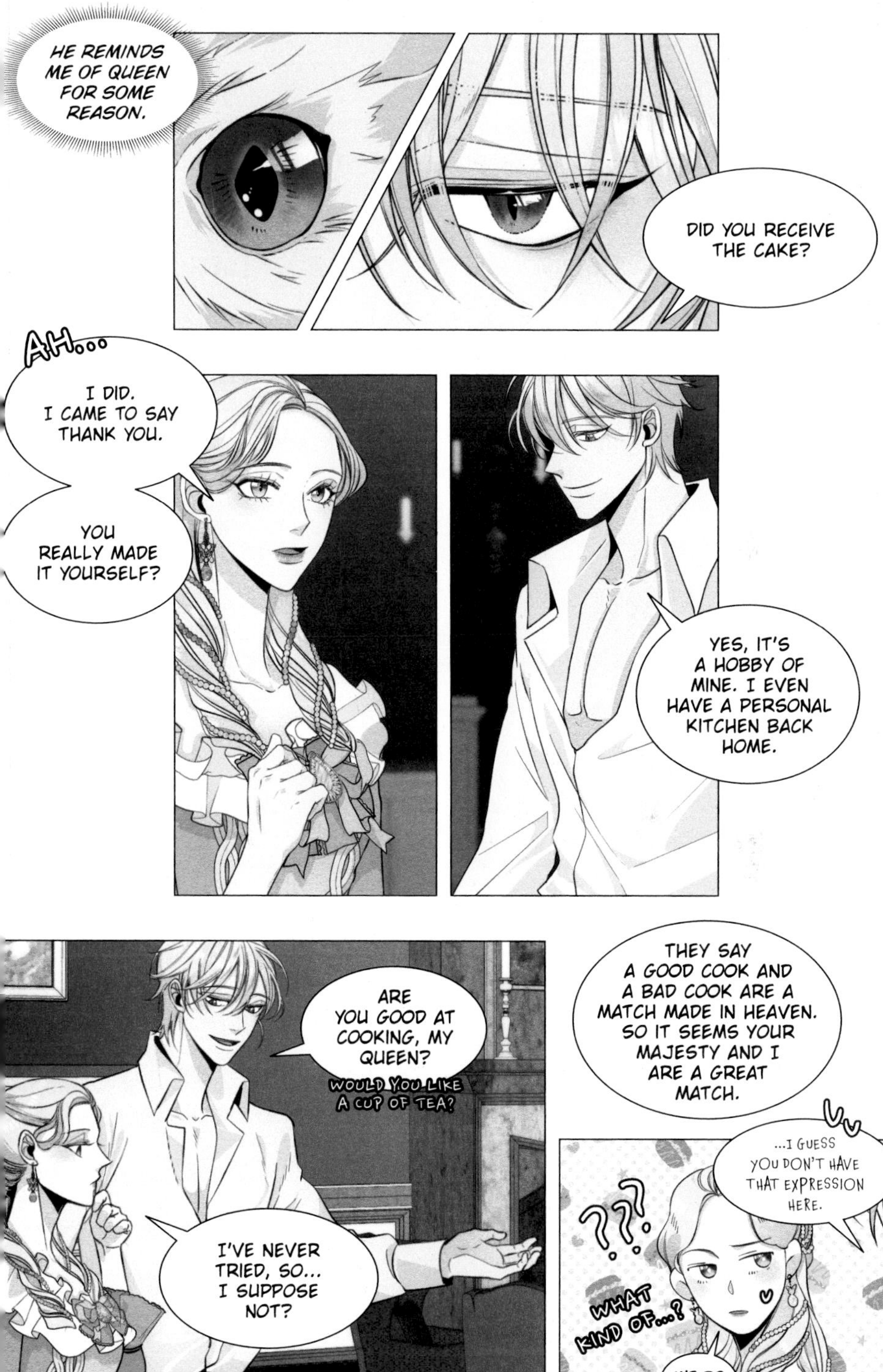
HE REMINDS ME OF QUEEN FOR SOME REASON.
DID YOU RECEIVE THE CAKE?
AH...
I DID. I CAME TO SAY THANK YOU.
YOU REALLY MADE IT YOURSELF?
YES, IT'S A HOBBY OF MINE. I EVEN HAVE A PERSONAL KITCHEN BACK HOME.
ARE YOU GOOD AT COOKING, MY QUEEN?
WOULD YOU LIKE A CUP OF TEA?
I'VE NEVER TRIED, SO... I SUPPOSE NOT?
THEY SAY A GOOD COOK AND A BAD COOK ARE A MATCH MADE IN HEAVEN. SO IT SEEMS YOUR MAJESTY AND I ARE A GREAT MATCH.
...I GUESS YOU DON'T HAVE THAT EXPRESSION HERE.
???
WHAT KIND OF...?
WE DO NOT.

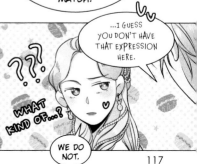

WON'T EVEN HUMOR ME, HUH?

ACTUALLY, I WANTED TO SEE QUEEN...HE LEFT IN TEARS.

I'M AFRAID HE'S OUT HUNTING. HE WAS CRYING A BIT WHEN HE RETURNED, BUT HE WAS FINE SOON AFTER.

IS THAT SO...?

BUT HIS KNIGHT JUST NOW WAS WORRIED ABOUT QUEEN...

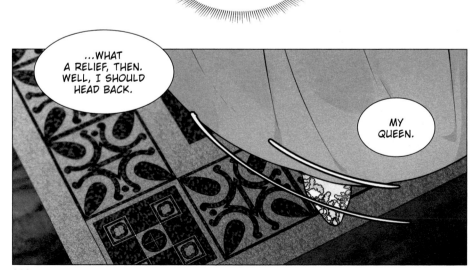

...WHAT A RELIEF, THEN. WELL, I SHOULD HEAD BACK.

MY QUEEN.

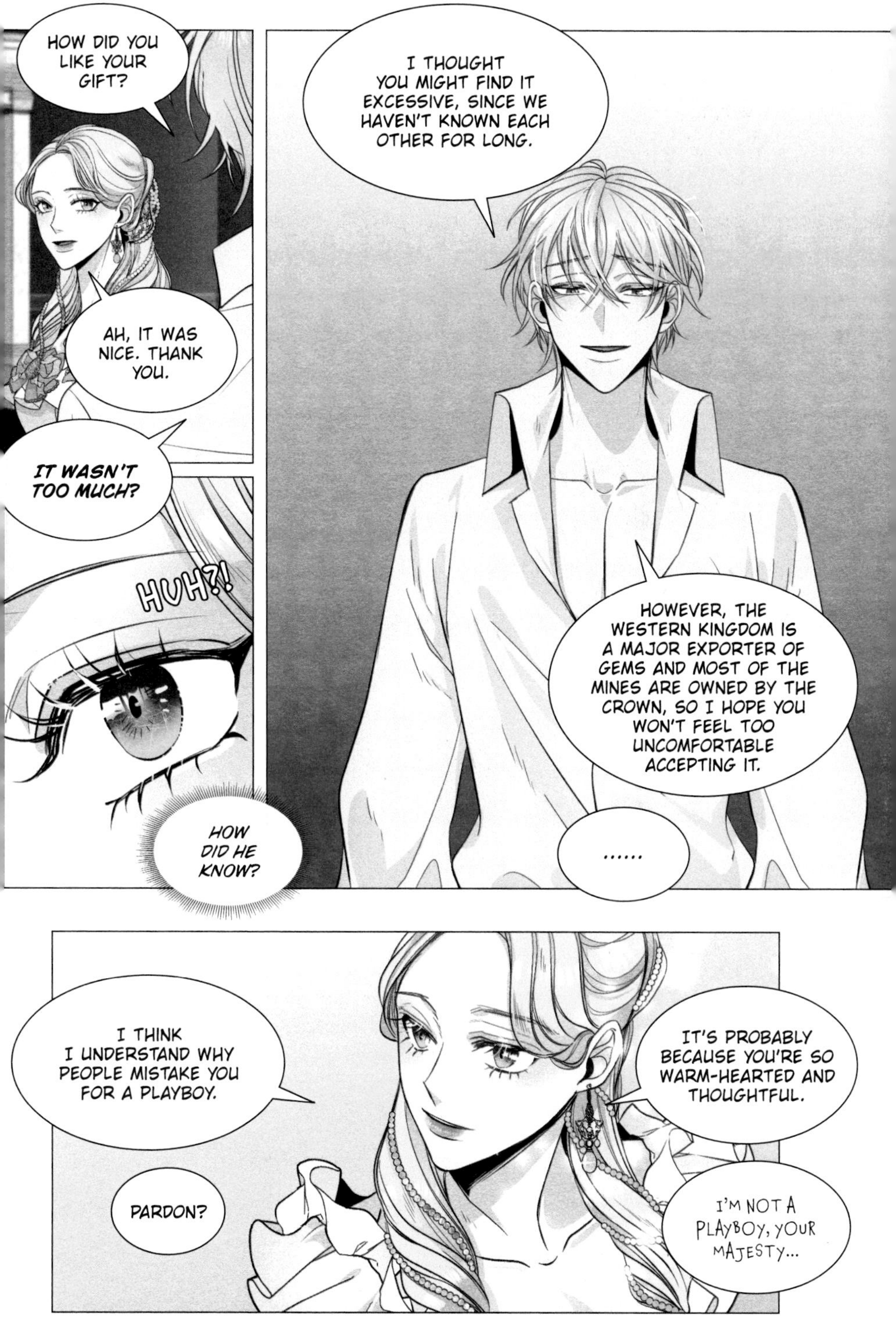
HOW DID YOU LIKE YOUR GIFT?
AH, IT WAS NICE. THANK YOU.
I THOUGHT YOU MIGHT FIND IT EXCESSIVE, SINCE WE HAVEN'T KNOWN EACH OTHER FOR LONG.
IT WASN'T TOO MUCH?
HUH?!
HOWEVER, THE WESTERN KINGDOM IS A MAJOR EXPORTER OF GEMS AND MOST OF THE MINES ARE OWNED BY THE CROWN, SO I HOPE YOU WON'T FEEL TOO UNCOMFORTABLE ACCEPTING IT.
HOW DID HE KNOW?
......
I THINK I UNDERSTAND WHY PEOPLE MISTAKE YOU FOR A PLAYBOY.
IT'S PROBABLY BECAUSE YOU'RE SO WARM-HEARTED AND THOUGHTFUL.
PARDON?
I'M NOT A PLAYBOY, YOUR MAJESTY...

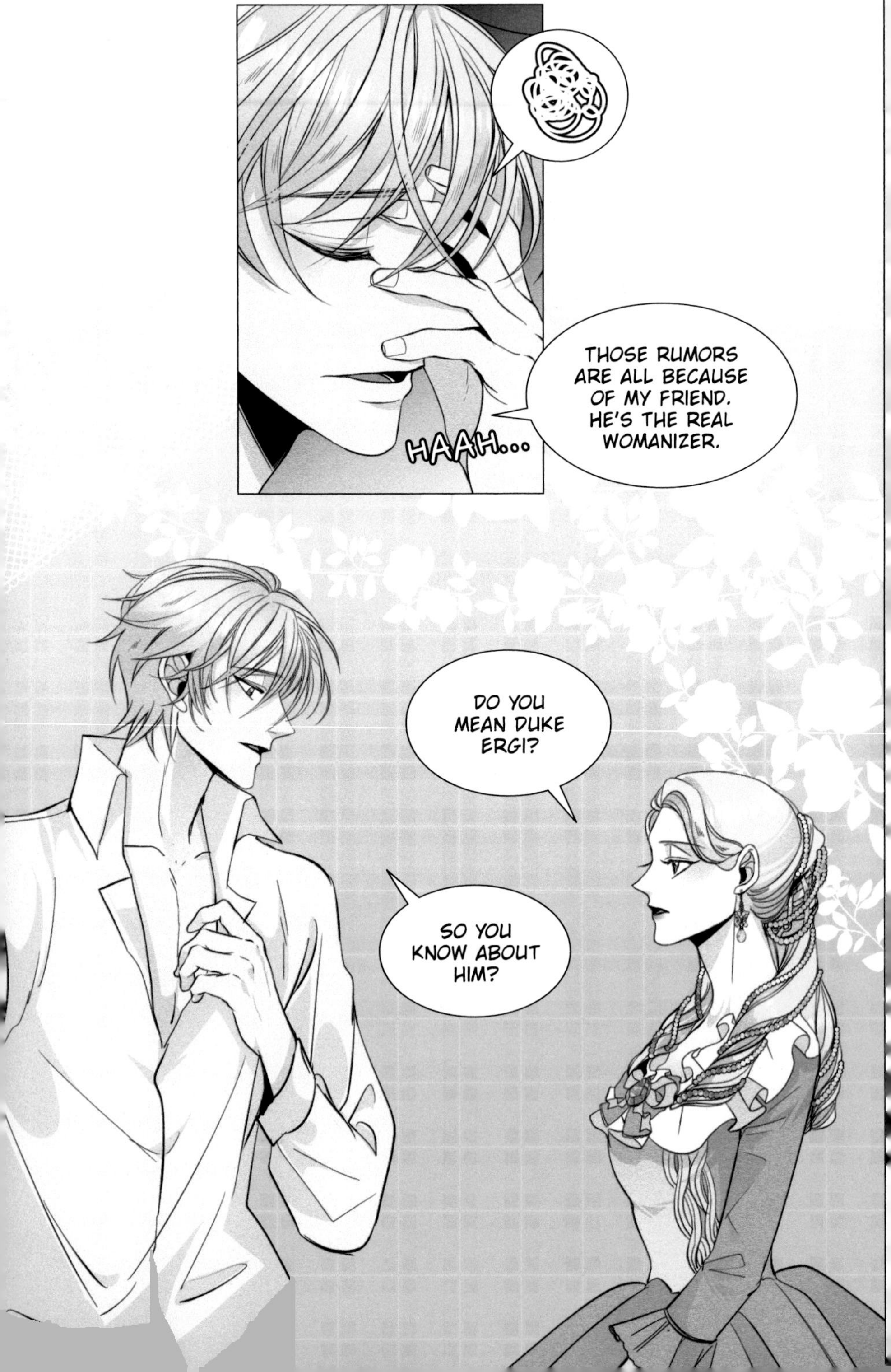
THOSE RUMORS ARE ALL BECAUSE OF MY FRIEND. HE'S THE REAL WOMANIZER.
HAAAH...
DO YOU MEAN DUKE ERGI?
SO YOU KNOW ABOUT HIM?

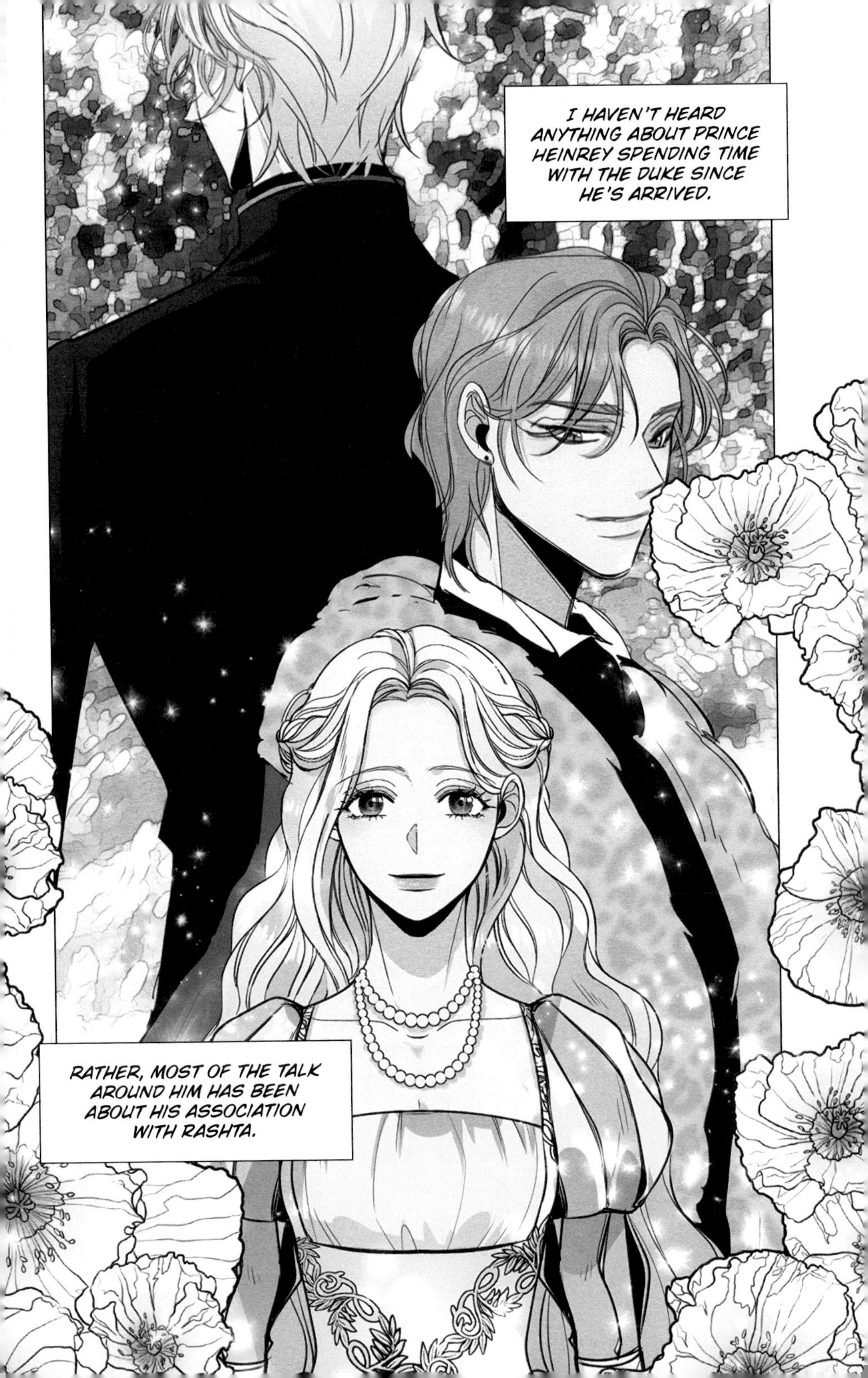
I HAVEN'T HEARD ANYTHING ABOUT PRINCE HEINREY SPENDING TIME WITH THE DUKE SINCE HE'S ARRIVED.
RATHER, MOST OF THE TALK AROUND HIM HAS BEEN ABOUT HIS ASSOCIATION WITH RASHTA.

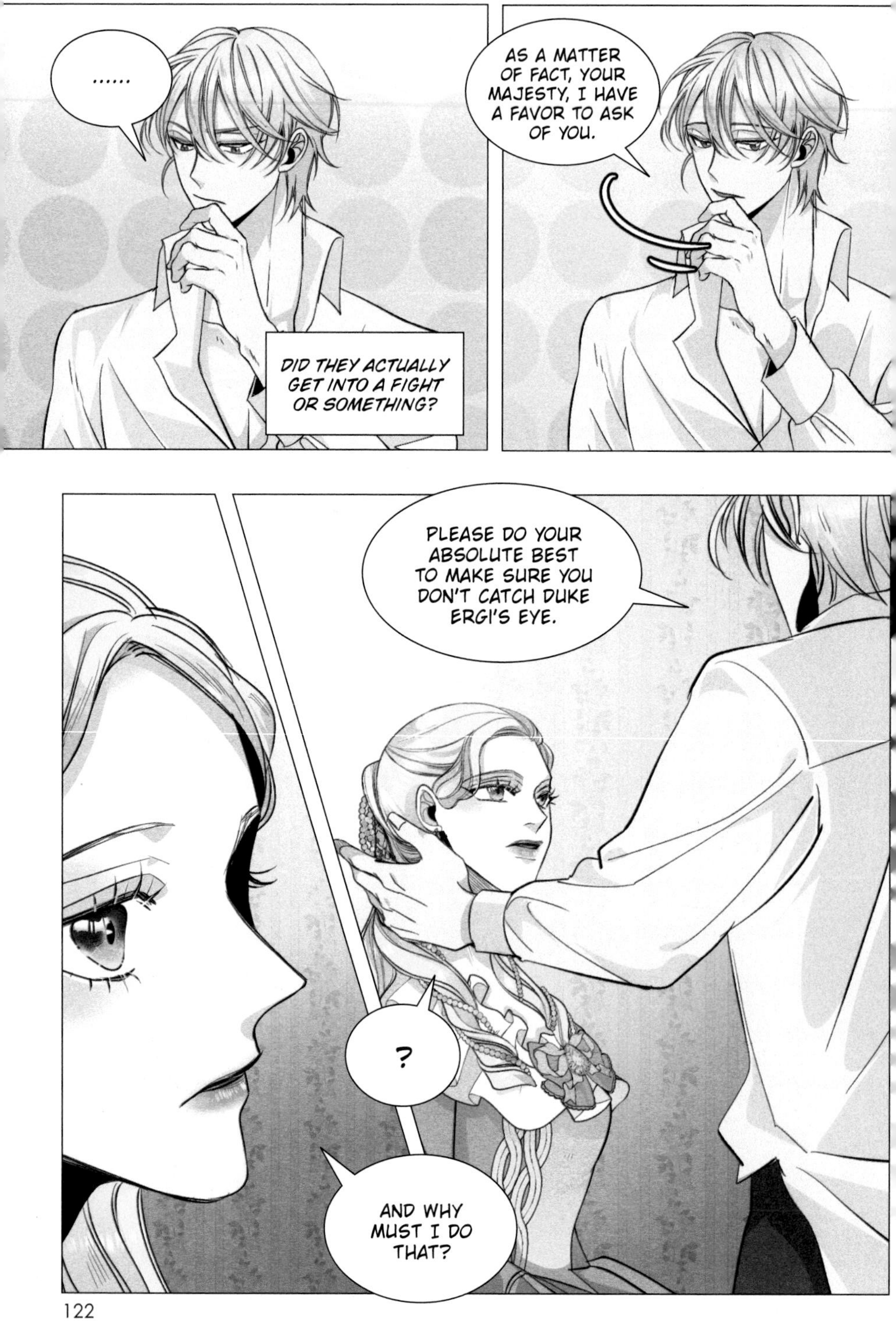
......
DID THEY ACTUALLY GET INTO A FIGHT OR SOMETHING?
AS A MATTER OF FACT, YOUR MAJESTY, I HAVE A FAVOR TO ASK OF YOU.
PLEASE DO YOUR ABSOLUTE BEST TO MAKE SURE YOU DON'T CATCH DUKE ERGI'S EYE.
?
AND WHY MUST I DO THAT?

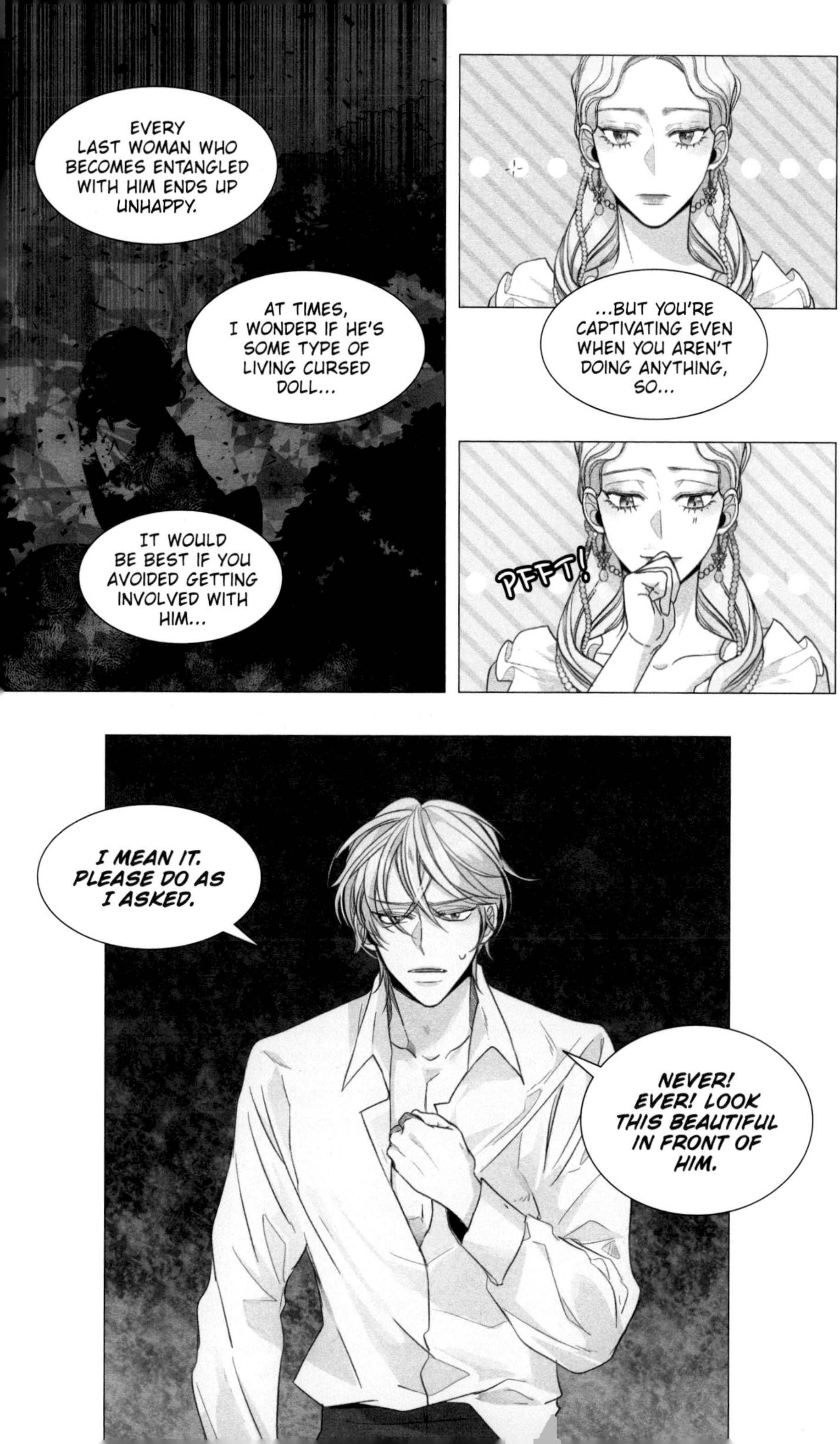
EVERY LAST WOMAN WHO BECOMES ENTANGLED WITH HIM ENDS UP UNHAPPY.
AT TIMES, I WONDER IF HE'S SOME TYPE OF LIVING CURSED DOLL...
IT WOULD BE BEST IF YOU AVOIDED GETTING INVOLVED WITH HIM...
...BUT YOU'RE CAPTIVATING EVEN WHEN YOU AREN'T DOING ANYTHING, SO...
PFFT!
I MEAN IT. PLEASE DO AS I ASKED.
NEVER! EVER! LOOK THIS BEAUTIFUL IN FRONT OF HIM.

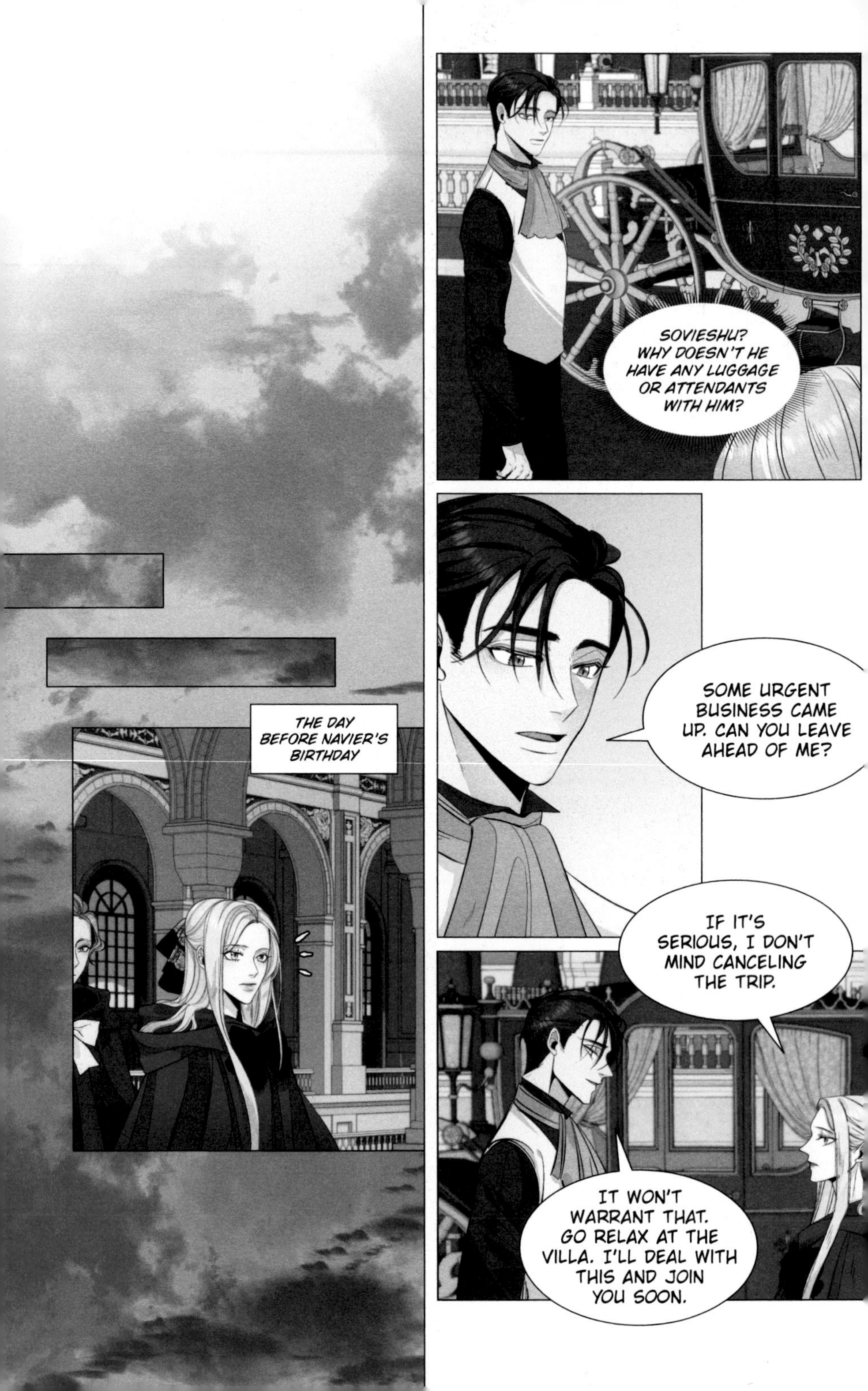
THE DAY BEFORE NAVIER'S BIRTHDAY
SOVIESHU? WHY DOESN'T HE HAVE ANY LUGGAGE OR ATTENDANTS WITH HIM?
SOME URGENT BUSINESS CAME UP. CAN YOU LEAVE AHEAD OF ME?
IF IT'S SERIOUS, I DON'T MIND CANCELING THE TRIP.
IT WON'T WARRANT THAT. GO RELAX AT THE VILLA. I'LL DEAL WITH THIS AND JOIN YOU SOON.

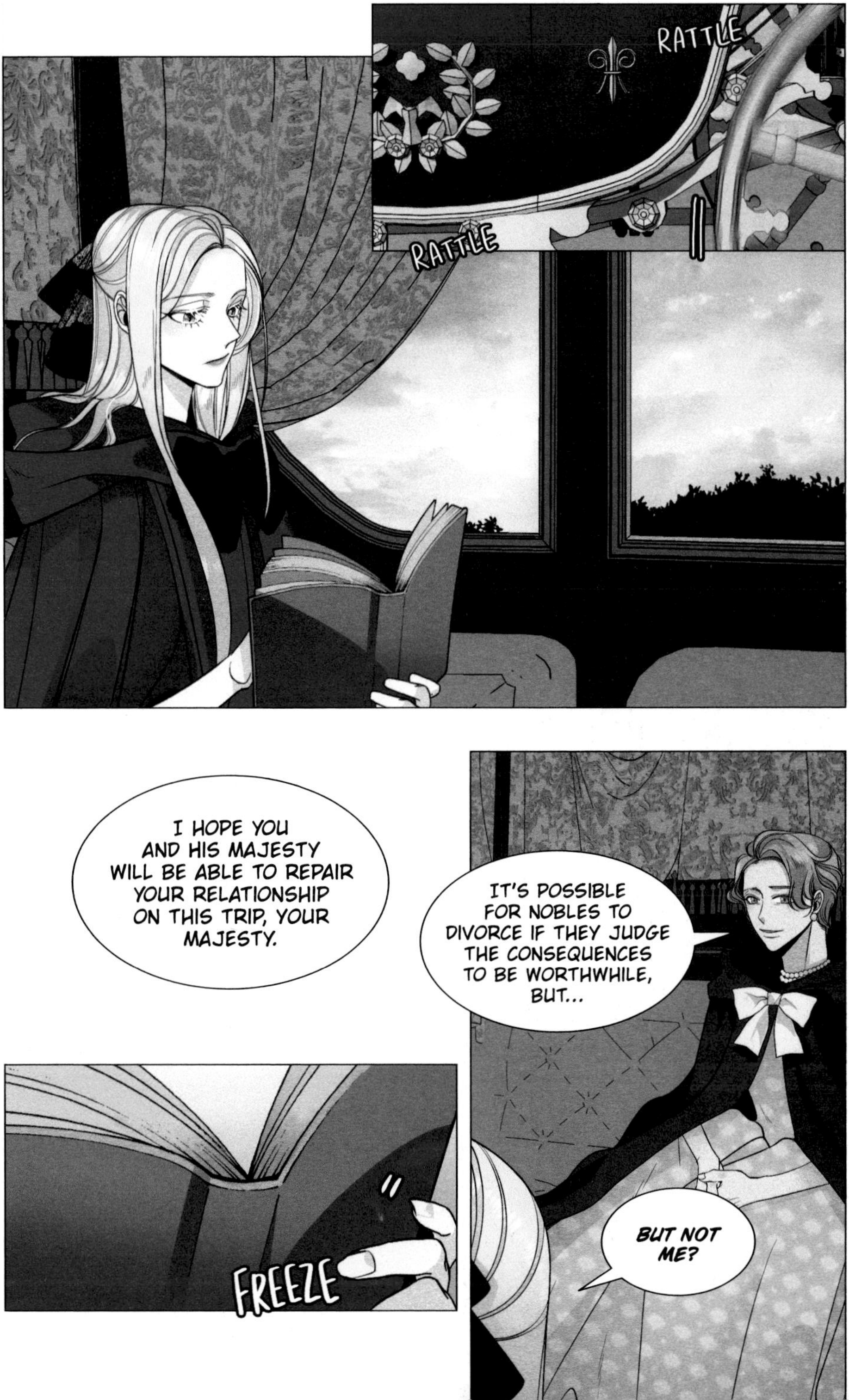
RATTLE
RATTLE
I HOPE YOU AND HIS MAJESTY WILL BE ABLE TO REPAIR YOUR RELATIONSHIP ON THIS TRIP, YOUR MAJESTY.
IT'S POSSIBLE FOR NOBLES TO DIVORCE IF THEY JUDGE THE CONSEQUENCES TO BE WORTHWHILE, BUT...
FREEZE
BUT NOT ME?

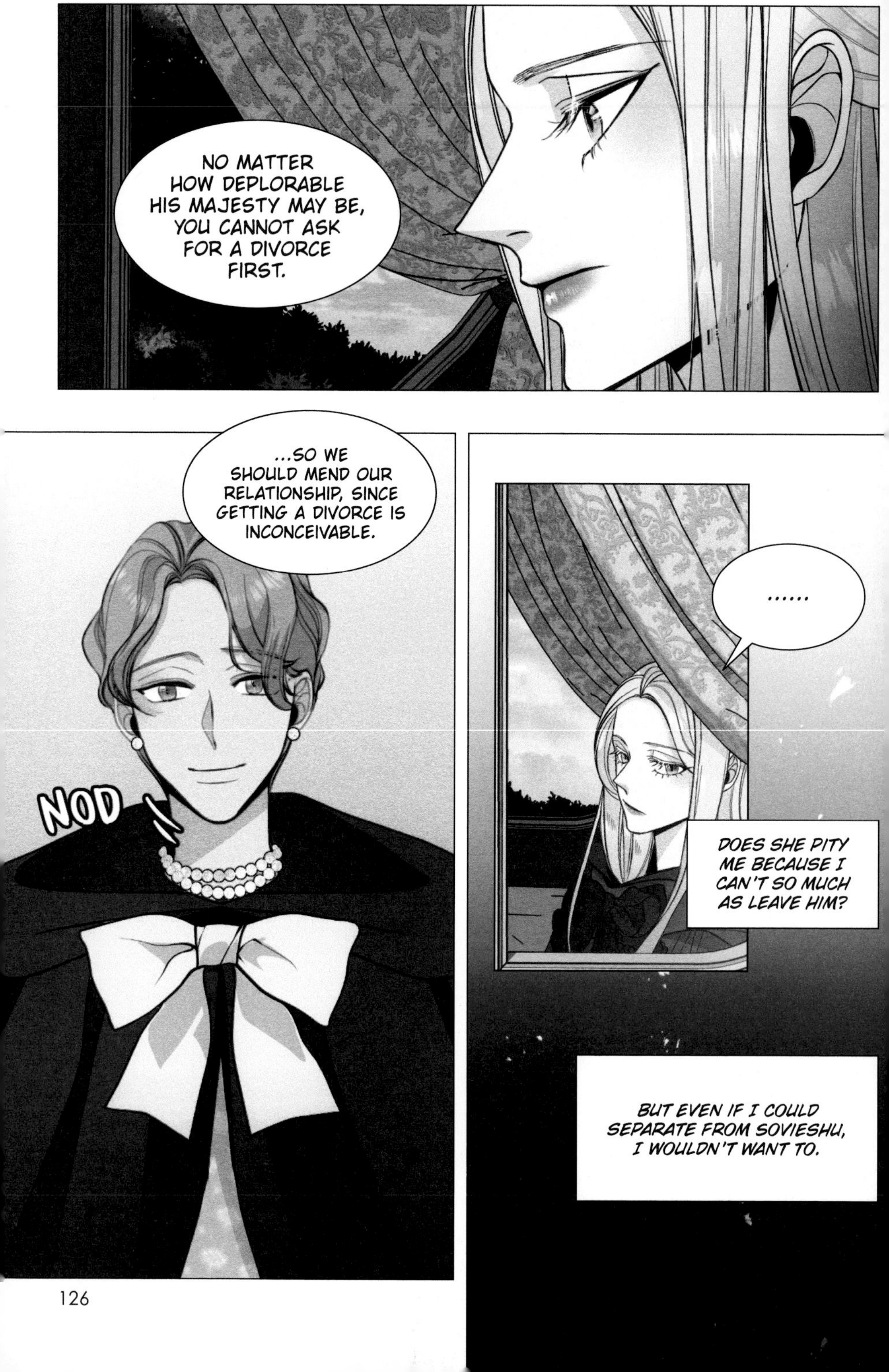
NO MATTER HOW DEPLORABLE HIS MAJESTY MAY BE, YOU CANNOT ASK FOR A DIVORCE FIRST.
...SO WE SHOULD MEND OUR RELATIONSHIP, SINCE GETTING A DIVORCE IS INCONCEIVABLE.
NOD
......
DOES SHE PITY ME BECAUSE I CAN'T SO MUCH AS LEAVE HIM?
BUT EVEN IF I COULD SEPARATE FROM SOVIESHU, I WOULDN'T WANT TO.

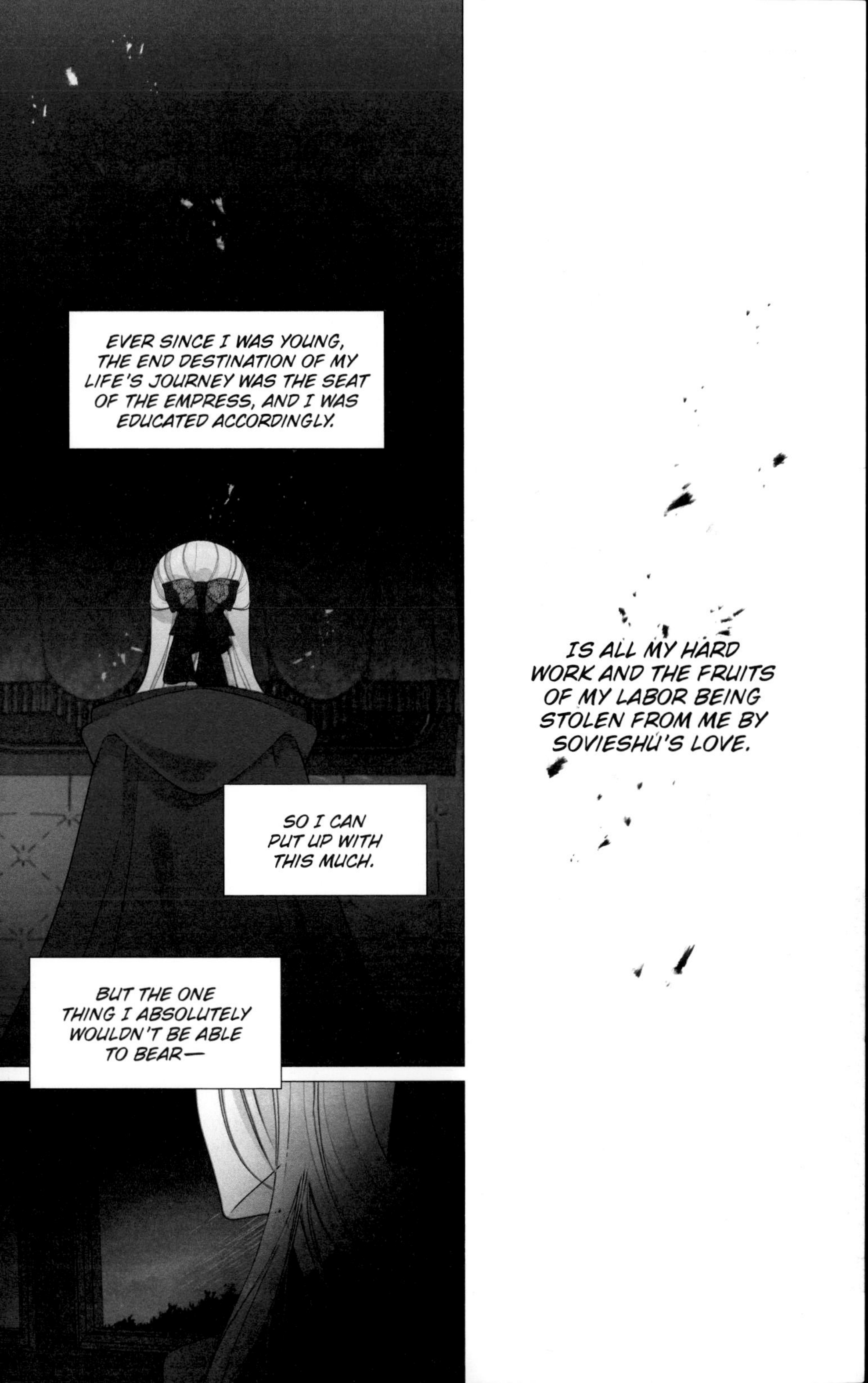
EVER SINCE I WAS YOUNG, THE END DESTINATION OF MY LIFE'S JOURNEY WAS THE SEAT OF THE EMPRESS, AND I WAS EDUCATED ACCORDINGLY.
SO I CAN PUT UP WITH THIS MUCH.
BUT THE ONE THING I ABSOLUTELY WOULDN'T BE ABLE TO BEAR—
IS ALL MY HARD WORK AND THE FRUITS OF MY LABOR BEING STOLEN FROM ME BY SOVIESHU'S LOVE.

The Remarried Empress

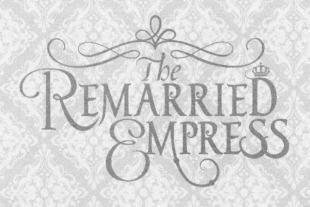

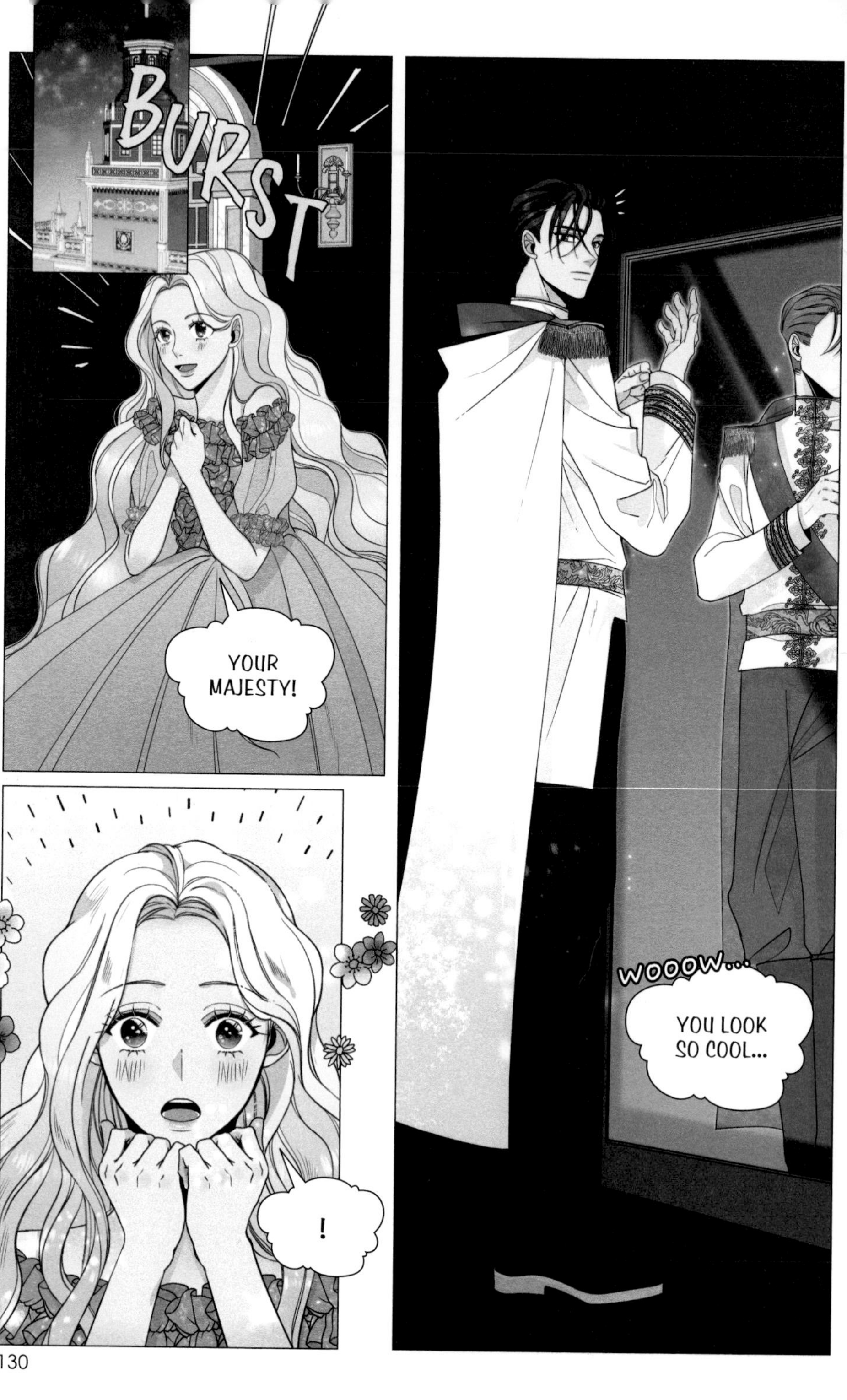
BURST
YOUR MAJESTY!
!
WOOOW...
YOU LOOK SO COOL...

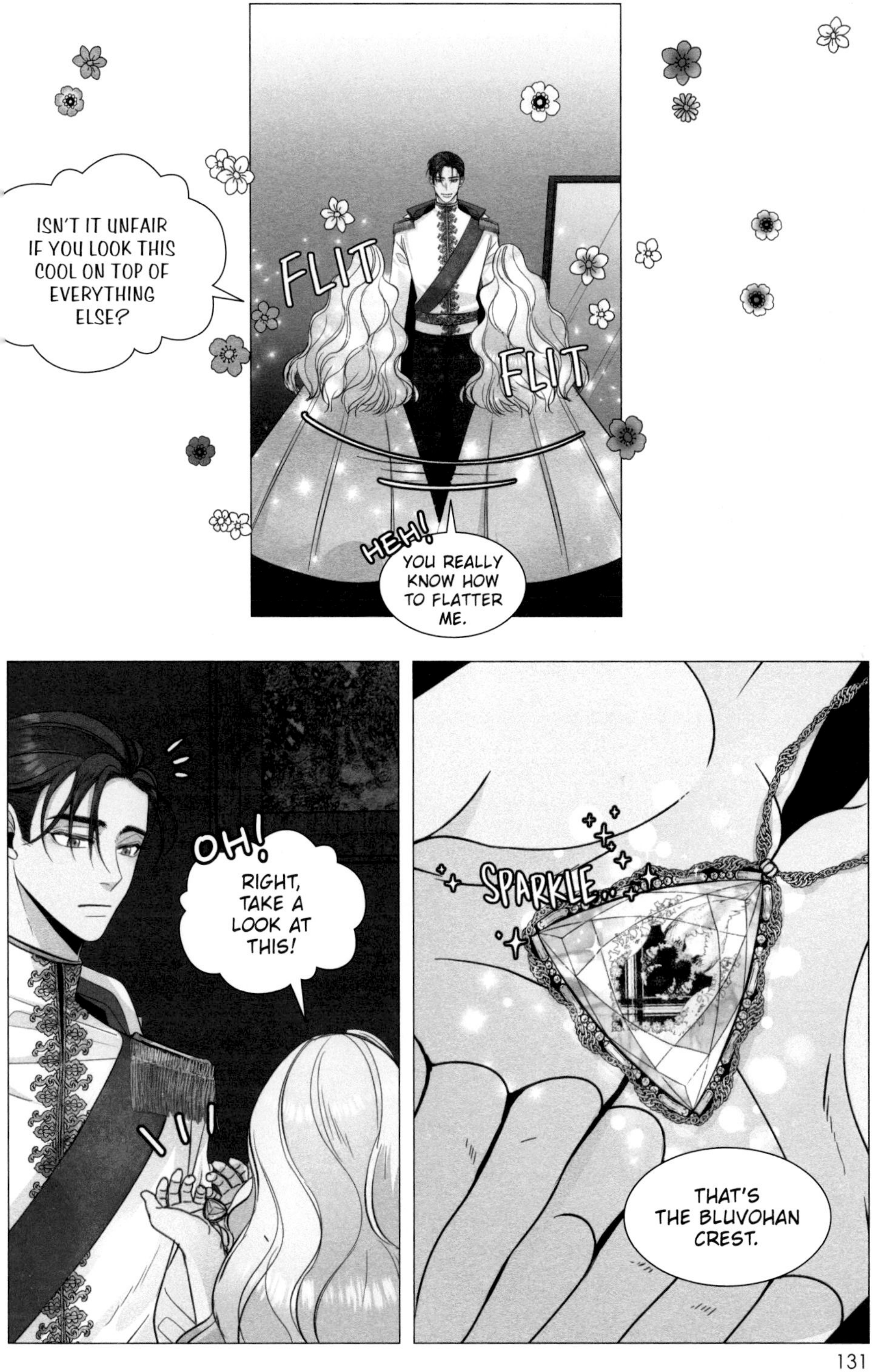
ISN'T IT UNFAIR IF YOU LOOK THIS COOL ON TOP OF EVERYTHING ELSE?
FLIT
FLIT
HEH!
YOU REALLY KNOW HOW TO FLATTER ME.
OH!
RIGHT, TAKE A LOOK AT THIS!
SPARKLE...
THAT'S THE BLUVOHAN CREST.

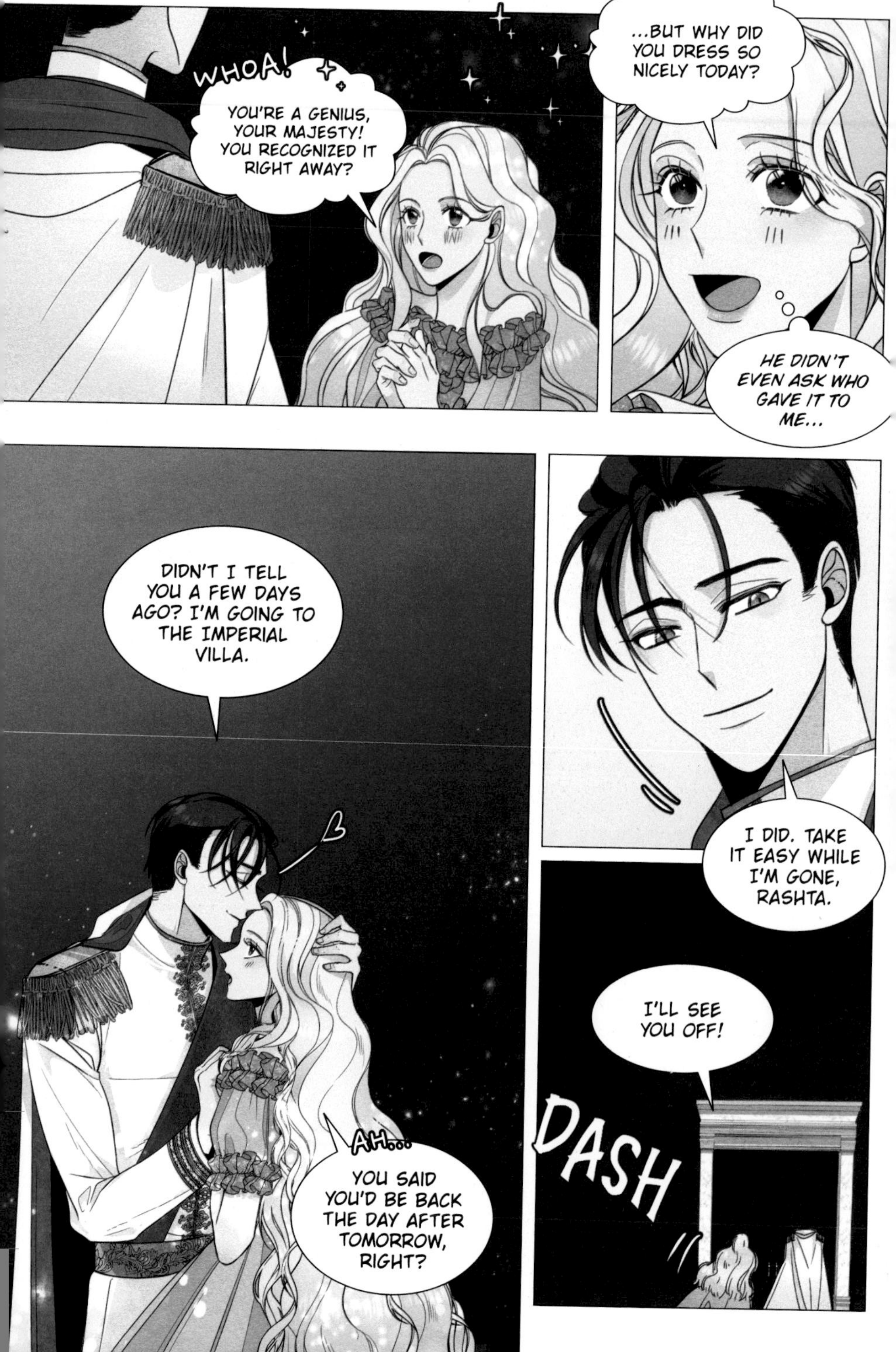
WHOA!
YOU'RE A GENIUS, YOUR MAJESTY! YOU RECOGNIZED IT RIGHT AWAY?
...BUT WHY DID YOU DRESS SO NICELY TODAY?
HE DIDN'T EVEN ASK WHO GAVE IT TO ME...
DIDN'T I TELL YOU A FEW DAYS AGO? I'M GOING TO THE IMPERIAL VILLA.
AH...
YOU SAID YOU'D BE BACK THE DAY AFTER TOMORROW, RIGHT?
I DID. TAKE IT EASY WHILE I'M GONE, RASHTA.
I'LL SEE YOU OFF!
DASH

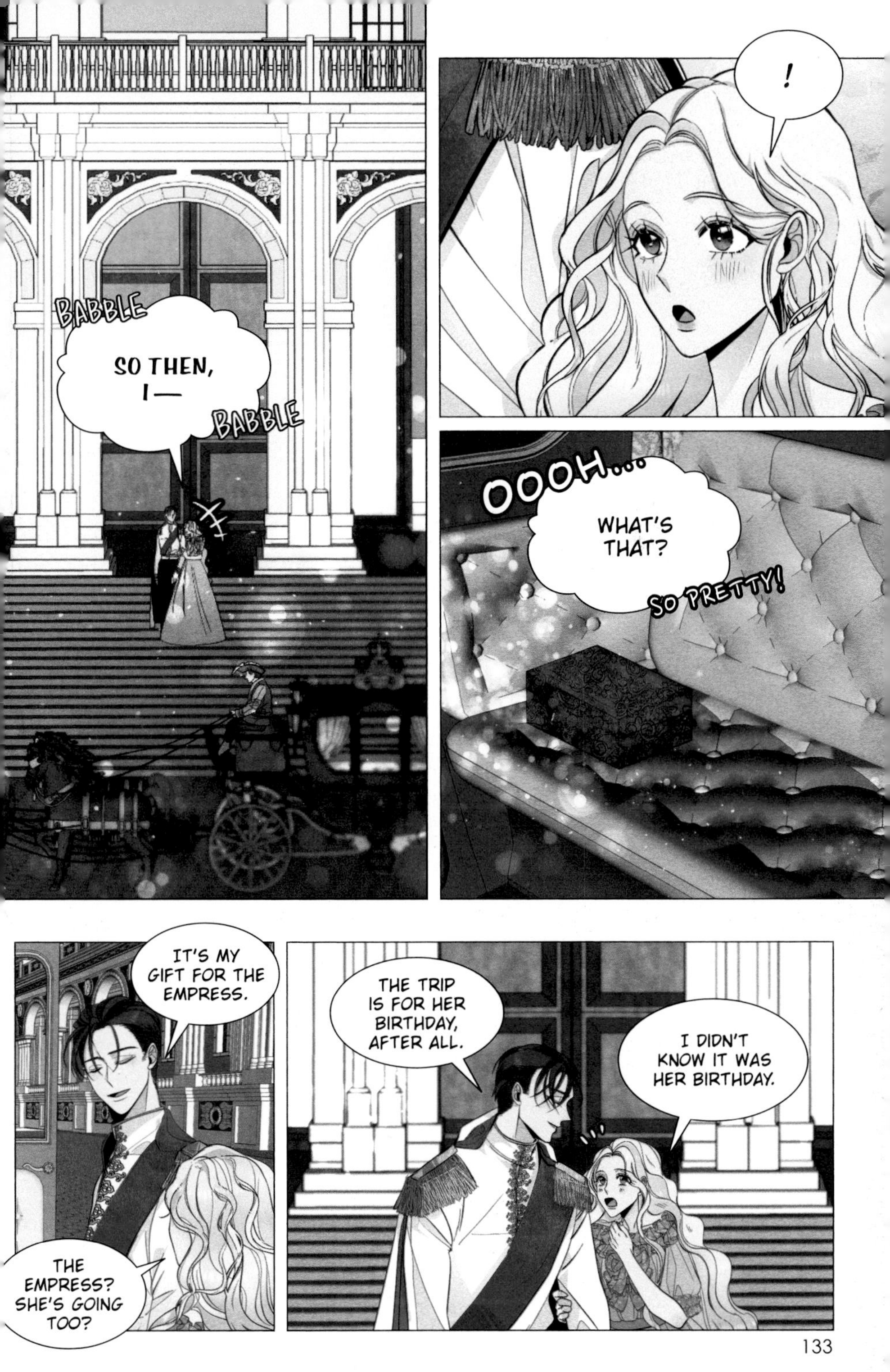
BABBLE
SO THEN, I—
BABBLE
!
OOOH...
WHAT'S THAT?
SO PRETTY!
IT'S MY GIFT FOR THE EMPRESS.
THE EMPRESS? SHE'S GOING TOO?
THE TRIP IS FOR HER BIRTHDAY, AFTER ALL.
I DIDN'T KNOW IT WAS HER BIRTHDAY.

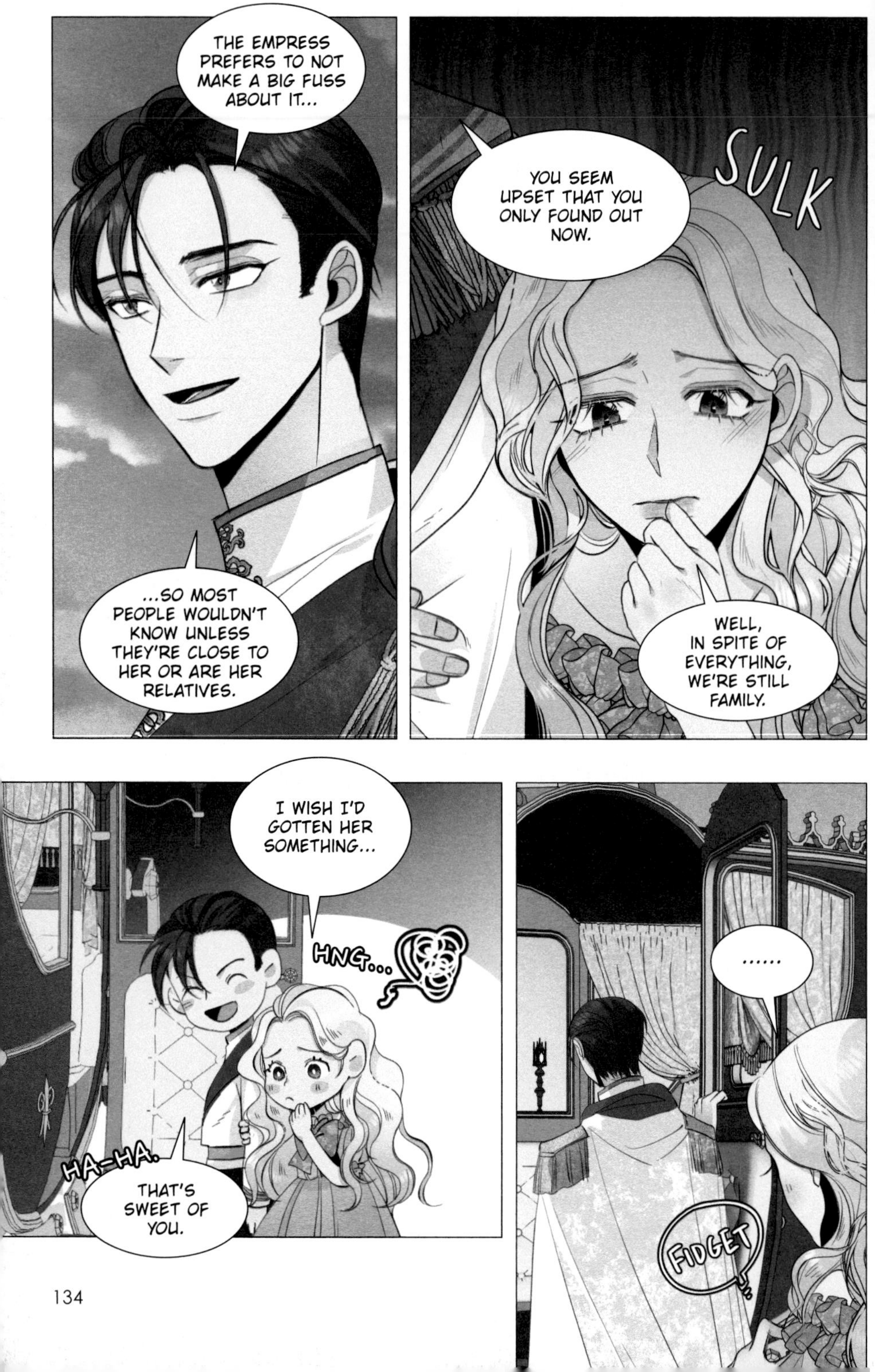
THE EMPRESS PREFERS TO NOT MAKE A BIG FUSS ABOUT IT...
...SO MOST PEOPLE WOULDN'T KNOW UNLESS THEY'RE CLOSE TO HER OR ARE HER RELATIVES.
SULK
YOU SEEM UPSET THAT YOU ONLY FOUND OUT NOW.
WELL, IN SPITE OF EVERYTHING, WE'RE STILL FAMILY.
I WISH I'D GOTTEN HER SOMETHING...
HNG...
HA-HA.
THAT'S SWEET OF YOU.
......
FIDGET

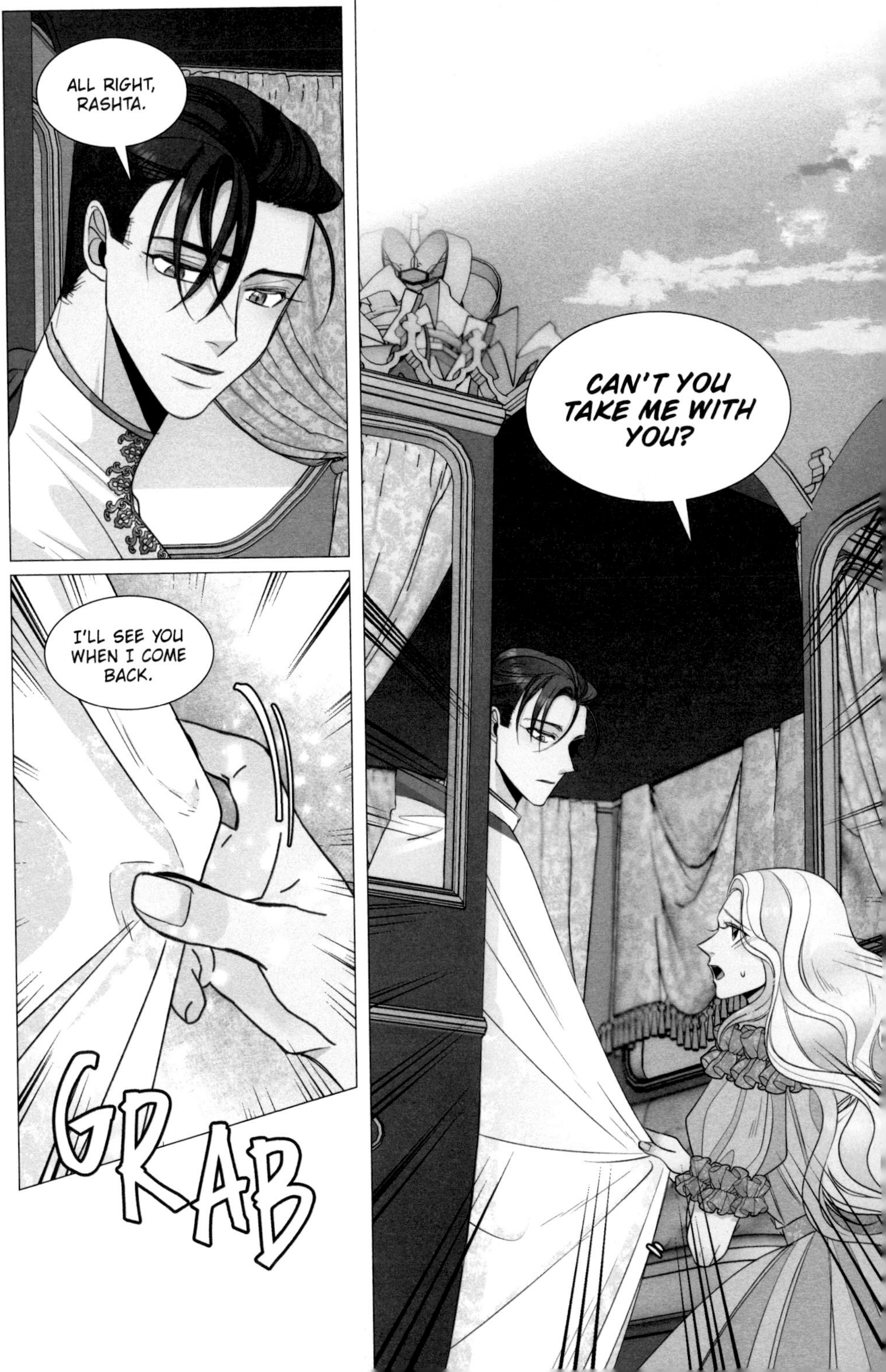
ALL RIGHT, RASHTA.
CAN'T YOU TAKE ME WITH YOU?
I'LL SEE YOU WHEN I COME BACK.
GRAB

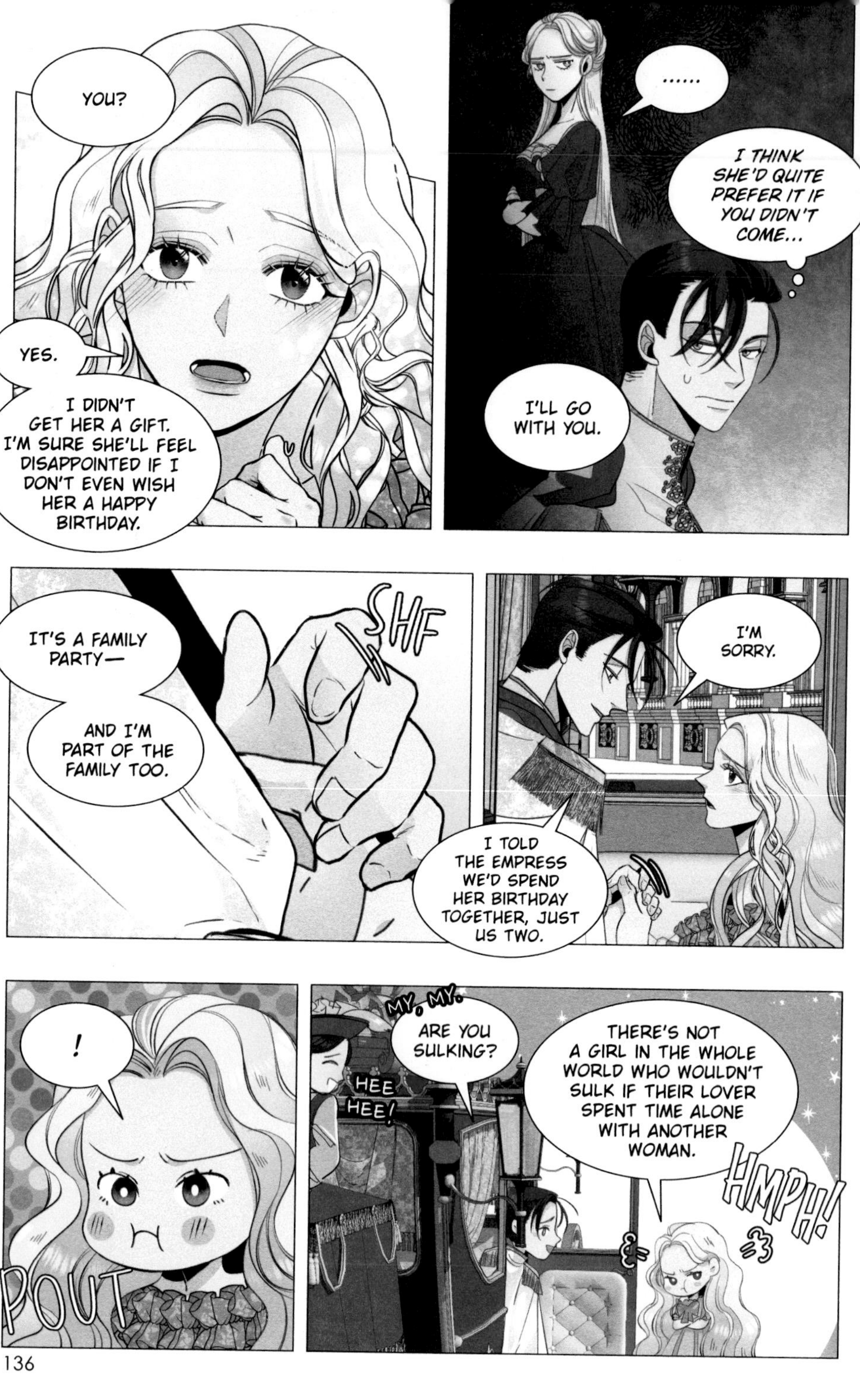
YOU?
YES.
I DIDN'T GET HER A GIFT. I'M SURE SHE'LL FEEL DISAPPOINTED IF I DON'T EVEN WISH HER A HAPPY BIRTHDAY.
......
I THINK SHE'D QUITE PREFER IT IF YOU DIDN'T COME...
I'LL GO WITH YOU.
IT'S A FAMILY PARTY—
AND I'M PART OF THE FAMILY TOO.
SHF
I'M SORRY.
I TOLD THE EMPRESS WE'D SPEND HER BIRTHDAY TOGETHER, JUST US TWO.
!
POUT
MY, MY.
ARE YOU SULKING?
HEE HEE!
THERE'S NOT A GIRL IN THE WHOLE WORLD WHO WOULDN'T SULK IF THEIR LOVER SPENT TIME ALONE WITH ANOTHER WOMAN.
HMPH!

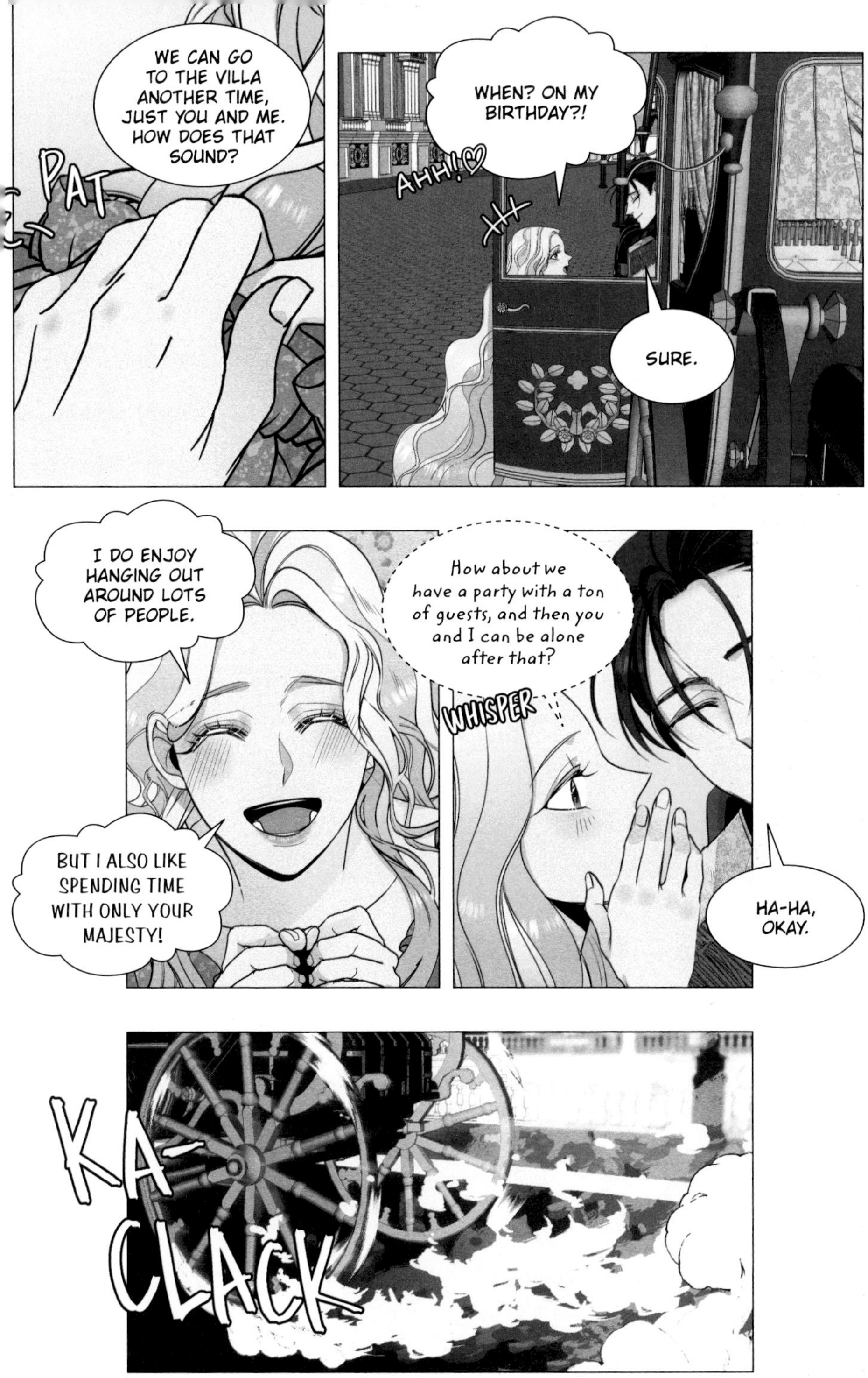
WE CAN GO TO THE VILLA ANOTHER TIME, JUST YOU AND ME. HOW DOES THAT SOUND?
PAT
WHEN? ON MY BIRTHDAY?!
AHH!
SURE.
I DO ENJOY HANGING OUT AROUND LOTS OF PEOPLE.
BUT I ALSO LIKE SPENDING TIME WITH ONLY YOUR MAJESTY!
How about we have a party with a ton of guests, and then you and I can be alone after that?
WHISPER
HA-HA, OKAY.
KA-CLACK

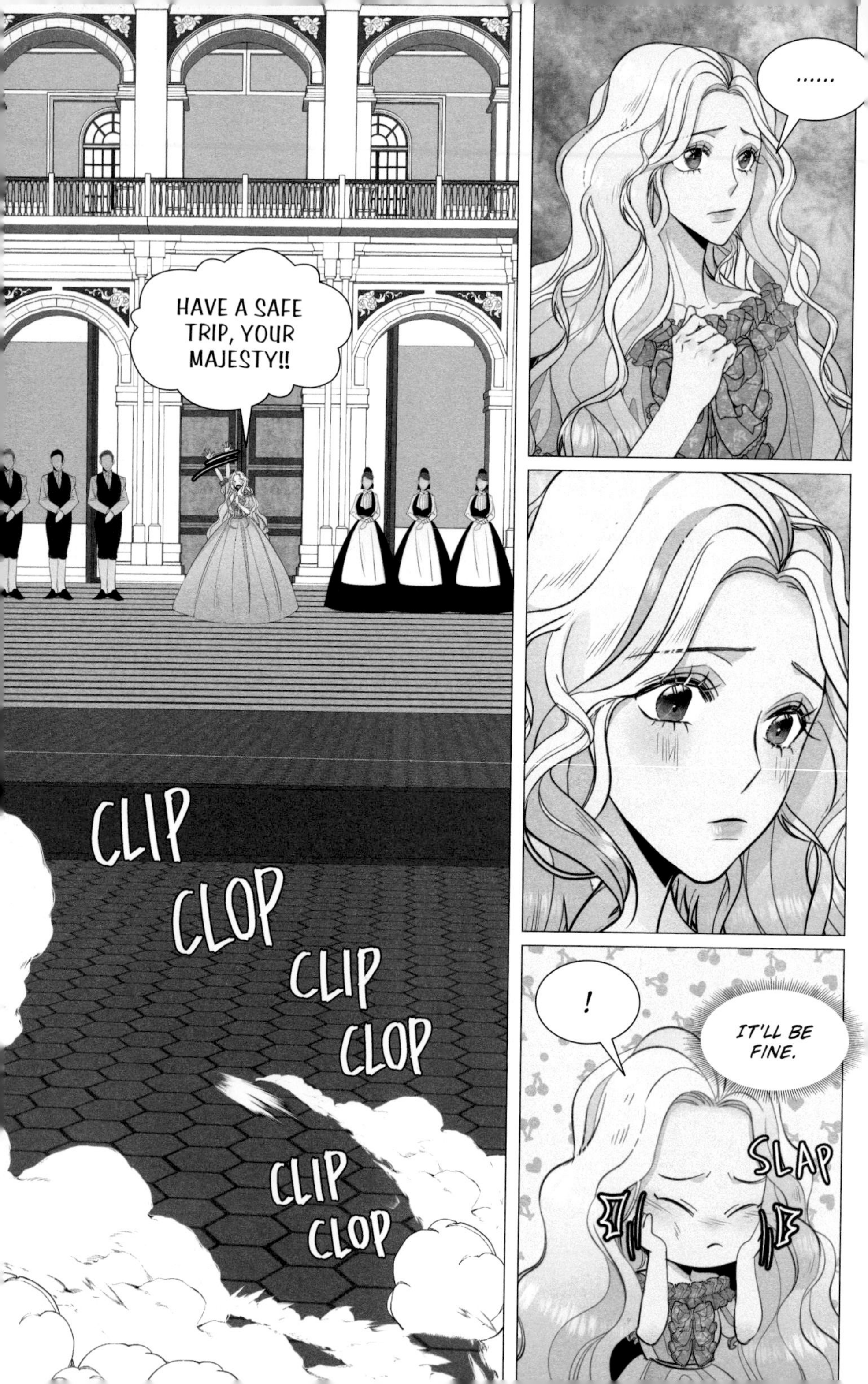

HAVE A SAFE TRIP, YOUR MAJESTY!!
CLIP
CLOP
CLIP
CLOP
CLIP
CLOP
......
!
IT'LL BE FINE.
SLAP

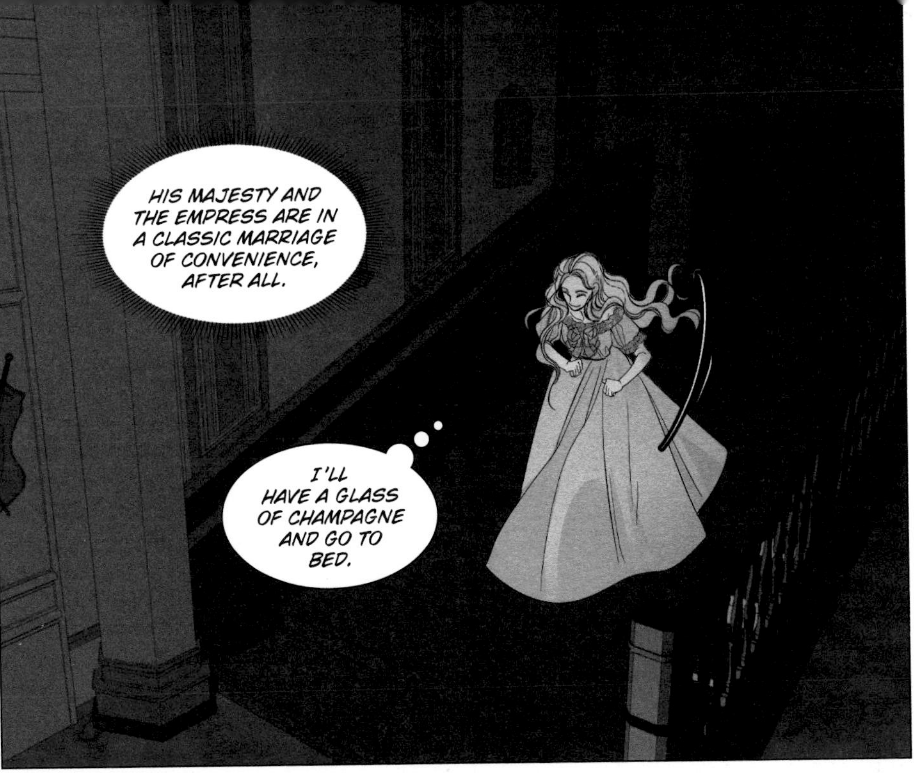
HIS MAJESTY AND THE EMPRESS ARE IN A CLASSIC MARRIAGE OF CONVENIENCE, AFTER ALL.
I'LL HAVE A GLASS OF CHAMPAGNE AND GO TO BED.

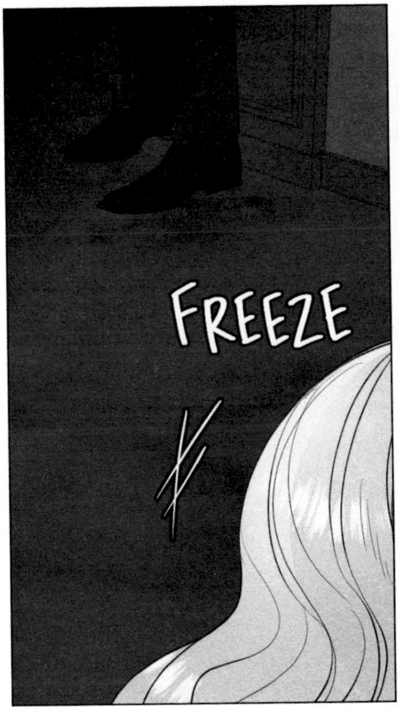
FREEZE

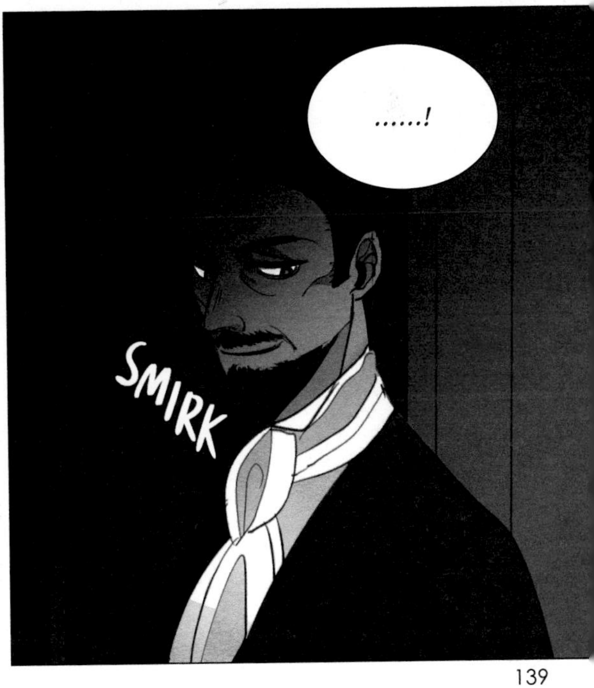
......!
SMIRK

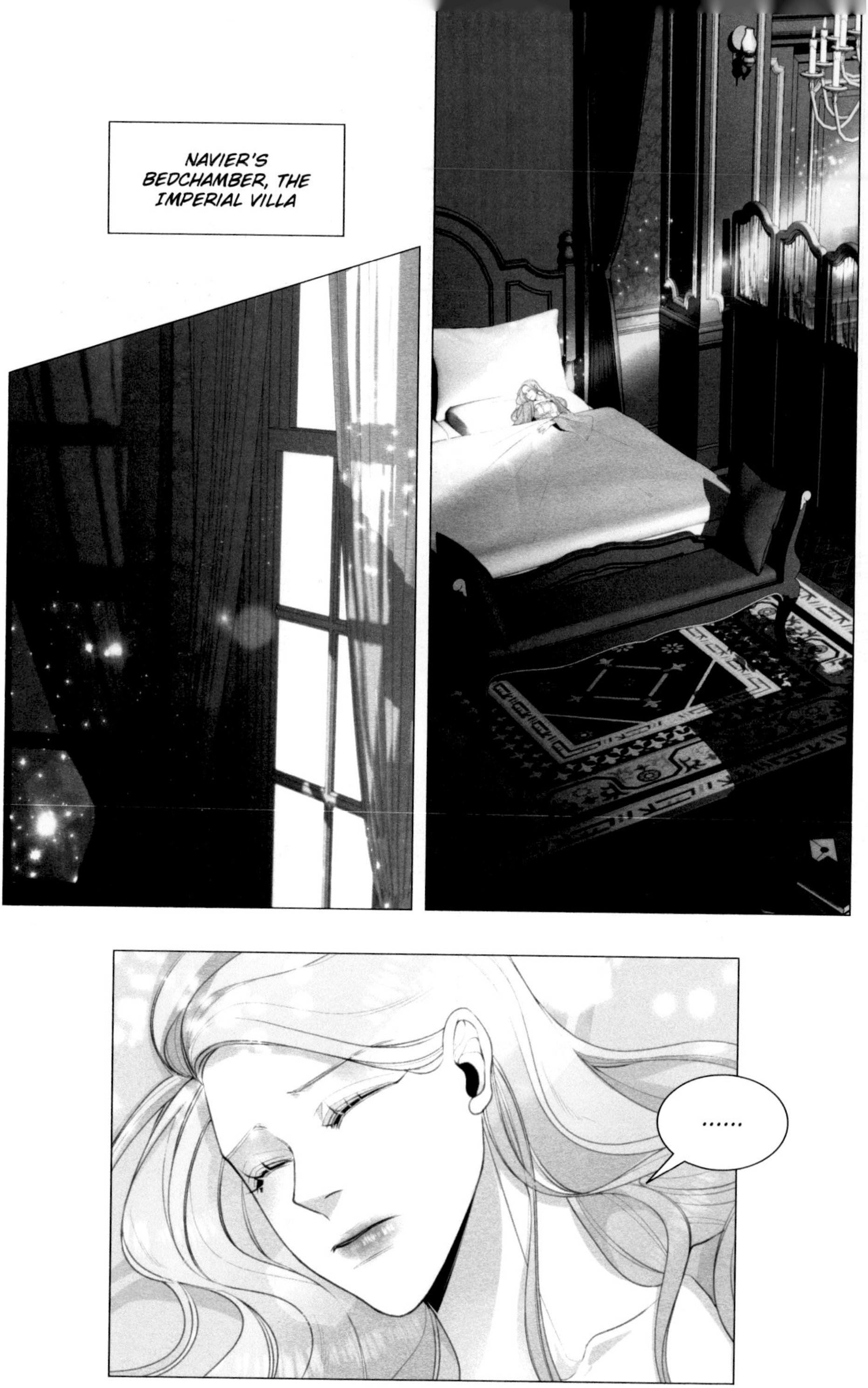
NAVIER'S BEDCHAMBER, THE IMPERIAL VILLA
......

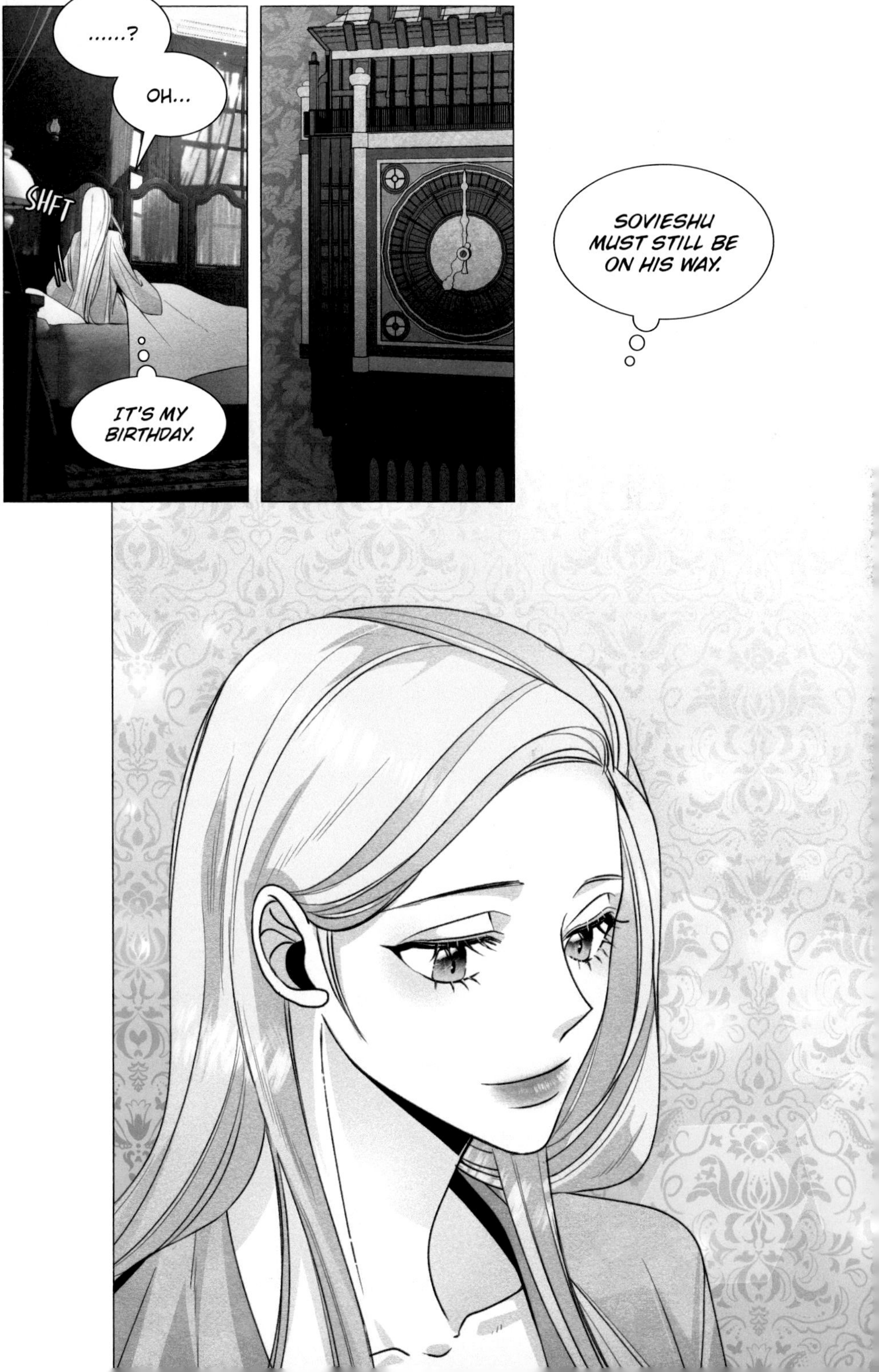
......?
OH...
SHFT
IT'S MY BIRTHDAY.
SOVIESHU MUST STILL BE ON HIS WAY.

EVEN ON VACATION, YOU'RE READING?

YOUR MAJESTY.

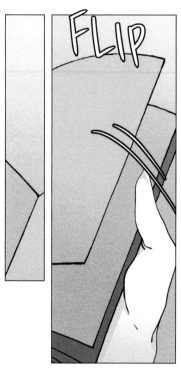

FLIP

DID YOU JUST ARRIVE?

STAND

NOD

MM-HMM.

I'M EXHAUSTED...

PLOP

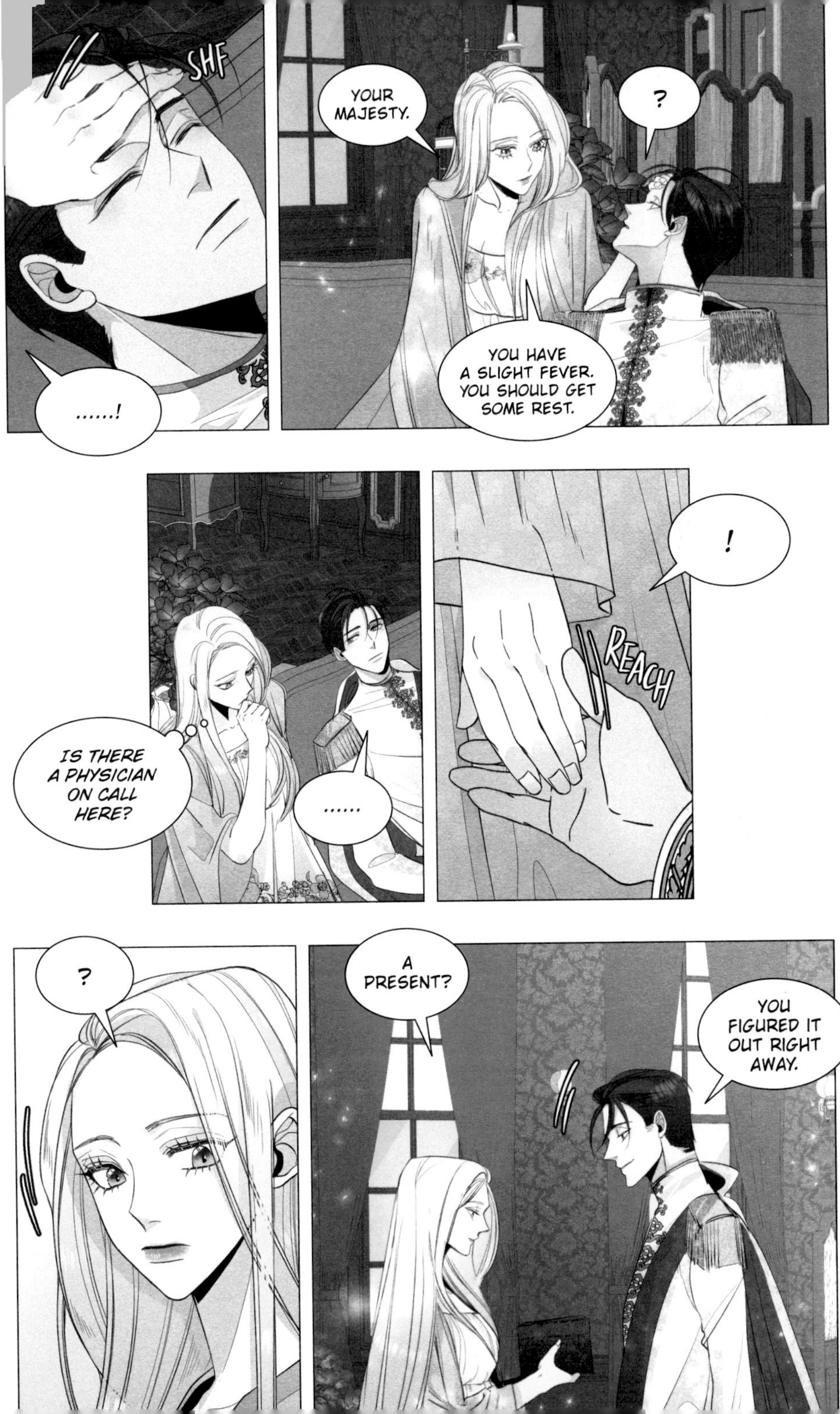
SHF
......!
YOUR MAJESTY.
?
YOU HAVE A SLIGHT FEVER. YOU SHOULD GET SOME REST.
IS THERE A PHYSICIAN ON CALL HERE?
......
!
REACH
?
A PRESENT?
YOU FIGURED IT OUT RIGHT AWAY.

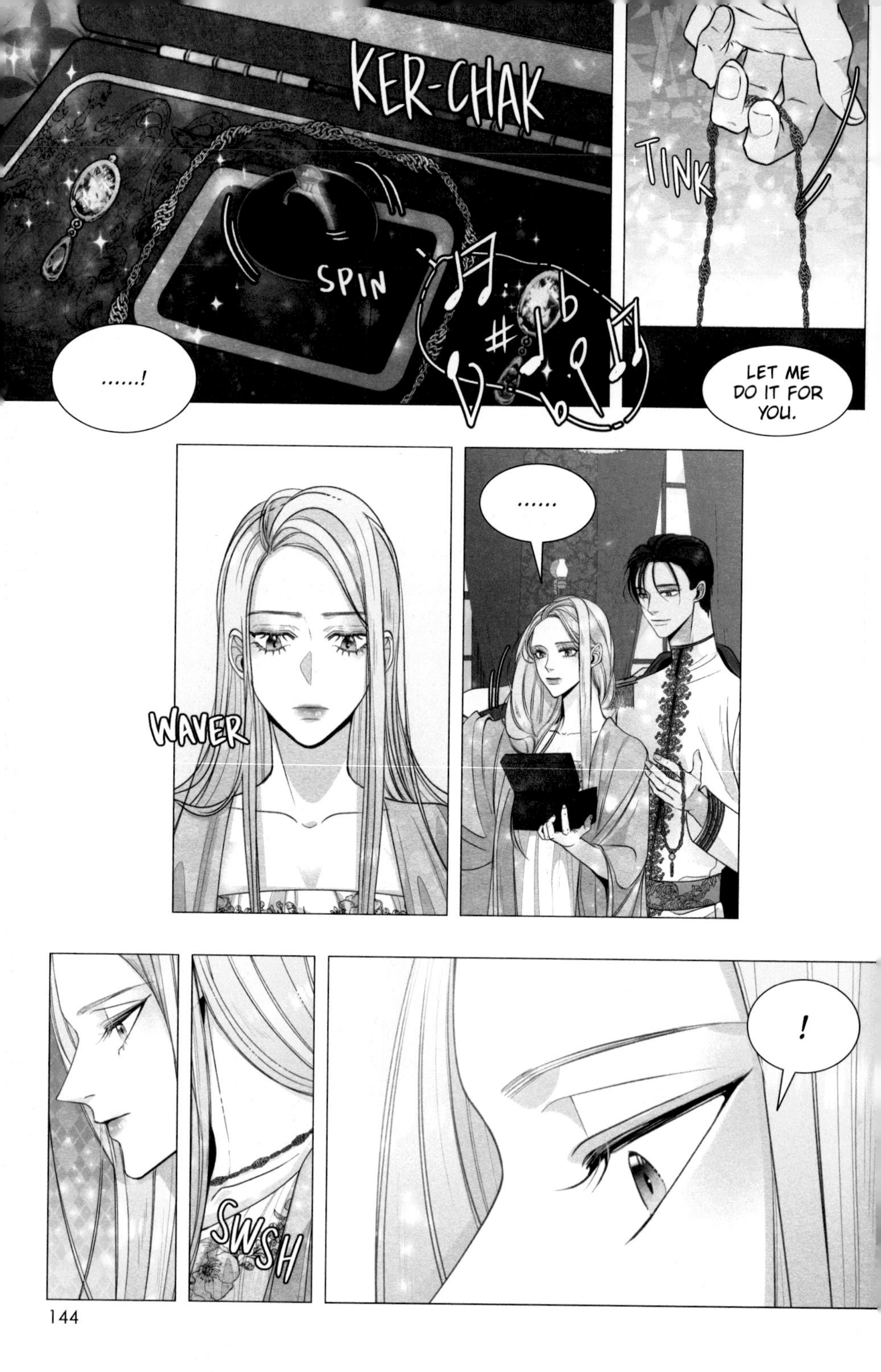
KER-CHAK
SPIN
......!
TINK
LET ME DO IT FOR YOU.
......
WAVER
SWSH
!

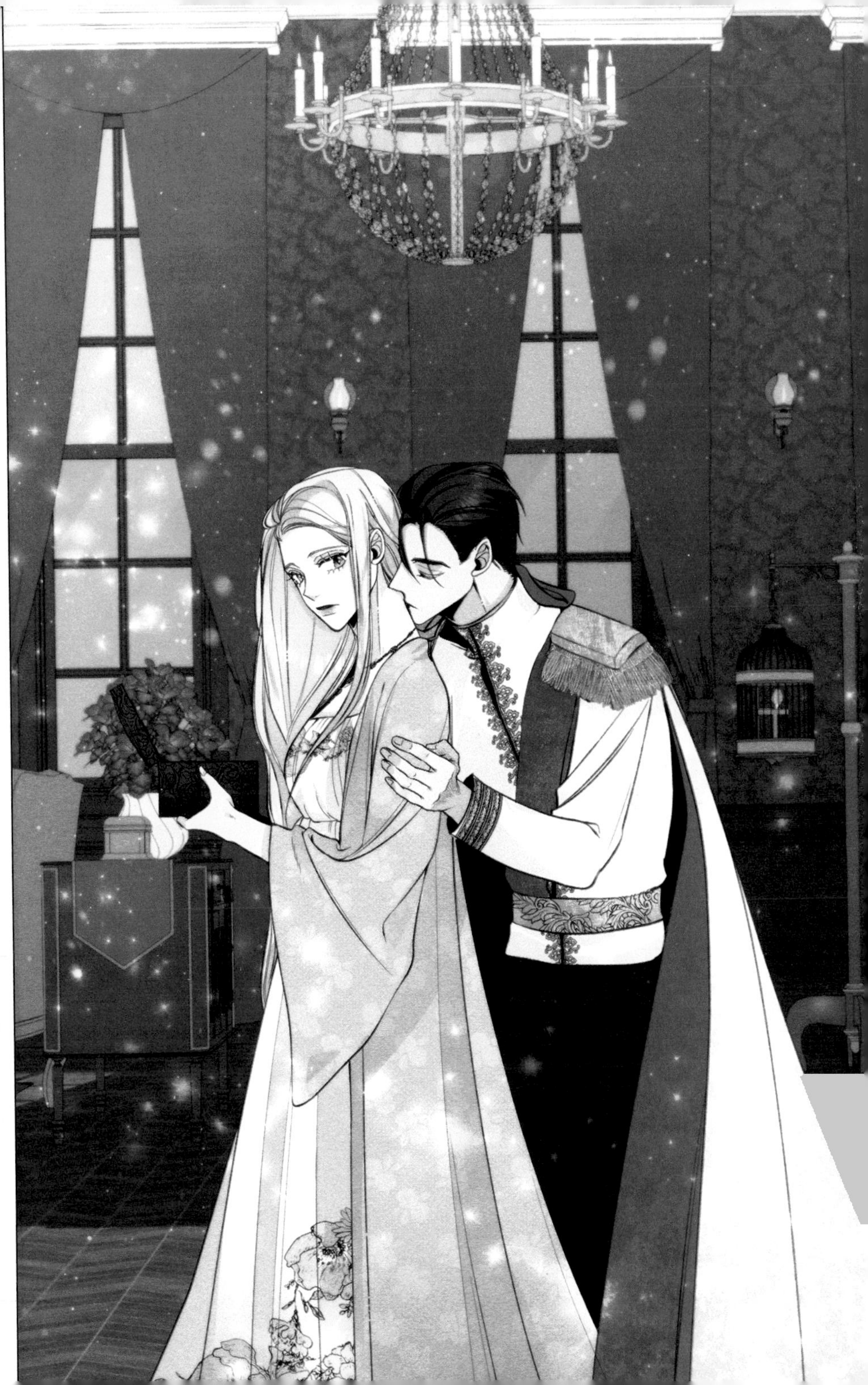

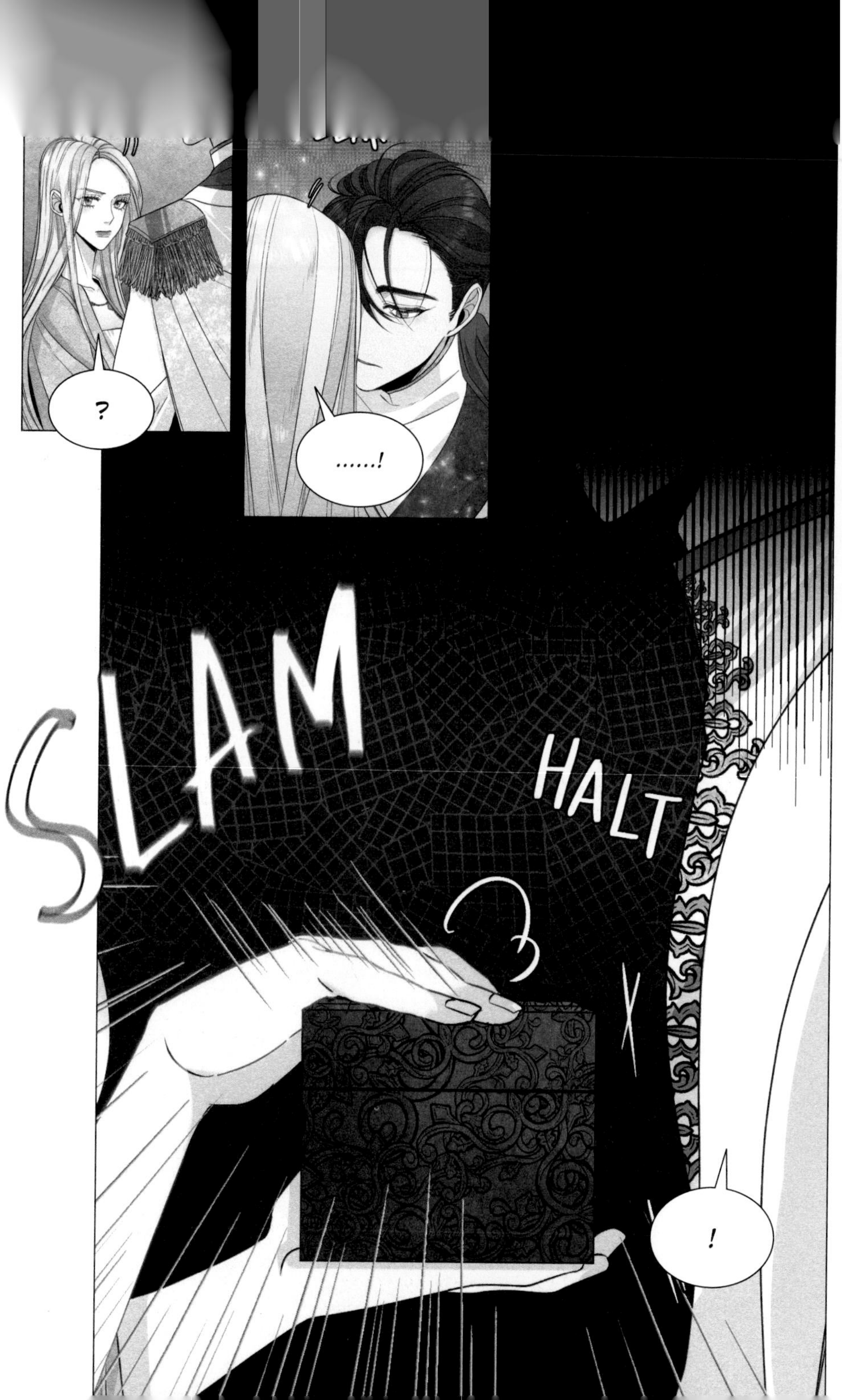
?
......!
SLAM
HALT
!

EMPRESS?

......

...I SEE.

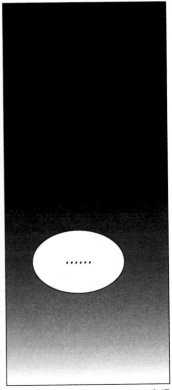

......

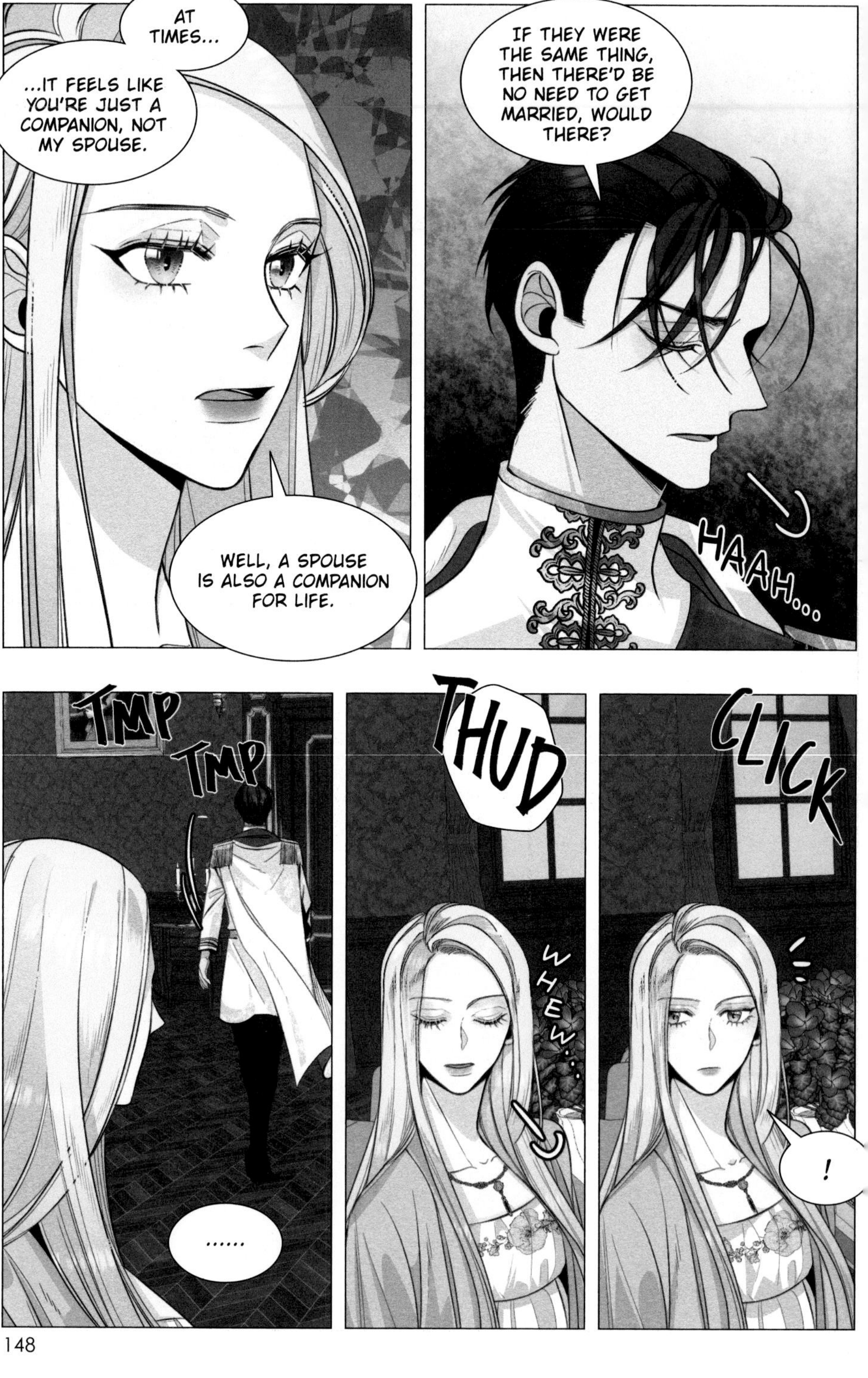

AT TIMES...
...IT FEELS LIKE YOU'RE JUST A COMPANION, NOT MY SPOUSE.
WELL, A SPOUSE IS ALSO A COMPANION FOR LIFE.
IF THEY WERE THE SAME THING, THEN THERE'D BE NO NEED TO GET MARRIED, WOULD THERE?
HAAH...
TMP
TMP
......
THUD
WHEW...
CLICK
!

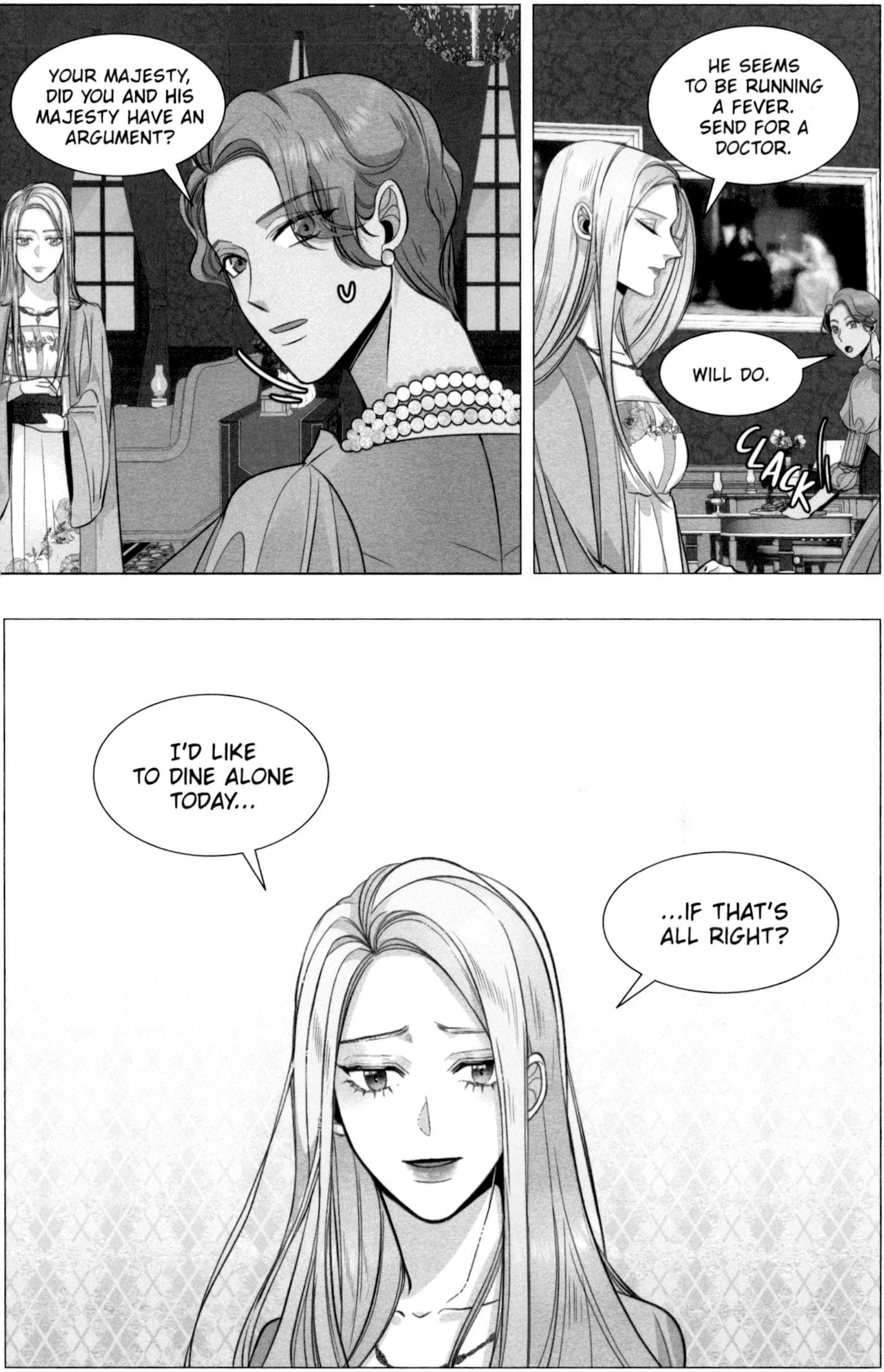
YOUR MAJESTY, DID YOU AND HIS MAJESTY HAVE AN ARGUMENT?
HE SEEMS TO BE RUNNING A FEVER. SEND FOR A DOCTOR.
WILL DO.
CLACK
I'D LIKE TO DINE ALONE TODAY...
...IF THAT'S ALL RIGHT?

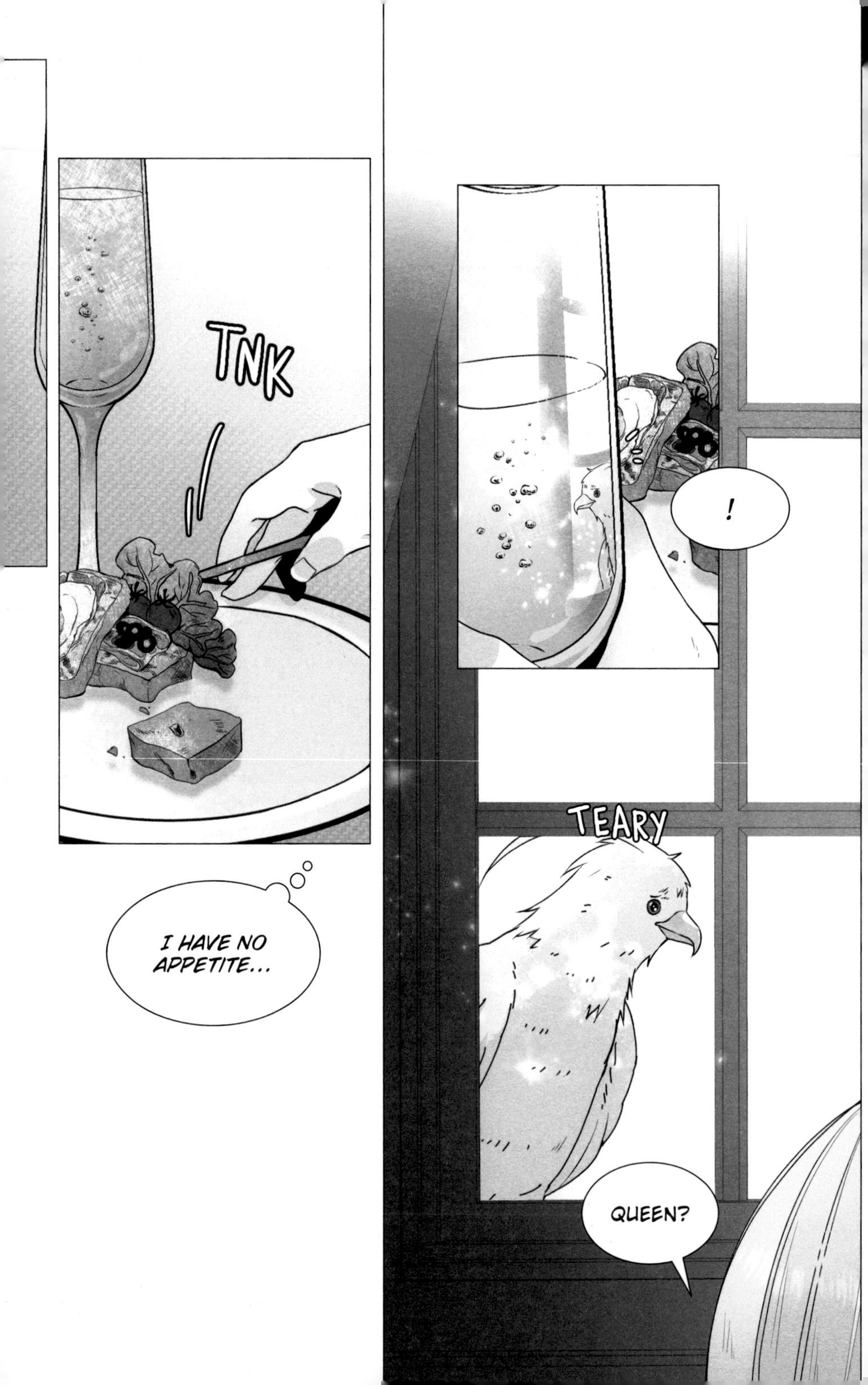
TNK
I HAVE NO APPETITE...
!
TEARY
QUEEN?

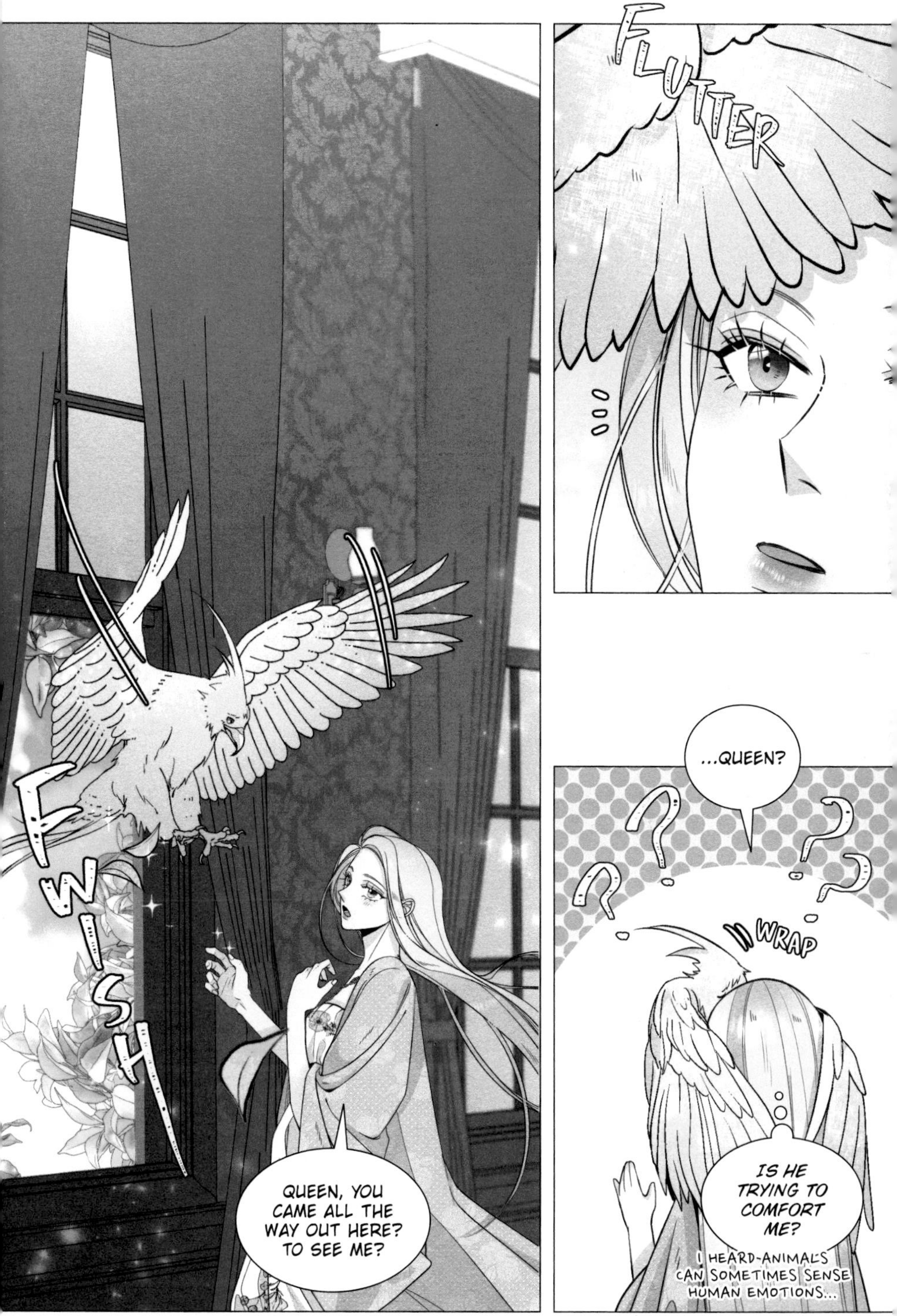
FLUTTER
FWISH
QUEEN, YOU CAME ALL THE WAY OUT HERE? TO SEE ME?
...QUEEN?
WRAP
IS HE TRYING TO COMFORT ME?
I HEARD ANIMALS CAN SOMETIMES SENSE HUMAN EMOTIONS...

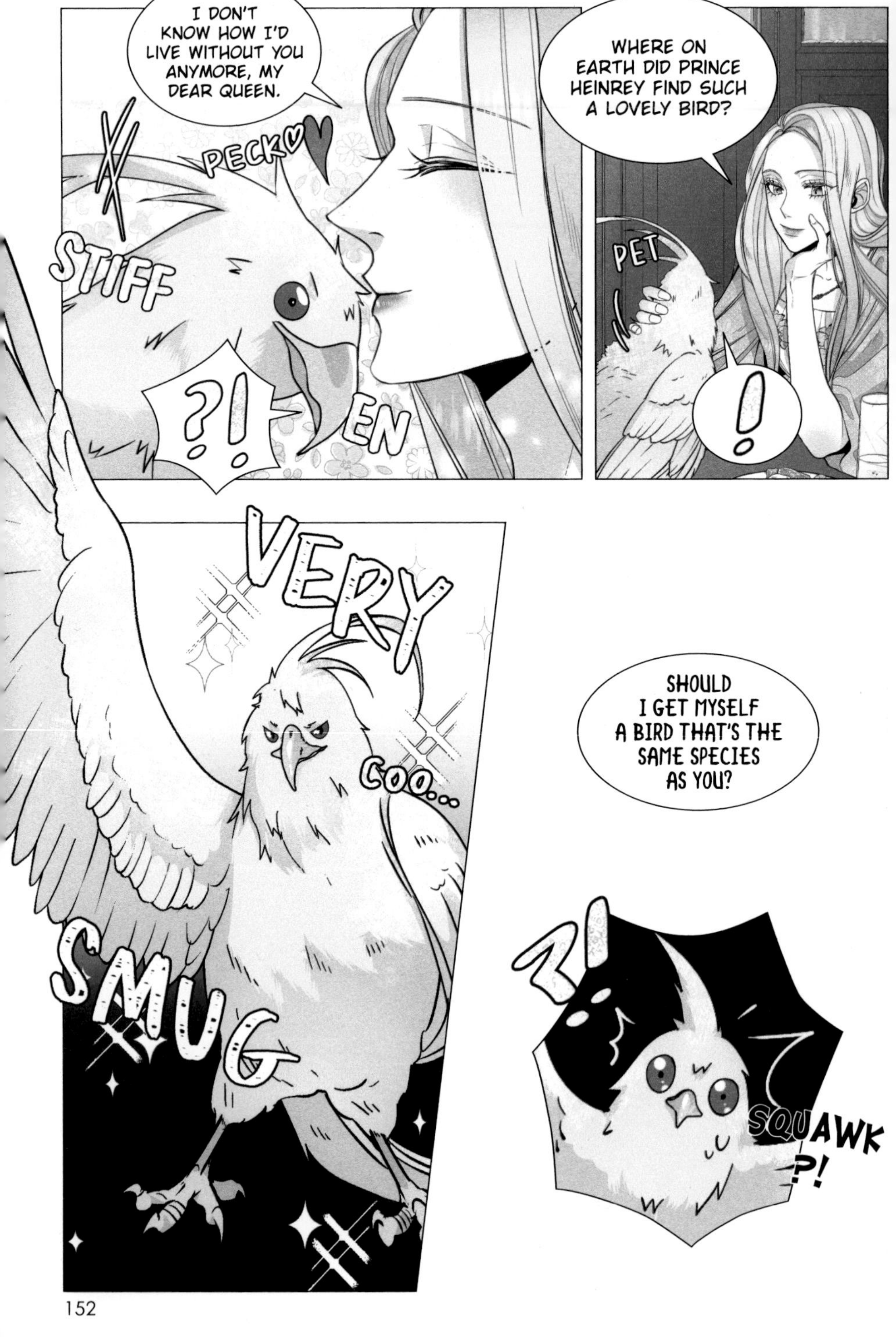
I DON'T KNOW HOW I'D LIVE WITHOUT YOU ANYMORE, MY DEAR QUEEN.
PECK
STIFF
?!
EN
WHERE ON EARTH DID PRINCE HEINREY FIND SUCH A LOVELY BIRD?
PET
!
VERY
COO...
SMUG
SHOULD I GET MYSELF A BIRD THAT'S THE SAME SPECIES AS YOU?
?!
SQUAWK ?!

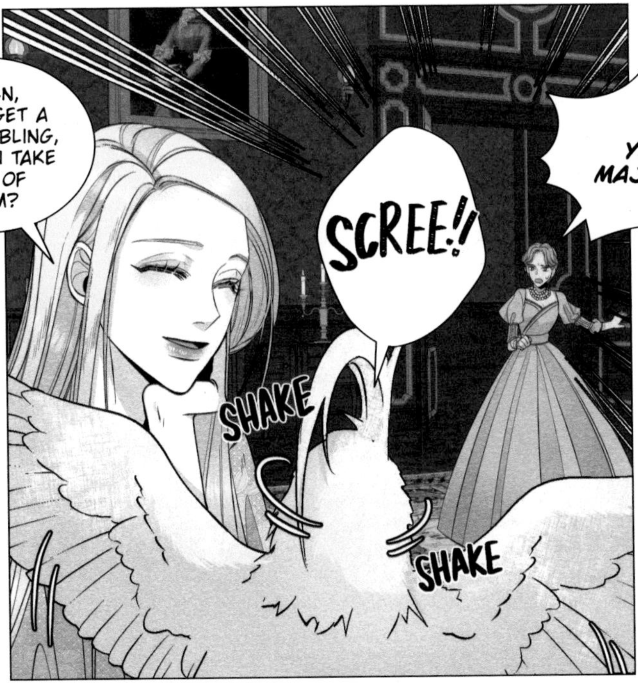
QUEEN, IF YOU GET A LITTLE SIBLING, WILL YOU TAKE CARE OF THEM?
SCREE!!
YOUR MAJESTY!
SHAKE
SHAKE

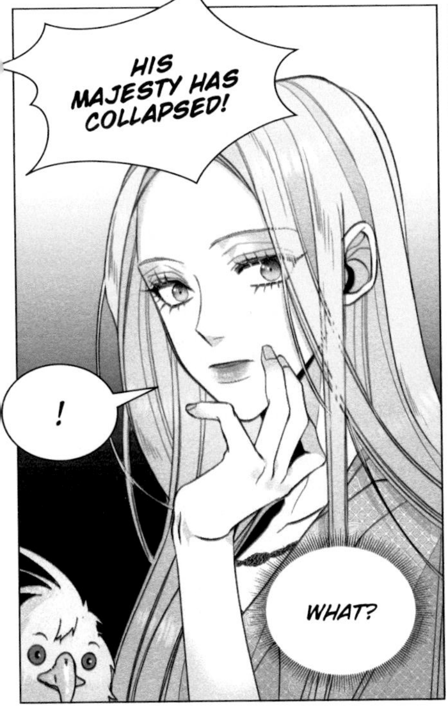
HIS MAJESTY HAS COLLAPSED!
!
WHAT?

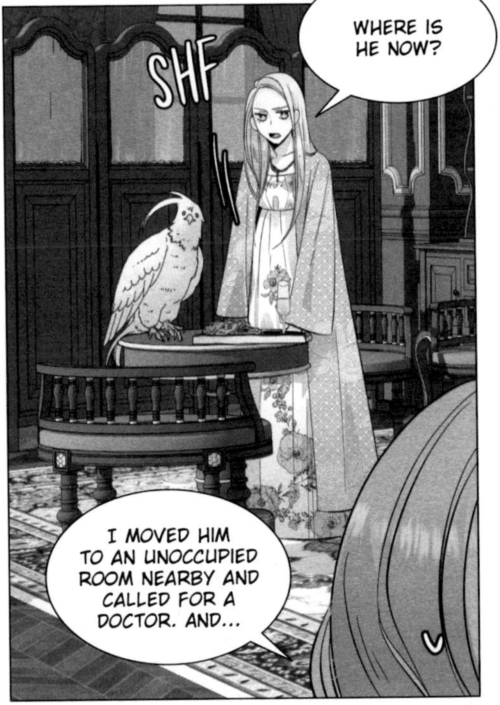
SHF
WHERE IS HE NOW?
I MOVED HIM TO AN UNOCCUPIED ROOM NEARBY AND CALLED FOR A DOCTOR. AND...

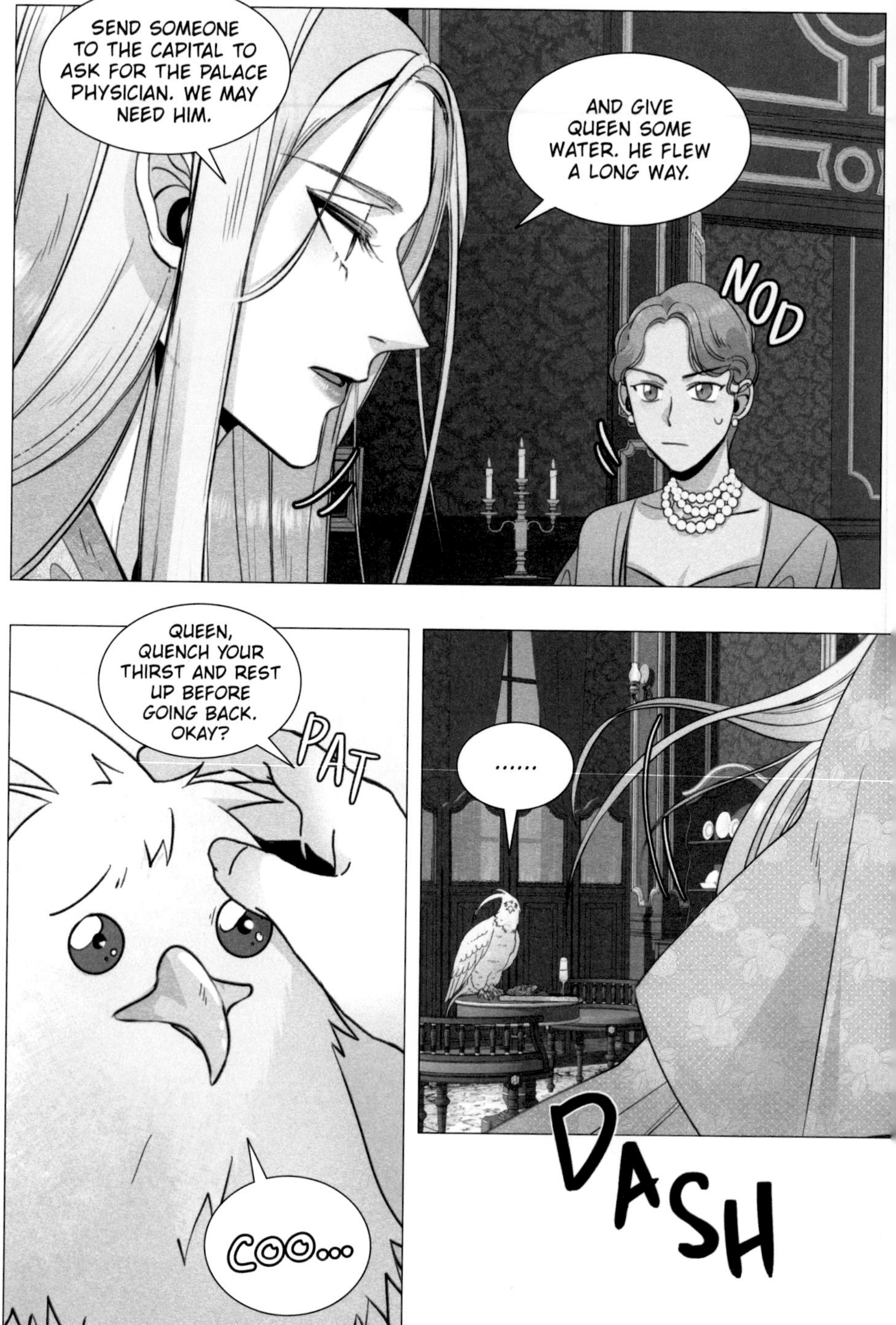
SEND SOMEONE TO THE CAPITAL TO ASK FOR THE PALACE PHYSICIAN. WE MAY NEED HIM.
AND GIVE QUEEN SOME WATER. HE FLEW A LONG WAY.
NOD
QUEEN, QUENCH YOUR THIRST AND REST UP BEFORE GOING BACK. OKAY?
PAT
COO...
......
DASH

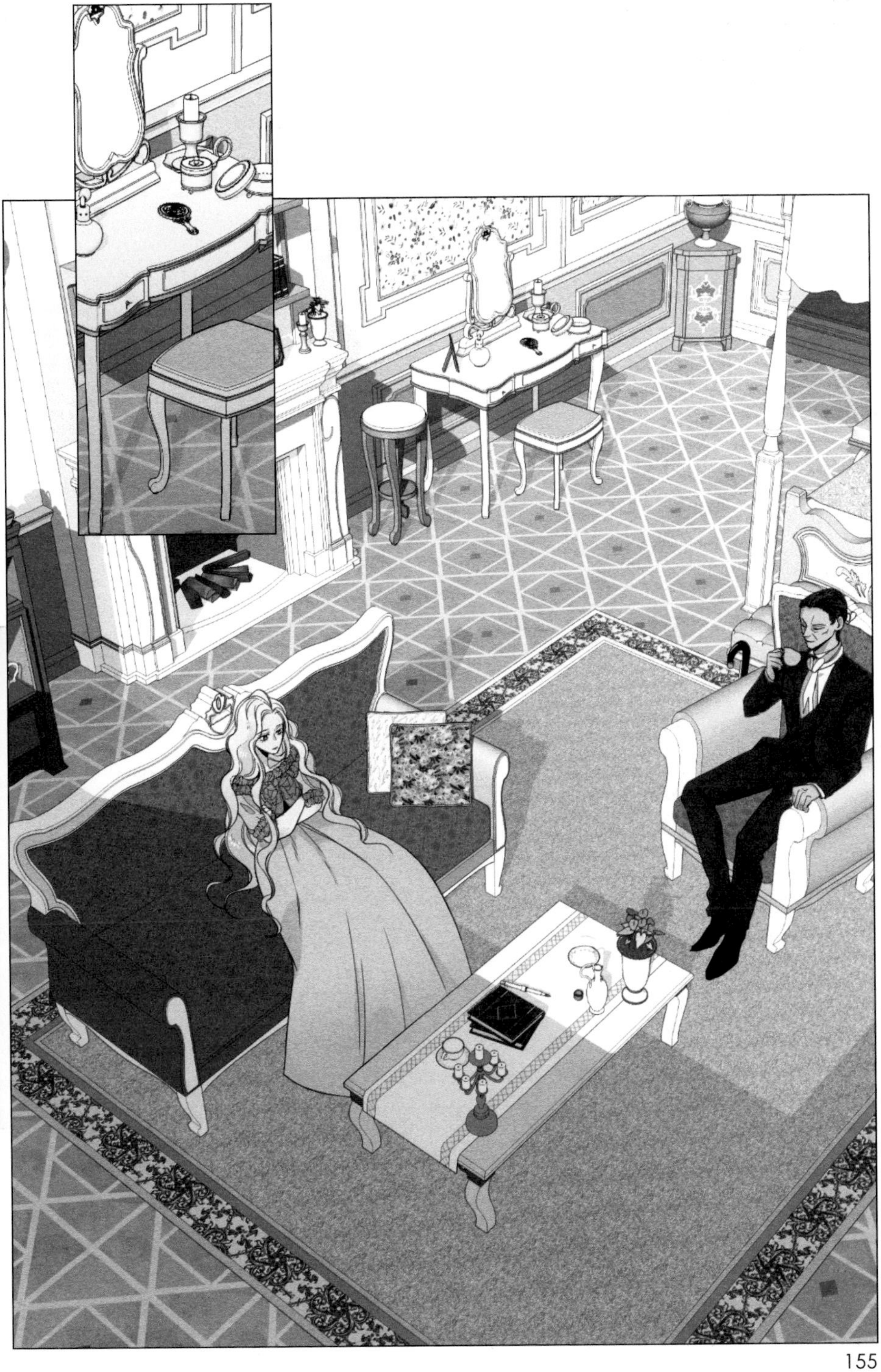

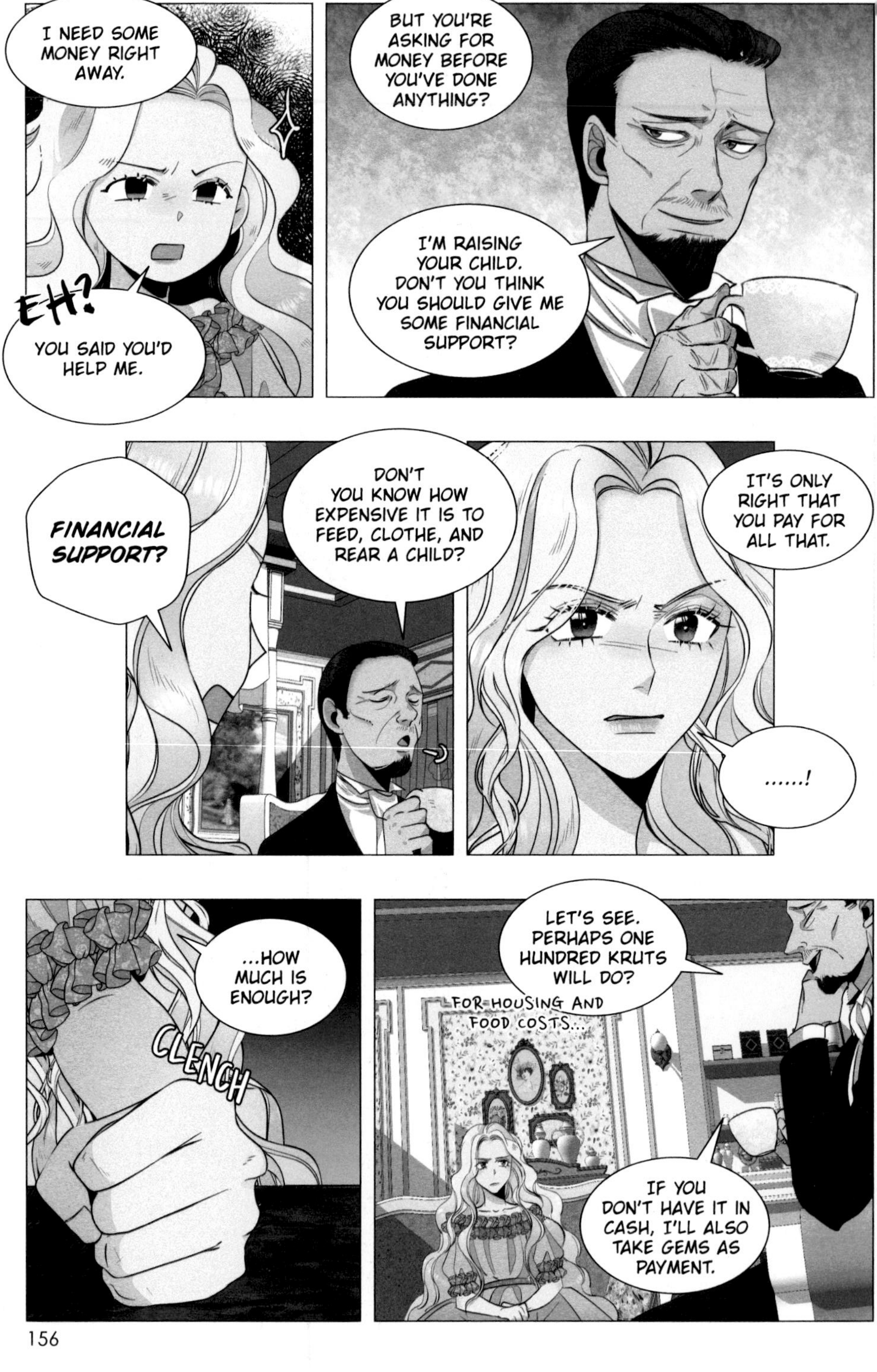
I NEED SOME MONEY RIGHT AWAY.
EH?
YOU SAID YOU'D HELP ME.
BUT YOU'RE ASKING FOR MONEY BEFORE YOU'VE DONE ANYTHING?
I'M RAISING YOUR CHILD. DON'T YOU THINK YOU SHOULD GIVE ME SOME FINANCIAL SUPPORT?
FINANCIAL SUPPORT?
DON'T YOU KNOW HOW EXPENSIVE IT IS TO FEED, CLOTHE, AND REAR A CHILD?
IT'S ONLY RIGHT THAT YOU PAY FOR ALL THAT.
......!
...HOW MUCH IS ENOUGH?
CLENCH
LET'S SEE. PERHAPS ONE HUNDRED KRUTS WILL DO?
FOR HOUSING AND FOOD COSTS...
IF YOU DON'T HAVE IT IN CASH, I'LL ALSO TAKE GEMS AS PAYMENT.

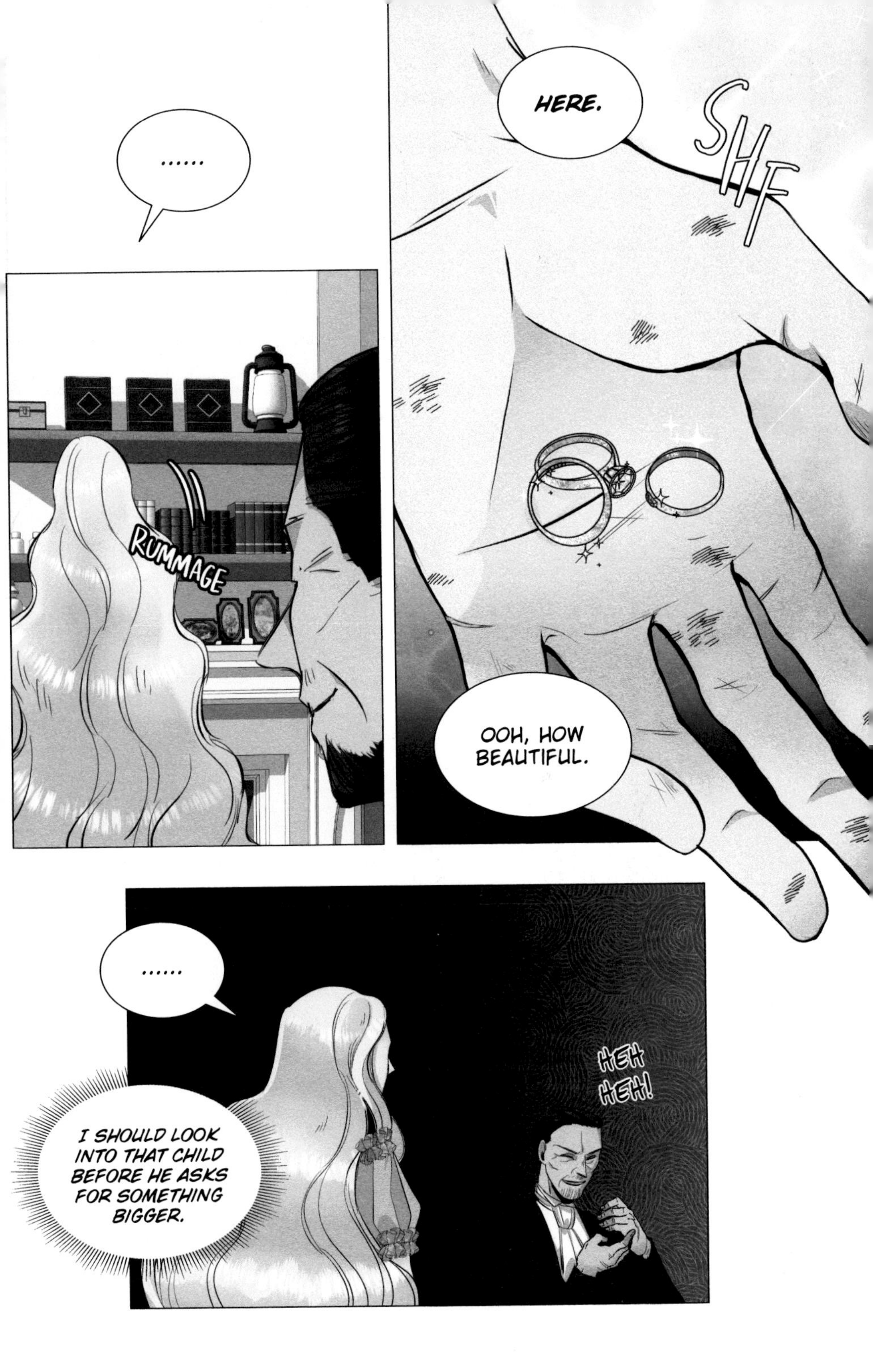
......
RUMMAGE
HERE.
SHF
OOH, HOW BEAUTIFUL.
......
I SHOULD LOOK INTO THAT CHILD BEFORE HE ASKS FOR SOMETHING BIGGER.
HEH HEH!

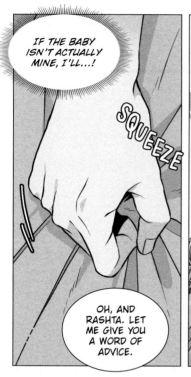

IF THE BABY ISN'T ACTUALLY MINE, I'LL...!

SQUEEZE

OH, AND RASHTA. LET ME GIVE YOU A WORD OF ADVICE.

?

THE EMPEROR AND EMPRESS LEFT FOR THE IMPERIAL VILLA YESTERDAY, YES?

I'M SURE THEY'LL HAVE A GREAT TIME TOGETHER.

POOR RASHTA. YOU HAVE NO ONE LOOKING OUT FOR YOU.

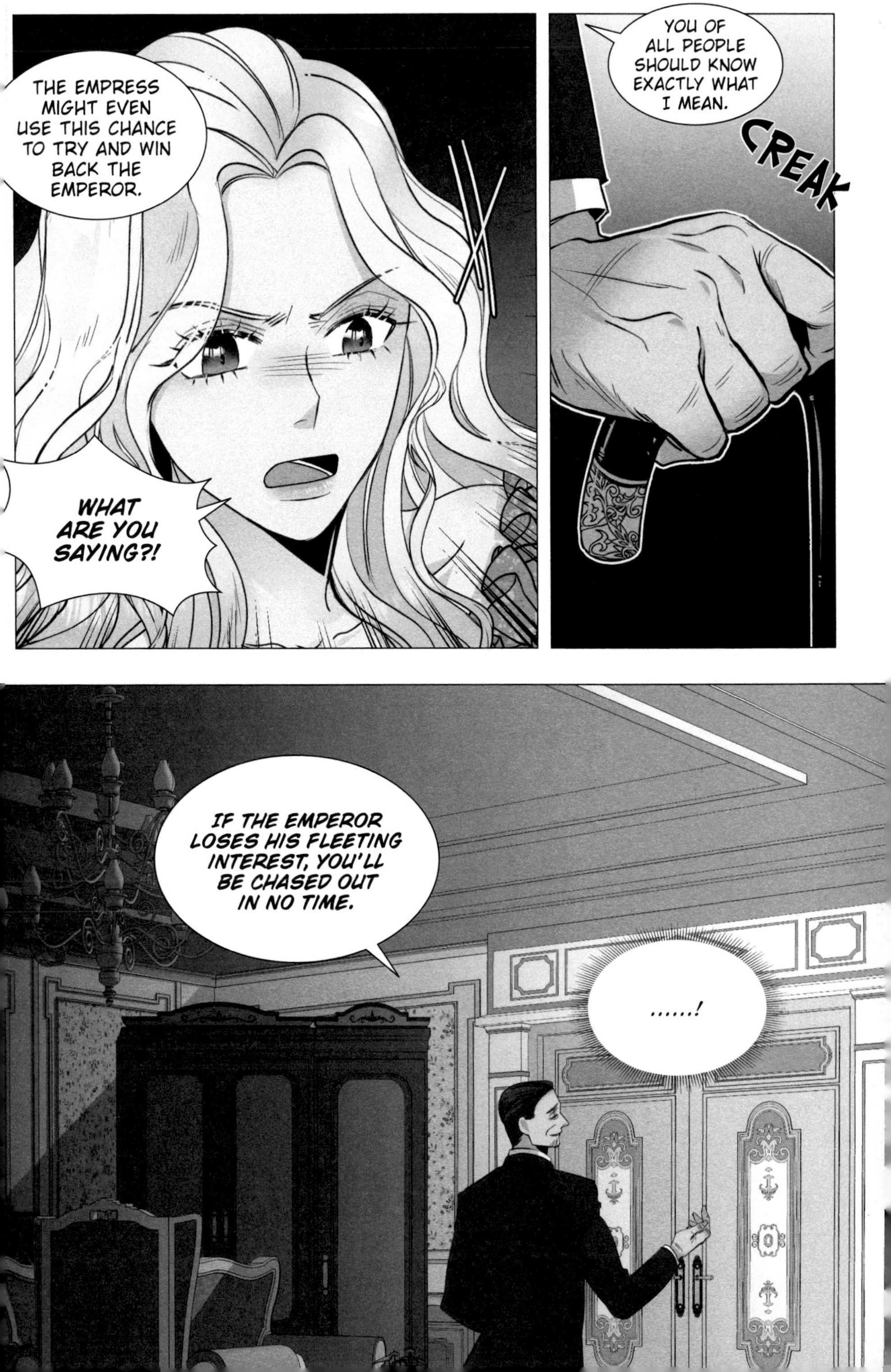
THE EMPRESS MIGHT EVEN USE THIS CHANCE TO TRY AND WIN BACK THE EMPEROR.
WHAT ARE YOU SAYING?!
YOU OF ALL PEOPLE SHOULD KNOW EXACTLY WHAT I MEAN.
CREAK
IF THE EMPEROR LOSES HIS FLEETING INTEREST, YOU'LL BE CHASED OUT IN NO TIME.
......!

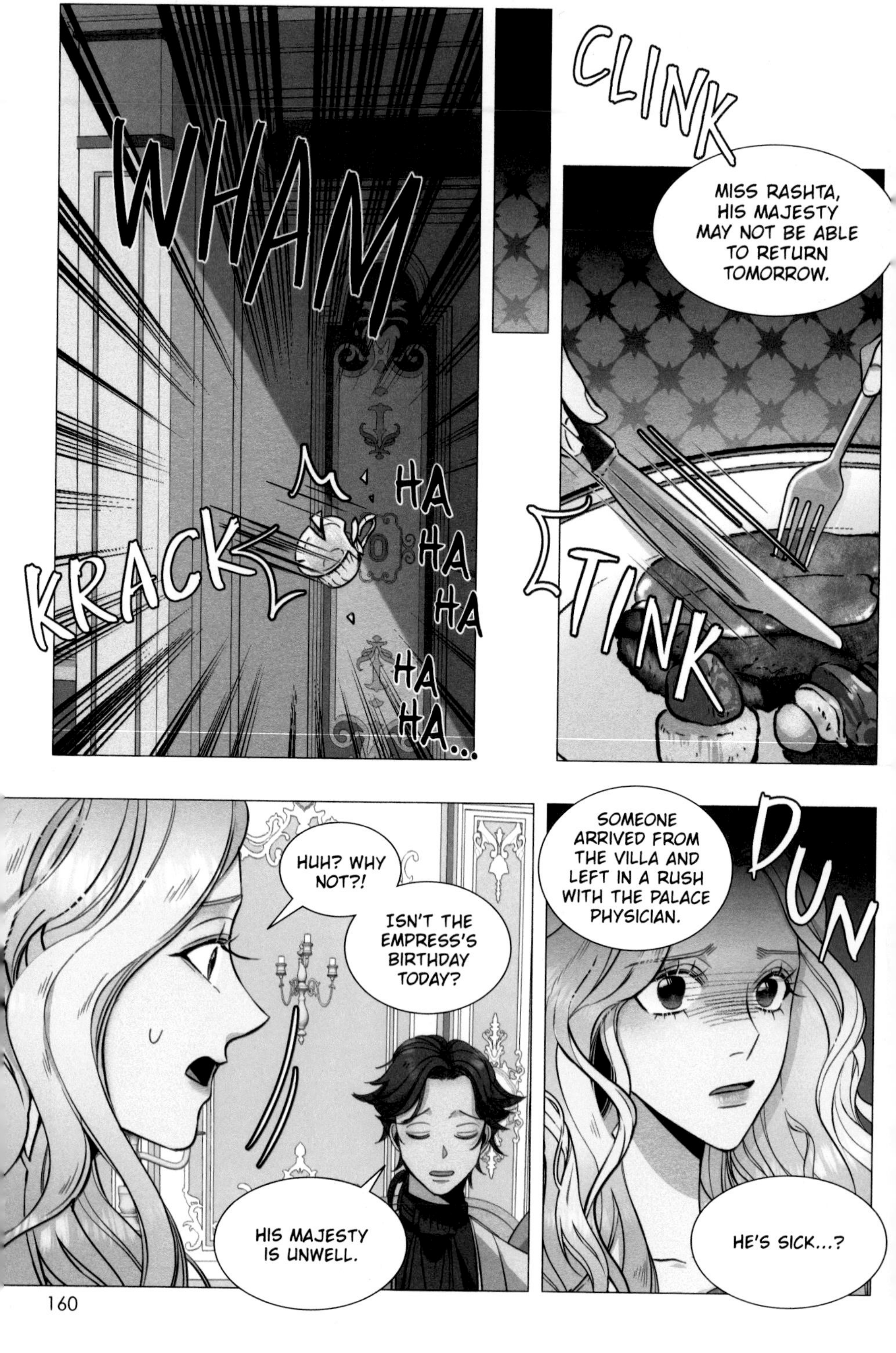
WHAM
KRACK
M
HA HA HA HA HA...
CLINK
MISS RASHTA, HIS MAJESTY MAY NOT BE ABLE TO RETURN TOMORROW.
TINK
HUH? WHY NOT?!
ISN'T THE EMPRESS'S BIRTHDAY TODAY?
HIS MAJESTY IS UNWELL.
SOMEONE ARRIVED FROM THE VILLA AND LEFT IN A RUSH WITH THE PALACE PHYSICIAN.
DUN
HE'S SICK...?

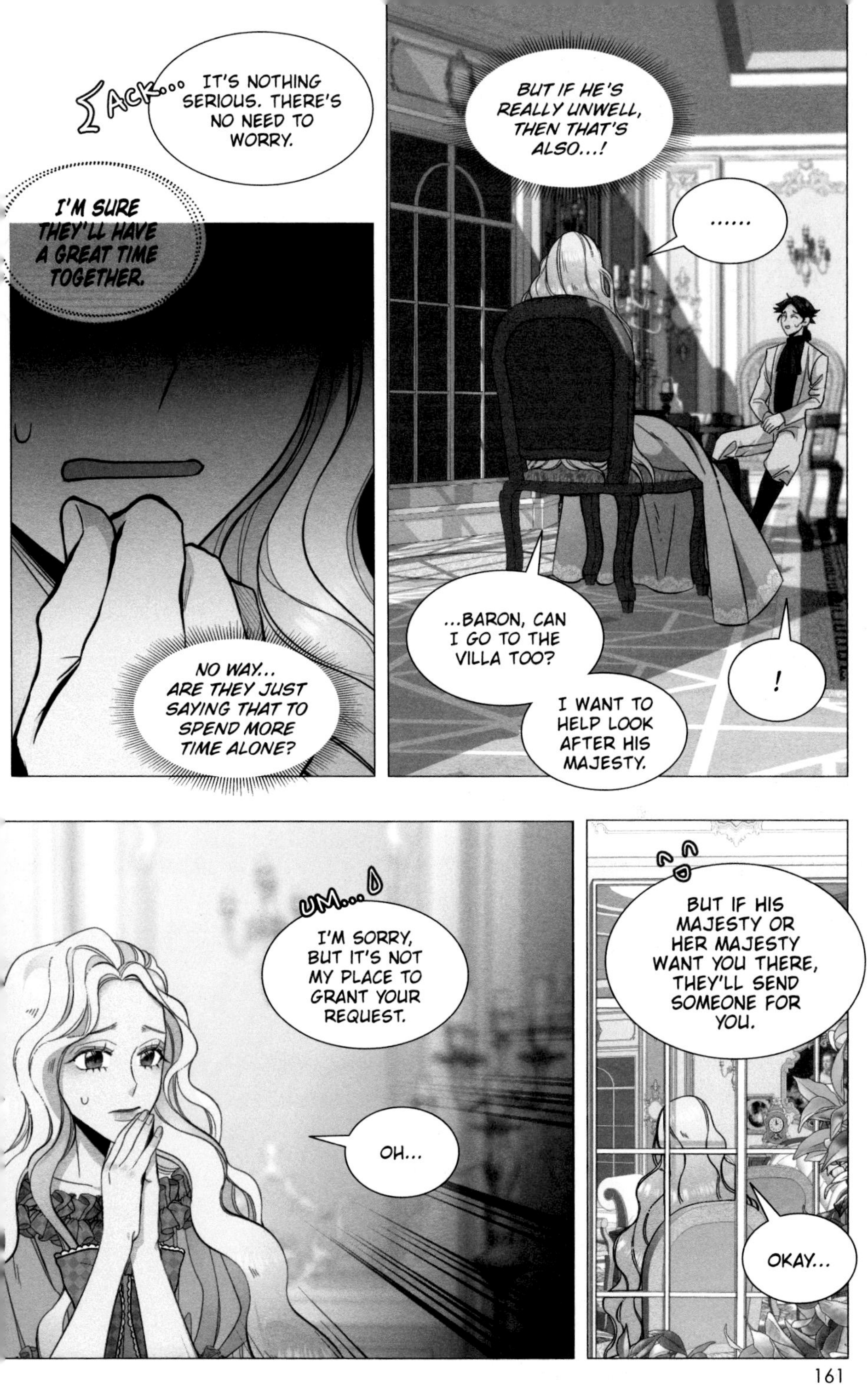
ACK... IT'S NOTHING SERIOUS. THERE'S NO NEED TO WORRY.
I'M SURE THEY'LL HAVE A GREAT TIME TOGETHER.
NO WAY... ARE THEY JUST SAYING THAT TO SPEND MORE TIME ALONE?
BUT IF HE'S REALLY UNWELL, THEN THAT'S ALSO...!
......
...BARON, CAN I GO TO THE VILLA TOO?
I WANT TO HELP LOOK AFTER HIS MAJESTY.
!
UM...
I'M SORRY, BUT IT'S NOT MY PLACE TO GRANT YOUR REQUEST.
OH...
BUT IF HIS MAJESTY OR HER MAJESTY WANT YOU THERE, THEY'LL SEND SOMEONE FOR YOU.
OKAY...

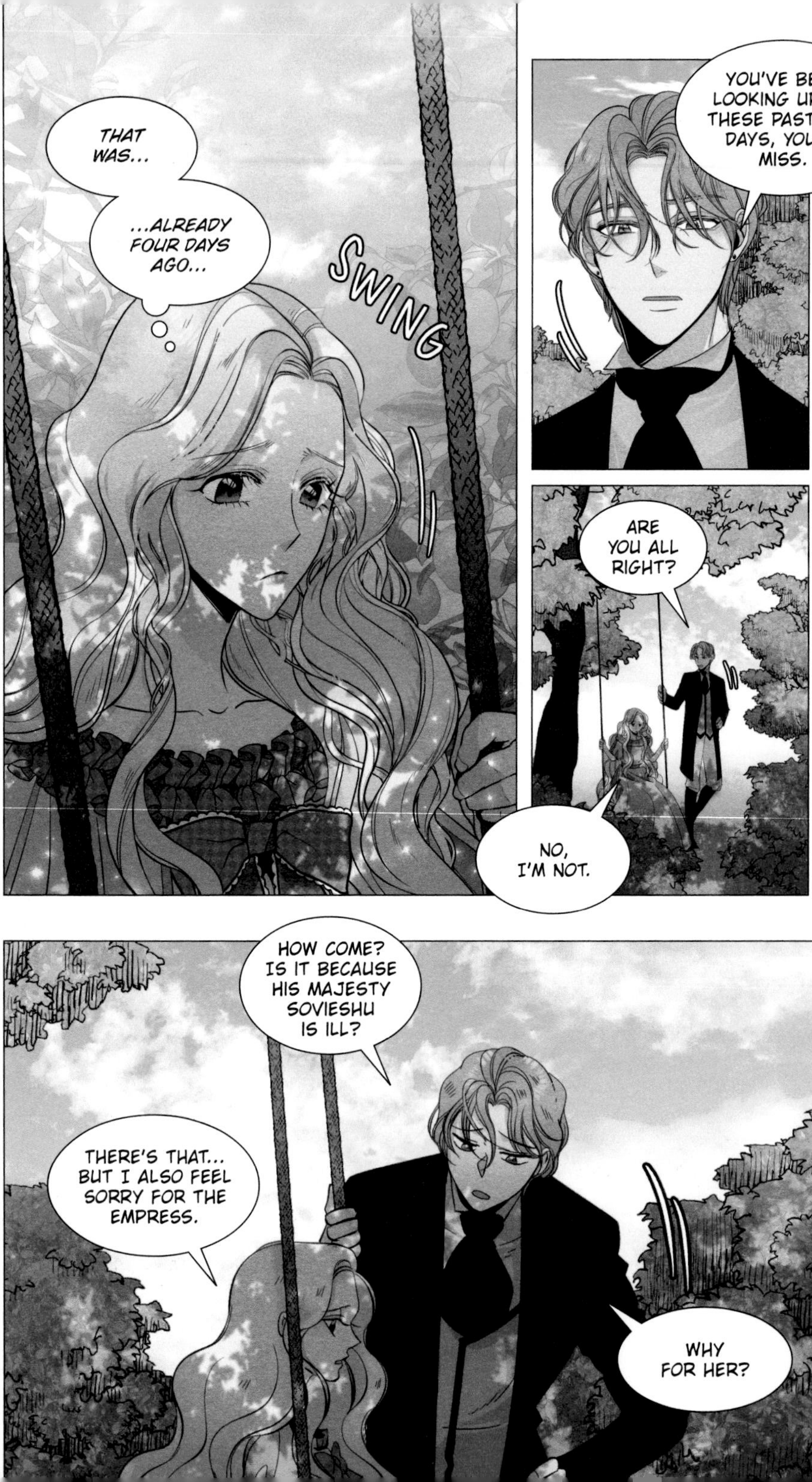
THAT WAS...
...ALREADY FOUR DAYS AGO...
SWING
YOU'VE BEEN LOOKING UPSET THESE PAST FEW DAYS, YOUNG MISS.
ARE YOU ALL RIGHT?
NO, I'M NOT.
HOW COME? IS IT BECAUSE HIS MAJESTY SOVIESHU IS ILL?
THERE'S THAT... BUT I ALSO FEEL SORRY FOR THE EMPRESS.
WHY FOR HER?

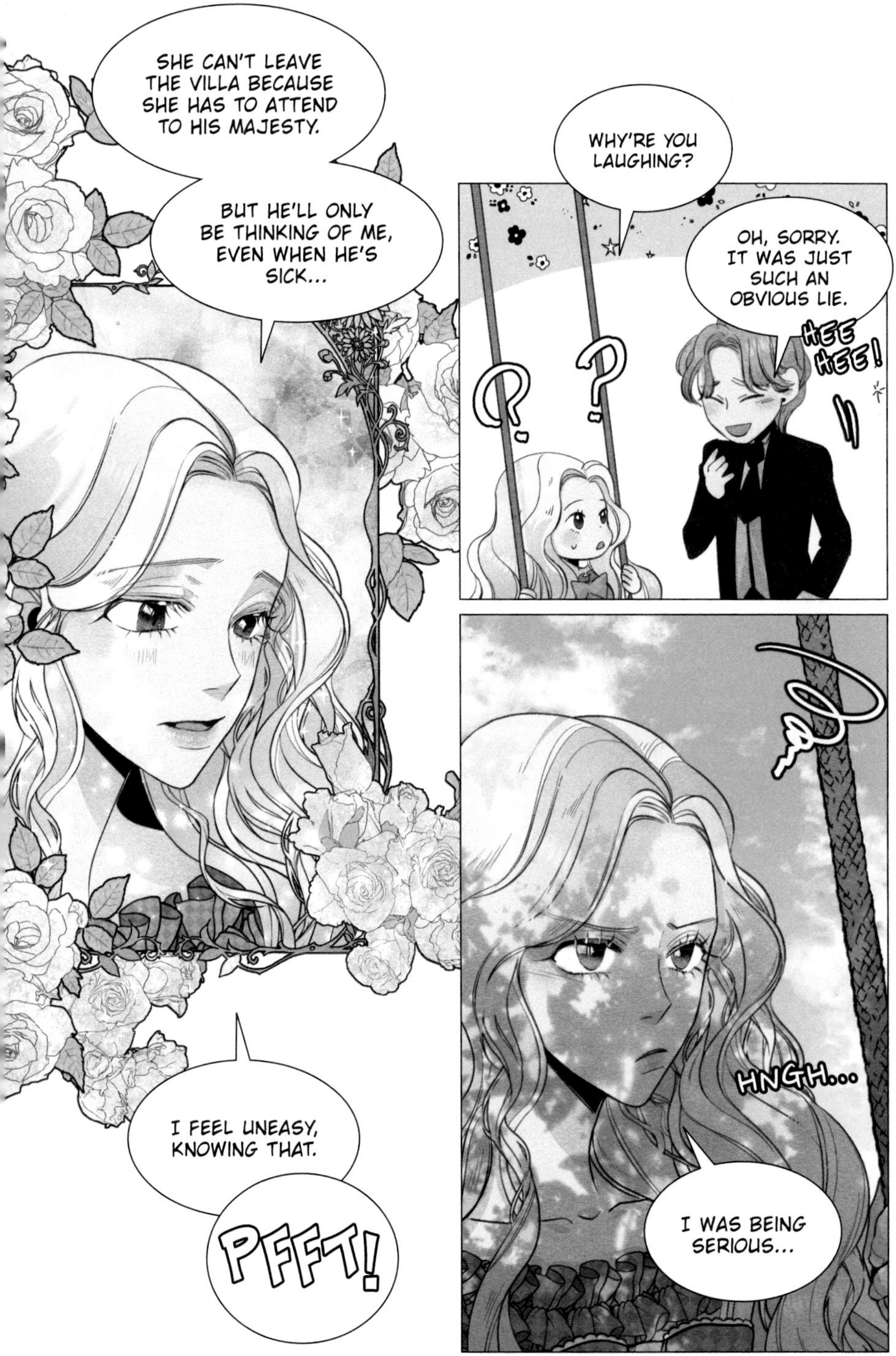
SHE CAN'T LEAVE THE VILLA BECAUSE SHE HAS TO ATTEND TO HIS MAJESTY.
BUT HE'LL ONLY BE THINKING OF ME, EVEN WHEN HE'S SICK...
I FEEL UNEASY, KNOWING THAT.
PFFT!
WHY'RE YOU LAUGHING?
OH, SORRY. IT WAS JUST SUCH AN OBVIOUS LIE.
HEE HEE!
I WAS BEING SERIOUS...
HNGH...

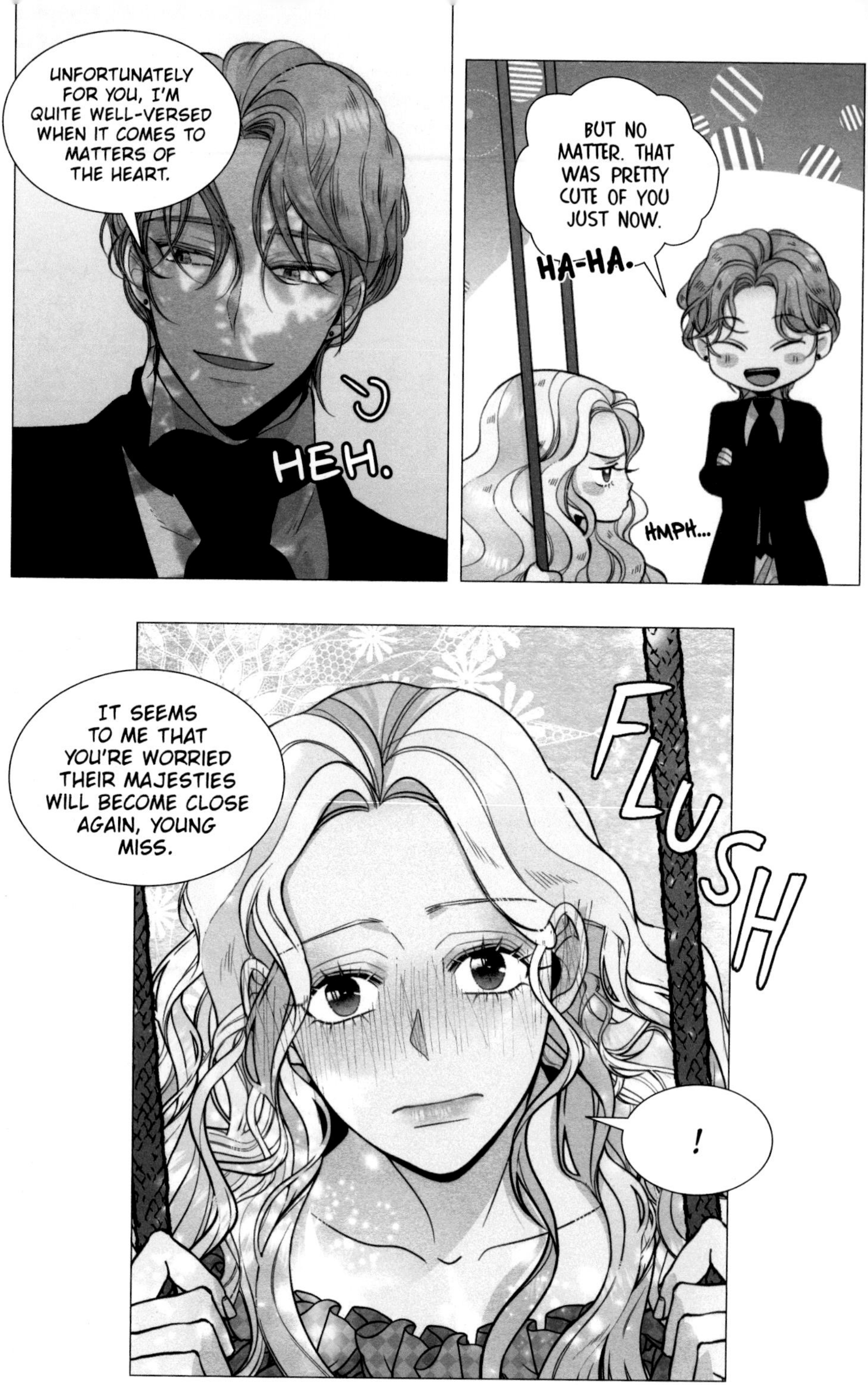
UNFORTUNATELY FOR YOU, I'M QUITE WELL-VERSED WHEN IT COMES TO MATTERS OF THE HEART.
HEH.
BUT NO MATTER. THAT WAS PRETTY CUTE OF YOU JUST NOW.
HA-HA.
HMPH...
IT SEEMS TO ME THAT YOU'RE WORRIED THEIR MAJESTIES WILL BECOME CLOSE AGAIN, YOUNG MISS.
FLUSH
!

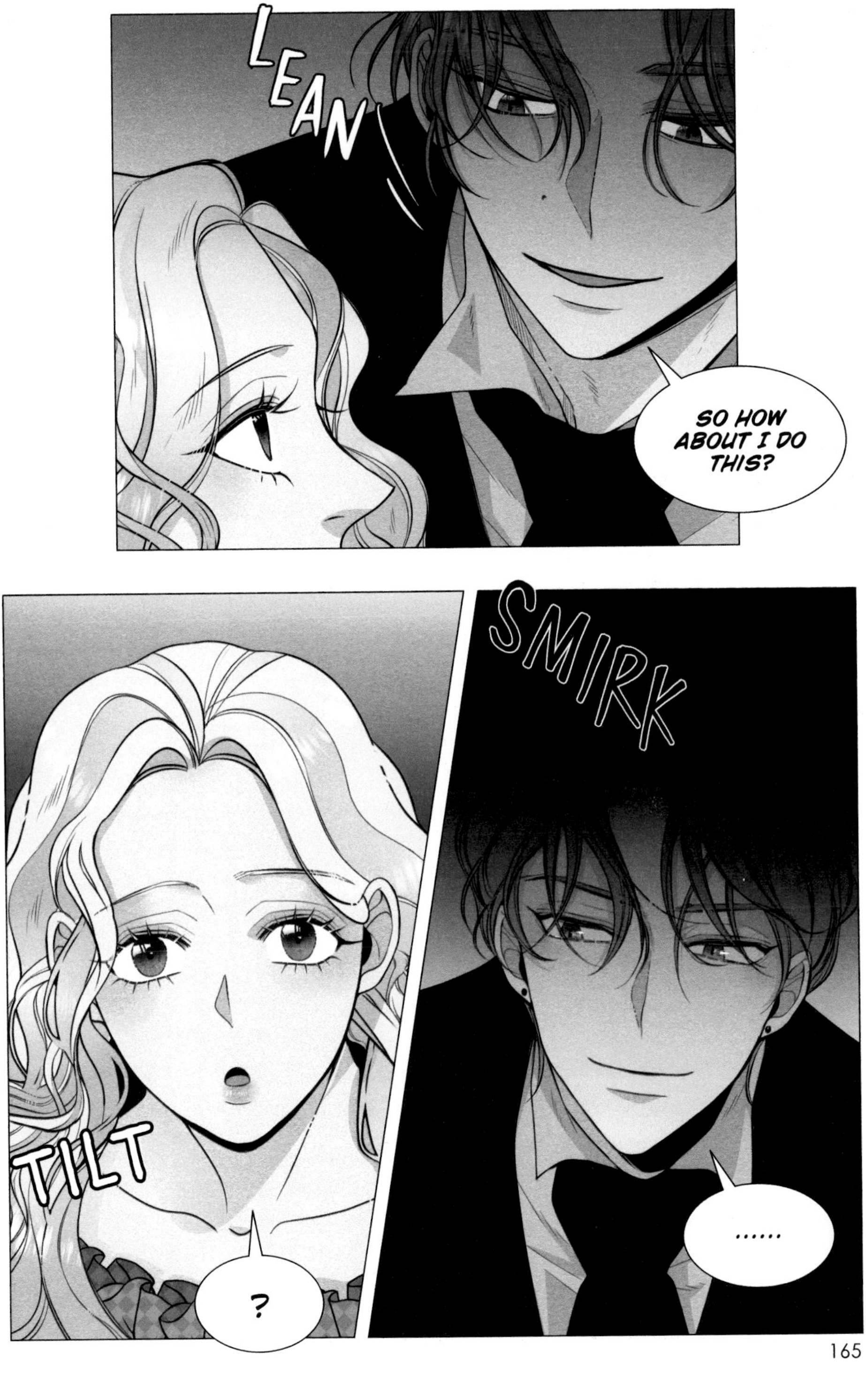
LEAN
SO HOW ABOUT I DO THIS?
SMIRK
TILT
?
......

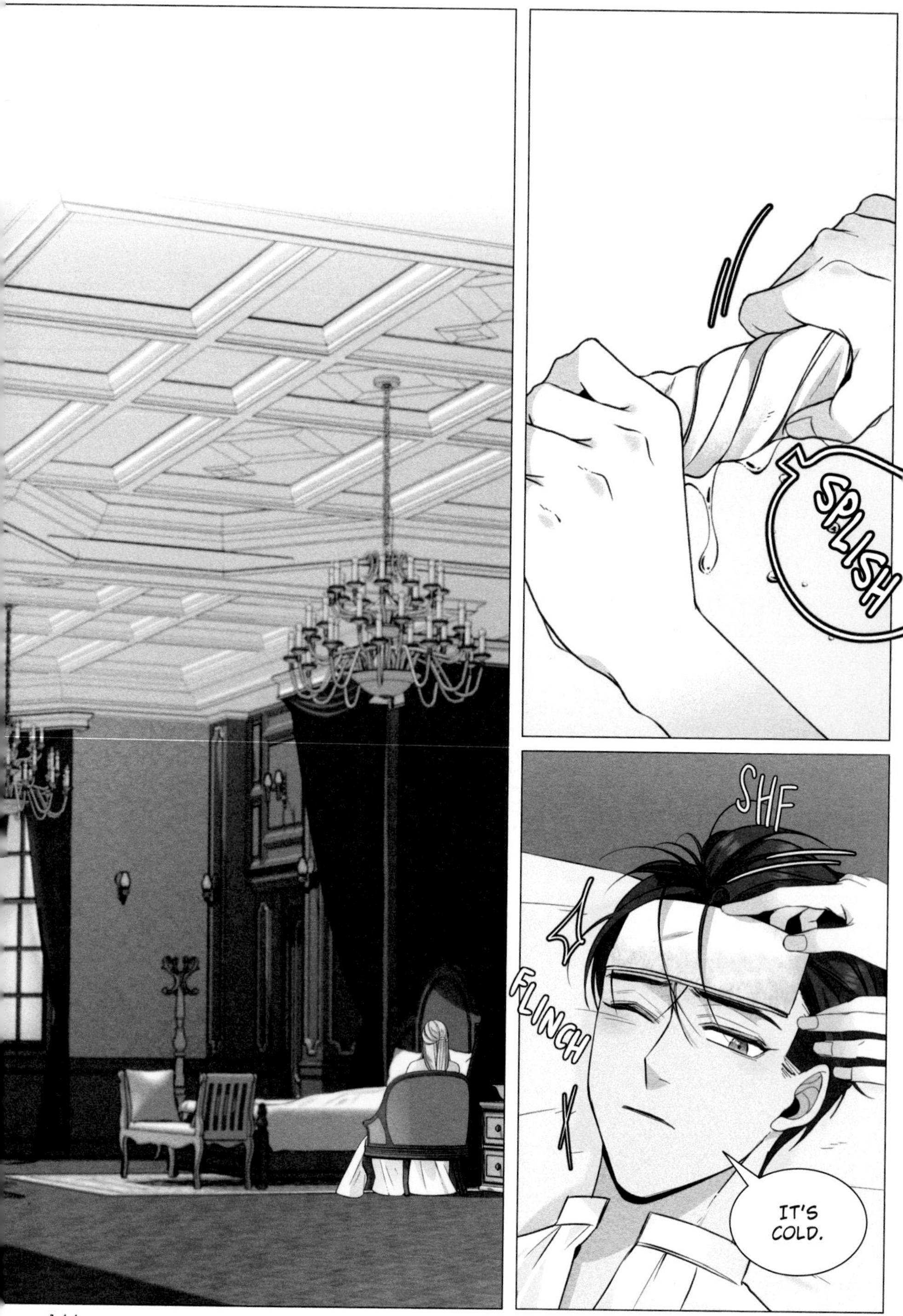
SPLISH
SHF
FLINCH
IT'S COLD.

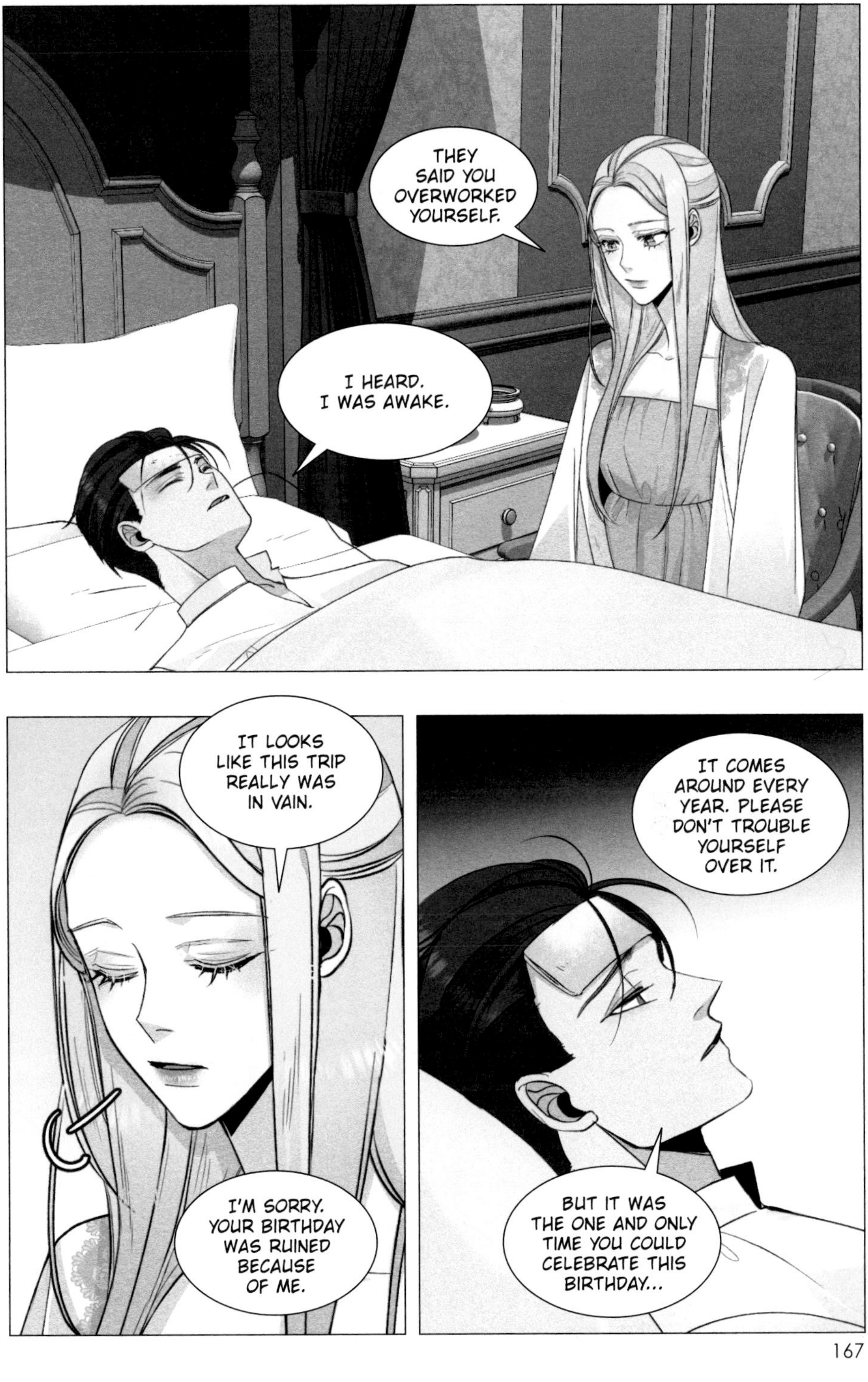
THEY SAID YOU OVERWORKED YOURSELF.
I HEARD. I WAS AWAKE.
IT LOOKS LIKE THIS TRIP REALLY WAS IN VAIN.
I'M SORRY. YOUR BIRTHDAY WAS RUINED BECAUSE OF ME.
IT COMES AROUND EVERY YEAR. PLEASE DON'T TROUBLE YOURSELF OVER IT.
BUT IT WAS THE ONE AND ONLY TIME YOU COULD CELEBRATE THIS BIRTHDAY...

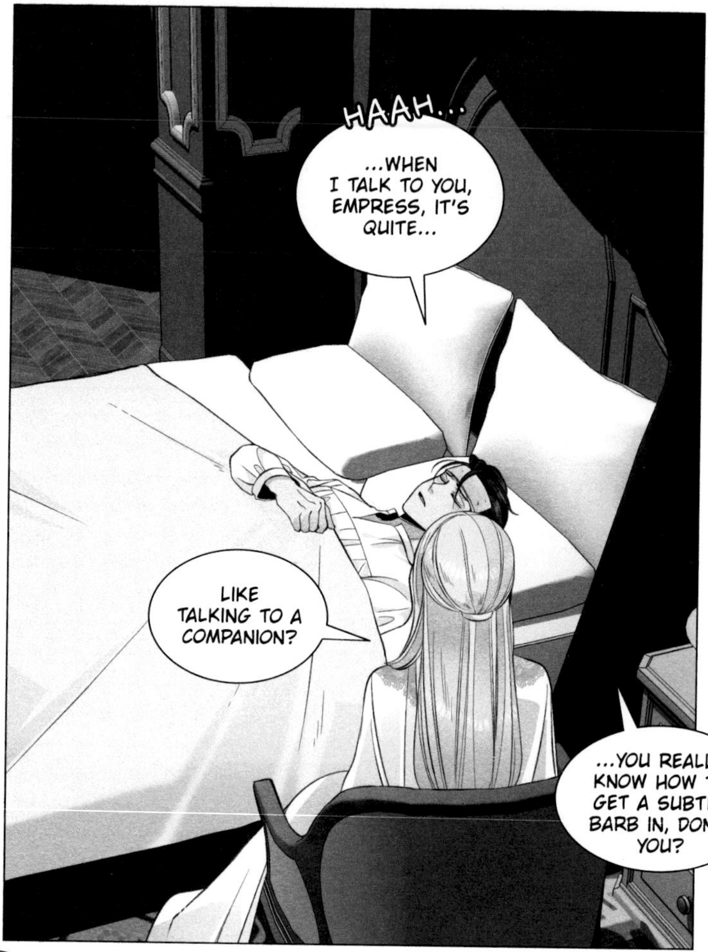
HAAH...
...WHEN I TALK TO YOU, EMPRESS, IT'S QUITE...
LIKE TALKING TO A COMPANION?
...YOU REALLY KNOW HOW TO GET A SUBTLE BARB IN, DON'T YOU?

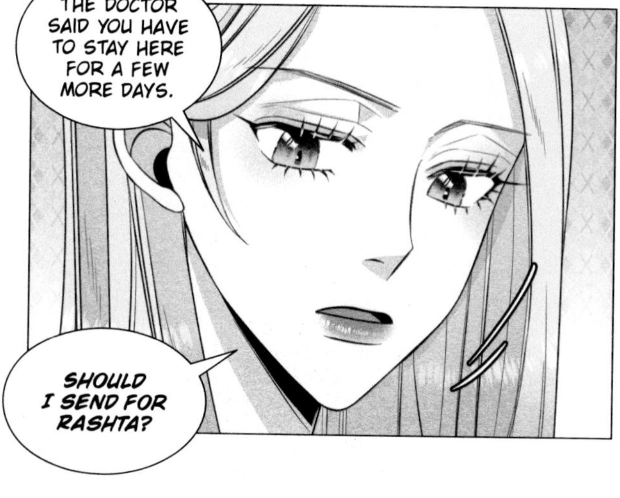
THE DOCTOR SAID YOU HAVE TO STAY HERE FOR A FEW MORE DAYS.
*SHOULD I SEND FOR RASHTA?*

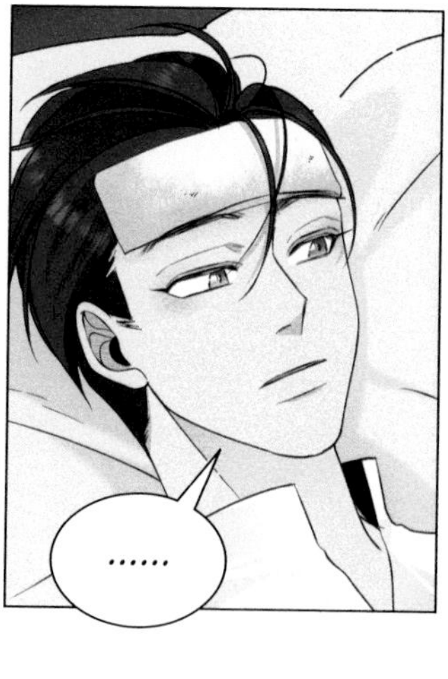
......

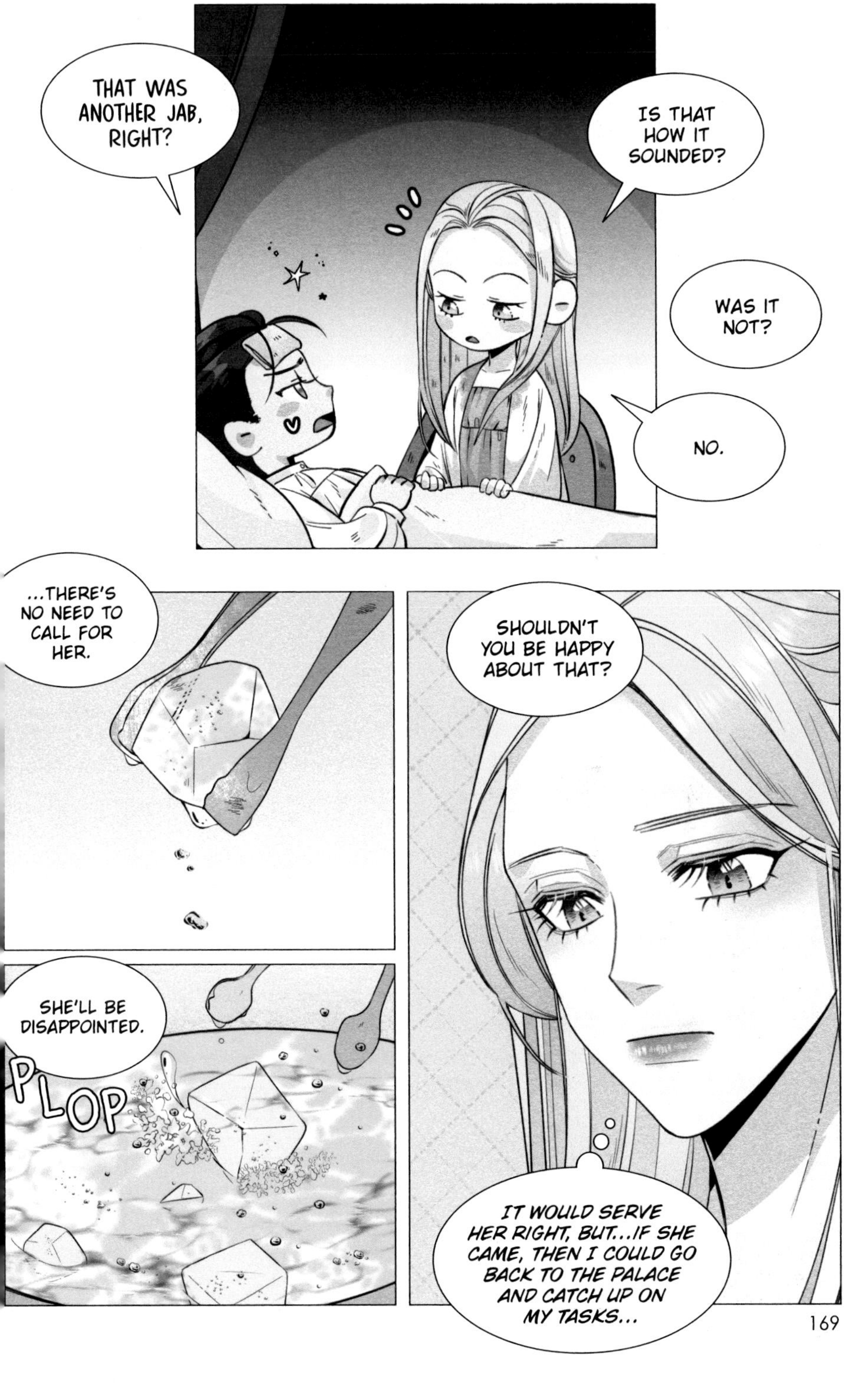
THAT WAS ANOTHER JAB, RIGHT?
IS THAT HOW IT SOUNDED?
WAS IT NOT?
NO.
...THERE'S NO NEED TO CALL FOR HER.
SHOULDN'T YOU BE HAPPY ABOUT THAT?
SHE'LL BE DISAPPOINTED.
PLOP
IT WOULD SERVE HER RIGHT, BUT...IF SHE CAME, THEN I COULD GO BACK TO THE PALACE AND CATCH UP ON MY TASKS...

THE THINGS SHE SAYS MAY BE CUTE AND FASCINATING, BUT...

SHF

...I DON'T FEEL AT PEACE WHEN I'M WITH HER.

SPLISH

SPLOSH

I JUST WANT SOME QUIET RIGHT NOW.

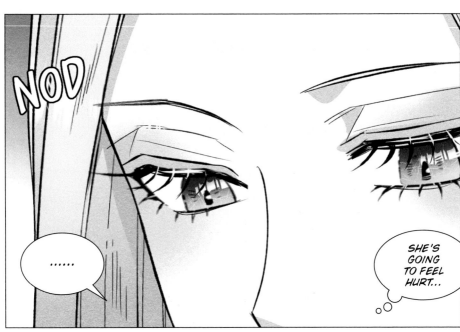

NOD

......

SHE'S GOING TO FEEL HURT...

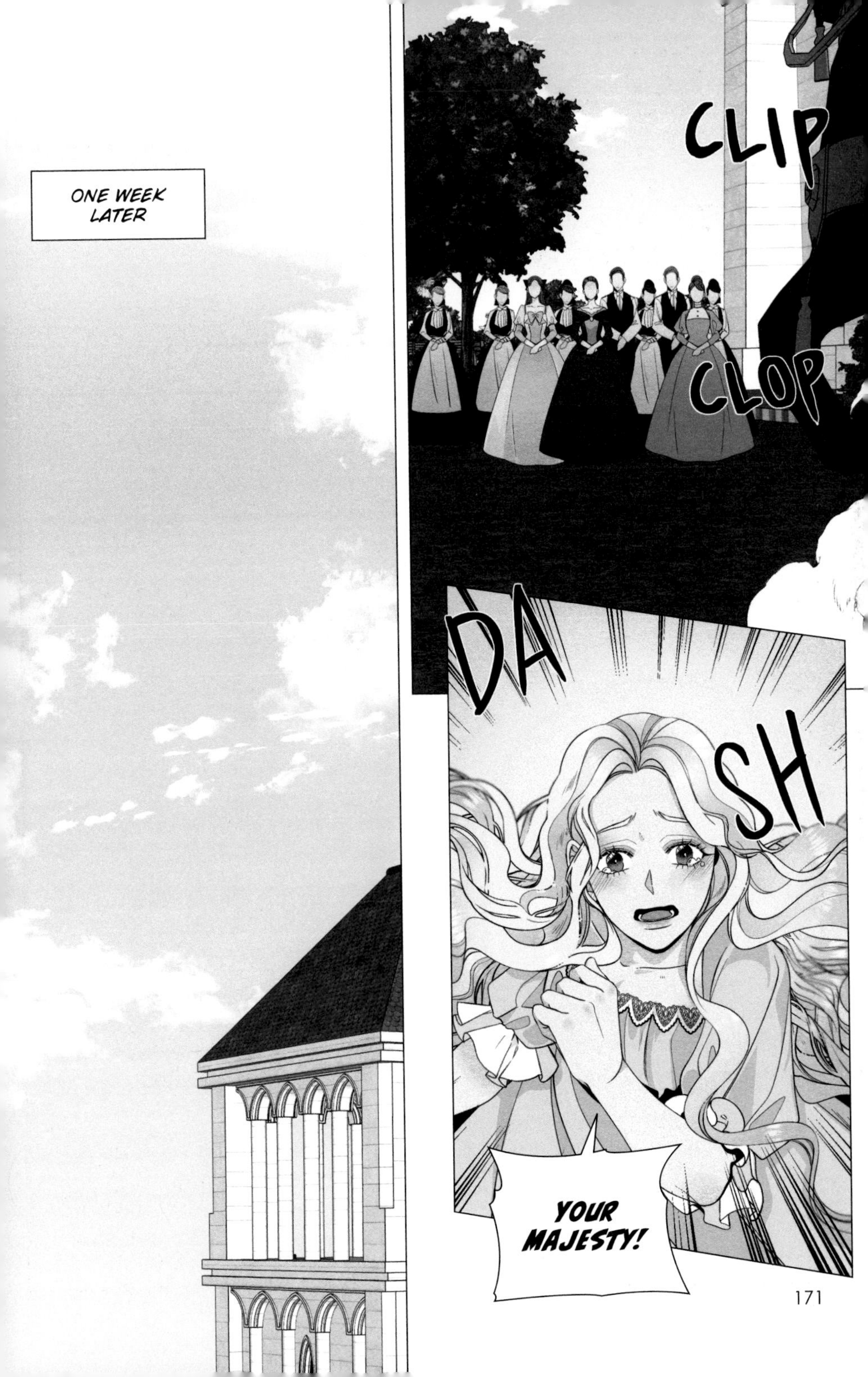
ONE WEEK LATER
CLIP
CLOP
DASH
YOUR MAJESTY!

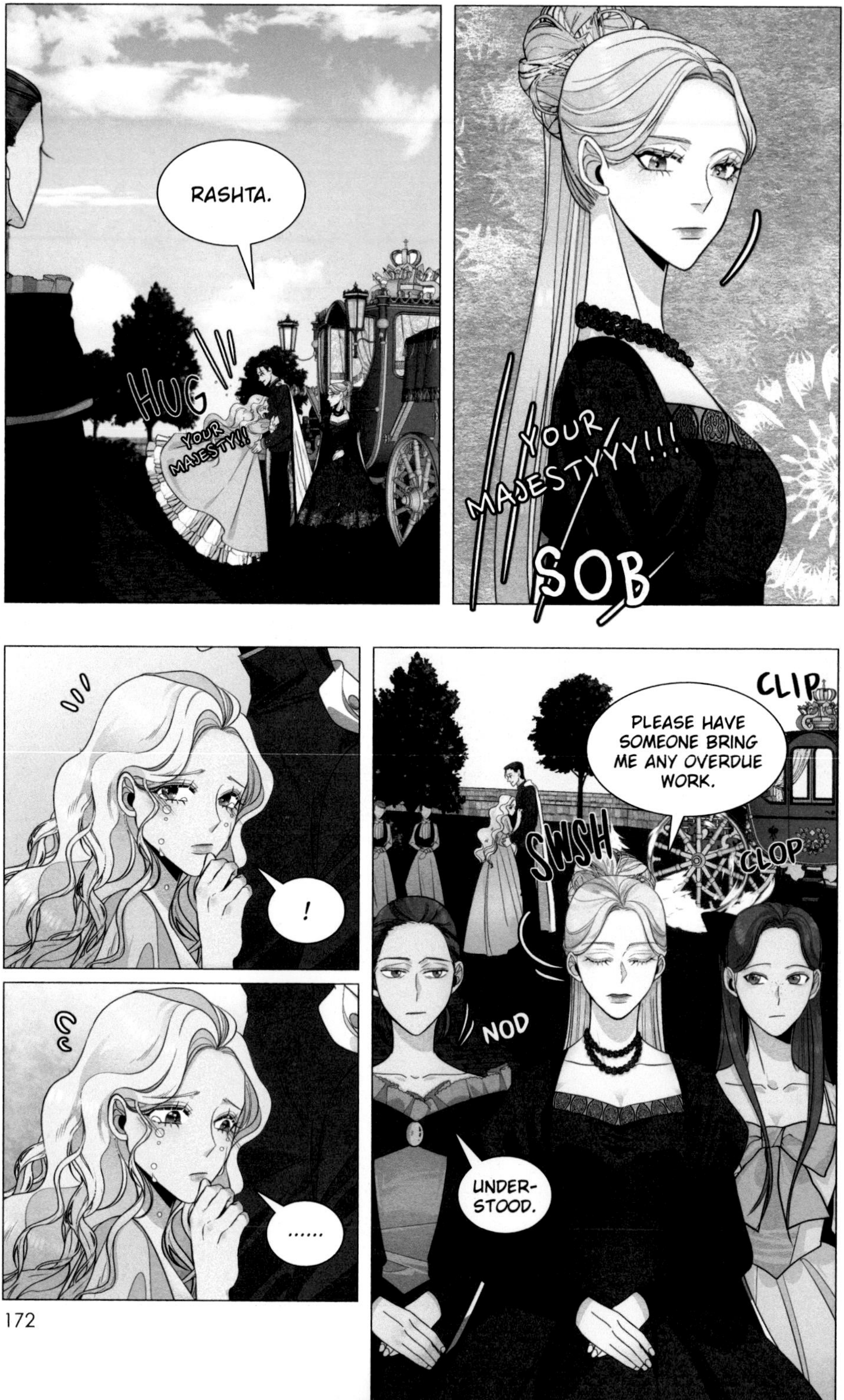
RASHTA.
HUG
YOUR MAJESTY!!
YOUR MAJESTYYY!!!
SOB
!
......
CLIP
PLEASE HAVE SOMEONE BRING ME ANY OVERDUE WORK.
SWSH
CLOP
NOD
UNDER-STOOD.

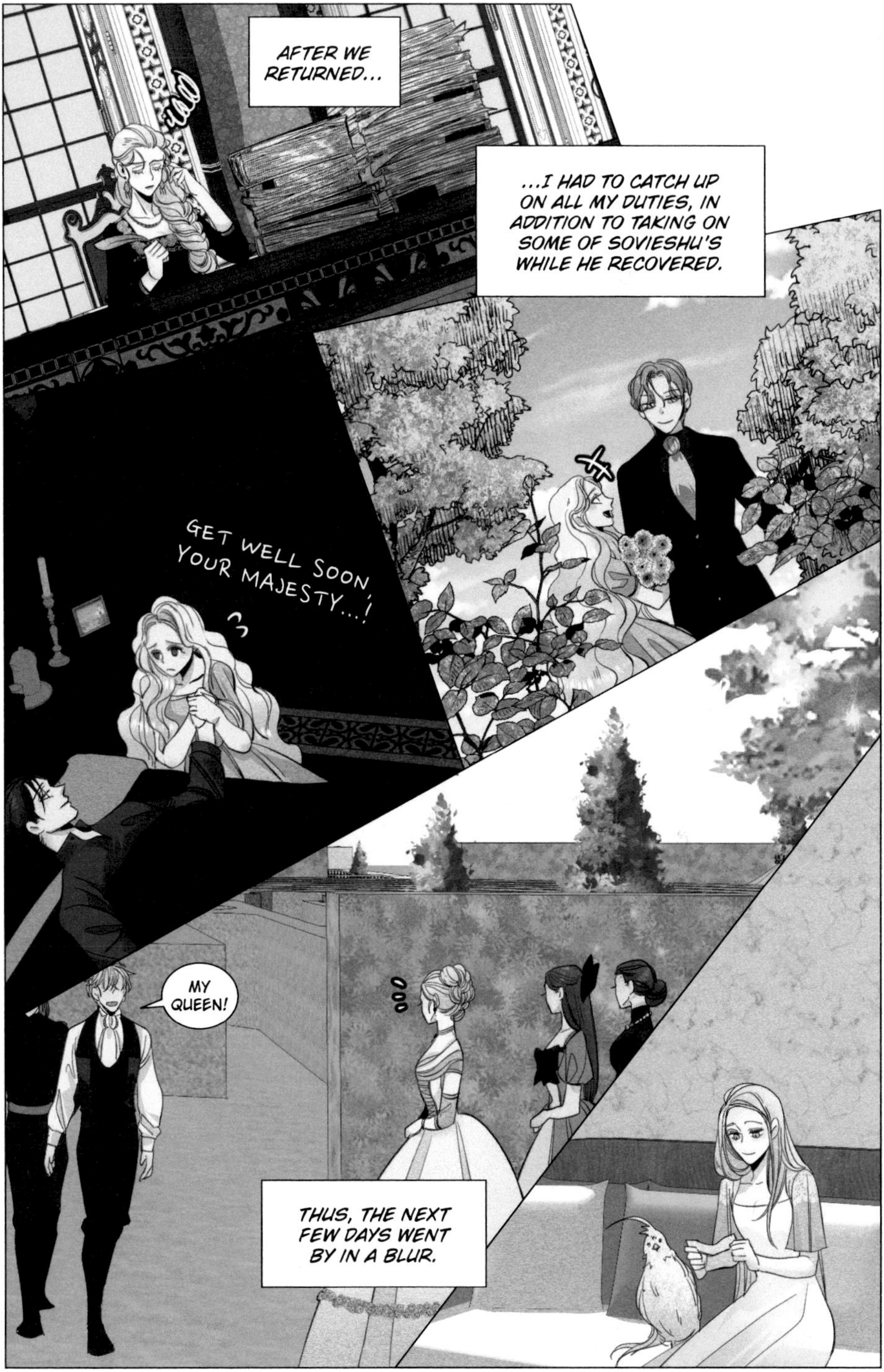
AFTER WE RETURNED...
...I HAD TO CATCH UP ON ALL MY DUTIES, IN ADDITION TO TAKING ON SOME OF SOVIESHU'S WHILE HE RECOVERED.
GET WELL SOON, YOUR MAJESTY...!
MY QUEEN!
THUS, THE NEXT FEW DAYS WENT BY IN A BLUR.

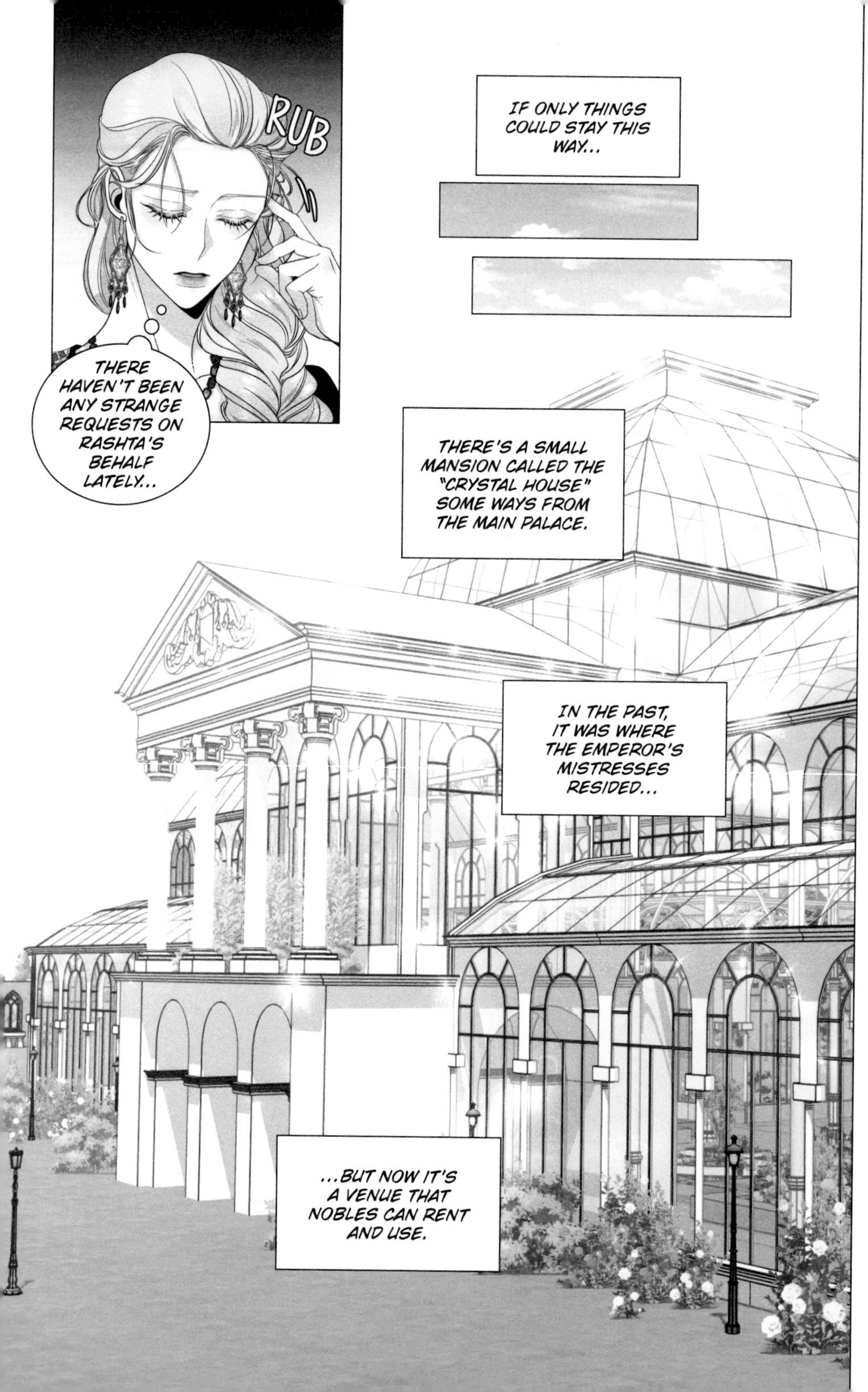

RUB
THERE HAVEN'T BEEN ANY STRANGE REQUESTS ON RASHTA'S BEHALF LATELY...
IF ONLY THINGS COULD STAY THIS WAY...
THERE'S A SMALL MANSION CALLED THE "CRYSTAL HOUSE" SOME WAYS FROM THE MAIN PALACE.
IN THE PAST, IT WAS WHERE THE EMPEROR'S MISTRESSES RESIDED...
...BUT NOW IT'S A VENUE THAT NOBLES CAN RENT AND USE.

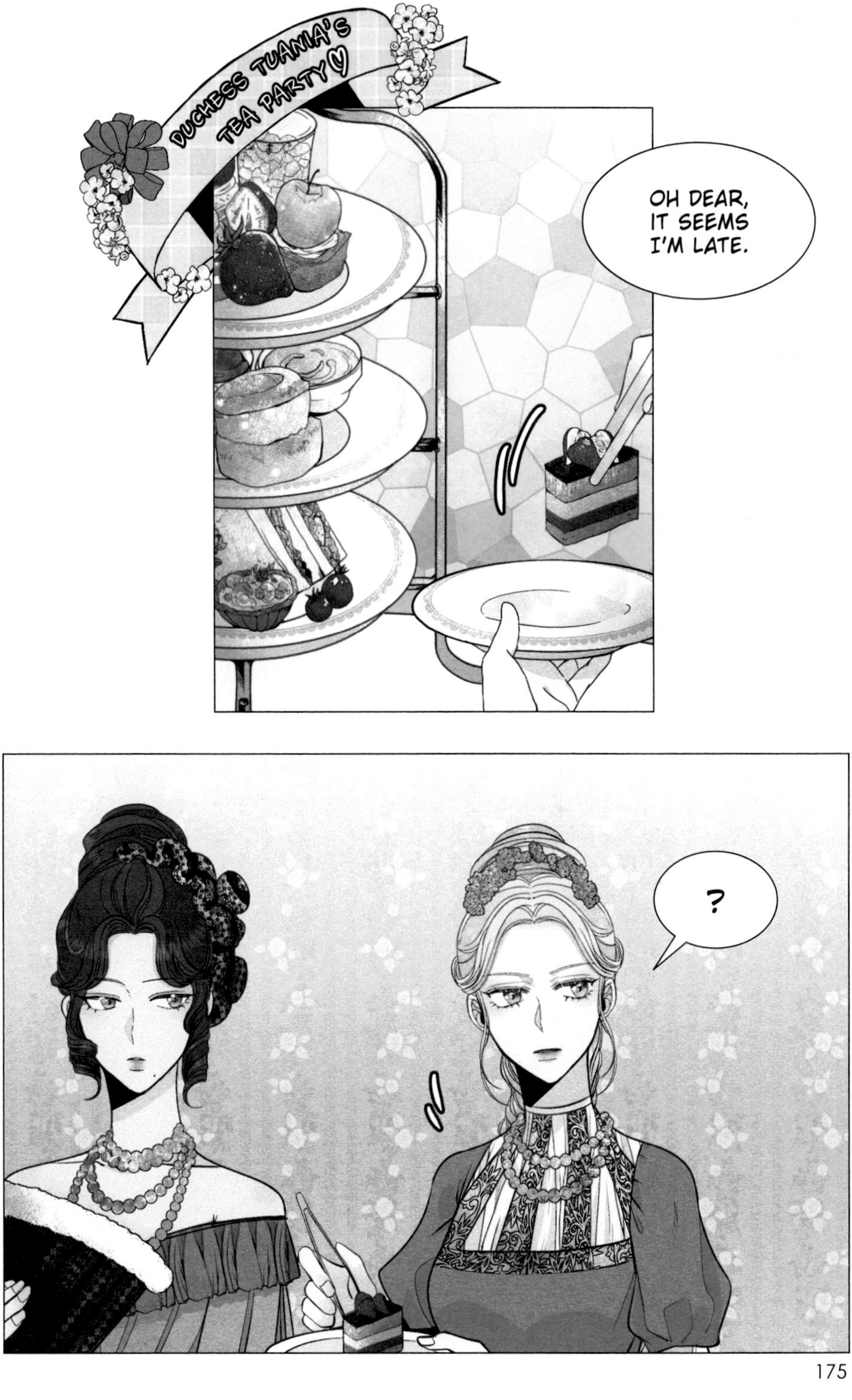
DUCHESS TUANIA'S TEA PARTY♡
OH DEAR, IT SEEMS I'M LATE.
?

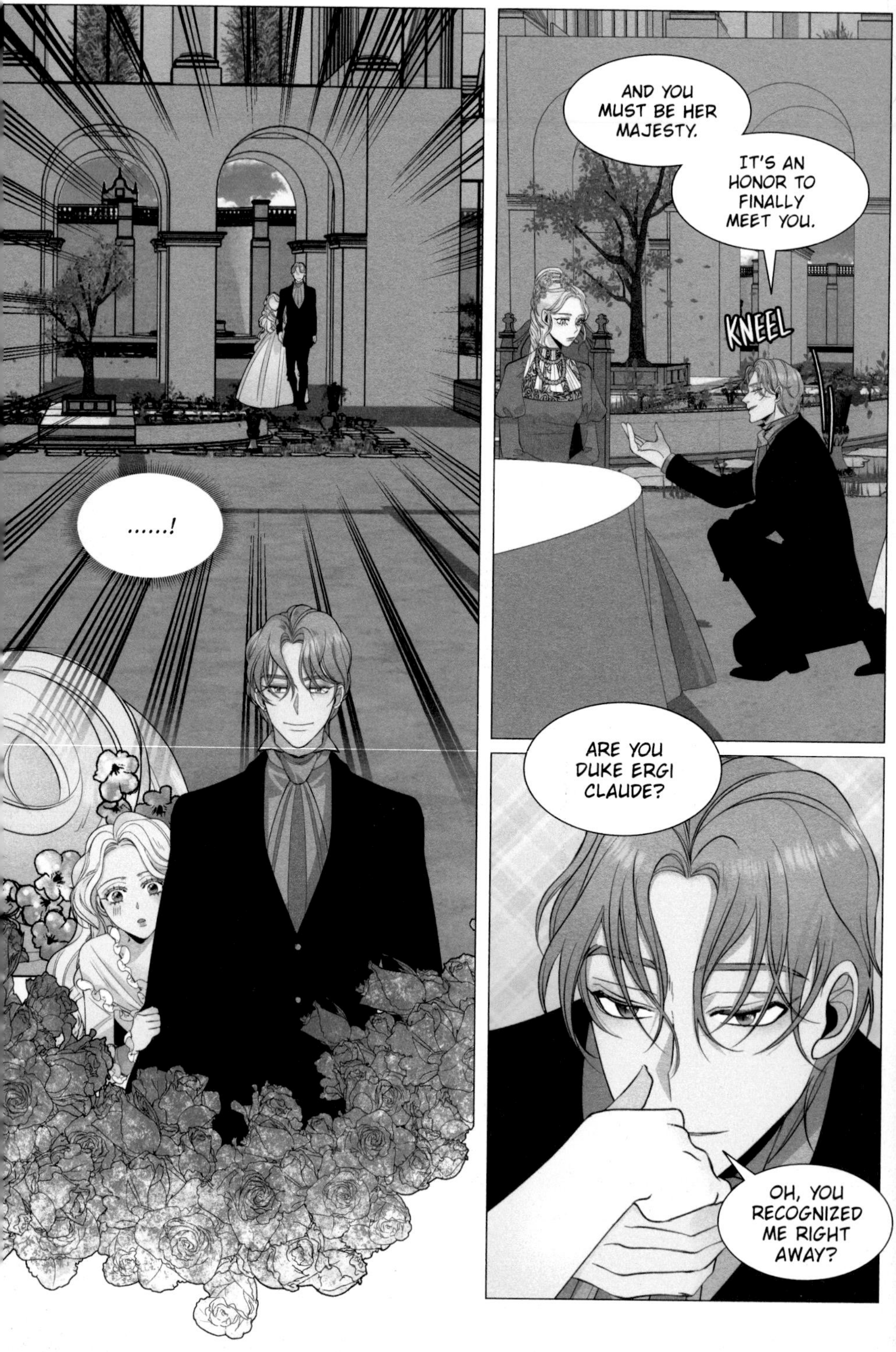
......!
AND YOU MUST BE HER MAJESTY.
IT'S AN HONOR TO FINALLY MEET YOU.
KNEEL
ARE YOU DUKE ERGI CLAUDE?
OH, YOU RECOGNIZED ME RIGHT AWAY?

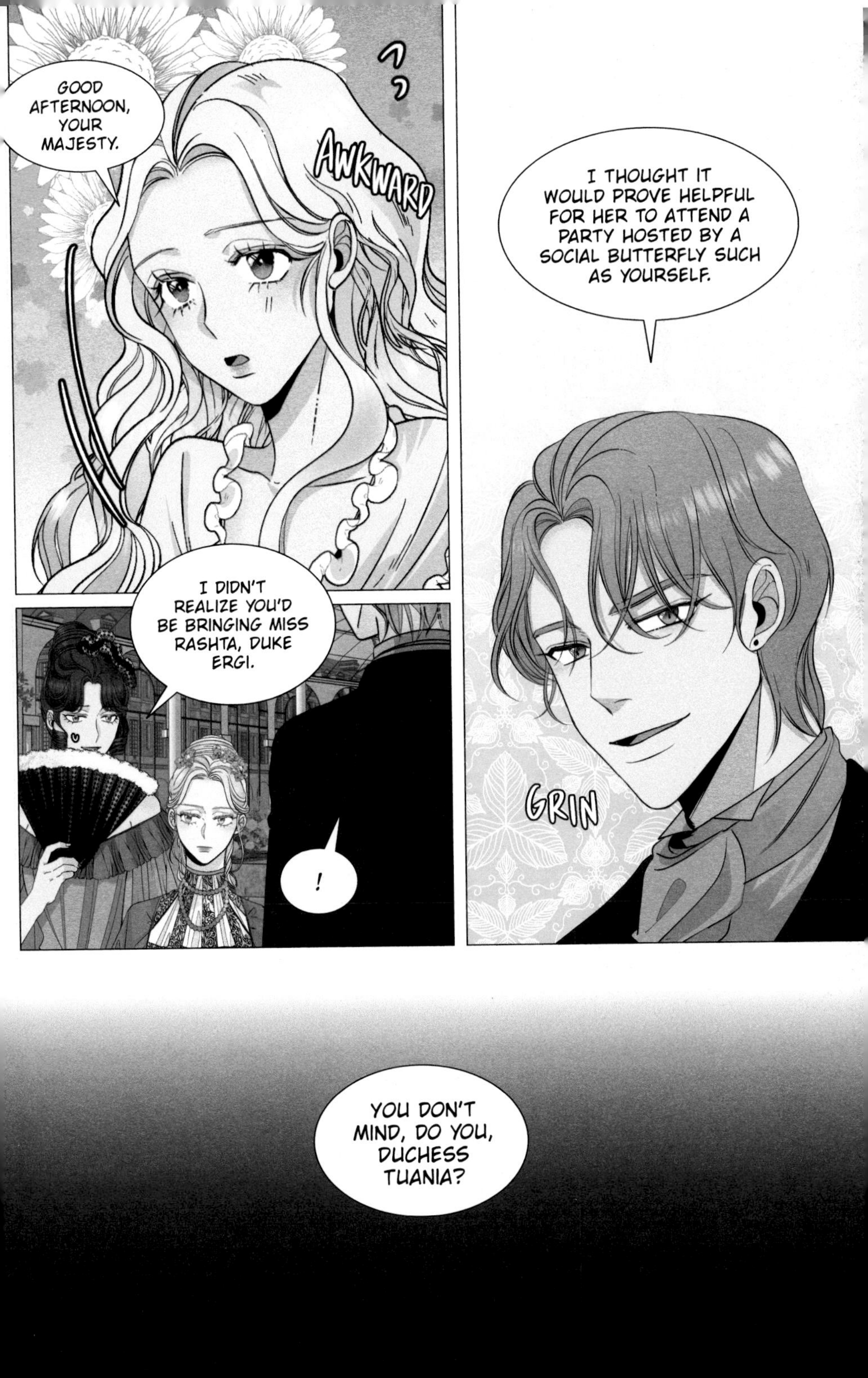
GOOD AFTERNOON, YOUR MAJESTY.
AWKWARD
I DIDN'T REALIZE YOU'D BE BRINGING MISS RASHTA, DUKE ERGI.
!
I THOUGHT IT WOULD PROVE HELPFUL FOR HER TO ATTEND A PARTY HOSTED BY A SOCIAL BUTTERFLY SUCH AS YOURSELF.
GRIN
YOU DON'T MIND, DO YOU, DUCHESS TUANIA?

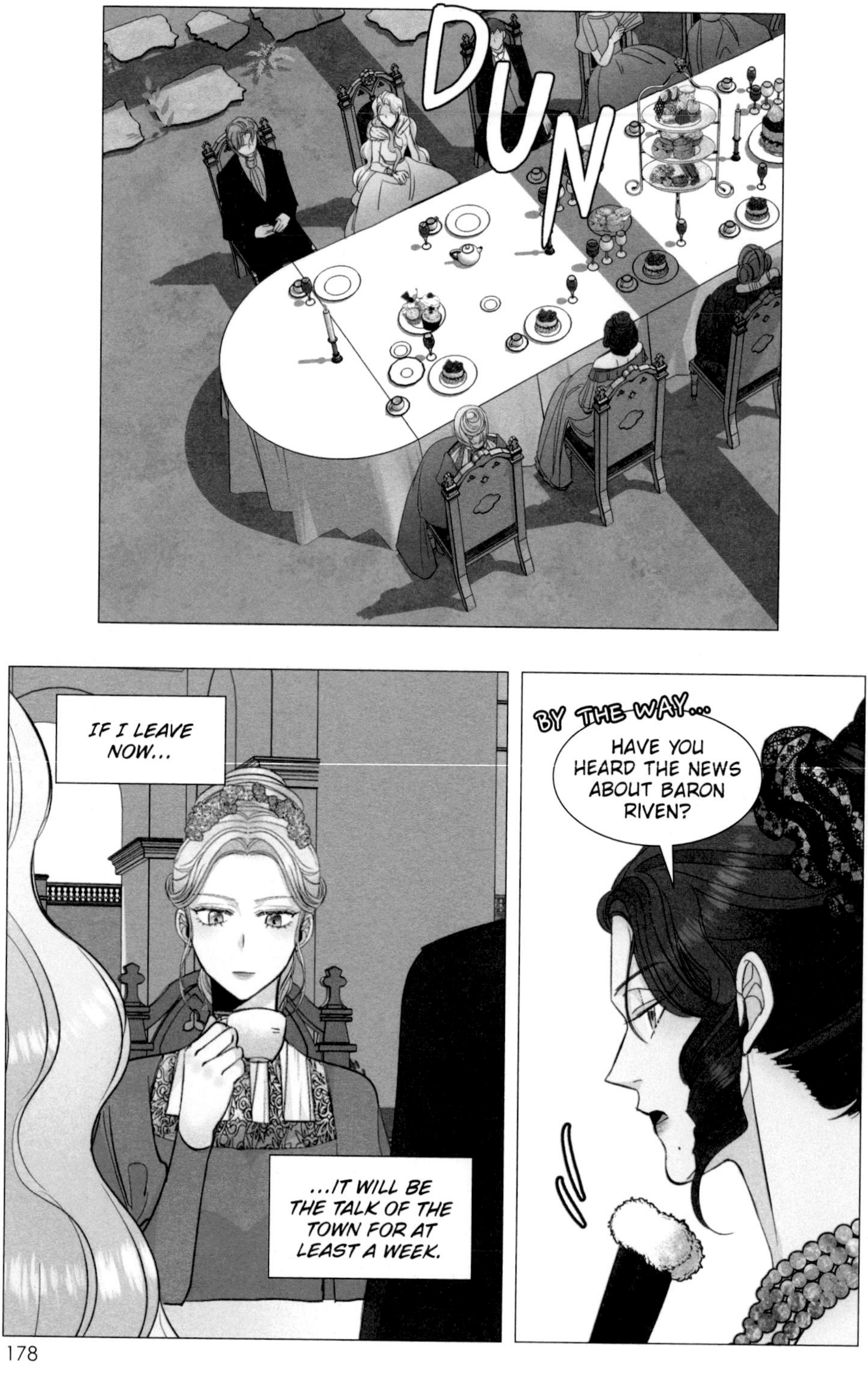
DUN
IF I LEAVE NOW...
...IT WILL BE THE TALK OF THE TOWN FOR AT LEAST A WEEK.
BY THE WAY...
HAVE YOU HEARD THE NEWS ABOUT BARON RIVEN?

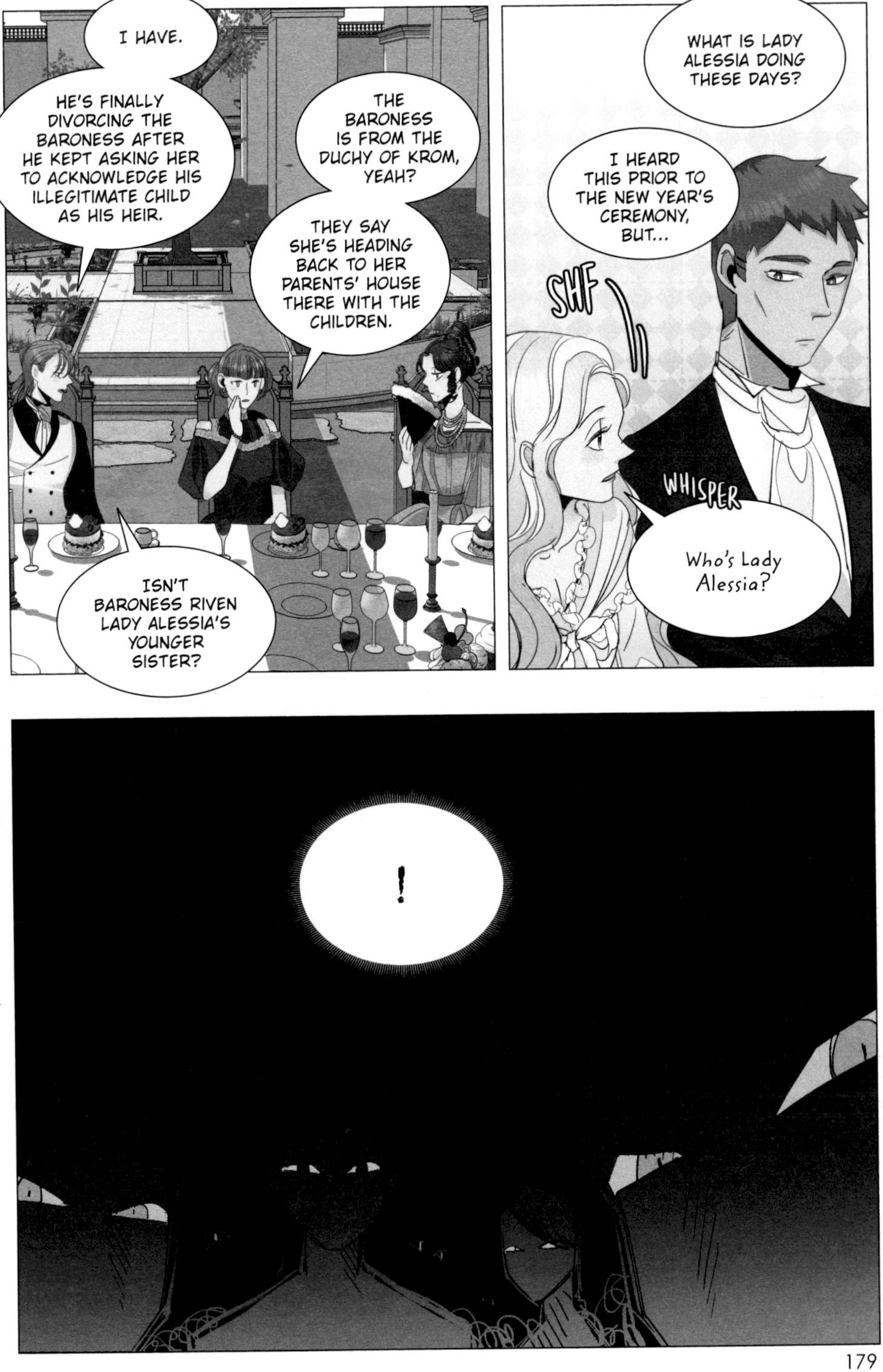
I HAVE.
HE'S FINALLY DIVORCING THE BARONESS AFTER HE KEPT ASKING HER TO ACKNOWLEDGE HIS ILLEGITIMATE CHILD AS HIS HEIR.
THE BARONESS IS FROM THE DUCHY OF KROM, YEAH?
THEY SAY SHE'S HEADING BACK TO HER PARENTS' HOUSE THERE WITH THE CHILDREN.
ISN'T BARONESS RIVEN LADY ALESSIA'S YOUNGER SISTER?
WHAT IS LADY ALESSIA DOING THESE DAYS?
I HEARD THIS PRIOR TO THE NEW YEAR'S CEREMONY, BUT...
SHF
WHISPER
Who's Lady Alessia?
!

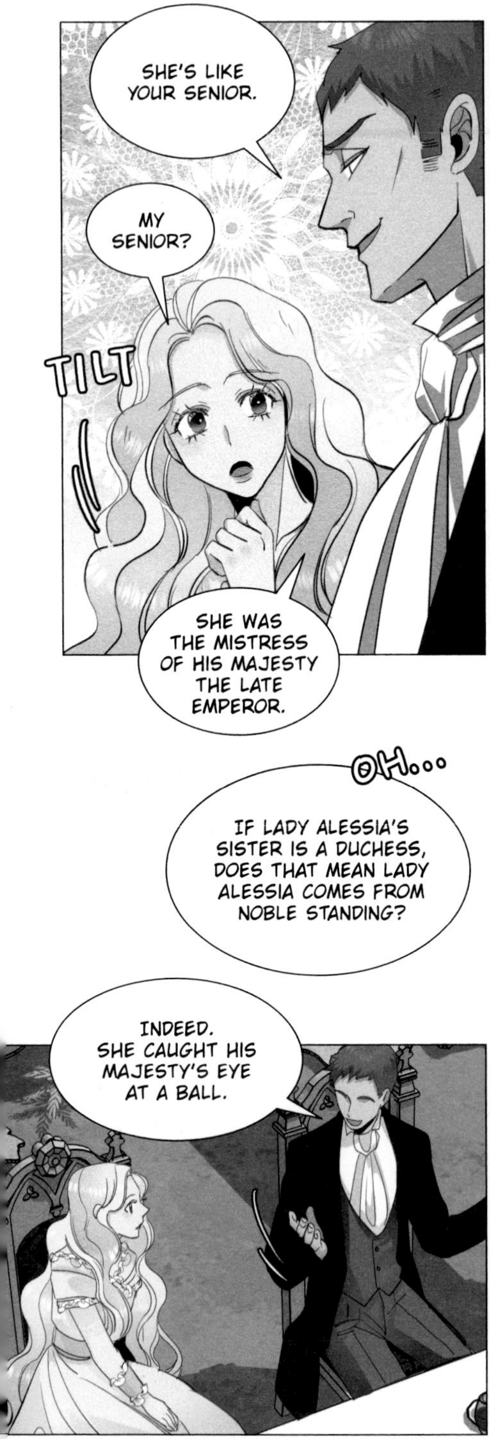

SHE'S LIKE YOUR SENIOR.
MY SENIOR?
TILT
SHE WAS THE MISTRESS OF HIS MAJESTY THE LATE EMPEROR.
OH...
IF LADY ALESSIA'S SISTER IS A DUCHESS, DOES THAT MEAN LADY ALESSIA COMES FROM NOBLE STANDING?
INDEED. SHE CAUGHT HIS MAJESTY'S EYE AT A BALL.


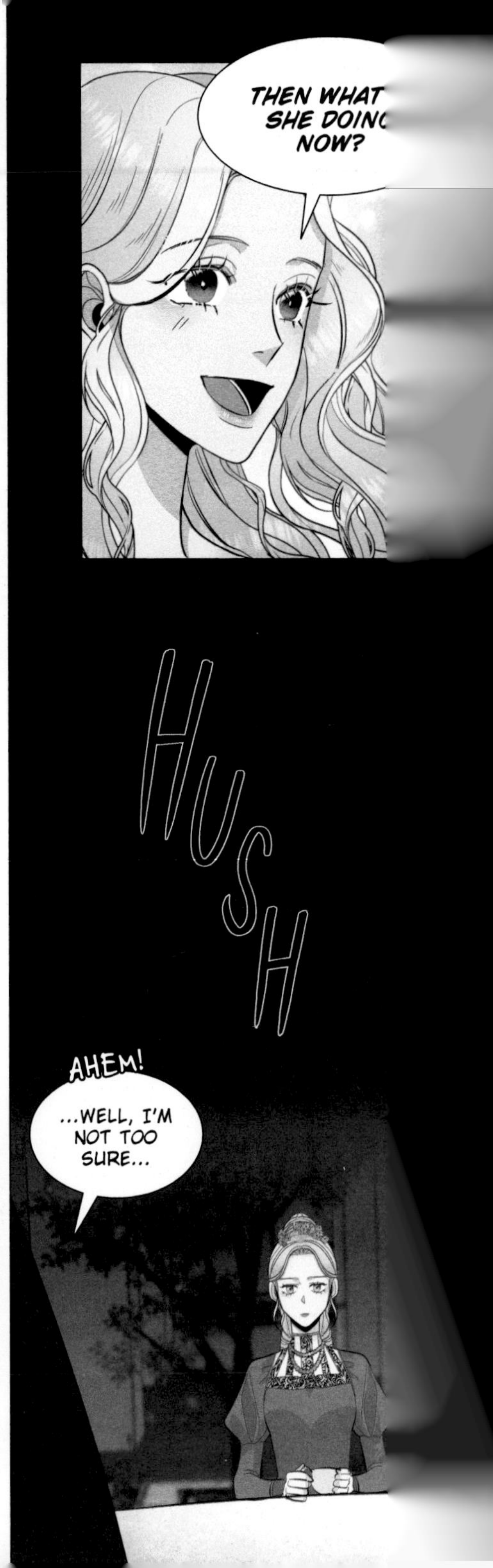

THEN WHAT SHE DOIN NOW?
HUSH
AHEM!
...WELL, I'M NOT TOO SURE...

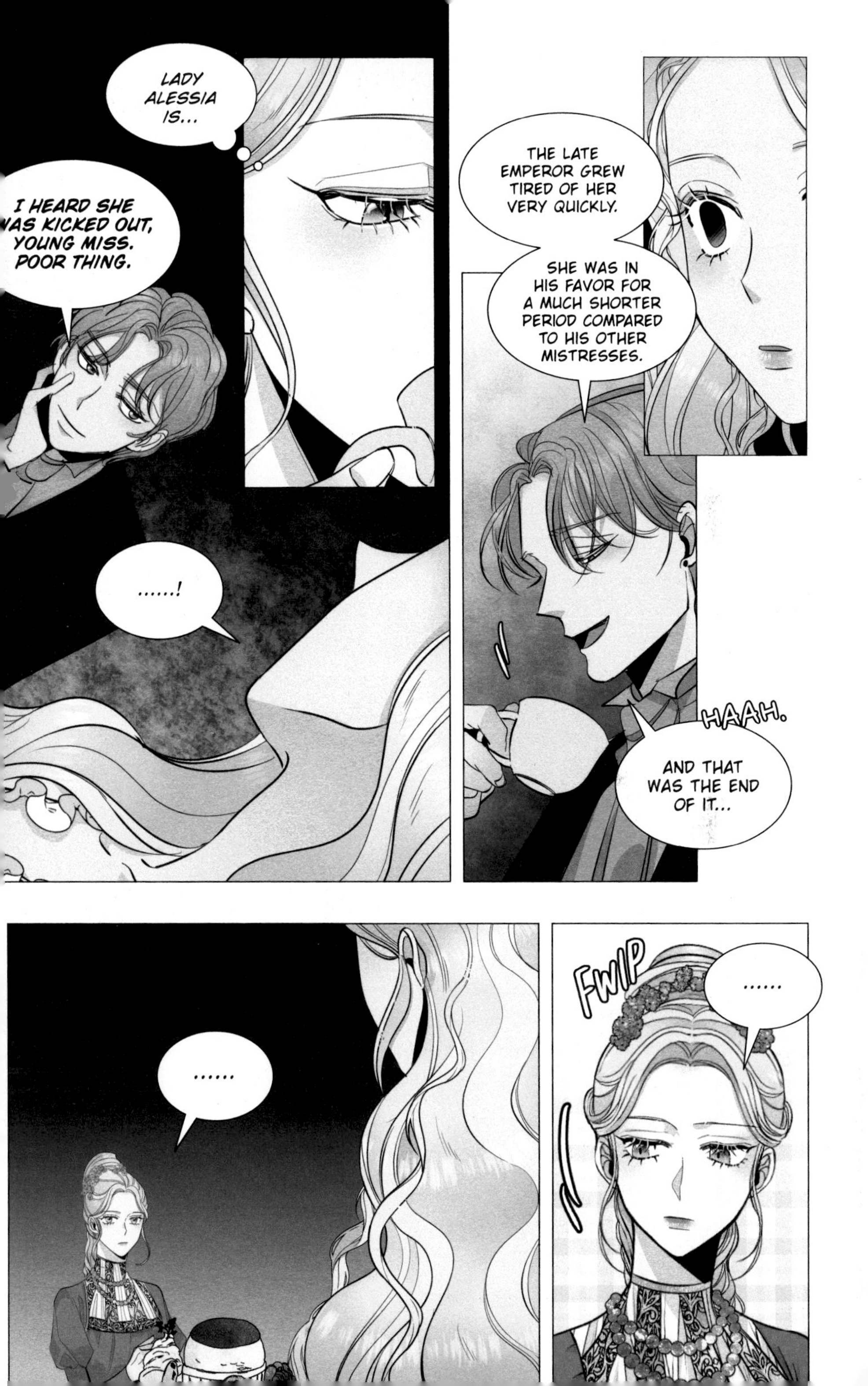
LADY ALESSIA IS...
I HEARD SHE WAS KICKED OUT, YOUNG MISS. POOR THING.
THE LATE EMPEROR GREW TIRED OF HER VERY QUICKLY.
SHE WAS IN HIS FAVOR FOR A MUCH SHORTER PERIOD COMPARED TO HIS OTHER MISTRESSES.
......!
HAAH.
AND THAT WAS THE END OF IT...
......
FWIP
......

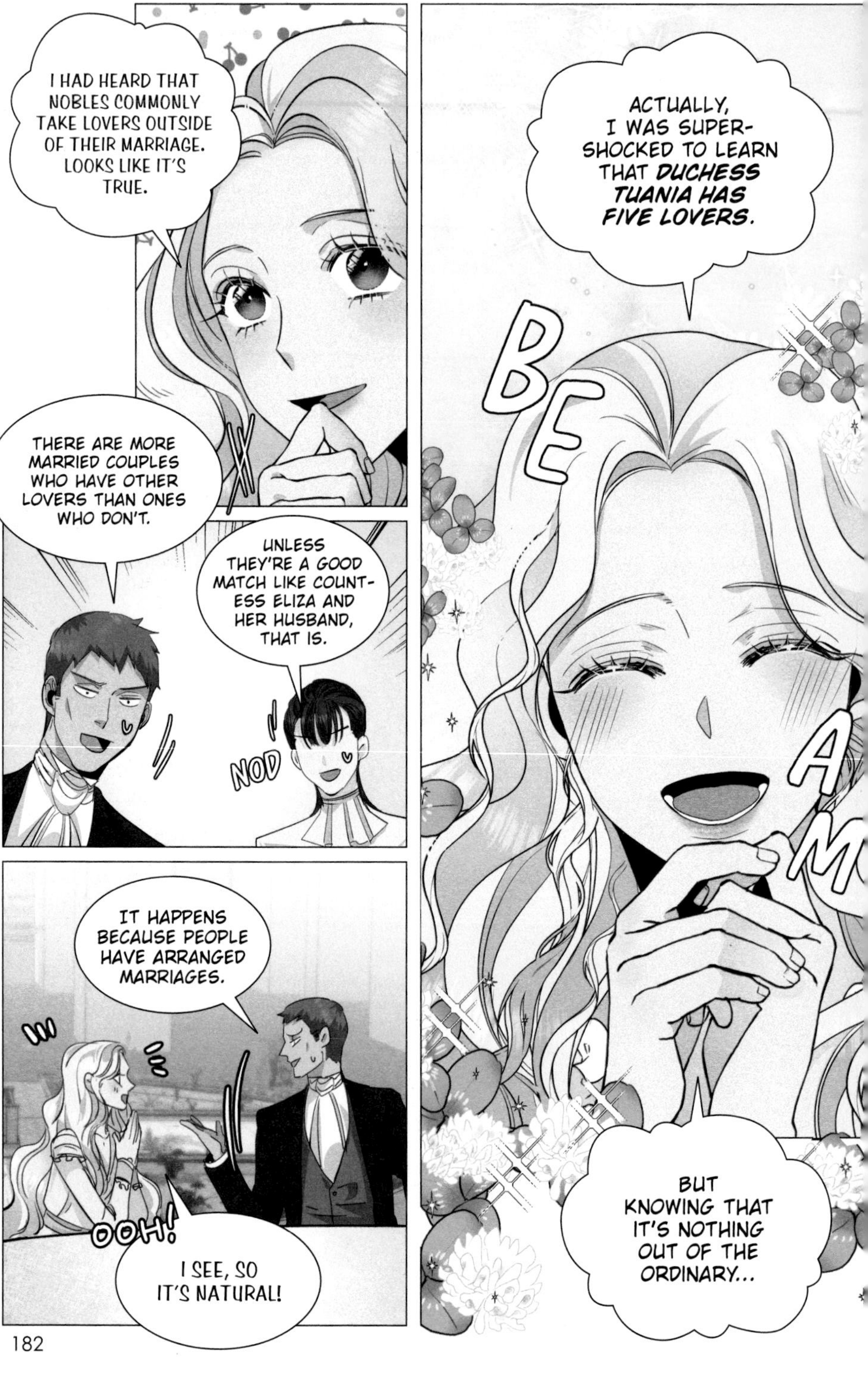
I HAD HEARD THAT NOBLES COMMONLY TAKE LOVERS OUTSIDE OF THEIR MARRIAGE. LOOKS LIKE IT'S TRUE.
THERE ARE MORE MARRIED COUPLES WHO HAVE OTHER LOVERS THAN ONES WHO DON'T.
UNLESS THEY'RE A GOOD MATCH LIKE COUNTESS ELIZA AND HER HUSBAND, THAT IS.
NOD
IT HAPPENS BECAUSE PEOPLE HAVE ARRANGED MARRIAGES.
OOH!
I SEE, SO IT'S NATURAL!
ACTUALLY, I WAS SUPER-SHOCKED TO LEARN THAT ***DUCHESS TUANIA HAS FIVE LOVERS.***
BE
AM
BUT KNOWING THAT IT'S NOTHING OUT OF THE ORDINARY...

...I FEEL LIKE I'VE STEPPED INTO A WHOLE NEW WORLD—

CLINK

......

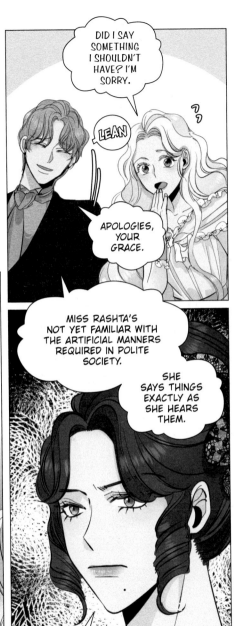

DID I SAY SOMETHING I SHOULDN'T HAVE? I'M SORRY.

LEAN

APOLOGIES, YOUR GRACE.

MISS RASHTA'S NOT YET FAMILIAR WITH THE ARTIFICIAL MANNERS REQUIRED IN POLITE SOCIETY.

SHE SAYS THINGS EXACTLY AS SHE HEARS THEM.

......!

183

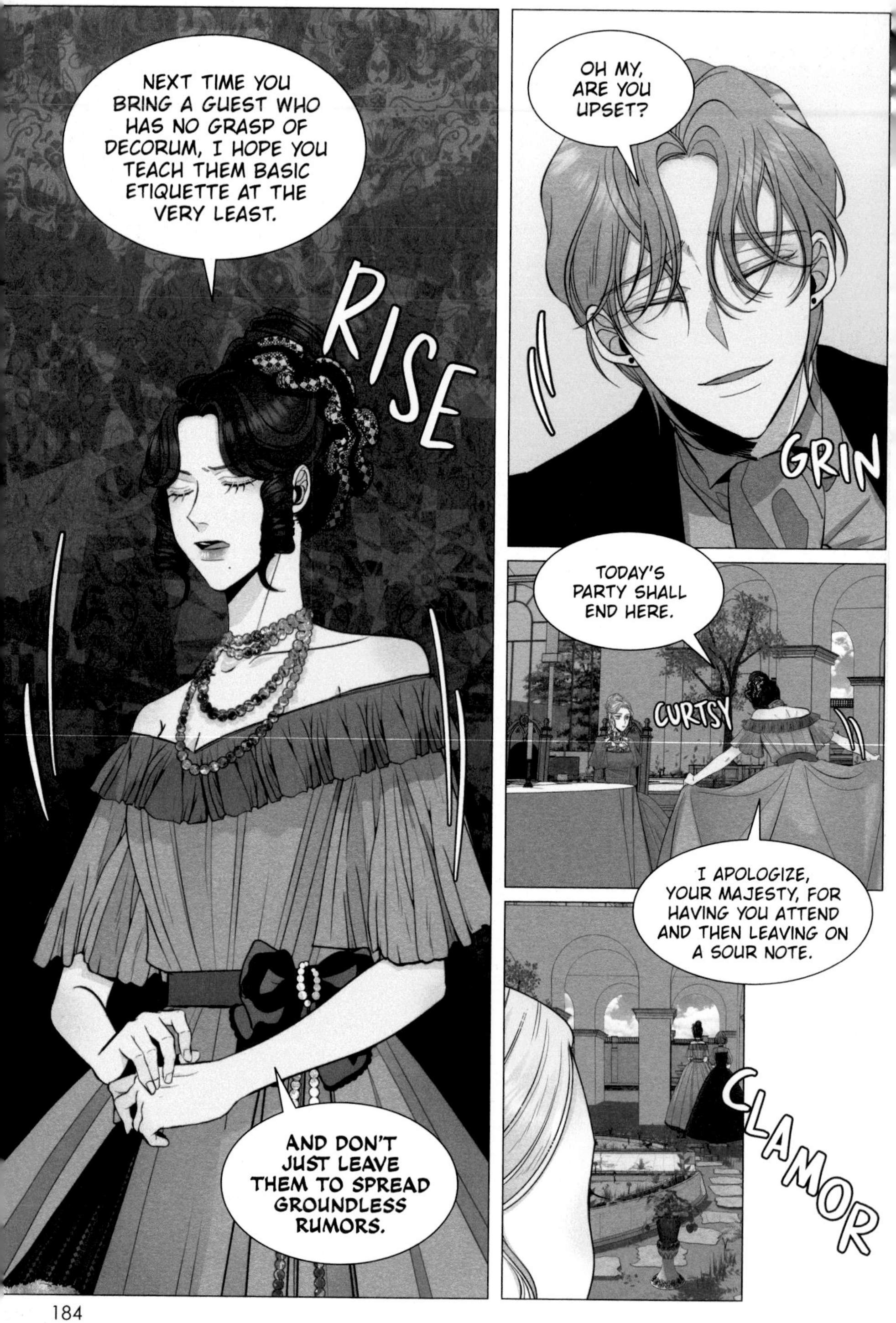
NEXT TIME YOU BRING A GUEST WHO HAS NO GRASP OF DECORUM, I HOPE YOU TEACH THEM BASIC ETIQUETTE AT THE VERY LEAST.
RISE
AND DON'T JUST LEAVE THEM TO SPREAD GROUNDLESS RUMORS.
OH MY, ARE YOU UPSET?
GRIN
TODAY'S PARTY SHALL END HERE.
CURTSY
I APOLOGIZE, YOUR MAJESTY, FOR HAVING YOU ATTEND AND THEN LEAVING ON A SOUR NOTE.
CLAMOR

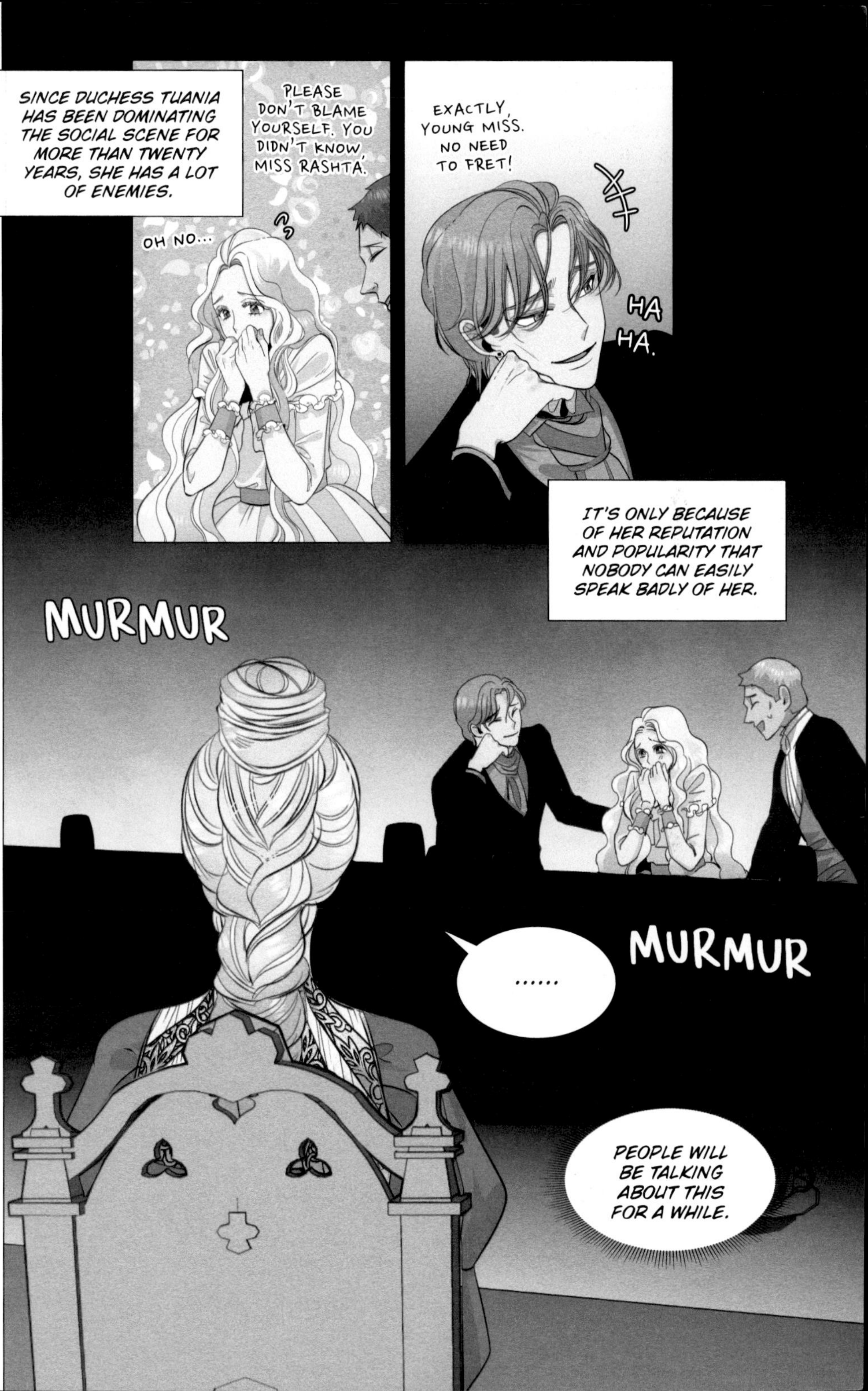
SINCE DUCHESS TUANIA HAS BEEN DOMINATING THE SOCIAL SCENE FOR MORE THAN TWENTY YEARS, SHE HAS A LOT OF ENEMIES.
PLEASE DON'T BLAME YOURSELF. YOU DIDN'T KNOW MISS RASHTA.
OH NO...
EXACTLY, YOUNG MISS. NO NEED TO FRET!
HA HA.
IT'S ONLY BECAUSE OF HER REPUTATION AND POPULARITY THAT NOBODY CAN EASILY SPEAK BADLY OF HER.
MURMUR
MURMUR
......
PEOPLE WILL BE TALKING ABOUT THIS FOR A WHILE.

The Remarried Empress

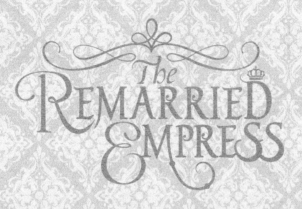

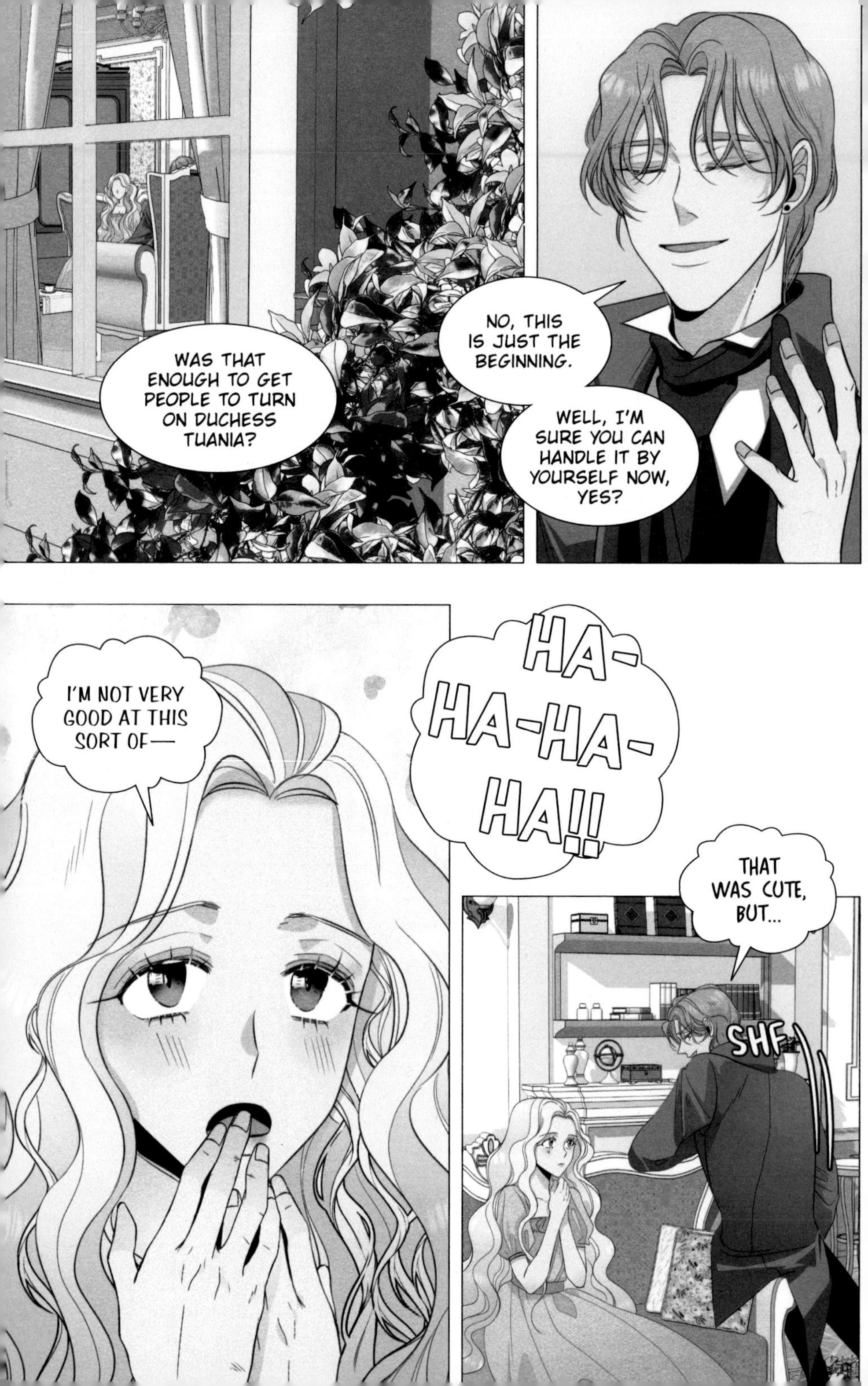
WAS THAT ENOUGH TO GET PEOPLE TO TURN ON DUCHESS TUANIA?
NO, THIS IS JUST THE BEGINNING.
WELL, I'M SURE YOU CAN HANDLE IT BY YOURSELF NOW, YES?
I'M NOT VERY GOOD AT THIS SORT OF—
HA-HA-HA-HA-HA!!
THAT WAS CUTE, BUT...
SHF

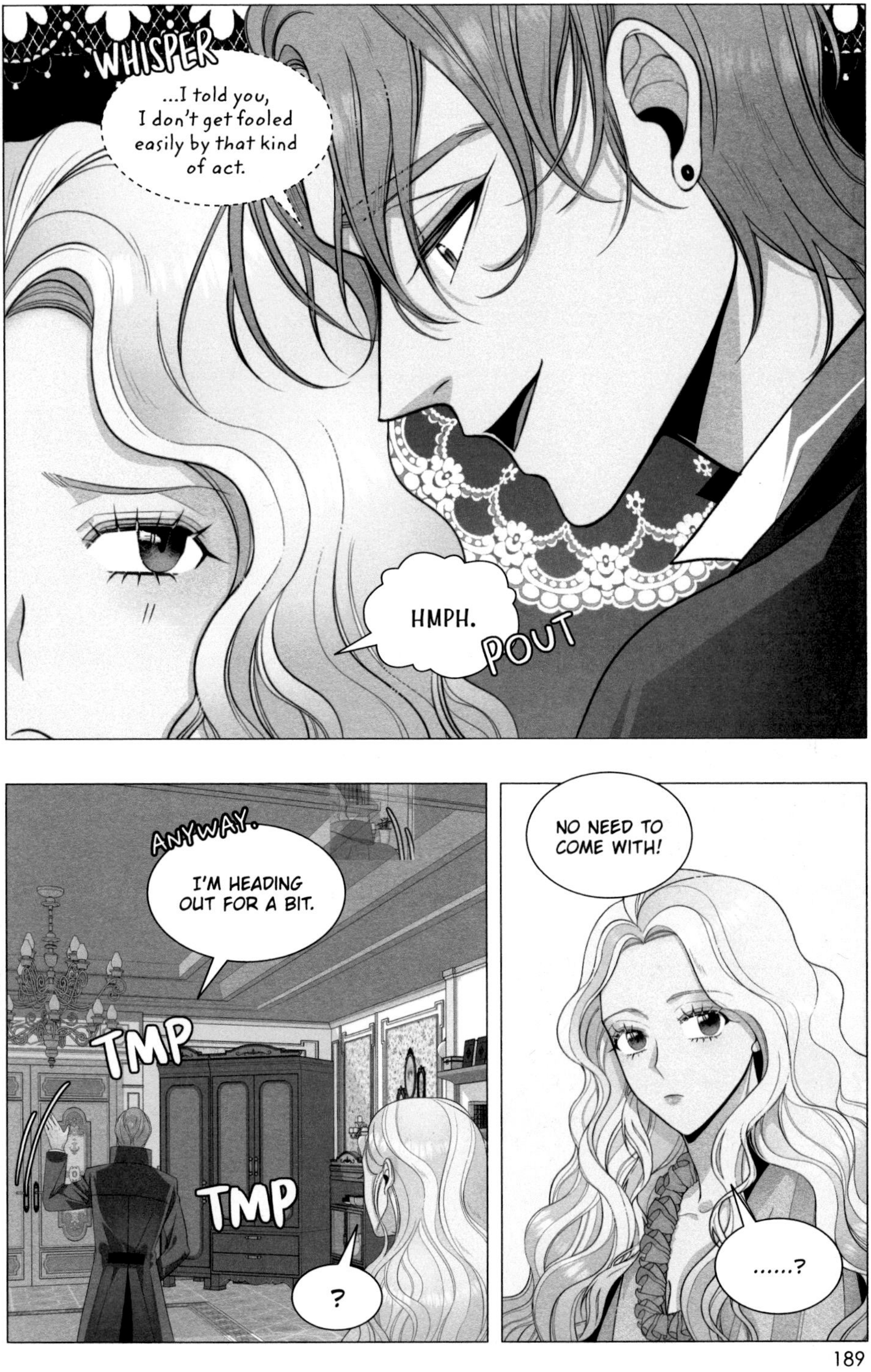
WHISPER
...I told you, I don't get fooled easily by that kind of act.
HMPH.
POUT
ANYWAY.
I'M HEADING OUT FOR A BIT.
TMP
TMP
?
NO NEED TO COME WITH!
......?

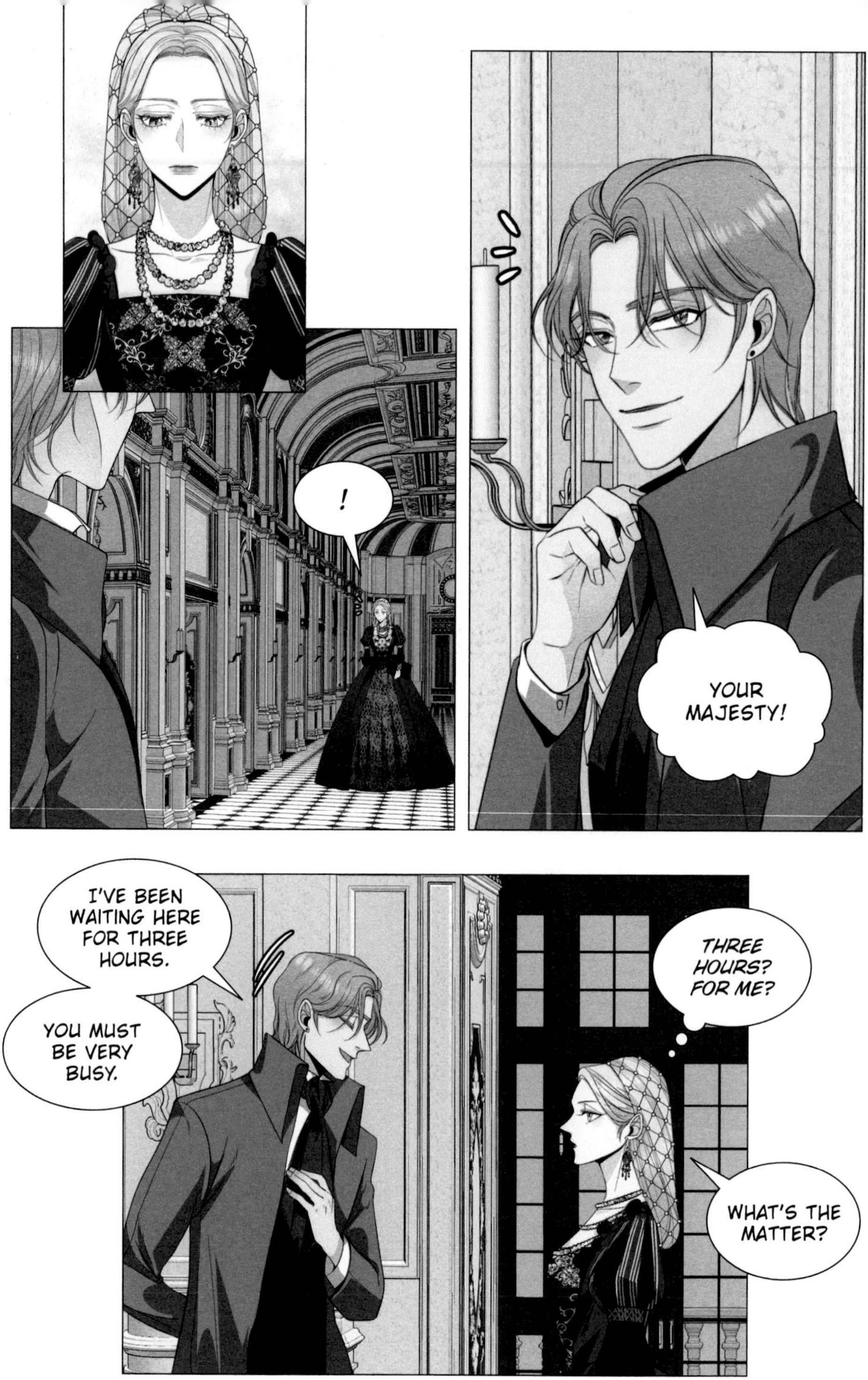
!
YOUR MAJESTY!
I'VE BEEN WAITING HERE FOR THREE HOURS.
YOU MUST BE VERY BUSY.
THREE HOURS? FOR ME?
WHAT'S THE MATTER?

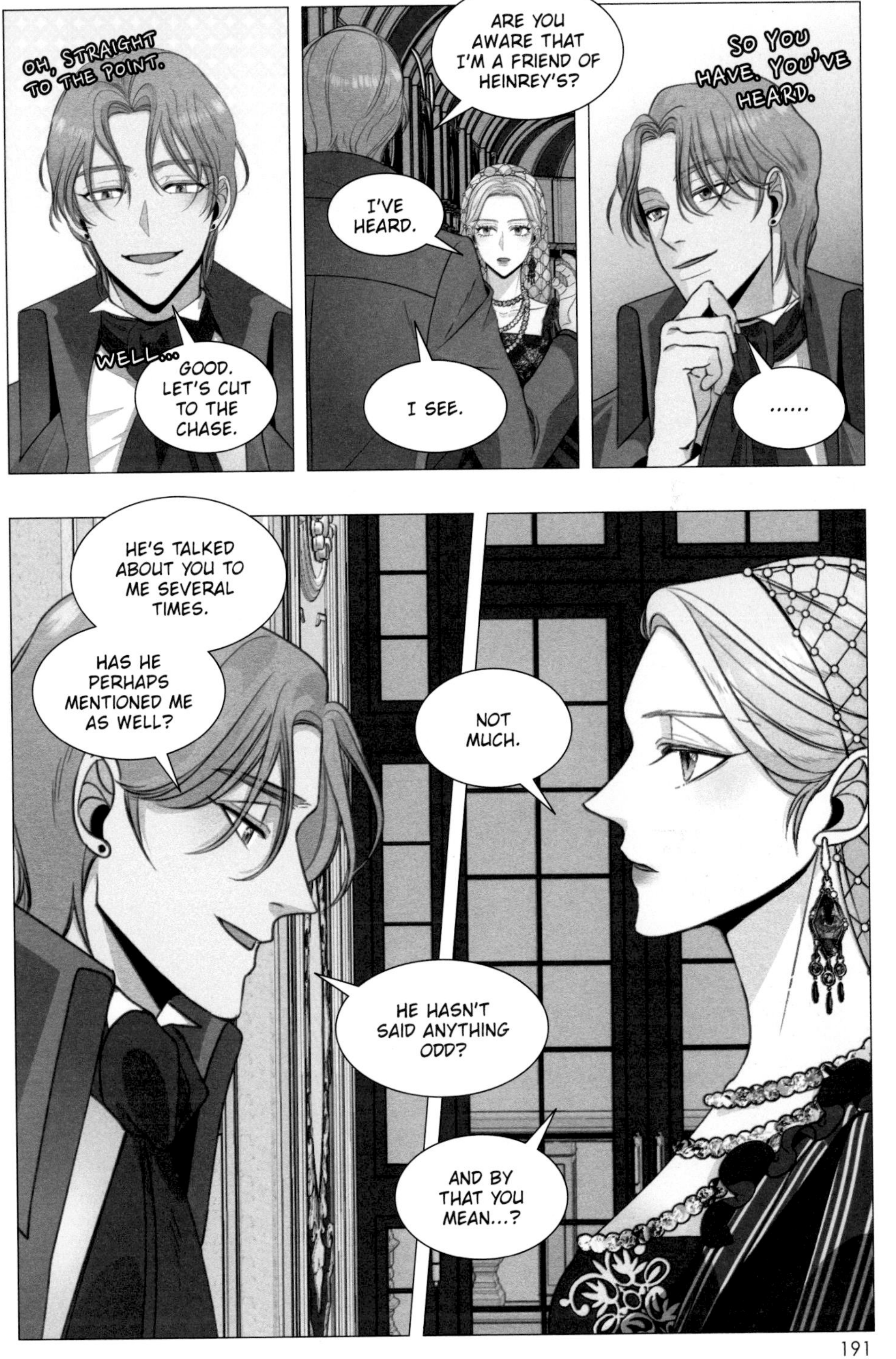
OH, STRAIGHT TO THE POINT.
WELL...
GOOD. LET'S CUT TO THE CHASE.
ARE YOU AWARE THAT I'M A FRIEND OF HEINREY'S?
I'VE HEARD.
I SEE.
SO YOU HAVE. YOU'VE HEARD.
......
HE'S TALKED ABOUT YOU TO ME SEVERAL TIMES.
HAS HE PERHAPS MENTIONED ME AS WELL?
NOT MUCH.
HE HASN'T SAID ANYTHING ODD?
AND BY THAT YOU MEAN...?

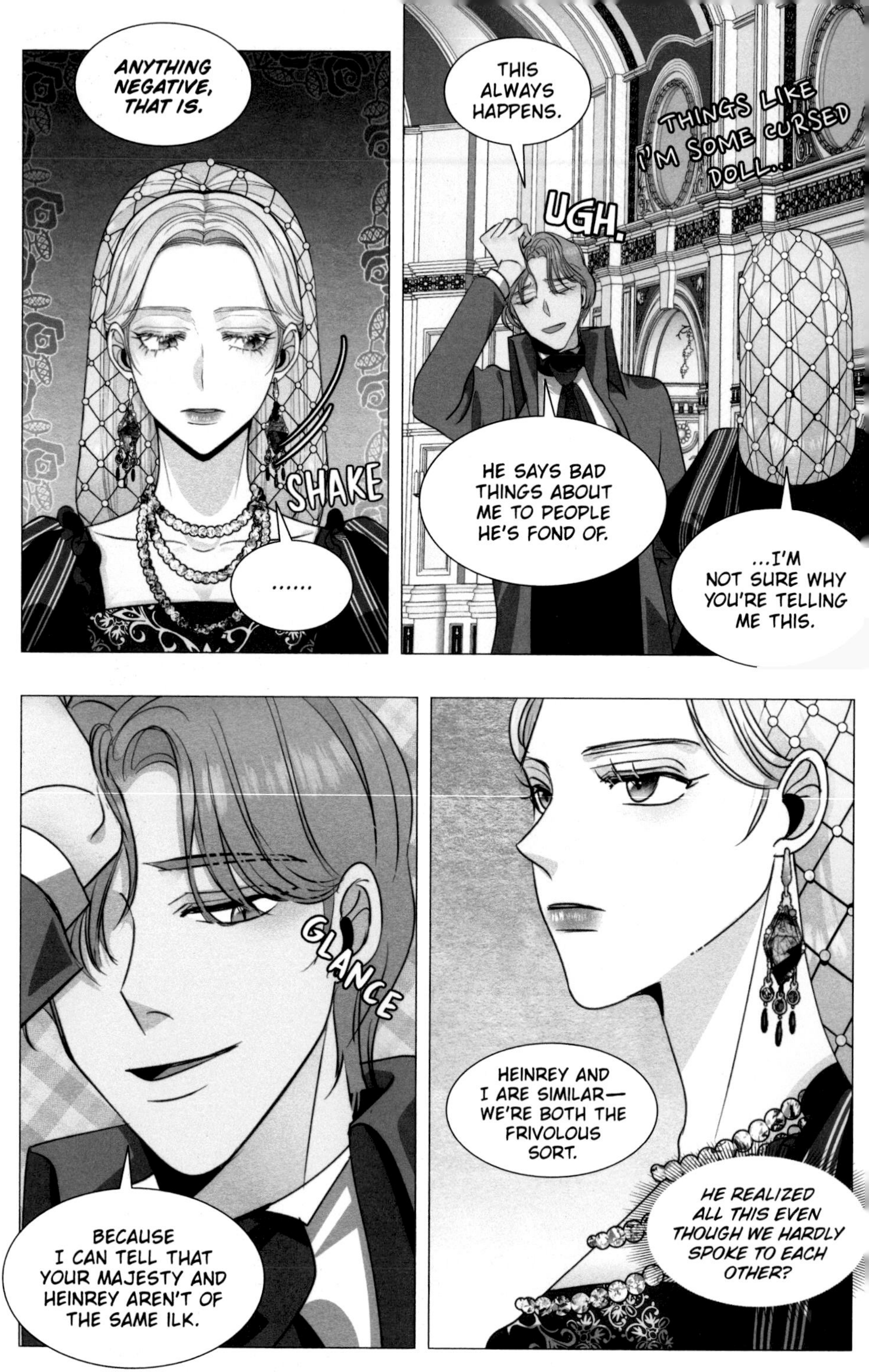
ANYTHING NEGATIVE, THAT IS.
SHAKE
......
THIS ALWAYS HAPPENS.
THINGS LIKE I'M SOME CURSED DOLL...
UGH.
HE SAYS BAD THINGS ABOUT ME TO PEOPLE HE'S FOND OF.
...I'M NOT SURE WHY YOU'RE TELLING ME THIS.
GLANCE
BECAUSE I CAN TELL THAT YOUR MAJESTY AND HEINREY AREN'T OF THE SAME ILK.
HEINREY AND I ARE SIMILAR— WE'RE BOTH THE FRIVOLOUS SORT.
HE REALIZED ALL THIS EVEN THOUGH WE HARDLY SPOKE TO EACH OTHER?

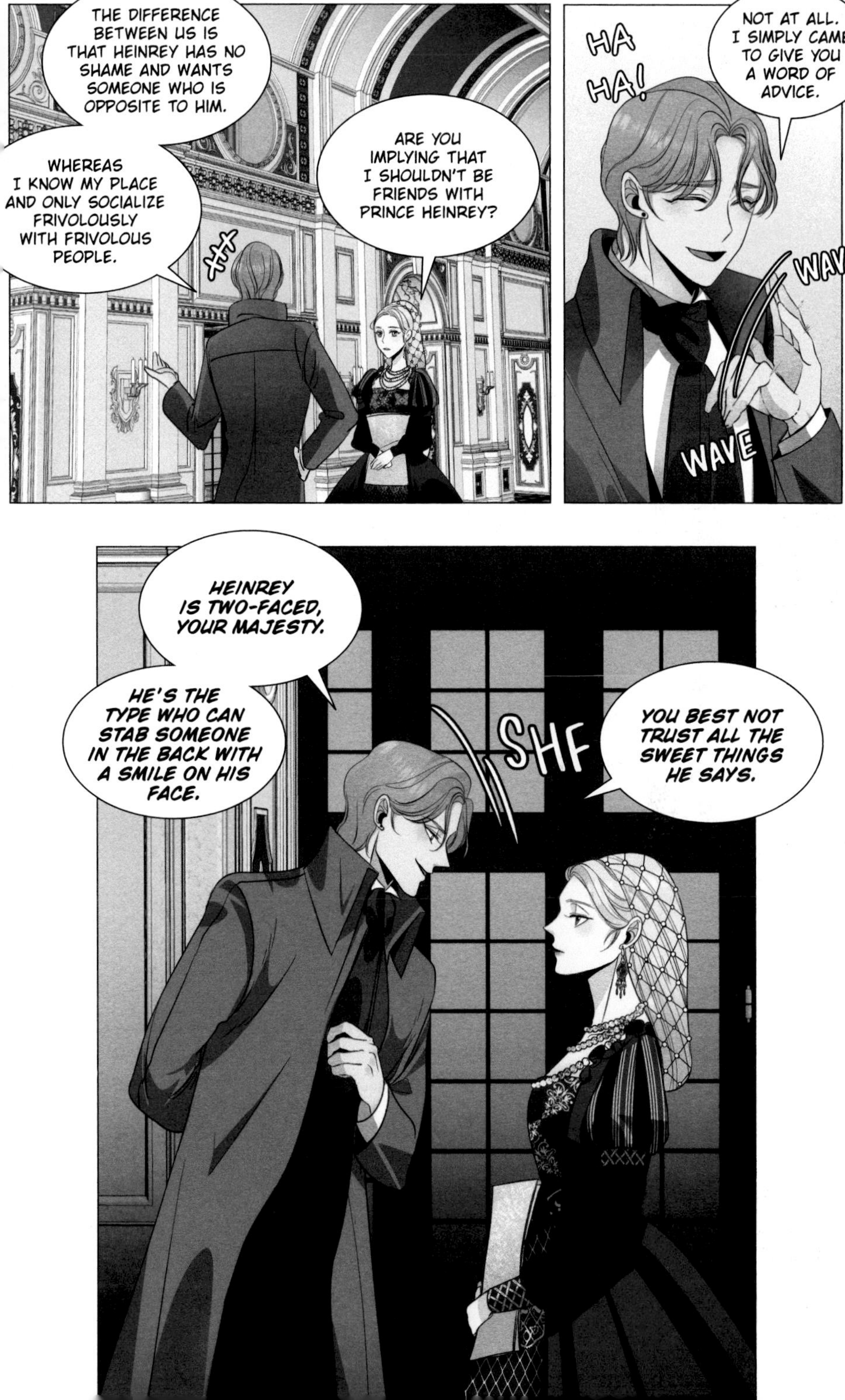
THE DIFFERENCE BETWEEN US IS THAT HEINREY HAS NO SHAME AND WANTS SOMEONE WHO IS OPPOSITE TO HIM.
WHEREAS I KNOW MY PLACE AND ONLY SOCIALIZE FRIVOLOUSLY WITH FRIVOLOUS PEOPLE.
ARE YOU IMPLYING THAT I SHOULDN'T BE FRIENDS WITH PRINCE HEINREY?
HA HA!
NOT AT ALL. I SIMPLY CAME TO GIVE YOU A WORD OF ADVICE.
WAVE
WAVE
HEINREY IS TWO-FACED, YOUR MAJESTY.
HE'S THE TYPE WHO CAN STAB SOMEONE IN THE BACK WITH A SMILE ON HIS FACE.
SHF
YOU BEST NOT TRUST ALL THE SWEET THINGS HE SAYS.

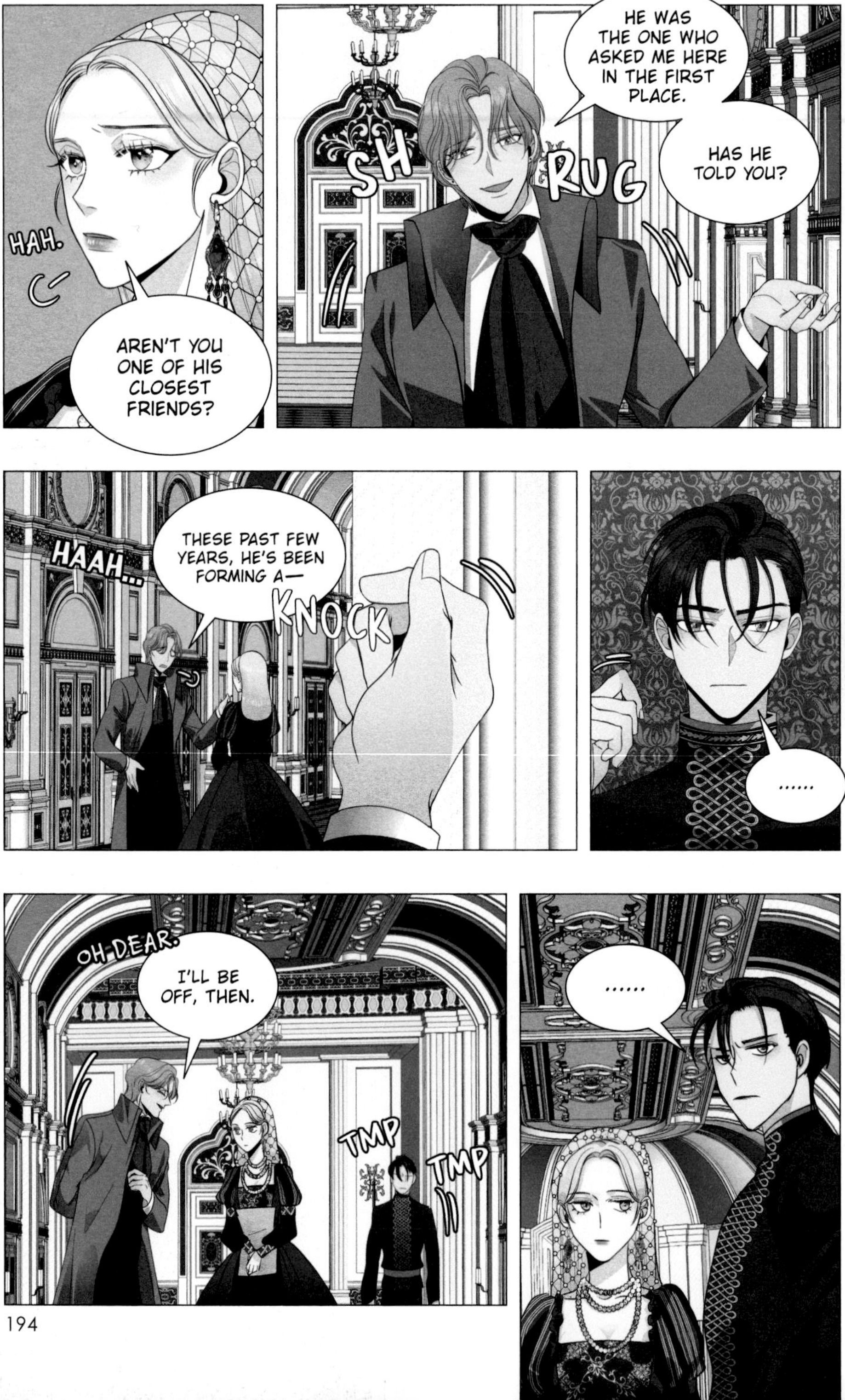
HAH.
AREN'T YOU ONE OF HIS CLOSEST FRIENDS?
HE WAS THE ONE WHO ASKED ME HERE IN THE FIRST PLACE.
SHRUG
HAS HE TOLD YOU?
HAAAH...
THESE PAST FEW YEARS, HE'S BEEN FORMING A—
KNOCK
......
OH DEAR.
I'LL BE OFF, THEN.
TMP
TMP
......

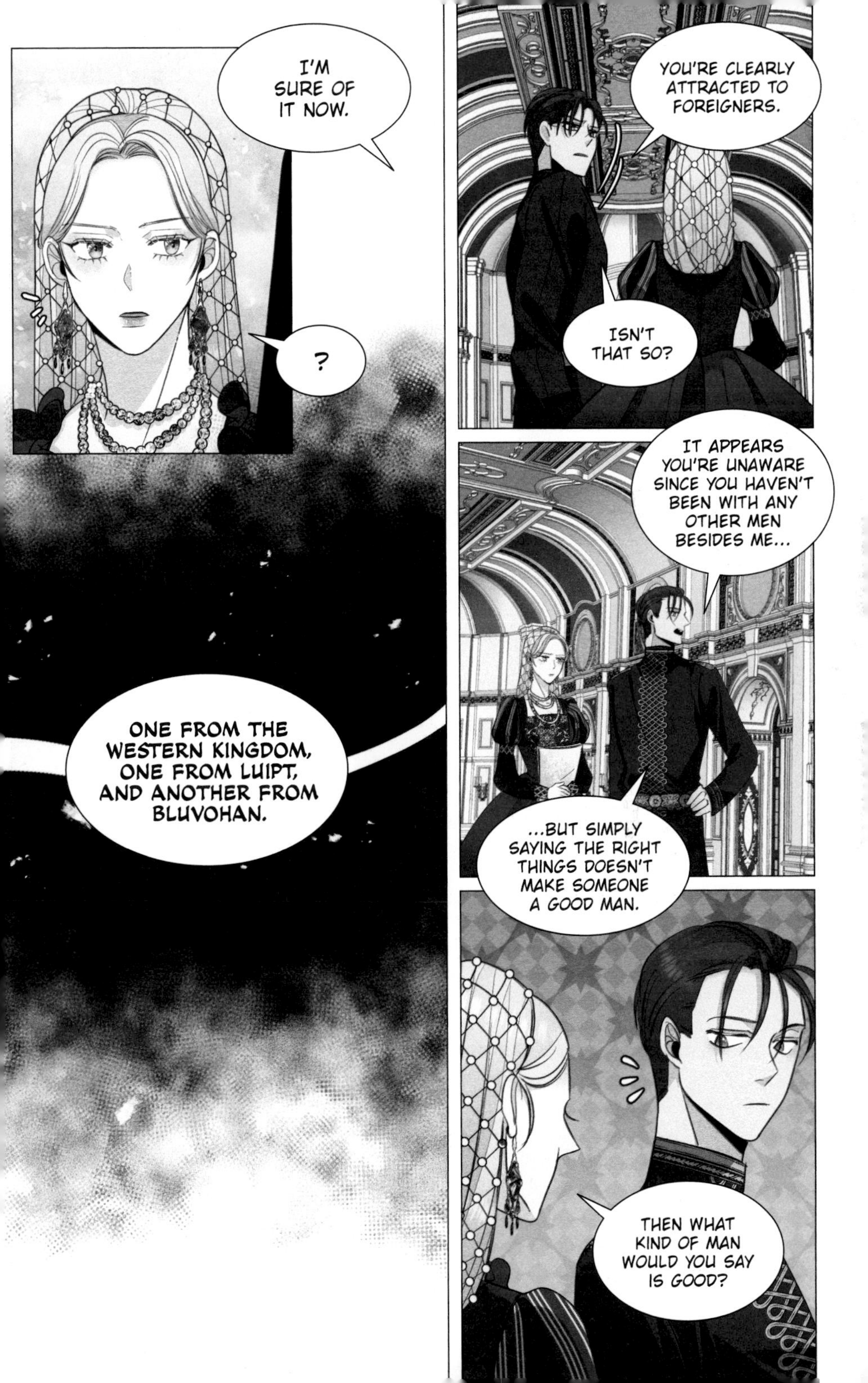
I'M SURE OF IT NOW.
?
ONE FROM THE WESTERN KINGDOM, ONE FROM LUIPT, AND ANOTHER FROM BLUVOHAN.
YOU'RE CLEARLY ATTRACTED TO FOREIGNERS.
ISN'T THAT SO?
IT APPEARS YOU'RE UNAWARE SINCE YOU HAVEN'T BEEN WITH ANY OTHER MEN BESIDES ME...
...BUT SIMPLY SAYING THE RIGHT THINGS DOESN'T MAKE SOMEONE A GOOD MAN.
THEN WHAT KIND OF MAN WOULD YOU SAY IS GOOD?

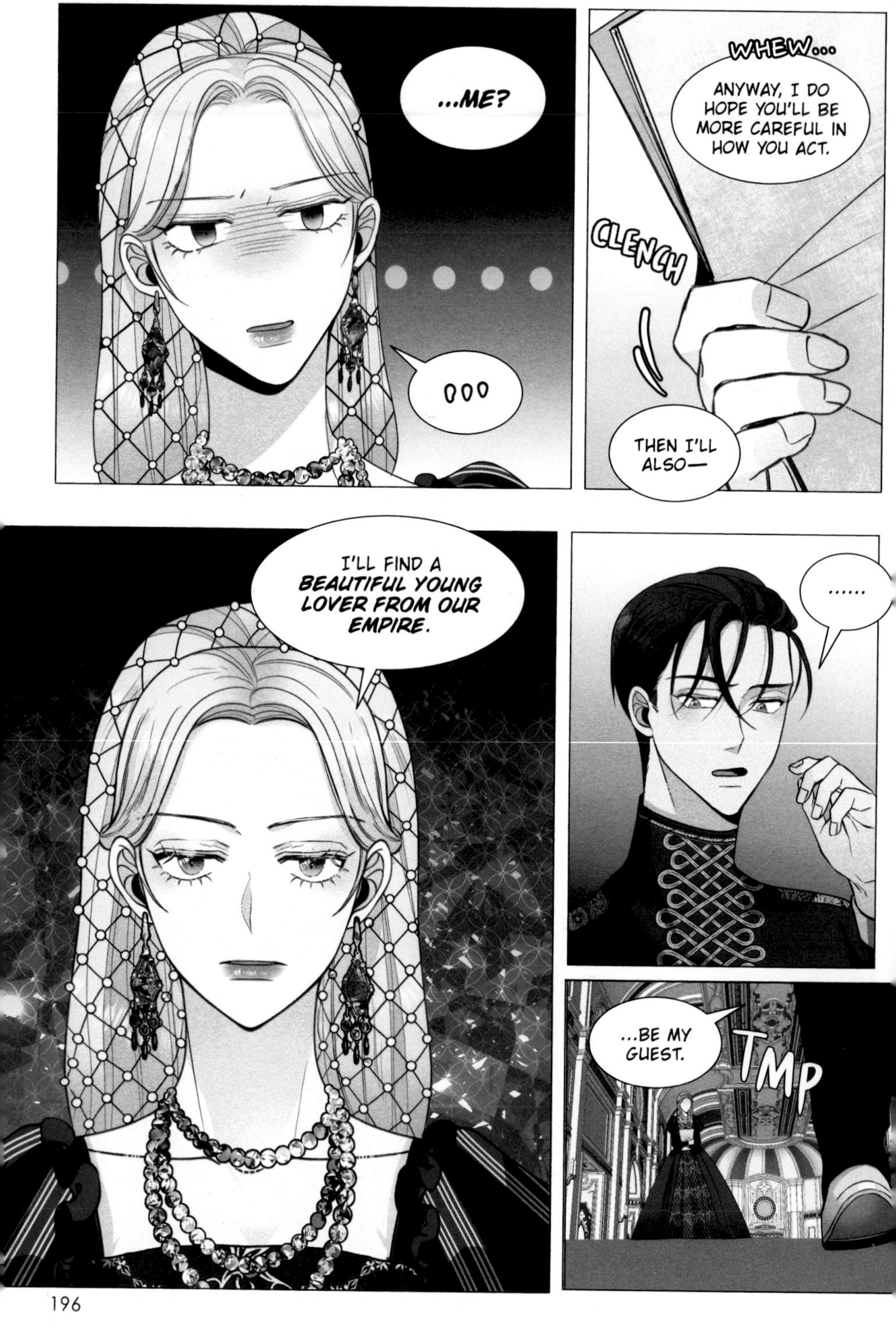
...ME?
OOO
WHEW...
ANYWAY, I DO HOPE YOU'LL BE MORE CAREFUL IN HOW YOU ACT.
CLENCH
THEN I'LL ALSO—
I'LL FIND A BEAUTIFUL YOUNG LOVER FROM OUR EMPIRE.
......
...BE MY GUEST.
TMP

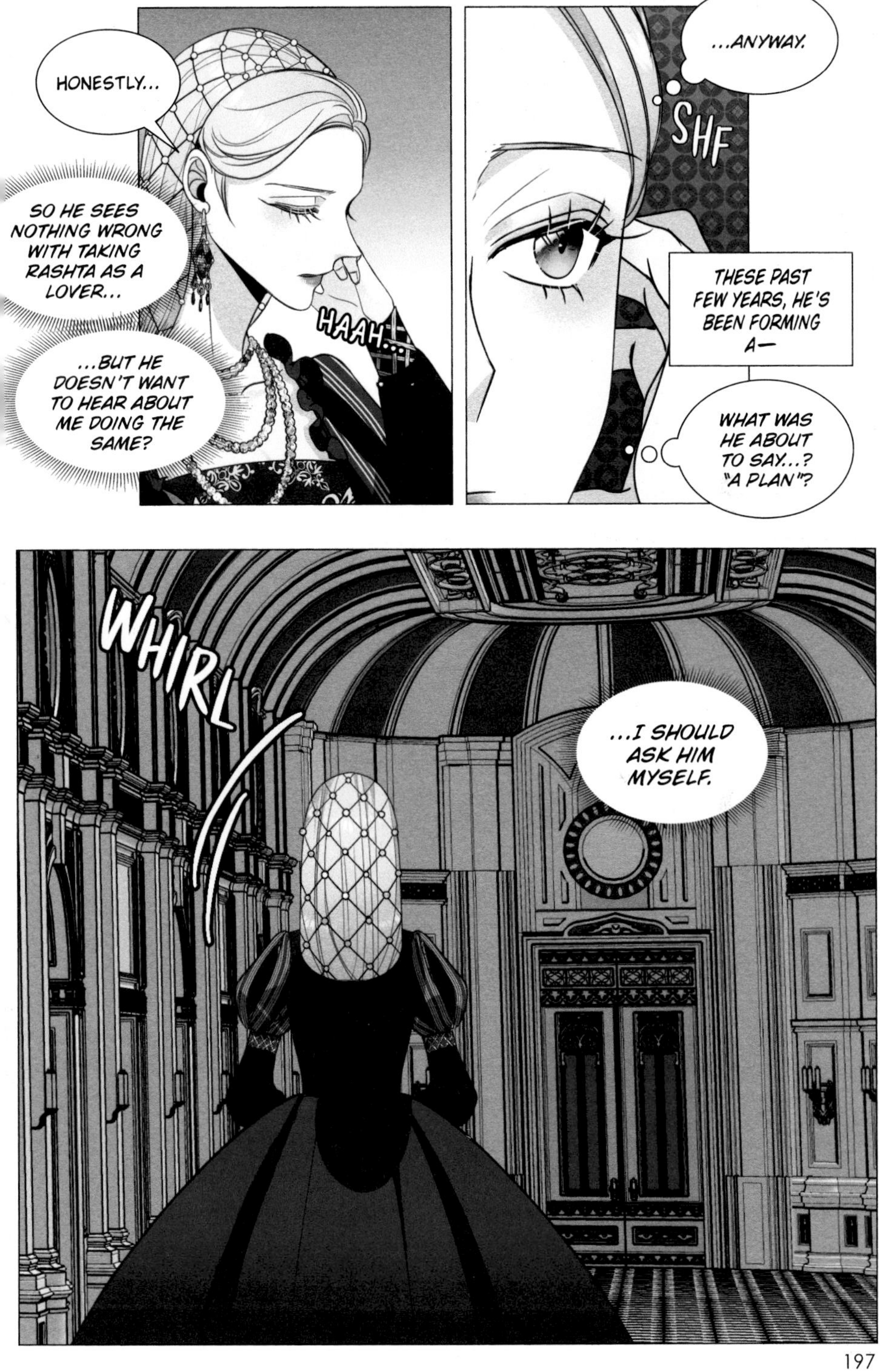
HONESTLY...
SO HE SEES NOTHING WRONG WITH TAKING RASHTA AS A LOVER...
...BUT HE DOESN'T WANT TO HEAR ABOUT ME DOING THE SAME?
HAAAH...
...ANYWAY.
SHF
THESE PAST FEW YEARS, HE'S BEEN FORMING A—
WHAT WAS HE ABOUT TO SAY...? "A PLAN"?
WHIRL
...I SHOULD ASK HIM MYSELF.

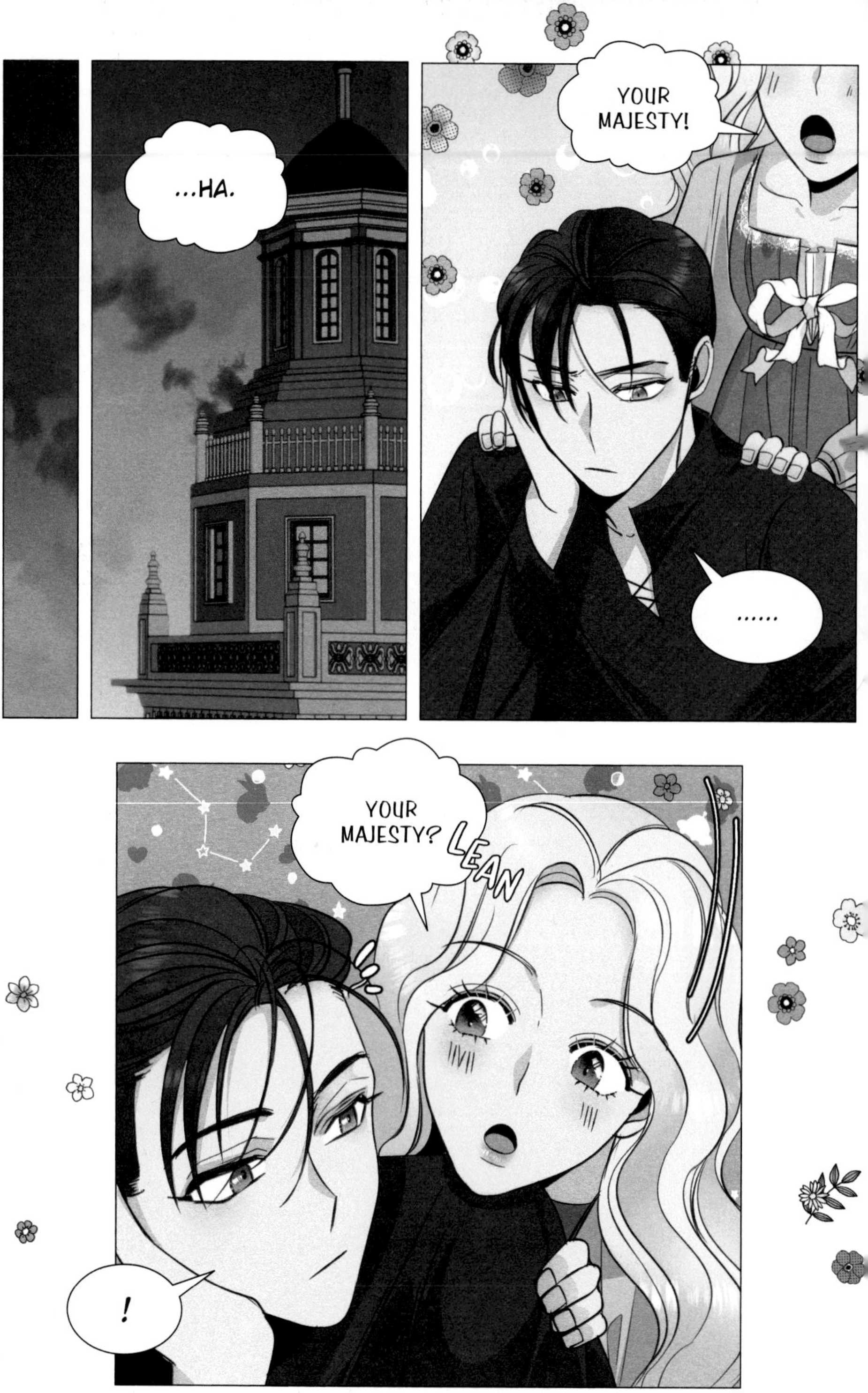
...HA.
YOUR MAJESTY!
......
YOUR MAJESTY?
LEAN
!

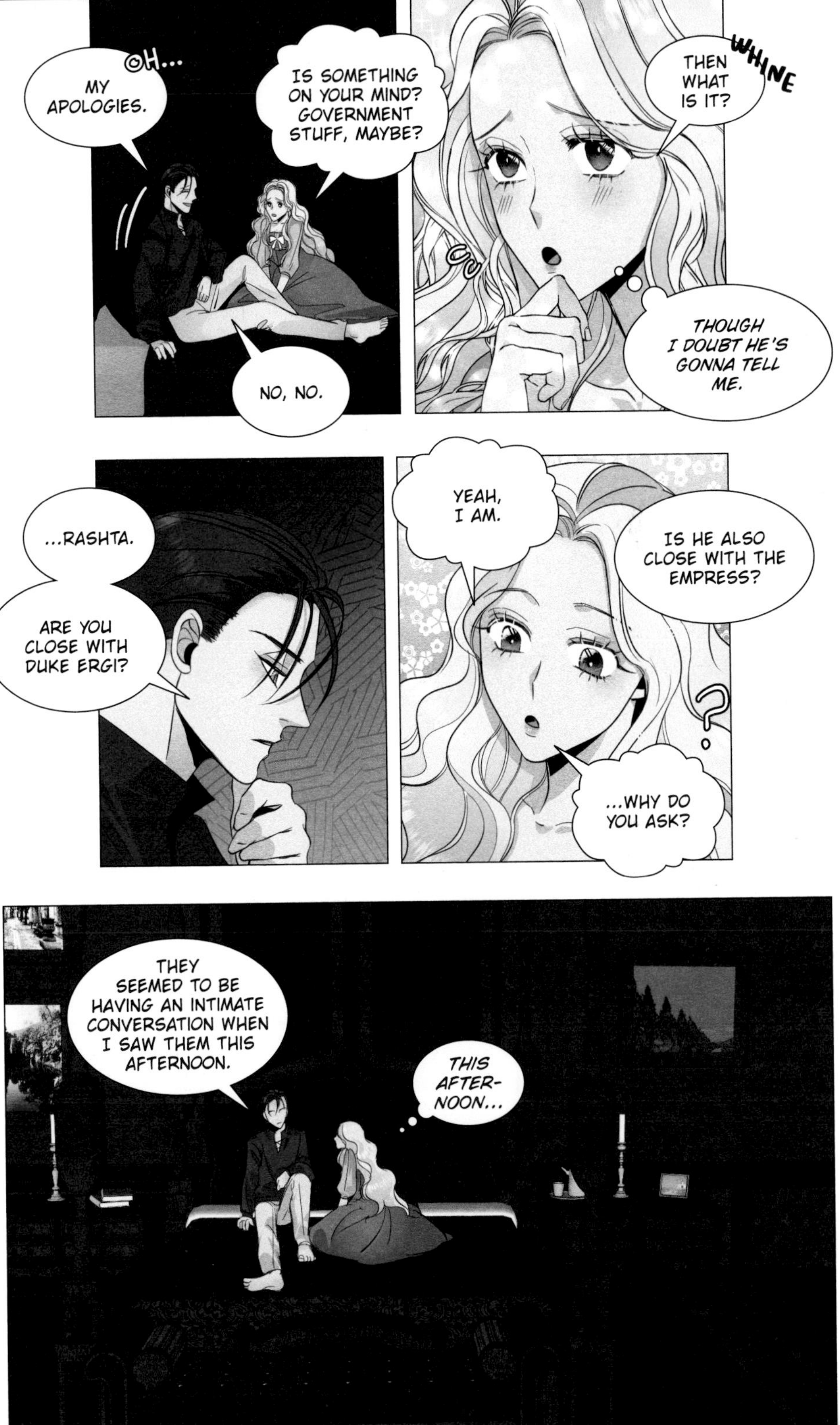
OH...
MY APOLOGIES.
IS SOMETHING ON YOUR MIND? GOVERNMENT STUFF, MAYBE?
NO, NO.
THEN WHAT IS IT?
WHINE
THOUGH I DOUBT HE'S GONNA TELL ME.
...RASHTA.
ARE YOU CLOSE WITH DUKE ERGI?
YEAH, I AM.
IS HE ALSO CLOSE WITH THE EMPRESS?
...WHY DO YOU ASK?
THEY SEEMED TO BE HAVING AN INTIMATE CONVERSATION WHEN I SAW THEM THIS AFTERNOON.
THIS AFTER-NOON...

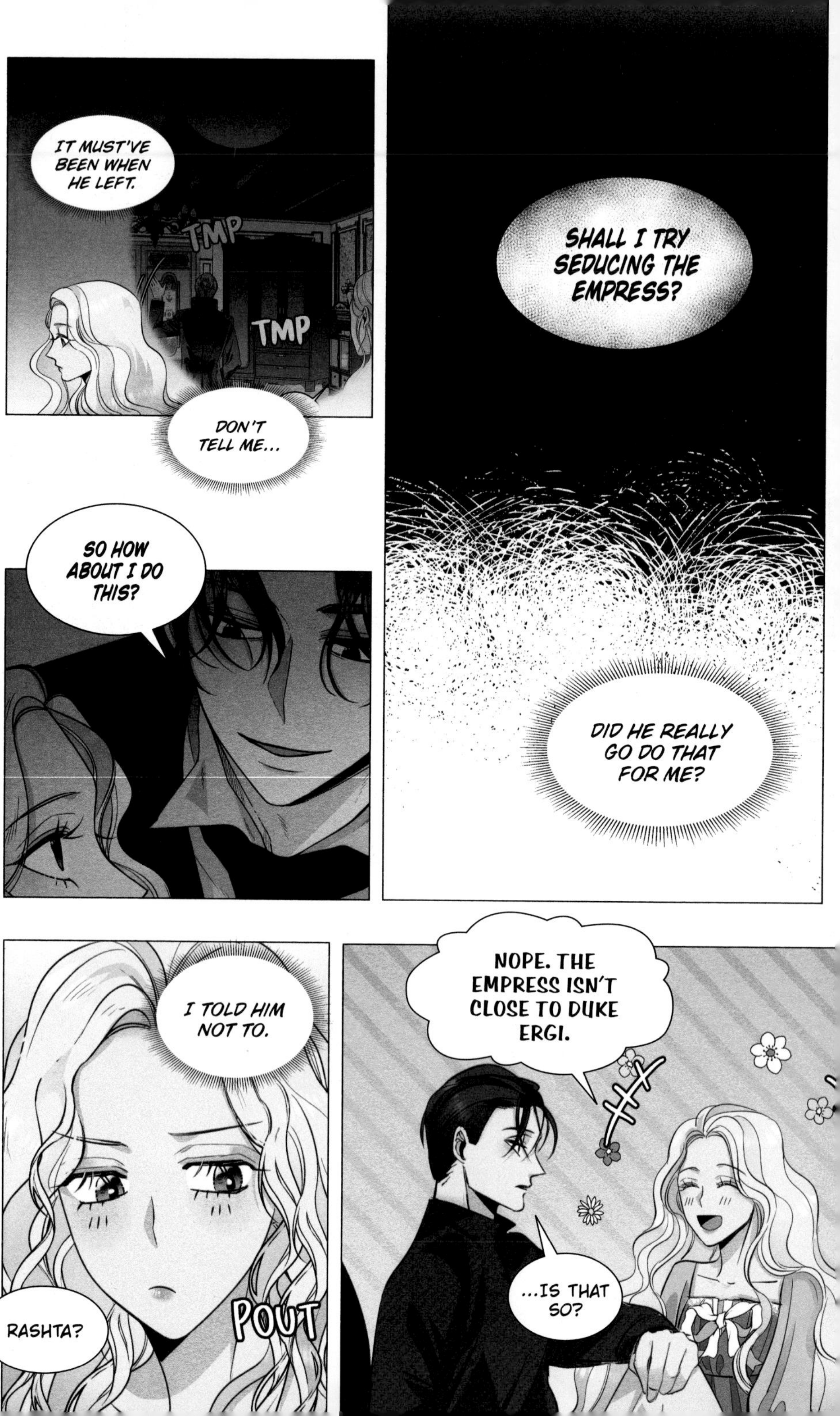
IT MUST'VE BEEN WHEN HE LEFT.
TMP
TMP
DON'T TELL ME...
SO HOW ABOUT I DO THIS?
SHALL I TRY SEDUCING THE EMPRESS?
DID HE REALLY GO DO THAT FOR ME?
I TOLD HIM NOT TO.
POUT
RASHTA?
NOPE. THE EMPRESS ISN'T CLOSE TO DUKE ERGI.
...IS THAT SO?

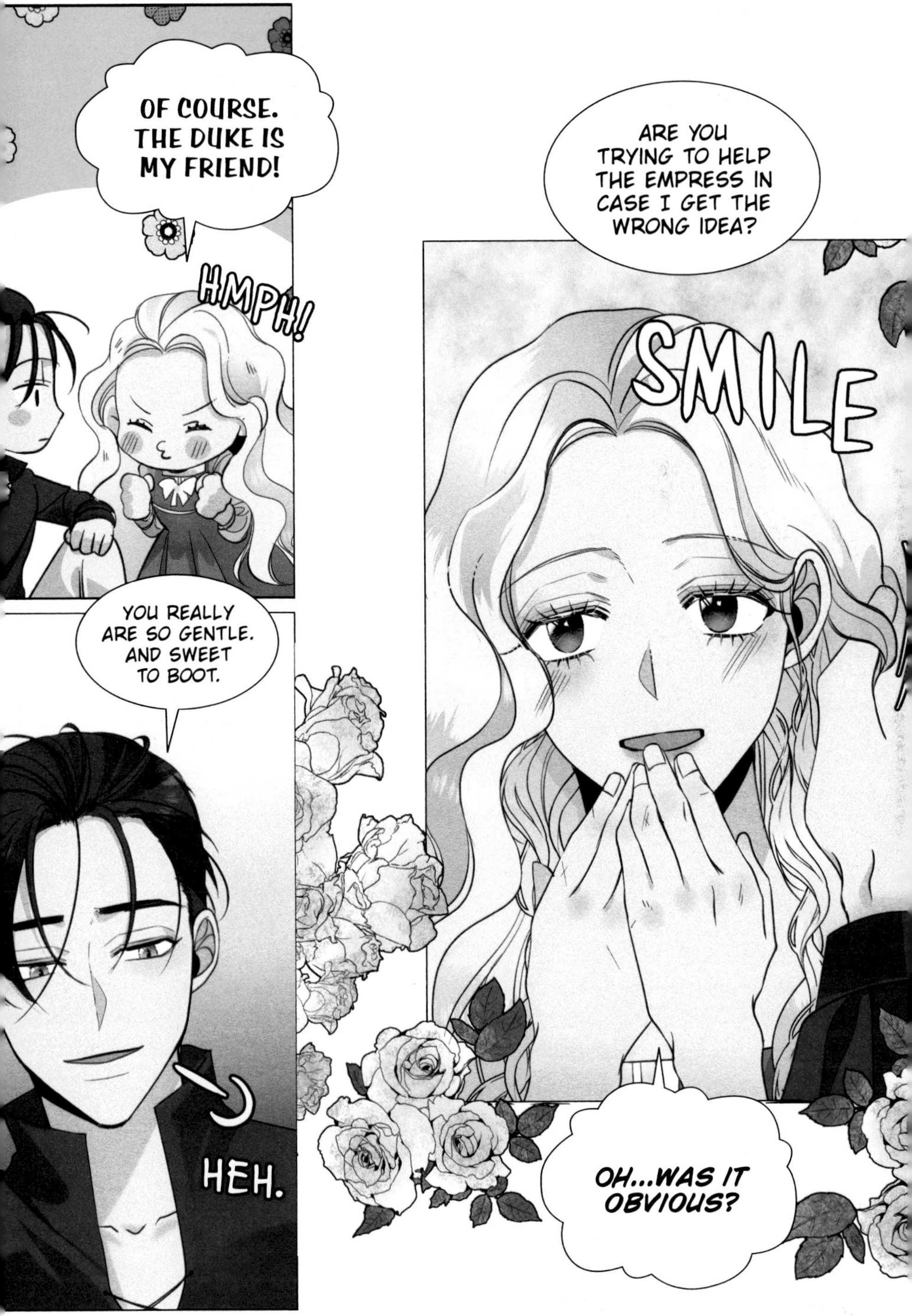
OF COURSE. THE DUKE IS MY FRIEND!
HMPH!
YOU REALLY ARE SO GENTLE. AND SWEET TO BOOT.
HEH.
ARE YOU TRYING TO HELP THE EMPRESS IN CASE I GET THE WRONG IDEA?
SMILE
OH...WAS IT OBVIOUS?

BY THE WAY, I SEE YOU'RE NOT WEARING THE RING I GAVE YOU THESE DAYS.

HIDE

THE... RING?

THE ONE WITH THE RED JEWEL EMBEDDED IN IT. DON'T YOU REMEMBER?

HUH? OH, YES.

THAT MEANS HE'S TALKING ABOUT...

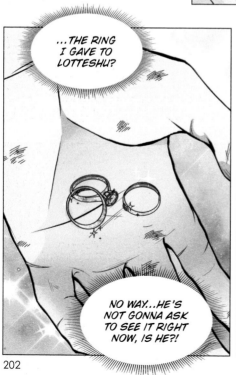

...THE RING I GAVE TO LOTTESHU?

NO WAY...HE'S NOT GONNA ASK TO SEE IT RIGHT NOW, IS HE?!

ACTUALLY, THAT GEM HAS A SPELL ON IT.

YOUR SCARS WILL DISAPPEAR IF YOU WEAR IT CONSISTENTLY.

WHAT...?!

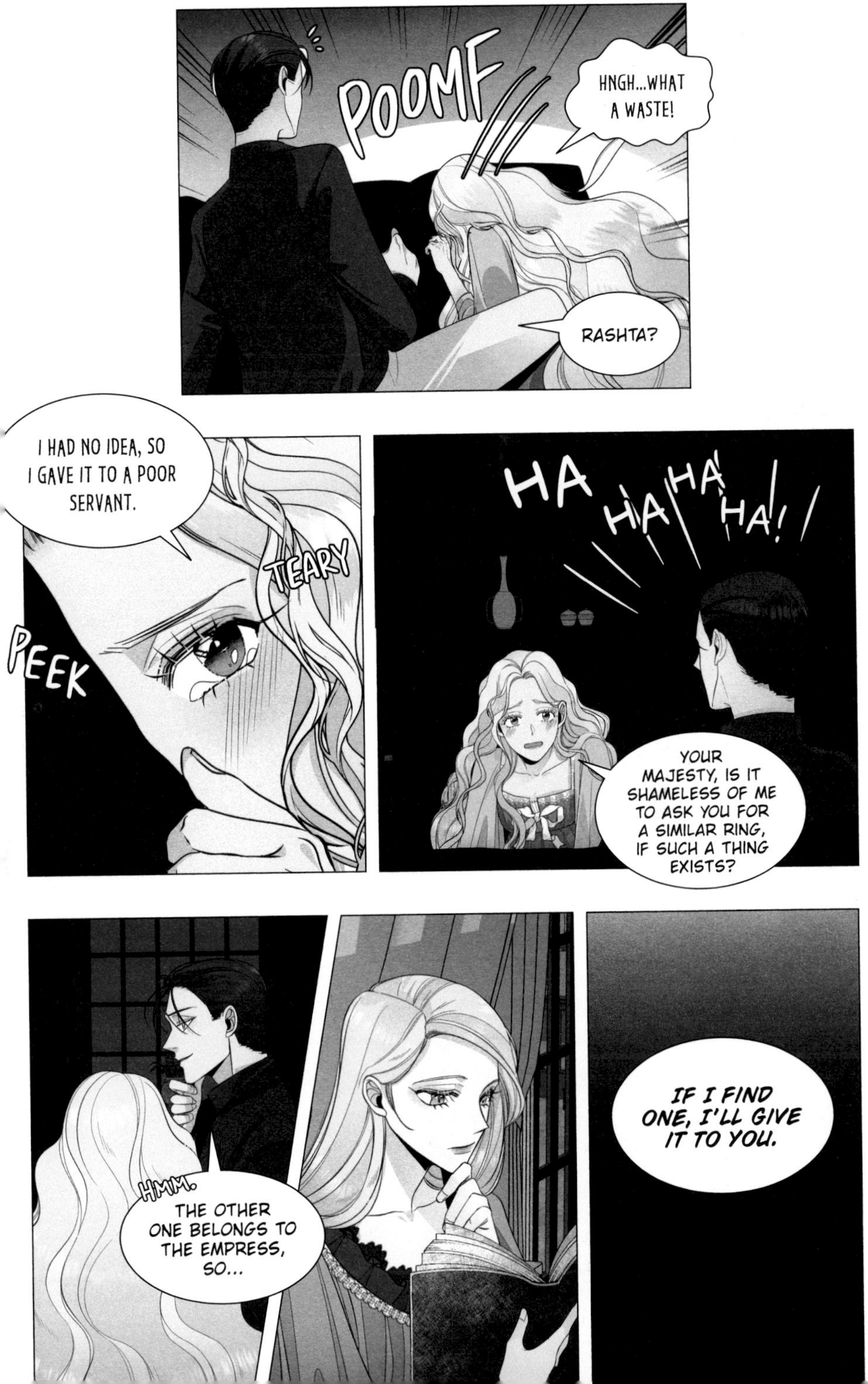
POOMF
HNGH...WHAT A WASTE!
RASHTA?
I HAD NO IDEA, SO I GAVE IT TO A POOR SERVANT.
TEARY
PEEK
HA HA HA HA HA!
YOUR MAJESTY, IS IT SHAMELESS OF ME TO ASK YOU FOR A SIMILAR RING, IF SUCH A THING EXISTS?
HMM.
THE OTHER ONE BELONGS TO THE EMPRESS, SO...
IF I FIND ONE, I'LL GIVE IT TO YOU.

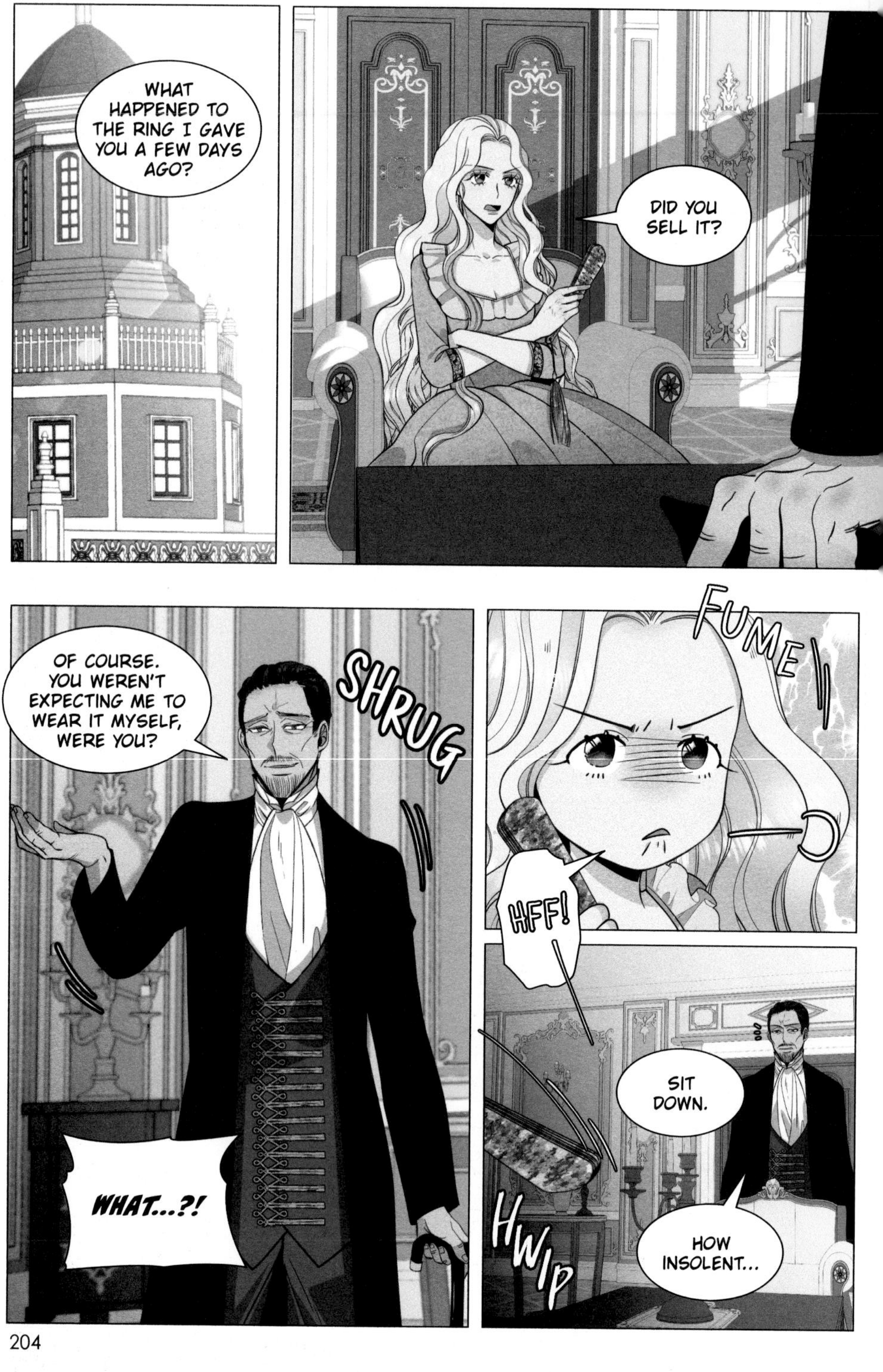
WHAT HAPPENED TO THE RING I GAVE YOU A FEW DAYS AGO?
DID YOU SELL IT?
OF COURSE. YOU WEREN'T EXPECTING ME TO WEAR IT MYSELF, WERE YOU?
SHRUG
WHAT...?!
FUME
HFF!
SIT DOWN.
HOW INSOLENT...
HWIP

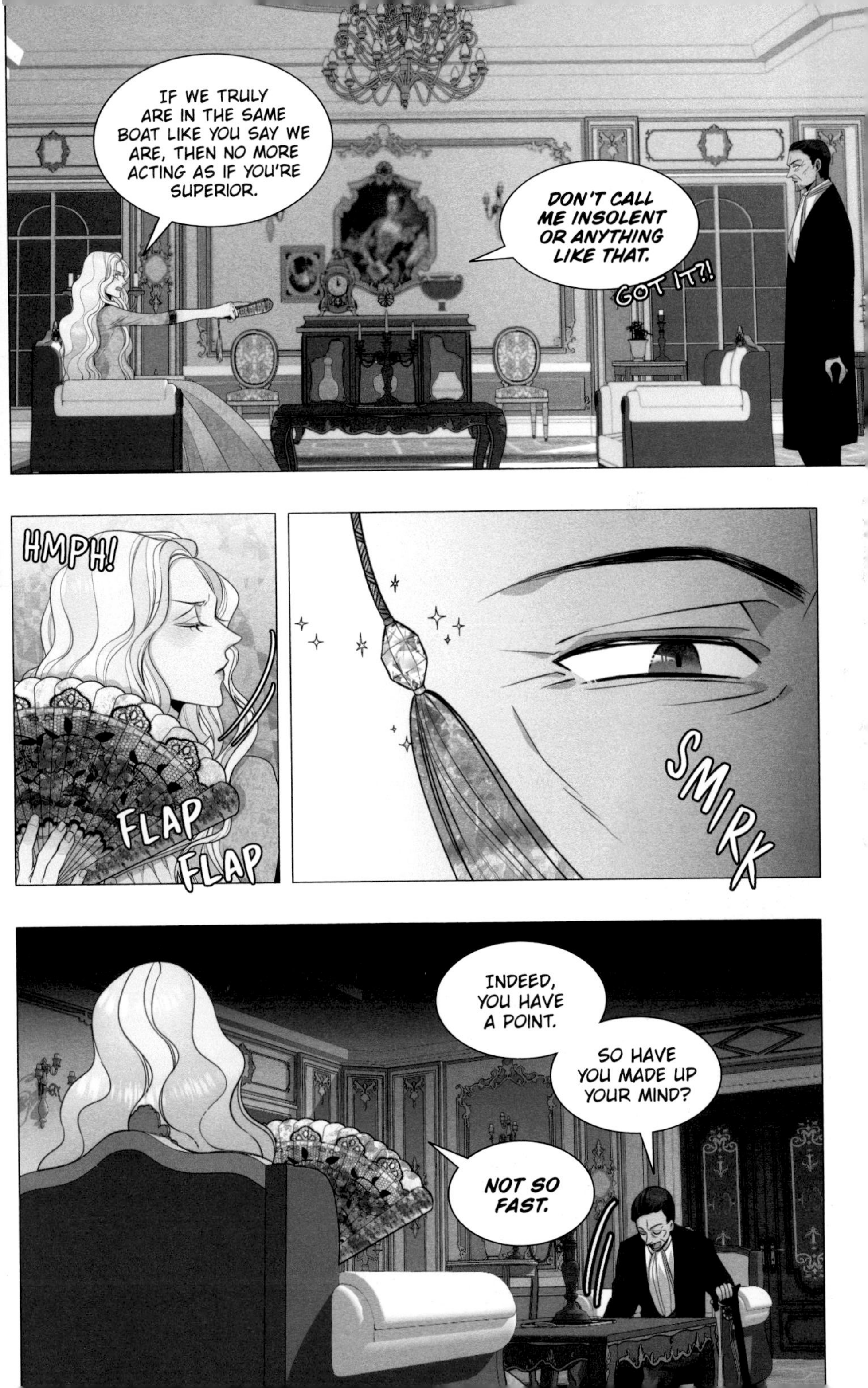
IF WE TRULY ARE IN THE SAME BOAT LIKE YOU SAY WE ARE, THEN NO MORE ACTING AS IF YOU'RE SUPERIOR.
DON'T CALL ME INSOLENT OR ANYTHING LIKE THAT.
GOT IT?!
HMPH!
FLAP
FLAP
SMIRK
INDEED, YOU HAVE A POINT.
SO HAVE YOU MADE UP YOUR MIND?
NOT SO FAST.

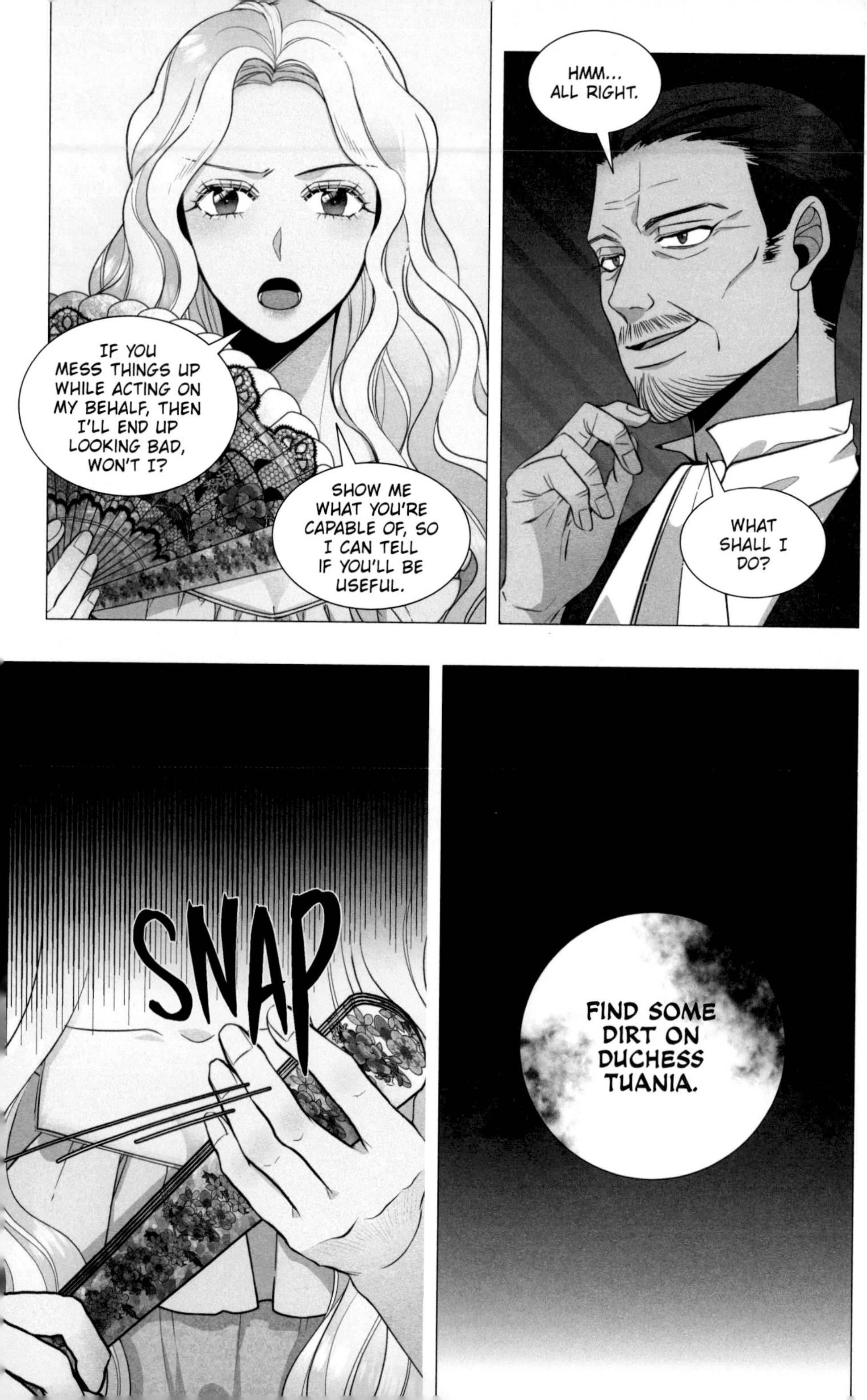
IF YOU MESS THINGS UP WHILE ACTING ON MY BEHALF, THEN I'LL END UP LOOKING BAD, WON'T I?
SHOW ME WHAT YOU'RE CAPABLE OF, SO I CAN TELL IF YOU'LL BE USEFUL.
HMM... ALL RIGHT.
WHAT SHALL I DO?
SNAP
FIND SOME DIRT ON DUCHESS TUANIA.

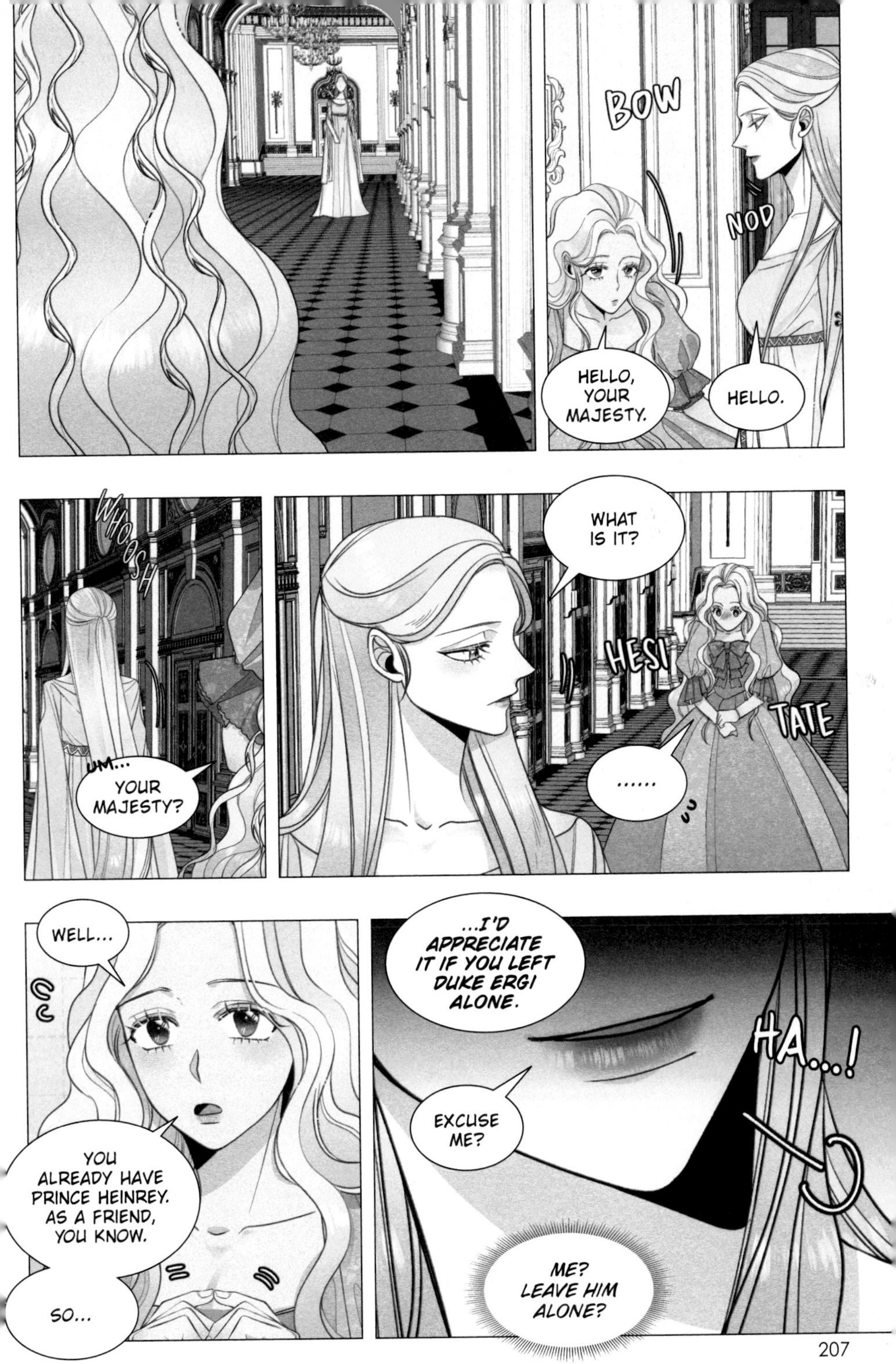
BOW
NOD
HELLO, YOUR MAJESTY.
HELLO.
WHOOSH
UM...
YOUR MAJESTY?
WHAT IS IT?
HESI
TATE
......
WELL...
YOU ALREADY HAVE PRINCE HEINREY. AS A FRIEND, YOU KNOW.
SO...
...I'D APPRECIATE IT IF YOU LEFT DUKE ERGI ALONE.
HA...!
EXCUSE ME?
ME? LEAVE HIM ALONE?

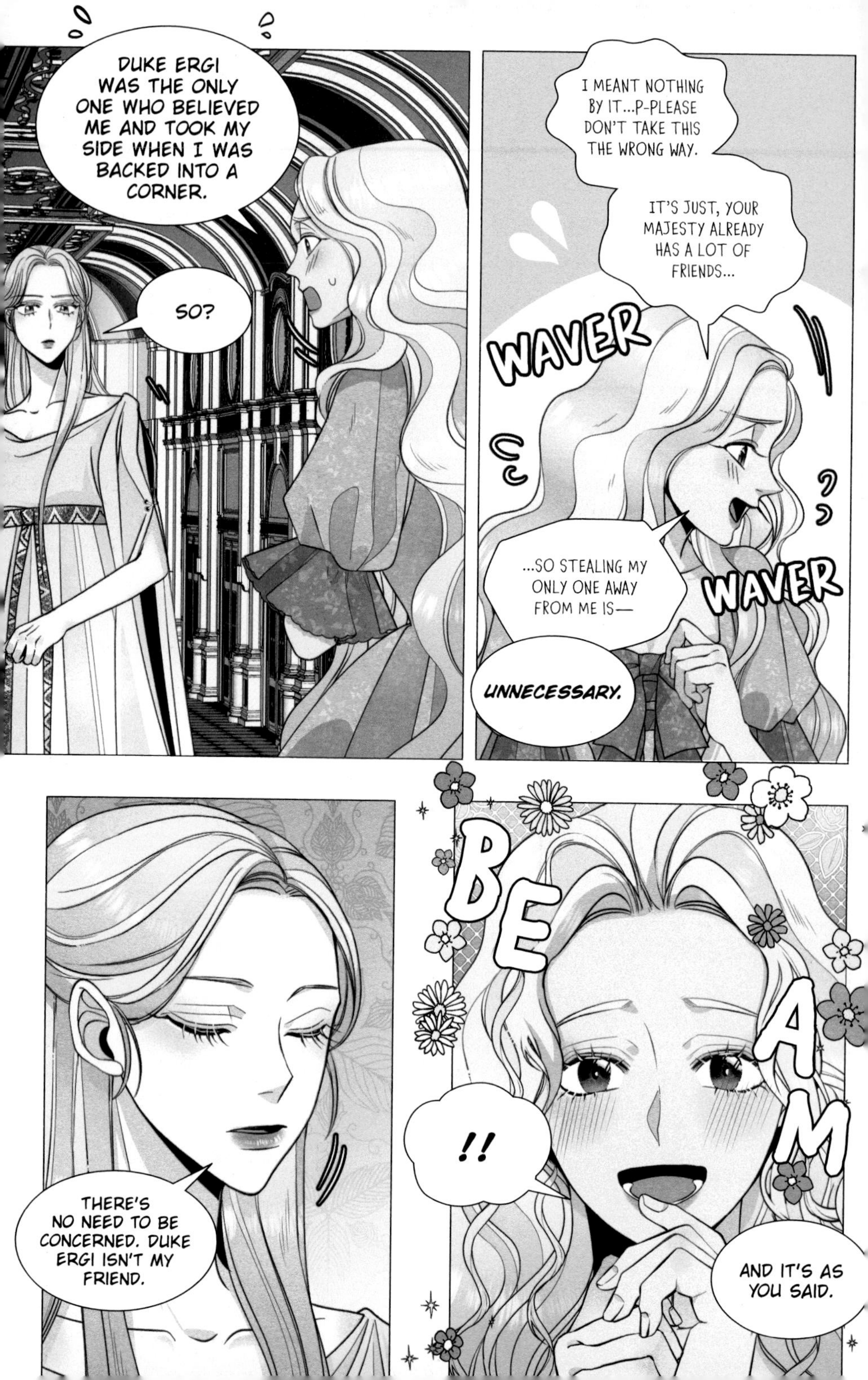
DUKE ERGI WAS THE ONLY ONE WHO BELIEVED ME AND TOOK MY SIDE WHEN I WAS BACKED INTO A CORNER.
SO?
I MEANT NOTHING BY IT...P-PLEASE DON'T TAKE THIS THE WRONG WAY.
IT'S JUST, YOUR MAJESTY ALREADY HAS A LOT OF FRIENDS...
WAVER
...SO STEALING MY ONLY ONE AWAY FROM ME IS—
WAVER
UNNECESSARY.
THERE'S NO NEED TO BE CONCERNED. DUKE ERGI ISN'T MY FRIEND.
BEAM
!!
AND IT'S AS YOU SAID.

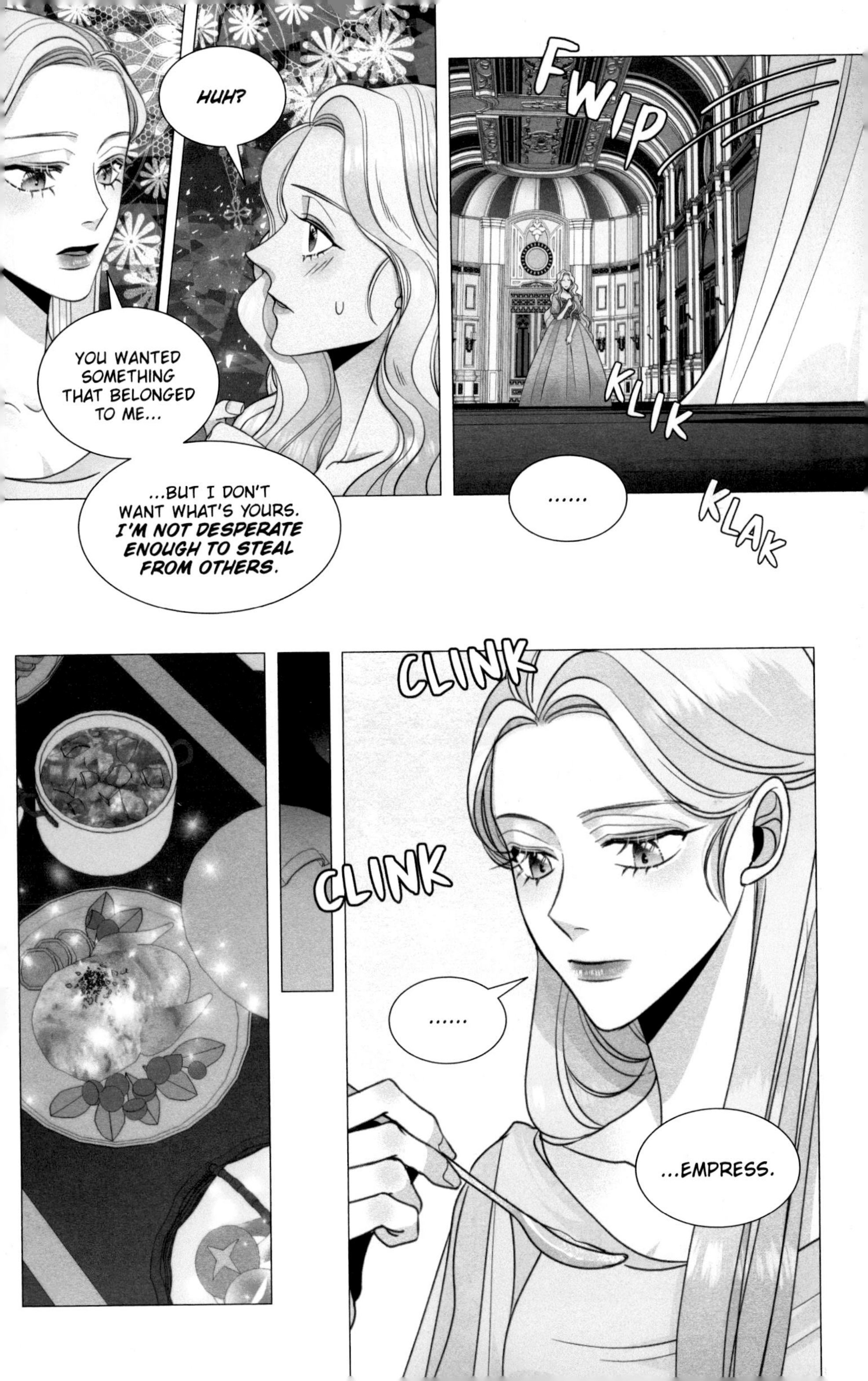
HUH?
YOU WANTED SOMETHING THAT BELONGED TO ME...
...BUT I DON'T WANT WHAT'S YOURS. I'M NOT DESPERATE ENOUGH TO STEAL FROM OTHERS.
FWIP
KLIK
KLAK
......
CLINK
CLINK
......
...EMPRESS.

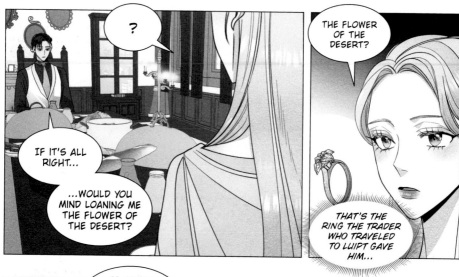

? 

THE FLOWER OF THE DESERT?

IF IT'S ALL RIGHT...

...WOULD YOU MIND LOANING ME THE FLOWER OF THE DESERT?

THAT'S THE RING THE TRADER WHO TRAVELED TO LUIPT GAVE HIM...

IF YOU'RE LOOKING FOR AN ENCHANTED RING WITH HEALING PROPERTIES, I BELIEVE YOU ALREADY HAVE ONE, NO?

WELL.

I DO, BUT NOT AT THIS VERY MOMENT, YOU SEE.

I'D LIKE TO LEND IT BRIEFLY TO SOMEONE WHO HAS INJURED THEIR HANDS.

I PROMISE TO RETURN IT, SO LET ME BORROW IT FOR A LITTLE WHILE.

MISS RASHTA'S HANDS MUST FEEL ROUGH.

TIDY

...YOU REALLY NEED IT?

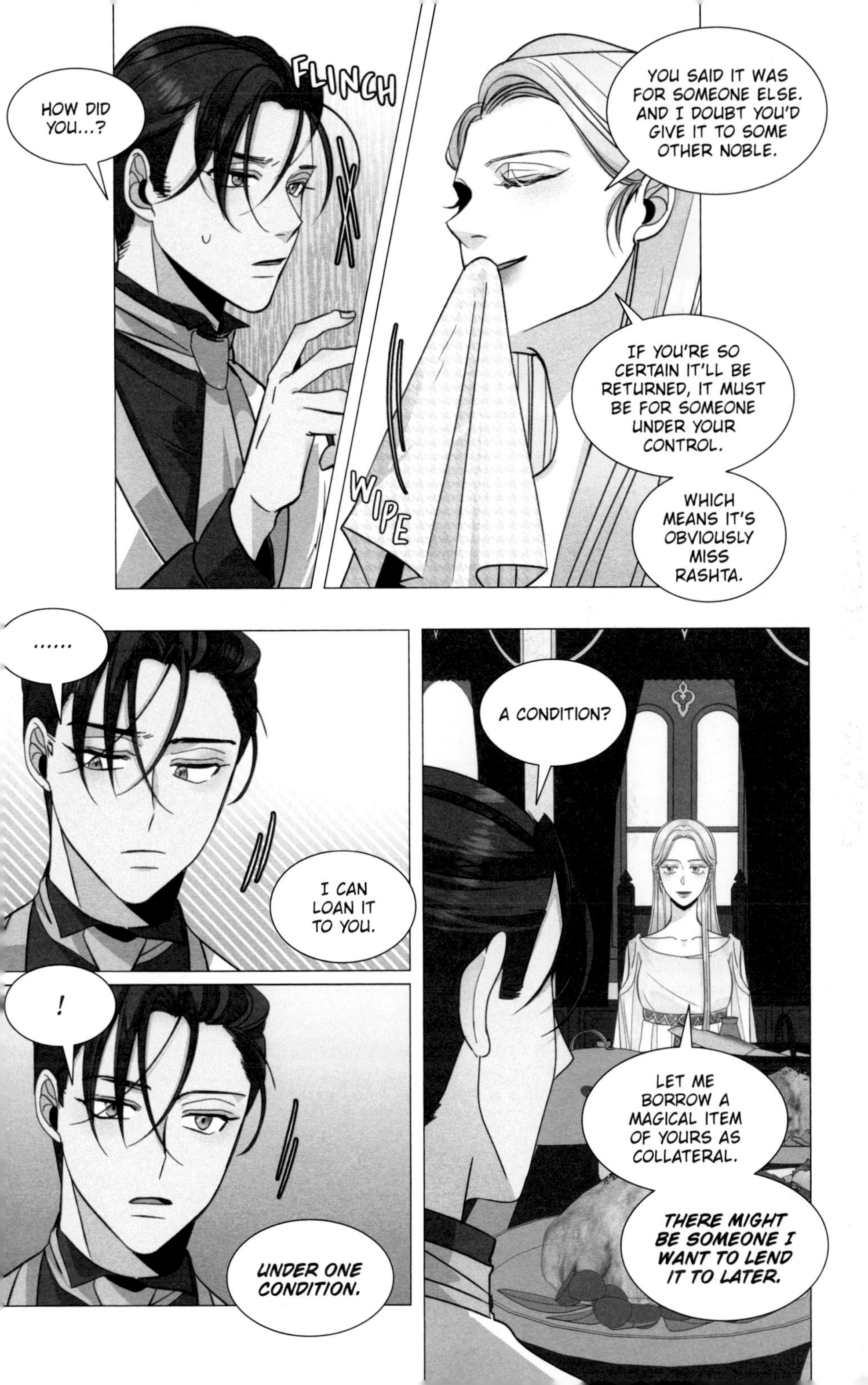
HOW DID YOU...?
FLINCH
YOU SAID IT WAS FOR SOMEONE ELSE. AND I DOUBT YOU'D GIVE IT TO SOME OTHER NOBLE.
WIPE
IF YOU'RE SO CERTAIN IT'LL BE RETURNED, IT MUST BE FOR SOMEONE UNDER YOUR CONTROL.
WHICH MEANS IT'S OBVIOUSLY MISS RASHTA.
......
I CAN LOAN IT TO YOU.
!
UNDER ONE CONDITION.
A CONDITION?
LET ME BORROW A MAGICAL ITEM OF YOURS AS COLLATERAL.
THERE MIGHT BE SOMEONE I WANT TO LEND IT TO LATER.

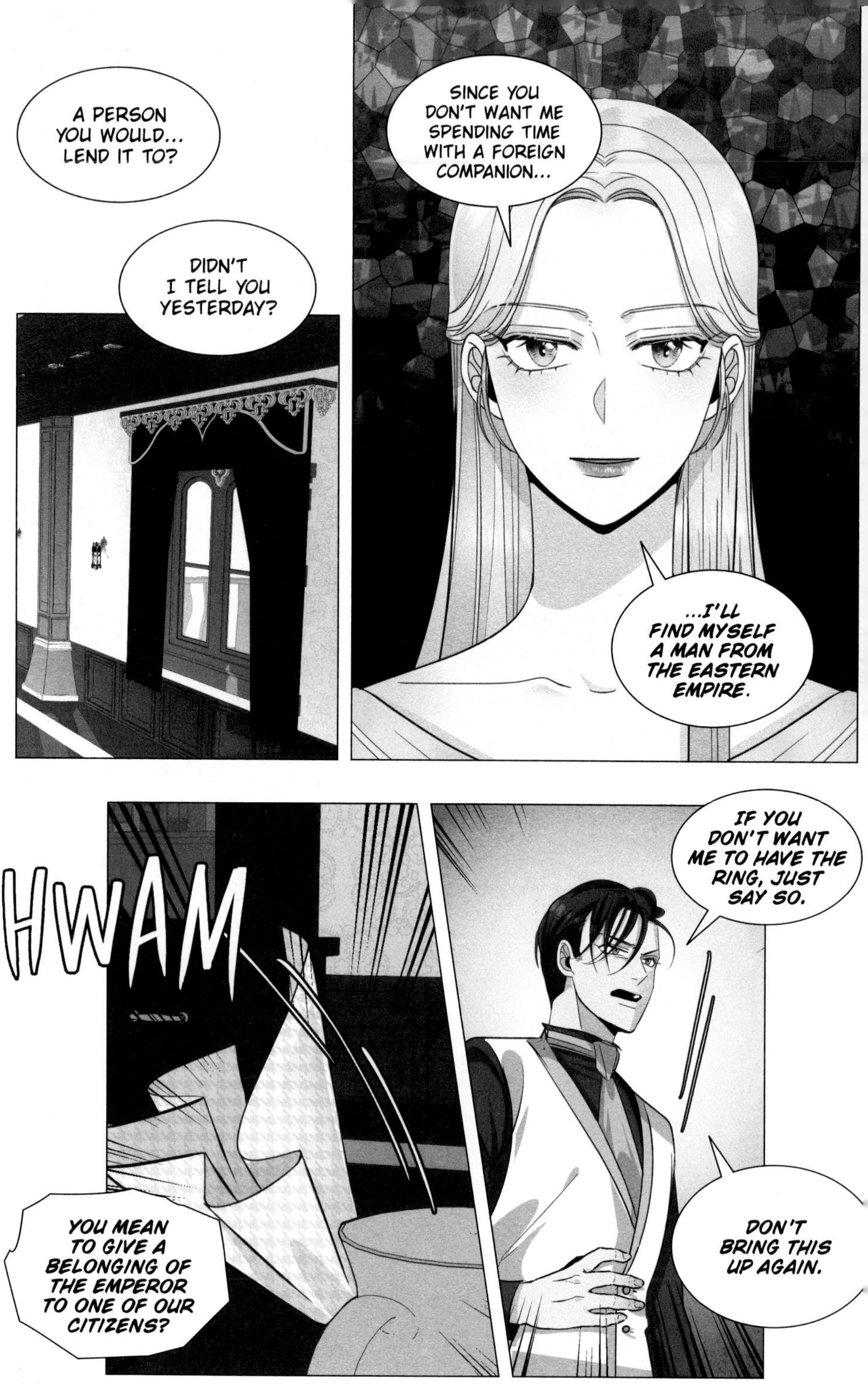
A PERSON YOU WOULD... LEND IT TO?
DIDN'T I TELL YOU YESTERDAY?
SINCE YOU DON'T WANT ME SPENDING TIME WITH A FOREIGN COMPANION...
...I'LL FIND MYSELF A MAN FROM THE EASTERN EMPIRE.
HWAM
YOU MEAN TO GIVE A BELONGING OF THE EMPEROR TO ONE OF OUR CITIZENS?
IF YOU DON'T WANT ME TO HAVE THE RING, JUST SAY SO.
DON'T BRING THIS UP AGAIN.

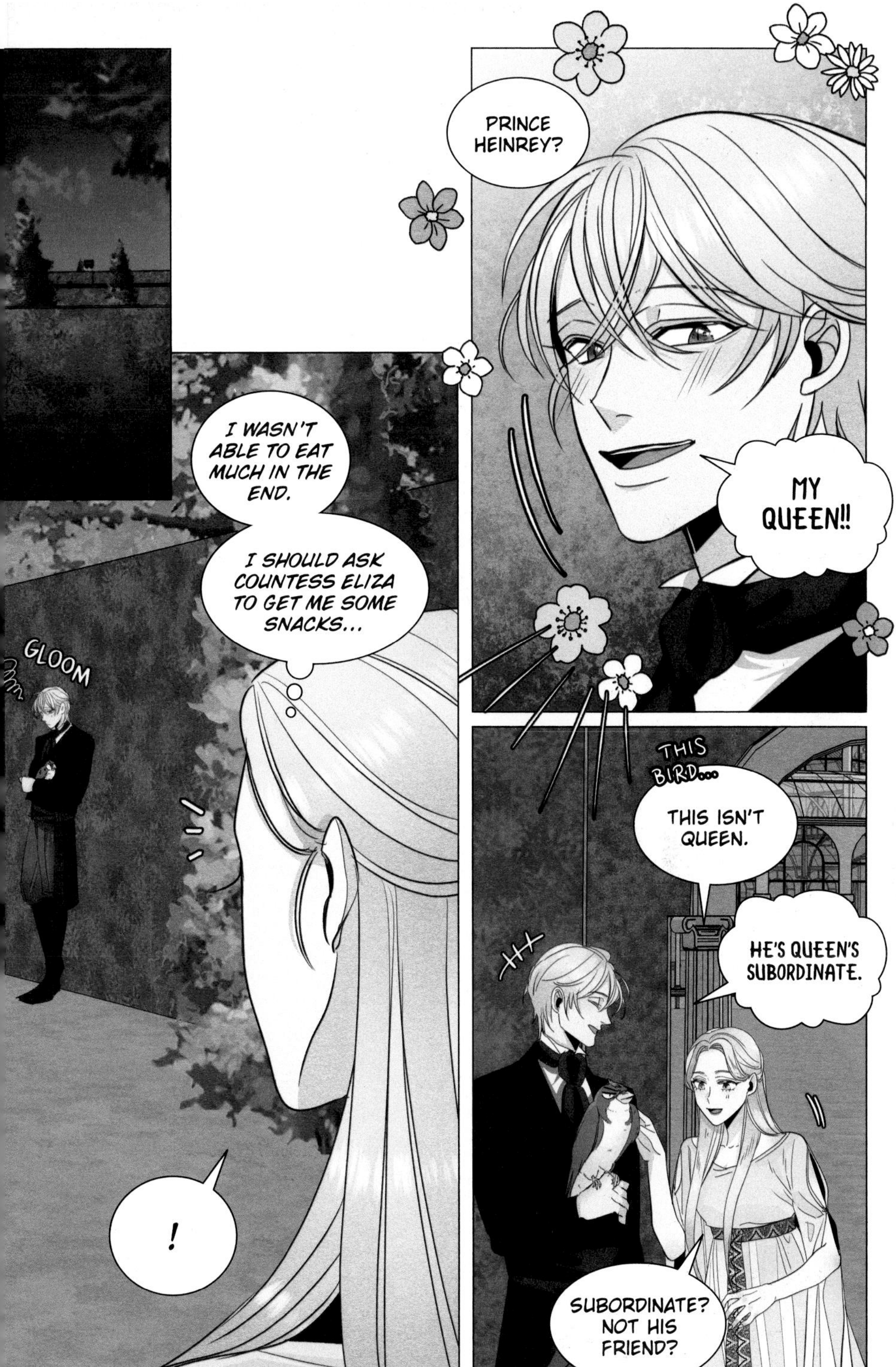

I WASN'T ABLE TO EAT MUCH IN THE END.
I SHOULD ASK COUNTESS ELIZA TO GET ME SOME SNACKS...
GLOOM
!
PRINCE HEINREY?
MY QUEEN!!
THIS BIRD...
THIS ISN'T QUEEN.
HE'S QUEEN'S SUBORDINATE.
SUBORDINATE? NOT HIS FRIEND?

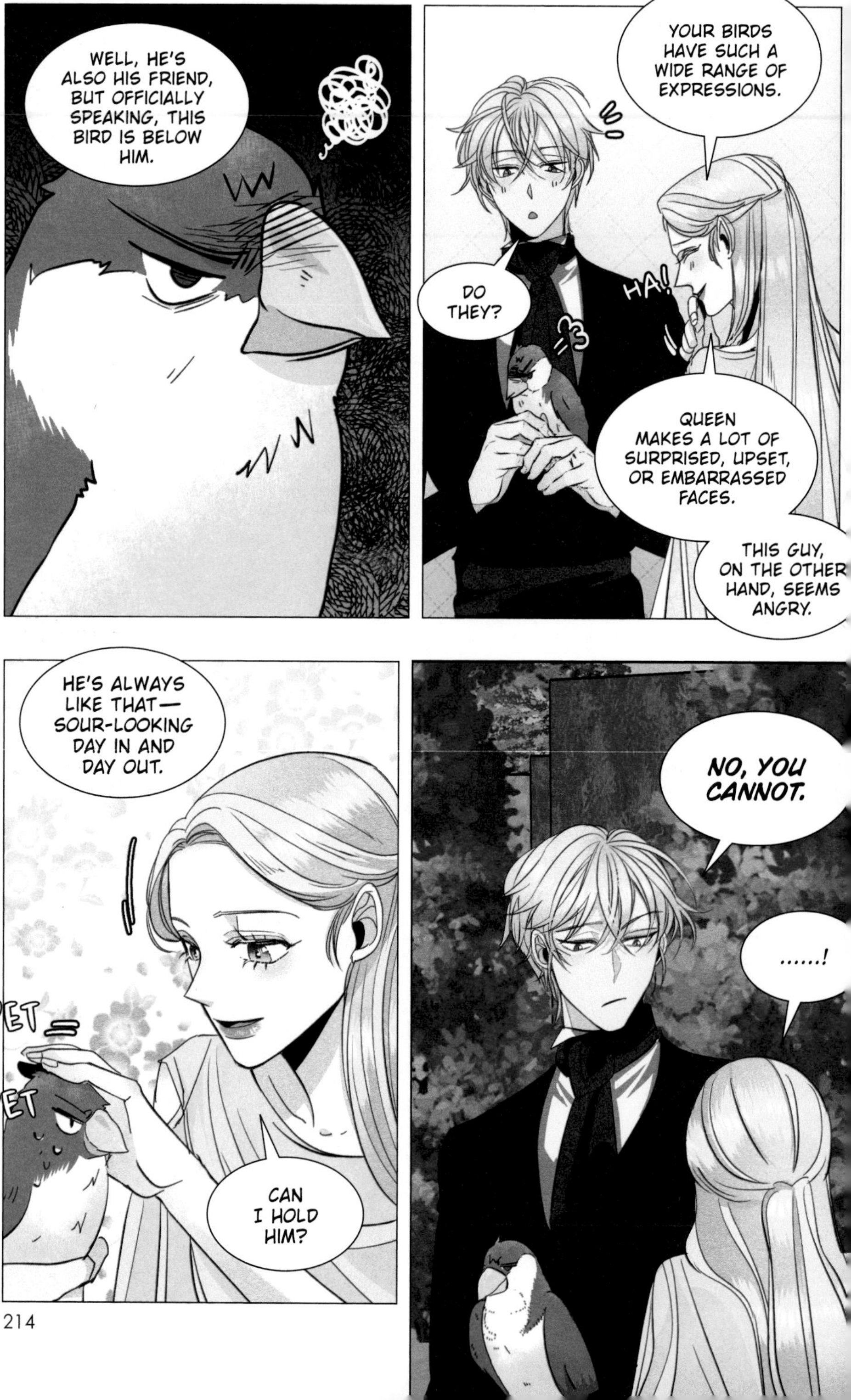
WELL, HE'S ALSO HIS FRIEND, BUT OFFICIALLY SPEAKING, THIS BIRD IS BELOW HIM.
YOUR BIRDS HAVE SUCH A WIDE RANGE OF EXPRESSIONS.
DO THEY?
HA!
QUEEN MAKES A LOT OF SURPRISED, UPSET, OR EMBARRASSED FACES.
THIS GUY, ON THE OTHER HAND, SEEMS ANGRY.
HE'S ALWAYS LIKE THAT— SOUR-LOOKING DAY IN AND DAY OUT.
PET
PET
CAN I HOLD HIM?
NO, YOU CANNOT.
......!

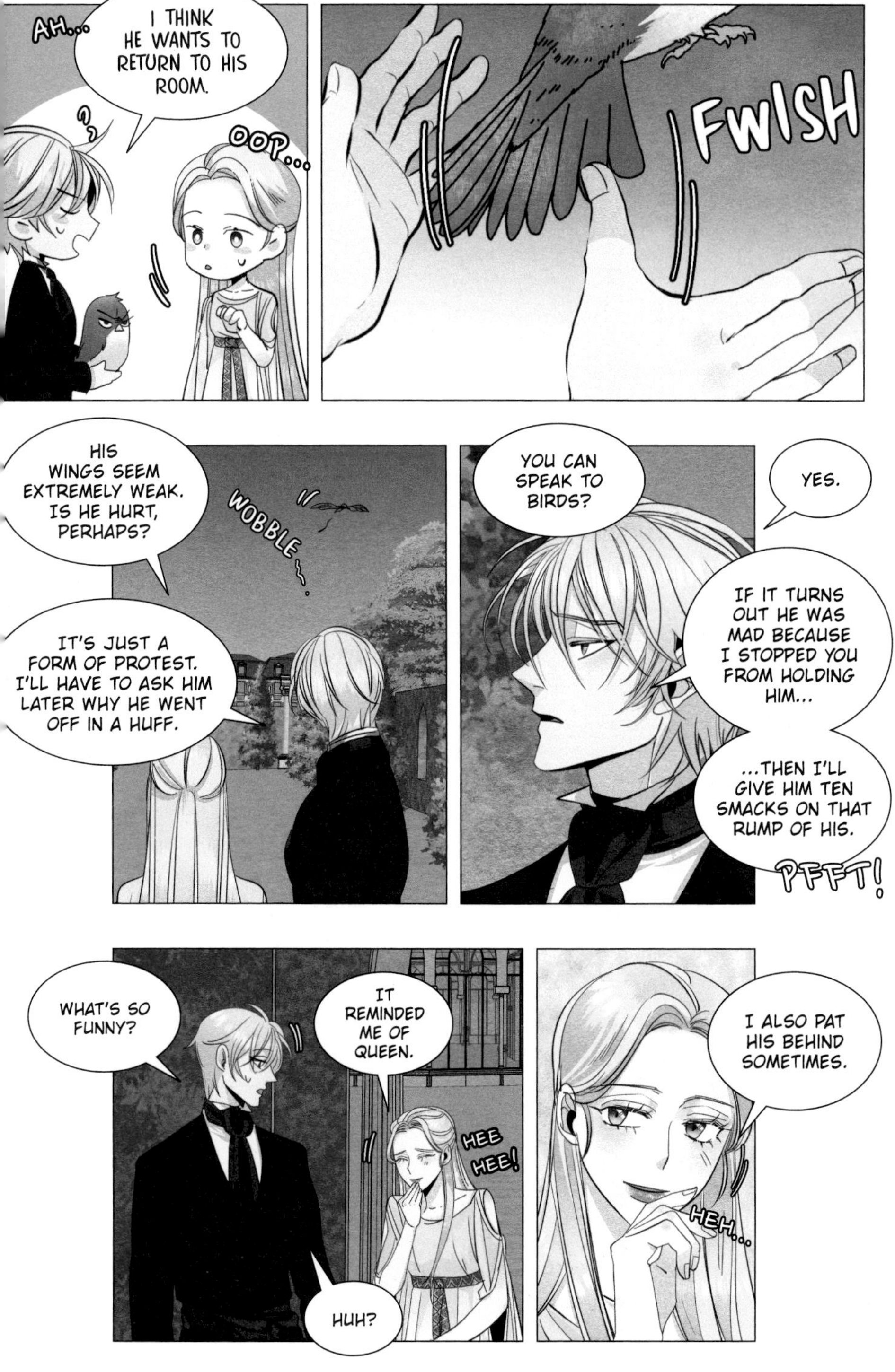
AH...
I THINK HE WANTS TO RETURN TO HIS ROOM.
OOP...
FWISH
HIS WINGS SEEM EXTREMELY WEAK. IS HE HURT, PERHAPS?
WOBBLE~
IT'S JUST A FORM OF PROTEST. I'LL HAVE TO ASK HIM LATER WHY HE WENT OFF IN A HUFF.
YOU CAN SPEAK TO BIRDS?
YES.
IF IT TURNS OUT HE WAS MAD BECAUSE I STOPPED YOU FROM HOLDING HIM...
...THEN I'LL GIVE HIM TEN SMACKS ON THAT RUMP OF HIS.
PFFT!
WHAT'S SO FUNNY?
IT REMINDED ME OF QUEEN.
HEE HEE!
HUH?
I ALSO PAT HIS BEHIND SOMETIMES.
HEH...

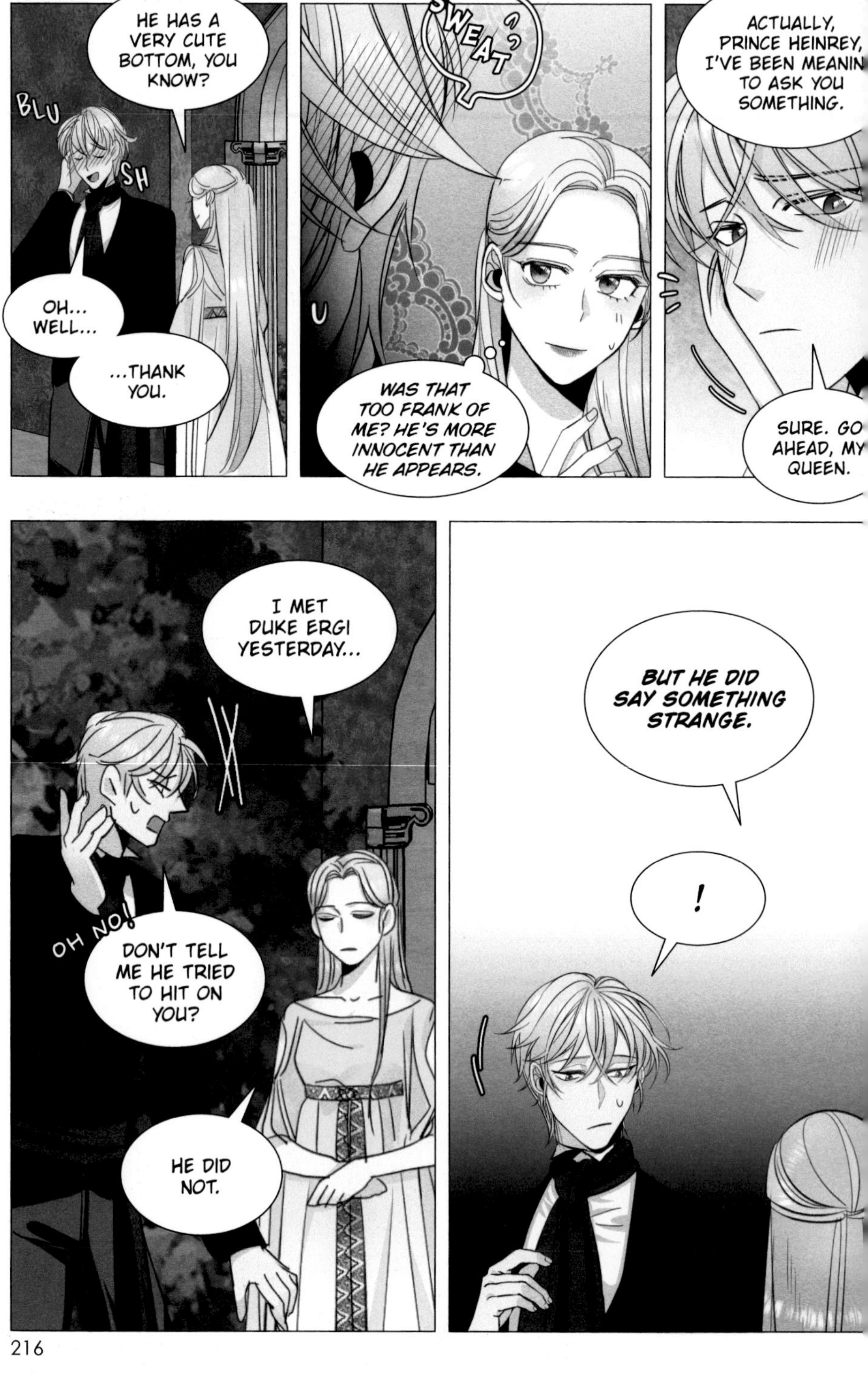
HE HAS A VERY CUTE BOTTOM, YOU KNOW?
BLUSH
OH... WELL...
...THANK YOU.
SWEAT
WAS THAT TOO FRANK OF ME? HE'S MORE INNOCENT THAN HE APPEARS.
ACTUALLY, PRINCE HEINREY, I'VE BEEN MEANIN TO ASK YOU SOMETHING.
SURE. GO AHEAD, MY QUEEN.
I MET DUKE ERGI YESTERDAY...
OH NO!
DON'T TELL ME HE TRIED TO HIT ON YOU?
HE DID NOT.
BUT HE DID SAY SOMETHING STRANGE.
!

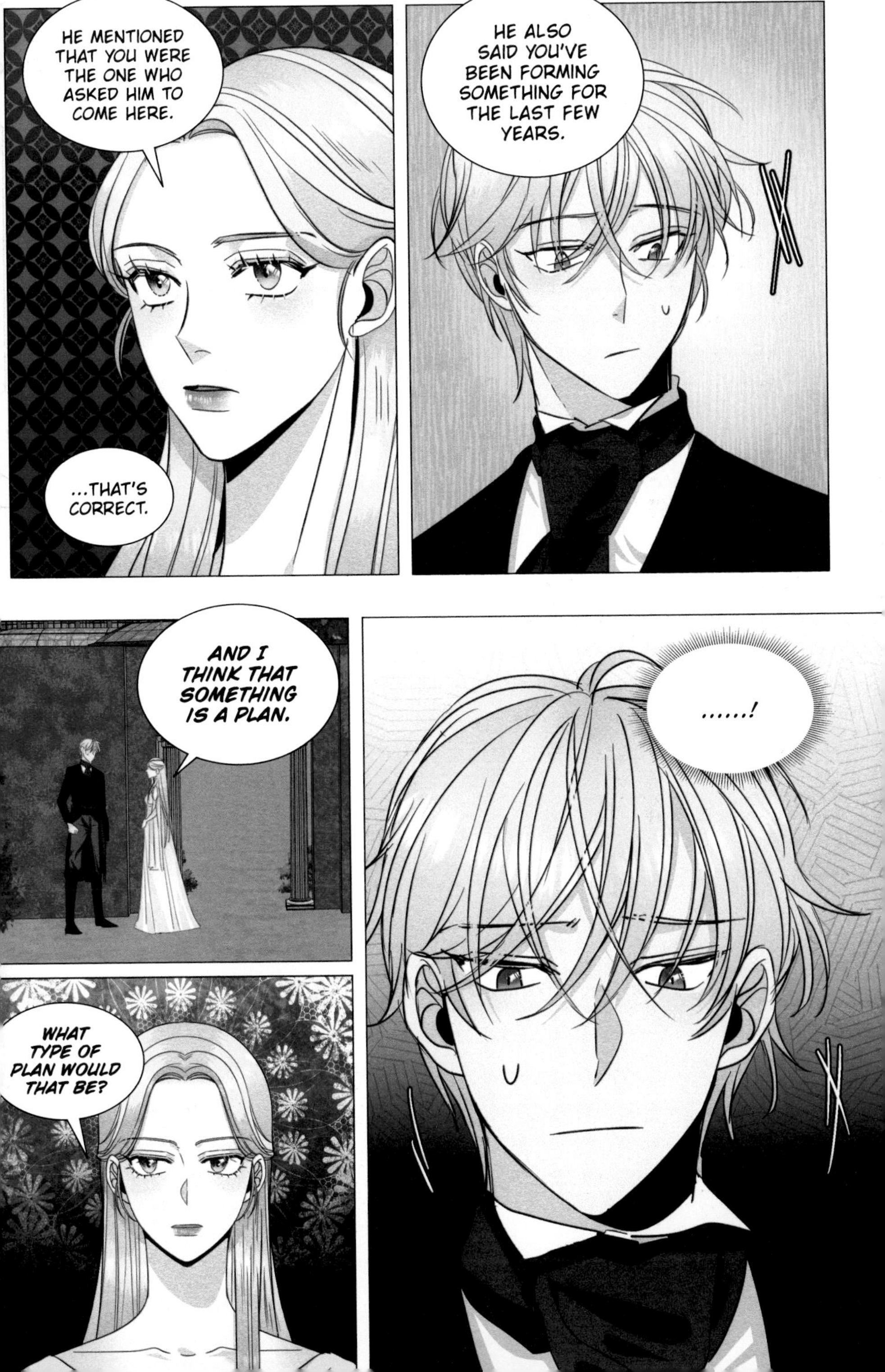
HE MENTIONED THAT YOU WERE THE ONE WHO ASKED HIM TO COME HERE.
...THAT'S CORRECT.
HE ALSO SAID YOU'VE BEEN FORMING SOMETHING FOR THE LAST FEW YEARS.
AND I THINK THAT SOMETHING IS A PLAN.
......!
WHAT TYPE OF PLAN WOULD THAT BE?

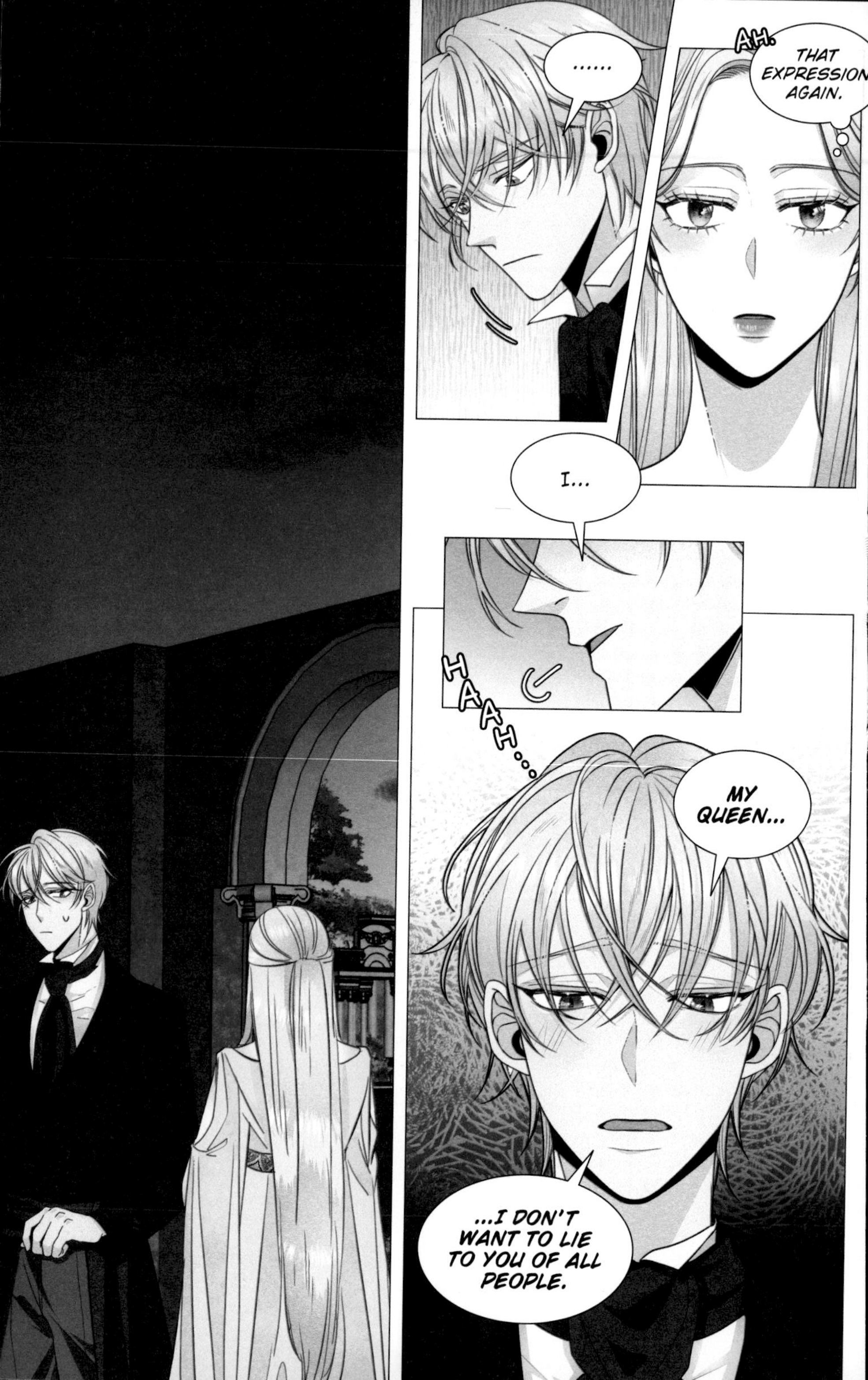
......
AH.
THAT EXPRESSION AGAIN.
I...
HAAAH...
MY QUEEN...
...I DON'T WANT TO LIE TO YOU OF ALL PEOPLE.

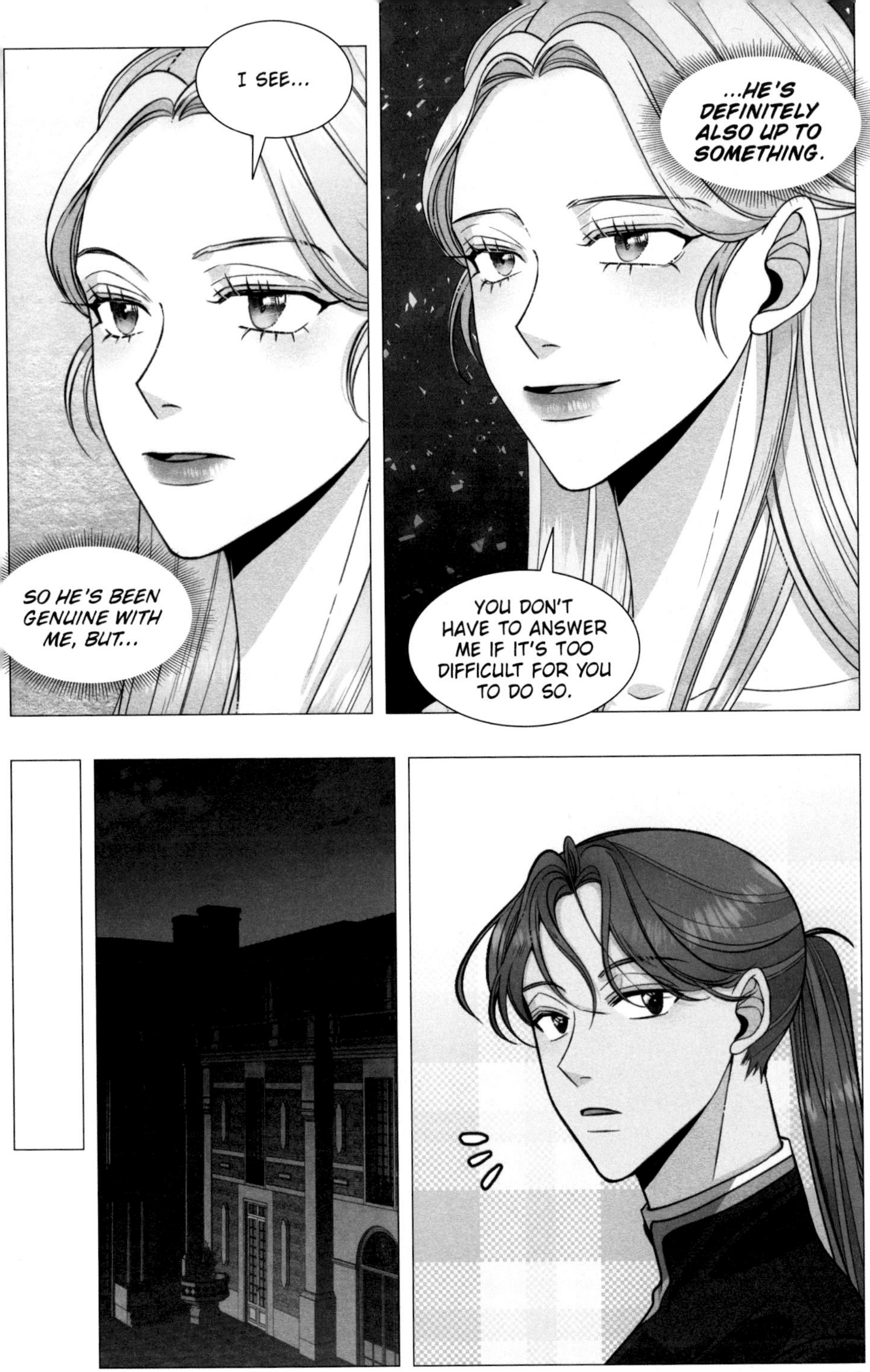
I SEE...
SO HE'S BEEN GENUINE WITH ME, BUT...
...HE'S DEFINITELY ALSO UP TO SOMETHING.
YOU DON'T HAVE TO ANSWER ME IF IT'S TOO DIFFICULT FOR YOU TO DO SO.

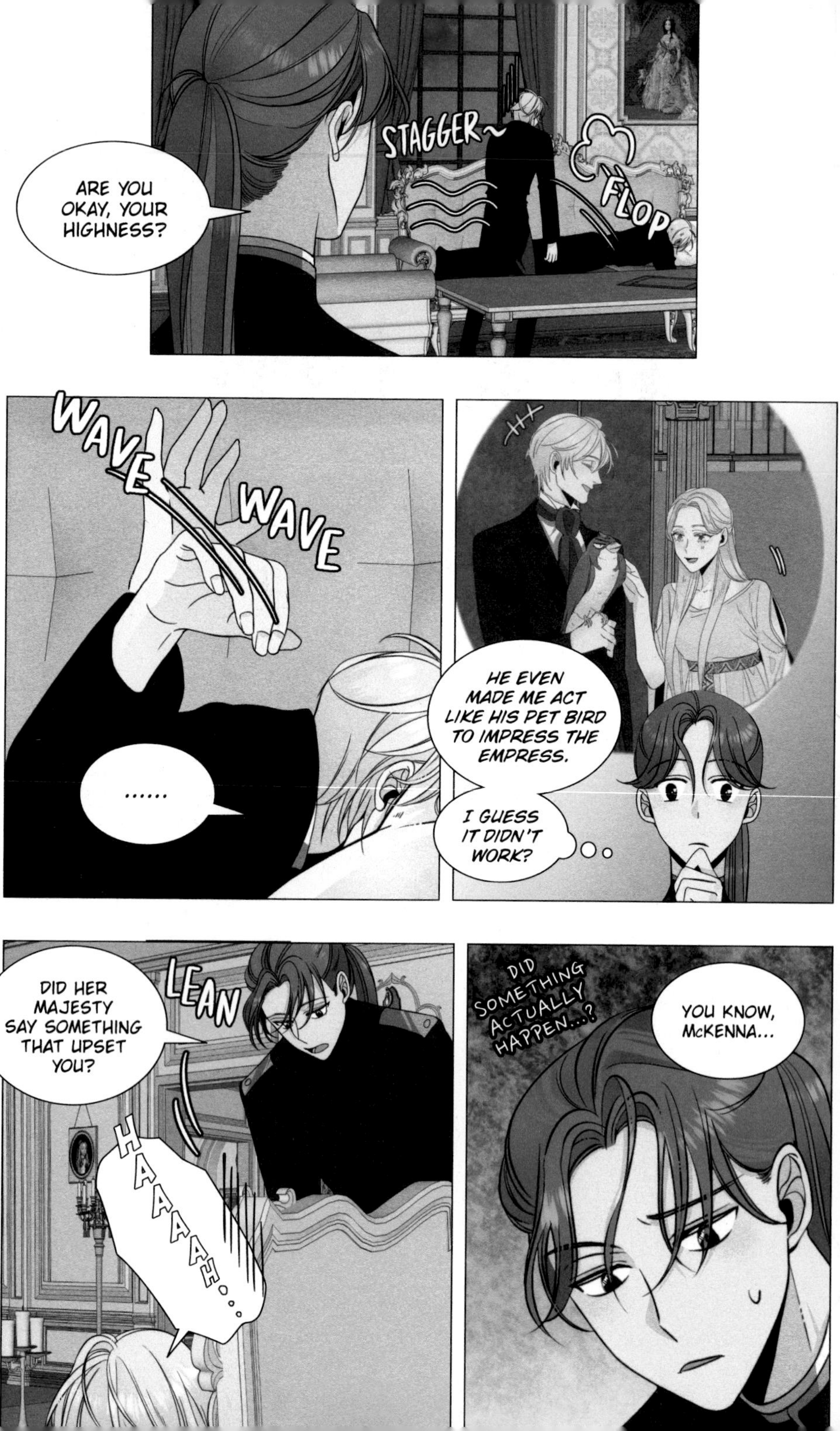
STAGGER~
FLOP
ARE YOU OKAY, YOUR HIGHNESS?
WAVE
WAVE
......
HE EVEN MADE ME ACT LIKE HIS PET BIRD TO IMPRESS THE EMPRESS.
I GUESS IT DIDN'T WORK?
LEAN
DID HER MAJESTY SAY SOMETHING THAT UPSET YOU?
HAAAAAH...
DID SOMETHING ACTUALLY HAPPEN...?
YOU KNOW, McKENNA...

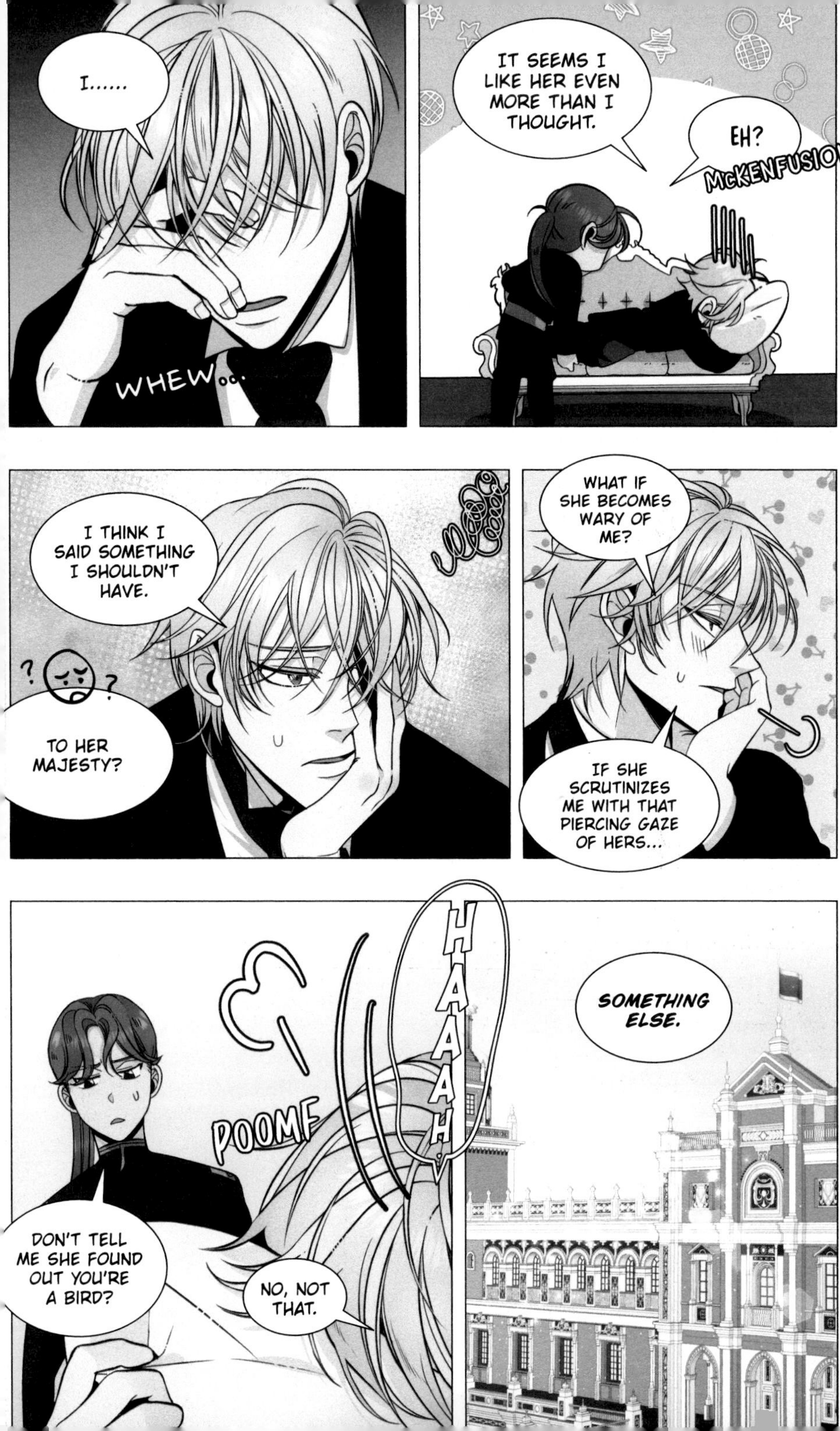

I......
WHEW...
IT SEEMS I LIKE HER EVEN MORE THAN I THOUGHT.
EH?
McKENFUSION
I THINK I SAID SOMETHING I SHOULDN'T HAVE.
TO HER MAJESTY?
WHAT IF SHE BECOMES WARY OF ME?
IF SHE SCRUTINIZES ME WITH THAT PIERCING GAZE OF HERS...
HAAAAH
POOMF
DON'T TELL ME SHE FOUND OUT YOU'RE A BIRD?
NO, NOT THAT.
SOMETHING ELSE.

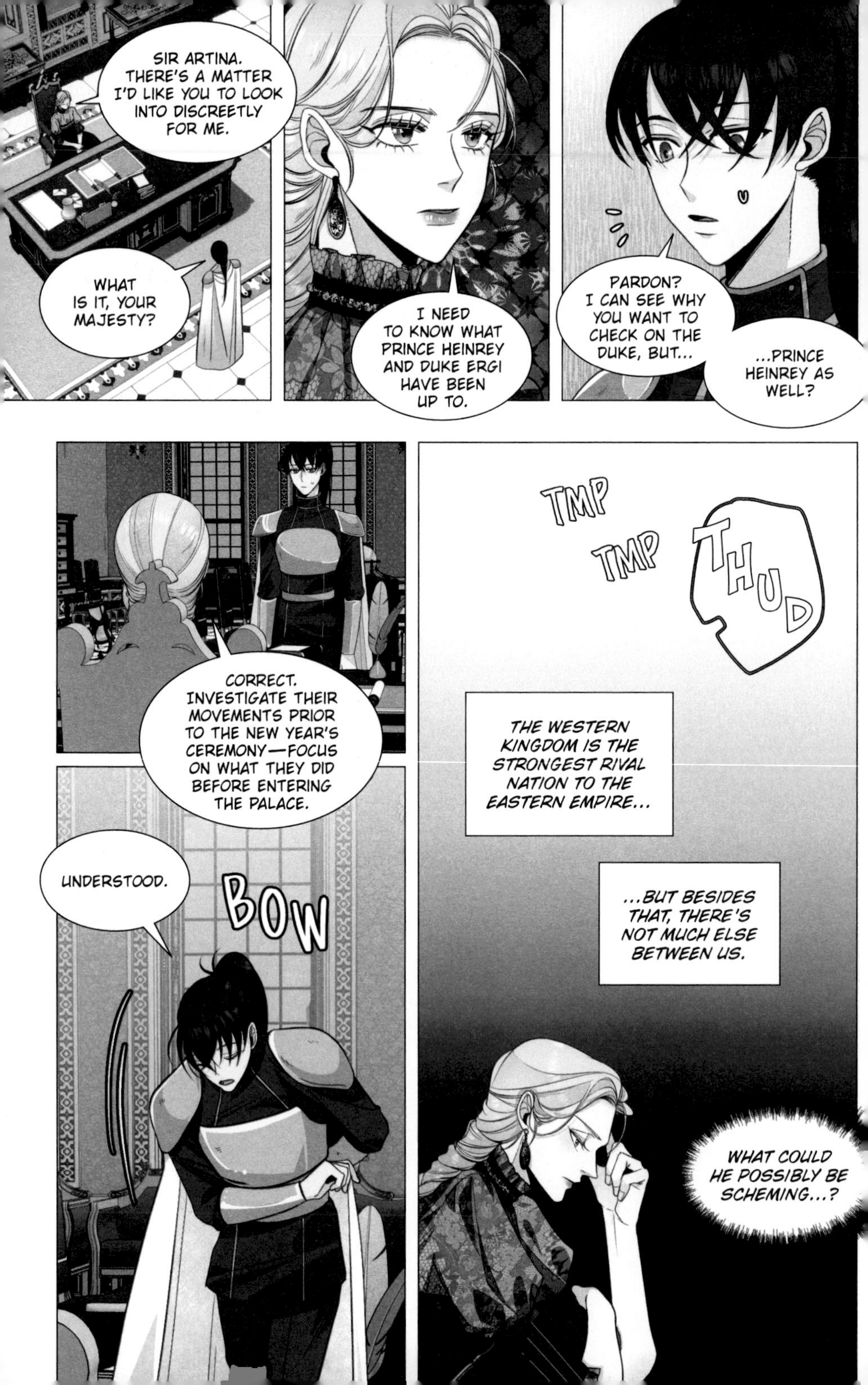
SIR ARTINA. THERE'S A MATTER I'D LIKE YOU TO LOOK INTO DISCREETLY FOR ME.
WHAT IS IT, YOUR MAJESTY?
I NEED TO KNOW WHAT PRINCE HEINREY AND DUKE ERGI HAVE BEEN UP TO.
PARDON? I CAN SEE WHY YOU WANT TO CHECK ON THE DUKE, BUT...
...PRINCE HEINREY AS WELL?
CORRECT. INVESTIGATE THEIR MOVEMENTS PRIOR TO THE NEW YEAR'S CEREMONY—FOCUS ON WHAT THEY DID BEFORE ENTERING THE PALACE.
UNDERSTOOD.
BOW
TMP
TMP
THUD
THE WESTERN KINGDOM IS THE STRONGEST RIVAL NATION TO THE EASTERN EMPIRE...
...BUT BESIDES THAT, THERE'S NOT MUCH ELSE BETWEEN US.
WHAT COULD HE POSSIBLY BE SCHEMING...?

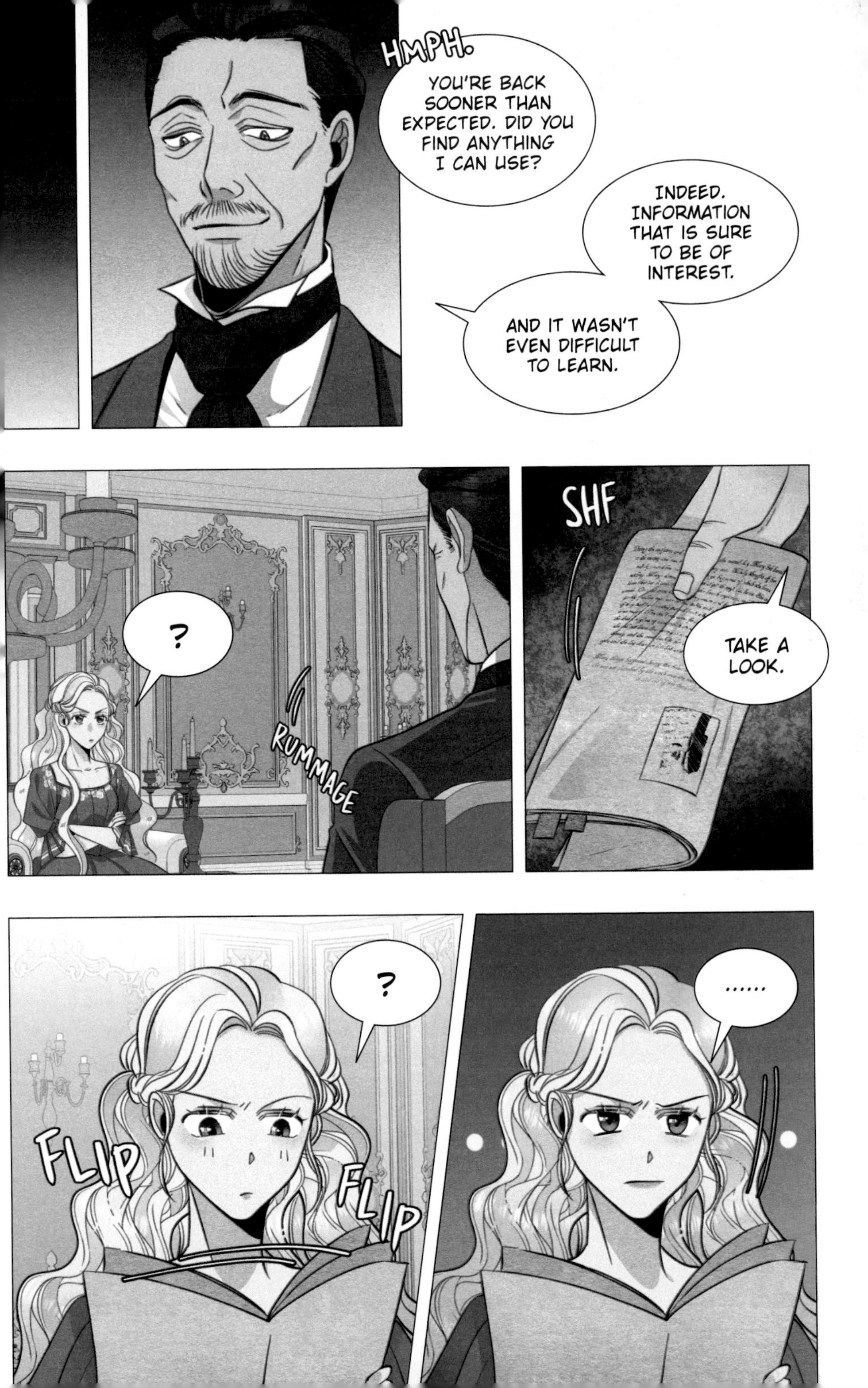
HMPH.
YOU'RE BACK SOONER THAN EXPECTED. DID YOU FIND ANYTHING I CAN USE?
INDEED. INFORMATION THAT IS SURE TO BE OF INTEREST.
AND IT WASN'T EVEN DIFFICULT TO LEARN.
?
RUMMAGE
SHF
TAKE A LOOK.
FLIP
FLIP
?
......

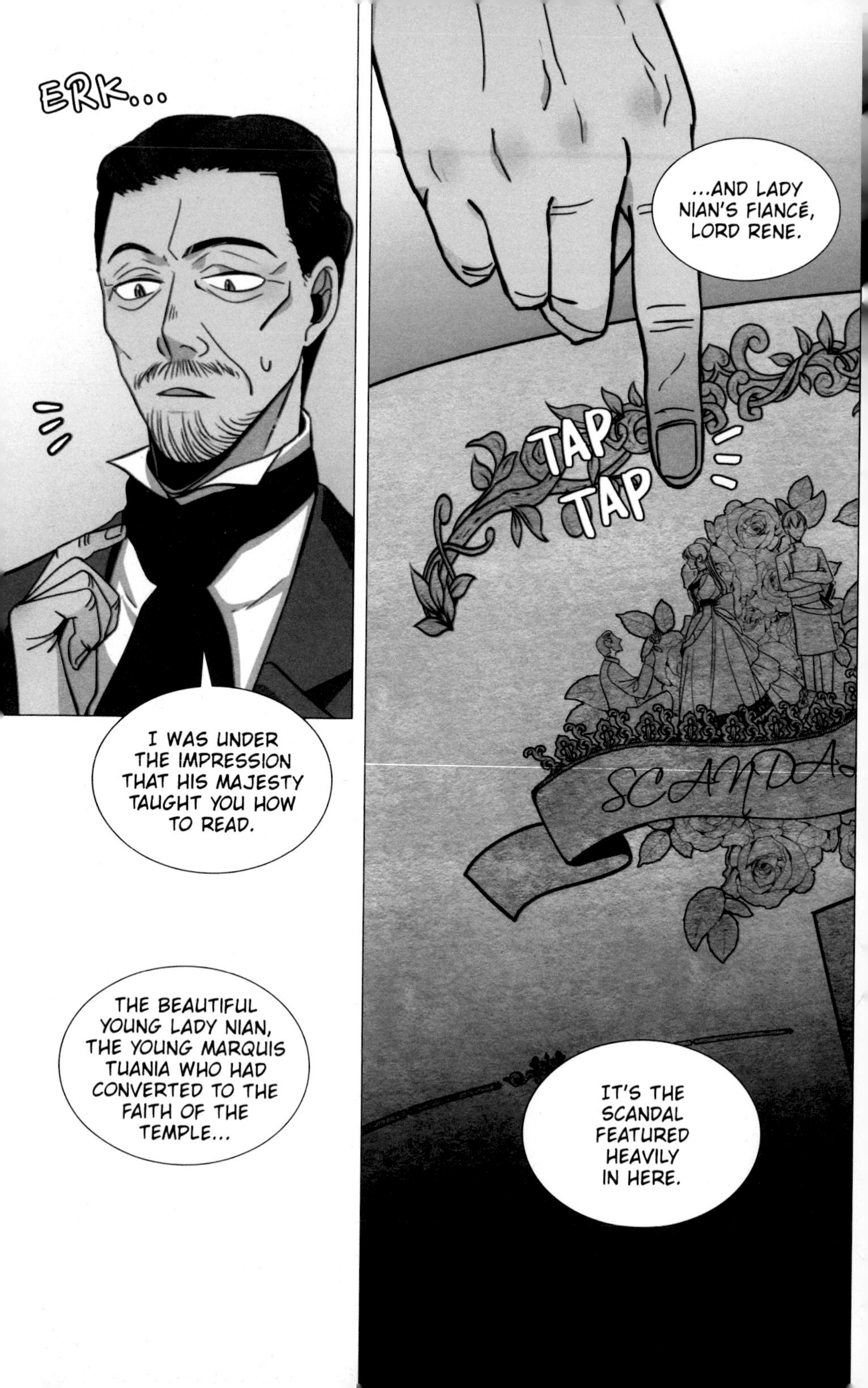
ERK...
I WAS UNDER THE IMPRESSION THAT HIS MAJESTY TAUGHT YOU HOW TO READ.
THE BEAUTIFUL YOUNG LADY NIAN, THE YOUNG MARQUIS TUANIA WHO HAD CONVERTED TO THE FAITH OF THE TEMPLE...
...AND LADY NIAN'S FIANCÉ, LORD RENE.
TAP TAP
SCANDA
IT'S THE SCANDAL FEATURED HEAVILY IN HERE.

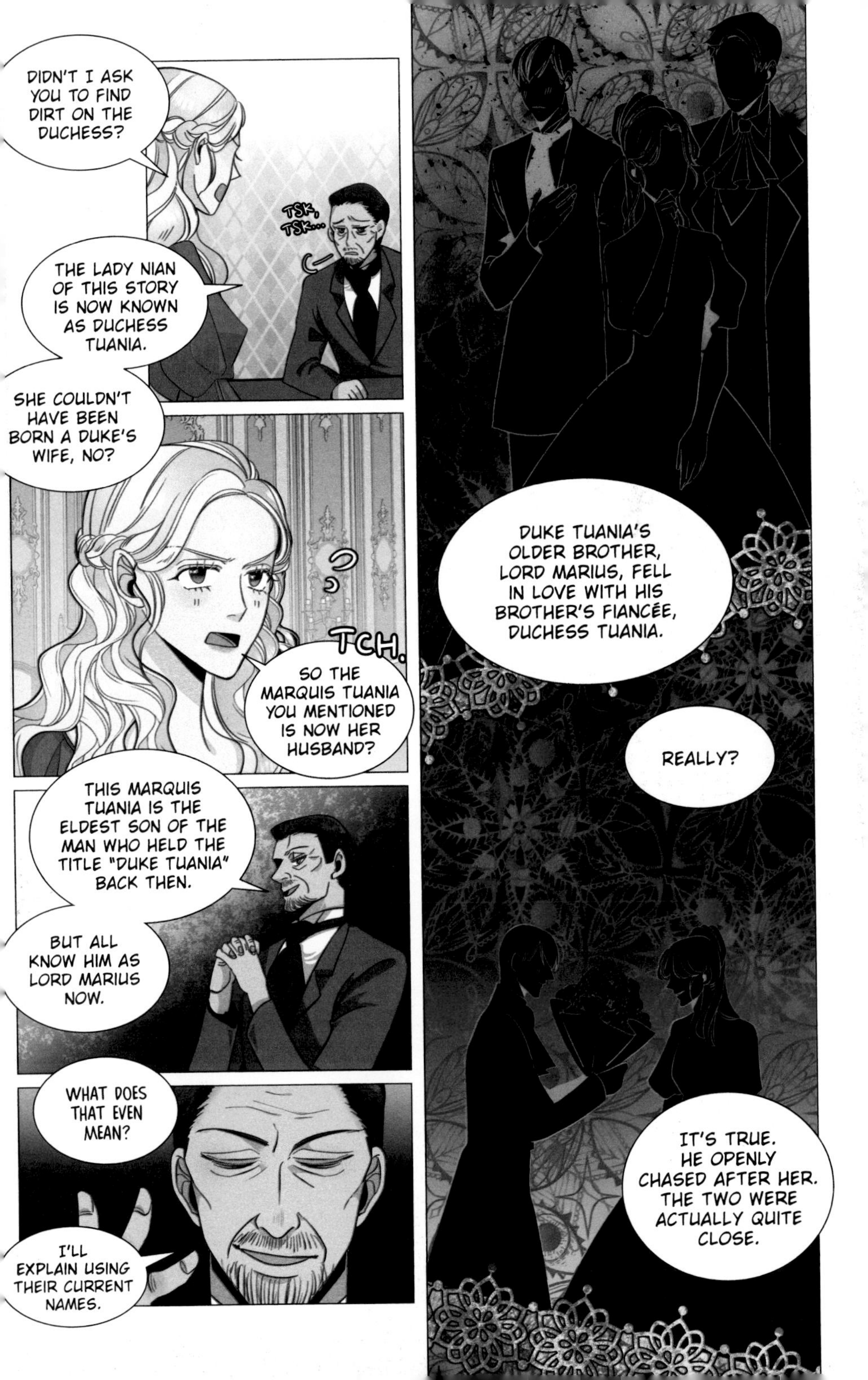
DIDN'T I ASK YOU TO FIND DIRT ON THE DUCHESS?
TSK, TSK...
THE LADY NIAN OF THIS STORY IS NOW KNOWN AS DUCHESS TUANIA.
SHE COULDN'T HAVE BEEN BORN A DUKE'S WIFE, NO?
TCH.
SO THE MARQUIS TUANIA YOU MENTIONED IS NOW HER HUSBAND?
THIS MARQUIS TUANIA IS THE ELDEST SON OF THE MAN WHO HELD THE TITLE "DUKE TUANIA" BACK THEN.
BUT ALL KNOW HIM AS LORD MARIUS NOW.
WHAT DOES THAT EVEN MEAN?
I'LL EXPLAIN USING THEIR CURRENT NAMES.
DUKE TUANIA'S OLDER BROTHER, LORD MARIUS, FELL IN LOVE WITH HIS BROTHER'S FIANCÉE, DUCHESS TUANIA.
REALLY?
IT'S TRUE. HE OPENLY CHASED AFTER HER. THE TWO WERE ACTUALLY QUITE CLOSE.

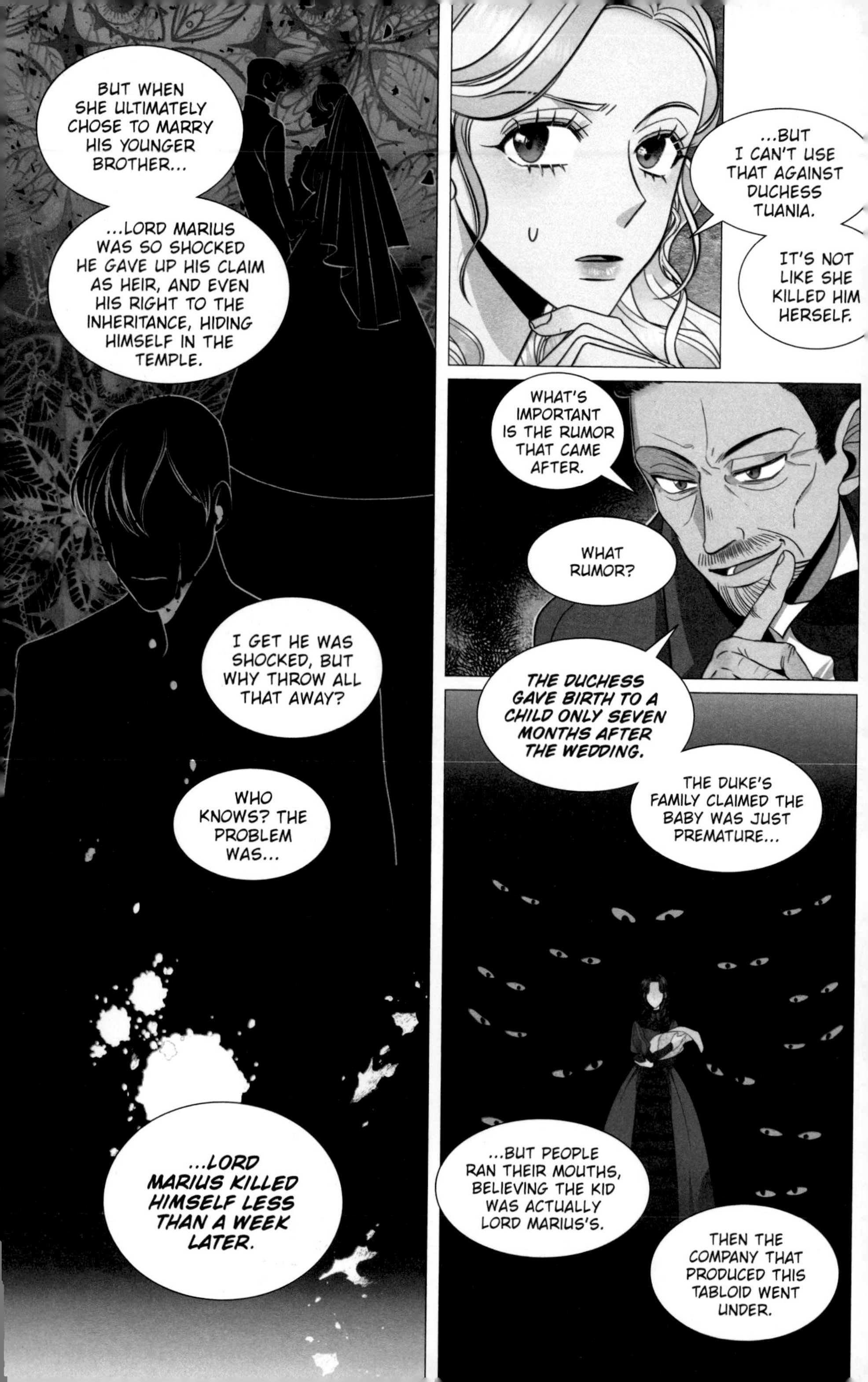
BUT WHEN SHE ULTIMATELY CHOSE TO MARRY HIS YOUNGER BROTHER...
...LORD MARIUS WAS SO SHOCKED HE GAVE UP HIS CLAIM AS HEIR, AND EVEN HIS RIGHT TO THE INHERITANCE, HIDING HIMSELF IN THE TEMPLE.
I GET HE WAS SHOCKED, BUT WHY THROW ALL THAT AWAY?
WHO KNOWS? THE PROBLEM WAS...
...LORD MARIUS KILLED HIMSELF LESS THAN A WEEK LATER.
...BUT I CAN'T USE THAT AGAINST DUCHESS TUANIA.
IT'S NOT LIKE SHE KILLED HIM HERSELF.
WHAT'S IMPORTANT IS THE RUMOR THAT CAME AFTER.
WHAT RUMOR?
THE DUCHESS GAVE BIRTH TO A CHILD ONLY SEVEN MONTHS AFTER THE WEDDING.
THE DUKE'S FAMILY CLAIMED THE BABY WAS JUST PREMATURE...
...BUT PEOPLE RAN THEIR MOUTHS, BELIEVING THE KID WAS ACTUALLY LORD MARIUS'S.
THEN THE COMPANY THAT PRODUCED THIS TABLOID WENT UNDER.

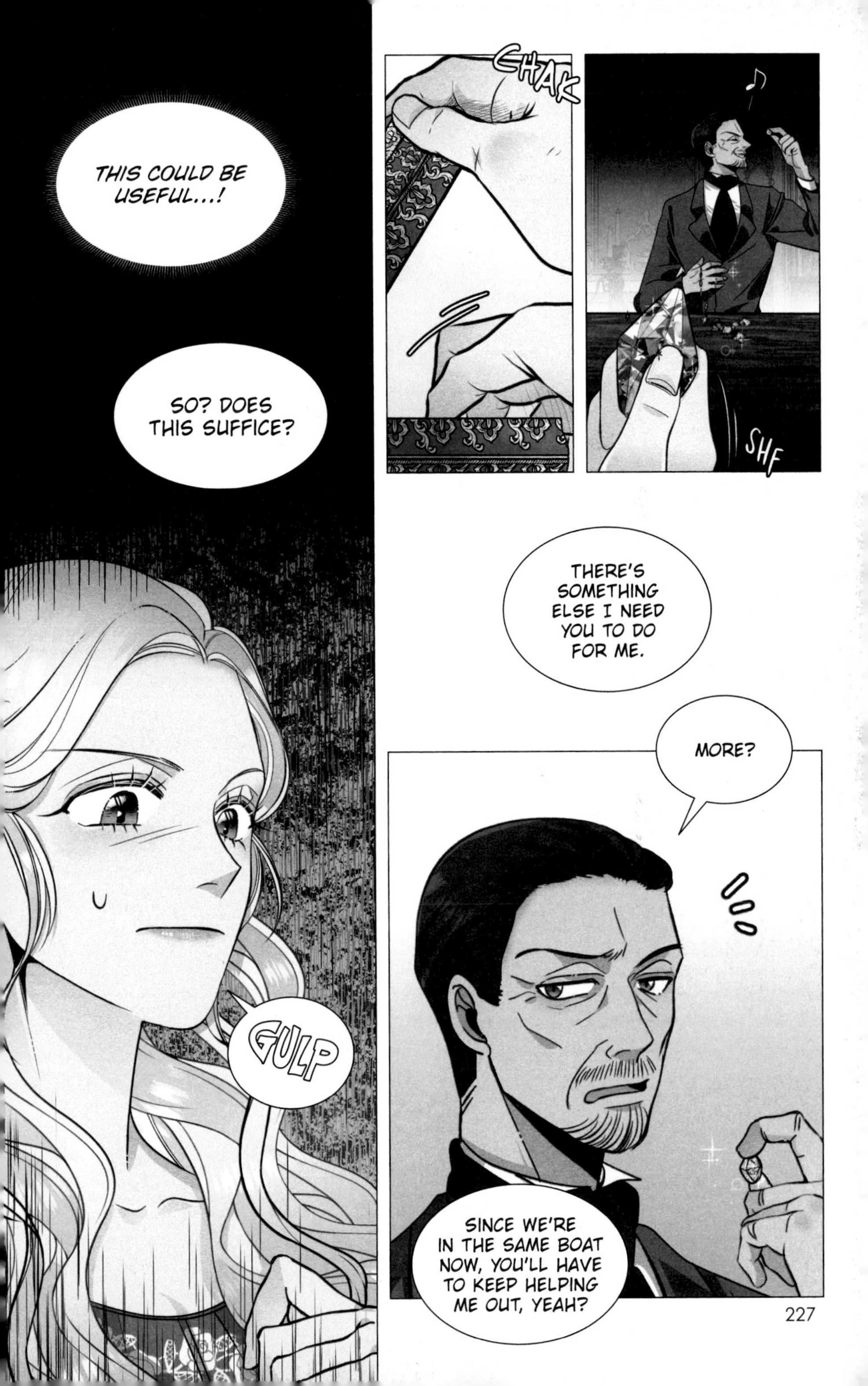
THIS COULD BE USEFUL...!
SO? DOES THIS SUFFICE?
CHAK
SHF
THERE'S SOMETHING ELSE I NEED YOU TO DO FOR ME.
GULP
MORE?
SINCE WE'RE IN THE SAME BOAT NOW, YOU'LL HAVE TO KEEP HELPING ME OUT, YEAH?

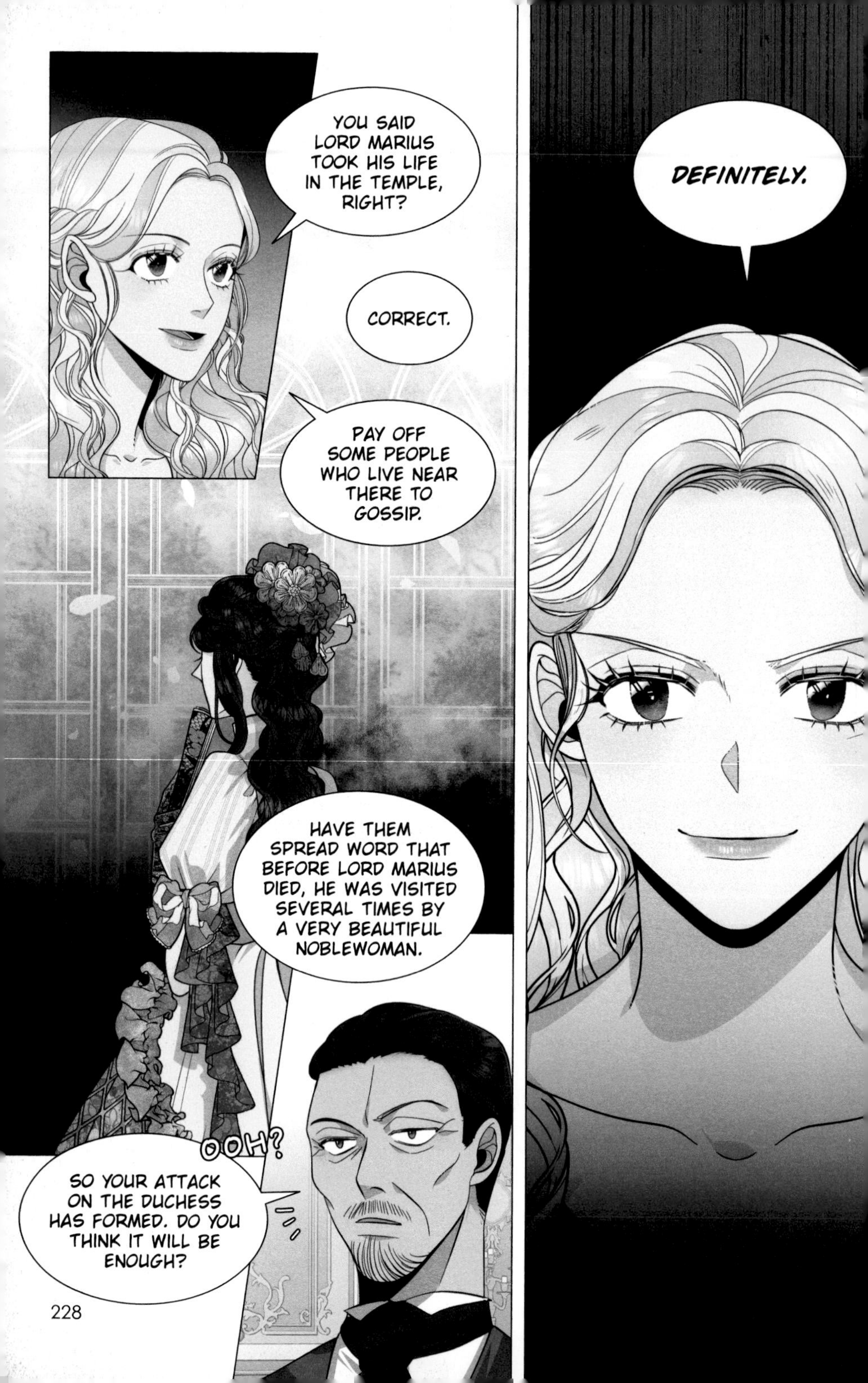
YOU SAID LORD MARIUS TOOK HIS LIFE IN THE TEMPLE, RIGHT?
CORRECT.
PAY OFF SOME PEOPLE WHO LIVE NEAR THERE TO GOSSIP.
HAVE THEM SPREAD WORD THAT BEFORE LORD MARIUS DIED, HE WAS VISITED SEVERAL TIMES BY A VERY BEAUTIFUL NOBLEWOMAN.
OOH?
SO YOUR ATTACK ON THE DUCHESS HAS FORMED. DO YOU THINK IT WILL BE ENOUGH?
DEFINITELY.

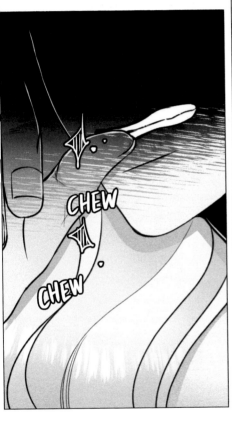

CHEW

CHEW

......

THE MAN WHO'S ALWAYS LOOKING AT DUCHESS TUANIA WITH DISPLEASURE AT PARTIES...

THAT HAS TO BE THE DUKE.

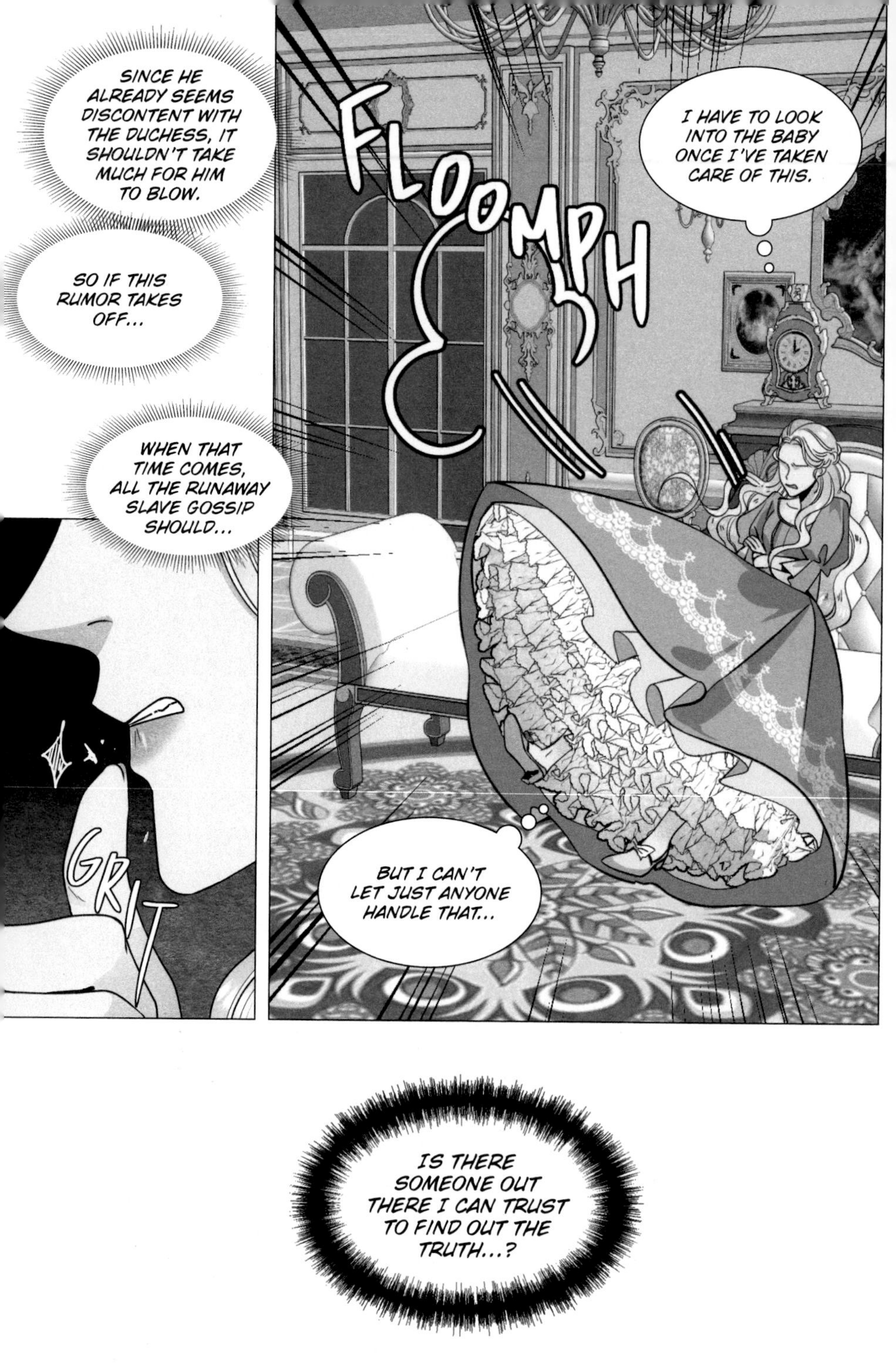
SINCE HE ALREADY SEEMS DISCONTENT WITH THE DUCHESS, IT SHOULDN'T TAKE MUCH FOR HIM TO BLOW.
SO IF THIS RUMOR TAKES OFF...
WHEN THAT TIME COMES, ALL THE RUNAWAY SLAVE GOSSIP SHOULD...
GRIT
FLOOMPH
I HAVE TO LOOK INTO THE BABY ONCE I'VE TAKEN CARE OF THIS.
BUT I CAN'T LET JUST ANYONE HANDLE THAT...
IS THERE SOMEONE OUT THERE I CAN TRUST TO FIND OUT THE TRUTH...?

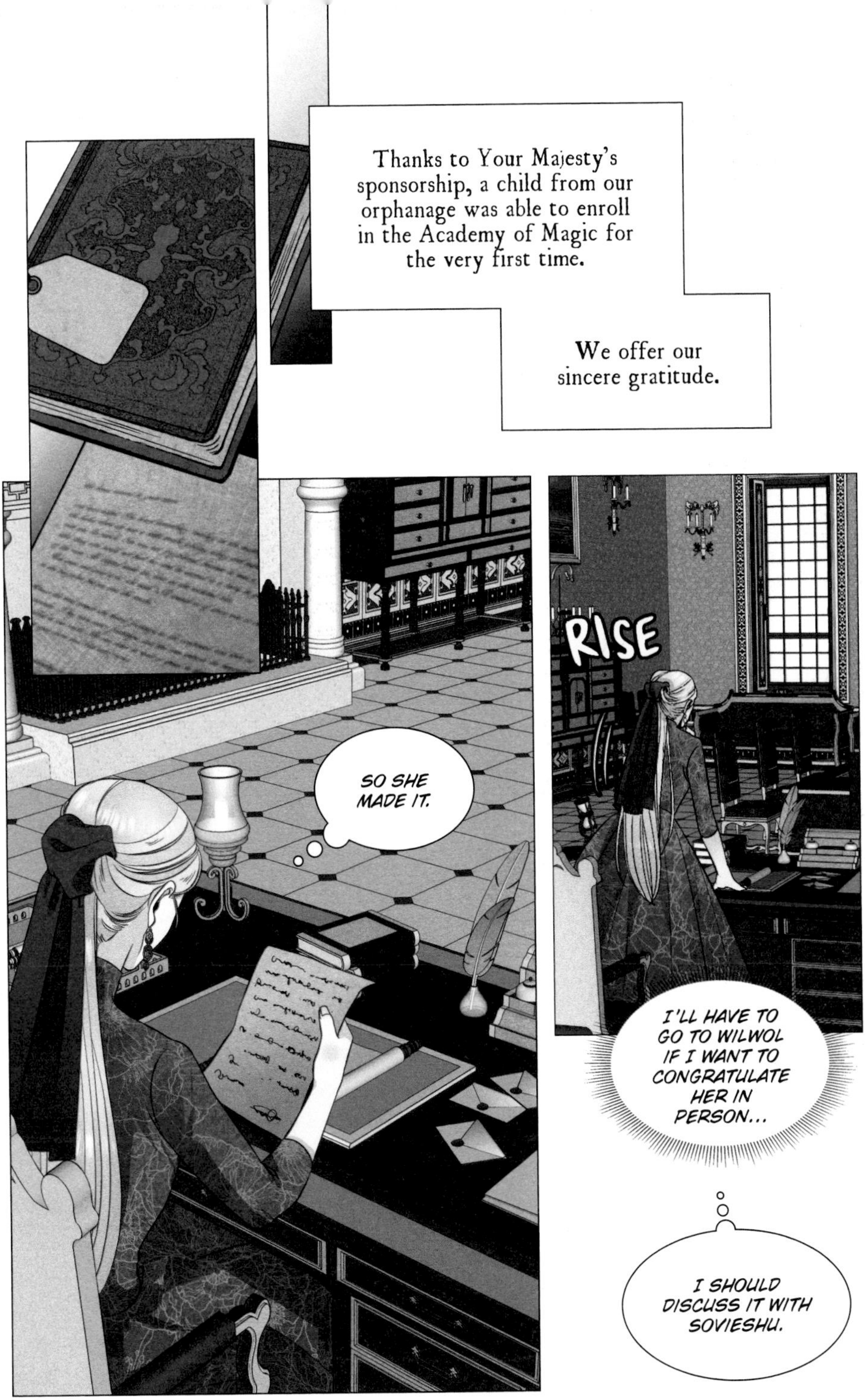
Thanks to Your Majesty's sponsorship, a child from our orphanage was able to enroll in the Academy of Magic for the very first time.
We offer our sincere gratitude.
SO SHE MADE IT.
RISE
I'LL HAVE TO GO TO WILWOL IF I WANT TO CONGRATULATE HER IN PERSON...
I SHOULD DISCUSS IT WITH SOVIESHU.

HAVE YOU FOUND THE STAR OF RED FLAMES?

!

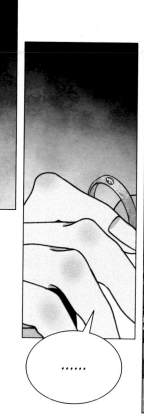

......

I DON'T KNOW IF "FOUND" IS THE RIGHT WORD.

I DID GIVE THE RING TO RASHTA, BUT IT TURNS OUT SHE GIFTED IT TO SOME POOR SERVANT GIRL, UNAWARE OF WHAT IT WAS.

SHE DIDN'T KNOW ABOUT ITS EFFECTS?

MM-HMM.

SO I TOLD COUNT FIRNIR TO LOOK FOR A SIMILAR RING...

...AND HE BROUGHT ME THIS.

HE SAID HE WON THE RING AT AN AUCTION LAST NIGHT.

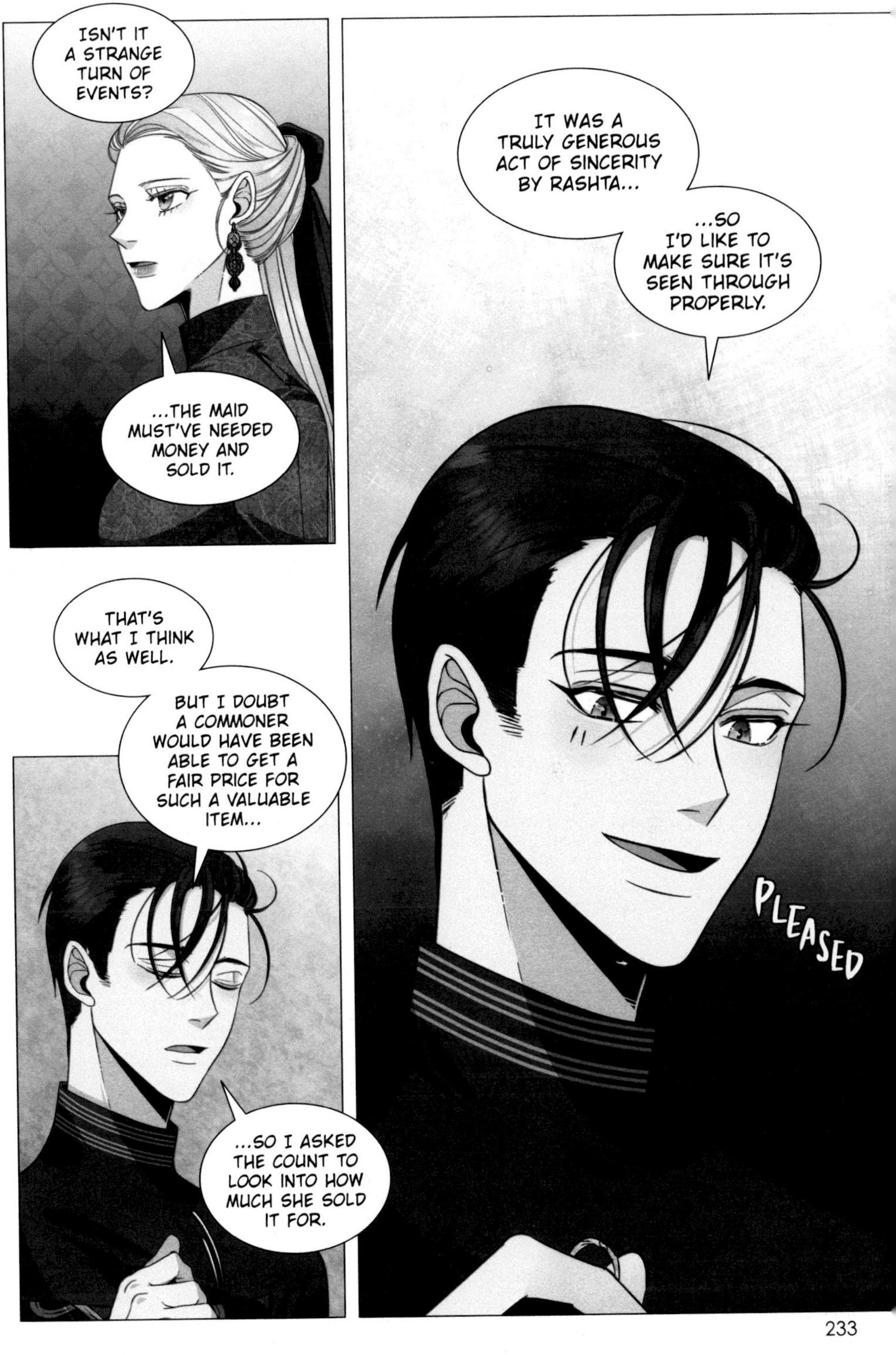
ISN'T IT A STRANGE TURN OF EVENTS?
...THE MAID MUST'VE NEEDED MONEY AND SOLD IT.
THAT'S WHAT I THINK AS WELL.
BUT I DOUBT A COMMONER WOULD HAVE BEEN ABLE TO GET A FAIR PRICE FOR SUCH A VALUABLE ITEM...
...SO I ASKED THE COUNT TO LOOK INTO HOW MUCH SHE SOLD IT FOR.
IT WAS A TRULY GENEROUS ACT OF SINCERITY BY RASHTA...
...SO I'D LIKE TO MAKE SURE IT'S SEEN THROUGH PROPERLY.
PLEASED

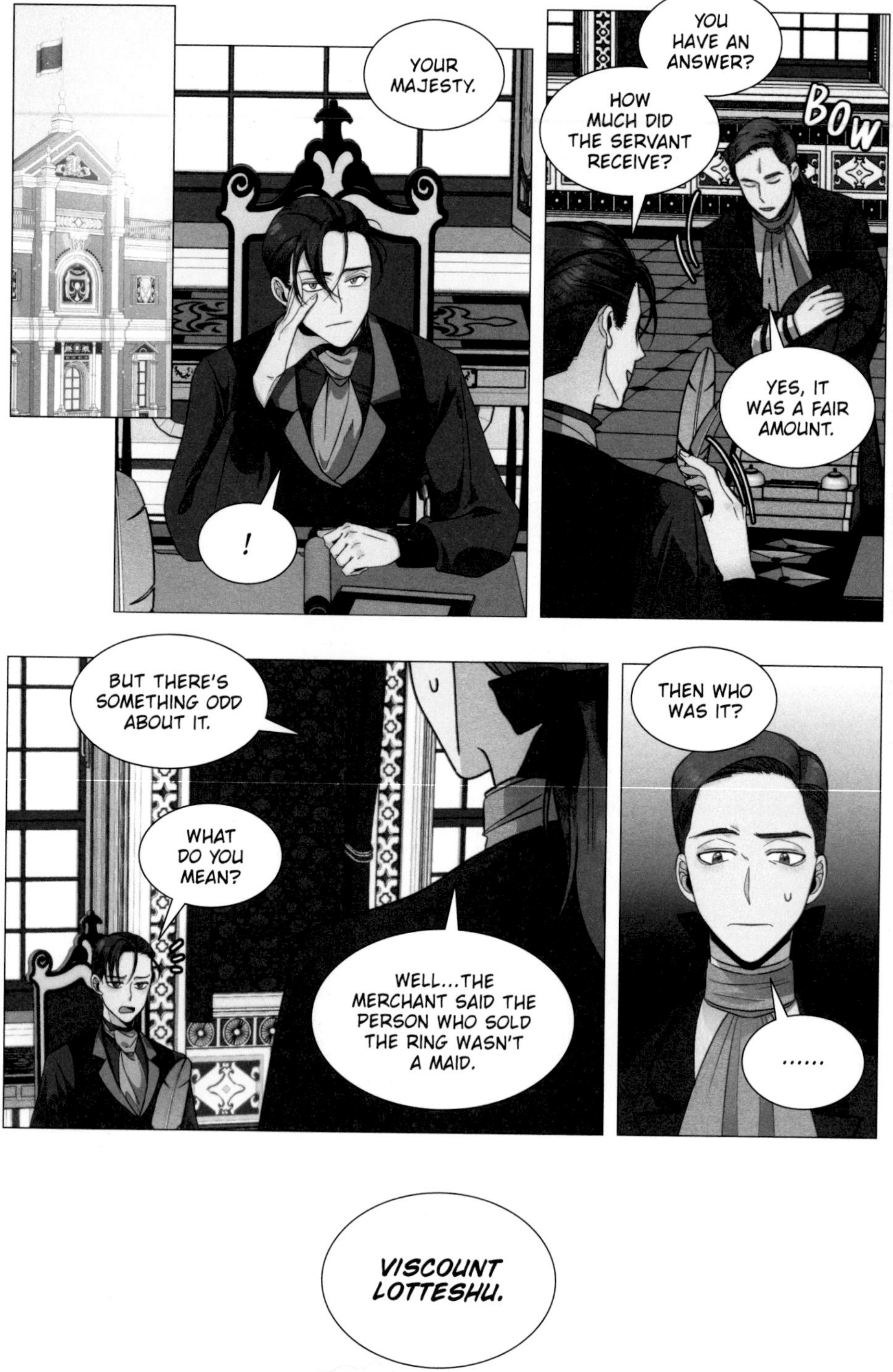
YOUR MAJESTY.
!
YOU HAVE AN ANSWER?
HOW MUCH DID THE SERVANT RECEIVE?
BOW
YES, IT WAS A FAIR AMOUNT.
BUT THERE'S SOMETHING ODD ABOUT IT.
WHAT DO YOU MEAN?
WELL...THE MERCHANT SAID THE PERSON WHO SOLD THE RING WASN'T A MAID.
THEN WHO WAS IT?
......
VISCOUNT LOTTESHU.

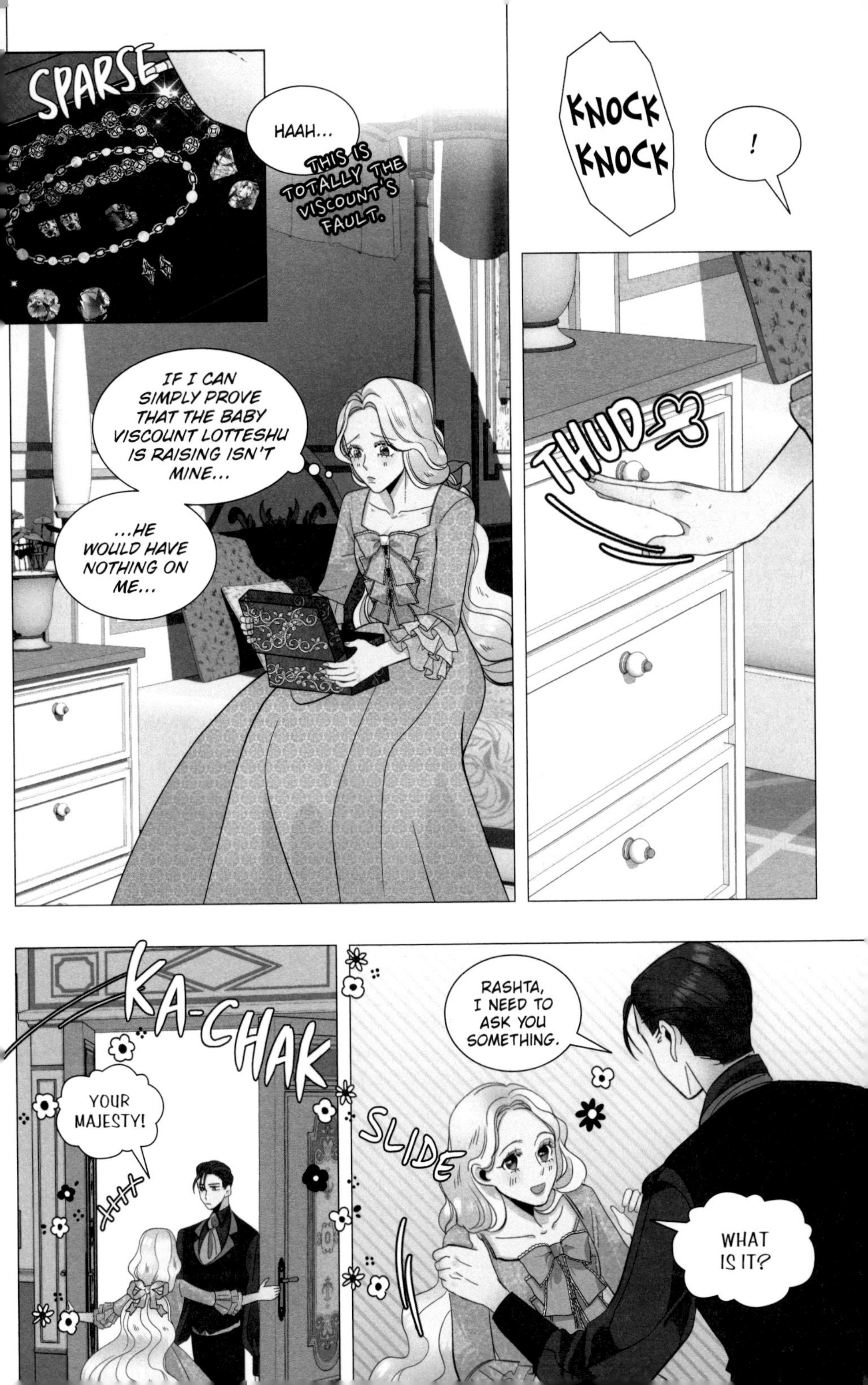
SPARSE
HAAH...
THIS IS TOTALLY THE VISCOUNT'S FAULT.
IF I CAN SIMPLY PROVE THAT THE BABY VISCOUNT LOTTESHU IS RAISING ISN'T MINE...
...HE WOULD HAVE NOTHING ON ME...
KNOCK KNOCK
!
THUD
KA-CHAK
YOUR MAJESTY!
RASHTA, I NEED TO ASK YOU SOMETHING.
SLIDE
WHAT IS IT?

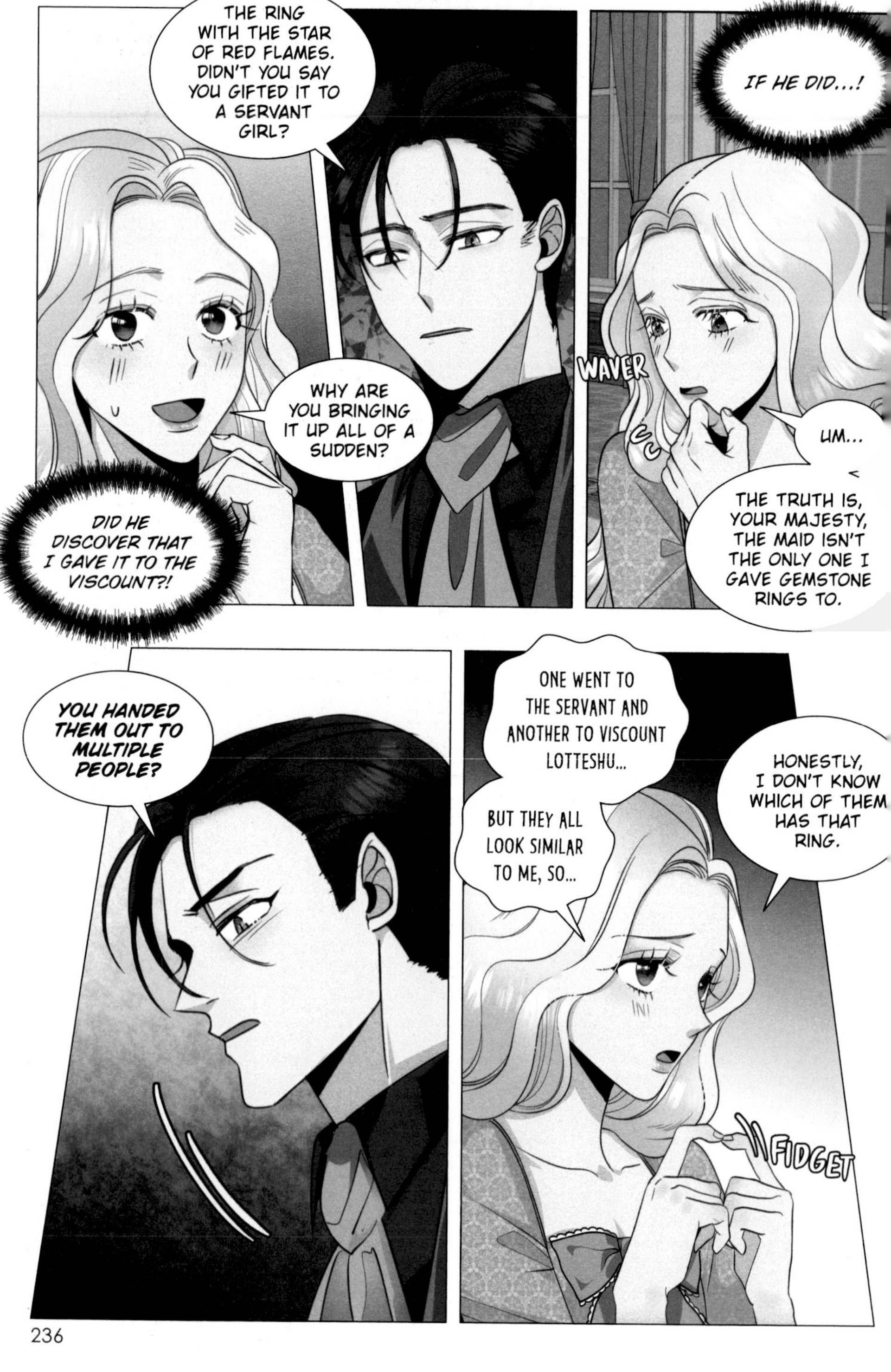

THE RING WITH THE STAR OF RED FLAMES. DIDN'T YOU SAY YOU GIFTED IT TO A SERVANT GIRL?
WHY ARE YOU BRINGING IT UP ALL OF A SUDDEN?
DID HE DISCOVER THAT I GAVE IT TO THE VISCOUNT?!
IF HE DID...!
WAVER
UM...
THE TRUTH IS, YOUR MAJESTY, THE MAID ISN'T THE ONLY ONE I GAVE GEMSTONE RINGS TO.
YOU HANDED THEM OUT TO MULTIPLE PEOPLE?
ONE WENT TO THE SERVANT AND ANOTHER TO VISCOUNT LOTTESHU...
BUT THEY ALL LOOK SIMILAR TO ME, SO...
HONESTLY, I DON'T KNOW WHICH OF THEM HAS THAT RING.
FIDGET

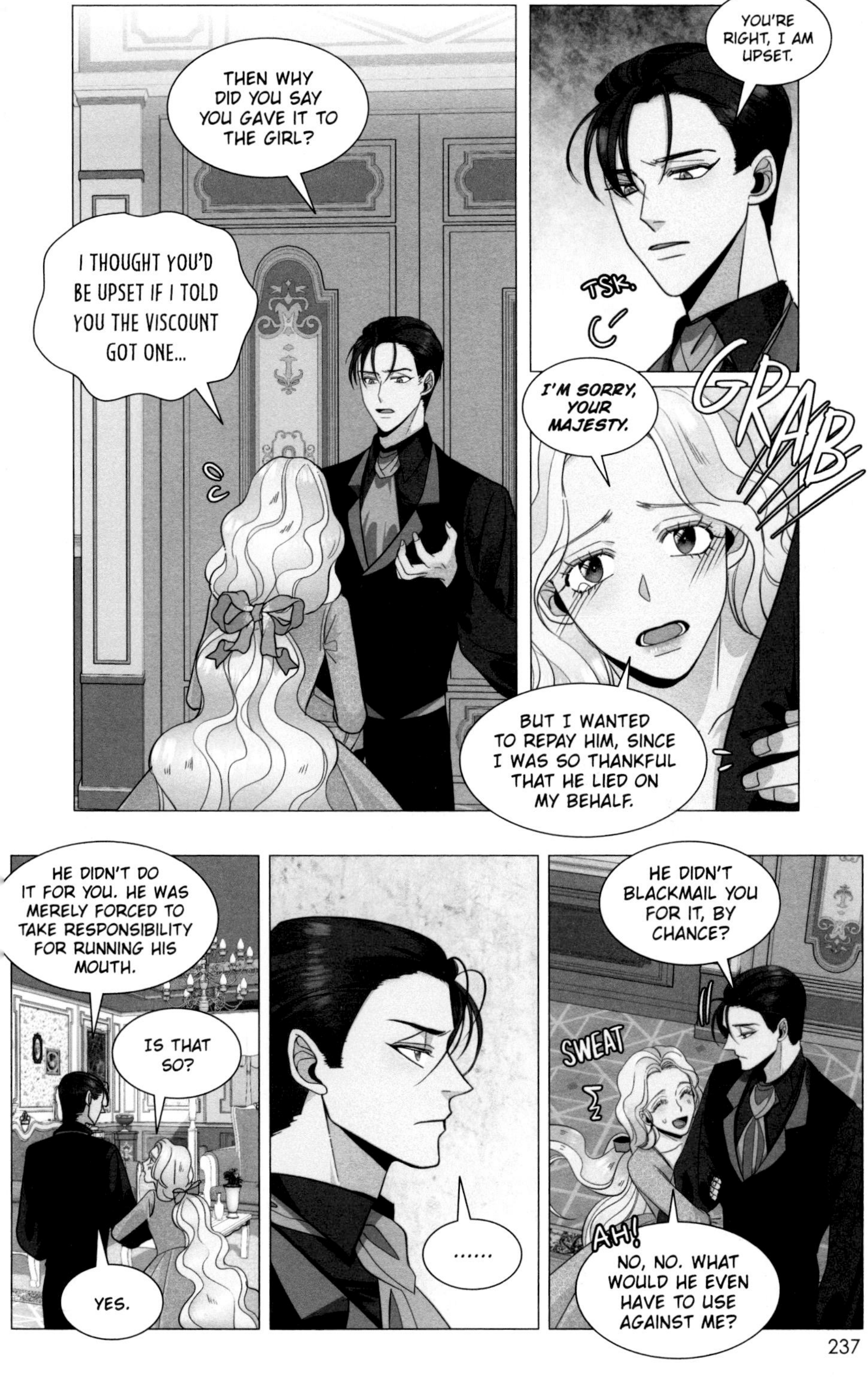
THEN WHY DID YOU SAY YOU GAVE IT TO THE GIRL?
I THOUGHT YOU'D BE UPSET IF I TOLD YOU THE VISCOUNT GOT ONE...
YOU'RE RIGHT, I AM UPSET.
TSK.
I'M SORRY, YOUR MAJESTY.
GRAB
BUT I WANTED TO REPAY HIM, SINCE I WAS SO THANKFUL THAT HE LIED ON MY BEHALF.
HE DIDN'T DO IT FOR YOU. HE WAS MERELY FORCED TO TAKE RESPONSIBILITY FOR RUNNING HIS MOUTH.
IS THAT SO?
YES.
......
HE DIDN'T BLACKMAIL YOU FOR IT, BY CHANCE?
SWEAT
AH!
NO, NO. WHAT WOULD HE EVEN HAVE TO USE AGAINST ME?

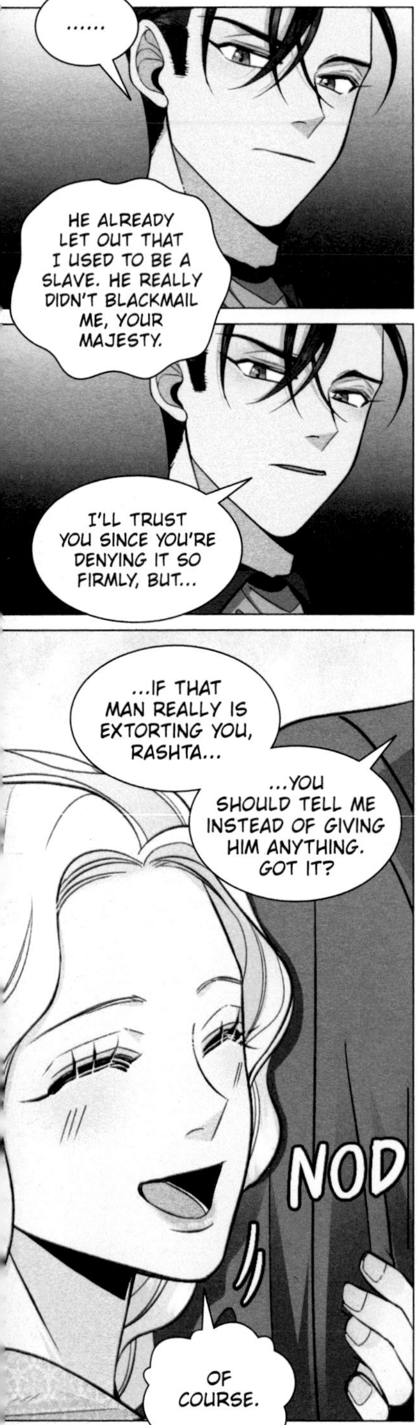

......
HE ALREADY LET OUT THAT I USED TO BE A SLAVE. HE REALLY DIDN'T BLACKMAIL ME, YOUR MAJESTY.
I'LL TRUST YOU SINCE YOU'RE DENYING IT SO FIRMLY, BUT...
...IF THAT MAN REALLY IS EXTORTING YOU, RASHTA...
...YOU SHOULD TELL ME INSTEAD OF GIVING HIM ANYTHING. GOT IT?
NOD
OF COURSE.




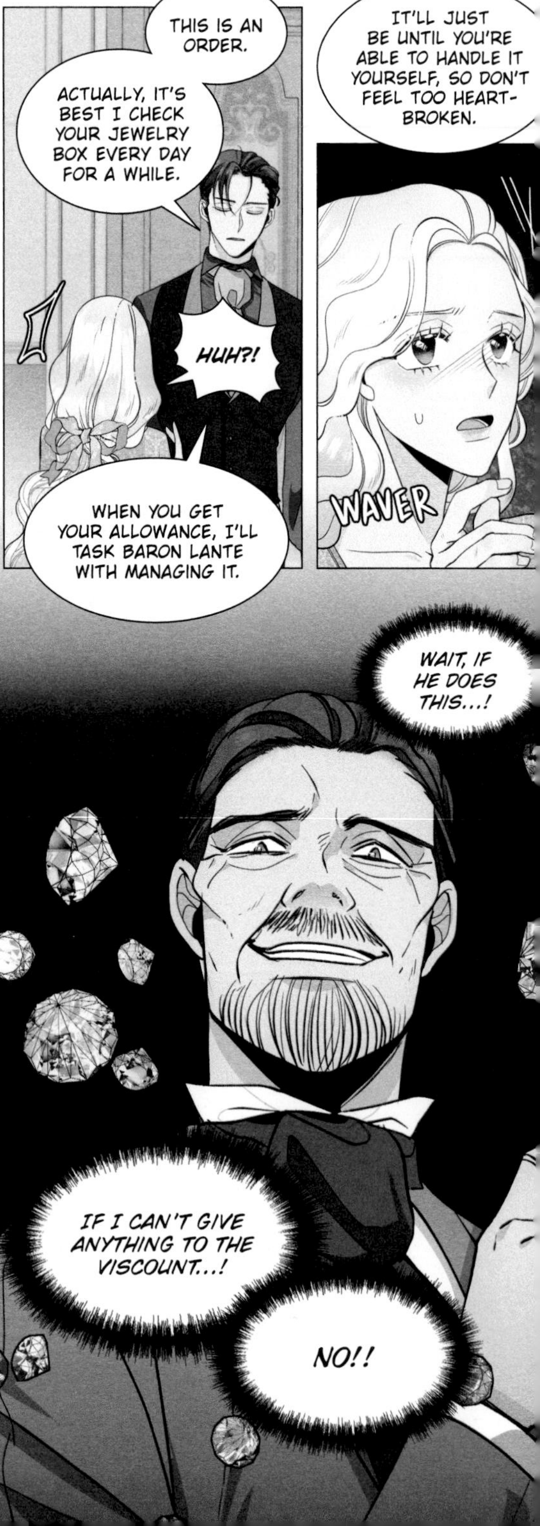

THIS IS AN ORDER.
ACTUALLY, IT'S BEST I CHECK YOUR JEWELRY BOX EVERY DAY FOR A WHILE.
HUH?!
WHEN YOU GET YOUR ALLOWANCE, I'LL TASK BARON LANTE WITH MANAGING IT.
IT'LL JUST BE UNTIL YOU'RE ABLE TO HANDLE IT YOURSELF, SO DON'T FEEL TOO HEART-BROKEN.
WAVER
WAIT, IF HE DOES THIS...!
IF I CAN'T GIVE ANYTHING TO THE VISCOUNT...!
NO!!

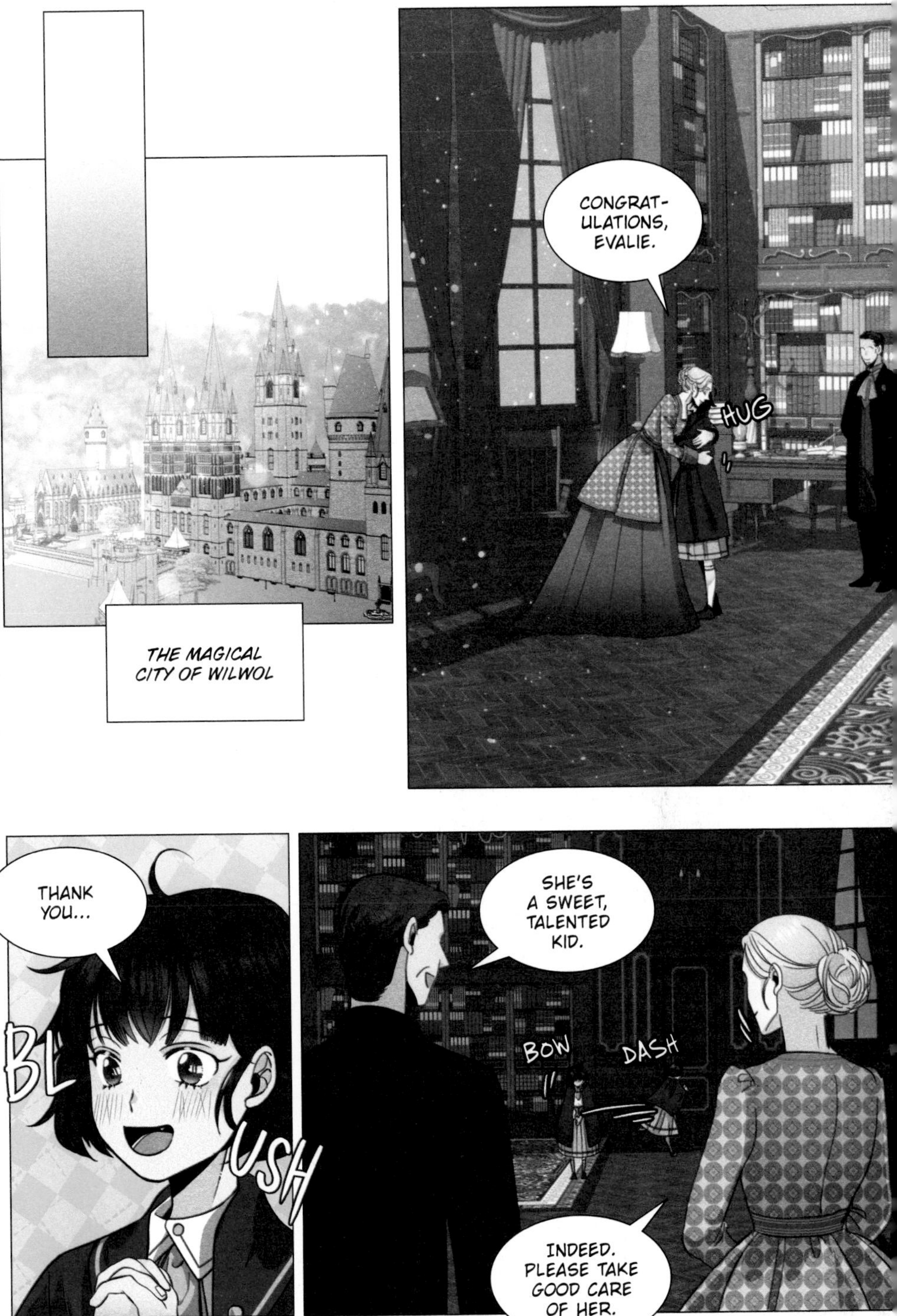
THE MAGICAL CITY OF WILWOL
CONGRAT-ULATIONS, EVALIE.
HUG
THANK YOU...
BLUSH
SHE'S A SWEET, TALENTED KID.
BOW
DASH
INDEED. PLEASE TAKE GOOD CARE OF HER.

TMP

TMP

I RECEIVED THE REPORT. DO WE STILL NOT KNOW THE CAUSE?

I'M AFRAID NOT. WE'RE INVESTIGATING HIGH AND LOW, BUT THE RATE OF THOSE MANIFESTING MAGIC IS FALLING.

AS MAGES BECOME RARER AND RARER, THEIR NUMBER WILL BECOME A HUGE VARIABLE FOR OUR NATIONAL DEFENSE.

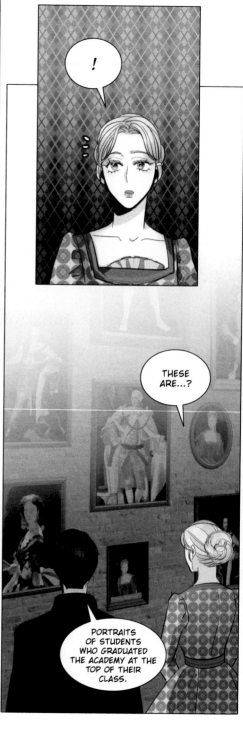

!

THESE ARE...?

PORTRAITS OF STUDENTS WHO GRADUATED THE ACADEMY AT THE TOP OF THEIR CLASS.

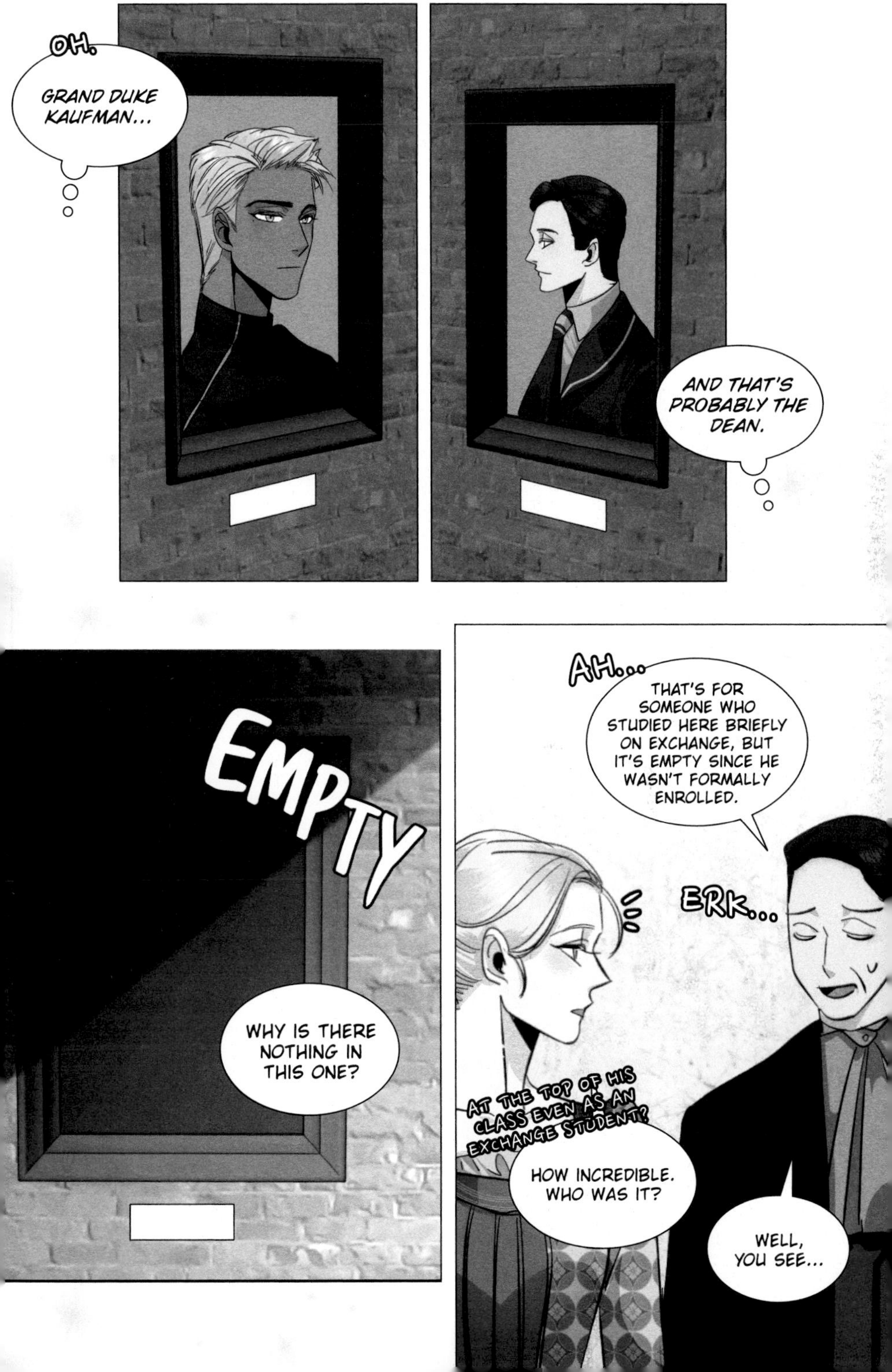
OH.
GRAND DUKE KAUFMAN...
AND THAT'S PROBABLY THE DEAN.
EMPTY
WHY IS THERE NOTHING IN THIS ONE?
AH...
THAT'S FOR SOMEONE WHO STUDIED HERE BRIEFLY ON EXCHANGE, BUT IT'S EMPTY SINCE HE WASN'T FORMALLY ENROLLED.
ERK...
AT THE TOP OF HIS CLASS EVEN AS AN EXCHANGE STUDENT?
HOW INCREDIBLE. WHO WAS IT?
WELL, YOU SEE...

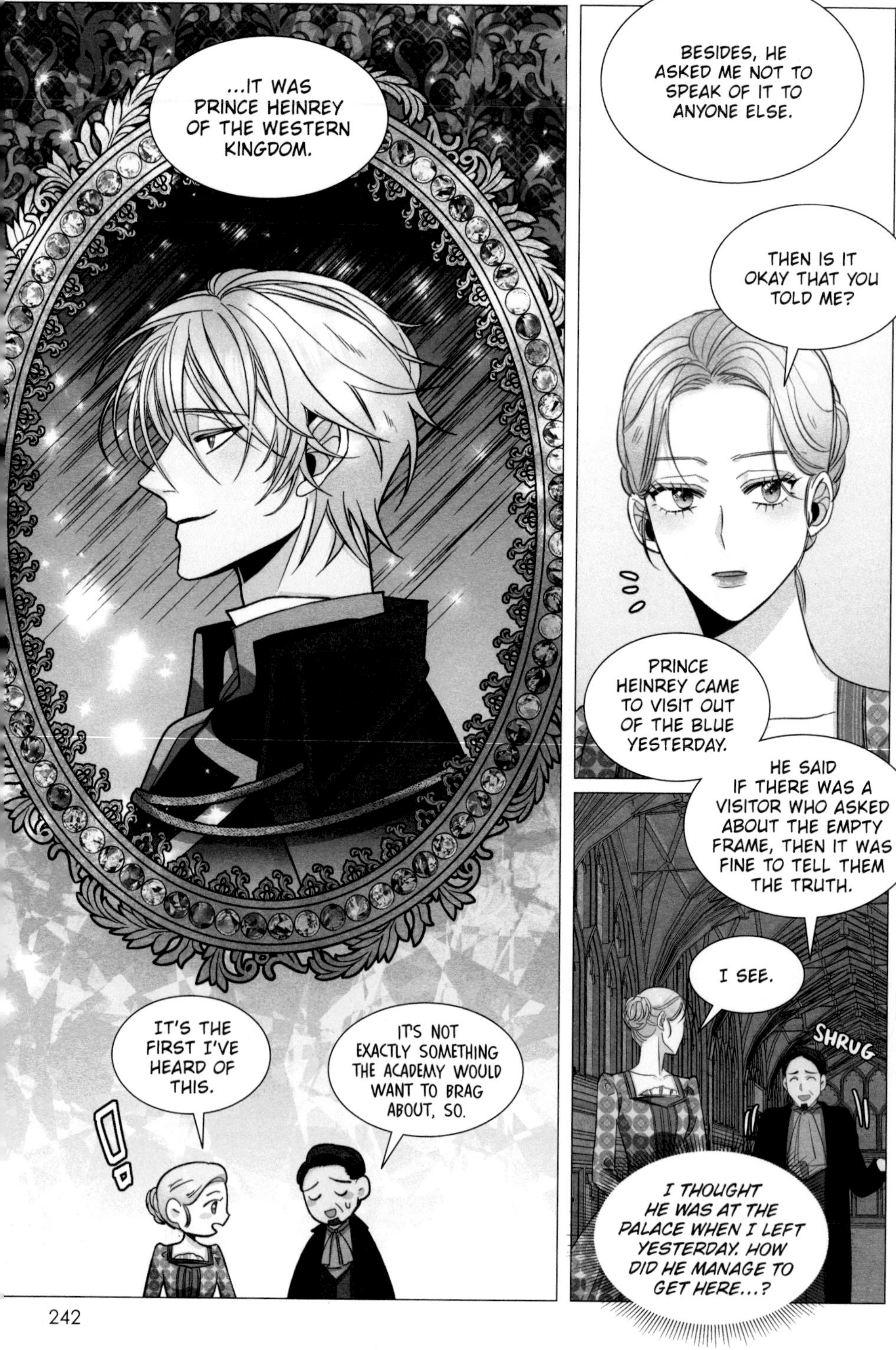
...IT WAS PRINCE HEINREY OF THE WESTERN KINGDOM.
IT'S THE FIRST I'VE HEARD OF THIS.
IT'S NOT EXACTLY SOMETHING THE ACADEMY WOULD WANT TO BRAG ABOUT, SO.
BESIDES, HE ASKED ME NOT TO SPEAK OF IT TO ANYONE ELSE.
THEN IS IT OKAY THAT YOU TOLD ME?
PRINCE HEINREY CAME TO VISIT OUT OF THE BLUE YESTERDAY.
HE SAID IF THERE WAS A VISITOR WHO ASKED ABOUT THE EMPTY FRAME, THEN IT WAS FINE TO TELL THEM THE TRUTH.
I SEE.
SHRUG
I THOUGHT HE WAS AT THE PALACE WHEN I LEFT YESTERDAY. HOW DID HE MANAGE TO GET HERE...?

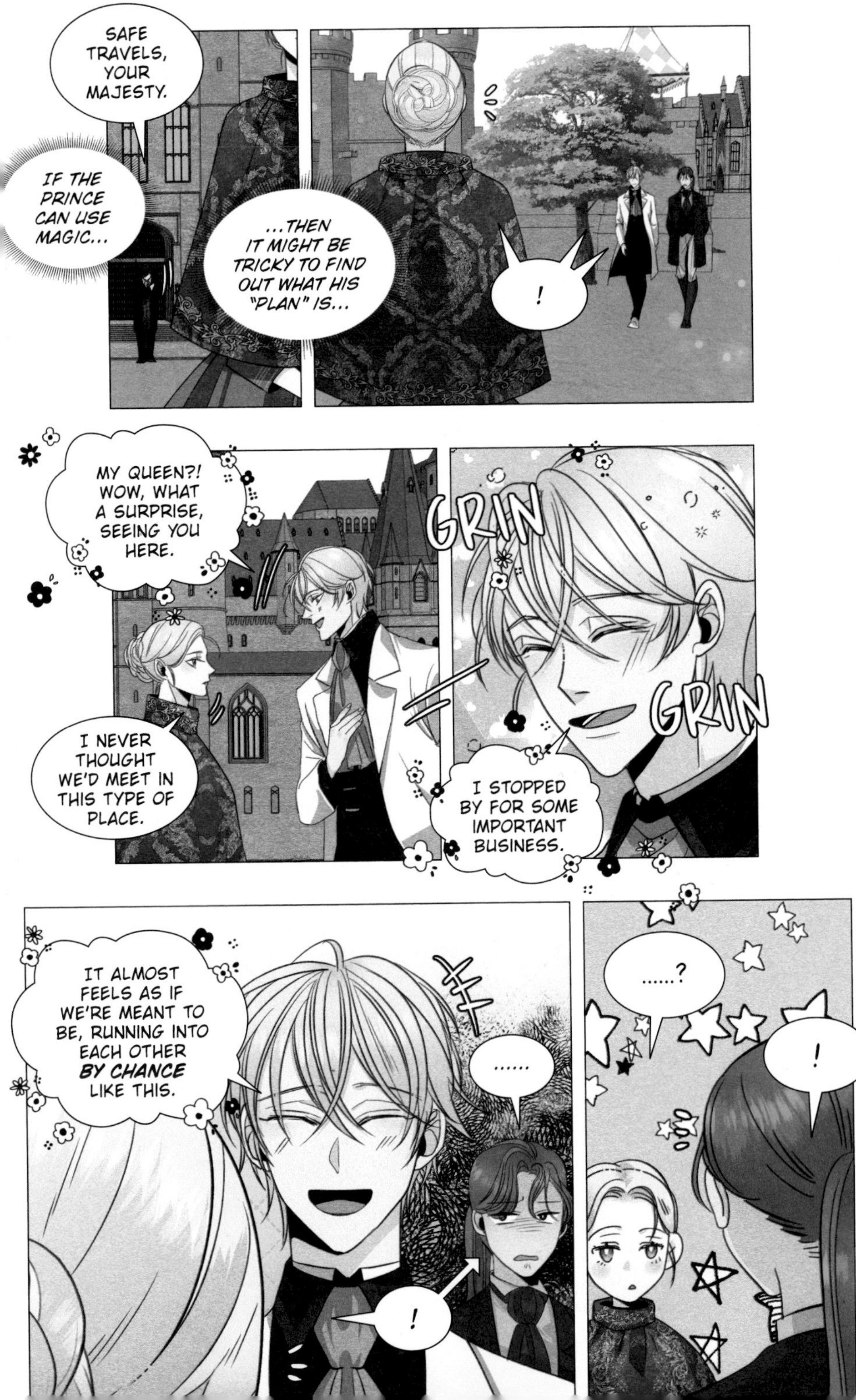
SAFE TRAVELS, YOUR MAJESTY.
IF THE PRINCE CAN USE MAGIC...
...THEN IT MIGHT BE TRICKY TO FIND OUT WHAT HIS "PLAN" IS...
!
MY QUEEN?! WOW, WHAT A SURPRISE, SEEING YOU HERE.
I NEVER THOUGHT WE'D MEET IN THIS TYPE OF PLACE.
GRIN
GRIN
I STOPPED BY FOR SOME IMPORTANT BUSINESS.
IT ALMOST FEELS AS IF WE'RE MEANT TO BE, RUNNING INTO EACH OTHER BY CHANCE LIKE THIS.
......
!
......?
!

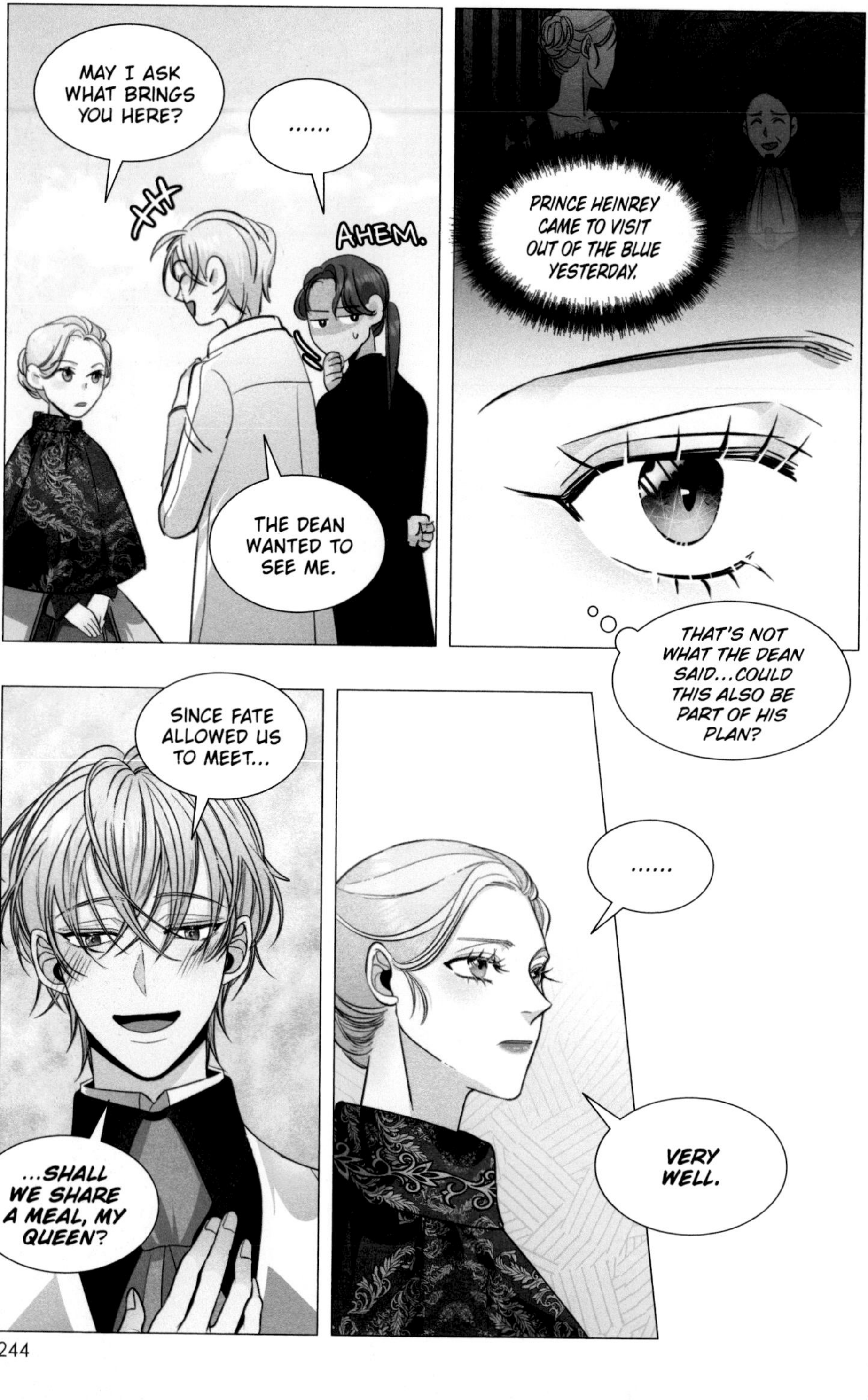
MAY I ASK WHAT BRINGS YOU HERE?
......
AHEM.
THE DEAN WANTED TO SEE ME.
PRINCE HEINREY CAME TO VISIT OUT OF THE BLUE YESTERDAY.
THAT'S NOT WHAT THE DEAN SAID...COULD THIS ALSO BE PART OF HIS PLAN?
SINCE FATE ALLOWED US TO MEET...
...SHALL WE SHARE A MEAL, MY QUEEN?
......
VERY WELL.

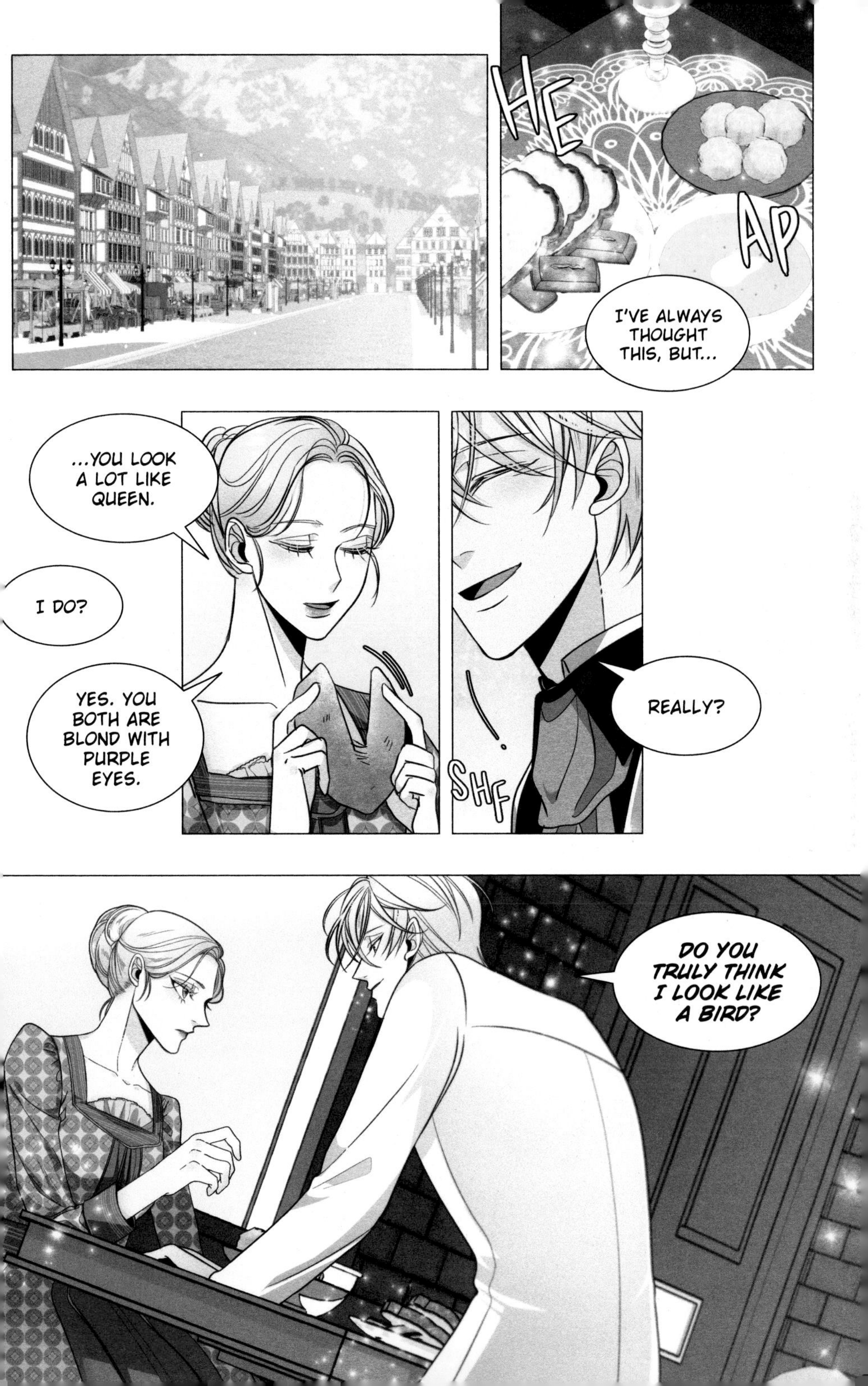
HEAP
I'VE ALWAYS THOUGHT THIS, BUT...
...YOU LOOK A LOT LIKE QUEEN.
I DO?
YES. YOU BOTH ARE BLOND WITH PURPLE EYES.
REALLY?
SHF
DO YOU TRULY THINK I LOOK LIKE A BIRD?

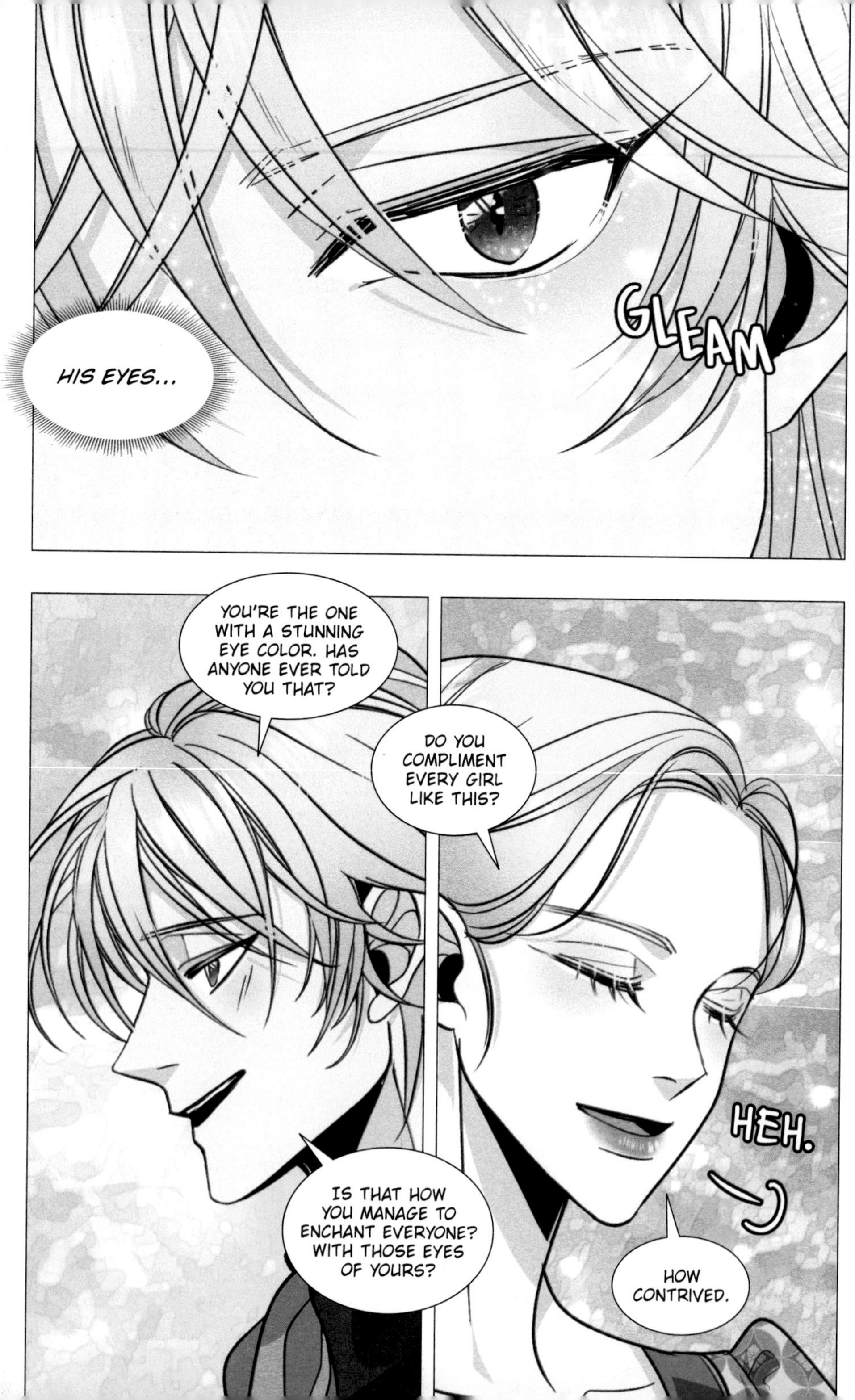
HIS EYES...
GLEAM
YOU'RE THE ONE WITH A STUNNING EYE COLOR. HAS ANYONE EVER TOLD YOU THAT?
DO YOU COMPLIMENT EVERY GIRL LIKE THIS?
IS THAT HOW YOU MANAGE TO ENCHANT EVERYONE? WITH THOSE EYES OF YOURS?
HEH.
HOW CONTRIVED.

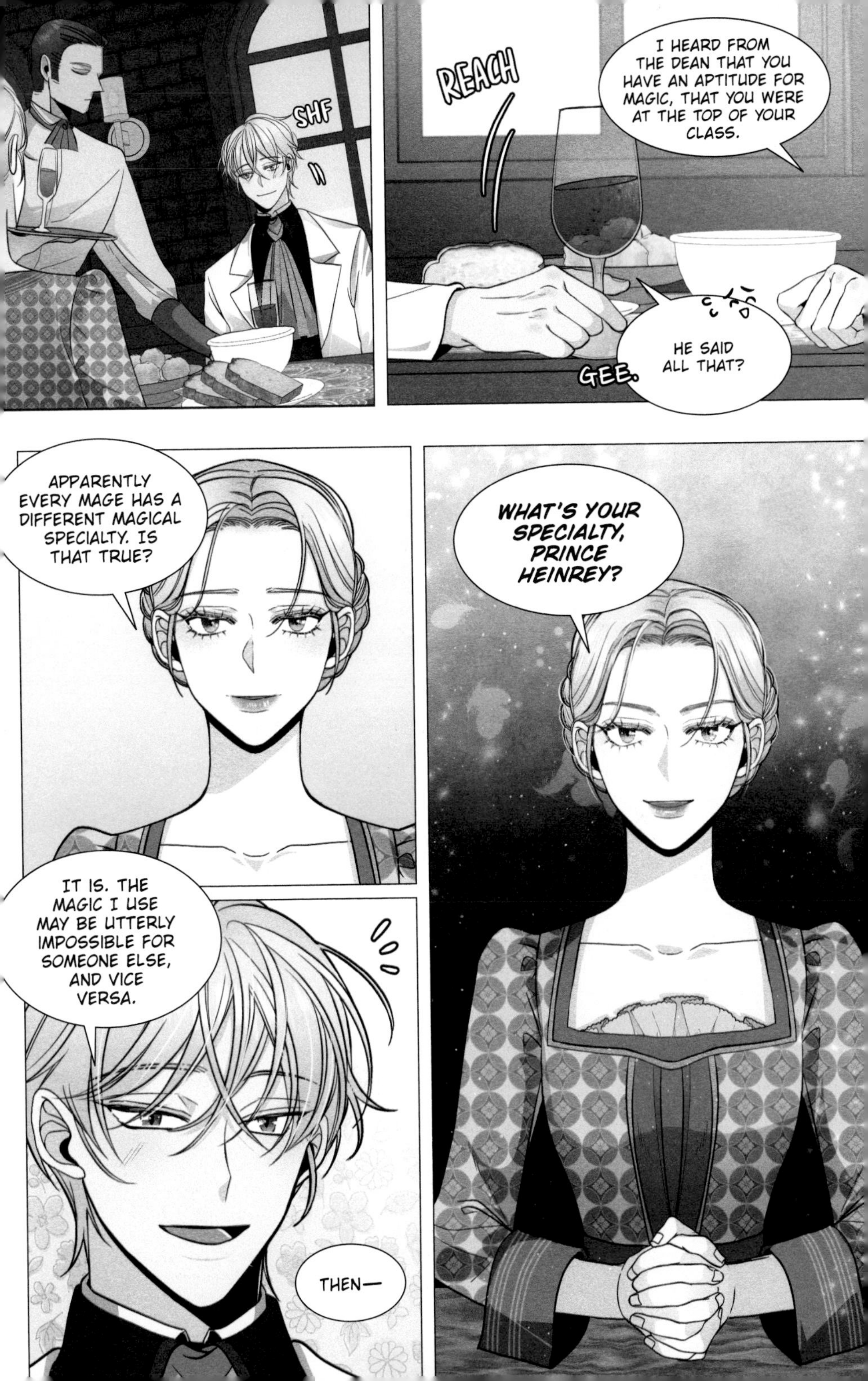
SHF
REACH
I HEARD FROM THE DEAN THAT YOU HAVE AN APTITUDE FOR MAGIC, THAT YOU WERE AT THE TOP OF YOUR CLASS.
GEE.
HE SAID ALL THAT?
APPARENTLY EVERY MAGE HAS A DIFFERENT MAGICAL SPECIALTY. IS THAT TRUE?
WHAT'S YOUR SPECIALTY, PRINCE HEINREY?
IT IS. THE MAGIC I USE MAY BE UTTERLY IMPOSSIBLE FOR SOMEONE ELSE, AND VICE VERSA.
THEN—

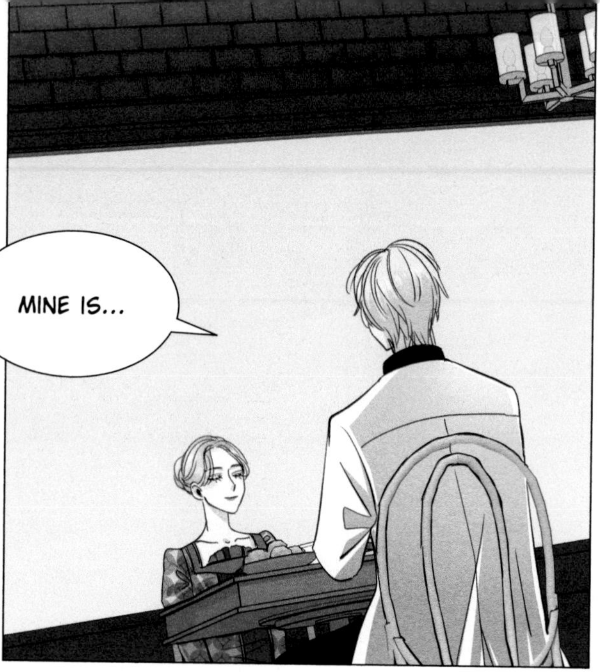
MINE IS...

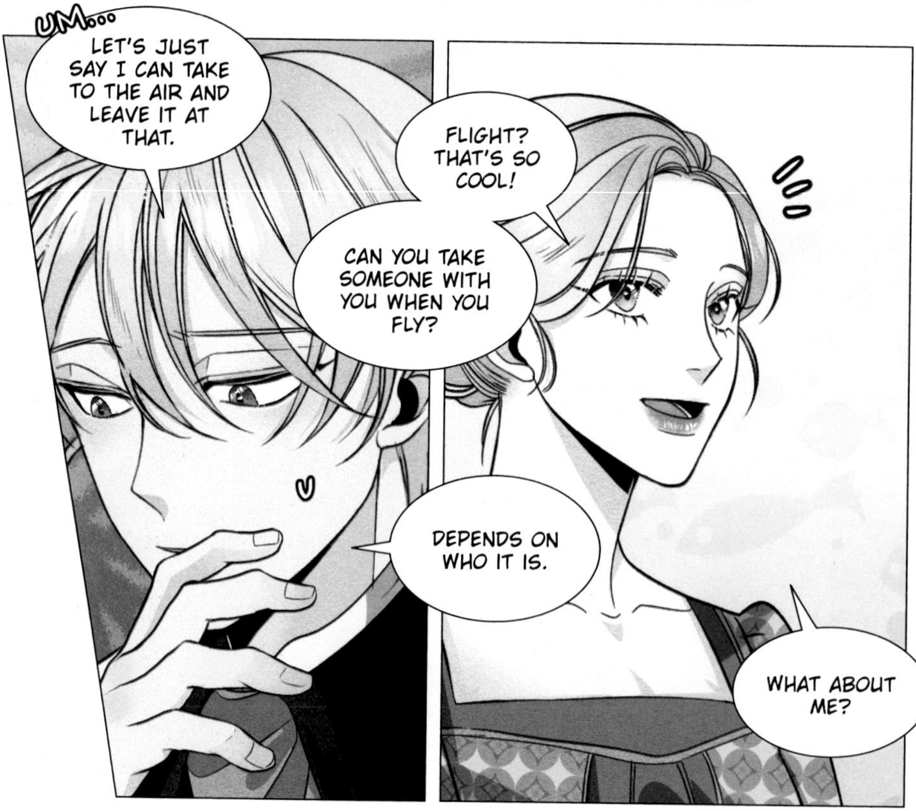
UM...
LET'S JUST SAY I CAN TAKE TO THE AIR AND LEAVE IT AT THAT.
FLIGHT? THAT'S SO COOL!
CAN YOU TAKE SOMEONE WITH YOU WHEN YOU FLY?
DEPENDS ON WHO IT IS.
WHAT ABOUT ME?

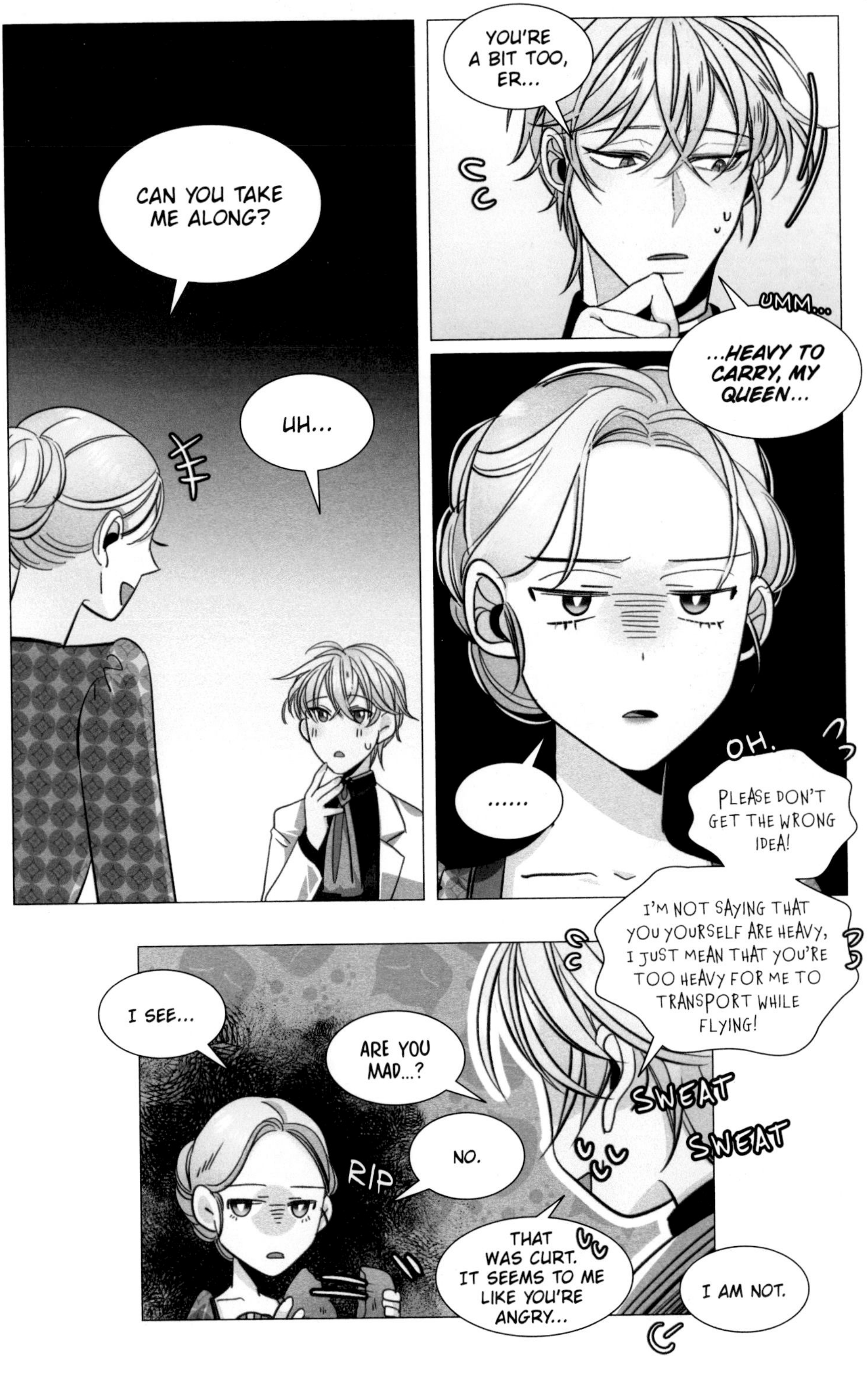
CAN YOU TAKE ME ALONG?
UH...
YOU'RE A BIT TOO, ER...
UMM...
...HEAVY TO CARRY, MY QUEEN...
......
OH.
PLEASE DON'T GET THE WRONG IDEA!
I'M NOT SAYING THAT YOU YOURSELF ARE HEAVY, I JUST MEAN THAT YOU'RE TOO HEAVY FOR ME TO TRANSPORT WHILE FLYING!
I SEE...
ARE YOU MAD...?
SWEAT
SWEAT
NO.
RIP
THAT WAS CURT. IT SEEMS TO ME LIKE YOU'RE ANGRY...
I AM NOT.

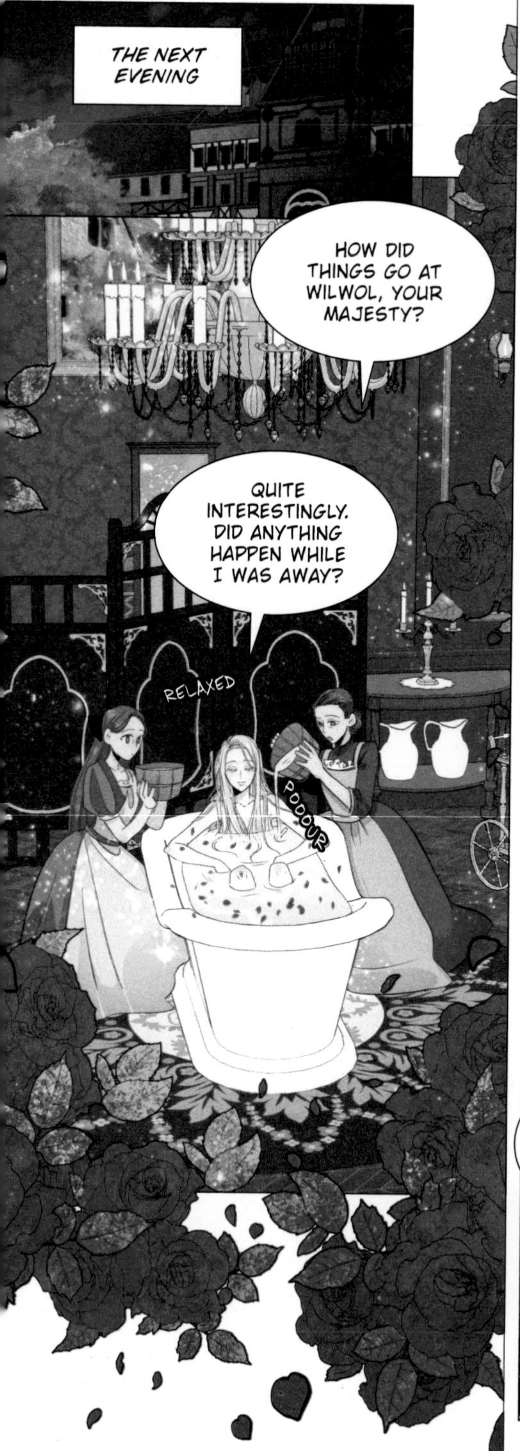
THE NEXT EVENING
HOW DID THINGS GO AT WILWOL, YOUR MAJESTY?
QUITE INTERESTINGLY. DID ANYTHING HAPPEN WHILE I WAS AWAY?
RELAXED
PODOUR

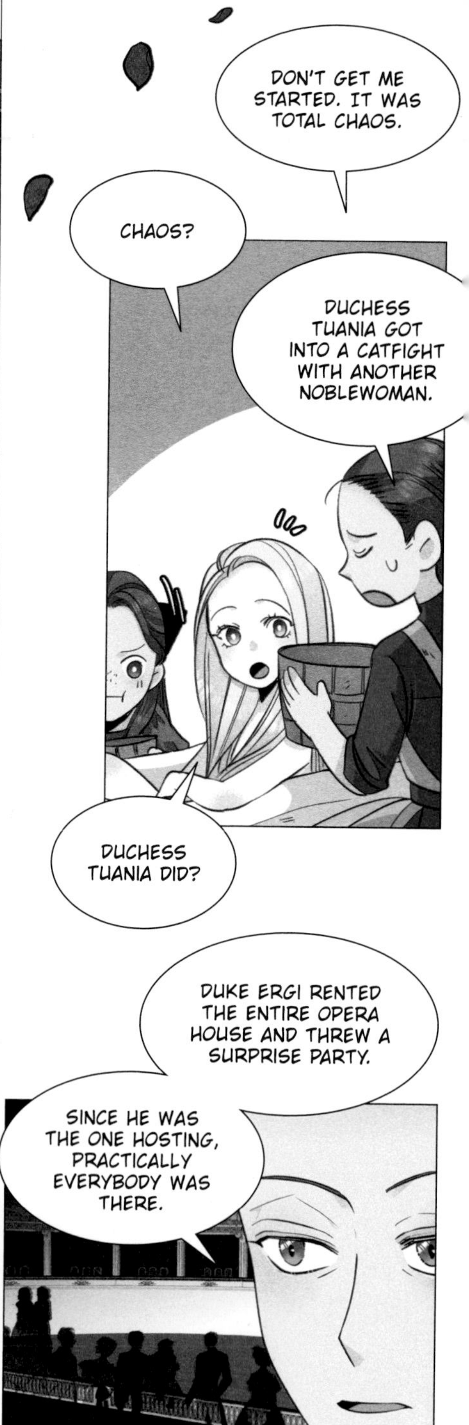
DON'T GET ME STARTED. IT WAS TOTAL CHAOS.
CHAOS?
DUCHESS TUANIA GOT INTO A CATFIGHT WITH ANOTHER NOBLEWOMAN.
DUCHESS TUANIA DID?
DUKE ERGI RENTED THE ENTIRE OPERA HOUSE AND THREW A SURPRISE PARTY.
SINCE HE WAS THE ONE HOSTING, PRACTICALLY EVERYBODY WAS THERE.

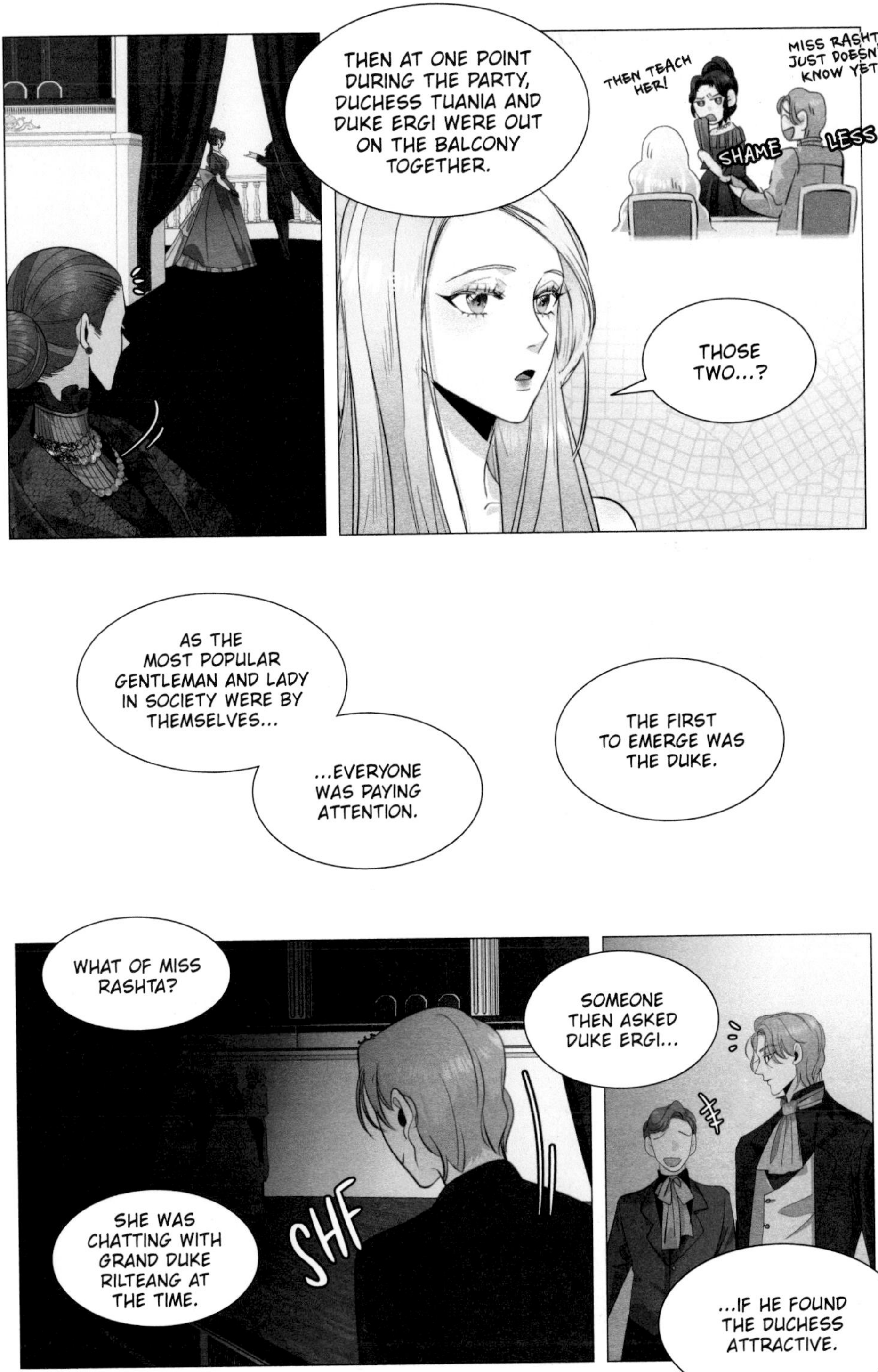

THEN AT ONE POINT DURING THE PARTY, DUCHESS TUANIA AND DUKE ERGI WERE OUT ON THE BALCONY TOGETHER.
THEN TEACH HER!
MISS RASHTA JUST DOESN'T KNOW YET!
SHAME LESS
THOSE TWO...?
AS THE MOST POPULAR GENTLEMAN AND LADY IN SOCIETY WERE BY THEMSELVES...
...EVERYONE WAS PAYING ATTENTION.
THE FIRST TO EMERGE WAS THE DUKE.
WHAT OF MISS RASHTA?
SHE WAS CHATTING WITH GRAND DUKE RILTEANG AT THE TIME.
SHF
SOMEONE THEN ASKED DUKE ERGI...
...IF HE FOUND THE DUCHESS ATTRACTIVE.

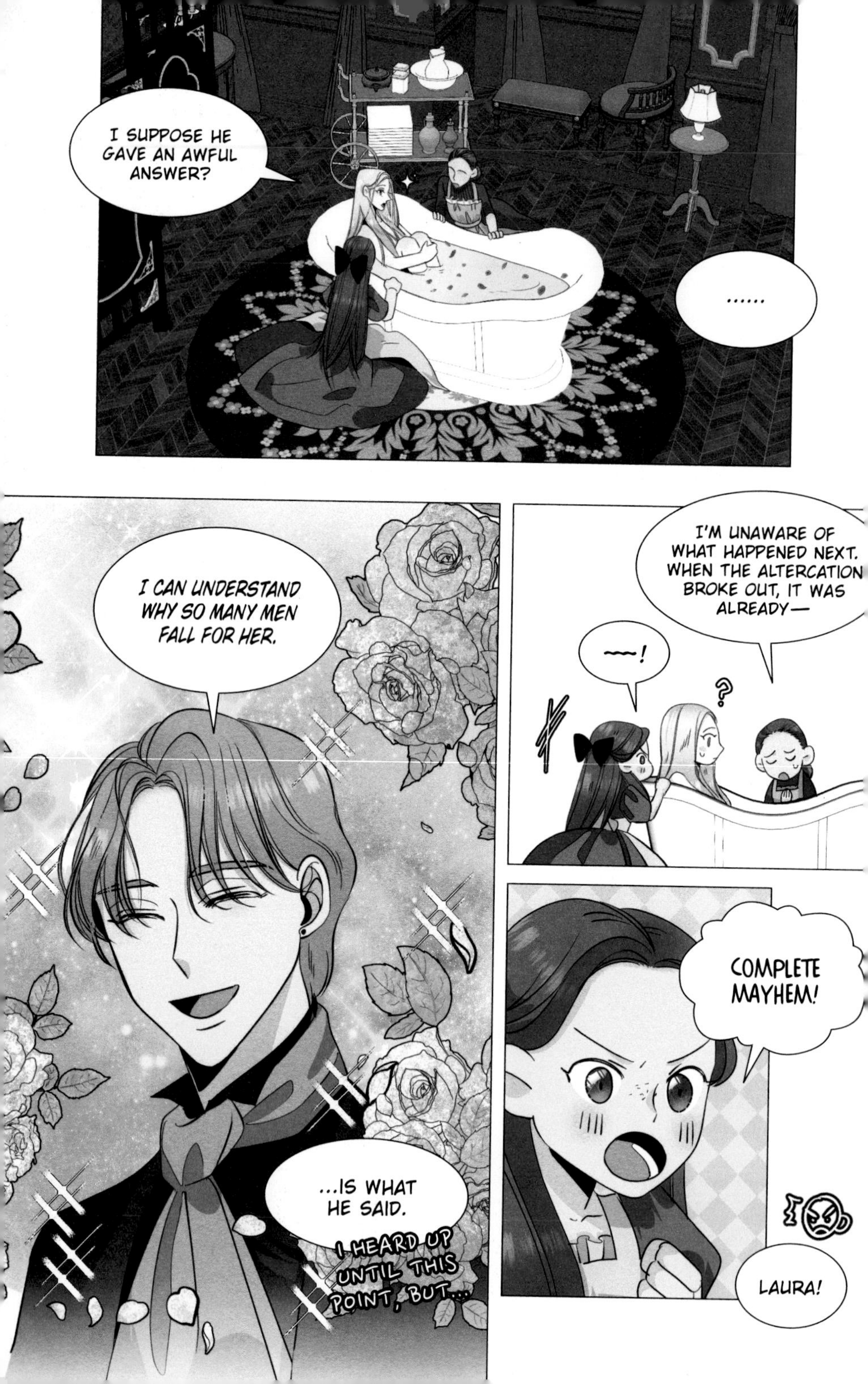
I SUPPOSE HE GAVE AN AWFUL ANSWER?
......
I CAN UNDERSTAND WHY SO MANY MEN FALL FOR HER.
...IS WHAT HE SAID.
I HEARD UP UNTIL THIS POINT, BUT...
I'M UNAWARE OF WHAT HAPPENED NEXT. WHEN THE ALTERCATION BROKE OUT, IT WAS ALREADY—
~~~!
?
COMPLETE MAYHEM!
LAURA!
~~~

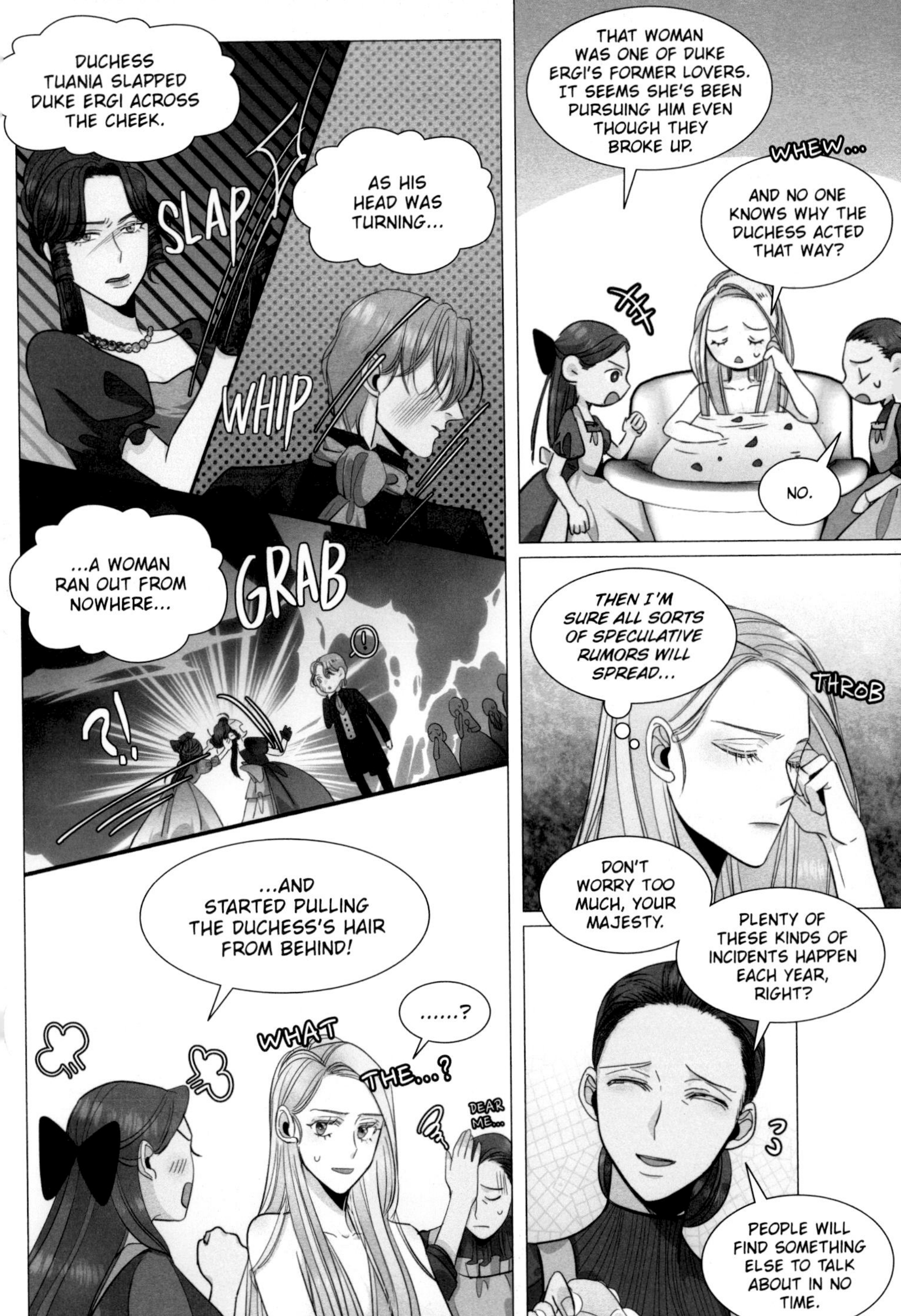
DUCHESS TUANIA SLAPPED DUKE ERGI ACROSS THE CHEEK.
SLAP
AS HIS HEAD WAS TURNING...
WHIP
...A WOMAN RAN OUT FROM NOWHERE...
GRAB
?!
!
...AND STARTED PULLING THE DUCHESS'S HAIR FROM BEHIND!
WHAT THE...?
......?
DEAR ME...
THAT WOMAN WAS ONE OF DUKE ERGI'S FORMER LOVERS. IT SEEMS SHE'S BEEN PURSUING HIM EVEN THOUGH THEY BROKE UP.
WHEW...
AND NO ONE KNOWS WHY THE DUCHESS ACTED THAT WAY?
NO.
THEN I'M SURE ALL SORTS OF SPECULATIVE RUMORS WILL SPREAD...
THROB
DON'T WORRY TOO MUCH, YOUR MAJESTY.
PLENTY OF THESE KINDS OF INCIDENTS HAPPEN EACH YEAR, RIGHT?
PEOPLE WILL FIND SOMETHING ELSE TO TALK ABOUT IN NO TIME.

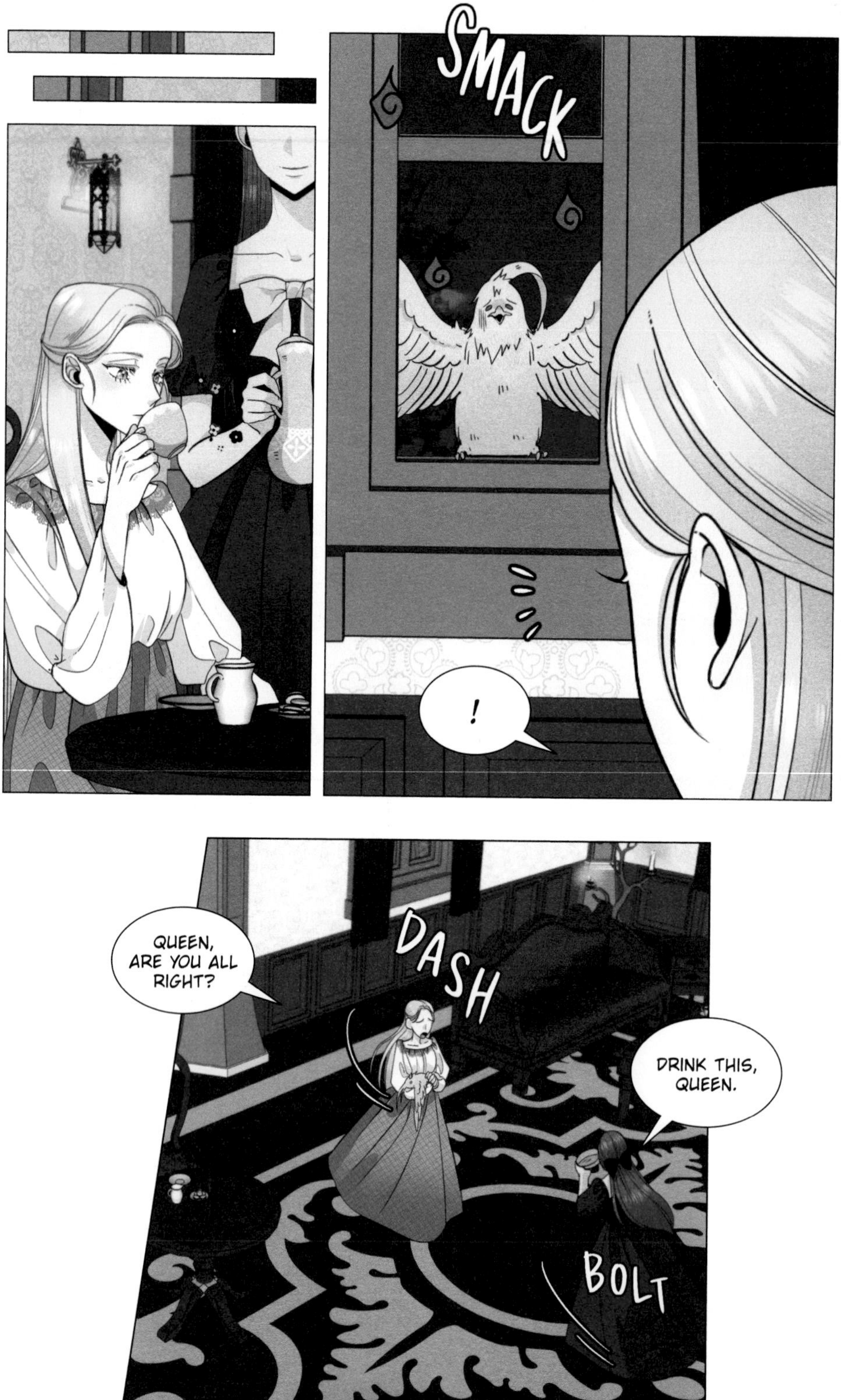
SMACK
!
QUEEN, ARE YOU ALL RIGHT?
DASH
DRINK THIS, QUEEN.
BOLT

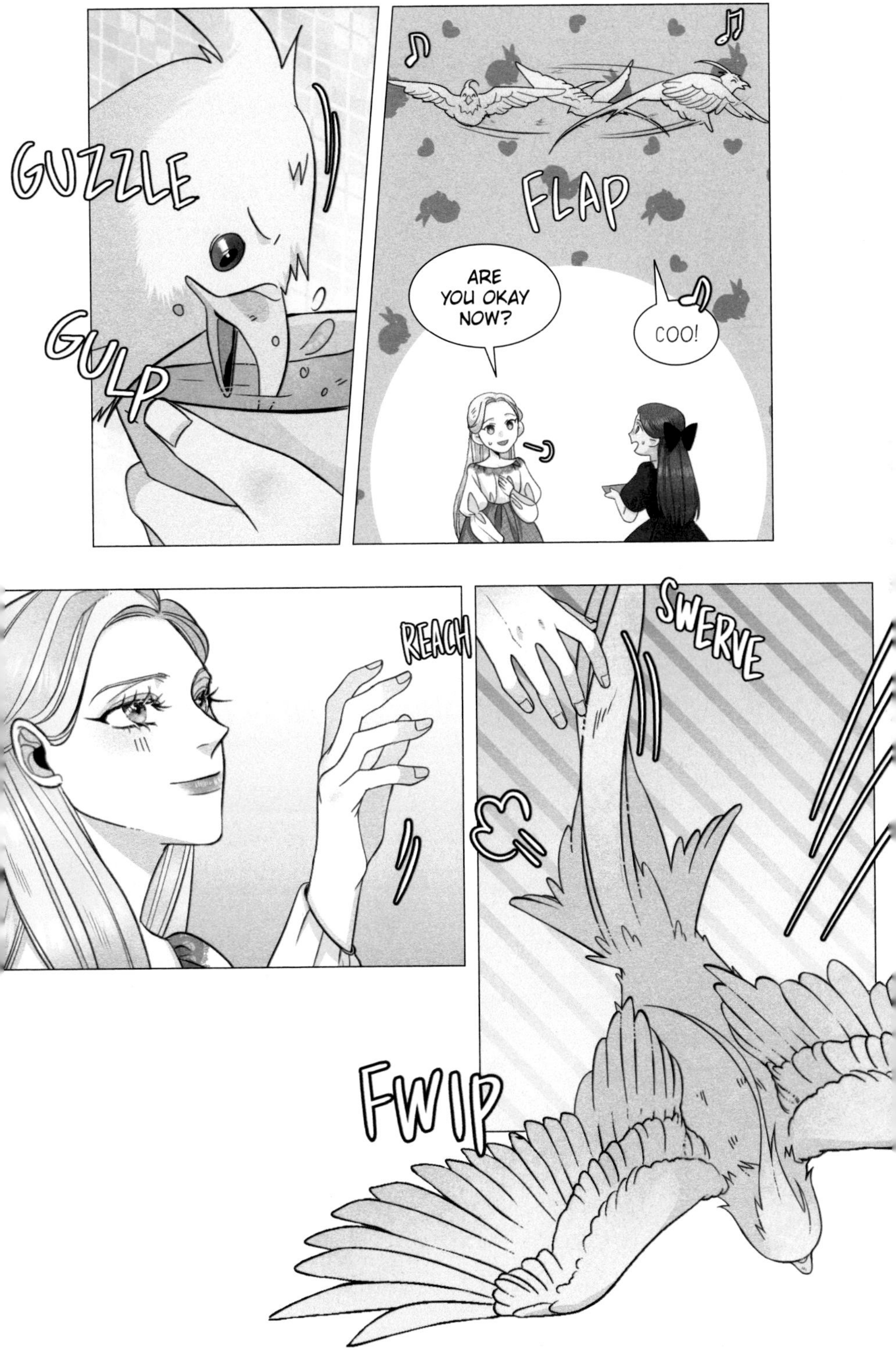
GUZZLE
GULP
FLAP
ARE YOU OKAY NOW?
COO!
REACH
SWERVE
FWIP

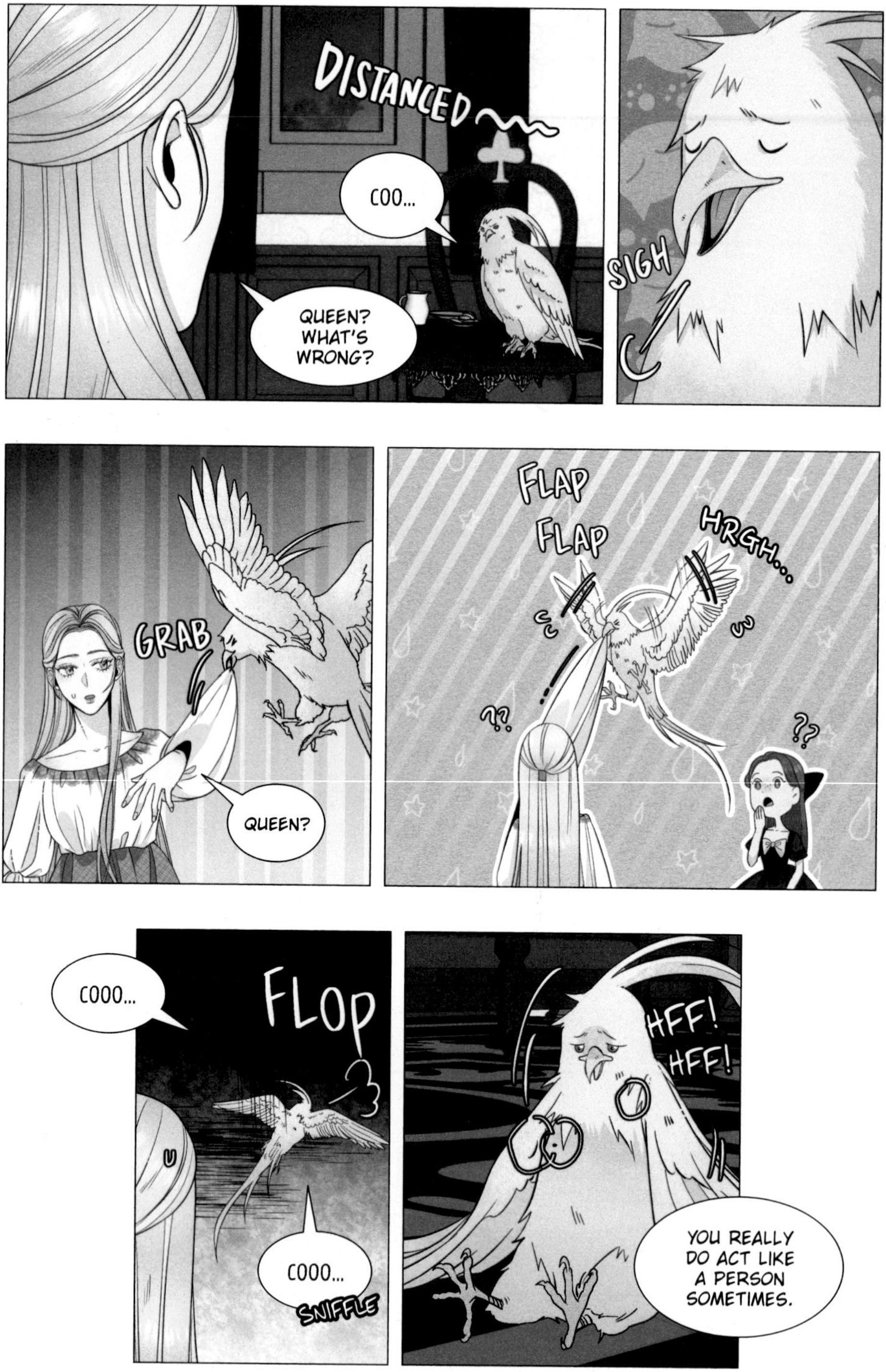
DISTANCED
COO...
QUEEN? WHAT'S WRONG?
SIGH
GRAB
QUEEN?
FLAP
FLAP
HRGH...
??
??
COOO...
FLOP
COOO...
SNIFFLE
HFF!
HFF!
YOU REALLY DO ACT LIKE A PERSON SOMETIMES.

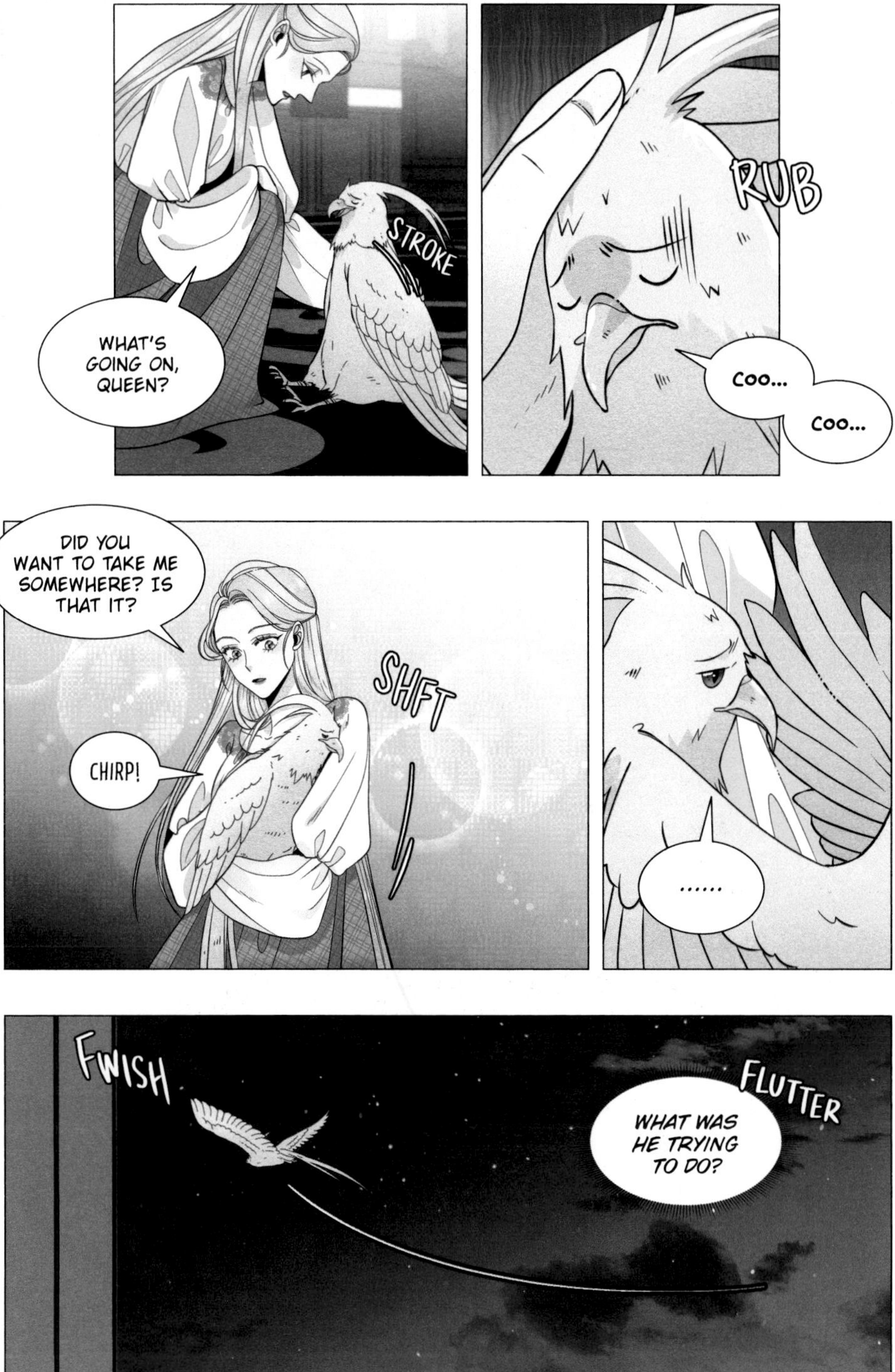
STROKE
WHAT'S GOING ON, QUEEN?
RUB
COO...
COO...
DID YOU WANT TO TAKE ME SOMEWHERE? IS THAT IT?
SHFT
CHIRP!
......
FWISH
FLUTTER
WHAT WAS HE TRYING TO DO?

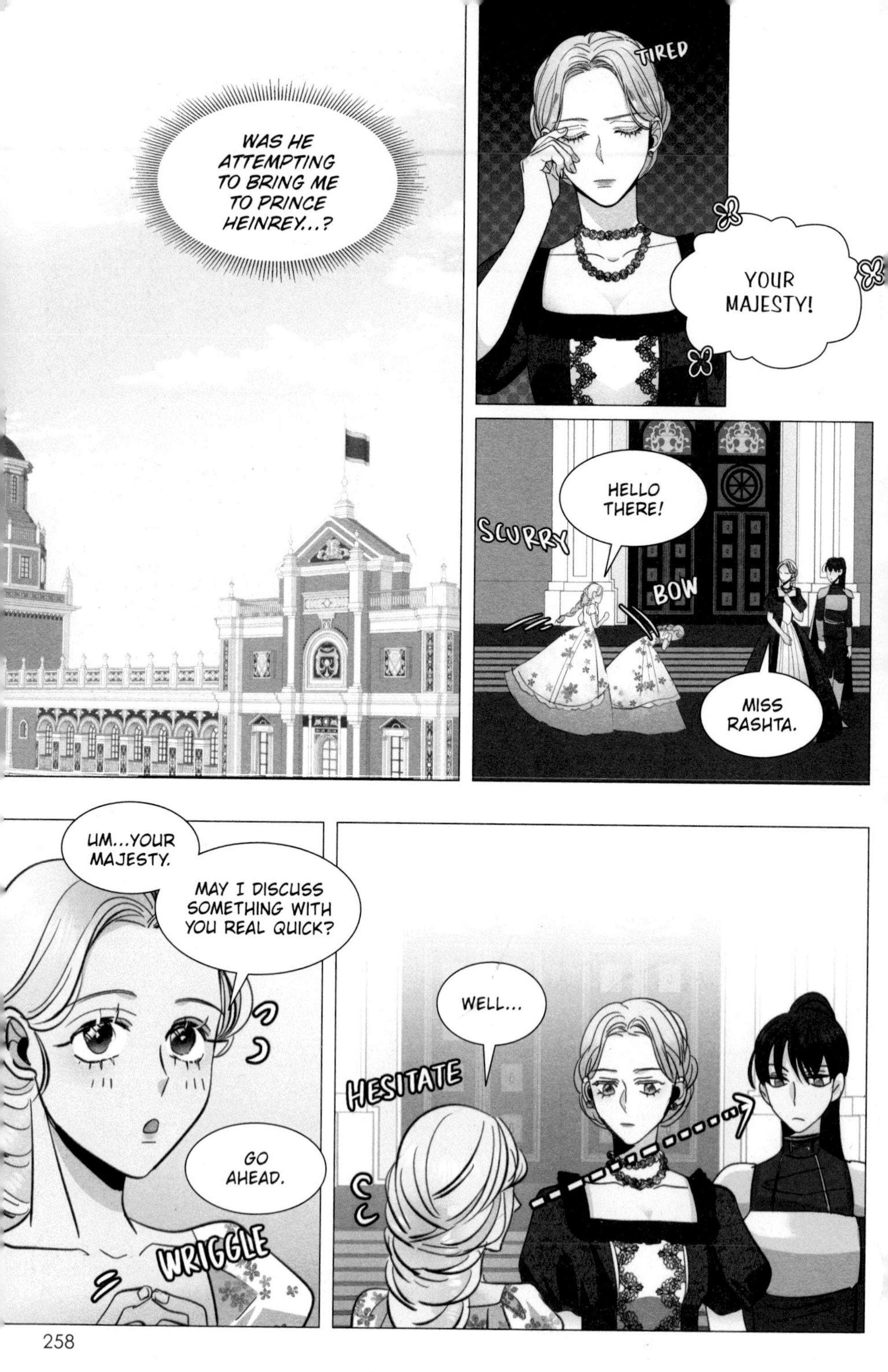
WAS HE ATTEMPTING TO BRING ME TO PRINCE HEINREY...?
TIRED
YOUR MAJESTY!
SCURRY
HELLO THERE!
BOW
MISS RASHTA.
UM...YOUR MAJESTY.
MAY I DISCUSS SOMETHING WITH YOU REAL QUICK?
GO AHEAD.
WRIGGLE
WELL...
HESITATE